Ford Pick-ups & Bronco Automotive Repair Manual

D1561010

by John B Raffa
and John H Haynes   Member of the Guild of Motoring Writers

Models covered

F-100, F-150, F-250, F-350 and Bronco with 300 cu in
in-line six-cylinder, 232 cu in V6, and 255, 302, 351, 400
and 460 cu in V8 engines. Manual and automatic transmissions.
Two-wheel drive and four-wheel drive. 1980 thru 1991.

Does not include diesel engine or Super Duty vehicles

ISBN 1 56392 009 3

Printed in the USA   *(11V9 – 880)*

ABCDE
FGHIJ
K.   2

Haynes Publishing Group
Sparkford Nr Yeovil
Somerset BA22 7JJ England

Haynes North America, Inc
861 Lawrence Drive
Newbury Park
California 91320 USA

Acknowledgments

Special thanks are due to Ford Motor Company for the supply of technical information and certain illustrations. Champion Spark Plug Company supplied the illustrations showing the various spark plug conditions,

About this manual

Its purpose

The purpose of this manual is to help you get the best value from your vehicle. It can do so in several ways. It can help you decide what work must be done even if you choose to get it done by a dealer service department or a repair shop; it provides information and procedures for routine maintenance and servicing; and it offers diagnostic and repair procedures to follow when trouble occurs.

It is hoped that you will use the manual to tackle the work yourself. For many simpler jobs, doing it yourself may be quicker than arranging an appointment to get the vehicle into a shop and making the trips to leave it and pick it up. More importantly, a lot of money can be saved by avoiding the expense the shop must pass on to you to cover its labor and overhead costs. An added benefit is the sense of satisfaction and accomplishment that you feel after having done the job yourself.

Using the manual

The manual is divided into Chapters. Each Chapter is divided into numbered Sections, which are headed in bold type between horizontal lines. Each Section consists of consecutively numbered paragraphs.

The two types of illustrations used (figures and photographs) are referenced by a number preceding their captions. Figure reference numbers denote Chapter and numerical sequence in the Chapter; i.e. Fig. 12.4 means Chapter 12, figure number 4. Figure captions are followed by a Section number which ties the figure to a specific portion of the text. All photographs apply to the Chapter in which they appear, and the reference number pinpoints the pertinent Section and paragraph.

Procedures, once described in the text, are not normally repeated. When it is necessary to refer to another Chapter, the reference will be given as Chapter and Section number, i.e. Chapter 1/16. Cross references given without use of the word, 'Chapter' apply to Sections and/or paragraphs in the same Chapter. For example, 'see Section 8' means in the same Chapter.

Reference to the left or right of the vehicle is based on the assumption that one is sitting in the driver's seat facing forward.

Even though extreme care has been taken during the preparation of this manual, neither the publisher nor the author can accept responsibility for any errors in, or omissions from, the information given.

Introduction to the Ford Pick-ups and Bronco

The Ford F100, F250, F350 and Bronco are available in a variety of trim options.

Engine options include a 300 cubic inch in-line six-cylinder, a 232 cubic inch V6 and V8s of 255, 302, 351, 400 and 460 cubic inch displacements.

Chassis layout is conventional with the engine mounted at the front and the power being transmitted through either a manual or automatic transmission by a driveshaft to the solid rear axle on 4x2 models. On 4x4 models, a transfer case transmits power to the front axle by way of a driveshaft. Models are equipped with three or four speed manual, four speed manual overdrive, three speed automatic and automatic overdrive transmissions.

F100 – F350 4x2 vehicles employ two I-beam type front axles and coil springs. The F150 4x4 and Bronco vehicles employ an independent front suspension system composed of a two-piece front driving axle assembly, two coil springs and two radius arms. The F250 – F350 vehicles also employ an independent front suspension system, but use semi-elliptic leaf springs rather than coils. All vehicles employ leaf springs in the rear suspension and double-acting shock absorbers at each wheel.

All vehicles are equipped with front disc and drum rear brakes, with vacuum booster assistance available as either standard or optional equipment.

Contents

1981 Ford F150 2-wheel drive pick-up

1981 Ford Bronco 4-wheel drive

General dimensions

Wheelbase	Inches
F100	117, 133
F150	117, 133, 139, 155
F250	
1980 and 1981	133, 139, 155
1982	133, 137, 139, 155, 161
1983	133, 137, 155, 161
F350	
1980 and 1981	133, 137, 155, 161
1982	133, 137, 161
1983	133, 137, 161, 168
Bronco	105

Buying parts

Replacement parts are available from many sources, which generally fall into one of two categories – authorized dealer parts departments and independent retail auto parts stores. Our advice concerning these parts is as follows:

Retail auto parts stores: Good auto parts stores will stock frequently needed components which wear out relatively fast, such as clutch components, exhaust systems, brake parts, tune-up parts, etc. These stores often supply new or reconditioned parts on an exchange basis, which can save a considerable amount of money. Discount auto parts stores are often very good places to buy materials and parts needed for general vehicle maintenance such as oil, grease, filters, spark plugs, belts, touch-up paint, bulbs, etc. They also usually sell tools and general accessories, have convenient hours, charge lower prices and can often be found not far from home.

Authorized dealer parts department: This is the best source for parts which are unique to the vehicle and not generally available elsewhere (such as major engine parts, transmission parts, trim pieces, etc.).

Warranty information: If the vehicle is still covered under warranty, be sure that any replacement parts purchased – regardless of the source – do not invalidate the warranty!

To be sure of obtaining the correct parts, have engine and chassis numbers available and, if possible, take the old parts along for positive identification.

Vehicle identification numbers

The Vehicle Identification Number (VIN) is stamped on a metal tag that appears near the bottom of the windshield on the driver's side. It is visible through the windshield from outside the vehicle.

The Safety Compliance Certificate Label is attached to the driver's door lock pillar. This label contains the name of the manufacturer, the month and year of manufacture, the certification statement and the VIN. The label also contains Gross Vehicle Weight Rating and Gross Axle Weight Ratings, wheel and tire data and information codes for additional vehicle data.

For specific and exact engine identification, a decal type label is attached to each engine. This label is attached to the front of the rocker arm cover on six-cylinder engines and the front of the *right* rocker arm cover on V6 and V8 engines. **Note**: *Exceptions may occur if brackets or equipment would prevent an unobstructed view of the label.* Always refer to this label when replacement parts are required, as parts often are different within engine families.

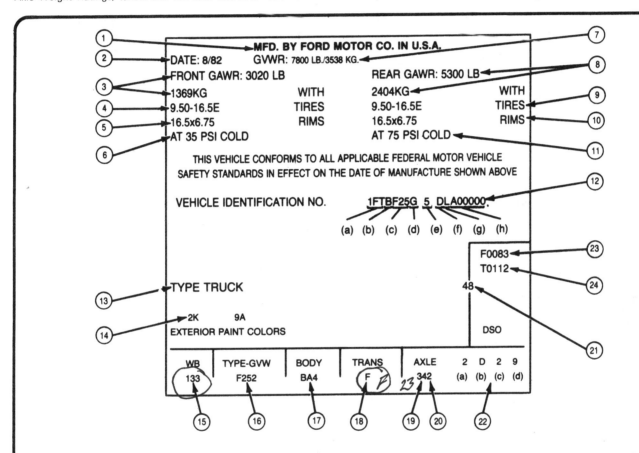

The Truck Safety Compliance Certification Label, located on the driver's door lock pillar, contains the following information:

1 Name and location of manufacturer
2 Date of manufacture
3 Front Gross Axle Weight Rating in pounds (LB) and kilograms (KG)
4 Front tire size
5 Front rim size
6 Front tire cold psi
7 Gross Vehicle Weight Rating in pounds (LB) and kilograms (KG)
8 Rear Gross Axle Weight Rating in pounds (LB) and kilograms (KG)
9 Rear tire size
10 Rear rim size
11 Rear tire cold psi
12 Vehicle Identification Number (VIN)
  A World manufacturer identifier
  B Brake type and Gross Vehicle Weight Rating (GVWR) class
  C Model or line, series chassis cab or body type
  D Engine type
  E Check digit
  F Model year
  G Assembly plant code
  H Sequential serial number
13 Type vehicle
14 Exterior paint codes (two sets of figures designates a two-tone)
15 Wheelbase in inches
16 Model code and GVW
17 Interior trim, seat and body/cab type
18 Transmission code
19 Rear axle code
20 Front axle code (if so equipped)
21 District/special order codes
22 Suspension identification codes
  A Auxiliary/option usage code (front)
  B Front spring code
  C Auxiliary/option usage code (rear)
  D Rear spring code
23 Front axle accessory reserve capacity in pounds
24 Total accessory reserve capacity in pounds

Maintenance techniques, tools and working facilities

Maintenance techniques

There are a number of techniques involved in maintenance and repair that will be referred to throughout this manual. Application of these techniques will enable the home mechanic to be more efficient, better organized and capable of performing the various tasks properly, which will ensure that the repair job is thorough and complete.

Fasteners

Fasteners, are nuts, bolts, studs and screws used to hold two or more parts together. There are a few things to keep in mind when working with fasteners. Almost all of them use a locking device of some type; either a lock washer, locknut, locking tab or thread adhesive. All threaded fasteners should be clean and straight, with undamaged threads and undamaged corners on the hex head where the wrench fits. Develop the habit of replacing damaged nuts and bolts with new ones. Special locknuts with nylon or fiber inserts can only be used once. If they are removed, they lose their locking ability and must be replaced with new ones.

Rusted nuts and bolts should be treated with a penetrating fluid to ease removal and prevent breakage. Some mechanics use turpentine in a spout-type oil can, which works quite well. After applying the rust penetrant, let it "work" for a few minutes before trying to loosen the nut or bolt. Badly rusted fasteners may have to be chiseled or sawed off or removed with a special nut breaker, available at tool stores.

If a bolt or stud breaks off in an assembly, it can be drilled and removed with a special tool commonly available for this purpose. Most automotive machine shops can perform this task, as well as other repair procedures (such as repair of threaded holes that have been stripped out).

Flat washers and lock washers, when removed from an assembly should always be replaced exactly as removed. Replace damaged washers with new ones. Always use a flat washer between a lock washer and any soft metal surface (such as aluminum), thin sheet metal or plastic.

Fastener sizes

For a number of reasons, automobile manufacturers are making wider and wider use of metric fasteners. Therefore, it is important to be able to tell the difference between standard (sometimes called U.S.,

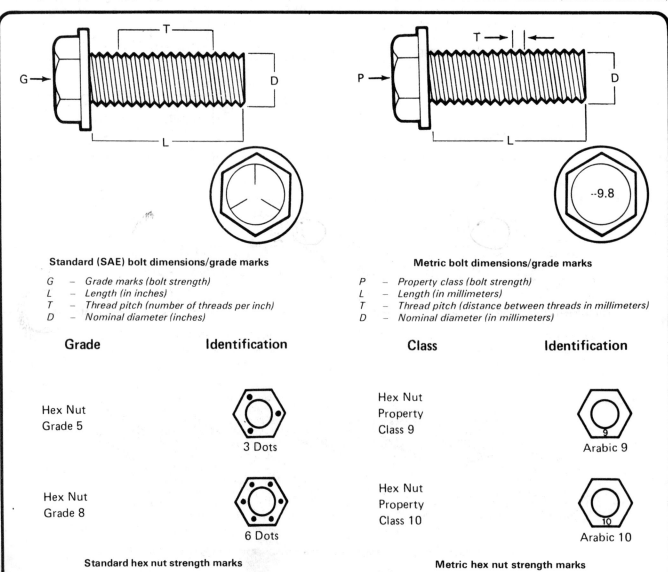

Standard (SAE) bolt dimensions/grade marks

G – Grade marks (bolt strength)
L – Length (in inches)
T – Thread pitch (number of threads per inch)
D – Nominal diameter (inches)

Grade	Identification
Hex Nut Grade 5	3 Dots
Hex Nut Grade 8	6 Dots

Standard hex nut strength marks

Metric bolt dimensions/grade marks

P – Property class (bolt strength)
L – Length (in millimeters)
T – Thread pitch (distance between threads in millimeters)
D – Nominal diameter (in millimeters)

Class	Identification
Hex Nut Property Class 9	Arabic 9
Hex Nut Property Class 10	Arabic 10

Metric hex nut strength marks

English or SAE) and metric hardware, since they cannot be interchanged.

All bolts, whether standard or metric, are sized according to diameter, thread pitch and length. For example, a standard $\frac{1}{2}$ – 13 x 1 bolt is $\frac{1}{2}$ inch in diameter, has 13 threads per inch and is 1 inch long. An M12 – 1.75 x 25 metric bolt is 12 mm in diameter, has a thread pitch of 1.75 mm (the distance between threads) and is 25 mm long. The two bolts are nearly identical, and easily confused, but they are not interchangeable.

In addition to the differences in diameter, thread pitch and length, metric and standard bolts can also be distinguished by examining the bolt heads. To begin with, the distance across the flats on a standard bolt head is measured in inches, while the same dimension on a metric bolt is measured in millimeters (the same is true for nuts). As a result, a standard wrench should not be used on a metric bolt and a metric wrench should not be used on a standard bolt. Also, standard bolts have slashes radiating out from the center of the head to denote the grade or strength of the bolt (which is an indication of the amount of torque that can be supplied to it). The greater the number of slashes, the greater the strength of the bolt (grades 0 through 5 are commonly used on automobiles). Metric bolts have a property class (grade) number, rather than a slash, molded into their heads to indicate bolt strength. In this case, the higher the number the stronger the bolt (property class numbers 8.8, 9.8 and 10.9 are commonly used on automobiles).

Strength markings can also be used to distinguish standard hex nuts from metric hex nuts. Standard nuts have dots stamped into one side, while metric nuts are marked with a number. The greater the number of dots, or the higher the number, the greater the strength of the nut.

Metric studs are also marked on their ends according to property class (grade). Larger studs are numbered (the same as metric bolts), while smaller studs carry a geometric code to denote grade.

It should be noted that many fasteners, especially Grades 0 through 2, have no distinguishing marks on them. When such is the case, the only way to determine whether it is standard or metric is to measure the thread pitch or compare it to a known fastener of the same size.

Since fasteners of the same size (both standard and metric) may have different strength ratings, be sure to reinstall any bolts, studs or nuts removed from your vehicle in their original locations. Also, when replacing a fastener with a new one, make sure that the new one has a strength rating equal to or greater than the original.

Tightening sequences and procedures

Most threaded fasteners should be tightened to a specific torque value (torque is basically a twisting force). Over-tightening the fastener can weaken it and lead to eventual breakage, while under-tightening can cause it to eventually come loose. Bolts, screws and studs, depending on the materials they are made of and their thread diameters, have specific torque values (many of which are noted in the Specifications at the beginning of each Chapter). Be sure to follow the torque recommendations closely. For fasteners not assigned a specific torque, a general torque value chart is presented here as a guide. As was previously mentioned, the sizes and grade of a fastener determine the amount of torque that can safely be applied to it. The figures listed here are approximate for Grade 2 and Grade 3 fasteners (higher grades can tolerate higher torque values).

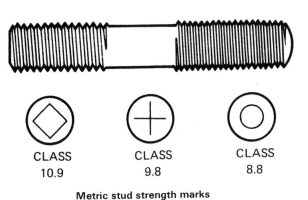

CLASS 10.9   CLASS 9.8   CLASS 8.8

Metric stud strength marks

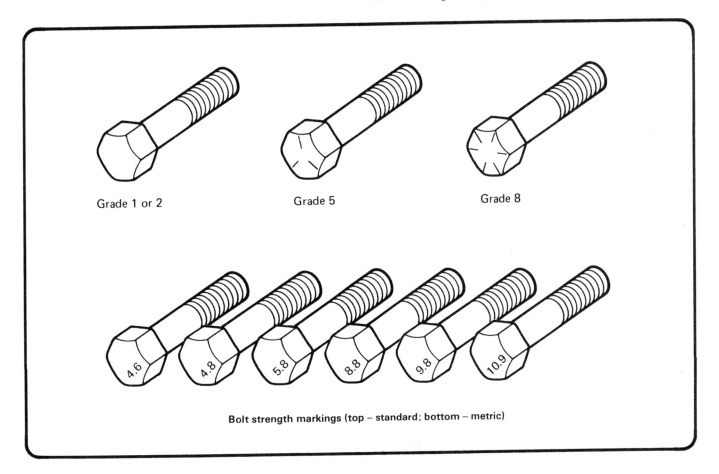

Grade 1 or 2   Grade 5   Grade 8

4.6   4.8   5.8   8.8   9.8   10.9

Bolt strength markings (top – standard; bottom – metric)

General torque values

	Ft-lb	Nm
Metric thread sizes		
M-6	6 to 9	9 to 12
M-8	14 to 21	19 to 28
M-10	28 to 40	38 to 54
M-12	50 to 71	68 to 96
M-14	80 to 140	109 to 154
Pipe thread sizes		
$\frac{1}{8}$	5 to 8	7 to 10
$\frac{1}{4}$	12 to 18	17 to 24
$\frac{3}{8}$	22 to 33	30 to 44
$\frac{1}{2}$	25 to 35	34 to 47
U.S. thread sizes		
$\frac{1}{4}$ - 20	6 to 9	9 to 12
$\frac{5}{16}$ - 18	12 to 18	17 to 24
$\frac{5}{16}$ - 24	14 to 20	19 to 27
$\frac{3}{8}$ - 16	22 to 32	30 to 43
$\frac{3}{8}$ - 24	27 to 38	37 to 51
$\frac{7}{16}$ - 14	40 to 55	55 to 74
$\frac{7}{16}$ - 20	40 to 60	55 to 81
$\frac{1}{2}$ - 13	55 to 80	75 to 108

Fasteners laid out in a pattern (i.e. cylinder head bolts, oil pan bolts, differential cover bolts, etc.) must be loosened and tightened in a definite sequence to avoid warping the component. This sequence will normally be shown in the appropriate Chapter. If a specific pattern is not given, the following procedures can be used to prevent warping. Initially, the bolts or nuts should be assembled finger-tight only. Next, they should be tightened one full turn each, in a crisscross or diagonal pattern. After each one has been tightened one full turn, return to the first one and tighten them all one-half turn, following the same pattern. Finally, tighten each of them one-quarter turn at a time until they all have been tightened to the proper torque value. To loosen and remove them the procedure would be reversed.

Component disassembly

Component disassembly should be done with care and purpose to help ensure that the parts go back together properly. Always keep track of the sequence in which parts are removed. Make note of special characteristics or marks on parts that can be installed more than one way (such as a grooved thrust washer on a shaft). It is a good idea to lay the disassembled parts out on a clean surface in the order that they were removed. It may also be helpful to make simple sketches or take instant photos of components before removal.

When removing fasteners from an assembly, keep track of their locations. Sometimes threading a bolt back in a part or putting the washers and nut back on a stud can prevent mixups later. If nuts and bolts cannot be returned to their original locations, they should be kept in a compartmented box or a series of small boxes. A cupcake or muffin tin is ideal for this purpose, since each cavity can hold the bolts and nuts from a particular area (i.e. oil pan bolts, valve cover bolts, engine mount bolts, etc.). A pan of this type is especially helpful when working on assemblies with very small parts such as the carburetor, alternator, valve train or interior dash and trim pieces. The cavities can be marked with paint or tape to identify the contents.

Whenever wiring looms, harnesses or connectors are separated, it's a good idea to identify them with numbered pieces of masking tape so that they can be easily reconnected.

Gasket sealing surfaces

Throughout any vehicle, gaskets are used to seal the mating surfaces between two parts and keep lubricants, fluids, vacuum or pressure contained in an assembly.

Many times these gaskets are coated with a liquid or paste-type gasket sealing compound before assembly. Age, heat and pressure can sometimes cause the two parts to stick together so tightly that they are very difficult to separate. Often, the assembly can be loosened by striking it with a soft-faced hammer near the mating surfaces. A regular hammer can be used if a block of wood is placed between the hammer and the part. Do not hammer on cast parts or parts that could be easily damaged. With any particularly stubborn part, always recheck to see that every fastener has been removed.

Avoid using a screwdriver or bar to pry apart an assembly, as they can easily mar the gasket sealing surfaces of the parts (which must remain smooth). If prying is absolutely necessary, use an old broom handle, but keep in mind that extra clean-up will be necessary if the wood splinters.

After the parts are separated, the old gasket must be carefully scraped off and the gasket surfaces cleaned. Stubborn gasket material can be soaked with rust penetrant or treated with a special chemical to soften it so that it can be easily scraped off. A scraper can be fashioned from a piece of copper tubing by flattening and sharpening one end. Copper is recommended because it is usually softer than the surfaces to be scraped, which reduces the chance of gouging the part. Some gaskets can be removed with a wire brush, but regardless of the method used, the mating surfaces must be left clean and smooth. If, for some reason the gasket surface is gouged, then a gasket sealer thick enough to fill scratches will have to be used upon reassembly of the components. For most applications, a non-drying (or semi-drying) gasket sealer should be used.

Hose removal tips

Caution: *If the vehicle is equipped with air conditioning, do not disconnect any of the a/c hoses without first having the system depressurized by a dealer service department or air conditioning specialist.*

Hose removal precautions closely parallel gasket removal precautions. Avoid scratching or gouging the surface that the hose mates against or the connection may leak. This is especially true for radiator hoses. Because of various chemical reactions, the rubber in hoses can bond itself to the metal spigot that the hose fits over. To remove a hose, first loosen the hose clamps that secure it to the spigot. Then, with slip-joint pliers, grab the hose at the clamp and rotate it around the spigot. Work it back and forth until it is completely free, then pull it off. Silicone or other lubricants will ease removal if they can be applied between the hose and the spigot. Apply the same lubricant to the inside of the hose and the outside of the spigot to simplify installation.

As the last resort (and if the hose is to be replaced with a new one anyway), the rubber can be slit with a knife and the hose peeled from its spigot. If this must be done, be careful that the metal connection is not damaged.

If a hose clamp is broken or damaged, do not re-use it. Wire-type clamps usually weaken with age, so it is a good idea to replace them with screw-type clamps whenever a hose is removed.

Tools

A selection of good tools is a basic requirement for anyone who plans to maintain and repair his or her own vehicle. For the owner who has few tools, if any, the initial investment might seem high, but when compared to the spiraling costs of professional auto maintenance and repair, it is a wise one.

To help the owner decide which tools are needed to perform the tasks detailed in this manual, the following tool lists are offered: *Maintenance and minor repair, Repair and overhaul* and *Special*. The newcomer to practical mechanics should start off with the *Maintenance and minor repair* tool kit, which is adequate for the simpler jobs performed on a vehicle. Then, as his confidence and experience grow, he can tackle more difficult tasks, buying additional tools as they are needed. Eventually the basic kit will be expanded into the *Repair and overhaul* tool set. Over a period of time, the experienced do-it-yourselfer will assemble a tool set complete enough for most repair and overhaul procedures and will add tools from the *Special* category when he feels the expense is justified by the frequency of use.

Maintenance and minor repair tool kit

The tools in this list should be considered the minimum for performance of routine maintenance, servicing and minor repair work. We recommend the purchase of combination wrenches (box-end and open-end combined in one wrench); while more expensive than open-ended ones, they offer the advantages of both types of wrench.

> Combination wrench set ($\frac{1}{4}$ in to 1 in or 6 mm to 19 mm)
> Adjustable wrench – 8 in
> Spark plug wrench (with rubber insert)
> Spark plug gap adjusting tool
> Feeler gauge set
> Brake bleeder wrench
> Standard screwdriver ($\frac{5}{16}$ in x 6 in)
> Phillips screwdriver (No.2 x 6 in)
> Combination pliers – 6 in
> Hacksaw and assortment of blades
> Tire pressure gauge
> Grease gun
> Oil can
> Fine emery cloth
> Wire brush
> Battery post and cable cleaning tool
> Oil filter wrench
> Funnel (medium size)
> Safety goggles
> Jack stands (2)
> Drain pan

Note: *If basic tune-ups are going to be a part of routine maintenance, it will be necessary to purchase a good quality stroboscopic timing light and a combination tachometer/dwell meter. Although they are included in the list of Special tools, they are mentioned here because they are absolutely necessary for tuning most vehicles properly.*

Repair and overhaul tool set

These tools are essential for anyone who plans to perform major repairs and are in addition to those in the *Maintenance and minor repair tool kit*. Included is a comprehensive set of sockets which, though expensive, are invaluable because of their versatility (especially when various extensions and drives are available). We recommend the $\frac{1}{2}$ in drive over the $\frac{3}{8}$ in drive. Although the larger drive is bulky and more expensive, it has the capability of accepting a very wide range of large sockets (ideally, the mechanic would have a $\frac{3}{8}$ in drive set and a $\frac{1}{2}$ in drive set).

> Socket set(s)
> Reversible ratchet
> Extension – 10 in

> Universal joint
> Torque wrench (same size drive as sockets)
> Ballpein hammer – 8 oz
> Soft-faced hammer (plastic/rubber)
> Standard screwdriver ($\frac{1}{4}$ in x 6 in)
> Standard screwdriver (stubby – $\frac{5}{16}$ in)
> Phillips screwdriver (No.3 x 8 in)
> Phillips screwdriver (stubby – No.2)
> Pliers – vise grip
> Pliers – lineman's
> Pliers – needle nose
> Pliers – spring clip (internal and external)
> Cold chisel – $\frac{1}{2}$ in
> Scriber
> Scraper (made from flattened copper tubing)
> Center punch
> Pin punches ($\frac{1}{16}$, $\frac{1}{8}$, $\frac{3}{16}$ in)
> Steel rule/straightedge – 12 in
> Allen wrench set ($\frac{1}{8}$ to $\frac{3}{8}$ in or 4 mm to 10 mm)
> A selection of files
> Wire brush (large)
> Jack stands (second set)
> Jack (scissor or hydraulic type)

Note: *Another tool which is often useful is an electric drill motor with a chuck capacity of $\frac{3}{8}$ in (and a set of good quality drill bits).*

Special tools

The tools in this list include those which are not used regularly, are expensive to buy, or which need to be used in accordance with their manufacturer's instructions. Unless these tools will be used frequently, it is not very economical to purchase many of them. A consideration would be to split the cost and use between yourself and a friend or friends. In addition, most of these tools can be obtained from a tool rental shop on a temporary basis.

This list contains only those tools and instruments widely available to the public, and not those special tools produced by vehicle manufacturers for distribution to dealer service departments. Occasionally, references to the manufacturer's special tools are included in the text of this manual. Generally, an alternate method of doing the job without the special tool is offered. However, sometimes there is no alternative to their use. Where this is the case, and the tool cannot be purchased or borrowed, the work should be turned over to the dealer, a repair shop or an automotive machine shop.

> Valve spring compressor
> Piston ring groove cleaning tool
> Piston ring compressor
> Piston ring installation tool
> Cylinder compression gauge
> Cylinder ridge reamer
> Cylinder surfacing hone
> Cylinder bore gauge
> Micrometer(s) and/or dial calipers
> Hydraulic lifter removal tool
> Balljoint separator
> Universal-type puller
> Impact screwdriver

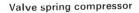

Valve spring compressor

Piston groove cleaning tool ring

Piston ring compressor

Piston ring removal/installation tool

Cylinder ridge reamer

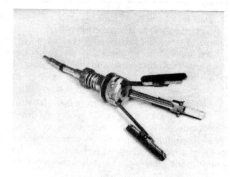

Cylinder surfacing hone

Cylinder bore gauge

Micrometer set

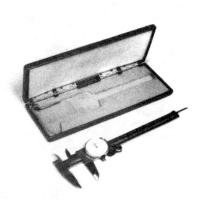

Dial caliper

Hydraulic lifter removal tool

Universal-type puller

Dial indicator set

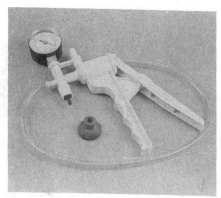

Hand-operated vacuum pump

Brake shoe spring tool

Dial indicator set
Stroboscopic timing light (inductive pickup)
Hand-operated vacuum/pressure pump
Tachometer/dwell meter
Universal electrical multimeter
Cable hoist
Brake spring removal and installation tools
Floor jack

Buying tools

For the do-it-yourselfer who is just starting to get involved in vehicle maintenance and repair, there are a couple of options available when purchasing tools. If maintenance and minor repair is the extent of the work to be done, the purchase of individual tools is satisfactory. If, on the other hand, extensive work is planned, it would be a good idea to purchase a modest tool set from one of the large retail chain stores. A set can usually be bought at substantial savings over the individual tool prices (and they often come with a tool box). As additional tools are needed, add-on sets, individual tools and a larger tool box can be purchased to expand the tool selection. Building a tool set gradually allows the cost of the tools to be spread over a longer period of time and gives the mechanic the freedom to choose only those tools that will actually be used.

Tool stores will often be the only source of some of the special tools that are needed, but regardless of where tools are bought, try to avoid cheap ones (especially when buying screwdrivers and sockets) because they won't last very long. The expense involved in replacing cheap tools will eventually be greater than the initial cost of quality tools.

Care and maintenance of tools

Good tools are expensive, so it makes sense to treat them with respect. Keep them in a clean and usable condition and store them properly when not in use. Always wipe off any dirt, grease or metal chips before putting them away. Never leave tools lying around in the work area. Upon completion of a job, always check closely under the hood for tools that may have been left there (so they don't get lost during a test drive).

Some tools, such as screwdrivers, pliers, wrenches and sockets, can be hung on a panel mounted on the garage or workshop wall, while others should be kept in a tool box or tray. Measuring instruments, gauges, meters, etc. must be carefully stored where they cannot be damaged by weather or impact from other tools.

When tools are used with care and stored properly, they will last a very long time. Even with the best of care, tools will wear out if used frequently. When a tool is damaged or worn out, replace it; subsequent jobs will be safer and more enjoyable if you do.

Working facilities

Not to be overlooked when discussing tools is the workshop. If anything more than routine maintenance is to be carried out, some sort of suitable work area is essential.

It is understood, and appreciated, that many home mechanics do not have a good workshop or garage available and end up removing an engine or doing major repairs outside. It is recommended, however, that the overhaul or repair be completed under the cover of a roof.

A clean, flat workbench or table of comfortable working height is an absolute necessity. The workbench should be equipped with a vise that has a jaw opening of at least four inches.

As mentioned previously, some clean, dry storage space is also required for tools, as well as the lubricants, fluids, cleaning solvents, etc. which soon become necessary.

Sometimes waste oil and fluids, drained from the engine or transmission during normal maintenance or repairs, present a disposal problem. To avoid pouring oil on the ground or into the sewage system, simply pour the used fluids into large containers, seal them with caps and deliver them to a local recycling center or disposal facility. Plastic jugs (such as old antifreeze containers) are ideal for this purpose.

Always keep a supply of old newspapers and clean rags available. Old towels are excellent for mopping up spills. Many mechanics use rolls of paper towels for most work because they are readily available and disposable. To keep the area under the vehicle clean, a large cardboard box can be cut open and flattened to protect the garage or shop floor.

Whenever working over a painted surface (such as when leaning over a fender to service something under the hood), always cover it with an old blanket or bedspread to protect the finish. Vinyl covered pads, made especially for this purpose, are available at auto parts stores.

Jacking and towing

Jacking

The jack supplied with the vehicle should be used for raising the vehicle during a tire change or when placing jackstands under the frame. **Under no circumstances should work be performed beneath the vehicle or the engine started while this jack is being used as the only means of support.**

All vehicles are supplied with a scissors-type jack which fits into a notch in the vertical rocker panel flange nearest to the wheel being changed.

The vehicle should be on level ground with the wheels blocked and the transmission in Park (automatic) or Reverse (manual). Pry off the hub cap (if equipped) using the tapered end of the lug wrench. Loosen the wheel nuts one half turn and leave them in place until the wheel is raised off the ground.

Place the jack under the side of the vehicle in the jacking notch. Use the supplied wrench to turn the jackscrew clockwise until the wheel is raised off the ground. Remove the wheel nuts, pull off the wheel and replace it with the spare.

With the beveled side in, replace the wheel nuts and tighten them until snug. Lower the vehicle by turning the jackscrew counterclockwise. Remove the jack and tighten the nuts in a diagonal fashion. Replace the hubcap by placing it into position and using the heel of your hand or a rubber mallet to seat it.

Towing

The vehicle can be towed with all four wheels on the ground provided speeds do not exceed 35 mph and the distance is not over 50 miles, otherwise transmission damage can result.

Towing equipment specifically designed for that purpose should be used and should be attached to the main structural members of the vehicle and not the bumper or brackets.

Safety is a major consideration when towing a vehicle and all applicable state and local laws must be obeyed. A safety chain system must be used for all towing.

While towing, the parking brake should be fully released and the transmission should be in Neutral. The steering must be unlocked (ignition switch in the Off position). Remember that power steering and power brakes will not work with the engine off.

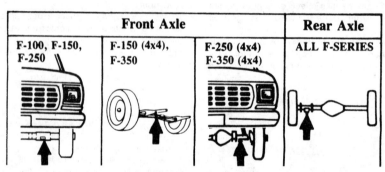

Pick-up truck jacking points

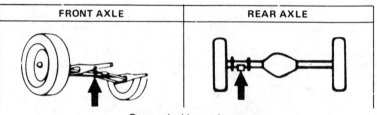

Bronco jacking points

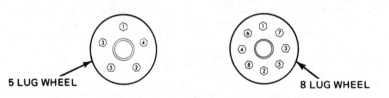

Wheel lug nut tightening sequence

Automotive chemicals and lubricants

A number of automotive chemicals and lubricants are available for use in vehicle maintenance and repair. They include a wide variety of products ranging from cleaning solvents and degreasers to lubricants and protective sprays for rubber, plastic and vinyl.

Contact point/spark plug cleaner is a solvent used to clean oily film and dirt from points, grime from electrical connectors and oil deposits from spark plugs. It is oil free and leaves no residue. It can also be used to remove gum and varnish from carburetor jets and other orifices.

Carburetor cleaner is similar to contact point/spark plug cleaner but it is a stronger solvent and may leave a slight oily residue. It is not recommended for cleaning electrical components or connections.

Brake system cleaner is used to remove grease or brake fluid from brake system components where clean surfaces are absolutely necessary and petroleum-based solvents cannot be used. It also leaves no residue.

Silicone-based lubricants are used to protect rubber parts such as hoses, weatherstripping and grommets and are used as lubricants for hinges and locks.

Multi-purpose grease is an all-purpose lubricant used whenever grease is more practical than a liquid lubricant such as oil. Some multi-purpose grease is white and specially formulated to be more resistant to water than ordinary grease.

Bearing grease/wheel bearing grease is a heavy grease used where increased loads and friction are encountered (i.e. wheel bearings, universal joints, etc.).

High temperature wheel bearing grease is designed to withstand the extreme temperatures encountered by wheel bearings in disc brake equipped vehicles. It usually contains molybdenum disulfide, which is a 'dry' type lubricant.

Gear oil (sometimes called gear lube) is a specially designed oil used in differentials, manual transmissions and transfer cases, as well as other areas where high friction, high temperature lubrication is required. It is available in a number of viscosities (weights) for various applications.

Motor oil, of course, is the lubricant specially formulated for use in the engine. It normally contains a wide variety of additives to prevent corrosion and reduce foaming and wear. Motor oil comes in various weights (viscosity ratings) of from 5 to 80. The recommended weight of the oil depends on the seasonal temperature and the demands on the engine. Light oil is used in cold climates and under light load conditions; heavy oil is used in hot climates and where high loads are encountered. Multi-viscosity oils are designed to have characteristics of both light and heavy oils and are available in a number of weights from 5W-20 to 20W-50.

Oil additives range from viscosity index improvers to slick chemical treatments that purportedly reduce friction. It should be noted that most oil manufacturers caution against using additives with their oils.

Gas additives perform several functions, depending on their chemical makeup. They usually contain solvents that help dissolve gum and varnish that build up on carburetor and intake parts. They also serve to break down carbon deposits that form on the inside surfaces of the combustion chambers. Some additives contain upper cylinder lubricants for valves and piston rings.

Brake fluid is a specially formulated hydraulic fluid that can withstand the heat and pressure encountered in brake systems. Care must be taken that this fluid does not come in contact with painted surfaces or plastics. An opened container should always be resealed to prevent contamination by water or dirt.

Undercoating is a petroleum-based, tar-like substance that is designed to protect metal surfaces on the underside of a vehicle from corrosion. It also acts as a sound deadening agent by insulating the bottom of the vehicle.

Weatherstrip cement is used to bond weatherstripping around doors, windows and trunk lids. It is sometimes used to attach trim pieces as well.

Degreasers are heavy-duty solvents used to remove grease and grime that accumulate on engine and chassis components. They can be sprayed or brushed on and, depending on the type, are rinsed with either water or solvent.

Solvents are used alone or in combination with degreasers to clean parts and assemblies during repair and overhaul. The home mechanic should use only solvents that are non-flammable and that do not produce irritating fumes.

Gasket sealing compounds may be used in conjunction with gaskets, to improve their sealing capabilities, or alone, to seal metal-to-metal joints. Many gaskets can withstand extreme heat, some are impervious to gasoline and lubricants, while others are capable of filling and sealing large cavities. Depending on the intended use, gasket sealers either dry hard or stay relatively soft and pliable. They are usually applied by hand, with a brush, or are sprayed on the gasket sealing surfaces.

Thread cement is an adhesive locking compound that prevents threaded fasteners from loosening because of vibration. It is available in a variety of types for different applications.

Moisture dispersants are usually sprays that can be used to dry out electrical components such as the distributor, fuse block and wiring connectors. Some types can also be used as a treatment for rubber and as a lubricant for hinges, cables and locks.

Waxes and polishes are used to help protect painted and plated surfaces from the weather. Different types of paint may require the use of different types of wax or polish. Some polishes utilize a chemical or abrasive cleaner to help remove the top layer of oxidized (dull) paint in older vehicles. In recent years, many non-wax polishes that contain a wide variety of chemicals such as polymers and silicones have been introduced. These non-wax polishes are usually easier to apply and last longer than conventional waxes and polishes.

Safety first!

Regardless of how enthusiastic you may be about getting on with the job at hand, take the time to ensure that your safety is not jeopardized. A moment's lack of attention can result in an accident, as can failure to observe certain simple safety precautions. The possibility of an accident will always exist, and the following points should not be considered a comprehensive list of all dangers. Rather, they are intended to make you aware of the risks and to encourage a safety conscious approach to all work you carry out on your vehicle.

Essential DOs and DON'Ts

DON'T rely on a jack when working under the vehicle. Always use approved jackstands to support the weight of the vehicle and place them under the recommended lift or support points.

DON'T attempt to loosen extremely tight fasteners (i.e. wheel lug nuts) while the vehicle is on a jack — it may fall.

DON'T start the engine without first making sure that the transmission is in Neutral (or Park where applicable) and the parking brake is set.

DON'T remove the radiator cap from a hot cooling system — let it cool or cover it with a cloth and release the pressure gradually.

DON'T attempt to drain the engine oil until you are sure it has cooled to the point that it will not burn you.

DON'T touch any part of the engine or exhaust system until it has cooled sufficiently to avoid burns.

DON'T siphon toxic liquids such as gasoline, antifreeze and brake fluid by mouth, or allow them to remain on your skin.

DON'T inhale brake lining dust — it is potentially hazardous (see *Asbestos* below)

DON'T allow spilled oil or grease to remain on the floor — wipe it up before someone slips on it.

DON'T use loose fitting wrenches or other tools which may slip and cause injury.

DON'T push on wrenches when loosening or tightening nuts or bolts. Always try to pull the wrench toward you. If the situation calls for pushing the wrench away, push with an open hand to avoid scraped knuckles if the wrench should slip.

DON'T attempt to lift a heavy component alone — get someone to help you.

DON'T rush or take unsafe shortcuts to finish a job.

DON'T allow children or animals in or around the vehicle while you are working on it.

DO wear eye protection when using power tools such as a drill, sander, bench grinder, etc. and when working under a vehicle.

DO keep loose clothing and long hair well out of the way of moving parts.

DO make sure that any hoist used has a safe working load rating adequate for the job.

DO get someone to check on you periodically when working alone on a vehicle.

DO carry out work in a logical sequence and make sure that everything is correctly assembled and tightened.

DO keep chemicals and fluids tightly capped and out of the reach of children and pets.

DO remember that your vehicle's safety affects that of yourself and others. If in doubt on any point, get professional advice.

Asbestos

Certain friction, insulating, sealing, and other products — such as brake linings, brake bands, clutch linings, torque converters, gaskets, etc. — contain asbestos. *Extreme care must be taken to avoid inhalation of dust from such products since it is hazardous to health.* If in doubt, assume that they *do* contain asbestos.

Fire

Remember at all times that gasoline is highly flammable. Never smoke or have any kind of open flame around when working on a vehicle. But the risk does not end there. A spark caused by an electrical short circuit, by two metal surfaces contacting each other, or even by static electricity built up in your body under certain conditions, can ignite gasoline vapors, which in a confined space are highly explosive. Do not, under any circumstances, use gasoline for cleaning parts. Use an approved safety solvent.

Always disconnect the battery ground (–) cable *at the battery* before working on any part of the fuel system or electrical system. Never risk spilling fuel on a hot engine or exhaust component.

It is strongly recommended that a fire extinguisher suitable for use on fuel and electrical fires be kept handy in the garage or workshop at all times. Never try to extinguish a fuel or electrical fire with water.

Fumes

Certain fumes are highly toxic and can quickly cause unconsciousness and even death if inhaled to any extent. Gasoline vapor falls into this category, as do the vapors from some cleaning solvents. Any draining or pouring of such volatile fluids should be done in a well ventilated area.

When using cleaning fluids and solvents, read the instructions on the container carefully. Never use materials from unmarked containers.

Never run the engine in an enclosed space, such as a garage. Exhaust fumes contain carbon monoxide, which is extremely poisonous. If you need to run the engine, always do so in the open air, or at least have the rear of the vehicle outside the work area.

If you are fortunate enough to have the use of an inspection pit, never drain or pour gasoline and never run the engine while the vehicle is over the pit. The fumes, being heavier than air, will concentrate in the pit with possibly lethal results.

The battery

Never create a spark or allow a bare light bulb near the battery. The battery normally gives off a certain amount of hydrogen gas, which is highly explosive.

Always disconnect the battery ground (–) cable *at the battery* before working on the fuel or electrical systems.

If possible, loosen the filler caps or cover when charging the battery from an external source. Do not charge at an excessive rate or the battery may burst.

Take care when adding water and when carrying a battery. The electrolyte, even when diluted, is very corrosive and should not be allowed to contact clothing or skin.

Always wear eye protection when cleaning the battery to prevent the caustic deposits from entering your eyes.

Household current

When using an electric power tool, inspection light, etc., which operates on household current, always make sure that the tool is correctly connected to its plug and that, where necessary, it is properly grounded. Do not use such items in damp conditions and, again, do not create a spark or apply excessive heat in the vicinity of fuel or fuel vapor.

Secondary ignition system voltage

A severe electric shock can result from touching certain parts of the ignition system (such as the spark plug wires) when the engine is running or being cranked, particularly if components are damp or the insulation is defective. In the case of an electronic ignition system, the secondary system voltage is much higher and could prove fatal.

Troubleshooting

Contents

This section provides an easy-reference guide to the more common faults which may occur during the operation of your vehicle. These faults and their probable causes are grouped under their respective systems i.e. Engine, Cooling system, etc., and also refer to the Chapter and/or Section which deals with the problem.

Remember that successful troubleshooting is not a mysterious 'black art' practiced only by professional mechanics, it's simply the result of a bit of knowledge combined with an intelligent, systematic approach to the problem. Always work by a process of elimination, starting with the simplest solution and working through to the most complex – and never overlook the obvious. Anyone can forget to fill the gas tank or leave the lights on overnight, so don't assume that you are above such oversights.

Finally, always get clear in your mind why a problem has occurred and take steps to ensure that it doesn't happen again. If the electrical system fails because of a poor connection, check all other connections in the system to make sure that they don't fail as well; if a particular fuse continues to blow, find out why – don't just go on replacing fuses. Remember, failure of a small component can often be indicative of potential failure or incorrect functioning of a more important component or system.

Engine

1 Engine will not rotate when attempting to start

1 Battery terminal connection loose or corroded. Check the cable terminals at the battery; tighten or clean off corrosion as necessary.
2 Battery discharged or faulty. If the cable connectors are clean and tight on the battery posts, turn the key to the On position and switch on the headlights and/or windshield wipers. If these fail to function, the battery is discharged.
3 Automatic transmission not fully engaged in Park or clutch not fully depressed.
4 Broken, loose or disconnected wiring in the starting circuit. Inspect all wiring and connectors at the battery, starter solenoid (at lower right side of engine) and ignition switch (on steering column).
5 Starter motor pinion jammed on flywheel ring gear. If manual transmission, place shift in gear and rock the vehicle to manually turn the engine. Remove starter and inspect pinion (Chapter 5) and flywheel (Chapter 5) at earliest convenience.
6 Starter solenoid faulty (Chapter 5).
7 Starter motor faulty (Chapter 5).
8 Ignition switch faulty (Chapter 10).

2 Engine rotates but will not start

1 Fuel tank empty.
2 Battery discharged (engine rotates slowly). Check the operation of electrical components as described in previous Section (Chapter 1).
3 Battery terminal connections loose or corroded. See previous Section.
4 Carburetor flooded and/or fuel level in carburetor incorrect. This will usually be accompanied by a strong fuel odor from under the hood. Wait a few minutes, depress the accelerator pedal all the way to the floor and attempt to start the engine.
5 Choke control inoperative (Chapters 1 and 4).
6 Fuel not reaching carburetor. With ignition switch in Off position, open hood, remove the top plate of air cleaner assembly and observe the top of the carburetor (manually move choke plate back if necessary). Have an assistant depress the accelerator pedal fully and make sure that fuel spurts into carburetor. If not, check fuel filter (Chapters 1 and 4), fuel lines and fuel pump (Chapter 4).
7 Excessive moisture on, or damage to, ignition components (Chapter 5).
8 Worn, faulty or incorrectly adjusted spark plugs (Chapter 1).
9 Broken, loose or disconnected wiring in the starting circuit (see previous Section).
10 Distributor loose, causing ignition timing to change. Turn the distributor as necessary to start the engine, then set ignition timing as soon as possible (Chapter 1).
11 Broken, loose or disconnected wires at the ignition coil, or faulty coil (Chapter 5).

3 Starter motor operates without rotating engine

1 Starter pinion sticking. Remove the starter (Chapter 5) and inspect.
2 Starter pinion or engine flywheel teeth worn or broken. Remove the inspection cover at the rear of the engine and inspect.

4 Engine hard to start when cold

1 Battery discharged or low. Check as described in Section 1.
2 Choke control inoperative or out of adjustment (Chapter 4).
3 Carburetor flooded (see Section 2).
4 Fuel supply not reaching the carburetor (see Section 4).
5 Carburetor worn and in need of overhauling (Chapter 4).

5 Engine hard to start when hot

1 Choke sticking in the closed position (Chapter 4).
2 Carburetor flooded (see Section 2).
3 Air filter in need of replacement (Chapter 1).
4 Fuel not reaching the carburetor (see Section 4).

6 Starter motor noisy or excessively rough in engagement

1 Pinion or flywheel gear teeth worn or broken. Remove the inspection cover at the rear of the engine and inspect.
2 Starter motor retaining bolts loose or missing.

7 Engine starts but stops immediately

1 Loose or faulty electrical connections at distributor, coil or alternator.
2 Insufficient fuel reaching the carburetor. Disconnect the fuel line at the carburetor and remove the filter (Chapter 1). Place a container under the disconnected fuel line. Observe the flow of fuel from the line. If little or none at all, check for blockage in the lines and/or replace the fuel pump (Chapter 4).
3 Vacuum leak at the gasket surfaces of the intake manifold and/or carburetor. Make sure that all mounting bolts (nuts) are tightened to specifications and that all vacuum hoses connected to the carburetor and manifold are positioned properly and in good condition.

8 Engine 'lopes' while idling or idles erratically

1 Vacuum leakage. Check mounting bolts (nuts) at the carburetor and intake manifold for tightness. Check that all vacuum hoses are connected and in good condition. Use a doctor's stethoscope or a length of fuel line hose held against your ear to listen for vacuum leaks while the engine is running. A hissing sound will be heard. A soapy water solution will also detect leaks. Check the carburetor and intake manifold gasket surfaces.
2 Leaking EGR valve or plugged PCV valve (see Chapters 1 and 6).
3 Air filter clogged and in need of replacement (Chapter 1).
4 Fuel pump not delivering sufficient fuel to the carburetor (see Section 4).
5 Carburetor out of adjustment (Chapter 4).
6 Leaking head gasket. If this is suspected, take the vehicle to a repair shop or dealer where this can be pressure checked without the need to remove the heads.
7 Timing chain or timing gears worn and in need of replacement (Chapter 1).
8 Camshaft lobes worn, necessitating the removal of the camshaft for inspection (Chapter 2).

9 Engine misses at idle speed

1 Spark plugs faulty or not gapped properly (Chapter 1 or 5).
2 Faulty spark plug wires (Chapter 1).
3 Carburetor choke not operating properly (Chapter 1).

4 Sticking or faulty emissions systems (Chapter 6).
5 Clogged fuel filter and/or foreign matter in fuel. Remove the fuel filter (Chapter 1) and inspect.
6 Vacuum leaks at carburetor, intake manifold or hose connections. Check as described in Section 8.
7 Incorrect speed (Chapter 1) or idle mixture (Chapter 1).
8 Incorrect ignition timing (Chapter 1).
9 Uneven or low cylinder compression. Remove plugs and use compression tester as per manufacturer's instructions.

10 Engine misses throughout driving range

1 Carburetor fuel filter clogged and/or impurities in the fuel system (Chapter 1). Also check fuel output at the carburetor (see Section 7).
2 Faulty or incorrectly gapped spark plugs (Chapter 1).
3 Incorrectly set ignition timing (Chapter 1).
4 Check for a cracked distributor cap, disconnected distributor wires or damage to the distributor components (Chapter 1).
5 Leaking spark plug wires (Chapter 1).
6 Emission system components faulty (Chapter 6).
7 Low or uneven cylinder compression pressures. Remove spark plugs and test compression with gauge (Chapter 1).
8 Weak or faulty ignition system (see Chapter 5).
9 Vacuum leaks at carburetor, intake manifold or vacuum hoses (see Section 8).

11 Engine stalls

1 Carburetor idle speed incorrectly set (Chapter 1).
2 Carburetor fuel filter clogged and/or water and impurities in the fuel system (Chapter 1).
3 Choke improperly adjusted or sticking (Chapter 1).
4 Distributor components damp, points out of adjustment or damage to distributor cap, rotor etc. (Chapter 5).
5 Emission system components faulty (Chapter 6).
6 Faulty or incorrectly gapped spark plugs (Chapter 1). Also check spark plug wires (Chapter 1).
7 Vacuum leak at the carburetor, intake manifold or vacuum hoses. Check as described in Section 8.
8 Valve clearances incorrectly set (Chapter 2).

12 Engine lacks power

1 Incorrect ignition timing (Chapter 1).
2 Excessive play in distributor shaft. At the same time check for worn rotor, faulty distributor cap, wires, etc. (Chapter 5).
3 Faulty or incorrectly gapped spark plugs (Chapter 1).
4 Carburetor not adjusted or excessively worn (Chapter 4).
5 Faulty system coil (Chapter 5).
6 Brakes binding (Chapter 1).
7 Automatic transmission fluid level incorrect, causing slippage (Chapter 1).
8 Manual transmission clutch slipping (Chapter 8).
9 Fuel filter clogged and/or impurities in the fuel system (Chapter 1).
10 Emissions control system not functioning properly (Chapter 6).
11 Use of sub-standard fuel. Fill tank with proper octane fuel.
12 Low or uneven cylinder compression pressures. Test with compression tester, which will detect leaking valves and/or blown head gasket (Chapter 1).

13 Engine backfires

1 Emissions system not functioning properly (Chapter 6).
2 Ignition timing incorrect (Section 1).
3 Carburetor in need of adjustment or worn excessively (Chapter 4).
4 Vacuum leak at carburetor, intake manifold or vacuum hoses. Check as described in Section 8.
5 Valve clearances incorrectly set, and/or valves sticking (Chapter 2).

14 Pinging or knocking engine sounds during acceleration or uphill

1 Incorrect grade of fuel. Fill tank with fuel of the proper octane rating.
2 Ignition timing incorrect (Chapter 1).
3 Carburetor in need of adjustment (Chapter 4).
4 Improper spark plugs. Check plug type with that specified on tune-up decal located inside engine compartment. Also check plugs and wires for damage (Chapter 1).
5 Worn or damaged distributor components (Chapter 5).
6 Faulty emissions system (Chapter 6).
7 Vacuum leak (check as described in Section 8).

15 Engine 'diesels' (continues to run) after switching off

1 Idle speed too fast (Chapter 1).
2 Electrical solenoid at side of carburetor not functioning properly (not all models, see Chapter 4).
3 Ignition timing incorrectly adjusted (Chapter 1).
4 Air cleaner valve not operating properly (Chapter 6).
5 Excessive engine operating temperatures. Probable causes of this are malfunctioning thermostat, clogged radiator, faulty water pump (see Chapter 3).

Engine electrical

16 Battery will not hold a charge

1 Alternator drivebelt defective or not adjusted properly (Chapter 1).
2 Electrolyte level too low or too weak (Chapter 1).
3 Battery terminals loose or corroded (Chapter 1).
4 Alternator not charging properly (Chapter 5).
5 Loose, broken or faulty wiring in the charging circuit (Chapter 10).
6 Short in vehicle circuitry causing a continual drain on battery.
7 Battery internal defect.

17 Ignition light fails to go out

1 Fault in alternator or charging circuit (Chapter 5).
2 Alternator drivebelt defective or not properly adjusted (Chapter 1).

18 Ignition light fails to come on when key is turned on

1 Ignition light bulb faulty (Chapter 10).
2 Alternator faulty (Chapter 5).
3 Fault in the printed circuit, dash wiring or bulb holder (Chapter 10).

Engine fuel system

19 Excessive fuel consumption

1 Dirty or choked air filter element (Chapter 1).
2 Incorrectly set ignition timing (Chapter 1).
3 Choke sticking or improperly adjusted (Chapter 1).
4 Emission system not functioning properly (not all vehicles, see Chapter 6).
5 Carburetor idle speed and/or mixture not adjusted properly (Chapter 1).
6 Carburetor internal parts excessively worn or damaged (Chapter 4).
7 Low tire pressure or incorrect tire size (Chapter 1).

20 Fuel leakage and/or fuel odor

1 Leak in a fuel feed or vent line (Chapter 4).
2 Tank overfilled. Fill only to automatic shut-off.
3 Emissions system filter in need of replacement (Chapter 6).
4 Vapor leaks from system lines (Chapter 4).

5 Carburetor internal parts excessively worn or out of adjustment (Chapter 4).

Engine cooling system

21 Overheating

1 Insufficient coolant in system (Chapter 1).
2 Fanbelt defective or not adjusted properly (Chapter 1).
3 Radiator core blocked or radiator grille dirty and restricted (Chapter 3).
4 Thermostat faulty (Chapter 3).
5 Fan blades broken or cracked (Chapter 3).
6 Radiator cap not maintaining proper pressure. Have cap pressure tested by gas station or repair shop.
7 Ignition timing incorrect (Chapter 1).

22 Overcooling

1 Thermostat faulty (Chapter 3).
2 Inaccurate temperature gauge (Chapter 10).

23 External coolant leakage

1 Deteriorated or damaged hoses. Loose clamps at hose connections (Chapter 3).
2 Water pump seals defective. If this is the case, water will drip from the 'weep' hole in the water pump body (Chapter 3).
3 Leakage from radiator core or header tank. This will require the radiator to be professionally repaired (see Chapter 3 for removal procedures).
4 Engine drain plugs or water jacket freeze plugs leaking (Chapters 2 or 3).

24 Coolant water leakage

Note: *Internal coolant leaks can usually be detected by examining the oil. Check the dipstick and inside of valve cover for water deposits and an oil consistency like that of a milkshake.*
1 Faulty cylinder head gasket. Have the system pressure-tested professionally or remove the cylinder heads (Chapter 2) and inspect.
2 Cracked cylinder bore or cylinder head. Dismantle engine and inspect (Chapter 2).

25 Coolant loss

1 Overfilling system (Chapter 3).
2 Coolant boiling away due to overheating (see Section 15).
3 Internal or external leakage (see Sections 22 and 33).
4 Faulty radiator cap. Have the cap pressure tested.

26 Poor coolant circulation

1 Inoperative water pump. A quick test is to pinch the top radiator hose closed with your hand while the engine is idling, then let it loose. You should feel a surge of coolant if the pump is working properly (Chapter 3).
2 Restriction in cooling system. Drain, flush and refill the system (Chapter 1). If necessary, remove the radiator (Chapter 3) and have it reverse-flushed or professionally cleaned.
3 Fan drivebelt defective or not adjusted properly (Chapter 1).
4 Thermostat sticking (Chapter 3).

Clutch

27 Fails to release (pedal pressed to the floor) – shift lever does not move freely in and out of Reverse

1 Improper linkage adjustment (Chapter 1).
2 Clutch fork off ball stud. Look under the vehicle, on the left side of the transmission.
3 Clutch disc warped, bent or excessively damaged (Chapter 7).

28 Clutch slips (engine speed increases with no increase in vehicle speed)

1 Linkage in need of adjustment (Chapter 1).
2 Clutch disc oil soaked or lining worn. Remove disc (Chapter 7) and inspect.
3 Clutch disc not seated. It may take 30 or 40 normal starts for a new disc to seat.

29 Grabbing while releasing clutch

1 Oil on clutch disc lining. Remove disc (Chapter 7) and inspect. Correct any leakage source.
2 Worn or loose engine or transmission mounts. These units move slightly when clutch is released. Inspect mounts and bolts.
3 Worn splines on clutch disc hub. Remove clutch components (Chapter 7) and inspect.
4 Warped pressure plate or flywheel. Remove clutch components and inspect.

30 Squeal or rumble with clutch fully engaged (pedal released)

1 Improper adjustment; no freeplay (Chapter 1).
2 Release bearing binding on transmission bearing retainer. Remove clutch components (Chapter 7) and check bearing. Remove any burrs or nicks, clean and relubricate before reinstallation.
3 Weak linkage return spring. Replace the spring.

31 Squeal or rumble with clutch fully disengaged (pedal depressed)

1 Worn, faulty or broken release bearing (Chapter 7).
2 Worn or broken pressure plate springs (or diaphragm fingers) (Chapter 7).

32 Clutch pedal stays on floor when disengaged

1 Bind in leakage or release bearing. Inspect linkage or remove clutch components as necessary.
2 Linkage springs being over-traveled. Adjust linkage for proper freeplay. Make sure proper pedal stop (bumper) is installed.

Manual transmission
Note: *Refer to Chapter 7 concerning the following problems (unless otherwise noted).*

33 Noisy in Neutral with engine running

1 Input shaft bearing worn.
2 Damaged main drivegear bearing.
3 Worn countergear bearings.
4 Worn or damaged countergear anti-lash shims.

34 Noisy in all gears

1 Any of the above causes, and/or:
2 Insufficient lubricant (see checking procedures in Chapter 1).

35 Noisy in one particular gear

1   Worn, damaged or chipped gear teeth for that particular gear.
2   Worn or damaged synchronizer for that particular gear.

36 Slips out of high gear

1   Transmission loose on clutch housing.
2   Shift rods interfering with engine mounts or clutch lever.
3   Shift rods not working freely.
4   Damaged mainshaft pilot bearing.
5   Dirt between transmission case and clutch housing, or misalignment of transmission.
6   Worn or improperly adjusted linkage.

37 Difficulty in engaging gears

1   Clutch not releasing completely (see clutch adjustment. Chapter 1).
2   Loose, damaged or out of adjustment shift linkage. Make a thorough inspection, replacing parts as necessary. (Chapter 7).

38 Oil leakage

1   Excessive amount of lubricant in transmission (see Chapter 1) for correct checking procedures. Drain lubricant as required.
2   Side cover loose or gasket damaged.
3   Rear oil seal or speedometer oil seal in need of replacement (Section 7).

Automatic transmission
Note: *Due to the complexity of the automatic transmission, it is difficult for the home mechanic to properly diagnose and service this component. For problems other than the following, the vehicle should be taken to a reputable mechanic.*

39 Fluid leakage

1   Automatic transmission fluid is a deep red color. Fluid leaks should not be confused with engine oil which can easily be blown by air flow to the transmission.
2   To pinpoint a leak, first remove all built-up dirt and grime from around the transmission. Degreasing agents and/or steam cleaning will achieve this. With the underside clean, drive the vehicle at low speeds so that air flow will not blow the leak far from its source. Raise the vehicle and determine where the leak is coming from. Common areas of leakage are:

   a)   Fluid pan: tighten mounting bolts and/or replace pan gasket as necessary (see Chapter 7)
   b)   Rear extension: tighten bolts and/or replace oil seal as necessary (Chapter 7)
   c)   Filler pipe: replace the rubber seal where pipe enters transmission case
   d)   Transmission oil lines: tighten connectors where lines enter transmission case and/or replace lines
   e)   Vent pipe: transmission over-filled and/or water in fluid (see checking procedures, Chapter 1)
   f)   Speedometer connector: replace the O-ring where speedometer cable enters transmission case

40 General shift mechanism problems

1   Chapter 7 deals with checking and adjusting the shift linkage on automatic transmissions. Common problems which may be attributed to poorly adjusted linkage are:

   a)   Engine starting in gears other than Park or Neutral
   b)   Indicator on quadrant pointing to a gear other than the one actually being used

   c)   Vehicle will not hold firm when in Park position
2   Refer to Chapter 7 to adjust the manual linkage.

41 Transmission will not downshift with the accelerator pedal pressed to the floor

Chapter 7 deals with adjusting the downshift cable or downshift switch to enable the transmission to downshift properly.

42 Engine will start in gears other than Park or Neutral

Chapter 7 deals with adjusting the Neutral start switches used with automatic transmissions.

43 Transmission slips, shifts rough, is noisy or has no drive in forward or reverse gears

1   There are many probable causes for the above problems, but the home mechanic should concern himself with only one possibility: fluid level.
2   Before taking the vehicle to a specialist, check the level of the fluid and condition of the fluid as described in Chapter 1. Correct fluid level as necessary or change the fluid and filter if needed. If the problem persists, have a professional diagnose the probable cause.

Driveshaft

44 Leakage of fluid at front of driveshaft

Defective transmission rear oil seal. See Chapter 7 for replacement procedures. While this is done, check the splined yoke for burrs or a rough condition which may be damaging the seal. If found, these can be dressed with crocus cloth or a fine stone.

45 Knock or clunk when the transmission is under initial load (just after transmission is put into gear)

1   Loose or disconnected rear suspension components. Check all mounting bolts and bushings (Chapter 11).
2   Loose driveshaft bolts. Inspect all bolts and nuts and tighten to specified torque (Chapter 8).
3   Worn or damaged universal joint bearings. Test for wear (Chapter 8).

46 Metallic grating sound consistent with vehicle speed

Pronounced wear in the universal joint bearings. Check for wear (Chapter 8).

47 Vibration

Note: *Before it can be assumed that the driveshaft is at fault, make sure the tires are perfectly balanced and perform the following test.*
1   Install a tachometer inside the vehicle to monitor engine speed as the vehicle is driven. Drive the vehicle and note the engine speed at which the vibration (roughness) is most pronounced. Now, shift the transmission to a different gear and bring the engine speed to the same point.
2   If the vibration occurs at the same engine speed (rpm) regardless of which gear the transmission is in, the driveshaft is NOT at fault since the driveshaft speed varies.
3   If the vibration decreases or is eliminated when the transmission is in a different gear at the same engine speed, refer to the following probable causes.
4   Bent or dented driveshaft. Inspect and replace as necessary (Chapter 8).
5   Undercoating or built-up dirt, etc. on the driveshaft. Clean the

shaft thoroughly and test.

6   Worn universal joint bearings. Remove and inspect (Chapter 8).

7   Driveshaft and/or companion flange out of balance. Check for missing weights on the shaft. Remove driveshaft (Chapter 8) and reinstall 180° from original position. Retest. Have driveshaft professionally balanced if problem persists.

48 Noise – same when in Drive as when vehicle is coasting

1   Road noise. No corrective procedures available.

2   Tire noise. Inspect tires and tire pressures (Chapter 1).

3   Front wheel bearings loose, worn or damaged (Chapters 1 and 8).

49 Vibration

See probable causes under *Driveshaft*. Proceed under the guidelines listed for the driveshaft. If the problem persists, check the rear wheel bearings by raising the rear of the vehicle and spinning the wheels by hand. Listen for evidence of rough (noisy) bearings. Remove and inspect (Chapter 8).

50 Oil leakage

1   Pinion oil seal damaged (Chapter 8).

2   Axle shaft oil seals damaged (Chapter 8).

3   Differential inspection cover leaking. Tighten mounting bolts or replace the gasket as required (Chapter 8).

Brakes

Note: *Before assuming a brake problem exists, check that the tires are in good condition and properly inflated (see Chapter 1), the front end alignment is correct and that the vehicle is not loaded with weight in an unequal manner.*

51 Vehicle pulls to one side during braking

1   Defective, damaged or oil contaminated brake pad on one side. Inspect as described in Chapter 9.

2   Excessive wear of brake pad material or disc on one side. Inspect and correct as necessary.

3   Loose or disconnected front suspension components. Inspect and tighten all bolts to specifications (Chapter 11).

4   Defective caliper assembly. Remove caliper and inspect for stuck piston or damage (Chapter 9).

52 Noise (high-pitched squeal without the brakes applied)

Front brake pads worn out. This noise comes from the wear sensor rubbing against the disc. Replace pads with new ones immediately (Chapter 9).

53 Excessive brake pedal travel

1   Partial brake system failure. Inspect entire system (Chapter 9) and correct as required.

2   Insufficient fluid in master cylinder. Check and add fluid (Chapter 1) and bleed system if necessary (Chapter 9).

3   Rear brakes not adjusting properly. Make a series of starts and stops while the vehicle is in Reverse. If this does not correct the situation, remove drums and inspect self-adjusters (Chapter 9).

54 Brake pedal feels spongy when depressed

1   Air in hydraulic lines. Bleed the brake system (Chapter 9).

2   Faulty flexible hoses. Inspect all system hoses and lines. Replace parts as necessary.

3   Master cylinder mountings insecure. Inspect master cylinder nuts and torque-tighten to specifications.

4   Master cylinder faulty (Chapter 9).

55 Excessive effort required to stop vehicle

1   Power brake booster not operating properly (Chapter 9).

2   Excessively worn linings or pads. Inspect and replace if necessary (Chapter 9).

3   One or more caliper pistons (front wheels) or wheel cylinders (rear wheels) seized or sticking. Inspect and rebuild as required (Chapter 9).

4   Brake linings or pads contaminated with oil or grease. Inspect and replace as required (Chapter 9).

5   New pads or linings installed and not yet 'bedded in'. It will take awhile for the new material to seat against the drum (or rotor).

56 Pedal travels to the floor with little resistance

Little or no fluid in the master cylinder reservoir caused by leaking wheel cylinder(s), leaking caliper piston(s), loose, damaged or disconnected brake lines. Inspect entire system and correct as necessary.

57 Brake pedal pulsates during brake application

1   Wheel bearings not adjusted properly or in need of replacement (Chapters 1 and 8).

2   Caliper not sliding properly due to improper installation or obstructions. Remove and inspect (Chapter 9).

3   Rotor not within specifications. Remove the rotor (Chapter 9) and check for excessive lateral runout and parallelism. Have the rotor professionally machined or replace it with a new one.

Suspension and steering

58 Vehicle pulls to one side

1   Tire pressures uneven (Chapter 1).

2   Defective tire (Chapter 1).

3   Excessive wear in suspension or steering components (Chapter 11).

4   Front end in need of alignment. Take vehicle to a qualified specialist.

5   Front brakes dragging. Inspect braking system as described in Chapter 9.

59 Shimmy, shake or vibration

1   Tire or wheel out of balance or out of round. Have professionally balanced.

2   Loose, worn or out-of-adjustment wheel bearings (Chapters 1 and 8).

3   Shock absorbers and/or suspension components worn or damaged (Chapter 11).

60 Excessive pitching and/or rolling around corners or during braking

1   Defective shock absorbers. Replace as a set (Chapter 11).

2   Broken or weak springs and/or suspension components. Inspect as described in Chapter 11.

61 Excessively stiff steering

1   Lack of lubricant in steering gearbox (manual) or power steering fluid reservoir (Chapter 1).

2   Incorrect tire pressures (Chapter 1).

3   Lack of lubrication at steering joints (Chapter 1).

4   Front end out of alignment.

5   See also section titled *Lack of power assistance.*

62 Excessive play in steering

1   Loose wheel bearings (Chapters 1 and 8).
2   Excessive wear in suspension or steering components (Chapter 11).
3   Steering gearbox out of adjustment (Chapter 11).

63 Lack of power assistance

1   Steering pump drivebelt faulty or not adjusted properly (Chapter 1).
2   Fluid level low (Chapter 1).
3   Hoses or pipes restricting the flow. Inspect and replace parts as necessary.
4   Air in power steering system. Bleed system (Chapter 11).

64 Excessive tire wear (not specific to one area)

1   Incorrect tire pressures (Chapter 1).
2   Tires out of balance. Have professionally balanced.
3   Wheels damaged. Inspect and replace as necessary.

4   Suspension or steering components excessively worn (Chapter 11).

65 Excessive tire wear on outside edge

1   Inflation pressures not correct (Chapter 1).
2   Excessive speed on turns.
3   Front end alignment incorrect (excessive toe-in). Have professionally aligned.
4   Suspension arm bent or twisted (Chapter 11).

66 Excessive tire wear on inside edge

1   Inflation pressures incorrect (Chapter 1).
2   Front end alignment incorrect (toe-out). Have professionally aligned.
3   Loose or damaged steering components (Chapter 11).

67 Tire tread worn in one place

1   Tires out of balance. Balance tires professionally.
2   Damaged or buckled wheel. Inspect and replace if necessary.
3   Defective tire (Chapter 1).

Chapter 1 Tune-up and routine maintenance

Refer to Chapter 13 for Specifications and information on 1984 and later models

Contents

Specifications

Note: *Additional specifications and torque recommendations can be found in each individual Chapter.*

Recommended lubricants and fluids

Engine oil type .... SAE grade SE or better
Automatic transmission fluid type
    C4, C6, AOD
        1980 .... Dexron II (Ford part no. D7-AZ-19582-A, B)
        1981 through 1983 .... Dexron II (Ford part no. XT-2-QDX)
    C5 .... Type H (Ford part no. XT-4-H)
Manual transmission lubricant .... SAE 80W gear lube
Transfer case lubricant .... Dexron II automatic transmission fluid
Engine coolant .... 50/50 mixture of Ethylene-glycol based antifreeze and water
Differential lubricant
    Ford rear axles – conventional and Traction-Lok .... Hypoid gear lubricant (Ford part no. EOAZ-19580-A; See note below)
    Front and rear Dana axles and Dana limited slip front and
      rear axles .... Hypoid gear lubricant (Ford part no. C6AZ-19580-E). **Note:** *Add friction modifier – Ford part no. C8AZ-19B546-A or equivalent – for complete refill of Ford Traction-Lok and Dana limited slip axles. Add four ounces for F250 and F350 limited slip rear axles. Add two ounces for Bronco, F150 and F250 limited slip front axles.*

Front axle spindle pins, front and rear spring shackle pins, steering column U-joints, clutch linkage fittings, driveshaft U-joints, joints with Zerk fittings, slip yoke pivots, parking brake linkage pivots and clevises, transmission control linkage pivots, front wheel bearings, rear wheel bearings (F350), brake and clutch pedal shaft, clutch linkage, F150/250 4X4 spindle needle bearings, accelerator control kickdown (automatic six-cylinder), accelerator ball socket linkage, transmission throttle valve lever (AOD only), spring stud shackles, double Carden joint center ball and transfer case shift linkage .... Lithium base grease NLG1 no. 2 (Ford part no. C1AZ-19590-B or equivalent)

Body hinges, latches, door striker plates and rotor, seat tracks, door tracks and checks, hood latch and auxiliary latch, spare tire carrier latch and automatic transmission shift linkage .... Polyethylene grease (Ford part no. D7AZ-19584-A or equivalent)
Lock cylinders and outside spare tire lock .... Lock lubricant (Ford part no. D8AZ-19550A or B or equivalent)
Manual steering gear lubricant .... Steering gear grease (Ford part no. C3AZ-19578-A or equivalent)
Power steering fluid .... Type F automatic transmission fluid
Speedometer and parking brake cable .... Speedometer cable lubricant (Ford part no. D2AZ-19581-A or equivalent)
Disc brake caliper rails .... Caliper side grease (Ford part no. D7AZ-19590-A or equivalent)
Brake and clutch master cylinders .... DOT 3 heavy-duty brake fluid
Brake and clutch pedal pivots and clevises .... SAE 10W engine oil
Exhaust control valve .... Rust penetrant fluid (Ford part no. D7AZ-19A501-A or equivalent)
Door weatherstrips .... Silicone spray (Ford part no. D7AZ-19553-A or equivalent)
Automatic locking hubs – 4X4 .... Darmex brake band lubricant (Ford part no. DX-123 LT or equivalent)

Engine oil capacity (with new filter) .... 6.0 U.S. quarts

Coolant capacities – 1980

	U.S. qts
300 cu in in-line six-cylinder (F100/350)	
Manual transmission	13
Automatic transmission	14
Manual/automatic transmission with air conditioning	17
302 cu in V8 (F100/150)	
Manual/automatic transmission with standard cooling;	
manual transmission with extra cooling	15
Automatic transmission with extra cooling;	
manual/automatic transmission with air conditioning	18
351 cu in V8	
F100	
Manual transmission with standard and extra cooling	17
F150/350	
Manual transmission with standard cooling	15
Manual transmission with extra cooling; automatic	
transmission with standard and extra cooling	17
Manual/automatic transmission with air conditioning	18
F100/350	
Manual/automatic transmission with super cooling	24
Bronco	
Manual transmission with standard cooling	20
All vehicles with super cooling	24
All vehicles not noted above	22
400 cu in V8	
F100/350	
Manual transmission with standard and extra cooling	
and air conditioning	18
Manual transmission with super cooling	24
Automatic transmission with standard and extra	
cooling and air conditioning	18
Automatic transmission with super cooling	24
Bronco	
All except super cooling	22
Super cooling	24

Coolant capacities – 1981 through 1983

300 cu in in-line six-cylinder (F100/350 and Bronco)	
Manual/automatic transmission with standard and extra cooling ..	13
Manual/automatic transmission with air conditioning	
and/or super cooling	14
255 cu in (1981 and 1982 F100 only) and 302 cu in V8 (F100/250)	
Manual/automatic transmission with standard cooling; manual	
transmission with extra cooling	13
Automatic transmission with extra cooling;	
manual/automatic transmission with air conditioning and	
super cooling	14
232 cu in V6 (F100)	
Standard and extra cooling	11
Air conditioning and super cooling	12
351 cu in V8 (F100/350 and Bronco)	
Manual/automatic transmission with standard and extra cooling ..	15
Manual/automatic transmission with air conditioning	
and/or super cooling	16
400 cu in V8 (1981 and 1982 only) (F350)	
Manual transmission with standard and extra cooling	15
All other vehicles	16
460 cu in V8 (1983 only) (F250 HD and F350)	
Manual transmission with extra cooling	16.5
All other vehicles	17.5

Fuel tank capacities

Note: *The standard fuel tank on all F100/350 vehicles is the front (midships) unit. A rear (aft/axle) tank is available as an option on all F100/350 models. The standard tank on Bronco vehicles is located in the rear (aft/axle) with a larger tank mounted in the same location available as an option (RPO).*

F100	U.S. gals
117 in wheelbase	
Midship tank	16.5
Aft/axle tank	19.0
133 in wheelbase	
Midship tank	16.5
Aft/axle tank	19.0

F150 4X2   U.S. gals
   117 in wheelbase
      Midship tank 16.5
      Aft/axle tank 19.0
   133 in wheelbase — each tank 19.0
   139 in wheelbase
      Midship tank 16.5
      Aft/axle tank 19.0
   155 in wheelbase — each tank 19.0
F150 4X4
   117 in wheelbase
      Midship tank 16.5
      Aft/axle tank 19.0
   133 in wheelbase — each tank 19.0
   155 in wheelbase — each tank 19.0
F250 4X2
   133 in wheelbase — each tank 19.0
   139 in wheelbase
      Midship tank 16.5
      Aft/axle tank 19.0
   155 in wheelbase — each tank 19.0
F250 4X4 — each tank 19.0
F350 — each tank 19.0
Bronco
   Aft/axle tank with RPO skid plate 25.0
   Aft/axle tank with steel auxiliary tank and standard skid plate 32.0

Manual transmission capacities

	U.S. pints
Ford 3-speed	3.5
Ford 4-speed overdrive	4.5
Ford 4-speed single-rail overdrive	4.5
New Process 435 4-speed with extension	7.0
New Process 435 4-speed without extension	6.5
Warner T-18 and T18B 4-speed	7.0
Warner T-19B 4-speed	7.0

Transfer case capacities

	U.S. pts
1980	
New Process 2-speed part-time	6.0
Warner 1345 full-time	6.0
1981 and 1982	
New Process 2-speed part-time	6.5
Warner 1345 full-time	6.5
1983	
New Process 2-speed part-time	7.0
Warner 1345 full-time	6.5

Automatic transmission capacities
Note: *Capacities given in the chart below are approximate dry capacities, including cooler and lines. Fluid level indicator should be used to determine actual fluid requirements. Check levels at normal operating temperatures. Do not overfill.*

	U.S. qts
1980	
C6	
F100/350 4X2	11.7
F100/350 4X4 and Bronco	13.5
C4	10.0
1981	
C6	
F100/350 4X2	11.7
F100/350 4X4 and Bronco	13.5
C4	9.6
AOD	12.0
1982 and 1983	
C6	
F100/350 4X2	11.7
F100/350 4X4 and Bronco	13.5
C5	11.0
AOD	12.0

Differential capacities
Note: *See note in Recommended lubricants and fluids chart at the beginning of this Section concerning complete refills of Ford Traction-Lok and Dana limited slip axles.*

	U.S. pts
1980	
Ford – F100/150 and Bronco	6.5

	U.S. pts
Dana 44 IFS (front axle) – F150 4X4 and Bronco	4.0
Dana 44 IFS HD (front axle) – F250 4X4	4.0
Dana 50 IFS (front axle) – F350 4X4	5.0
Dana 60 – F250	5.0
Dana 61-1 – F350	6.0
Dana 61-2 – F250	6.0
Dana 70 – F350	6.5
Dana 70 HD – F350	6.0

1981 and 1982

Ford – F100/150 and Bronco	6.5
Dana 44 IFS (front axle) – F150 4X4 and Bronco	3.9
Dana 44 IFS HD (front axle) – F250 4X4	3.8
Dana 50 IFS (front axle) – F350 4X4	4.1
Dana 60 – F250	6.0
Dana 6-1 – F350	6.6
Dana 6-2 – F250	6.0
Dana 70 – F350	6.6
Dana 70 HD – F350	6.6

1983

Ford 8.8-in ring gear – F100, 150, 250 and Bronco	5.5
Ford 9.0-in ring gear – F100, 150, 250	5.5
Dana 44 IFS (front axle) – F250 4X4 and Bronco	3.6
Dana 44 IFS HD (front axle) – F250 4X4	3.6
Dana 50 IFS (front axle) – F350 4X4	3.8
Dana 60 – F100/350 4X2 and F150/350 4X4	6.0
Dana 60-5 – F100/350	6.0
Dana 61-2 – F250	6.0
Dana 70 – F350 4X2	6.5
Dana 70 HD – F350 4X2	7.4

Ignition system

Spark plug type and gap	See Emissions Control Information label in the engine compartment
Distributor type	
1980	Breakerless, Duraspark II
1981 through 1983	Breakerless, Duraspark II or Duraspark III, depending on engine calibration
Distributor direction of rotation	
Six-cylinder in-line engines	Clockwise
V6 engines	Counterclockwise
V8 engines	Counterclockwise
Firing order (see Fig. 1.29 on page 54 for cylinder locations/distributor cap terminal numbers)	
Six-cylinder in-line engines	1-5-3-6-2-4
V6 engines	1-4-2-5-3-6
255, 302 and 460 cu in V8 engines	1-5-4-2-6-3-7-8
351 and 400 cu in V8 engines	1-3-7-2-6-5-4-8
Spark plug wire resistance	Less than 5000 ohms per inch
Ignition timing	See Emission Control Information label in the engine compartment
Battery electrolyte specific gravity	1.230 at 80-degrees F (27-degrees C)

Drivebelt tension (measured with Burroughs-type gauge)

$\frac{1}{4}$ in belts

New (before being rotated more than once)	50 to 80 lbs
Used (less than 10 minutes operation)	40 to 80 lbs
Belts having more than 10 minutes operation	40 to 60 lbs

$\frac{3}{8}$, $\frac{15}{32}$ and $\frac{1}{2}$ in belts

New (before being rotated more than once)	120 to 160 lbs
Used (less than 10 minutes operation)	90 to 160 lbs
Belts (more than 10 minutes operation)	72 to 120 lbs

Accessory belt tension (measured with Burroughs-type gauge)

Thermactor belt

300 cu in-line 6-cylinder engine without air conditioning

New	50 to 90 lbs
Used (more than 10 minutes operation)	40 to 60 lbs

All other engines

New	90 to 130 lbs
Used (more than 10 minutes operation)	80 to 100 lbs

Air conditioning compressor, power steering and alternator belts

New	120 to 160 lbs
Used (more than 10 minutes operation)	110 to 130 lbs

Serpentine belt (V6 only)

New	150 to 190 lbs
Used (more than 10 minutes operation)	140 to 160 lbs

Clutch pedal free play .... $\frac{1}{2}$ to 2 in

Brakes

Front disc brake pad minimum thickness (above rivet heads on single
   piston types or above backing plate on dual piston types) .... $\frac{1}{32}$ in
Rear (drum) brake lining thickness (above rivet heads) .... $\frac{1}{32}$ in

Torque specifications   Ft-lb

Spark plug	
300 cu in in-line 6-cylinder engine	17 to 22
460 cu in V8	5 to 10
All others	10 to 15
Oil pan drain plug	15 to 25
Manual transmission drain and fill plugs	
New Process 435	25 to 35
Borg-Warner 4-speed (all)	25 to 40
All others	10 to 20
Transfer case drain and fill plugs	
New Process 208	30 to 40
Borg-Warner 1345	
Drain plug	6 to 14
Fill plug	15 to 25
Automatic transmission pan bolts	12 to 16
Automatic transmission converter drain plug	
C4	15 to 26
C5	12 to 17
AOD and C6	8 to 28
Automatic transmission filter screen-to-main body bolts	
C4 and C6	40 to 55 in-lb
C5	25 to 40 in-lb
AOD	80 to 100 in-lb
Differential fill plug	
Conventional	15 to 30
Dana	20 to 30
Wheel lug nut	
$\frac{1}{2}$ in nut	90
$\frac{9}{16}$ in nut (single rear wheels)	145
$\frac{9}{16}$ in nut (dual rear wheels)	220
Front wheel bearing adjusting nut (4x2 only)	22 to 25 (back-off $\frac{1}{8}$ turn)

1 Introduction

This Chapter was designed to help the home mechanic maintain
his or her vehicle for peak performance, economy, safety and longevity.

On the following pages you will find a maintenance schedule
along with Sections which deal specifically with each item on the
schedule. Included are visual checks, adjustments and item replace-
ments.

Servicing your vehicle using the time/mileage maintenance schedule and the sequenced Sections involves a planned program of
maintenance. Keep in mind that it is a complete plan, and maintaining
only a few items at the specified intervals will not produce the same
results.

You will find as you service your vehicle that many of the
procedures can, and should, be grouped together due to the nature of
the job at hand. Examples of this are as follows:

If the vehicle is raised for a chassis lubrication, for example, this is
the ideal time for the following checks: manual transmission oil,
exhaust system, suspension, steering and the fuel system.

If the tires and wheels are removed, as during a routine tire
rotation, go ahead and check the brakes and wheel bearings at the
same time.

If you must borrow or rent a torque wrench, it would be advisable
to service the spark plugs and repack (or replace) the wheel bearings
all in the same day to save time and money.

The first step of this or any maintenance plan is to prepare yourself
before the actual work begins. Read through the appropriate Sections
for all work that is to be performed before you begin. Gather together
all necessary parts and tools. If it appears you could have a problem
during a particular job, don't hesitate to ask advice from your local
parts man or dealer service department.

2 Routine maintenance intervals

The following recommendations are given with the assumption
that the vehicle owner will be doing the maintenance or service work
(as opposed to a dealer service department). They are based on factory
service/maintenance recommendations, but the time and/or mileage
intervals have been shortened in most cases, to ensure that the service
is thorough and complete. Not all maintenance checks or operations
apply to every vehicle.

When the vehicle is new, it should be serviced initially by a factory
authorized dealer service department to protect the factory warranty.
In most cases the initial maintenance check is done at no cost to the
owner.

Every 250 miles (400 km), weekly, and before long trips

Steering
   Check tire pressures (cold) (Sec 5)
   Inspect tires for wear and damage (Sec 5)
   Check power steering fluid level (Sec 3)
   Check steering for smooth and responsive operation (Sec 9)

Brakes
   Check the fluid level in the reservoir; if fluid level has dropped
   noticeably since the last check, inspect all brake lines and hoses
   for leakage (Sec 7)
   Check for satisfactory brake operation (Sec 7)

Lights, wipers, horns, instruments
   Check all lights for proper operation

Fig. 1.1 Engine compartment components (typical)

1 Automatic transmission fluid dipstick
2 PCV valve
3 Air filter housing
4 Engine oil dipstick
5 Brake fluid reservoir
6 Windshield washer fluid reservoir
7 Power steering fluid reservoir
8 Radiator cap
9 Oil filler cap
10 Distributor
11 Valve cover
12 Spark plugs
13 Upper radiator hose
14 Air cleaner duct
15 Battery

1

Check the operation of the windshield wipers and washers
Check the windshield wiper blade condition (Sec 14)
Check the horn operation
Check the operation of all instruments

Engine

Check the oil level and add oil as required (Sec 3)
Check the radiator coolant level and add coolant as required (Sec 3)
Check the battery electrolyte level, adding water as necessary (Sec 4)

Every 3000 miles (5000 km) or 3 months, whichever comes first

Change the engine oil and filter (Sec 16)
Check the throttle solenoid positioner (TSP) (Chapter 6)
Check the exhaust heat control valve operation (Chapter 6)
Check and replace if necessary, the air cleaner filter element (Sec 15).
Clean and refill the oil bath-type air cleaner (Sec 15).
Check the curb idle speed (Sec 33).
Check the fast idle speed (Sec 33).

Every 6000 miles (10 000 km) or 6 months, whichever comes first

Check carburetor TSP off-idle speed (Chapter 4)
Lubricate the universal joints and slip yoke (if equipped with grease fittings) (Sec 19)
Lubricate the steering column universal joints (4-wheel drive) (Sec 19)
Check cooling system clamps and hoses (Sec 12)
Lubricate the front axle spindle pins (2-wheel drive) (Sec 19)
Check the exhaust system for loose or damaged components (Sec 8)
Check the power steering fluid level, adding fluid as necessary (Sec 3)
Lubricate the steering linkage (Sec 19)
Lubricate the clutch linkage (Sec 19)
Check the disc brake linings, piston boots and pivot pins (Sec 7)
Check the front differential lubricant level (4-wheel drive), adding oil as necessary (Sec 3)
Check the rear differential lubricant level, adding oil as necessary (Sec 3)
Check the transfer case lubricant level (4-wheel drive), adding oil as necessary (Sec 3)
Check the clutch linkage free play and adjust as necessary (Sec 20)
Check the manual transmission lubricant level, adding oil as necessary (Sec 3)
Check all drivebelts for proper tension (Sec 6)
Inspect the drivebelts for wear and damage, replacing as necessary (Sec 6)
Check the deceleration fuel valve (Sec 32)
Check the automatic transmission bands (Chapter 7)
Check the carburetor throttle, choke and deceleration valves, adjusting or replacing as necessary (Chapters 4 and 6)
Adjust the idle fuel mixture (if applicable) (Sec 33)
Replace the fuel filter element (Sec 17)

Every 12 000 miles (20 000 km) or 12 months, whichever comes first

Lubricate the parking brake linkages, pivots and clevises (Sec 19)
Clean and repack the front free-running hubs (4-wheel drive) (Chapter 8)
Check the spark plug wires (Sec 27)
Check the operation of the EGR system and delay valve (if equipped) (Chapter 6)
Check the operation of the spark control system (if equipped) (Chapter 6)
Replace the spark plugs (engines using leaded fuel) (Sec 29)
Check and clean the crankcase breather cap (Sec 16)
Inspect the drum brake lining, lines and hoses (Sec 7)
Check the PCV valve, replacing it as necessary (Sec 13)
Drain the chassis mounted fuel filter system (Sec 17)
Check the engine coolant condition (Sec 12)
Check the operation of the temperature controlled air cleaner (Chapter 6)

Every 18 000 miles (30 000 km) or 18 months, whichever comes first

Replace the spark plugs (engines using unleaded fuel) (Sec 29)
Adjust the ignition timing (Sec 31)
Check the distributor cap and rotor (Sec 28)
Tighten the intake manifold nuts and bolts to the specified torque (Chapter 2)
Check the Thermactor system (Chapter 6)
Replace the crankcase ventilation filter (Sec 13)
Check the choke system (Sec 32)

Every 24 000 miles (40 000 km) or 24 months, whichever comes first

Drain and refill the cooling system with the specified coolant (Sec 25)
Repack and adjust the rear wheel bearings (Dana axles) (Chapter 8)
Drain and refill the manual transmission with the specified lubricant (Sec 21)
Drain and refill the front differential (4-wheel drive) (Sec 24)
Drain and refill the transfer case (4-wheel drive) (Sec 22)
Drain and refill the rear differential (Sec 24)
Check the evaporative system hoses, vapor line and fuel filler cap (Sec 18)
Check the evaporative emissions canister, replacing it as necessary (Sec 18)
Check the engine compression (Sec 30)

Severe operating conditions

Severe operating conditions are defined as follows:

Extended periods of idling or low-speed operation
Towing any trailers up to 1000 lb (450 kg) for long distances
Operating when the outside temperatures remain below 10°F (-12°C) for 60 days or more and most trips are less than 10 miles (16 km)
Operation in severe dust conditions
The automatic transmission is also considered to be part of the systems under severe operating conditions and must be serviced at closer intervals on vehicles which accumulate 2000 miles (3200 km) per month

If your vehicle falls into the severe operating conditions category, the maintenance schedule must be amended as follows:

a)　Change engine oil and filter every 2 months or 2000 miles (3200 km)
b)　Check, clean and regap spark plugs every 4000 miles (6400 km)
c)　Service the automatic transmission bands every 5000 miles (8000 km) (Chapter 7) and drain and refill the transmission with fresh fluid every 20 000 miles (32 000 km)
d)　Dana rear differentials must be drained and refilled every 6000 miles if a Class II or III trailer is towed
e)　Check the paper-type air cleaner element every 1000 miles
f)　Lubricate the universal joints, slip yoke, front axle spindle pins, steering linkage, spring shackles and pins daily or as soon as possible when operating in mud and/or water or every 1000 miles (1600 km) when operating off road
g)　Check and replace the cartridge-type fuel filter frequently when operating in dusty conditions

3　Fluid level checks

1　There are a number of components on a vehicle which rely on the use of fluids to perform their jobs. Through the normal operation of the vehicle, these fluids are used up and must be replenished before damage occurs. See the *Recommended lubricants and fluids* Section for the specific fluid to be used when adding is required. When checking fluid levels make sure that the vehicle is on a level surface.

Engine oil

2   The engine oil level is checked with a dipstick located on the left side of the engine block.

3   The oil level should be checked when the engine is cold or at least 10 minutes after it has been shut off. Make sure that the vehicle is sitting on level ground. Any deviations in level can cause a major variation in the actual fluid level.

4   Pull the dipstick from the tube and wipe all the oil from the end with a clean rag. Insert the dipstick all the way back into the oil pan and pull it out again (photo). Check the dipstick at the end and note the oil level in relationship to the marks on the dipstick. Some dipsticks have an Add mark followed by a number to help indicate how much oil to add to the engine. In any case, the oil should be kept within the safe reading on the dipstick.

5   Oil is added to the engine by removing the cap located on the rocker arm cover. Use an oil spout or funnel to reduce any chance of oil being poured on the outside of the engine.

6   Checking the oil level can also be an important preventative maintenance step. If the oil level is dropping abnormally, it indicates an oil leak or internal engine wear problems which should be checked and corrected. If there are water droplets in the oil, or if it has a milky-looking color, this also indicates internal engine problems that should be looked into immediately.

7   The condition of the oil is also important and can be observed when checking the level. With the dipstick removed from the engine, take your thumb and index finger and wipe oil from the dipstick onto your fingers. Look for small dirt particles or metal particles which will show up on the dipstick or feel gritty to the touch. This is an indication that the oil should be drained and fresh oil added. If this condition persists, abnormal engine wear is occurring and should be checked and corrected.

Automatic transmission fluid

8   The fluid inside the transmission must be at normal operating temperature to get an accurate reading on the dipstick. This is done by driving the vehicle for several miles, making frequent starts and stops to allow the transmission to shift through all gears.

9   Park the vehicle on a level surface, place the selector lever in Park and leave the engine running at an idle.

10   Remove the transmission dipstick (located on the right side, near the rear of the engine) (photo) and wipe all the fluid from the end of the dipstick with a clean rag.

11   Push the dipstick back into the transmission until the cap seats firmly on the dipstick tube. Now remove the dipstick again and observe the fluid on the end. The upper level of the fluid should be between the Add and Don't Add marks.

12   If the fluid level is at or below the Add mark on the dipstick, add sufficient fluid to raise the level to the top hole, just below the Don't Add mark. One pint of fluid will raise the level to this point. Fluid should be added directly into the dipstick guide tube, using a funnel to prevent spills.

13   It is important that the transmission not be overfilled. Under no circumstances should the fluid level be above the Don't Add mark on the dipstick, as this could cause internal damage to the transmission. The best way to prevent overfilling is to add fluid a little at a time, driving the vehicle and checking the level between additions.

14   Use only transmission fluid specified by Ford. This information can be found in the *Recommended lubricants and fluids* Section of the Specifications.

15   The condition of the fluid should also be checked. If the fluid at the end of the dipstick is a dark reddish-brown color, or if the fluid has a burnt smell, the transmission fluid should be changed. If you are in doubt about the condition of the fluid, purchase some new fluid and compare the two for color and smell.

Manual transmission oil

16   To check the manual transmission oil, access to the transmission must be possible from under the vehicle.

17   Locate the fill plug at the side of the transmission case. Clean all dirt from the area adjacent to the plug. Slowly withdraw the plug. If oil starts to come out as the plug is withdrawn, immediately reinsert it into the transmission, as the level is correct.

18   Remove the fill plug if the oil does not run out and check that the level is up to the bottom of the plug hole. If it is not, fill the transmission through this hole to the correct level.

19   Visually check the transmission for any signs of leakage at either

3.4 Removing the engine oil level dipstick

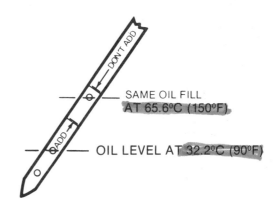

Fig. 1.2 Typical markings on an engine oil dipstick (Sec 3)

3.10 Removing the automatic transmission fluid level dipstick

the front or rear seal or near such components as the speedometer drive.

Transfer case (4x4) oil

20   To check the oil level in the transfer case (if so equipped), locate

the fill plug on the side (just as you did for the transmission).
21 Check the transfer case oil level in the same manner as the manual transmission.

Differential oil
22 Differentials are checked by withdrawing the fill plug from either the rear cover (Dana differentials) or from the side of the removable differential assembly (all others). Use the same procedure as was used to check the oil level in the manual transmission.

Engine coolant
Caution: *Do not attempt to check the engine coolant under any circumstances while the engine is running or immediately after it has been shut off. Damage to the cooling system, and to the engine, and personal injury can result from attempting to check the coolant while the engine is hot. If the engine has been run, turn it off and wait until it has cooled. Use extreme caution when removing the radiator cap even after the engine has cooled, as steam and pressure can be released from the cooling system.*

23 To check the engine coolant with a non-recovery type system, remove the radiator cap. Check the coolant level by looking down the neck and observing the fluid level below the cap seat. Add sufficient coolant to bring the level to between $\frac{3}{4}$ and $1\frac{1}{2}$ inches below the neck.
24 If the vehicle is equipped with a closed cooling system, the radiator cap should not be removed for checking. A coolant reservoir located to the side of the radiator should indicate a level within itself. If the level in the reservoir is between the Low and Full marks it is correct. If the level is below the Low mark, check the radiator after the system has completely cooled. For this check, the radiator cap must be removed.
25 If the radiator is very low on fluid, check the cooling system for any leaks, using a pressure-type checker.

Brake fluid
26 The brake fluid reservoir is located directly above the brake master cylinder, which is attached to either the firewall at the left of the engine or to the brake vacuum booster in that same location. Remove any accumulation of dirt or loose particles from the cover. If checking the brake fluid on a vehicle with water or snow on it, be sure to clean the hood and cowling area completely of any liquid. Serious contamination of the brake fluid can result if even one drop of water is allowed to enter the brake fluid reservoir.
27 Snap the retaining clip to the side to release the cover from the master cylinder reservoir.
28 Remove the cover (photo) being very careful not to let any type of contamination enter the reservoir.
29 Observe the fluid level inside the dual chambers. Check that it is within $\frac{1}{4}$ inch of the top of the cylinder.
30 Small amounts of fluid can be added to the system to make up for any fluid lost due to evaporation or brake component wear. If a large amount of fluid is necessary to bring the system back up to the proper level, check the system for any signs of leakage. Loss of braking capability can result from leakage in the brake hydraulic system.
31 Clean the cover carefully and replace it on the cylinder. Be careful not to allow any contaminants to fall into the reservoir.
32 Snap the retaining clip back into place.

Power steering fluid
33 The power steering pump is located to the left front of the engine. The dipstick for the power steering system is located in the cap on the filler neck of the power steering pump (photo).
34 With the engine running and at its normal operating temperature, turn the steering wheel in both directions (to the stops) several times to stabilize the fluid level within the system.
35 Stop the engine and check the fluid level. Remove the cap from the pump and see if the level is between the bottom of the dipstick and the Full mark on the Full-Hot side of the dipstick. If the fluid is being checked when the vehicle is cold, check the fluid on the Full-Cold side.

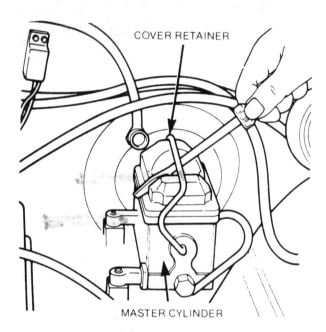

Fig. 1.3 Removing the lock clip from the brake master cylinder fluid reservoir (Sec 3)

3.28 Removing the brake fluid reservoir cover

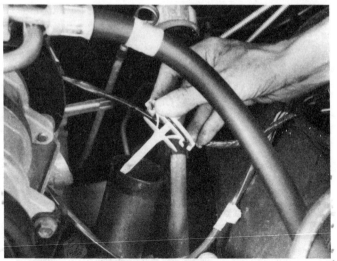

3.33 Checking the power steering reservoir fluid level

Windshield washer fluid

36 Check the clear windshield washer reservoir for the proper fluid level.

37 If necessary to add liquid, water may be used in warm climates. In climates where the temperature gets below the freezing level, fill the reservoir with a special cleaning and antifreeze washer solution manufactured for this purpose.

4 Battery – servicing

Checking

1 Certain precautions must be followed when checking or servicing the battery. Hydrogen gas, which is highly flammable, is always present in the battery cells, so keep lighted tobacco and any other open flames away from the battery. The electrolyte inside the battery is actually diluted sulfuric acid, which can be hazardous to your skin and cause damage if splashed in the eyes. It will also ruin clothes and painted surfaces.

2 Check the battery case for cracks and evidence of leakage.

3 To check the electrolyte level in the battery (non-maintenance-free batteries only), remove all the vent caps (photo). If the battery water level is low, add distilled water until the level is above the cell plates. There is an indicator in each cell to help you judge when enough water has been added. Do not overfill.

4 Periodically check the specific gravity of the electrolyte with a hydrometer. This is especially important during cold weather. If the reading is below the Specification, the battery should be recharged.

5 Check the tightness of the battery terminals to ensure good electrical connections. The terminals can be cleaned with a stiff wire brush. Corrosion (photo) can be kept to a minimum by applying a layer of petroleum jelly or grease to the terminal and cable connectors after they are assembled.

6 Inspect the entire length of the battery cables for corrosion, cracks and frayed conductors.

7 Check that the rubber protector over the positive terminal (if equipped) is not torn or missing. It should completely cover the terminal.

8 Make sure that the battery is securely mounted.

9 The battery case and caps should be kept clean and dry. If corrosion is evident, clean the battery as described below.

10 If the vehicle is not being used for an extended period, disconnect the battery cables and have it charged approximately every six weeks.

Cleaning

11 Corrosion on the battery hold-down components and inner fender panels can be removed by washing with a solution of water and baking soda. Once the area has been thoroughly cleaned, rinse it with clear water.

12 Corrosion on the battery case and terminals can also be removed with a solution of water and baking soda and a stiff brush. Be careful that none of the solution is splashed into your eyes or onto your skin (wear protective gloves). Do not allow any of the baking soda and water solution to get into the battery cells. Rinse the battery thoroughly once it is clean.

13 To thoroughly clean a battery cable terminal, the cables must be removed. When removing and installing the battery cables, always use a puller tool as the battery posts can be easily damaged by twisting or pulling on the cable ends. After removing the cables, thoroughly clean both the battery posts and the insides of the cable ends with a special battery cleaning tool (photos).

14 Metal parts of the vehicle which have been damaged by spilled battery acid should be painted with a zinc-based primer and paint. Do this only after the area has been thoroughly cleaned and dried.

Charging

15 As was mentioned before, if the battery's specific gravity is below the specified amount, the battery must be recharged.

16 If the battery is to remain in the vehicle during charging, disconnect the cables from the battery to prevent damage to the electrical system.

17 When batteries are being charged, hydrogen gas (which is very explosive and flammable) is produced. Do not smoke or allow an open

1

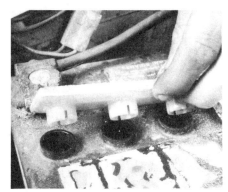

4.3 Checking the electrolyte level in a non-maintenance-free battery

4.5 Battery terminal corrosion usually appears as light fluffy crystals

14.13A Removing the ground cable from the battery post (always remove this cable first and replace it last)

14.13B Clean the battery posts with a special tool

14.13C Cleaning the battery cable clamps with the wire brush end of the special tool

flame near a charging or a recently charged battery. Also, do not plug in the battery charger until the connections have been made at the battery posts.

18 The average time necessary to charge a battery at the normal rate is from 12 to 16 hours (sometimes longer). Always charge the battery slowly. A quick charge or boost charge is hard on a battery and will shorten its life. Use a battery charger that is rated at no more than $3\frac{1}{2}$ amperes.

19 Remove all of the vent caps and cover the vent holes with a clean cloth to prevent the spattering of electrolyte. Hook the battery charger leads to the battery posts (positive to positive, negative to negative), then plug in the charger. Make sure it is set at 12 volts if it has a selector switch.

20 Check the battery often during charging to make sure that it does not overheat.

21 The battery can be considered fully charged when it is gassing freely and there is no increase in specific gravity during three successive readings taken at hourly intervals.

22 Overheating of the battery during charging at normal charging rates, excessive gassing and continual low specific gravity readings are an indication that the battery should be replaced with a new one.

5 Tires and wheels – checking and rotation

Checking

1 Periodically inspecting the tires can not only prevent you from being stranded with a flat tire, but can also give you clues as to possible problems with the steering and suspension systems before major damage occurs.

2 Proper tire inflation adds miles to the life of the tires, allows the vehicle to achieve maximum gas mileage and contributes to overall riding comfort.

3 When inspecting each tire, first check the wear on the tread. Irregularities in the tread pattern (cupping, flat spots, more wear on one side than the other) are indications of front end alignment and/or balance problems. If any of these conditions are found, you should take the vehicle to a wheel alignment shop to correct the problem. Tires with tread marker indicators showing should be replaced. Truck tires without tread markers should be replaced if there is less than $\frac{1}{32}$ inch of tread left on any part of the tire.

4 Also check the tread area for cuts or punctures. Many times a nail or tack will imbed itself into the tire tread and yet the tire will hold its air pressure for a short time. In most cases, a repair shop or gas station can repair the punctured tire.

5 It is also important to check the sidewalls of the tire, both inside and outside. Check for the rubber being deteriorated, cut or punctured. Also inspect the inboard side of the tire for signs of brake fluid leakage, indicating a thorough brake inspection is needed immediately (Section 7).

6 Incorrect tire pressure cannot be determined merely by looking at the tire. This is especially true for radial tires. A tire pressure gauge must be used. If you do not already have a reliable gauge, it is a good idea to purchase one and keep it in the glove box. Built-in pressure gauges at gas stations are often unreliable.

7 Always check tire inflation when the tires are cold. Cold, in this case, means that the vehicle has not been driven more than one mile after sitting for three hours or more. It is normal for the pressure to increase four to eight pounds or more when the tires are hot.

8 Unscrew the valve cap protruding from the wheel and firmly press the gauge onto the valve stem. Observe the reading on the gauge and check this figure against the recommended tire pressure for your vehicle.

9 The recommended pressures are listed on a tag attached to the driver's door latch post under the striker plate or in the back of your owner's manual. Be sure to set the pressure in accordance with both the size of tire on your particular vehicle and with the load you are planning to carry with it. These specifications will vary widely so be careful when looking them up. Overloaded and/or underinflated tires on a truck are one of the most common areas of break-down as well as being potentially dangerous.

10 Check all tires and add air as necessary to bring all tires up to the recommended pressure levels. Do not forget the spare tire. Be sure to reinstall the valve caps, which will keep dirt and moisture out of the valve stem mechanism.

11 Carefully inspect the wheels for damage and signs of deterioration.

Wheels that have been scraped or hit against a curb are especially susceptible to cracking or bending. If a wheel is damaged in any way it is a good idea to replace it with a new one.

12 Check the wheel lug nuts for tightness. Wheel nuts should be tightened to the correct specification with a torque wrench. If the bolt holes have become elongated or flattened, replace the wheel. Tighten the lug nuts in the proper sequence as shown in a crisscross pattern.

13 A very thorough examination of the wheel and tire requires removal of the wheel from the vehicle. If the wheel has been balanced on the vehicle, mark one wheel stud and one bolt hole on the wheel so it can be installed in the same relative position.

14 Clean the inner surface of the wheel and pay particular attention to the mating face of the wheel where it contacts the brake drum or hub assembly. Any corrosion on this surface can prevent the wheel from seating flat against the drum or hub.

15 Some F250 and F350 model trucks will have two-piece or 'split-rim' type wheels. Check these types of wheels very carefully for any signs of incorrect seating between the outer ring and the main center of the wheel. This type of wheel can come apart with the power of a small explosion and has been known to cause injury and even death. If you have a wheel of this type that appears to be incorrectly assembled or is coming apart, take it immediately to a truck-tire service facility. **Warning:** *Do not attempt to do any type of work on these wheels as they require a safety cage as well as other special equipment to be handled properly.*

Rotation

16 The tires should be rotated at the specified intervals and whenever uneven wear is noticed. Tire rotation can contribute significantly to increased life from a set of tires. Tires should be rotated only if they are the same size, tread type, ply rating and load range. All of this information is included on the sidewall of the tire.

17 Since the vehicle will be raised and the tires removed anyway, this is a good time to check the brakes and/or repack the wheel bearings (Sec 26). Read these Sections through first to determine if you will be

Fig. 1.4 Built-in tire wear indicators make it possible to tell at a glance when a tire is due for replacement (Sec 5)

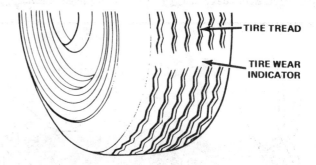

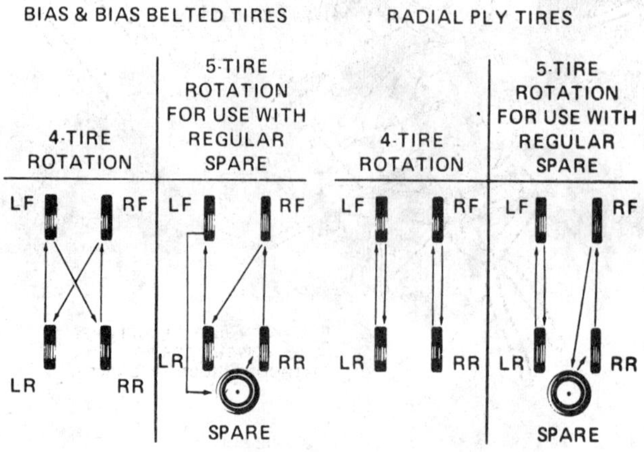

Fig. 1.5 Tire rotation diagram (Sec 5)

performing these operations at the same time you rotate the tires.

18 The position of each tire in the rotation sequence depends on the type of tire used on your vehicle. Radial tires use a different rotation pattern than bias ply tires. Do not use any other rotation pattern than the type shown, or else handling, ride and other problems can occur, particularly with radial tires.

19 See the information in *Jacking and towing* at the front of this manual for the proper procedures to follow in raising the vehicle and changing a tire; however, if the brakes are to be checked, do not apply the parking brake as stated. Make sure the tires are blocked to prevent the vehicle from rolling.

20 Preferably, the entire vehicle should be raised at the same time. This can be done on a hoist or by jacking up each corner of the vehicle and then lowering it onto jackstands placed under the frame rails. Always use four jackstands and make sure the vehicle is firmly supported all around.

21 After rotation, check and adjust the tire pressures as necessary and be sure to check wheel nut tightness.

---

6 Engine drivebelts(s) – check, adjustment and replacement

1 The drivebelts, or V-belts at the front of the engine play an important role in the overall operation of the engine and its components. Due to their function and material make-up, the belts will wear and stretch after a period of time and should be inspected and adjusted periodically to prevent major engine damage.

2 The number of belts used on a vehicle depends on the accessories installed. Drivebelts are used to turn the alternator, air pump, power steering pump, water pump, fan, and air conditioning compressor. Depending on the pulley arrangement, a single belt may be used for more than one of these components.

3 With the engine off, open the hood and locate the various belts at the front of the engine. Using your fingers (and a flashlight if necessary), move along the belts checking for cracks and separation. Also check for fraying and glazing, which gives the belt a shiny appearance. Both sides of the belts should be inspected, which means

you will have to twist the belt to check the underside.

4 Drivebelt tension should be checked using a special gauge designed for this purpose. On dual belt systems, check one belt at a time. Compare the reading on the drivebelt gauge with the Specifications at the front of the Chapter.

5 **Note:** *Steps 6 through 10 pertain to all engines except the 232 cu in V6. If your vehicle is equipped with a V6, refer to Steps 11 through 13.*

6 If space limitations do not permit the use of a tensioning tool, drive belt tension can be checked by pushing on the belt at a distance halfway between the pulleys. Push firmly with your thumb and see how much the belt moves down (deflects). A rule of thumb is that if the distance (pulley center-to-pulley center) is between 7 inches and 11 inches, the belt should deflect $\frac{1}{4}$ in. If the belt is longer and travels between pulleys spaced 12 in to 16 in apart, the belt should deflect $\frac{1}{2}$ in (photo).

7 If it is necessary to adjust the belt tension, either to make the belt tighter or looser, it is done by moving the belt-driven accessory on its bracket.

8 For each component there will be an adjustment or strap bolt and a pivot bolt. Both bolts must be loosened slightly to enable you to move the component.

9 After the two bolts have been loosened, move the component away from the engine (to tighten the belt) or toward the engine (to loosen the belt). Hold the accessory in this position and check the belt tension. If it is correct, tighten the two bolts until snug, the recheck the tension. If it is all right tighten the two bolts completely.

10 It will often be necessary to use some sort of pry bar to move the accessory while the belt is adjusted. If this must be done to gain the proper leverage, be very careful not to damage the component being moved, or the part being pried against.

11 On V6 engines, loosen the two idler bracket bolts (refer to Fig. 1.10) and turn the adjusting bolt until the belt is adjusted properly. Turning the wrench to the right tightens the belt and turning the wrench to the left loosens the belt.

12 Tighten the two idler pulley bolts and recheck the belt tension.

13 If the belt tension is still incorrect, repeat Steps 11 and 12.

1

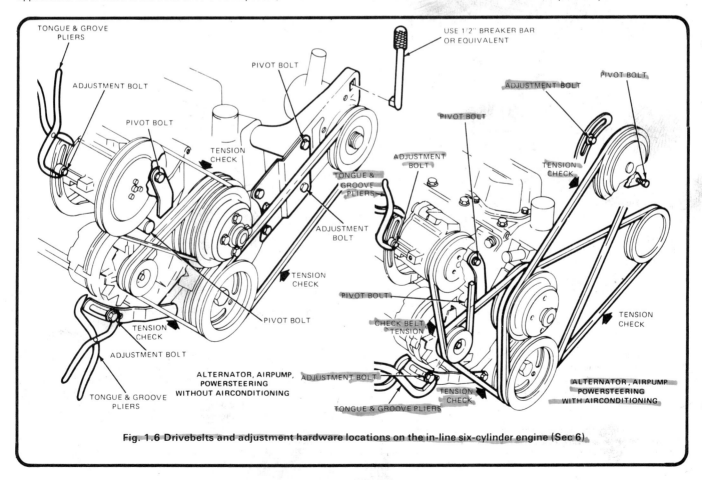

Fig. 1.6 Drivebelts and adjustment hardware locations on the in-line six-cylinder engine (Sec 6)

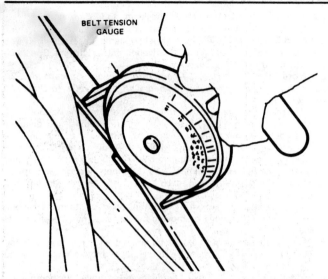

Fig. 1.7 Checking drivebelt tension with a special belt tension
gauge (Sec 6)

6.6 Checking drivebelt tension by depressing it at the center of the run

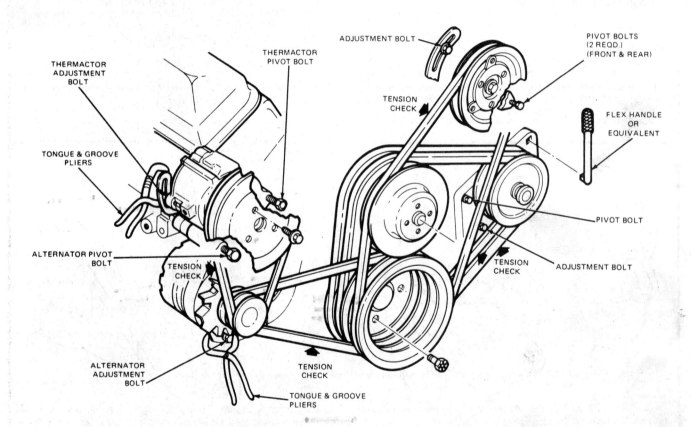

Fig. 1.8 Drivebelts and adjustment hardware locations on the 460 V8 engine (Sec 6)

14   Replacement procedures for drivebelts are basically the same as the adjustment procedures. When installing new belts, make sure they are properly seated in their pulley grooves. On V6 engines, make sure that all V grooves make proper contact with the pulleys (refer to Fig. 1.11).

7   Brake system – inspection and adjustment

1   The brakes should be inspected at the specified intervals, as well

as every time the wheels are removed or whenever a problem is suspected. Indications of a potential problem in the braking systems are: the vehicle pulls to one side when the brake pedal is depressed; noises coming from the brakes when they are applied; excessive brake pedal travel; pulsating pedal; and leakage of fluid (usually seen on the inside of the tire or wheel).

Disc brakes – inspection
2   Using a wrench of the proper size, break loose the lug nuts on the front wheels but do not unscrew them any farther at this point.

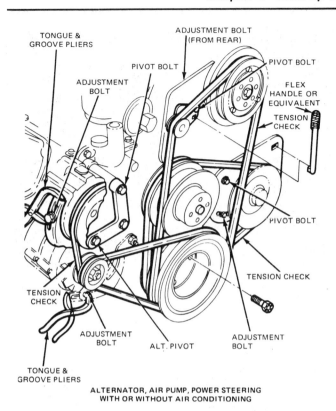

Fig. 1.9 Drivebelts and adjustment hardware locations on V8 engines (255, 302 and 350W engines shown, others similar except 460) (Sec 6)

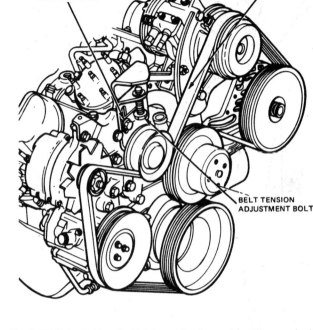

Fig. 1.10 Drivebelt and adjustment hardware locations on the V6 engine (Sec 6)

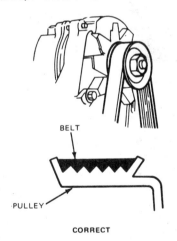 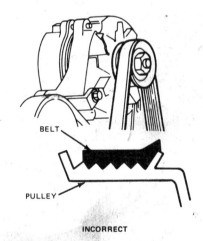

Fig. 1.11 The V6 drivebelt must fully engage the pulley (left) to prevent slippage and excess wear (Sec 6)

3   Raise the front end of the vehicle and support it securely on jackstands. Be sure the parking brake is set.
4   Unscrew the lug nuts and remove the wheel.
5   Turn the steering all the way to the right to enable the brake inspection hole of the left brake to be observed more easily. The inspection hole appears as an oval-shaped window squarely in the center of the brake caliper bracket. We recommend that the brake pads be replaced if they are worn within the tolerances listed at the beginning of this Chapter. It is also advisable to replace them if any difference in wear is apparent between the two sides.
6   If there is a question about whether to replace the pads or not, a more accurate measurement can be made by removing the pads as described in Chapter 9. Remember, disc brake pads are relatively inexpensive and easy to replace, other brake parts such as discs are not.
7   Perform the same inspection on the right brake after turning the

steering all the way to the left for better viewing access. If any deviation is noted between the four front brake pads (two per side), all of the pads should be replaced at the same time. Do not mix different types of replacement pads or use pads of a different material type than original equipment.
8   While checking the pad linings, also inspect the rotor (disc) surface for scoring or hot spots indicated by small discolored blemishes. Light scoring is acceptable but if the damage is excessive, the rotor should be resurfaced or replaced with a new one. Always replace rotors in pairs.

Hydraulic lines and parking brake cables — inspection

9   Before installing the wheels, check for any leakage around the brake hose connections leading to the caliper. Also check for damage (cracking, splitting, etc.) to the brake hose and lines.
10 Replace the hose, lines or fittings if any sign of hydraulic leakage

is present.

11 Inspect the hydraulic system throughout the vehicle by first supporting the vehicle to allow access to the undercarriage. Trace the hydraulic lines from the master cylinder to the combination valve and then out to each individual wheel. Pay particular attention to the rubber-coated brake hoses that lead to the front calipers and to the flexible rubber line that connects the brake line at the rear of the vehicle's frame to the T-fitting located on the rear axle housing.

12 Carefully observe the parking brake system cables, linkage and connecting points. If any fraying or damage is noted to any of the cables, replace the affected parts.

Drum brakes — inspection and cleaning

Note: *The following procedure requires a special large deep socket if your vehicle is equipped with the full-floating type of axle hub (identified by 8-lug wheels and a protruding center hub). Additionally you will need new lock washers for the axle retaining nuts as well as a new gasket and axle bearing nut lock washer.*

13 The brake drum must be removed in order to inspect the condition of the linings and hardware.

14 Loosen the lug nuts approximately $\frac{1}{2}$ turn. On models with full-floating axle hubs, loosen the axle retaining bolts on the center hub.

15 Raise the vehicle and support it securely.

16 Remove the lug nuts and the wheel(s).

17 On vehicles equipped with semi-floating axles (5-lug wheels and no protruding center hub) unthread the spring clips from the lug studs and pull the drum off the axle flange. **Note:** *If the drum will not come off the flange easily, check to make sure the emergency brake is fully released. If the drum still won't come off, it will be necessary to back off the brake shoe adjustment.*

18 **Note:** *Steps 18 through 22 apply to full-floating hubs only. Refer to Fig. 1.12 for component identification.* Heavy-duty vehicles equipped with full-floating rear axles require removal of the axle. Remove the previously loosened axle retaining nuts and washers and remove the axle and gasket.

19 Remove the locking wedge from the adjusting nut keyway slot with a screwdriver. **Note:** *This must be done before the adjusting nut is removed or even turned.*

20 Remove the wheel bearing adjusting nut with the deep socket.

21 Pull the drum off the spindle approximately two to three inches and then push it back on. This will pull the outer wheel bearing out

onto the spindle for easier removal. (See Chapter 9 for instructions on backing off the brake adjustment for drum removal if it won't pull off easily.)

22 Remove the brake drum. Notice that the inner wheel bearing will be retained to the drum with the inner wheel bearing seal. Use caution not to damage this seal.

23 With the drum removed, carefully vacuum or brush away any accumulations of brake lining material and dust. Do not blow this material out with compressed air as asbestos is hazardous to breathe.

24 Check the thickness of the lining material. If the thickness is at the minimum specification or close to it, the brake shoes should be replaced with new ones. The shoes should also be replaced if they are cracked, glazed (shiny surface) or wet from brake fluid or oil.

25 Check the brake return springs, parking brake cable (rear brakes), and self-adjusting brake mechanisms for condition and position.

26 Carefully check the brake components for any signs of fluid leakage. Use your finger to carefully pry back the lip of the rubber wheel cylinder cups. These are located at the top of the brake assembly. Any leakage at these cups is an indication that the wheel cylinders should be overhauled immediately (Chapter 9). Also check the connections at the rear of the brake backing plate for any signs of leakage or deterioration.

27 If the wheel cylinders are dry and there are signs of grease or oil in the brake assembly area, the axle seal is defective and should be replaced. Grease or oil will ruin asbestos and rubber parts so any accumulation of grease or oil requires replacement of the brake shoes and/or rubber parts affected by it. See Chapter 8 for seal replacement procedures.

28 Wipe off the inside of the drum with a clean rag and brake cleaning solvent or denatured alcohol. Again, be careful not to breathe or spread the dangerous asbestos dust.

29 Check the inside of the drum for cracks, scores, deep grooves or hot spots which will appear as small discoloured areas. If these imperfections cannot be removed with fine emery cloth and light rubbing, the drum must be taken to an automotive machine shop, parts house or brake specialist with the equipment necessary to machine the drums.

30 If, after the inspection and cleaning process, all parts are in good working condition, reinstall the brake drum, retaining clips and wheel (semi-floating axle type only).

31 On full floating-type axle assemblies only, refer to Chapter 8, Section 3 and perform Steps 12 through 19.

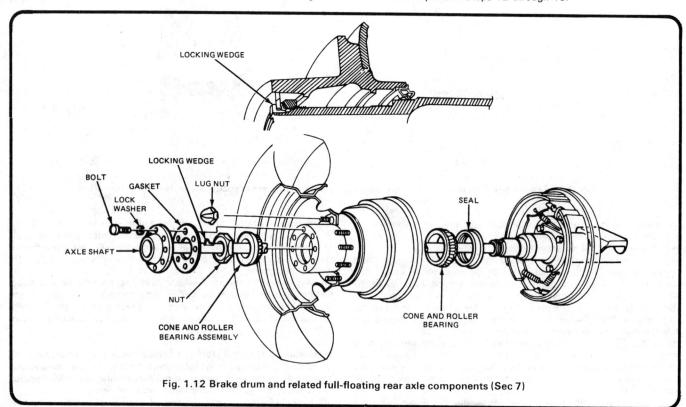

Fig. 1.12 Brake drum and related full-floating rear axle components (Sec 7)

Drum brake adjustment

32 Adjust the brakes (if they have been replaced or had to be retracted for removal purposes) by removing the rubber plug at the rear of the brake backing plate.

33 Use a brake adjustment tool inserted through the slot in the backing plate to rotate the star wheel adjuster until the brakes drag against the drums. You will have to keep rotating the wheel assembly while you are performing this operation.

34 Finally, loosen the star wheel adjuster to a point where the dragging just stops. If the drum drags heavily in one spot, it is out-of-round and will have to be resurfaced or replaced for proper braking operation.

35 Install the wheel(s) and tighten the retaining nuts to the correct torque. Lower the vehicle to the ground and pump the brake pedal several times to ascertain correct brake operation and 'feel' before attempting to drive the vehicle.

8 Exhaust system – inspection

1 With the engine cold (at least three hours after the vehicle has been driven), check the complete exhaust system from its starting point at the engine to the end of the tailpipe. This should done on a hoist where full access is available.

2 Check the pipes and connections for signs of leakage and/or corrosion, indicating a potential failure. Make sure that all brackets and hangers are in good condition and tight.

3 At the same time, inspect the underside of the body for holes, corrosion, open seams, etc. which may allow exhaust gases to enter the passenger compartment. Seal all body openings with silicone or body putty.

4 Rattles and other noises can often be traced to the exhaust system, especially the mounts and hangers. Try to move the pipes, muffler and catalytic converter (if equipped). If the components can come into contact with the body or driveline parts, secure the exhaust system with new mounts.

5 This is also an ideal time to check the running condition of the engine by inspecting inside the very end of the tailpipe. The exhaust deposits here are an indication of engine state-of-tune. If the pipe is black and sooty or coated with white deposits, the engine is in need of a tune-up (including a thorough carburetor inspection and adjustment).

9 Suspension and steering – inspection

1 Whenever the front of the vehicle is raised for service it is a good idea to visually check the suspension and steering components for wear.

2 Indications of a fault in these systems are excessive play in the steering wheel before the front wheels react, excessive sway around corners or body movement over rough roads and binding at some point as the steering wheel is turned.

3 Before the vehicle is raised for inspection, test the shock absorbers by pushing down to rock the vehicle at each corner. If you push the vehicle down and it does not come back to a level position within one or two bounces, the shocks are worn and need to be replaced. As this is done, check for squeaks and strange noises from the suspension components. Information on shock absorber and suspension components can be found in Chapter 11.

4 Now raise the front end of the vehicle and support it firmly on jackstands placed under the frame rails. Because of the work to be done, make sure the vehicle cannot fall from the stands.

5 Grab the top and bottom of the front tire with your hands and rock the tire/wheel on its spindle or balljoints. If there is any play or looseness, the wheel bearings should be serviced (see Section 26 or Chapter 8).

6 Crawl under the vehicle and check for loose bolts, broken or disconnected parts and deteriorated rubber bushings on all suspension and steering components. Look for grease or fluid leaking from around the steering box. Check the power steering hoses and connections for leaks.

7 If the wheel bearings have been adjusted or determined to be adjusted properly, again grasp the wheel assembly and move it up and down and side-to-side to check the spindle or balljoints for looseness. Any play or looseness in these components requires disassembly and

usually replacement. Improper lubrication usually causes failure of these components. If they are loose, steering control, shimmying at the steering wheel and other problems often crop up. Do not ignore these components as they are the major connecting points of the wheel/spindle assembly to the suspension of the vehicle.

10 Glass and mirrors – inspection

1 Vehicle cab glass as well as mirrors, particularly in vehicles with loads or bodies that restrict vision, are very important safety factors of a truck. All the glass should be examined and cleaned before each day's operation of the vehicle. If any glass within the driver's viewing area is cracked or broken, it is a good idea to replace it as soon as possible.

2 Mirrors play an important part in the operation of a truck, especially when high, wide loads restrict the driver's vision. Make sure that all mirrors are in good condition. Clean them daily. Make sure that the adjustment is correct and that all brackets and mounting hardware are tight.

11 Lighting system – inspection and adjustment

1 It is easiest to inspect the lighting system at night in an enclosed garage (do not run the engine inside an enclosed area).

2 First, turn on the lights to the first position on the headlight switch. This should activate all of the parking lights and various marker lights. Slowly walk around the vehicle and make sure that all lights are working properly. Trucks depend on certain marker light systems to indicate their size and height to other vehicles in traffic situations. It is important to keep these lighting systems working correctly.

3 If a light is found to be inoperative, check the bulb to determine if that is the problem. If a bulb replacement does not remedy the situation, see Chapter 10.

4 Turn the light switch on to the full headlight position. All the lights that were previously illuminated should still be lit along with the headlights. Make sure that the high beam works on the headlight system as well as the normal driving beam. Check the headlight aim for proper range and side angle. Adjust the headlights with a special headlight aimer or with the following temporary method, if necessary.

Headlight adjustment

5 You will need a screwdriver and a wall to shine your headlights on.

6 Park your vehicle approximately three feet from the wall you have selected (a garage door works well for this purpose). It is easier to do this at dusk or after dark for clear definition of where the lights are shining.

7 Mark the outlines of the beam pattern on the wall with a pencil or tape. Move the vehicle back about 25 feet from the wall. The top of the low beam should be no higher than the top of the circles you have inscribed on the wall. They should also be no lower than the center of the circles.

8 If the beam shines outside of the circle, use the screwdriver and locate one of the two headlight adjustment screws (see Chapter 10) which are accessible through slots provided in the headlight molding (the piece of plastic trim surrounding the headlight). These adjustment screws have tension springs. One screw will raise and lower the light beam and the other one will rotate it from side-to-side. Experiment with each screw until you move the beams in the direction that you want them to go.

9 Adjust the high beams in a similar manner. If you have a four-light system, the bright beams (center) are adjusted so the center of the beam is aimed at the top of the low beam marks.

10 As this procedure is less than perfect, it it best to have the headlights adjusted by your local dealer or other possible service facility.

12 Cooling system – inspection

1 Many major engine failures can be attributed to a faulty cooling system. If your vehicle is equipped with an automatic transmission, the cooling system also plays an integral role in transmission longevity.

2 The cooling system should be checked with the engine cold. Do this before the vehicle is driven for the day or after it has been shut off

for one or two hours.

3   Remove the radiator cap and thoroughly clean the cap (inside and out) with clean water. Also clean the filler neck on the radiator. All traces of corrosion should be removed.

4   Carefully check the upper and lower radiator hoses along with the smaller diameter heater hoses. Inspect the entire length of each hose, replacing any hose which is cracked, swollen or shows signs of deterioration. Cracks may become more apparent if the hose is squeezed (photo).

5   Also check that all hose connections are tight. A leak in the cooling system will usually show up as white or rust colored deposits on the areas adjoining the leak.

6   Use compressed air or a soft brush to remove bugs, leaves etc. from the front of the radiator or air conditioning condenser. Be careful not to damage, or cut yourself on the delicate cooling fins.

13 PCV system – inspection and valve and filter replacement

Inspection

Note: *The following tests are to be performed with the engine idling and at normal operating temperature. Refer to Figs. 1.14 and 1.15 for component location and identification.*

1   Remove the PCV valve from the grommet located in the rocker arm cover (photo). Make sure the connection to the PCV valve at the inlet side remains connected.

2   Check for a strong suction which will be accompanied by a hissing noise at the valve. You can place a finger over the valve inlet to feel the suction. At the same time your finger is blocking the valve, any vacuum leaks should become apparent in the connections and the hose.

3   Install the PCV valve back into its correct position.

4   Loosely plug the air inlet hose after removing it from the air cleaner connection. Use a small piece of stiff paper over the opening to block it. After approximately a minute, the paper should be held against the hose opening by a strong suction.

5   **Note**: *The following tests will be made with the engine shut off.* Remove the PCV valve from its grommet and shake it. It should make a clicking, metallic noise, which indicates the valve is operating.

6   Observe the hose leading to the PCV valve as well as the air inlet connections, PCV valve grommet and air inlet gasket at the oil filler cap (if so equipped). If any loose connections are found, tighten the connections or replace the clamps.

7   If the hoses are found to be leaking, replace the hoses.

Valve replacement

8   Replace the PCV valve if it fails any of the above tests. PCV replacement valves are of two types: high flow and standard flow. The type required for your vehicle is indicated in the 'Engine Family' box at the upper left corner of the Emissions Control Information label in the engine compartment. If the box contains the designation PCV, use a high flow valve; if there is no designation, use a standard flow valve.

9   Disconnect the crankcase ventilation tube from the PCV valve and remove the valve from the grommet in the rocker arm cover.

10 If an adaptor elbow is required, install it on the replacement PCV valve.

11 Install the valve in the grommet and connect the crankcase ventilation tube.

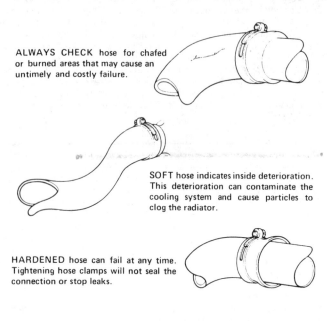

ALWAYS CHECK hose for chafed or burned areas that may cause an untimely and costly failure.

SOFT hose indicates inside deterioration. This deterioration can contaminate the cooling system and cause particles to clog the radiator.

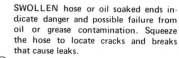

HARDENED hose can fail at any time. Tightening hose clamps will not seal the connection or stop leaks.

SWOLLEN hose or oil soaked ends indicate danger and possible failure from oil or grease contamination. Squeeze the hose to locate cracks and breaks that cause leaks.

Fig. 1.13 Radiator hose inspection procedure (Sec 12)

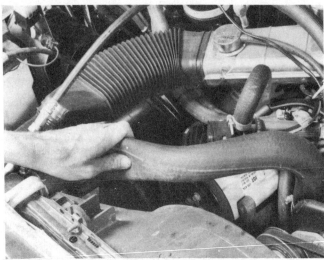

12.4 Checking a radiator hose for cracks by squeezing it

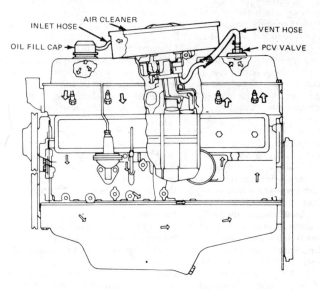

Fig. 1.14 Component layout of the in-line six-cylinder PCV system (Sec 13)

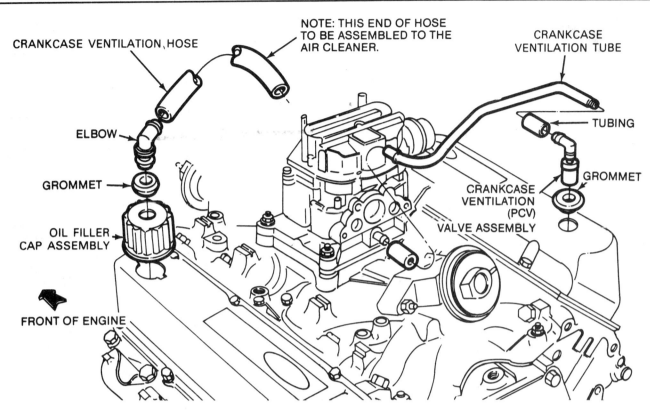

CRANKCASE VENTILATION HOSE

NOTE: THIS END OF HOSE
TO BE ASSEMBLED TO THE
AIR CLEANER.

CRANKCASE
VENTILATION TUBE

ELBOW

GROMMET

OIL FILLER
CAP ASSEMBLY

FRONT OF ENGINE

TUBING

GROMMET

CRANKCASE
VENTILATION
(PCV)
VALVE ASSEMBLY

Fig. 1.15 Component layout of a typical V8 PCV system (Sec 13)

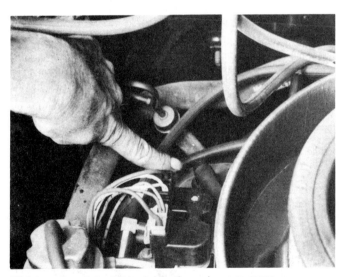

13.1 Location of the PCV valve in the rocker arm cover

13.14 Location of the crankcase ventilation filter inside the air filter housing

12 If the replacement valve requires a plastic fitting for additional vacuum lines, soak the fitting in hot water prior to installing the new PCV valve.

13 **Note:** *Replacing a PCV valve could cause a leaner air-fuel mixture and a change in idle speed. If your engine uses a high flow PCV valve, check and adjust both the curb idle speed and the idle mixture to the specifications given on the Emissions Control Information label. With a standard flow PCV valve, it is only necessary to check and adjust curb idle speed to the specified rpm.*

14 Replace the crankcase ventilation filter in the air cleaner housing. To do this, remove the air cleaner top plate, lift out the filter (it is a small, rectangular filter) and replace it with a new one (photo).

14 Windshield wipers – inspection and blade replacement

1 Windshield wiper blades will require replacement depending on the amount of use, weather conditions, chemical reactions from environmental conditions and age. Keep the blades clean and lubricated with a light silicone spray.

2 If the wiper blades cease to do an effective job of wiping the windshield clean, make sure that the blades and the windshield are cleaned properly before replacement. Look at the blades closely while they are still installed on the vehicle without manually moving the wiper arms across the windshield. Make sure that the blades are in

good condition and have not started to deteriorate or split.

3   If the windshield wiper blades do not prove effective and they have been cleaned along with the windshield (a film-like coating on the windshield can also cause streaking or poor wiping), replace the blades with new ones.

4   Cycle the arm and blade assembly to a position on the windshield where removal of the assembly can be performed without difficulty. Turn the ignition key off when the blade is in the desired position.

Blade replacement – Trico type

5   With the blade assembly resting on the windshield, grasp either end of the wiper blade frame and pull it away from the windshield, then pull the blade assembly from the pin. **Note:** *The rubber element extends past the frame so, to prevent damage to the blade element, be sure to grasp the blade frame and not the end of the blade element.*

6   To install, push the blade assembly onto the pin until it is fully seated, making sure the blade is securely attached to the wiper arm.

Blade replacement – Tridon type

7   To remove the blade assembly from the wiper arm, pull up on the spring lock and pull the blade assembly from the pin. Be sure the spring lock is not pulled up excessively or it will become distorted.

8   To install, push the blade assembly onto the pin so that the spring lock engages the pin. Be sure the blade assembly is securely attached to the pin.

Rubber wiper replacement

9   Most rubber wiper blade elements can be replaced without replacing the entire wiper blade assembly, Due to the differences in various manufacturers' models and retaining techniques, you will need to refer to the specific manufacturer's instructions to replace the rubber blade element.

15 Air filter – inspection and replacement

1   At the specified intervals the air filter should be replaced with a new one. A thorough program of preventative maintenance would call for the filter to be inspected periodically between changes.

2   The air filter is located inside the air cleaner housing on the top of the engine. To remove the filter, unscrew the wing nut at the top of the air cleaner and lift off the top plate. If the top plate is connected to emissions control devices, tilt it back far enough to allow access to the filter element.

3   While the top plate is off, be careful not to drop anything down into the carburetor.

4   Lift the air filter out of the housing (photo).

5   To check the filter, hold it up to strong sunlight, or place a flashlight or droplight on the inside of the ring-shaped filter. If you can see light coming through the paper element, the filter is all right. Check

all the way around the filter.

6   Wipe the inside of the air cleaner housing with a rag. Be careful not to drop any debris down the carburetor.

7   Place the old filter (if in good condition) or the new filter (if specified interval has elapsed) back into the air cleaner housing. Make sure it seats properly in the bottom of the housing.

8   Reinstall the top plate with the wing nut.

16 Engine oil and filter change

1   Frequent oil changes may be the best form of preventative maintenance available to the home mechanic. When engine oil ages, it gets diluted and contaminated which ultimately leads to premature parts wear.

2   Although some sources recommend oil filter changes every other oil change, we feel that the minimal cost of an oil filter and the relative ease with which it is installed dictate that a new filter be used whenever the oil is changed.

3   The tools necessary for a normal oil and filter change are a wrench to fit the drain plug at the bottom of the oil pan, an oil filter wrench to remove the old filter, a container with at least an eight quart capacity to drain the old oil into and a funnel or oil can spout to help pour fresh oil into the engine.

4   In addition, you should have plenty of clean rags and newspapers handy to mop up any spills. Access to the underside of the vehicle is greatly improved if it can be lifted on a hoist, driven onto ramps or supported by jackstands. Do not work under a vehicle which is supported only by a bumper, hydraulic or scissors-type jack.

5   If this is your first oil change, it is a good idea to crawl underneath and familiarize yourself with the locations of the oil drain plug and the oil filter (photo). Since the engine and exhaust components will be warm during the actual work, it is best to figure out any potential problems before the engine and its accessories are hot.

6   Allow the engine to warm up to normal operating temperature. If the new oil or any tools are needed, use this warm-up time to gather everything necessary for the job. The correct type of oil to buy for your application can be found in *Recommended lubricants* near the front of this Chapter.

7   With the engine oil warm (warm engine oil will drain better and more built-up sludge will be removed with the oil), raise the vehicle for access beneath it. Make sure it is firmly supported. If jackstands are used they should be placed toward the front of the frame rails.

8   Move all necessary tools, rags and newspaper under the vehicle. Postion the drain pan under the drain plug. Keep in mind that the oil will initially flow from the pan with some force, so place the pan accordingly.

9   Being careful not to touch any of the hot exhaust pipe components, use the wrench to remove the drain plug near the bottom of the oil pan. Depending on how hot the oil has become, you may

15.4 Lifting the air filter out of the housing

16.5 Location of the oil filter (351 V8 engine shown)

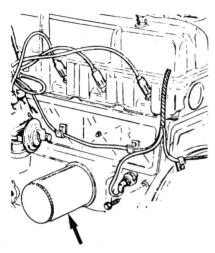

Fig. 1.16 Location of the oil filter on the in-line six-cylinder engine (Sec 16)

want to wear gloves while unscrewing the plug the final few turns.

10 Allow the old oil to drain into the pan. It may be necessary to move the pan further under the engine as the oil flow reduces to a trickle.

11 After all the oil has drained, clean the drain plug thoroughly with a clean rag. Small metal particles may cling to this plug (which could immediately contaminate your new oil).

12 Clean the area around the drain plug opening and reinstall the drain plug. Tighten the plug securely with your wrench. If a torque wrench is available, tighten the drain plug to the proper torque.

13 Move the drain pan in position under the oil filter.

14 Now use the filter wrench to loosen the oil filter. Chain or metal band-type filter wrenches may distort the filter canister, but don't worry too much about this as the filter will be discarded anyway.

15 Sometimes the oil filter is on so tight it cannot be readily loosened, or is in a position in the engine compartment that makes access difficult. If you run into such problems, you can increase the grip of the band-type filter remover by gluing a couple of strips of medium grit sandpaper to the inside of the band, applying some rough-surfaced electrical tape (not the shiny, plastic type) to the inside of the band or by wrapping the bottom of an old latex glove around the filter before applying the filter remover band.

16 Completely unscrew the old filter. Be careful, it is full of oil. Empty the old oil inside the filter into the drain pan.

17 Compare the old filter with the new one to make sure they are of the same type.

18 Use a clean rag to remove all oil, dirt and sludge from the area where the oil filter mounts to the engine. Check the old filter to make sure the rubber gasket is not stuck to the engine mounting surface (use a flashlight if necessary). If this gasket is stuck to the engine remove it.

19 Open a new can of oil and smear a light coat of this fresh oil onto the rubber gasket of the new oil filter.

20 Attach the new filter to the engine following the tightening directions printed on the filter canister or packing box. Filter manufacturers recommend against using a filter wrench due to possible overtightening or damage to the canister.

21 Remove all tools, rags, etc. from under the vehicle, being careful not to spill the oil in the drain pan. Lower the vehicle off its support devices.

22 Move to the engine compartment and locate the oil filler cap on the engine. In most cases there will be a twist-off cap on the rocker arm cover or a cap at the end of a fill tube at the front of the engine.

23 If an oil can spout is used, push the spout into the top of the oil can and pour fresh oil through the filler opening. A funnel placed into the opening may also be used.

24 Pour about three (3) quarts of fresh oil into the engine. Wait a few minutes to allow the oil to drain to the pan, then check the level on the oil dipstick (see Section 3 if necessary). If the oil level is at or near the lower Add mark, clean the filler cap, install it, start the engine and allow the new oil to circulate.

25 Run the engine for only about a minute and then shut it off. Immediately look under the vehicle and check for leaks at the oil pan drain plug and around the oil filter. If either is leaking, tighten with a bit more force.

26 With the new oil circulated and the filter now completely full, recheck the level on the dipstick and add enough oil to bring the level to the safe mark on the dipstick.

27 During the first few trips after an oil change, make it a point to check for leaks and keep track of the oil level.

28 The old oil drained from the engine cannot be reused in its present state and should be disposed of. Oil reclamation centers, auto repair shops and gas stations will normally accept the oil which can be refined and used again. After the oil has cooled, it can be drained into a suitable container (capped plastic jugs, topped bottles, milk cartons, etc.) for transport to one of these disposal sites.

17 Fuel filter – replacement

1 Fuel filters must be replaced according to the maintenance interval suggestions as well as when a blockage in the fuel line occurs due to excessive foreign material in the fuel.

2 Considering the volatile nature of gasoline, precautions should be exercised when a fuel filter is replaced. This work should be done on a cool engine. Never smoke or have any open flames around the work area. Do not work within an enclosed area. When removing a fuel system component, take care to clean up any spills which will inevitably occur when gasoline under pressure is released. Make sure that gasoline does not puddle or stand anywhere in the engine compartment or work area. Clean any spilled gasoline off the vehicle as well as yourself as it can burn your skin.

3 Fuel filters are located in a number of different positions depending on the year, engine size and weight rating of the vehicle. Most fuel filters can be found in-line somewhere between the fuel pump and the carburetor.

4 If a fuel filter is located in-line between the carburetor and the fuel pump, it is usually connected with rubber hoses. Release the clamps on the rubber hoses and slowly remove the filter from the system. Use caution, as gasoline will be under pressure at this point.

5 After removing the filter, drain it and discard it in a non-incendiary refuse container. Replace the filter with an exact duplicate replacement and push it in to new rubber connecting hoses which should be provided with the filter. Also replace the clamps if they appear weak.

6 Tighten all clamps. Start the vehicle and check for leaks.

7 If the filter is the type located in the inlet of the carburetor, first remove the line leading to the inlet by unthreading it, if it has a fitting, or by removing the clamp and hose if it is so equipped.

8 Carefully unscrew the carburetor inlet/filter unit from the carburetor. Be careful not to damage the threads in the carburetor.

9 Some filters in the carburetor are integral with the inlet connection. If this type is being replaced, simply screw in a new filter/inlet assembly after applying one drop of an approved hydraulic sealant to the external threads of the new filter.

10 If an internal filter is located inside the carburetor inlet, the spring, gasket and filter must be removed after the inlet is unscrewed.

11 Assemble the new filter, seal and spring in the reverse order of their removal.

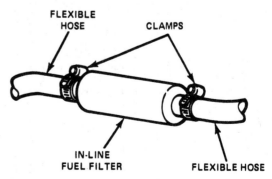

FLEXIBLE
HOSE   CLAMPS

IN-LINE
FUEL FILTER   FLEXIBLE HOSE

Fig. 1.17 Typical installation of an in-line fuel filter (Sec 17)

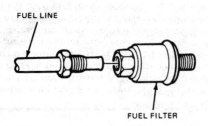

Fig. 1.18 Typical installation of an integral-type fuel filter (Sec 17)

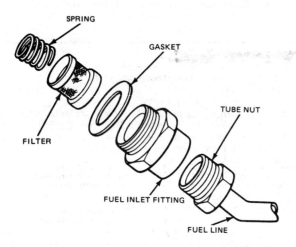

Fig. 1.19 Typical installation of a fuel filter inside the carburetor inlet (Sec 17)

12 Carefully screw in the inlet connector using caution not to damage the threads in the carburetor.
13 Some fuel filters are located in the bottom of the fuel pump. To remove this type of filter, unscrew the canister from the bottom of the fuel pump in the same way that an oil filter is removed.
14 Slowly drop the canister and filter assembly off the bottom of the fuel pump, being careful not to spill the gasoline contained within it.
15 Empty the container and then remove the filter and gasket assembly.
16 Insert a new filter and gasket assembly.

17 Screw the filter and filter housing assembly back on to the base of the fuel pump.
18 Start the vehicle and check the filter and surrounding area for leaks.

18 Evaporative emissions system – inspection

Note: *See illustrations in Chapter 6 for component location and identification.*
1 The evaporative emissions system consists of the charcoal carbon canister, the lines connecting the canister to the carburetor air cleaner and to the fuel tank, and the fuel tank filler cap.
2 Inspect the fuel filler cap(s) and make sure the gasket sealing the cap is in good condition. It should not be cracked, broken or show signs of leakage.
3 Inspect the lines leading to the charcoal canister from the fuel tank. They should be in good shape and the rubber should not show signs of cracking, checking or leakage.
4 Check all of the clamps and make sure they are sealing the system. Check the carbon-filled canister for any signs of leakage, over-filling or damage. In most cases, a carbon canister will last the lifetime of the vehicle; however, certain situations will require replacement. If the carbon canister shows signs of leakage or damage, replace it, as it is not a serviceable unit.
5 Check all the lines leading from the carbon canister to the air cleaner. In some cases there will be two lines, one leading from the carburetor fuel bowl to vent it, and one line leading from the carbon canister to the air cleaner for burning of the accumulated vapors.
6 Replace any lines in questionable condition and exercise the same precautions as are necessary when dealing with fuel lines or the fuel filter.

19 Lubrication – chassis, body and driveline components

1 A grease gun filled with the proper grease (see *Recommended lubricants* near the front of this Chapter) and some rags are the main pieces of equipment necessary to lubricate the chassis and steering components. Notice that different components require different types of grease so a grease gun with changeable cartridges or several grease guns will be necessary to correctly perform the lubrication process.
2 Carefully look over the accompanying illustration for the location of the lubrication fittings on the chassis and steering linkage. After you have familiarized yourself with these locations, look under the vehicle and relate the chart to the grease fittings, many of which are visible from under the vehicle's front bumper.
3 Easier access to some of these fittings will require raising and supporting the vehicle with a jack and jackstands. Be sure the vehicle

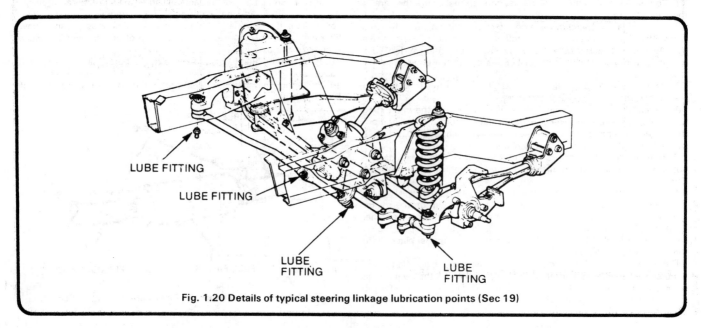

Fig. 1.20 Details of typical steering linkage lubrication points (Sec 19)

is firmly supported with jackstands and read the information on jacking instructions at the front of this book if you are unfamiliar with the correct procedures.

4   Before you do any greasing, force a little of the grease out the nozzle to remove any dirt from the end of the gun. Wipe the nozzle clean with a rag.

5   With the grease gun, plenty of clean rags and the location diagram, go under the vehicle to begin lubricating the components.

6   Wipe the grease fitting nipple clean and push the nozzle firmly over the fitting nipple. Squeeze the trigger on the grease gun to force grease into the component. **Note:** *When lubricating the steering linkage joints, pump only enough lubricant to fill the rubber cup to a firm-to-the-touch capacity.* If you pump in too much grease, the cups can rupture allowing grease to leak out and dirt to enter the joint. For all other suspension and steering fittings, continue pumping grease into the nipple until grease seeps out of the joint between the two

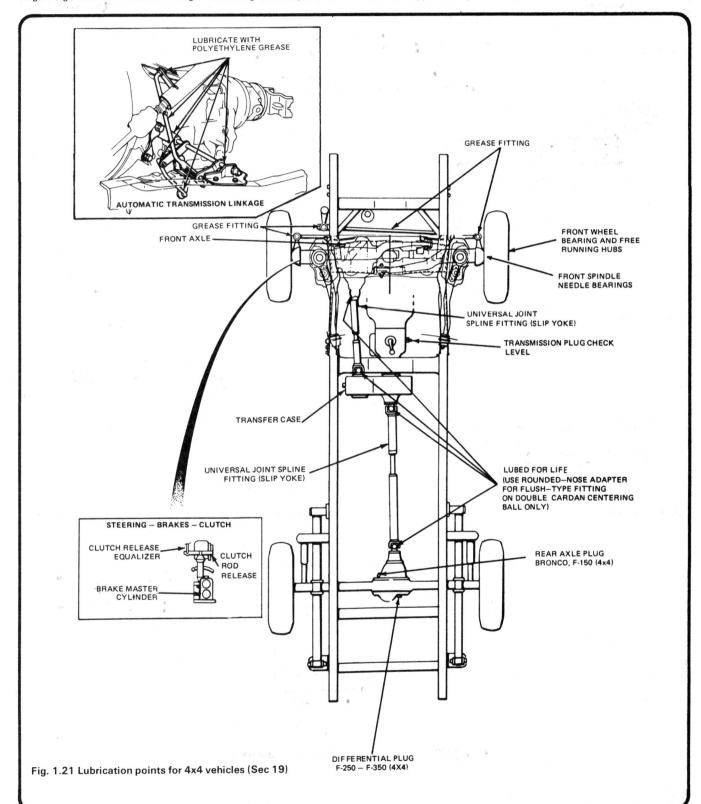

Fig. 1.21 Lubrication points for 4x4 vehicles (Sec 19)

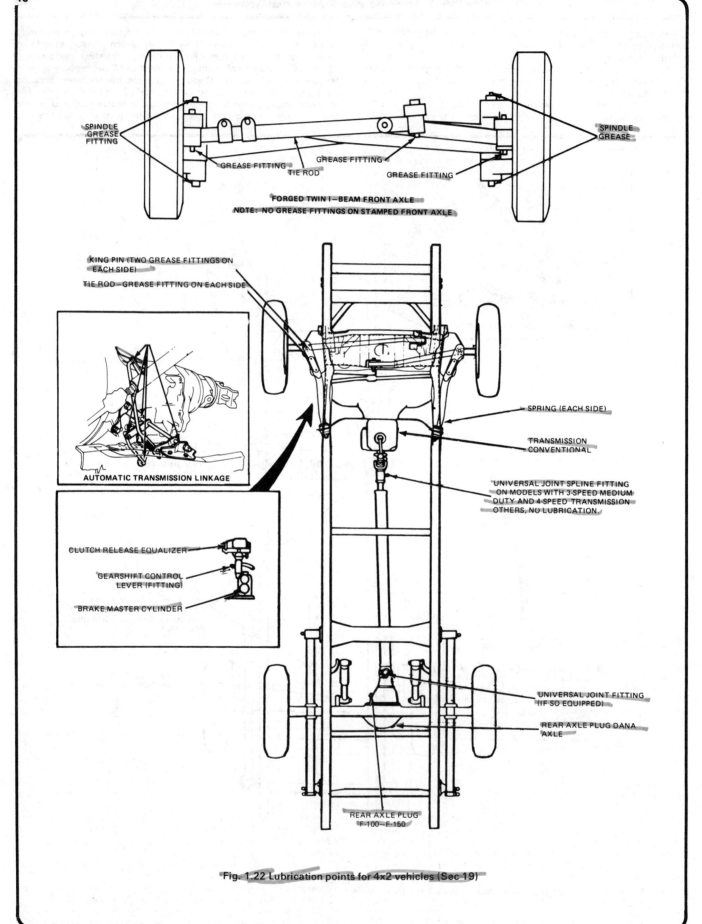

SPINDLE GREASE FITTING

SPINDLE GREASE

GREASE FITTING

TIE ROD

GREASE FITTING

GREASE FITTING

FORGED TWIN I—BEAM FRONT AXLE

NOTE: NO GREASE FITTINGS ON STAMPED FRONT AXLE

KING PIN (TWO GREASE FITTINGS ON EACH SIDE)

TIE ROD—GREASE FITTING ON EACH SIDE

AUTOMATIC TRANSMISSION LINKAGE

SPRING (EACH SIDE)

TRANSMISSION CONVENTIONAL

UNIVERSAL JOINT SPLINE FITTING ON MODELS WITH 3-SPEED MEDIUM DUTY AND 4-SPEED TRANSMISSION OTHERS, NO LUBRICATION.

CLUTCH RELEASE EQUALIZER

GEARSHIFT CONTROL LEVER (FITTING)

BRAKE MASTER CYLINDER

UNIVERSAL JOINT FITTING (IF SO EQUIPPED)

REAR AXLE PLUG DANA AXLE

REAR AXLE PLUG F-100—F-150

Fig. 1.22 Lubrication points for 4x2 vehicles (Sec 19)

components. If the grease seeps out around the grease gun nozzle, the nipple is clogged or the nozzle is not fully seated around the fitting nipple. Resecure the gun nozzle to the fitting and try again. If necessary, replace the fitting. Make sure the king pins have plenty of grease of the correct type.

7   Wipe the excess grease from the components and the grease fitting.

8   Check the universal joints on the driveshaft; some have fittings, some are factory sealed. About two pumps is all that is required for grease-type universal joints. While you are under the vehicle, clean and lubricate the parking brake cable along with its cable guides and levers. This can be done by smearing some of the chassis grease onto the cable and its related parts with your fingers. Place a few drops of light engine oil on the standard transmission and transfer case, if 4x4 or Bronco, shifting linkage rods and swivels. Lubricate 3-speed and AOD automatic transmission linkages with the lubricants specified at the beginning of this Chapter.

9   Lower the vehicle to the ground for the remaining body lubrication process.

10   Open the hood and smear a little chassis grease on the hood latch mechanism. If the hood has an inside release, have an assistant pull the release knob from inside the vehicle as you lubricate the cable at the latch.

11   Lubricate all the hinges (door, hood, tailgate) with a few drops of light engine oil to keep them in proper working order.

12   The key lock cylinders can be lubricated with spray-on graphite which is available at auto parts stores.

13   Spray silicone lubricant on the door seals to keep them pliable and effective.

14   Lubricate the accelerator linkage pivots with a multi-purpose lubricant, usually available in small spray cans.

15   Lubricate the clutch linkage (if the vehicle is stick-shift equipped) with the grease gun through the fitting provided on the cross-shaft linkage.

16   Use a rust penetrant and inhibitor on the manifold exhaust heat control valve if the vehicle is so equipped.

17   Spray some multi-purpose lubricant on the brake pedal (and clutch pedal) pivot shafts under the dash area for smooth, quiet operation of these pedal(s). Be sure to wipe off any excess so that the operator's shoes and clothing do not pick up any extra lubricant.

18   Some universal joints, particularly those found on 4X4 equipped vehicles, will require the use of a special 'needle' lubrication adapter for your grease gun. Do not overlook this part of the driveline lubrication as it is important for the continued service of these joints; they are relatively expensive and difficult to replace should they fail.

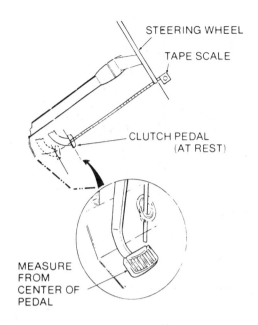

Fig. 1.23 Measuring points for determining clutch pedal free play (Sec 20)

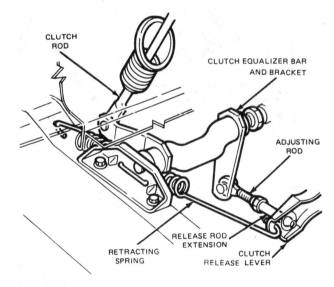

Fig. 1.24 Details of components involved in clutch pedal free play adjustment (Sec 20)

20 Clutch – adjustment

1   To adjust the clutch pedal free play, two measurements will have to be taken.

2   The first measurement is taken with the pedal fully released. The distance between the face of the clutch pedal and the bottom of the steering wheel should be taken for a base measurement.

3   Depress the clutch pedal until all of the free play is taken up and additional resistance is felt. This point is the beginning of the clutch being actuated at the release bearing.

4   In this depressed position, again measure the distance between the base of the steering wheel and the clutch pedal face. Subtract this distance from the original base measurement to find the clutch pedal free play.

5   If the clutch pedal play is more than the maximum, or less than the minimum specifications, the clutch must be adjusted to prevent premature failure of the throw-out bearing or damage to the clutch.

6   To adjust the clutch, remove the retracting spring at the clutch linkage near the bellhousing next to the clutch release lever.

7   Loosen the two jam nuts on the clutch release rod and back off both of the nuts several turns.

8   Turn the first jam nut against the swivel until the specified free play is achieved. Notice that one turn of the jam nut will move the play approximately $\frac{1}{4}$ in.

9   Hold the first jam nut with an open end wrench and tighten the second jam nut against the first. This locks the adjustment. Recheck your measurement.

10   Reinstall the clutch linkage retracting spring.

21 Manual transmission – oil change

1   Drive the vehicle for at least 15 minutes in stop-and-go traffic to warm the oil in the case. Use all of the gears including Reverse during this driving cycle to ensure that the lubricant is sufficiently warm to drain completely.

2   Raise the vehicle to a level position using either a suitable lift or four jackstands (see *Jacking and towing* at the front of this book). Remove the drain plug from the transmission. Allow plenty of time for the lubricant to drain.

3   After all of the lubricant has been drained, replace and retorque the case drain plug.

4   Using the proper grade and type of hypoid gear oil, refill the transmission case until the fluid reaches the filler hole level.

5   Replace the filler plug and tighten the plug to the correct torque specification. Drive the vehicle for a short distance and recheck the oil

level. In some cases a small amount of additional fluid will have to be added.

6 After driving the vehicle, recheck the drain and filler plugs for any signs of leakage.

22 Transfer case – oil change

1 Drive the vehicle for at least 15 minutes in stop-and-go traffic to warm the oil in the case. Perform the warm-up procedure in 4-wheel drive. The manual locking hubs should be in the Lock position if the vehicle is so equipped. Use all gears including Reverse to ensure that the lubricant is sufficiently warm to drain completely.

2 Remove the filler plug from the rear top case half (photo).

3 Remove the drain plug from the rear bottom case half and allow the old lubricant to drain completely.

4 Carefully clean and install the drain plug after the case is completely drained. Tighten the plug to the specified torque.

5 Fill the case with the specified lubricant until it is level with the lower edge of the filler hole.

6 Install the filler plug and tighten it to the specified torque.

7 Drive the vehicle for a short distance and recheck the oil level. In

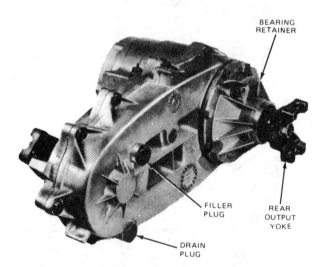

Fig. 1.25 Locations of the filler and drain plugs in a typical transfer case (B-W 1345 shown, others similar) (Sec 22)

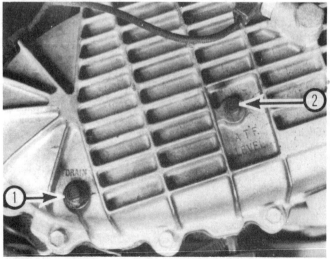

22.2 Locations of the transfer case drain plug (1) and fill plug (2)

some cases a small amount of additional oil will have to be added.

8 After driving the vehicle, recheck the drain and filler plugs for any signs of leakage, retorquing the plugs if necessary.

23 Automatic transmission – fluid change

1 At the specified time intervals, the transmission fluid should be changed and the filter replaced with a new one. Since there is no drain plug, the transmission oil pan must be removed from the bottom of the transmission to drain the fluid.

2 Before any draining, purchase the specified transmission fluid (see *Recommended lubricants* near the front of this Chapter) a new filter and all necessary gaskets. **Note:** *Due to the susceptibility of automatic transmissions to contamination, under no circumstances should the old filter or gaskets be reused.*

3 Other tools necessary for this job include jackstands to support the vehicle in a raised position, a wrench to remove the oil pan bolts, a standard screwdriver, a drain pan capable of holding at least 30 pints, newspapers and clean rags.

4 The fluid should be drained immediately after the vehicle has been driven. This will remove any built-up sediment better than if the fluid were cold. Because of this, it may be wise to wear protective gloves (fluid temperature can exceed 350°F in a hot transmission).

5 After the vehicle has been driven to warm up the fluid, raise it and place it on jackstands for access underneath. Make sure it is firmly supported by the four stands placed on the frame rails.

6 Move the necessary equipment under the vehicle, being careful not to touch any of the hot exhaust components.

7 Place the drain pan under the transmission oil pan and remove the oil pan bolts along the rear and sides of the pan. Loosen, but do not remove, the bolts at the front of the pan.

8 Carefully pry the pan down at the rear, allowing the hot fluid to drain into the drain pan. If necessary, use a screwdriver to break the gasket seal at the rear of the pan; however, do not damage the pan or transmission in the process.

9 Support the pan and remove the remaining bolts at the front of the pan. Lower the pan and drain the remaining fluid into the drain receptacle. As this is done, check the fluid for metal particles which may be an indication of transmission failure.

10 Now visible on the bottom of the transmission is the filter/strainer held in place by screws.

11 Remove the screws, the filter and the gasket.

12 Thoroughly clean the transmission oil pan with solvent. Inspect for metal particles and foreign matter. Dry with compressed air, if available. It is important that all remaining gasket material be removed from the oil pan mounting flange. Use a gasket scraper or putty knife for this.

13 Clean the filter mounting surface on the valve body. Again, this surface should be smooth and free of old gasket material.

14 Place the new filter into position with a new gasket between it and the transmission valve body. Install the mounting screws and tighten them to the specified torque.

15 Apply a bead of gasket sealant around the oil pan mounting surface, with the sealant to the inside of the bolt holes. Press the new gasket into place on the pan, making sure all bolt holes line up.

16 Lift the pan up to the bottom of the transmission and install the mounting bolts. Tighten the bolts in a diagonal fashion, working around the pan. Using a torque wrench, tighten the bolts to the specified torque.

17 Lower the vehicle off the jackstands.

18 Open the hood and remove the transmission fluid dipstick from its guide tube.

19 Since fluid capacities vary between the various transmission types, it is best to add a little fluid at a time, continually checking the level with the dipstick. Allow the fluid time to drain into the pan. Add fluid until the level just registers on the end of the dipstick. In most cases, a good starting point will be 4 to 5 pints (6 to 7 pints on 4x4 vehicles equipped with the C6 transmission) added to the transmission through the filler tube (use a funnel to prevent spills).

20 With the selector lever in Park apply the parking brake and start the engine without depressing the accelerator pedal (if possible). Do not race the engine at a high speed; run at a slow idle only, for at least two minutes.

21 Depress the brake pedal and shift the transmission through each gear. Place the selector in the Neutral position and (with the engine

still idling) still check the level on the dipstick. Look under the vehicle for leaks around the transmission oil pan mating surface.

22 Add more fluid through the dipstick tube until the level on the dipstick is just above the middle hole. Do not add any more fluid at this time.

23 Push the dipstick firmly back into its tube and drive the vehicle to reach normal operating temperature (15 miles of highway driving or its equivalent in the city). Park on a level surface and check the fluid level on the dipstick with the engine idling and the transmission in Neutral. The level should now be at or just below the Don't add mark on the dipstick. If not, add more fluid as necessary to bring the level up to this point. Again, do not overfill.

24 Differentials – oil change

Note: *Carefully read through this Section before undertaking this procedure. You will need to purchase the correct type and amount of differential lubricant before draining the old oil out of the vehicle. In some cases you will also need a differential cover gasket and an additive.*

1 The vehicle should be driven for several minutes before draining the differential oil. This practice will warm up the oil and ensure complete drainage.

2 Move a drain pan, rags, newspapers, and tools under the vehicle. With the drain pan under the differential, remove the drain plug from the bottom of the housing. On Dana-type differentials, no drain plug is provided which necessitates that the differential cover be removed to drain the fluid. Remove the inspection/fill plug to help vent the non-Dana type differentials.

3 After the oil has completely drained, wipe the area around the drain hole with a clean rag and install the drain plug. Reinstall the differential cover with a new gasket on Dana-type differentials. Tighten the cover retaining bolts to the proper torque.

4 Fill the housing (through the inspection hole) with the recommended lubricant until the level is even with the bottom of the inspection hole. Check the manufacturer's tag on the driver's door latch post or the tag attached to the differential to determine if your vehicle is equipped with a locking or equal-lock type of differential. These differentials require the use of an additional additive to supplement the normal differential lubricant (see *Recommended lubricants* at the beginning of this Chapter). Add the prescribed amount of the additive at this time. Install the inspection plug after cleaning it and the threads in the case or cover.

5 After driving the vehicle, check for leaks at the drain and inspection plugs.

6 When the job is complete, check for metal particles or chips in the drained oil, which indicate that the differential should be thoroughly inspected and repaired (see Chapter 8 for more information).

25 Cooling system – draining, flushing and refilling

1 Periodically, the cooling system should be drained, flushed and refilled. This is to replenish the antifreeze mixture and prevent rust and corrosion which can impair the performance of the cooling system and ultimately cause engine damage.

2 At the same time the cooling system is serviced, all hoses and the radiator cap should be inspected and replaced if faulty (see Section 12).

3 Antifreeze is a poisonous solution, so take care not to spill any of the cooling mixture on the vehicle's paint or your own skin. If this happens, rinse immediately with plenty of clear water. Also it is advisable to consult your local authorities about the dumping of antifreeze before draining the cooling system. In many areas reclamation centers have been set up to collect automobile oil and drained antifreeze/water mixtures rather than allowing these liquids to be added to the sewage and water facilities.

4 With the engine cold, remove the radiator cap.

5 Move a large container under the radiator to catch the coolant mixture as it is drained.

6 Drain the radiator. Most models are equipped with a drain plug at the bottom of the radiator which can be opened using a wrench to hold the fitting while the petcock is turned to the open position. If this drain has excessive corrosion and cannot be turned easily, or the radiator is not equipped with a drain, disconnect the lower radiator hose to allow

the coolant to drain. Be careful that none of the solution is splashed on your skin or in your eyes.

7 If accessible, remove the engine drain plugs. On V8 engines, there is one plug on each side of the block, about halfway back and on the lower edge near the oil pan rail. Six-cylinder engines have one drain plug, located at the left rear of the cylinder block.

8 On systems with an expansion reservoir, disconnect the overflow pipe and remove the reservoir. Flush it out with clean water.

9 Place a hose (a common garden hose is fine) in the radiator filler neck at the top of the radiator and flush the system until the water runs clean at all drain points.

10 In severe cases of contamination or clogging of the radiator, remove (see Chapter 3) and reverse flush. This involves simply inserting the hose in the bottom radiator outlet to allow the water to run against the normal flow, draining through the top. A radiator repair shop should be consulted if further cleaning or repair is necessary.

11 Where the coolant is regularly drained and the system refilled with the correct antifreeze mixture there should be no need to employ chemical cleaners or descalers.

12 To refill the system, reconnect the radiator hoses and install the drain plugs securely in the engine. Special thread sealing tape (available at auto parts stores) should be used on the drain plugs in the engine block. Install the expansion reservoir and the overflow hose where applicable.

13 On vehicles without an expansion reservoir, refill the system through the radiator filler cap until the level is about $\frac{3}{4}$ to $1\frac{1}{2}$ inches below the filler neck.

14 On vehicles with an expansion reservoir, fill the radiator to the base of the filler neck and then add more coolant to the expansion reservoir so that it reaches the Full cold mark.

15 Run the engine until normal operating temperature is reached and with the engine idling, add coolant up to the correct level (see Section 3), then install the radiator cap so that the arrows are in alignment with the overflow pipe. Install the reservoir cap.

16 Always refill the system with a mixture of high quality antifreeze and water in the proportion called for on the antifreeze container or in your owner's manual. Chapter 3 also contains information on antifreeze mixtures.

17 Keep a close watch on the coolant level and the various cooling hoses during the first few miles of driving. Tighten the hose clamps and/or add more coolant mixture as necessary.

26 Wheel bearings (front – 4x2) – check, repack and adjustment

Note: *This procedure applies only to 4x2 vehicles only. Information on Bronco and F150/350 4x4 models will be found in Chapter 8. Refer to Fig. 1.26 to locate pertinent 4x2 components.*

1 In most cases, the front wheel bearings will not need servicing until the brake pads are changed. However, these bearings should be checked whenever the front wheels are raised for any reason.

2 With the vehicle securely supported on jackstands, spin the wheel and check for noise, rolling resistance and free play. Now grab the top of the tire with one hand and the bottom of the tire with the other. Move the tire in and out on the spindle. If it moves more than 0.005 in, the bearings should be checked, then repacked with grease or replaced if necessary.

3 To remove the bearings for replacing or repacking, begin by removing the hub cap and wheel.

4 Remove the brake caliper as described in Chapter 9.

5 Use wire to hang the caliper assembly out of the way. Be careful not to kink or damage the brake hose.

6 Pry the grease cap off the hub using a screwdriver. This cap is located at the center of the hub.

7 Use needle-nose pliers to straighten the bent ends of the cotter pin and then pull the cotter pin out of the locking nut. Discard the cotter pin, as a new one should be used on reassembly.

8 Remove the spindle nut and washer from the end of the spindle.

9 Pull the hub assembly out slightly and then push it back into its original position. This should force the outer bearing off the spindle enough so that it can be removed with your fingers. Remove the outer bearing, noting how it is installed on the end of the spindle.

10 Now the hub assembly can be pulled off the spindle.

11 Use a screwdriver to pry out the inner bearing lip seal on the rear side of the hub. As this is done, note the direction in which the seal is installed.

1

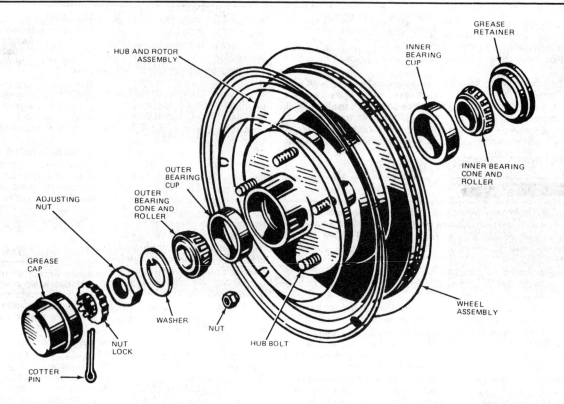

Fig. 1.26 Components of front wheel bearing assembly – exploded view (4x2 only) (Sec 26)

12 The inner bearing can now be removed from the hub, again noting how it is installed.

13 Use clean parts solvent to remove all traces of the old grease from the bearings, hub and spindle. A small brush may prove useful; however, make sure no bristles from the brush embed themselves inside the bearing rollers. Allow the parts to air dry.

14 Carefully inspect the bearings for cracks, heat discoloration, bent rollers, etc. Check the bearing races inside the hub for cracks, scoring, and uneven surfaces. If the bearing races are in need of replacement this job is best left to a repair shop which can press the new races into position.

15 Use an approved high-temperature front-wheel bearing grease to pack the bearings. Work the grease fully into the bearings, forcing it between the rollers, cone and cage.

16 Apply a thin coat of grease to the spindle at the outer bearing seat, inner bearing seat, shoulder and seal seat.

17 Put a small quantity of grease inboard of each bearing race inside the hub. Using your fingers, form a dam at these points to provide extra grease availability and to keep thinned grease from flowing out of the bearing.

18 Place the grease-packed inner bearing into the rear of the hub and put a little more grease outboard of the bearings.

19 Place a new seal over the inner bearing and tap the seal with a flat plate and a hammer until it is flush with the hub.

20 Carefully place the hub assembly onto the spindle and push the grease-packed outer bearing into position.

21 Install the washer and spindle nut. Tighten the nut only slightly (22 to 25 ft-lbs of torque).

22 Spin the hub in a forward direction to seat the bearings and remove any grease or burrs which would cause excessive bearing play later.

23 Put a little grease outboard of the outer bearing to provide extra grease availability.

24 Now check that the spindle nut is still tight (22 to 25 ft-lbs).

25 Loosen the spindle nut $\frac{1}{8}$ turn.

26 Using your hand (not a wrench of any kind), tighten the nut until it is snug. Install a new cotter pin through the hole in the spindle and spindle nut. If the nut slits do not line up, loosen the nut slightly until they do. From the hand-tight position the nut should not be loosened any more than one-half flat to install the cotter pin.

27 Bend the ends of the new cotter pin until they are flat against the nut. Cut off any extra length which could interfere with the dust cap.

28 Install the dust cap, tapping it into place with a rubber mallet.

29 Reinstall the brake caliper as described in Chapter 9.

30 Install the tire/wheel assembly and tighten the mounting nuts.

31 Grab the top and bottom of the tire and check the bearings in the same manner as described at the beginning of this Section.

32 Lower the vehicle to the ground and fully tighten the wheel nuts. Install the hub cap, using a rubber mallet to fully seat it.

27 Spark plug wires – checking and replacement

1 The spark plug wires should be checked at the recommended intervals or whenever new spark plugs are installed.

2 The wires should be inspected one at a time to prevent mixing up the order which is essential for proper engine operation. Each original spark plug wire is numbered to help identify its location. If any number is illegible, a piece of masking tape can be marked with the correct number and wrapped around the spark plug wire.

3 Disconnect the plug wire from the spark plug. A removal tool can be used for this, or you can grab the rubber boot, twist slightly and then pull the wire free. Do not pull on the wire itself, only on the rubber boot.

4 Inspect inside the boot for corrosion, which will look like a white crusty powder. Some vehicles use a conductive white grease which should not be mistaken for corrosion. **Note:** *When any spark plug wire on an electronic ignition system is detached from a spark plug, distributor or coil terminal, silicone grease (Ford No. D7AZ-19A331-A or equivalent electronic application grease) should be applied to the interior surface of the boot before reinstalling the wire onto the component.*

5 Now push the wire and boot back onto the end of the spark plug. It should be a tight fit on the plug end. If not, remove the wires and use a pair of pliers to carefully crimp the metal connector inside the wire boot until the fit is secure.

6 Now, using a clean rag, clean each wire along its entire length. Remove all built-up dirt and grease. As this is done, inspect for burns, cracks or any other form of damage.

7 Disconnect the wire at the distributor (again, pulling and twisting

CARBON DEPOSITS

Symptoms: Dry sooty deposits indicate a rich mixture or weak ignition. Causes misfiring, hard starting and hesitation.

Recommendation: Check for a clogged air cleaner, high float level, sticky choke and worn ignition points. Use a spark plug with a longer core nose for greater anti-fouling protection.

OIL DEPOSITS

Symptoms: Oily coating caused by poor oil control. Oil is leaking past worn valve guides or piston rings into the combustion chamber. Causes hard starting, misfiring and hesition.

Recommendation: Correct the mechanical condition with necessary repairs and install new plugs.

TOO HOT

Symptoms: Blistered, white insulator, eroded electrode and absence of deposits. Results in shortened plug life.

Recommendation: Check for the correct plug heat range, over-advanced ignition timing, lean fuel mixture, intake manifold vacuum leaks and sticking valves. Check the coolant level and make sure the radiator is not clogged.

PREIGNITION

Symptoms: Melted electrodes. Insulators are white, but may be dirty due to misfiring or flying debris in the combustion chamber. Can lead to engine damage.

Recommendation: Check for the correct plug heat range, over-advanced ignition timing, lean fuel mixture, clogged cooling system and lack of lubrication.

HIGH SPEED GLAZING

Symptoms: Insulator has yellowish, glazed appearance. Indicates that combustion chamber temperatures have risen suddenly during hard acceleration. Normal deposits melt to form a conductive coating. Causes misfiring at high speeds.

Recommendation: Install new plugs. Consider using a colder plug if driving habits warrant.

GAP BRIDGING

Symptoms: Combustion deposits lodge between the electrodes. Heavy deposits accumulate and bridge the electrode gap. The plug ceases to fire, resulting in a dead cylinder.

Recommendation: Locate the faulty plug and remove the deposits from between the electrodes.

NORMAL

Symptoms: Brown to grayish-tan color and slight electrode wear. Correct heat range for engine and operating conditions.

Recommendation: When new spark plugs are installed, replace with plugs of the same heat range.

ASH DEPOSITS

Symptoms: Light brown deposits encrusted on the side or center electrodes or both. Derived from oil and/or fuel additives. Excessive amounts may mask the spark, causing misfiring and hesitation during acceleration.

Recommendation: If excessive deposits accumulate over a short time or low mileage, install new valve guide seals to prevent seepage of oil into the combustion chambers. Also try changing gasoline brands.

WORN

Symptoms: Rounded electrodes with a small amount of deposits on the firing end. Normal color. Causes hard starting in damp or cold weather and poor fuel economy.

Recommendation: Replace with new plugs of the same heat range.

DETONATION

Symptoms: Insulators may be cracked or chipped. Improper gap setting techniques can also result in a fractured insulator tip. Can lead to piston damage.

Recommendation: Make sure the fuel anti-knock values meet engine requirements. Use care when setting the gaps on new plugs. Avoid lugging the engine.

SPLASHED DEPOSITS

Symptoms: After long periods of misfiring, deposits can loosen when normal combustion temperature is restored by an overdue tune-up. At high speeds, deposits flake off the piston and are thrown against the hot insulator, causing misfiring.

Recommendation: Replace the plugs with new ones or clean and reinstall the originals.

MECHANICAL DAMAGE

Symptoms: May be caused by a foreign object in the combustion chamber or the piston striking an incorrect reach (too long) plug. Causes a dead cylinder and could result in piston damage.

Recommendation: Remove the foreign object from the engine and/or install the correct reach plug.

1

only on the rubber boot). Check for corrosion and a tight fit in the same manner as the spark plug end.

28 Distributor cap and rotor — inspection and replacement

Note: *Refer to Fig. 1.27 for component location and identification.*

1   To check the distributor cap and rotor, first release the two clips retaining the distributor cap to adapter. Lift the cap from the distributor and turn it over to observe the contacts on the inside surface. Wipe the cap clean with a dry cloth and check that the contact points are not burned or scored. Also, carefully inspect, using a high-powered light if necessary, for any signs of carbon tracking which look like black pencil lines on the inside of the cap surface. If any of these conditions exist, replace the distributor cap with a new one.

2   Check the carbon contact located at the center of the cap and make sure that it is not worn down. It should protrude from the cap a small amount in order to make contact with the corresponding spring blade of the rotor.

3   Lift the rotor off of the distributor cam and check that the spring on the top of the rotor is effective and that the contact point is clean. It may be necessary to use a small file to brush away some of the carbon but do not wear away any of the metal. Check the outer rotating end of the contact on the rotor. Make sure that no excessive pitting, scoring or erosion is present. If any of these conditions exist, replace the rotor with a new one.

4   Installation of the rotor requires aligning the tang on the inside of the rotor with the corresponding notch on the distributor shaft. Push the rotor firmly onto the shaft until it bottoms on its seat once the notch and tang are aligned.

5   Install the cap over the top of the adapter and make sure that the notch in the cap fits the tang which protrudes on the side of the adapter. Clip the two retaining clips to each side of the cap and make sure that all of the wires are securely inserted into their respective terminals.

6   **Note:** *Because all 1980 through 1983 Ford trucks covered in this manual are equipped with electronic ignition systems, no further servicing of the ignition components is required. Refer to Section 27 regarding use of lubricant when reinstalling spark plug wires. Apply lubricant to the rotor as shown in the accompanying illustration.*

29 Spark plugs — replacement

1   The spark plugs are located on the left side of in-line six-cylinder engines and on both sides of V6 and V8 engines.

2   In most cases, the tools necessary for a spark plug replacement job are a plug wrench or spark plug socket which fits onto a ratchet wrench (this special socket will be insulated inside to protect the porcelain insulator) and a feeler gauge to check and adjust the spark plug gap.

3   The best procedure to follow when replacing the spark plugs is to purchase the new spark plugs beforehand, adjust them to the proper gap and then replace each plug one at a time. When buying the new spark plugs it is important to obtain the correct plugs for your specific engine. This information can be found on the Emissions Control Information label located under the hood of your vehicle or in the factory owner's manual. If differences exist between these sources, purchase the spark plug type specified on the emissions label as it was printed for your specific engine. Ford specifies that a special silicone grease (Ford part no. D7AZ-19A331-A) be applied inside the wire boot whenever one of the high-tension cables is disconnected.

4   .With the new spark plugs at hand, allow the engine to thoroughly cool before attempting the removal. During this cooling time, each of the new spark plugs can be inspected for defects and the gap can be checked.

5   The gap is checked by inserting the proper thickness gauge between the electrodes at the tip of the plug. The gap between these electrodes should be the same as that given on the Emission Control Information label. The wire should just touch each of the electrodes. If the gap is incorrect, use the notched adjuster on the feeler gauge body to bend the curved side electrode slightly until the proper gap is achieved. Also, at this time check for cracks in the spark plug body indicating the spark plug should not be used. If the side electrode is not exactly over the center one, use the notched adjuster to align the two.

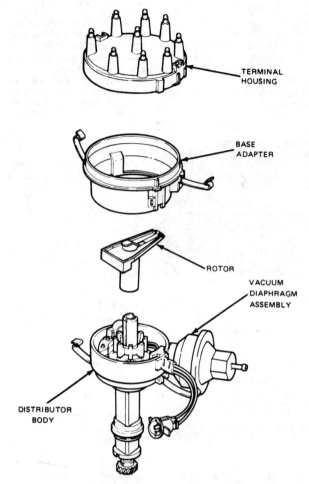

Fig. 1.27 Components of a typical electronic ignition system (Sec 28)

TERMINAL HOUSING

BASE ADAPTER

ROTOR

VACUUM DIAPHRAGM ASSEMBLY

DISTRIBUTOR BODY

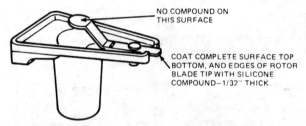

NO COMPOUND ON THIS SURFACE

COAT COMPLETE SURFACE TOP BOTTOM, AND EDGES OF ROTOR BLADE TIP WITH SILICONE COMPOUND—1/32" THICK.

Fig. 1.28 Lubricating points for a typical electronic distributor rotor (Sec 28)

6   Cover the fenders of the vehicle to prevent damage to the paint.

7   With the engine cool, remove the spark plug wire from one spark plug. Do this by grabbing the boot at the end of the wire, not the wire itself. Sometimes it is necessary to use a twisting motion while the boot and plug wire are pulled free. Using a plug wire removal tool is the easiest and safest method.

8   If compressed air is available, use it to blow any dirt or foreign material away from the spark plug area. A common bicycle pump will also work. The idea here is to eliminate the possibility of material falling into the engine cylinder as the spark plug is removed.

9   Now place the spark plug wrench or socket over the plug and remove it from the engine by turning in a counterclockwise motion.

10   Compare the spark plug with those shown in the photographs in this Chapter to get an indication of the overall running condition of the engine.

11   Carefully insert one of the new plugs into the spark plug hole and tighten it by hand. Be especially careful not to cross-thread the spark

plug in the hole. If resistance is felt as you thread the spark plug in by hand, back it out and start again. *Do not, under any circumstances, force the spark plug into the hole with a wrench or socket.*

12 Finally, tighten the spark plug with the wrench or socket. It is best to use a torque wrench for this to ensure the plug is seated correctly. The correct torque figure is given in the Specifications.

13 Before pushing the spark plug wire onto the end of the plug, inspect it following the procedures outlined in Section 27. Using a clean screwdriver, apply a thin layer of the silicone grease to the inside of the spark plug boot.

14 Attach the plug wire to the new spark plug, again using a twisting motion on the boot until it is firmly seated on the spark plug. Make sure the wire is routed through the loom clips.

15 Follow the above procedures for the remaining spark plugs, replacing them one at a time to prevent mixing up the spark plug wires.

30 Compression check

1 A compression check will tell you what mechanical condition the engine is in. Specifically, it can tell you if the compression is down due to leakage caused by worn piston rings, defective valves and seats or a blown head gasket. Make sure that the engine oil is of the correct viscosity and that the battery is fully charged.

2 Run the engine until it reaches normal operating temperature.

3 Turn the engine off. Set the carburetor throttle plates to the wide-open position. This may be verified by removing the top plate of the air cleaner and looking down into the carburetor throat. The throttle plates should be perpendicular to the ground.

4 Remove all spark plug wires from the spark plugs after marking them for position. Clean the area around the spark plugs before you remove them. This will keep dirt from falling into the cylinders while you are performing the compression test. Remove the spark plugs.

5 Install the compression gauge in the number one cylinder spark plug hole. On six-cylinder in-line engines, this is the cylinder nearest the front of the vehicle. On V6 and V8 engines, this is the cylinder nearest the front of the vehicle on the right-hand side (the driver's right as he sits in the vehicle). **Note:** *Make sure that the ignition switch is Off or the ignition coil is disconnected before proceeding with the next step.*

6 Crank the engine for approximately five revolutions with a remote starter or with an assistant operating the ignition switch from the driver's seat.

7 Observe the number of compression strokes required to reach the highest reading. Also, observe the pattern that the engine follows as it builds up to the highest compression reading (the compression should build up quickly in a healthy engine). Low compression on the first stroke, followed by gradually increasing pressure on successive strokes, indicates worn piston rings. A low compression reading on the first stroke, which does not build up during successive strokes, indicates leaking valves or a defective head gasket. Record the highest gauge reading obtained. Repeat the procedure for the remaining cylinders and compare the results. The compression is considered normal if the lowest cylinder reading is within 75 percent of the highest cylinder reading.

8 Variations exceeding 75 percent are a good indication of internal engine component problems. To further diagnose the engine using the compression gauge, select the low reading cylinder(s) for a further 'wet' compression test.

9 To perform a 'wet' compression test, pour a couple of teaspoons of engine oil (a squirt can work well) into each cylinder, through the spark plug hole, and repeat the test.

10 If the compression increases after the oil is added, the piston rings are definitely worn. If the compression does not increase significantly the leakage is occurring at the valves or head gasket.

11 If two adjacent cylinders have equally low compression, there is a strong possibility that the head gasket between them is blown. The appearance of coolant in the combustion chambers or the crankcase would verify this condition.

12 If the compression is higher than normal, the combustion chambers are probably coated with carbon deposits. If that is the case, the cylinder head (or heads) should be removed and decarbonized.

13 If compression is way down, or varies greatly between cylinders, it would be a good idea to have a 'leak-down' test performed by a reputable automotive repair shop. This test will pinpoint exactly where the leakage is occurring and how severe it is.

31 Ignition timing – checking and adjustment

Note: *Ignition timing on Duraspark III ignition systems is controlled by an Electronic Engine Control (EEC) and is not adjustable. The information which follows is applicable only to vehicles equipped with the Duraspark II ignition system. The process for checking and adjusting ignition timing requires the use of a stroboscopic-type timing light. These are available at auto parts stores as well as from rental agencies. Timing an engine 'by ear' and static timing procedures are not acceptable with today's tight emissions controls and should only be used to initially start and run an engine after it has been disassembled or the distributor has been removed.*

1 Start the engine and bring it to normal operating temperature.

2 Shut the engine off and connect the stroboscopic-type timing light according to the manufacturer's instructions. At the same time, refer to the Emissions Control Information label (located inside the engine compartment) for the proper engine timing specifications. Make sure the wiring leads for the timing light are not contacting any heat source such as an exhaust manifold and that they are routed away from any moving parts such as the vehicle's cooling fan.

3 Remove and block any vacuum hoses leading to the distributor if this is dictated by the instructions on the Emissions Control Information label. Use a golf-tee, pencil or other similar device to block off any removed vacuum lines. **Caution:** *Make sure that you have no dangling articles of clothing such as ties or jewelry which can be caught in the moving components of the engine.*

4 Start the engine, make sure that it is idling at the proper speed, according to the Emissions Control Information label. If not, see Chapter 4.

5 Aim the timing light at the timing marks. If the timing marks do not show up clearly, it may be necessary to stop the engine and clean the timing pointer and crankshaft pulley with a rag and a cleaning agent.

6 Compare the position of the timing marks with the timing specifications for your vehicle. If the marks line up, the ignition timing is correct and no adjustment is necessary. If the timing is incorrect, turn off the engine.

7 Loosen the distributor hold-down bolt with a wrench or special distributor bolt tool.

8 Restart the engine and rotate the distributor in either direction while pointing the timing light at the timing marks.

9 Be sure that the timing marks are aligned correctly and turn off the engine.

10 Tighten the distributor hold-down bolt.

11 Restart the engine and check the timing to make sure it has not moved while tightening down the clamp bolt.

12 Recheck the idle speed to make sure it has not changed significantly. If the idle speed has changed, reset the idle speed and recheck the timing, as timing will vary with engine rpm.

13 Reconnect all vacuum hoses and other connections removed for checking purposes.

32 Carburetor and choke system – inspection

Carburetor check

1 The first step in inspection of the carburetor is the removal of the air cleaner. The following instructions will apply to most vehicles; however, some variations may be encountered.

2 Remove the wing nut in the center of the top cover.

3 Remove the clamp and rubber fresh-air inlet hose from the air cleaner duct and valve assembly.

4 Remove the hose clamp and flexible hot air tube from the bottom of the duct and valve assembly. Be careful in this step if the engine is warm as this hose is used to duct hot air from the exhaust manifold area up to the carburetor.

5 Remove any vacuum hoses attached to the bottom of the air cleaner assembly. Mark them carefully so they may be reattached in the correct positions. Plug these hoses with a golf tee, pencil, or similar item to prevent vacuum leaks.

6 Remove the rocker cover vent hose from the side of the air cleaner (at the elbow). This is a rubber hose leading from the rocker cover and PCV valve.

54

PISTONS

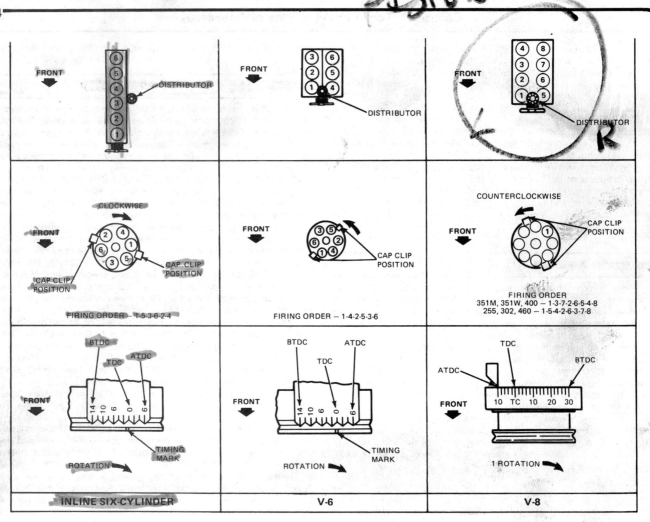

Fig. 1.29 Chart indicating cylinder numbering and distributor location (top row); distributor rotation and firing order (center), and crankshaft timing marks (bottom) (Sec 31)

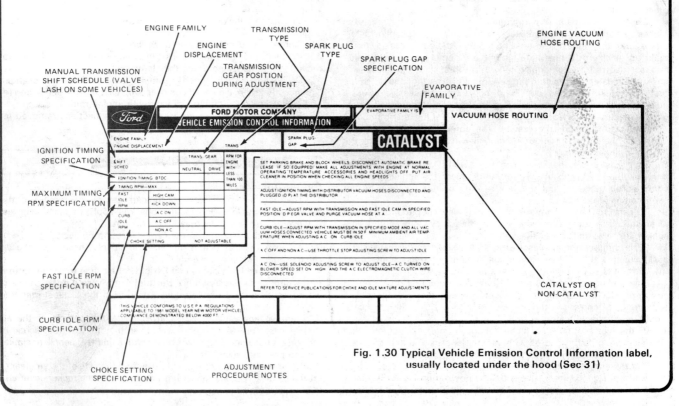

Fig. 1.30 Typical Vehicle Emission Control Information label, usually located under the hood (Sec 31)

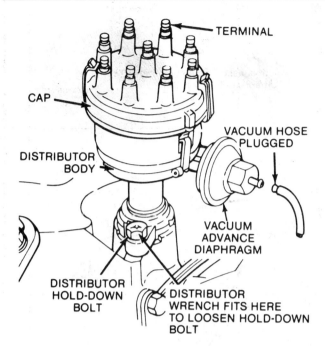

Fig. 1.31 Details of a typical ignition distributor installation (eight-cylinder shown, others similar) (Sec 31)

compartment if it is connected to one or two vacuum hoses (optional). If you do this, place the cover where it will not be damaged or contact hot engine parts.

10   Once the air cleaner has been removed, a visible inspection of the carburetor is possible. The main item to look for is decaying and/or leaking hoses. It is not necessary to remove any hoses to check their condition, but flexing them with the fingers will usually reveal telltale cracks or splits. Check the carburetor body itself for any signs of leakage and/or built-up sludge which could hamper the operation of any moving parts. Take care not to knock loose any large pieces of residue which will fall down into the carburetor inlet and finally end up in the engine. If excessively dirty, the carburetor should be removed and thoroughly cleaned (see Chapter 4).

11   While looking for leaks, check the carburetor top plate hold-down screws for tightness. Often, over a period of time vibration will cause these screws to loosen, creating a major source of gasoline and vacuum leakage. If a leak is suspected at any other point in the carburetor system, but it is not readily identifiable, clean the entire area and then prepare to run the vehicle without the air cleaner. **Note:** *Do not drive the vehicle in this condition as the engine is heavily dependent on filtered air for its continued service. This is a test procedure and should be performed only long enough to pinpoint any leaks which may occur under pressure or with the engine running.* Before starting the engine, disconnect and plug the small vacuum hose(s) which connect to the base of the air cleaner. Place these hoses out of the way from any heat sources or from the drivebelts and pulleys.

12   Check the accelerator linkage or the cable that connects the carburetor to the accelerator pedal. A helper working the throttle from the driver's seat will allow you to make close observation of the moving components of the accelerator system. Perform this procedure with the engine off.

13   Have an assistant slowly depress the accelerator to its full travel, then allow it to return while observing the cable or linkage and attending moving parts. Lubrication of these parts can be accomplished at the same time. Use a lightweight penetrating oil for the cable and pivot points.

14   If any major leaks or problems are noticed in the carburetor, refer to Chapter 4 for further information. **Note:** *Always use caution to see that nothing is dropped into the carburetor air intake, as it will eventually end up in the engine and cause serious damage.*

7   Remove the flexible air purge hose leading from the charcoal canister to the air cleaner.

8   Lift the air cleaner assembly off of the carburetor. **Note:** *Make sure that the gasket at the base of the air cleaner assembly either remains with the air cleaner or stays on the inlet flange of the carburetor. It sometimes can come loose and fall into the carburetor intake as the air cleaner is removed.*

9   The air cleaner cover may be set to the side of the engine

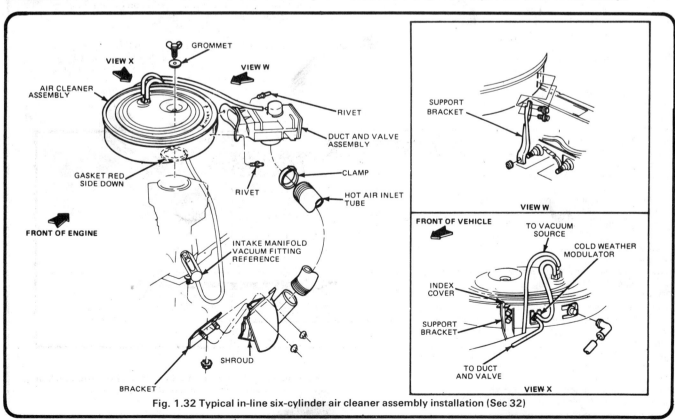

Fig. 1.32 Typical in-line six-cylinder air cleaner assembly installation (Sec 32)

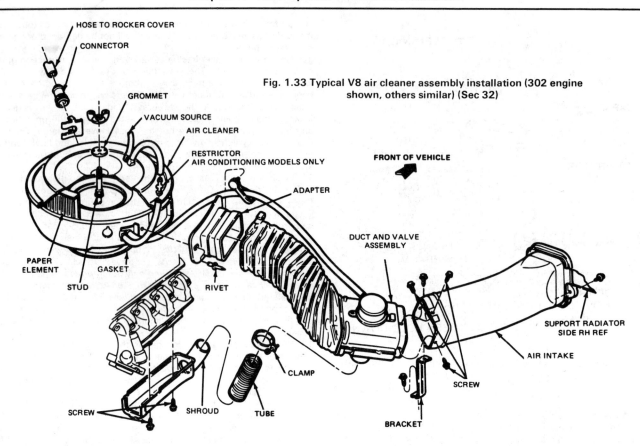

HOSE TO ROCKER COVER
CONNECTOR
GROMMET
VACUUM SOURCE
AIR CLEANER
RESTRICTOR
AIR CONDITIONING MODELS ONLY
ADAPTER
FRONT OF VEHICLE
DUCT AND VALVE ASSEMBLY
PAPER ELEMENT
GASKET
STUD
RIVET
SUPPORT RADIATOR SIDE RH REF
AIR INTAKE
CLAMP
SCREW
SCREW
SHROUD
TUBE
BRACKET

Fig. 1.33 Typical V8 air cleaner assembly installation (302 engine shown, others similar) (Sec 32)

Choke system check

15 The choke operates only when the engine is cold, so this check should be performed before the engine has been started for the day. The vehicle should be allowed to sit at least four hours at a temperature under 68°F since the last time it was run.

16 The air cleaner need not be removed for this check, but the top cover must be opened up. Take the top off by removing the wing nut and washer. Set the top cover aside, making sure you place it in a position where it is out of the way of any moving parts and is not in contact with any heat sources.

17 Look at the top of the carburetor at the center of the air cleaner housing. You will notice a flat plate at the carburetor opening.

18 Have an assistant press the accelerator pedal to the floor. The plate should close off the inlet fully. (On four-barrel carburetors, the plate covers only the front two barrels of the carburetor). Start the engine while you observe the plate at the carburetor inlet. Do not position your face directly over the carburetor, as the engine could backfire, causing serious burns. When the engine starts, the choke plate should open slightly.

19 Allow the engine to continue running at a fast idle speed. As the engine warms up to operating temperature, the plate should slowly open, allowing more air to enter through the top of the carburetor. Some vehicles will not fully open the plate unless the accelerator pedal is once again quickly pushed to more than its half-way position and released. If, after a few moments, you notice that the plate is not moving, try this quick depression of the accelerator pedal to see if it does release the choke linkage.

20 After a few minutes of operation, the choke plate should be fully opened to the vertical position once the engine has warmed up to operating temperature (photo). You will notice that the engine speed corresponds with the plate opening. With the plate fully closed, the engine should run at a fast idle speed. As the plate opens, the engine speed should decrease and eventually arrive at its normal curb idle operation level.

21 If a fault is detected during the above checks, refer to Chapter 4 for specific information on adjusting and servicing the choke components. Chapter 6 also contains information on emissions control systems related to the carburetor.

32.20 Checking the choke plate for proper operation

33 Idle speed and mixture adjustment

1 Anti-pollution laws in this country have dictated that strict tune-up rules are applied to light-duty vehicles, including trucks. Idle speed and especially idle mixtures are covered under these regulations and strict adherence to the correct method of adjustment is required. Due to the wide range of vehicles, models and power train combinations covered in this book, it is impractical to describe every method of idle speed and mixture adjustment. Additionally, certain areas require that these adjustments be made only by qualified technicians using expensive, specialized exhaust sampling equipment.

2 If you feel that you are qualified to make these adjustments,

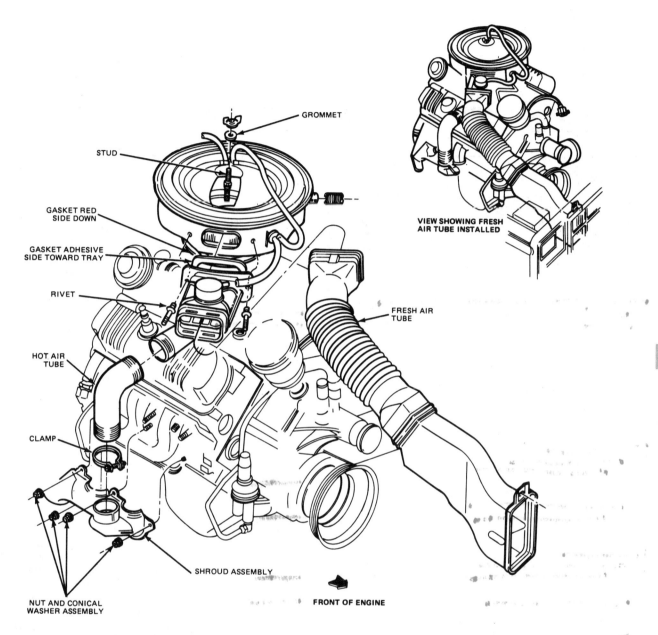

GROMMET

STUD

GASKET RED
SIDE DOWN

GASKET ADHESIVE
SIDE TOWARD TRAY

RIVET

HOT AIR
TUBE

CLAMP

NUT AND CONICAL
WASHER ASSEMBLY

SHROUD ASSEMBLY

FRONT OF ENGINE

VIEW SHOWING FRESH
AIR TUBE INSTALLED

FRESH AIR
TUBE

Fig. 1.34 Typical V6 air cleaner assembly installation (Sec 32)

please refer to Chapter 4 for the correct procedure involving your vehicle. The data for your particular vehicle should be clearly displayed on a decal or metal plate inside the engine compartment. The operation of various devices, such as throttle positioners, dash pots, solenoids and the connecting or disconnecting of vacuum lines to them, are all variables which must be controlled while making idle speed adjustments. Do not, under any circumstances, attempt to make any adjustments on carburetors or attempt to disable the limiter-type devices on the idle mixture screws in an effort to modify your vehicle's idle or performance characteristics. Following the factory designated procedures is the best way to achieve a satisfactorily performing engine and comply with federal and local motor vehicle laws.

3   If you are equipped to handle the correct procedure for adjusting idles, be sure to adhere strictly to the procedure involved for the vehicle and to the data provided on the Emissions Control Information label.

34 Valves – adjustment

1   All Ford truck light-duty engines are equipped with hydraulic valve lifters. Under normal circumstances these lifters maintain the ideal valve clearance for the valve train. Therefore, no adjustment is necessary.

2   In some instances, especially when repeated valve jobs have been performed on an engine, the valve clearance will have to be manually set. In these cases, a special procedure is required to bleed down the hydraulic lifter, check the clearance and replace the actual pushrod with a longer or shorter service unit. If you have a vehicle which is suspected of this condition, see Chapter 2 for the correct procedure to install a different size pushrod for correct valve lash adjustment.

Chapter 2 Part A Engine general

Contents

Specifications

Collapsed lifter gap

300 cu in in-line 6-cylinder and 255, 351, 400 cu in V8s	
Allowable	0.100 to 0.200 in
Desired	0.125 to 0.175 in
232 cu in V6	0.088 to 0.189 in
302 cu in V8	
Allowable	0.071 to 0.193 in
Desired	0.096 to 0.165 in
460 cu in V8	
Allowable	0.075 to 0.175 in
Desired	0.100 to 0.150 in

Torque specifications

	Ft-lb
Front motor mounts	
Insulator-to-engine bolts	
300 cu in in-line 6-cylinder, 232 cu in V6 and 460 cu in V8	60 to 80
255, 302, 351 and 400 cu in V8s	50 to 70
Insulator-to-frame bracket bolts	
300 cu in in-line 6-cylinder and 460 cu in V8	54 to 74
232 cu in V6	50 to 70
255, 302, 351 and 400 cu in V8s	48 to 64
Rear motor mount	
Insulator-to-transmission bolts	
300 cu in in-line 6-cylinder and 351M and 400 cu in V8s	50 to 70
232 cu in V6 and 255, 302, 351W and 460 cu in V8s	60 to 80
Insulator-to-support bolts (all)	50 to 70

1 General information

A wide variety of engines were installed in Ford pick-ups and Broncos, ranging from economical in-line six-cylinder engines to large displacement, high-powered V8s. All engines have cast iron blocks with cylinder bores machined directly into the block. Forged crankshafts run in replaceable bearing inserts.

Lubrication for these power plants is handled by full pressure oiling systems supplied by an oil pump driven from the base of the distributor. A flow-through oil filter with provision for oil bypass is part of this system.

The pistons are of the three-ring type with two compression rings and one oil control ring. Connecting rods have replaceable bearings in the big end (crankshaft) and replaceable bushings at the small end (piston).

All engines, except the 232 cu in V6, have cast iron heads with replaceable valve guide inserts. The V6 is equipped with aluminium heads. The valves are activated by a camshaft which runs within the block in replaceable bearings. Hydraulic lifters ride on the camshaft lobes and provide motion to the pushrods, which in turn act on rocker arms to move the valves.

The powerplants are all durably constructed for long service life and are fully serviceable for rebuilding.

2 Engine repair operations – general note

The following engine repair operations can be performed with the engine installed and still bolted to its mounts:

Removal of the intake and exhaust manifolds
Removal of the valve mechanism
Removal of the cylinder heads
Removal of the damper, crankcase front cover (timing cover), front oil seal, timing chain and timing gears
Removal of the flywheel (with the transmission removed)
Removal of the camshaft

The following engine repair operations can be performed with the engine installed but raised slightly off its mounts:

Removal of the oil pan
Removal of the oil pump
Removal of the rear main oil seal
Removal of the pistons, connecting rods and bearings
Removal of the engine mounts

The following engine repair operations can be performed only after

Fig. 2.1 Engine compartment bottom view – 4x4 (typical)

1 Front engine support bracket (above frame member)
2 Front crossmember
3 Axleshaft assembly
4 Front driveshaft
5 Exhaust pipe flanges
6 Transmission housing bolts
7 Engine oil pan
8 Starter

2A

the engine has been completely removed from the vehicle:

> *Removal of the crankshaft*
> *Removal of the main and camshaft bearings*

Whenever engine work is required, there are some basic steps which the home mechanic should perform before any work is begun. These preliminary steps will help prevent delays during the operation. They are as follows:

a) Read through the appropriate Sections in this manual to get an understanding of the processes involved, tools necessary and replacement parts which will be needed.

b) Contact your local dealer or auto parts store to check on replacement parts availability and cost. In many cases, a decision must be made beforehand whether to simply remove the faulty component and replace it with a new or rebuilt unit or to overhaul the existing part.

c) If the vehicle is equipped with air conditioning, it is absolutely necessary that a qualified specialist depressurize the system (if required to perform the necessary engine repair work). The home mechanic should never disconnect any of the air conditioning system lines while it is still pressurized, as this can cause serious personal injury as well as damage to the air conditioning system. Determine if depressurization is necessary while the vehicle is still operational.

3   Engine overhaul – general note

1   It is not always easy to determine when, or if, an engine should be completely overhauled, as a number of factors must be considered.
2   High mileage is not necessarily an indication that an overhaul is needed, while low mileage, on the other hand, does not preclude the need for an overhaul. Frequency of servicing is probably the single most important consideration. An engine that has regular (and frequent) oil and filter changes, as well as other required maintenance, will most likely give many thousands of miles of reliable service. Conversely, a neglected engine may require an overhaul very early in its life.
3   Excessive oil consumption is an indication that piston rings and/or valve guides are in need of attention (make sure that oil leaks are not responsible before deciding that the rings and guides are bad). Have a cylinder compression or leak-down test performed by an experienced tune-up mechanic to determine for certain the extent of the work required.
4   If the engine is making obvious 'knocking' or rumbling noises, the connecting rod and/or main bearings are probably at fault. Check the oil pressure with a gauge (installed in place of the oil pressure sending unit) and compare it to the Specifications. If it is extremely low, the bearings and/or pump are probably worn out.
5   Loss of power, rough running, excessive valve train noise and high fuel consumption rates may also point to the need for an overhaul (especially if they are all present at the same time). If a complete tune-up does not remedy the situation, major mechanical work is the only solution.
6   An engine overhaul generally involves restoring the internal parts to the specifications of a new engine. During an overhaul, the piston rings are replaced and the cylinder walls are reconditioned (rebored and/or honed). If a rebore is done, new pistons are required. The main and connecting rod bearings are replaced with new ones and, if necessary, the crankshaft may be reground to restore the journals. Generally, the valves are serviced as well, since they are usually in less-than-perfect condition at this point. While the engine is being overhauled, other components such as the carburetor, the distributor, the starter and the alternator can be rebuilt also. The end result should be a like-new engine that will give as many trouble-free miles as the original.
7   Before beginning the engine overhaul, read through the entire procedure to familiarize yourself with the scope and requirements of the job. Overhauling an engine is not that difficult, but it is time consuming. Plan on the vehicle being tied up for a considerable period of time, especially if parts must be taken to an automotive machine shop for repair or reconditioning. Most work can be done with typical shop hand tools, although a number of precision measuring tools are required for inspecting parts to determine if they must be replaced.

Often a reputable automotive machine shop will handle the inspection of parts and offer advice concerning reconditioning and replacement. As a general rule, time is the primary cost of an overhaul, so it doesn't pay to install worn or sub-standard parts.
8   As a final note, to ensure maximum life and minimum trouble from a rebuilt engine, everything must be assembled with care in a spotlessly clean environment.

4   Engine rebuilding alternatives

1   The home mechanic is faced with a number of options when performing an overhaul. The decision to replace the engine block, piston/rod assemblies and crankshaft depends on a number of factors with the number one consideration being the condition of the block. Other considerations are cost, availability of machine shop facilities, parts availability, time available to complete the project and experience.
2   Some of the rebuilding alternatives are as follows:
   Individual parts – If the inspection procedures prove that the engine block and most engine components are in reusable condition, they may be the most economical alternative. The block, crankshaft and piston/rod assemblies should be inspected carefully. Even if the block shows a little wear, the cylinder bores should receive a finish hone, a job for a machine shop.
   Master kit (crankshaft kit) – This rebuild package usually consists of a reground crankshaft and a matched set of pistons and connecting rods. The pistons will come already installed on the connecting rods. Piston rings and the necessary bearings may or may not be included in the kit. These kits are commonly available for standard cylinder bores, as well as for engine blocks which have been bored to a regular oversize.
   Short block – A short block consists of an engine block with a crankshaft and piston/rod assemblies already installed. All new bearings are incorporated and all clearances will be within tolerances. Depending on where the short block is purchased, a guarantee may be included. The existing camshaft, valve mechanism, cylinder heads and external parts can be bolted to this short block with little or no machine shop work necessary for the engine overhaul.
   Long block – A long block consists of a short block plus oil pump, oil pan, cylinder heads(s), valve cover(s), camshaft and valve mechanism, camshaft gear, timing gear, timing chain and crankcase front cover. All components are installed with new bearings, seals and gaskets incorporated throughout. The installation of manifolds and external parts is all that is necessary. Some form of guarantee is usually included with purchase.
3   Give careful thought to which method is best for your situation and discuss the alternatives with local automotive machine shops, auto parts dealer or dealership partsmen.

5   Engine overhaul – disassembly sequence

1   The Sections in this Chapter deal with removal, inspection, overhaul and installation of the various engine components. Reference should be made to the appropriate Chapters for removing and servicing the external engine components. These parts include the alternator, water pump, carburetor, etc.
2   If the engine is removed from the vehicle for major overhaul, the entire engine should be stripped. The exact order in which the engine parts are removed is to some degree a matter of personal preference. However, the following sequence can be used as a guide:
   a) Alternator (Chapter 5)
   b) Accessory drivebelts and pulleys (if not previously removed)
   c) Water pump and related hoses (Chapter 3)
   d) Fuel pump and filter assembly (Chapter 4)
   e) Distributor and coil (Chapter 5)
   f) Carburetor and fuel lines (Chapter 4)
   g) Clutch, pressure plate and disc (Chapter 7)
   h) Oil dipstick and dipstick tube (if so equipped)
   i) Spark plugs (Chapter 1)
3   With these components removed, the engine sub-assemblies can be removed, serviced and installed in the following order:
   a) Exhaust manifold(s)
   b) Intake manifold
   c) Rocker arm covers

d) Rocker arms and pushrods
e) Lifters
f) Cylinder head assembly
g) Front pulley and vibration damper assembly
h) Timing cover, timing chain and gears
i) Camshaft
j) Oil pan
k) Oil pump and pickup assembly
l) Piston and rod assemblies
m) Crankshaft and bearings

6 Engine removal – methods and precautions

If it has been decided that an engine needs to be removed for overhaul or major repair work, certain preliminary steps should be taken.

Locating a suitable work area is of greatest importance. A shop is, of course, the most desirable place to work. Adequate work space along with storage space for the vehicle is very important. If a shop or garage is not available, at the very least a flat, level, clean work surface made of concrete or asphalt is required.

Cleaning of the engine compartment and engine prior to removal will help you keep tools clean and organized.

A hoist such as an engine A-frame will also be necessary. Make sure that the equipment is rated in excess of the combined weight of the engine and its accessories. Safety is of primary importance, considering the potential hazards involved in lifting the engine out of the vehicle.

If the engine is being removed by a novice, a helper should be available. Advice and aid from someone more experienced would also be helpful. There are many instances when one person cannot simultaneously perform all of the operations which will be required when lifting the engine out of the vehicle.

Plan the operation ahead of time. Arrange for or obtain all of the tools and equipment you will need prior to beginning the job. Some of the equipment necessary to perform engine removal and installation safely and with relative ease are (in addition to an engine hoist) a heavy duty floor jack, complete sets of wrenches and sockets as described in the front of this book, wooden blocks and plenty of rags and cleaning solvent for mopping up the inevitable spills. If the hoist is to be rented, make sure that you arrange for it in advance and perform all of the operations possible without it beforehand. This will save you money and time.

Plan for the vehicle to be out of use for a considerable amount of time. A machine shop will be required to perform some of the work which the home mechanic cannot accomplish due to a lack of special equipment. These shops often have a busy schedule and it would be wise to consult them prior to removing the engine in order to accurately estimate the amount of time required to service or repair components that may need work.

Always use extreme caution when removing and installing the engine; serious injury can result from careless actions. Plan ahead. Take your time and a job of this nature, although major, can be accomplished successfully.

7 Engine – removal and installation

Note: *The engine must be removed alone, with the transmission left in place in the vehicle. Also, due to the wide range of vehicle models and engines covered by this manual, the following instructions are of a general nature and may cover some steps not applicable to your vehicle. If a step doesn't apply to your vehicle, move on to the next one.*

Removal

1 Remove the battery cables (negative first, then positive) from the battery.
2 Mark the position of the hood with a scribe or marking pen so it can be installed in the same position relative to the hinges and latch. Remove the hood. Cover the fenders for protection.
3 Remove the air cleaner along with the related emissions control and supply hoses from the carburetor. Cover the inlet of the carburetor with a clean cloth.
4 Remove all vacuum lines from the intake manifold area. Some of these lines will connect the automatic transmission modulator, speed

control and emission control related systems. Clearly mark all lines to prevent confusion when the engine is installed.
5 Remove the fuel feed hose from the fuel pump. Use caution when performing this step as gasoline is flammable and all precautions pertaining to flammable liquids should be observed. Plug the feed hose with a clamp and bolt if the fuel tank level is above the fuel feed line level.
6 **Note**: *Mark any electrical wires for proper installation before disconnecting them.* Disconnect the electrical connection(s) at the rear of the engine. In most cases, this will be a large multi-wire connector(s). However, some vehicles will be equipped with individual wires leading to components such as the engine operating sensors, ignition coil and emissions control related items like throttle positioners and choke heaters. Remove the starter cable from the starter. Position this cable out of the way. Remove the spark plug wires and the distributor cap as a unit.
7 Remove the speed control actuating cable from the carburetor linkage.
8 Remove the choke cable from the carburetor at its hold-down clamp and connecting linkage.
9 Disconnect the transmission kick-down cable or linkage from its connecting point at the carburetor linkage and at the transmission bellcrank connector.
10 Remove the throttle linkage from the carburetor connecting point and from the throttle pedal bellcrank (in some cases this is a cable system which will have a cable hold-down clamp on the intake manifold and a connector at the carburetor linkage). Remove the throttle linkage return spring.
11 Drain the engine oil and remove the oil filter.
12 Drain the coolant from the engine and radiator drain plugs.
13 Remove the heater hoses from their connecting points at the water pump and intake manifold. Position these heater hoses out of the way and secure them to the fender well.
14 Remove the radiator hoses from the engine. Remove the radiator hoses from the radiator if there is not enough clearance for the radiator to be removed with the hoses still in place.
15 Remove the fan shroud from the radiator and slide it back over the fan assembly.
16 Remove the transmission cooler lines from the chamber at the bottom of the radiator.
17 Loosen the alternator adjusting bolt and remove the drivebelt from the pulleys. Remove all other drivebelts attached to the water pump/fan drive pulley.
18 Remove the bolts retaining the fan and spacer (or fan clutch drive assembly) to the water pump.
19 Remove the assembly and fan shroud by lifting them straight up and out of the engine compartment.
20 Remove the radiator-to-radiator saddle retaining bolts.
21 Remove the radiator from the vehicle through the top of the engine compartment. Remove the alternator retaining bolt and position the alternator and wiring out of the way. It is important to secure the alternator in place with a wire or rope to prevent damage to the wiring connector at the rear of the alternator. Never allow the alternator to hang from the wiring.
22 In some cases the air conditioning system will not need discharging, since the hoses leading to the compressor unit are long enough for it to be swung out of the way and secured to the fender well. *Disconnect the air conditioning hoses only if the system has been discharged.* Remember that the system can only be discharged by a qualified specialist.
23 Remove the air conditioning compressor from the mounting brackets and secure it out of the way.
24 Remove the power steering pump belt.
25 Remove the power steering pump from the mounting bracket, position it out of the way and secure it. **Note**: *The following steps will be performed with the vehicle raised. Make sure that the vehicle is supported securely.*
26 Remove the starter (Chapter 5).
27 Remove the automatic transmission dipstick tube retaining bolt from the rear of the cylinder head or from the rear of the bellhousing retaining lug. Remove the automatic transmission dipstick and tube.
28 Remove the lower bellhousing retaining bolts.
29 Remove the engine mount-to-frame insulator retaining nuts and washers.
30 Support the transmission assembly securely using retaining straps and/or cables. It is possible to support the transmission with blocks or

2A

jacks but it must also be secured to prevent it from moving from side-to-side.

31 Remove the flywheel inspection cover.

32 Remove the torque converter drain plug cover.

33 Remove the torque converter-to-flexplate retaining nuts. They will be at the front of the torque converter flexplate and the crankshaft will need to be rotated 90° to position each retaining nut for removal.

34 Remove the bolt(s) retaining the inlet pipe(s) to the exhaust manifold(s). Remove the exhaust inlet pipe(s) from the exhaust manifold(s).

35 Remove the upper bellhousing-to-engine retaining bolts.

36 Lower the vehicle and make sure the transmission is supported solidly.

37 Install an engine lifting sling or chain. There are several methods which can be used to accomplish this. Metal eye hooks can be attached with bolts positioned at diagonally opposite corners of the cylinder heads on V8 engines. This method may also be used on V6 engines, but because the V6 heads are made of aluminum, special caution should be exercised. Make sure that the bolts attaching the eye hooks are threaded well into the heads, preventing thread damage when the engine is lifted. Six-cylinder engine diagonal mounting can be achieved by using a manifold-to-cylinder head retaining bolt at the right front of the engine and the accessory mounting boss at the left rear of the engine block to retain the eye hooks or bracket. A sling can be fashioned from a short piece of chain connected to open-end hooks. A cable and bracket arrangement would also work well.

38 Raise the engine high enough for the engine mount studs to clear the frame bracket insulators.

39 Double check all attachment points to ensure that all of the retaining bolts holding the engine to the transmission have been removed.

40 Separate the engine from the bellhousing (or torque-converter housing) making sure that the flywheel/clutch assembly (torque-converter flexplate) pulls straight out of the housing without binding. You may need to adjust the engine height and angle for the two components to separate cleanly. A small wedge-type tool can be used between the housing and the engine block to separate them. However, if resistance is felt, check to make sure no retaining bolts are left in the engine. Do not force any parts during this removal procedure. If the engine is stuck to the transmission assembly, a fastener is probably holding them together.

41 Pull the engine straight forward and away from the transmission. Take care not to damage the transmission input shaft while performing this step.

42 When the transmission input shaft or torque converter has completely cleared the clutch assembly or flexplate, raise the engine and remove it from the engine compartment. There should be no connections between the engine and the vehicle.

43 Place the engine on an engine stand or other suitable support for disassembly and further operations.

Installation

44 Lift the engine off the engine stand with a hoist. The chains should be positioned as on removal, with the engine sitting level.

45 Lower the engine into place inside the engine compartment, closely watching clearances. On manual transmissions, carefully guide the engine onto the transmission input shaft. The two components should be at the same angle, with the shaft sliding easily into the engine.

46 Install the engine mount through-bolts and the bellhousing bolts. Tighten them to the specified torque.

47 Install the remaining engine components in the reverse order of removal.

48 Fill the cooling system with the proper coolant and water mixture (Chapter 3).

49 Fill the engine with the correct grade of engine oil (Chapter 1)

50 Check the transmission fluid level, adding fluid as necessary.

51 Connect the positive battery cable, followed by the negative cable. If sparks or arcing occur as the negative cable is connected to the battery, check that all electrical accessories are turned off (check dome light first). If arcing still occurs, check that all electrical wiring is connected properly to the engine and transmission.

52 See Section 10 for the starting up sequence.

8 Engine mounts – replacement (engine in vehicle)

1 Disconnect the negative battery cable from the battery.

2 Disconnect the throttle linkage from the carburetor on vehicles equipped with mechanical linkage.

3 Disconnect the fuel supply hose from the fuel tank line at the fuel pump. **Caution:** *Observe all precautions for working with flammable liquids (gasoline) when performing this operation.*

4 On vehicles equipped with an automatic transmission, remove the transmission cooler lines from their mounting clips located on the side of the engine block. Make sure that the lines are free from the engine, as it will need to be raised several inches to replace the mounts. Disconnect the clutch cross-shaft on manual transmission equipped vehicles.

5 Disconnect the lower radiator hose from the radiator.

6 Disconnect the upper radiator hose from the radiator.

7 Disconnect the engine mount retaining nuts from the connecting studs at the insulator.

8 If the rear mount is being changed, make sure that the

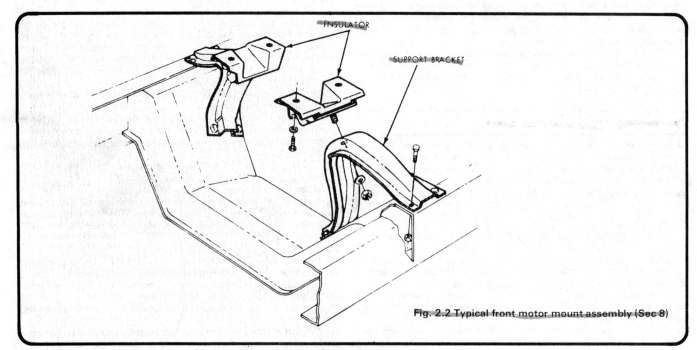

Fig. 2.2 Typical front motor mount assembly (Sec 8)

speedometer cable, driveshaft, transmission linkage and transfer case linkage (if so equipped) will not bind or contact the body as the transmission is being raised.

9   Raise the engine (or transmission) using a jack and a block of wood underneath the oil pan. Make sure that the engine mounts do not bind as the engine is raised up off the insulator assembly.

10 Disconnect the engine mounts from the engine.

11 Install the new mounts onto the engine, making sure that the bolts are tightened to the proper torque.

12 Lower the engine back onto the insulators making sure that the mount stud lines up with and falls into the hole provided in the engine mount insulator located on the frame crossmember.

13 Attach the insulator retaining nut and lock washer. Tighten this nut to the proper torque.

14 Assembly is the reverse of disassembly. Make certain that all linkages are attached securely and adjusted properly.

9   Valve adjustment

1   On V8 engines, the valve arrangement on the left band is E-I-E-I-E-I-E-I and on the right band is I-E-I-E-I-E-I-E. For the in-line six engine, the valve arrangement is E-I-I-E-I-E-E-I-E-I-I-E. On V6 engines, the valve arrangement is I-E-I-E-I-E on the right bank and E-I-E-I-E-I on the left bank.

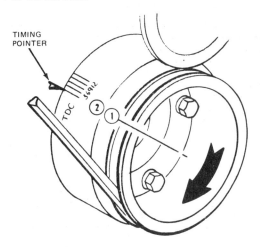

Fig. 2.3 Positioning the crankshaft for checking valve clearance and installing the rocker arms on the 460 V8 and 232 V6 engines (Sec 9)

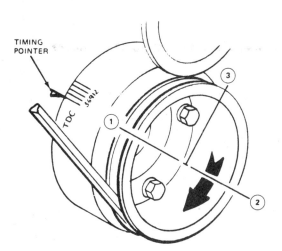

Fig. 2.4 Vibration damper markings for valve adjustment on all V8 engines except 460 (Sec 9)

2   Normally these engines do not need any valve adjustments because the lash is accounted for by the hydraulic lifter. If you have a running engine that has symptoms of valve clearance problems (such as excessive noise from a lifter), check for a defective part. Normally an engine will not reach a point at which it needs a valve adjustment unless a component malfunction has occurred. Hydraulic lifter failure and excessive rocker arm wear are two examples of likely component failure. Also, if major engine work is done, such as a valve job, which alters the relationship among valve train components, a means of compensating for the dimensional changes must be provided. Shorter and longer pushrods are available for this purpose. To determine whether a shorter or longer pushrod is necessary, proceed as follows.

3   Connect an auxiliary starter switch to the starter solenoid.

4   Position the piston in the number one cylinder at top dead center (TDC) on the compression stroke. To do this, remove all of the spark plugs from the engine, then locate the number one cylinder spark plug wire and trace it back to the distributor. Make a mark on the distributor body directly below the terminal where the number one spark plug wire attaches to the distributor cap, then remove the cap and wires from the distributor. Slip a wrench or socket over the large bolt at the front of the crankshaft and slowly turn it in a clockwise direction (viewed from the front) until the notch in the crankshaft pulley is aligned with the O on the timing mark tag, or until the pointer on the block is aligned with the zero mark on the pulley, depending upon how your particular engine is inscribed. At this point the rotor should be pointing at the mark you made on the distributor body. If it is not, turn the crankshaft one complete revolution (360°) in a clockwise direction. If the rotor is now pointing at the mark on the distributor body, then the number one piston is at TDC on the compression stroke.

5   On V6 and V8 engines, with the crankshaft in the position described in Step 4, mark a line from the zero mark across the pulley, representing the crankshaft center, and, on all V8s except the 460 cu in engine, mark another line 90 degrees from the timing mark.

6   On in-line six-cylinder engines, mark the pulley with two chalk marks spaced 120 degrees on either side of the zero timing mark.

7   Remove the rocker arm cover(s) (see the appropriate Chapter for your engine).

8   Make sure that the lifters are compressed (not pumped up with oil). This is accomplished during engine assembly by installing new lifters, or by compressing the lifters and relieving them of all internal oil pressure if they have been in service. A special tool is available for this procedure.

9   With the number one piston at TDC, position the lifter compressor tool on the intake rocker end and slowly apply pressure to bleed down the lifter until the plunger is completely bottomed. Hold the lifter in this

2A

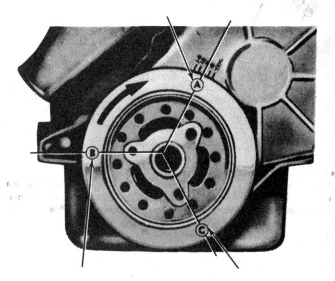

Fig. 2.5 Vibration damper markings (arrows) for valve adjustment on in-line six-cylinder engines (Sec 9)

Fig. 2.6 Bleeding the lifter down with a lifter compressing tool
(arrow) (Sec 9)

255 and 302 cu in V8 engines
14 After checking the clearances on both number one cylinder valves check the remaining valves as shown in Position 1 in Fig. 2.7.
15 Rotate the engine 180 degrees with the auxiliary starter switch to Position 2 and check the valves as indicated.
16 Rotate the engine 270 degrees to Position 3 and check the remaining valves as indicated.

351 and 400 cu in V8 engines
17 After checking the clearances on both number one cylinder valves, check the remaining valves as shown in Position 1 in Fig. 2.8.
18 Rotate the engine 180 degrees with the auxiliary starter switch to Position 2 and check the valves as indicated.
19 Rotate the engine 270 degrees to Position 3 and check the remaining valves as indicated.

460 cu in V8 engines
20 After checking the clearances on both number one cylinder valves, check the remaining valves as shown in Position 1 in Fig. 2.9.
21 Rotate the crankshaft 360 degrees with the auxiliary starter switch to Position 2 and check the remaining valves as indicated.
22 After completion of the entire valve adjustment procedure, install the remaining engine components and run the engine. It may be necessary for an engine to run several minutes for the clearance in the valve train to be taken up completely by the hydraulic lifter(s), particularly if new lifters were installed.
23 If the components are all in good shape and a valve lash problem is indicated by excessive noise or rough engine idling, use the special service tool to compress the lifter to recheck the valve clearance.

POSITION 1
No. 1 Intake   No. 1 Exhaust
No. 7 Intake   No. 5 Exhaust
No. 8 Intake   No. 4 Exhaust

POSITION 2
No. 5 Intake   No. 2 Exhaust
No. 4 Intake   No. 6 Exhaust

POSITION 3
No. 2 Intake   No. 7 Exhaust
No. 3 Intake   No. 3 Exhaust
No. 6 Intake   No. 8 Exhaust

Fig. 2.7 Vibration damper position and valve adjustment order for 255 and 302 engines (Sec 9)

POSITION 1
No. 1 Intake   No. 1 Exhaust
No. 4 Intake   No. 3 Exhaust
No. 8 Intake   No. 7 Exhaust

POSITION 2
No. 3 Intake   No. 2 Exhaust
No. 7 Intake   No. 6 Exhaust

POSITION 3
No. 2 Intake   No. 4 Exhaust
No. 5 Intake   No. 5 Exhaust
No. 6 Intake   No. 8 Exhaust

Fig. 2.8 Vibration damper position and valve adjustment order for 351M, 351W and 400 engines (Sec 9)

POSITION 1
No. 1 Intake   No. 1 Exhaust
No. 3 Intake   No. 8 Exhaust
No. 7 Intake   No. 5 Exhaust
No. 8 Intake   No. 4 Exhaust

POSITION 2
No. 2 Intake   No. 2 Exhaust
No. 4 Intake   No. 3 Exhaust
No. 5 Intake   No. 6 Exhaust
No. 6 Intake   No. 7 Exhaust

Fig. 2.9 Vibration damper position and valve adjustment order for 460 engines (Sec 9)

position and check the available clearance between the rocker arm and the valve stem tip with a feeler gauge. Compare the measurements to the Specifications. If the clearance is greater than specified, install a longer pushrod. If the clearance is less than specified, install a shorter pushrod. Repeat the procedure on the number one exhaust valve.
10 Employing the lifter bleed down and measuring procedures stated in Step 9, complete the valve clearance check as follows.

In-line six-cylinder engines
11 Rotate the crankshaft with the auxiliary starter, one-third revolution at a time, and adjust both intake and exhaust valves at each position in the remaining firing order sequence, 5-3-6-2-4.

V6 engines
12 After checking the clearances on both number one cylinder valves, check number 3 intake and number 2 exhaust, then number 6 intake and number 4 exhaust without rotating the crankshaft.
13 Rotate the crankshaft 360 degrees with the auxiliary starter switch and check, in order, number 2 intake and number 3 exhaust, number 4 intake and number 5 exhaust, and number 5 intake and number 6 exhaust.

10 Engine start-up after major repair or overhaul

1 With the engine in place in the vehicle and all components connected, make a final check that all lines and wires have been connected and that no rags or tools have been left in the engine compartment.
2 Connect the negative battery cable. If it sparks or arcs, power is being drawn from someplace and all accessories and wiring should be checked.
3 Fill the cooling system with the proper mixture and amount of coolant (Chapter 3).
4 Fill the crankcase with the correct quantity and grade of oil (Chapter 1).
5 Check the tension of all drivebelts (Chapter 1).
6 Remove the high tension wire from the center tower of the distributor cap to prevent the engine from starting. Now crank the engine over for about 15 to 30 seconds. This will allow the oil pump to distribute oil and the fuel pump to start pumping fuel to the carburetor.
7 Now connect the high tension lead at the distributor and start the engine. Immediately check all gauges and warning lights for proper readings and check for coolant or oil leaks.

8   If the engine does not start immediately, check to make sure fuel is reaching the carburetor. This may take a while.

9   After allowing the engine to run for a few minutes at low speed, turn it off and check the oil and coolant levels.

10 Start the engine again and check the ignition timing, emissions control settings and carburetor idle speeds (Chapter 1).

11 Run the vehicle easily during the first 500 to 1000 miles (break-in period) then check the torque settings on all major engine components, particularly the cylinder heads. Tighten any bolts which may have loosened.

2A

Chapter 2 Part B
300 cu in in-line six cylinder engines

Refer to Chapter 13 for information on 1987 and later models

Contents

Specifications

General
Bore and stroke	4.00 x 3.98 in
Compression pressure	Lowest cylinder must be within 75% of highest cylinder
Oil pressure (at 2000 rpm, normal operating temperature)	40 to 60 psi

Engine block
Cylinder bore
Diameter	4.000 to 4.0048 in
Taper limit	0.010 in
Out-of-round limit	0.005 in
Deck warpage limit	0.003 in per 6 in, or 0.006 in overall

Pistons and rings
Piston

Diameter
Coded red	3.9982 to 3.9988 in
Coded blue	3.9994 to 4.0000 in
Oversize available	0.003 in

Piston-to-cylinder bore clearance
Standard	0.0014 in
Service limit	0.0022 in

Piston ring-to-groove side clearance

Standard
Top ring	0.0019 to 0.0036 in
2nd ring	0.002 to 0.004 in
Oil ring	Snug fit in groove
Service limit	0.002 in maximum increase in clearance

Piston ring end gap
Top ring	0.010 to 0.020 in
2nd ring	0.010 to 0.020 in
Oil ring	0.015 to 0.055 in
Piston pin diameter (standard)	0.9749 to 0.9754 in
Piston pin-to-piston clearance	0.002 to 0.004 in; under 8500 GVW – 0.0003 to 0.0005 in
Piston pin-to-connecting rod fit	Interference fit

Crankshaft and flywheel
Main journal
Diameter	2.3982 to 2.3990 in
Taper limit	0.0005 in per inch
Out-of-round limit	0.006 in
Runout limit	0.002 in

Main bearing oil clearance
Standard	0.0008 to 0.0015 in
Service limit	0.0028 in

Connecting rod journal
Diameter	2.1228 to 2.1236 in
Taper limit	0.0006 in per inch
Out-of-round limit	0.0006 in

Connecting rod bearing oil clearance
Standard	0.0008 to 0.0015 in

Service limit	0.0024 in
Connecting rod side clearance	
Standard	0.006 to 0.013 in
Service limit	0.018 in
Crankshaft endplay	
Standard	0.004 to 0.008 in
Service limit	0.012 in
Flywheel clutch face runout limit	0.010 in
Flywheel ring gear lateral runout limit	
Manual transmission	0.040 in
Automatic transmission	0.060 in

Camshaft

Bearing journal	
Diameter	2.017 to 2.018 in
Journal runout	0.008 TIR max
Bearing oil clearance	
Standard	0.001 to 0.003 in
Service limit	0.006 in
Lobe lift	
Intake	
F100 and F150 4x2 with 2.47:1 or 2.75:1 axle ratio and manual transmission	0.247 in
All others	0.249 in
Exhaust	
F100 and F150 4x2 with 2.47:1 or 2.75:1 axle ratio and manual transmission	0.247 in
All others	0.249 in
Runout limit	0.008 in
Endplay	
Standard	0.001 to 0.007 in
Service limit	0.009 in
Cam gear-to-crankshaft gear backlash	0.004 to 0.100 in
Cam gear runout limit (assembled)	0.005 in
Crankshaft gear runout limit (assembled)	0.005 in

2B

Cylinder head and valve train

Head warpage limit	0.006 in per 6 in or 0.007 in overall
Valve seat angle	45°
Valve seat width	
Intake	0.060 to 0.080 in
Exhaust	0.070 to 0.090 in
Valve seat runout limit	0.002 TIR
Valve face angle	44°
Valve face runout limit	0.002 TIR
Valve margin width	1/32 in min
Valve stem diameter – standard	
Intake	0.3416 to 0.3423 in
Exhaust	0.3416 to 0.3423 in
Valve guide diameter	
Intake	0.3433 to 0.3443 in
Exhaust	0.3433 to 0.3443 in
Valve stem-to-guide clearance	
Intake	
Standard	0.0010 to 0.0027 in
Service limit	0.0055 in
Exhaust	
Standard	0.0010 to 0.0027 in
Service limit	0.0055 in
Valve spring free length	
Intake	1.99 in
Exhaust	1.87 in
Valve spring pressure (lbs. @ specified length)	
Intake (1st check)	
Standard	76 to 84 @ 1.700 in
Service limit	10% loss of pressure
Intake (2nd check)	
Standard	187 to 207 @ 1.300 in
Service limit	10% loss of pressure
Exhaust (1st check)	
Standard	77 to 85 @ 1.580 in
Service limit	10% loss of pressure
Exhaust (2nd check)	
Standard	182 to 202 @ 1.180 in
Service limit	10% loss of pressure

Valve spring installed height	
Intake	$1\frac{11}{16}$ to $1\frac{23}{32}$ in
Exhaust	$1\frac{9}{16}$ to $1\frac{19}{32}$ in
Valve spring out-of-square limit	0.078 ($\frac{5}{64}$) in
Collapsed lifter gap	See Chapter 2A, Specifications
Lifter diameter	0.8740 to 0.8745 in
Lifter bore diameter	0.8752 to 0.8767 in
Lifter-to-bore clearance	
Standard	0.007 to 0.0027 in
Service limit	0.005 in
Pushrod runout limit	0.015 TIR

Oil pump

Outer race-to-housing clearance	0.001 to 0.013 in
Rotor assembly end clearance	0.004 in max
Driveshaft-to-housing bearing clearance	0.0015 to 0.0030 in
Relief spring tension	20.6 to 22.6 lbs. @ 2.49 in
Relief valve clearance	0.0015 to 0.0030 in

Torque specifications

	Ft-lb (unless otherwise noted)
Connecting rod nut	40 to 45
Front cover	12 to 18
Head bolts	
Step 1	55
Step 2	65
Step 3	85
Damper-to-crankshaft bolts	130 to 150
EGR valve-to-carburetor spacer or intake manifold	12 to 18
Flywheel/flexplate-to-crankshaft bolts	75 to 85
Main bearing cap bolts	60 to 70
Intake manifold-to-cylinder head bolts	22 to 32
Intake manifold-to-exhaust manifold nuts	28 to 32
Exhaust manifold-to-cylinder head bolts	
1980 and 1981	28 to 33
1982 and 1983	22 to 32
Oil filter insert-to-cylinder block/adapter	20 to 30
Oil filter adapter-to-cylinder block	40 to 50
Oil filter-to-adapter or cylinder block	$\frac{1}{2}$ turn after gasket contacts sealing surface with oiled gasket
Oil inlet tube-to-pump	10 to 15
Oil pan drain plug	15 to 25
Oil pan-to-cylinder block bolts	
Through 1990	10 to 15
1991	15 to 18
Oil pump-to-cylinder block bolts	10 to 15
Oil inlet tube-to-main bearing cap	22 to 32
Pulley-to-damper bolt	35 to 50
Rocker arm stud nut	17 to 23
Spark plug-to-cylinder head	10 to 15
Valve rocker arm cover bolts	4 to 7
Valve pushrod cover-to-cylinder block bolts	15 to 20 in-lbs;
Water/coolant outlet housing bolts	12 to 18
Water pump-to-front cover bolts	12 to 18
Alternator bracket-to-cylinder block bolt	30 to 45
Alternator adjusting arm-to-cylinder block bolt	19 to 27
Alternator adjusting arm-to-alternator bolt	24 to 40
Thermactor pump pivot bolt	30 to 35
Thermactor pump adjusting arm-to-pump bolt	22 to 32
Thermactor pump pulley-to-pump hub bolt	150 to 220 in-lbs
Thermactor pump bracket-to-cylinder block bolt	22 to 32
Fuel filter-to-carburetor pump	80 to 100 in-lbs
Carburetor attaching nuts	12 to 15
Camshaft thrust plate-to-cylinder block screws	9 to 12
Fuel pump-to-front cover bolts	12 to 18
Carburetor mounting stud	5 to 10
Distributor clamp down bolt	17 to 25
Intake manifold vacuum fittings	6 to 10

11 General information

The 300 cu in in-line six-cylinder Ford engine block is made of cast iron. The crankshaft, which is supported by seven main bearings, is cast of nodular iron and the pistons are of aluminum alloy with integral steel struts. The valve rocker arms are ball pivot stud mounted employing positive stop studs. The lifters (tappets) are hydraulic and self-adjusting. Rotators are employed on the exhaust valves and timing gears are of the helical type. This engine is standard in all vehicles covered in this manual.

12 Valve spring, retainer and seal – replacement (on vehicle)

Note: *Broken valve springs and retainers or defective valve stem seals can be replaced without removing the cylinder head (on engines that have no damage to the valves or valve seats). Two special tools and a compressed air source are required to perform this operation, so read through this Section carefully and rent or buy the tools before beginning this job.*

1   Remove the air cleaner.

2   Remove the accelerator cable return spring.

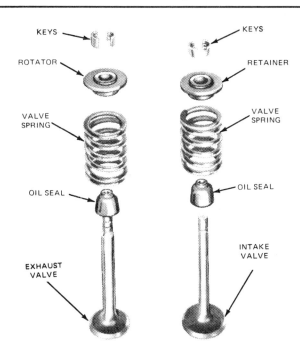

Fig. 2.10 Typical valve components (Sec 12)

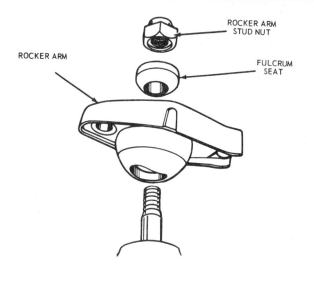

Fig. 2.11 Typical rocker arm assembly components (Sec 12)

3   Remove the accelerator cable linkage at the carburetor.
4   Disconnect the choke cable at the carburetor connecting point.
5   Remove the PCV valve from the rocker arm cover and remove the rocker arm cover.
6   Remove the spark plug from the cylinder which has the bad component.
7   Crank the engine until the piston in the cylinder with the bad component is at top dead center on the compression stroke (refer to Step 4 of Section 9 in Chapter 2A). Note that the distributor should be marked opposite the appropriate terminal; not necessarily number one.
8   Install a special air line adapter which will screw into the spark plug hole and connect to a compressed air source. Remove the valve rocker arm stud nut, fulcrum seat, rocker arm and pushrod.
9   Apply compressed air to the cylinder in question. If the engine rotates until the piston is at bottom dead center, be very careful that you do not drop the valve into the cylinder as it will fall all the way in. Do not release the air pressure or the valve will drop through the guide.
10 Compress the valve spring with the special tool designed for this purpose.
11 Remove the keepers, spring retainer and valve spring, then remove the valve stem seal. **Note:** *If air pressure fails to hold the valve in the closed position during this operation, there is apparently damage to the seat or valve. If this condition exists, remove the cylinder head for further repair operations.*
12 If air pressure has forced the piston to the bottom of the cylinder, wrap a rubber band, tape or string around the top of the valve stem so that the valve will not fall through into the combustion chamber if it is dropped. Release the air pressure.
13 Inspect the valve stem for damage. Rotate the valve in its guide and check the valve stem tip for eccentric movement (which would indicate a bent valve).
14 Move the valve up and down through its normal travel and make sure that the valve guide and stem do not bind. If the valve stem binds, either the valve is bent and/or the guide is damaged and the head will have to be removed for repair.
15 Reapply air pressure to the cylinder to retain the valve in the closed position.
16 Lubricate the valve stem with engine oil and install a new valve stem seal.
17 Install the spring in position over the valve. Make sure that the closed coil end of the spring is correctly positioned next to the cylinder head.
18 Install the valve spring retainer. Compress the valve spring, using

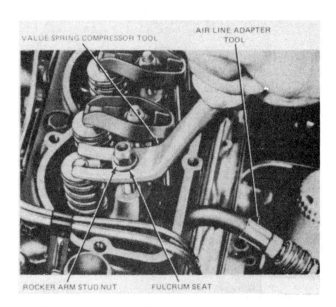

Fig. 2.12 Compressing a valve spring with the cylinder head on the engine (Sec 12)

the valve spring compressor, and install the valve spring keepers. Remove the compressor tool and make sure that the valve spring keepers are installed correctly.
19 Apply engine oil to both ends of the pushrod.
20 Install the pushrod in position.
21 Apply engine oil to the tip of the valve stem.
22 Apply engine oil to the fulcrum seats and socket.
23 Install the rocker arm, fulcrum seat and stud nut and adjust the stud nut to the specified torque.
24 Remove the air source and the adapter from the spark plug hole.
25 Install the spark plug and connect the spark plug wire to it.
26 Install a new rocker arm cover gasket and attach the rocker arm cover to the engine.
27 Connect the accelerator cable to the carburetor at its connecting point.
28 Install the accelerator cable return spring. Connect the choke cable to the carburetor.
29 Install the PCV valve in the rocker arm cover and make sure that the line connected to the PCV valve is positioned correctly on both ends.
30 Install the air cleaner.

CONVERTER HOUSING

Fig. 2.13 In-line six-cylinder engine external components – exploded view

1 Cylinder block
2 Timing cover
3 Timing cover gasket
4 Cylinder head
5 Cylinder head gasket
6 Cylinder head bolt
7 Crankshaft damper and pulley assembly
8 Flywheel assembly
9 Crankshaft pulley retaining washer
10 Flywheel ring gear
11 Flywheel clutch mounting surface
12 Pushrod cover
13 Pushrod cover gasket
14 Pushrod cover bolt grommet
15 Rocker arm cover
16 Rocker arm cover gasket
17 Oil pan
18 Timing cover front seal
19 Oil pan drain plug
20 Oil filter
21 Oil pan drain plug gasket
22 Oil dipstick
23 Oil dipstick tube
24 Oil pan gasket set
25 Oil filter mounting bolt insert
26 Engine torque plate
27 Flywheel/crankshaft mounting flange
28 Water outlet connection gasket
29 Water pump
30 Water pump housing gasket
31 Thermostat
32 Water outlet connection
33 Oil pressure gauge sending unit
34 Fuel pump
35 Fuel pump gasket
36 Intake manifold
37 Exhaust manifold
38 Manifold clamp
39 Carburetor gasket
40 Distributor cap
41 Distributor
42 Spark plug wire set
43 Distributor hold down clamp
44 Spark plug
45 Intake manifold-to-cylinder head gasket

31 Start and run the engine, making sure that there are no oil leaks and that there are no unusual sounds coming from the valve assembly.

13 Manifolds – removal and installation

Removal

1 Remove the air cleaner and related air cleaner attachments.
2 Disconnect the choke cable at its linkage connecting point at the carburetor.
3 Disconnect the accelerator cable or linkage at the connecting point of the carburetor. Remove the accelerator return spring.
4 Remove the kick-down rod return spring and the kick-down shaft from its linkage at the carburetor.
5 Disconnect the fuel inlet line from the carburetor.
6 Disconnect all vacuum lines from the carburetor.
7 Disconnect the muffler inlet pipe from the exhaust manifold and support it out of the way.
8 Disconnect the power brake booster vacuum line from the intake manifold.
9 Remove the ten bolts and three nuts retaining the manifolds to the cylinder head. Lift the manifold assemblies away from the engine.
10 Remove and scrape the gaskets from the mating surface of the manifolds. If the manifolds are to be replaced or changed, remove the nuts connecting the intake manifold to the exhaust manifold.

Installation

11 Install new studs in the exhaust manifold for the inlet pipe.
12 If the intake and the exhaust manifolds have been separated, coat the mating surfaces with graphite grease. Place the exhaust manifold over the studs on the intake manifold. Connect the two with the lock washers and nuts. Tighten the nuts finger tight.
13 Install a new intake manifold-to-head gasket.
14 Coat the mating surfaces lightly with graphite grease. Place the manifold assemblies against the mating surface of the cylinder head, making sure that the gaskets are positioned correctly. Install the attaching washers, bolts and nuts finger tight and make sure everything is positioned and aligned correctly. Tighten the nuts and bolts to the proper torque in the order shown. Tighten the exhaust-to-intake manifold nuts to the proper torque (if they were removed).
15 Attach a new gasket to the inlet pipe and fasten the pipe to the exhaust manifold. Tighten the nuts to the proper torque.
16 Install the crankcase vent hose to the intake manifold inlet tube and tighten the hose clamp.
17 Attach the fuel inlet line to the carburetor.
18 Install the distributor vacuum line on the fitting at the carburetor.
19 Connect the accelerator cable to the carburetor and install the return spring. Connect the choke cable to the carburetor and adjust the choke.
20 Install the bellcrank assembly and kick-down rod return spring.

2B

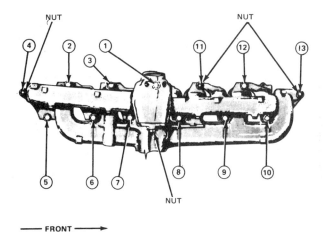

Fig. 2.14 In-line six-cylinder engine intake and exhaust manifold bolt tightening sequence (Sec 13)

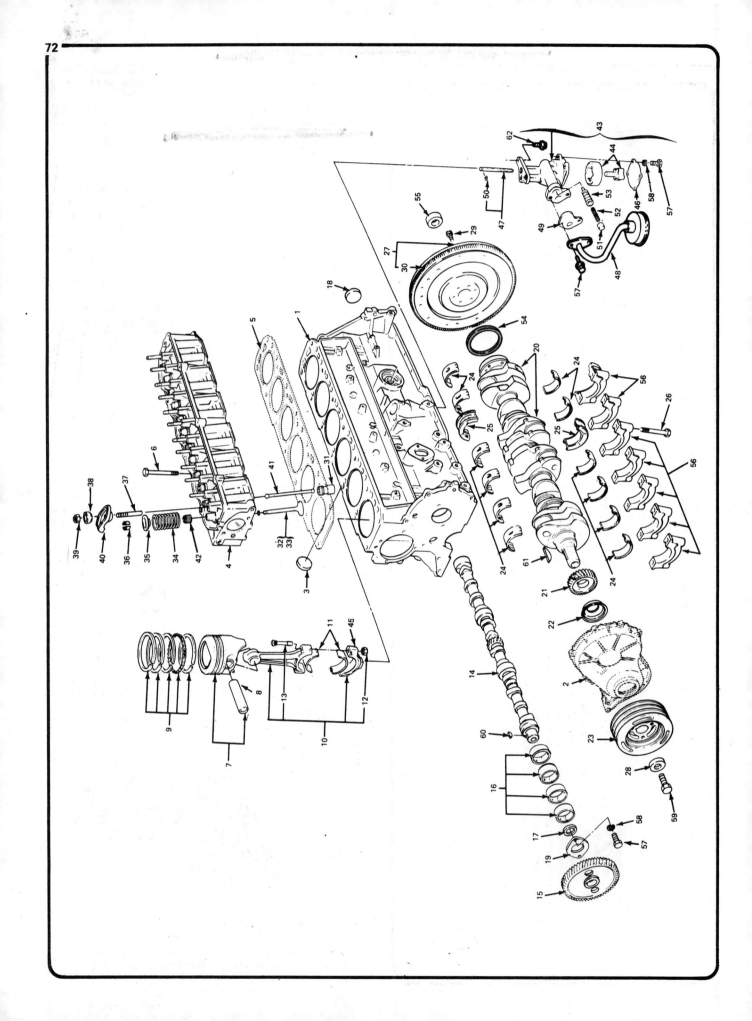

Fig. 2.15 In-line six-cylinder engine internal components – exploded view

1 Block assembly
2 Timing cover
3 Expansion plug
4 Cylinder head
5 Cylinder head gasket
6 Cylinder head bolt
7 Piston assembly
8 Piston pin
9 Piston ring set
10 Connecting rod assembly
11 Connecting rod bearing
12 Connecting rod nut
13 Connecting rod bolt
14 Camshaft
15 Camshaft timing gear
16 Camshaft bearing
17 Camshaft gear spacer
18 Camshaft rear bearing plug
19 Camshaft thrust plate
20 Crankshaft assembly
21 Crankshaft timing gear
22 Crankshaft oil slinger
23 Crankshaft pulley and damper assembly
24 Crankshaft main bearing
25 Crankshaft main thrust bearing
26 Crankshaft main bearing cap bolt
27 Flywheel assembly
28 Crankshaft pulley retaining washer
29 Flywheel-to-crankshaft bolt
30 Flywheel ring gear
31 Hydraulic lifter assembly
32 Exhaust valve
33 Intake valve
34 Valve spring
35 Valve spring retainer
36 Valve spring retainer key
37 Valve rocker arm support stud
38 Valve rocker arm fulcrum seat
39 Valve rocker arm stud
40 Valve rocker arm nut
41 Pushrod
42 Valve stem seal
43 Oil pump assembly
44 Oil pump drive rotor and shaft assembly
45 Connecting rod cap
46 Oil pump drive plate
47 Oil pump intermediate shaft
48 Oil pump screen, tube and cover assembly
49 Oil pump inlet tube gasket
50 Oil pump intermediate shaft ring
51 Oil pump relief valve plug
52 Oil pump relief valve spring
53 Oil pump relief valve plunger
54 Crankshaft rear packing
55 Clutch pilot bearing
56 Main bearing cap
57 Bolt $(\frac{5}{16}\text{-}18 \times 1)$
58 Lock washer $(\frac{5}{16}\ \frac{19}{32} \times \frac{5}{64})$
59 Bolt $(\frac{5}{8}\text{-}18 \times 2)$
60 Woodruff key $(\frac{3}{4} \times \frac{5}{32})$
61 Woodruff key $(\frac{5}{16} \times 1\frac{3}{4})$
62 Screw $(\frac{5}{16}\text{-}18 \times 1)$

21 Adjust the transmission control kick-down linkage as specified in Chapter 7.
22 Install the air cleaner. Readjust the engine idle speed and idle fuel mixture as described in Chapter 4.

14 Flywheel – removal, inspection and installation

Note: *These instructions are valid only if the engine has been removed from the vehicle. If the engine is still in the vehicle, the transmission, the bellhousing and clutch assembly must be removed to expose the flywheel (refer to Chapter 7). Automatic transmission equipped vehicles are equipped with a flexplate rather than a flywheel. It can be separated from the crankshaft by removing the mounting bolts. If the ring gear teeth are worn or damaged or if the flexplate is damaged, replace it with a new one and tighten the mounting bolts to the specified torque.*

1 Mark the flywheel and the crankshaft end with a center punch to ensure installation in the same relative position.
2 To keep the crankshaft from turning, wedge a large screwdriver or pry bar between the ring gear teeth and the engine block (it must be positioned so that as the crankshaft moves, the tool bears against the block). Make sure that the tool is not pushing against the oil pan. Another method of preventing crankshaft rotation involves holding the front pulley retaining bolt with a large wrench or socket and breaker bar. This method may require a helper. **Caution:** *Support the flywheel before performing the following step as it could fall off and be damaged or cause injury.*
3 Remove the flywheel retaining bolts from the crankshaft flange.
4 Remove the flywheel from the crankshaft by pulling straight back on it.
5 Inspect the flywheel clutch disc mating surface for scoring, heat marks, cracks and warpage. If any of these conditions exist, the flywheel should be taken to an automotive machine shop to be resurfaced (or replaced with a new one). If the flywheel is cracked, it must be replaced with a new one.
6 Installation is the reverse of removal. The retaining bolts should be coated with a thread-locking compound and tightened in a crisscross pattern to the prescribed torque.

15 Rocker arm and pushrod covers – removal and installation

Removal

1 Remove the positive crankcase ventilation hose from the top of the rocker arm cover.
2 Disconnect the air vent tube from the oil filler cap and remove the filler cap and tube from the rocker arm cover.
3 Disconnect the fuel supply hose at the fuel pump and at the carburetor. Remove the fuel supply hose.
4 Bring the engine to top dead center for the number one piston and mark the distributor as described in Chapter 5. Remove the distributor from the engine.
5 Remove the ignition coil and bracket from the side of the engine.

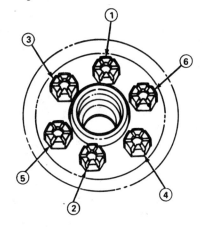

Fig. 2.16 Tightening sequence for flywheel bolts (Sec 14)

6   Remove the retaining screws holding the rocker arm cover to the cylinder head.
7   Remove the rocker arm cover from the cylinder head and clean the old gasket from the mating surfaces.
8   Remove the retaining bolts for the pushrod cover at the left side of the engine.
9   Remove the pushrod cover from the side of the engine and clean the old gasket from the cover and engine block.

Installation

10 Install a new gasket on the pushrod cover. RTV-type gasket sealant will keep it positioned.
11 Place the pushrod cover on the engine and tighten the retaining bolts.
12 Install a new rocker arm cover gasket in the rocker arm cover. RTV-type gasket sealant will hold it in place.
13 Install the rocker arm cover on the cylinder head, making sure that the bolt holes line up.
14 Install the rocker arm cover retaining bolts and tighten them to the proper torque.
15 Install the components listed in Steps 1 through 5 in reverse order.
16 After the engine has been started, run it until it reaches normal operating temperature. Check the pushrod cover and rocker arm cover for leaks.

16 Rocker arms and pushrods – removal, inspection and installation

1   Remove the rocker arm cover as described in the previous Section.
2   Remove the rocker arm stud nut, fulcrum seat and rocker arm from each cylinder. Keep them in order or mark them if they are to be re-installed so they can be replaced in their original positions.
3   Inspect the rocker arm cover bolt holes for worn or damaged seals where the bolt heads meet the cover.
4   Inspect the rocker arm for signs of excessive wear, galling or damage. Make sure the oil hole at the pushrod end of the rocker arm is open.
5   Inspect the rocker arm fulcrum for galling and check for wear on its face. If any of these conditions exist, replace the rocker arm and fulcrum as an assembly.
6   To remove the pushrods, pull them straight up through the cylinder head and out of the lifter pocket.
7   Inspect the pushrods to see if they are bent, cracked or excessively worn. If any of these conditions exist, replace the pushrods with new ones.
8   Apply engine oil or assembly lube to the top of the valve stem and the pushrod guide in the cylinder head.
9   Apply lubricant to the rocker arm fulcrum seat and the fulcrum seat socket in the rocker arm.

Fig. 2.17 Removing a pushrod from the cylinder head (Sec 16)

10 Install the pushrod (with lubricant applied to both ends).
11 Install the valve rocker arm, fulcrum seat and stud nut and tighten the stud nut to the proper torque.
12 Replace the rocker arm cover and gasket as described in the previous Section.

17 Valves – servicing

1   Because of the complex nature of the job and the special tools and equipment required, servicing of the valves, the valve seats and the valve guides (commonly known as a 'valve job') is best left to a professional.
2   The home mechanic can remove and disassemble the head, do the initial cleaning and inspection, then reassemble and deliver the head to a dealer service department or a reputable automotive machine shop for the actual valve servicing.
3   The dealer service department, or automotive machine shop, will remove the valves and springs, recondition or replace the valves and valve seats, recondition or replace the valve guides, check and replace the valve springs, spring retainers and keepers (as necessary), replace the valve seals with new ones, reassemble the valve components and make sure the installed spring height is correct. The cylinder head gasket surface will also be resurfaced if it is warped.
4   After the valve job has been performed by a professional, the head will be in like-new condition. When the head is returned, be sure to clean it again, very thoroughly (before installation on the engine), to remove any metal particles and abrasive grit that may still be present from the valve service or head resurfacing operations. Use compressed air, if available, to blow out all the holes and passages.

18 Cylinder head – removal, inspection and installation

Removal

Note: *If the engine has been removed from the vehicle, you may skip Steps 1 through 14 and begin with Step 15.*
1   Drain the cooling system.
2   Remove the air cleaner and connections leading to the air cleaner.
3   Disconnect the PCV valve from the rocker arm cover and remove the valve.
4   Disconnect the vent hose from the intake manifold inlet tube and remove it.
5   Disconnect and remove the carburetor fuel inlet line leading from the fuel pump.
6   Disconnect and remove all vacuum lines from the carburetor.
7   Disconnect the choke cable at its connection point to the carburetor and position the choke cable and housing out of the way. Secure the cable and housing to the firewall or fender well.
8   Disconnect the accelerator cable or accelerator linkage from the carburetor connecting point. Remove the accelerator return spring.
9   Disconnect the kick-down link at the carburetor connecting point.
10 Disconnect and remove the upper radiator hose from the thermostat outlet.
11 Remove the heater hose at the coolant outlet elbow.
12 Remove the nuts securing the muffler inlet pipe to the exhaust manifold and support the pipe out of the way.
13 Mark the wires leading to the coil and disconnect them. Remove the coil bracket attaching bolt. Secure the coil and bracket out of the way.
14 Remove the rocker arm cover.
15 Loosen the rocker arm stud nuts so the rocker arms can be rotated to one side.
16 Remove the pushrods in sequence and label them so they can be installed in their original locations. A numbered box or rack will keep them properly organized.
17 Disconnect the spark plug wires at the spark plugs.
18 Remove the cylinder head retaining bolts. If you have an engine hoist or similar device handy, attach eyelet bolts at the two ends of the cylinder head in the holes provided and lift the cylinder head off of the engine block. If equipment of this nature is not available, use a helper and pry the cylinder head up off of the engine block. **Caution**: *Do not wedge any tools between the cylinder head and block gasket mating surfaces.*
19 Turn the cylinder head upside down and secure it on a workbench or cylinder head holding device. **Note**: *New and rebuilt cylinder heads*

are commonly available for engines at dealerships and auto parts stores. Due to the fact that some specialized tools are necessary for the dismantling and inspection of the head, and replacement parts may not be readily available, it may be more practical and economical for the home mechanic to purchase a replacement head and install it.

20 Another alternative at this point is to take the cylinder heads to a competent automotive machine shop or shop specializing in cylinder heads and exchange them or leave your heads for the overhaul process.

21 If the complete engine is being overhauled at the same time, it may be wise to wait until the other components have been inspected.

22 If you are attempting to repair a part of the cylinder head assembly or you wish to inspect the components yourself, read the following procedure first to gain an understanding of the steps involved and the tools and replacement parts necessary for the job. Proceed as follows.

23 Using a valve spring compressor (available at tool or auto parts stores), compress each of the valve springs and remove the valve keepers. Work on one valve at a time, removing the keepers, then releasing the spring and removing the retainer, valve rotator (if equipped), spring and spring damper. Place these components together on the numbered box or rack used during cylinder head removal. All valve mechanism components must be kept separate so they can be returned to their original locations.

24 Remove the oil seals fom the stem of each valve. New seals should be used during reassembly.

25 Remove any spring shims used at the bottom of the valve spring.

26 Remove each valve, in turn, and place it in the numbered box or rack to complete the valve mechanism removal. Place the valve components in an area where they will not be mixed up.

27 Clean all old gasket material or sealant from the head gasket mating surface. Be careful not to scratch this sealing surface.

28 Clean the threads on all cylinder head attaching bolts thoroughly.

Inspection

29 Inspect each of the valve springs and dampers. Replace any spring which is deformed, cracked or broken. Check the valve spring tension using a special tool designed for this purpose. If you don't have access to this tool, take the springs to a shop that does. Weak valve springs may appear all right but can cause a poor running engine.

30 Carefully inspect the head for cracks around and inside the exhaust ports and combustion chambers or external cracks to the water jackets.

31 Check the cylinder head for warpage. Do this by placing a straightedge across the length of the head and measuring any gaps between the straightedge and the head surface with a feeler gauge. This should be done at three points across the head gasket surface and also in a diagonal fashion across this surface.

32 If warpage exceeds the specified limit at any point when a straightedge which spans the entire head is used, the cylinder head should be resurfaced.

33 At this point, even if you are doing the work yourself, you will have to take your cylinder head and related components to a shop with the necessary equipment for valve service work. If you choose not to reassemble the head yourself, omit steps 35 through 40 and begin the procedure at step 41 to reinstall the head on the engine block.

34 Make sure all valve mechanism components are perfectly clean and free from carbon and dirt. The bare cylinder head should also be clean and free from abrasive agents which may have been used for valve grinding, reaming, etc.

35 Insert a valve in the proper port. Install a new oil seal over the valve stem, using engine oil for lubricant.

36 Assemble the valve spring assembly for that cylinder. This will include the spring, seat, retainer and valve rotator (if so equipped). Notice that the closed coil end of the spring mates to the seat on the cylinder head.

37 Use the valve spring compressor to hold the spring assembly over the valve stem.

38 Install the valve keepers and release the compressor. Make sure the keepers seat properly in the upper groove of the valve stem.

39 Tap the retainers to ensure that the keepers are seated correctly.

40 Check the installed height of the valve springs using a caliper. Measure from the top of the shim (if present) or the spring seat to the top of the valve spring. Set the calipers next to a scale. Compare the spring height on the scale to the Specifications. If the springs are too long, shims can be used under the valve spring to bring the spring to the proper height. Shims are used to correct springs which are too

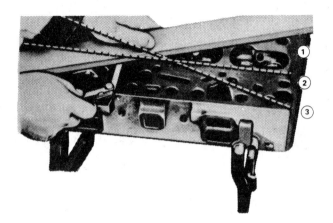

Fig. 2.18 Checking the cylinder head gasket surface for warpage with a straightedge and feeler gauge (check in the three positions indicated) (Sec 18)

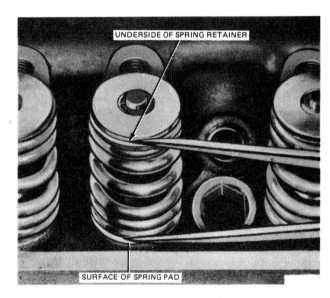

UNDERSIDE OF SPRING RETAINER

SURFACE OF SPRING PAD

Fig. 2.19 Checking the valve spring installed height with a caliper (Sec 18)

high, as the shims will act to compress the springs slightly. At no time should the spring be shimmed to give an installed height under the minimum specified length.

Installation

41 Make sure that the cylinder head and cylinder block mating surfaces are clean, flat and prepared for the new cylinder head gasket. Clean the exhaust manifold and muffler inlet pipe gasket surfaces.

42 Position the gasket over the dowel pins on the cylinder block, making sure that it is facing the right direction and that the correct surface is exposed. Gaskets are often marked 'front' and 'this side up' to aid the installer.

43 Using the previously installed lifting hooks (or two people) carefully lower the cylinder head into place on the block in its correct position. Take care not to move the head sideways or to scrape it across the surface as it can dislodge the gasket and/or damage the mating surfaces.

44 Coat the cylinder head retaining bolts with light engine oil and thread the bolts into the block. Tighten the bolts using the cylinder head bolt tightening sequence shown in the accompanying illustration. Work up to the final torque in three steps to avoid warping the head.

45 Apply a coat of engine oil to the rocker arm fulcrum seats and sockets in the rocker arms.

2B

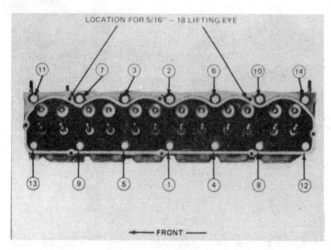

Fig. 2.20 In-line six-cylinder engine cylinder head bolt tightening sequence (Sec 18)

Fig. 2.21 Proper alignment of the camshaft and crankshaft gear timing marks on an in-line six-cylinder engine (Sec 19)

Fig. 2.22 Removing the camshaft gear from the camshaft with a gear puller (Sec 19)

46 Install the pushrods, the rocker arms, the rocker arm fulcrum seats and the retaining nuts.
47 Install the rocker arm cover. The remaining steps are the reverse of the removal procedure.
48 Start the engine and allow it to reach operating temperature. Shut it off, allow it to cool down and retorque the head bolts.

19 Timing cover and gears – removal and installation

Note: *The following procedure requires the use of a gear puller and gear installation tools.*

Removal
1   Drain the cooling system.
2   Remove the fan shroud and the radiator (Chapter 3).
3   Remove the alternator adjustment bolt.
4   Loosen the drivebelt and swing the adjusting arm up out of the way.
5   Remove the fan, drivebelts, fan spacer and pulley.
6   Remove the large bolt and washer from the crankshaft nose. It may be necessary to prevent the crankshaft from rotating by putting the transmission in gear (if the engine is still in the vehicle) or by holding the flywheel or crankshaft flange with a suitable tool if the engine is out of the vehicle.
7   Remove the vibration damper using a suitable puller.
8   Remove the front oil pan attaching bolts.
9   Remove the timing cover attaching bolts.
10 Remove the cover and scrape the old gasket from the mating surfaces of the cover and the engine block.
11 Remove the crankshaft oil seal by pushing it out of the front cover with a suitable sized drift. Be careful not to damage the front cover while performing this operation.
12 Remove any chemical sealants from the seal bore of the cover. Check the bore carefully for anything that would prevent the new seal from seating properly in the cover.
13 Before removing the gears, the camshaft endplay, timing gear backlash and timing gear runout should be inspected as described in Section 20.
14 Turn the crankshaft and/or camshaft until the timing marks of both gears can be aligned as shown in the accompanying illustration. **Caution:** *If the heads, valves and pistons remain in the engine while the gears are being installed, do not turn either the crankshaft or camshaft while the gears are removed. Serious internal engine damage can result from rotating either assembly independent of the other.*
15 Use a suitable gear puller to remove the gear from the camshaft.
16 Using a suitable puller, remove the timing gear from the crankshaft.

Installation
17 Make sure that the camshaft endplay, timing gear backlash and timing gear runout are within the Specifications. Do not install the camshaft gear until all of these camshaft related tolerances are correct (see Section 20 for the procedure).
18 Align the key spacer and thrust plate before installing the camshaft drivegear onto the camshaft. Make sure that the timing marks are properly aligned.
19 Install the crankshaft gear using the special drive tool. A substitute special tool can be fashioned by using a bolt and nut with a thread that matches the thread of the vibration damper retaining bolt. Use a bolt approximately $2\frac{1}{2}$ inches long. Place the crankshaft gear on the crankshaft. Position the damper on the crankshaft. Thread the bolt (with the nut run all the way up the bolt) into the crankshaft nose. After the bolt is threaded into the crankshaft as far as possible, use the nut to drive the damper onto the crankshaft. Make sure the damper is correctly aligned with the key on the crankshaft and check the internal bore of the damper as well as the outside surface of the crankshaft if resistance is felt. The damper will drive the crankshaft gear into position. Remove the damper with a puller. A large deep socket (if you have access to one) can also be used to drive the gear onto the crankshaft and will save having to pull the damper back off.
20 Install the crankshaft oil slinger in front of the crankshaft drivegear. Note that the cupped side faces away from the engine.
21 Coat the outside edge of the new crankshaft oil seal with grease and install the seal in the cover using an appropriate drive tool. Make

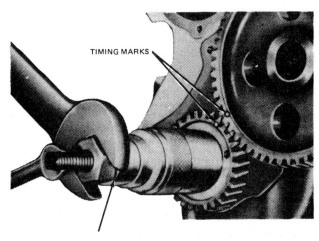

Fig. 2.23 Installing the crankshaft gear – note use of special tool (arrow) (Sec 19)

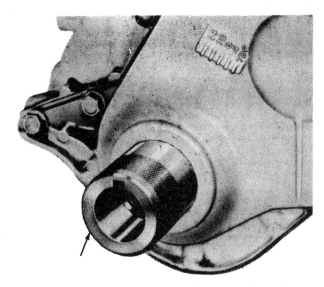

Fig. 2.24 Aligning the timing gear cover with an alignment tool (arrow) (Sec 19)

Fig. 2.25 Installing the crankshaft vibration damper with a sprocket replacement tool (arrow) (Sec 19)

sure the seal is seated completely in the bore.

22 If the oil pan is still on the engine, cut the old front oil pan seal flush at the cylinder block-to-pan junction. Remove the old seal.

23 Clean all gasket surfaces on the camshaft cover, block and oil pan.

24 If the oil pan is in place, cut and install a new pan seal so that it is flush with the engine block-to-oil pan junction.

25 Align the pan seal locating tabs with the holes in the oil pan. Make sure that the seal tabs pull all the way through so that the seal is completely seated. Apply RTV-type gasket sealant to the block and pan mating surfaces (particularly to the corner junctions of the block, oil pan and cover).

26 Position the cover over the end of the crankshaft and onto the cylinder block. Start the cover and pan retaining screws by hand.

27 Slide an alignment tool over the crank stub to make sure that the cover is located correctly before tightening the retaining bolts. If no alignment tool is available, try to locate a pipe to center the seal over the nose of the crankshaft. If the seal is not centered, the high spots will cause oil leakage around the vibration damper.

28 Tighten the retaining bolts for the cover and oil pan to the correct torque.

29 Install the alternator adjusting arm and tighten all the oil pan and front cover screws.

30 Make sure that the oil pan screws are tightened first to compress the pan seal so the alignment of the cover is retained.

31 Lubricate the nose of the crankshaft, the inner hub of the vibration damper and the seal surface with engine oil.

32 Align the damper keyway with the key on the crankshaft and install the damper.

33 Install the bolt and washer retaining the damper and tighten it to the proper torque.

34 Install the pulley(s), drivebelt(s), spacer and fan.

35 Adjust all drivebelt tensions.

36 Install the fan shroud, radiator and hoses.

37 Fill the cooling system.

38 Fill the engine with oil if the oil has been drained.

39 Start and operate the engine at a fast idle and check for leaks of any type.

2B

20 Camshaft and lifters – removal, inspection and installation

Removal

1 Remove the air cleaner.

2 Remove the PCV valve from the rocker arm cover.

3 Disconnect the choke cable at the connecting point of the carburetor.

4 Disconnect the throttle cable at the carburetor connecting point. Remove the accelerator return spring.

5 Remove the coil bracket retaining bolt and swing the coil out of the way. Support it securely and do not let it hang from the wires.

6 Remove the rocker arm cover.

7 Disconnect the spark plug wires from the spark plugs and the coil wire from the coil.

8 Remove the distributor cap and spark plug wire assembly.

9 Remove the pushrod cover from the side of the block.

10 Loosen the rocker arm stud nuts until the rocker arms are free of the pushrods. Turn the rocker arms to the side and remove the pushrods. Make sure that the pushrods are numbered or marked so that they can be installed in the same locations.

11 Remove the valve lifters with a special magnetic valve lifter tool.

12 Drain the cooling system and the oil from the crankcase.

13 Remove the radiator.

14 Remove the front timing cover.

15 Remove the oil pump and oil pan.

16 Disconnect the fuel lines at the fuel pump. Remove the fuel pump retaining bolts and secure the fuel pump out of the way.

17 Disconnect the vacuum lines at the distributor and remove all vacuum lines from the carburetor. **Note:** *The following checking procedures require the use of a magnetic base dial indicator.*

18 Check the camshaft endplay by pushing the camshaft all the way to the rear of its travel in the block.

19 Install a dial indicator so the indicator stem is on the camshaft sprocket retaining bolt. Zero the dial indicator in this position.

20 Using a large screwdriver between the camshaft gear and the block, pull the camshaft forward and release it. The reading on the dial indicator will give you the endplay measurement. Compare it to the

Fig. 2.26 Checking the camshaft endplay with a dial indicator (Sec 20)

Fig. 2.27 Checking the crankshaft endplay with a dial indicator (Sec 20)

Fig. 2.28 Checking the timing gear backlash with a dial indicator (Sec 20)

Specifications. If the endplay is excessive, check the spacer for correct installation. If the spacer is correctly installed, and the endplay is too great, replace the thrust plate with a new one.

21 Check the timing gear backlash by installing a dial indicator on the cylinder block and positioning the stem against the timing gear.

22 Zero the pointer on the dial indicator.

23 While holding the crankshaft still, move the camshaft timing gear until it takes up the slack in the gear train.

24 Read the dial indicator to obtain the gear backlash.

25 Compare the results to the Specifications.

26 If the backlash is excessive, replace the timing gear and the crankshaft gear with new ones.

27 To check the timing gear runout, install a dial indicator on the engine block with the stem touching the face of the timing gear.

28 Hold the camshaft gear against the camshaft thrust plate and zero the indicator.

29 Rotate the crankshaft to turn the camshaft while holding the camshaft gear against the thrust plate.

30 Rotate the gear through one complete revolution of the camshaft. Observe the reading on the dial indicator during this revolution.

31 If the runout exceeds the Specifications, remove the camshaft gear and check for foreign objects or burrs between the camshaft and gear flanges. If this condition does not exist and the runout is excessive, the gears must be replaced with new ones. Use a similar procedure to check the crankshaft gear runout. Make sure that the crankshaft is situated against one end of the thrust bearing (this will prevent you from obtaining a crankshaft endplay measurement as opposed to the actual runout of the crankshaft gear).

32 Turn the crankshaft until the timing marks are directly adjacent to each other.

33 Remove the camshaft thrust plate retaining screws.

34 Carefully withdraw the camshaft from the engine block, being careful that the lobes do not catch on the camshaft bearings (they can scrape and damage them easily).

35 Remove the camshaft from the gear using a special hydraulic press. This procedure will have to be handled by a suitably equipped automotive machine shop.

36 Remove the key, the thrust plate and the spacer.

Inspection

37 Visually inspect the hydraulic lifters for cupping on the camshaft mating face and for signs of excessive wear, galling or cracking.

38 The hydraulic valve lifter is tested using a special lifter tester and special testing fluid. This procedure must be handled by a suitably equipped automotive machine shop.

39 If you suspect that a lifter is defective, you will have to replace the lifter with a new one. It is not necessary to test the new lifter before installation.

40 Check the lift of each camshaft lobe in a special V-block cradle. Again, this is a procedure which should be handled by a suitably equipped machine shop.

41 Also, check the camshaft bearing surfaces for any signs of galling or excessive wear. If any of these conditions exist, replace the camshaft with a new one. If the bearing journals of the camshaft show any signs of wear or damage, check the cam bearings in the engine block. Do not install any camshaft in worn or damaged bearings.

Installation

42 Make sure that the camshaft endplay, timing gear backlash and/or timing gear runout are within Specifications before installing the camshaft.

43 Oil the camshaft bearing journals and apply engine assembly lubricant to all of the lobes.

44 Install the key, spacer and thrust plate into position on the front of the camshaft. Install the gear on the camshaft using the special tool. An alternative is to use a bolt that will fit the threaded hole in the end of the camshaft. Put a nut and large flat washer on the bolt. Thread the bolt into the camshaft with the gear in place. Hold the bolt stationary and turn the nut down the bolt to push the gear into place on the camshaft. Remove the bolt and nut combination after the cam gear is in place.

45 Install the camshaft into the engine. Be careful not to nick or damage the camshaft bearings. Install the camshaft retaining bolts, making sure the camshaft gear is aligned with the crankshaft gear.

46 Tighten the camshaft thrust plate bolts to the proper torque, using the access holes provided in the camshaft gear.

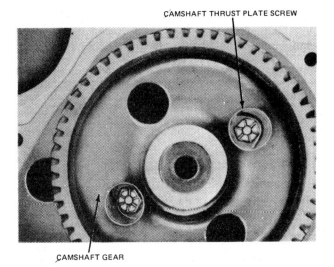

Fig. 2.29 Locations of the camshaft thrust plate screws (Sec 20)

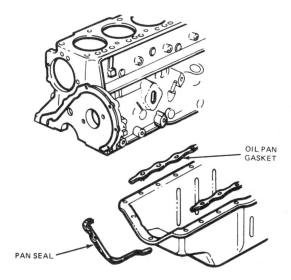

Fig. 2.30 Typical oil pan gasket and front pan seal installation (Sec 21)

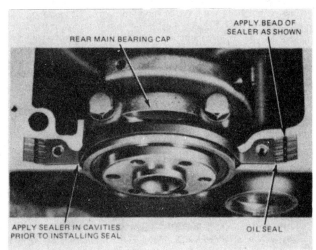

Fig. 2.31 Installing the rear oil pan seal (Sec 21)

47 Install the timing cover as described in Section 19.
48 Do not turn the engine until the distributor is installed, as the timing marks must remain aligned.
49 Install the oil pump and oil pan.
50 Lubricate the bottom of the lifters with engine assembly lube and install them into their proper positions. Install the pushrods, align the rocker arms and tighten the nuts, install the rocker arm and pushrod covers and hook up the throttle cable.
51 Install the distributor as described in Chapter 5.
52 Install the fuel pump as described in Chapter 4.
53 Install the vacuum line connecting the distributor to the carburetor.
54 Connect the fuel outlet line and the fuel feed line to the fuel pump.
55 Fill the crankcase with oil.
56 Install the radiator and fill the cooling system with the correct coolant.
57 Start the engine and check for oil and fuel leaks.
58 Adjust the ignition timing as described in Chapter 1.
59 Adjust the carburetor idle speed and mixture as described in Chapter 4.

21 Oil pan – removal and installation

Note: *This procedure is for removal and installation of the oil pan with the engine in the vehicle only. If the engine has been removed for an overhaul, use only Step 10 and Steps 14 through 26.*

Removal

1 Drain the engine oil and disconnect the negative battery cable from the battery.
2 Drain the cooling system.
3 Remove the radiator as described in Chapter 3.
4 Raise the vehicle and support it securely. Disconnect the starter cable at the starter.
5 Remove the starter from the bellhousing. It is attached with three bolts.
6 Remove the engine front insulator-to-support bracket retaining nuts and washers.
7 Raise the front of the engine with a jack. Place a thick wooden block between the jack and the oil pan.
8 Place one inch wood blocks between the front support insulators and the support brackets.
9 Lower the engine onto the spacer blocks and remove the jack.
10 Remove the oil pan attaching bolts.
11 Lower the pan to the crossmember.
12 Remove the two oil pump inlet tube-to-oil pump retaining bolts and washers.
13 Remove the oil pump inlet assembly and allow it to rest in the oil pan.
14 Remove the oil pan from the vehicle. It may be necessary to rotate the crankshaft so the counterweights clear the pan.
15 Clean all gaskets from the mating surfaces of the engine block and the pan.

Installation

16 Remove the rear main bearing cap-to-oil pan seal.
17 Remove the timing cover-to-oil pan seal.
18 Clean all mating surfaces and seal grooves.
19 Install new oil pan-to-cylinder front cover oil seals.
20 Install a new rear main bearing cap-to-oil pan seal.
21 Install new oil pan side gaskets on the block. Apply a thin, even coat of RTV-type gasket sealer to both sides of the gaskets.
22 Make sure the tabs of the front and rear seal fit properly into the mating slots on the oil pan side seals. A small amount of RTV-type gasket sealer at each mating junction will help prevent any leaks from these critical spots.
23 Clean the inlet tube and screen assembly and place it in the oil pan.
24 Position the oil pan underneath the engine.
25 Lift the inlet tube and screen assembly from the oil pan and secure it to the oil pump with a new gasket. Tighten the two retaining bolts to the proper torque.
26 Attach the oil pan to the engine block and install the retaining bolts. Tighten the bolts to the specified torque, starting from the center and working out in each direction.

2B

27 Raise the engine with a jack and a block of wood underneath the oil pan and remove the wood spacers previously installed under the support brackets.

28 Lower the engine to the correct installed position and install the washers and nuts on the insulator studs. Tighten the nuts to the specified torque (see Chapter 1A).

29 Install the starter and connect the starter cable.

30 Lower the vehicle.

31 Install the radiator according to the instructions in Chapter 3.

32 Fill the cooling system with coolant and check for leaks.

33 Fill the engine crankcase with oil and hook up the negative battery cable.

34 Start the engine and check carefully for leaks at the oil pan gasket sealing surfaces.

22 Oil pump – removal and installation

1   Remove the oil pan as described in Section 21.

2   Remove the bolts retaining the oil pump to the block.

3   Remove the oil pump assembly.

4   Clean the mating surfaces of the oil pump and the block.

5   Before installation, prime the pump by filling the inlet opening with oil and rotating the pump shaft until the oil spurts out of the outlet.

6   Attach the oil pump to the engine block using the two retaining bolts.

7   Tighten the bolts to the proper torque.

8   Install the oil pan by referring to Section 21.

23 Oil pump – disassembly, inspection and reassembly

1   Remove the two bolts securing the pick-up to the oil pump, then remove the pick-up.

2   Clean the oil pump with solvent and dry it thoroughly with compressed air.

3   Remove the oil pump housing cover. It is retained by four bolts.

4   Use a brush to clean the inside of the pump housing and the pressure relief valve chamber. Make sure that the interior of the oil pump is clean.

5   Visually check the inside of the pump housing and the outer race and rotor for excessive wear, scoring or damage. Check the mating surface of the pump cover for wear, grooves or damage. If any of these conditions exist, replace the pump with a new one.

6   Measure the outer race-to-housing clearance with a feeler gauge and compare the results with the Specifications.

7   Using a straightedge and feeler gauge, measure the end plate-to-rotor assembly clearance and compare the results with the Specificatons.

8   Check the driveshaft-to-housing bearing clearance by measuring the inside diameter of the housing bearing and subtracting that figure from the outside diameter of the driveshaft. Compare the results with the Specifications.

9   If any components fail the checks mentioned, replace the entire oil pump, as the components are not serviced as separate parts.

10 Inspect the relief valve spring for wear or a collapsed condition.

11 Check the relief valve piston for scoring, damage and free operation within its bore.

12 If the relief valve fails any of the above tests, replace the entire relief valve assembly with a new one.

13 Install the rotor, outer housing and race in the oil pump.

14 Install the rotor housing cover and the four retaining bolts and tighten them to the proper torque.

15 Attach the pick-up tube to the oil pump body using a new gasket. Tighten the bolts to the proper torque.

24 Piston/connecting rod assembly – removal

1   Prior to removing the piston/connecting rod assemblies, remove the cylinder head, the oil pan, and the oil pump by referring to the appropriate Sections.

2   Using a ridge reamer, completely remove the ridge at the top of each cylinder (photo). Follow the manufacturer's instructions provided with the ridge reaming tool. Failure to remove the ridge before

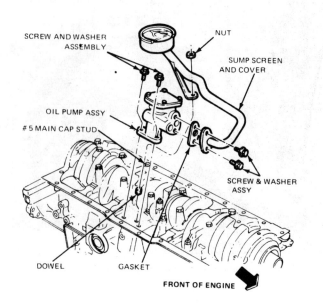

Fig. 2.32 Details of an in-line six-cylinder oil pump installation (Sec 23)

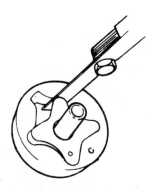

Fig. 2.33 Measuring the oil pump outer race-to-housing clearance with a feeler gauge (Sec 23)

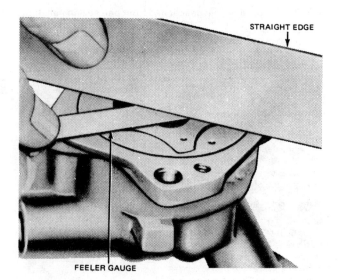

Fig. 2.34 Checking the oil pump rotor endplay with a feeler gauge and straightedge (Sec 23)

24.2 Removing the ridge at the top of the cylinder with a ridge reamer

attempting to remove the piston/connecting rod assemblies will result in piston breakage.

3   Mark each of the connecting rods and connecting rod bearing caps to ensure that they are properly mated during reassembly.

4   Loosen each of the connecting rod cap nuts approximately $\frac{1}{2}$ turn each. Remove the number one connecting rod cap and bearing insert. Do not drop the bearing insert out of the cap. Slip a short length of plastic or rubber hose over each connecting rod cap bolt (to protect the crankshaft journal when the piston is removed) and push the connecting rod/piston assembly out through the top of the engine. Use a wooden tool to push on the upper bearing insert in the connecting rod. If resistance is felt, double-check to make sure that all of the ridge was removed from the cylinder.

5   Repeat the procedure for the remaining cylinders. After removal, reassemble the connecting rod caps and bearing inserts to their respective connecting rods and install the cap nuts finger tight. Leaving the old bearing inserts in place until reassembly will help prevent the connecting rod bearing surfaces from being accidentally nicked or gouged.

25 Crankshaft and main bearings – removal

Note: *The crankshaft may be removed only after the engine has been removed from the vehicle.*

1   Remove the spark plugs from the cylinder head. Remove the cylinder head if the entire engine is going to be dismantled.

2   Remove the oil level dipstick.

3   Remove the bolt and lock washer retaining the vibration damper to the front of the crankshaft.

4   Remove the vibration damper with a suitable puller.

5   Remove the timing cover and gasket as described in Section 19.

6   Remove the flywheel.

7   Remove the engine rear cover plate.

8   Remove the oil pan and gaskets.

9   Remove the oil pump and inlet tube assembly.

10 Visually check all of the main bearing and rod bearing caps to see that they are marked for location. If they are not, mark them with a numbered die or a center punch.

11 If the engine is being entirely dismantled, remove the piston and rod assemblies.

12 If the crankshaft only is being removed from the engine, remove the connecting rod cap and bearing from the number one cylinder and then rotate it to the top dead center position. **Note:** *Use caution when turning the crankshaft for further connecting rod cap removal as the rod bolts can come in contact with the crankshaft bearing surfaces and damage the crank pin journals. It is a very good idea to slip a short section of rubber hose over each rod bolt to protect the journals.*

13 Follow the procedure in Step 12 for each remaining connecting rod cap and bearing.

14 Remove the main bearing caps and retaining bolts.

15 Remove the rear main bearing oil seal.

16 Remove the lower main bearing inserts if they did not stay with the main bearing caps.

17 Carefully lift the crankshaft out of the engine block taking care that all of the crank pins clear the exposed connecting rod bolts.

18 Replace the main bearings and caps in the block and tighten the bolts finger tight.

26 Engine block – cleaning and inspection

1   Remove the soft plugs from the engine block. To do this, knock the plugs into the block (using a hammer and punch), then grasp them with large pliers and pull them back through the holes.

2   Using a gasket scraper, remove all traces of gasket material from the engine block. Be very careful not to nick or gouge the gasket sealing surfaces.

3   Remove the main bearing caps and separate the bearing inserts from the caps and the engine block. Tag the bearings according to which cylinder they were removed from (and whether they were in the cap or the block) and set them aside.

4   Using a hex wrench of the appropriate size, remove the threaded oil gallery plugs from the front and back of the block.

5   If the engine is extremely dirty, it should be taken to an automotive machine shop to be steam cleaned or hot tanked.

6   After the block is returned, clean all oil holes and oil galleries one more time (brushes for cleaning oil holes and galleries are available at most auto parts stores). Flush the passages with warm water (until the water runs clear), dry the block thoroughly and wipe all machined surfaces with a light rust-preventative oil. If you have access to compressed air, use it to speed the drying process and to blow out all of the oil holes and galleries.

7   If the block is not extremely dirty or sludged up, you can do an adequate cleaning job with warm soapy water and a stiff brush. Take plenty of time and do a thorough job. Regardless of the cleaning method used, be very sure to thoroughly clean all oil holes and galleries, dry the block completely and coat all machined surfaces with light oil.

8   The threaded holes in the block must be clean to ensure accurate torque readings during reassembly. Run the proper size tap into each of the holes to remove any rust, corrosion, thread sealant or sludge and to restore any damaged threads. If possible, use compressd air to clear the holes of debris produced by this operation. Now is a good time to thoroughly clean the threads on the head bolts and the main bearing cap bolts as well.

9   Reinstall the main bearing caps and tighten the bolts finger tight.

10 After coating the sealing surfaces of the new soft plugs with a good quality gasket sealer, install them in the engine block. Make sure they are driven in straight and seated properly, or leakage could result. Special tools are available for this purpose, but equally good results can be obtained using a large socket (with an outside diameter slightly larger than the outside diameter of the soft plug) and a large hammer.

11 Double-check to make sure that the ridge at the top of the cylinders has been competely removed.

12 Visually check the block for cracks, rust and corrosion. Look for stripped threads in the threaded holes. It is also a good idea to have the block checked for hidden cracks by an automotive machine shop that has the special equipment to do this type of work. If defects are found, have the block repaired, if possible, or replaced.

13 Check the cylinder bores for scuffing and scoring.

14 Using the appropriate precision measuring tools, measure each cylinder's diameter at the top (just under the ridge), center and bottom of the cylinder bore, parallel to the crankshaft axis. Next, measure each cylinder's diameter at the same three locations across the crankshaft axis (photos). Compare the results to the Specifications. If the cylinder walls are badly scuffed or scored, or if they are out-of-round or tapered beyond the limits given in the Specifications, have the engine block rebored and honed at an automotive machine shop. If a rebore is done, oversized pistons and rings will be required as well.

15 If the cylinders are in reasonably good condition and not worn to the outside of the limits, and if the piston-to-cylinder clearances can be maintained properly, then they do not have to be rebored; honing is all that is necessary.

16 Before honing the cylinders, install the main bearing caps (without the bearings) and tighten the bolts to the specified torque.

2B

26.14A Determining the cylinder bore size with a telescoping gauge

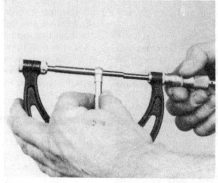

26.14B Measuring the telescoping gauge with a micrometer

27.2 Measuring the crankshaft main bearing journals with a micrometer

17 To perform the honing operation, you will need the proper size flexible hone (with fine stones), plenty of light oil or honing oil, some rags and an electric drill motor. Mount the hone in the drill motor, compress the stones and slip the hone into the first cylinder. Lubricate the cylinder thoroughly, turn on the drill and move the hone up and down in the cylinder at a pace which will produce a fine crosshatch pattern on the cylinder walls (with the crosshatch lines intersecting at approximately a 60° angle). Be sure to use plenty of lubricant, and do not take off any more material than is absolutely necessary to produce the desired finish. Do not withdraw the hone from the cylinder while it is running. Instead, shut off the drill and continue moving the hone up and down in the cylinder until it comes to a complete stop, then compress the stones and withdraw the hone. Wipe the oil out of the cylinder and repeat the procedure on the remaining cylinders. Remember, do not remove too much material from the cylinder wall. If you do not have the tools or do not desire to perform the honing operation, most automotive machine shops will do it for a reasonable fee.

18 After the honing job is complete, chamfer the top edges of the cylinder bores with a small file so that the rings will not catch when the pistons are installed.

19 Check the cylinder head mating surface (top deck) of the block using a straightedge and a feeler gauge. Have the deck surface of the block machined if the warpage exceeds the Specifications.

20 Next, the entire engine block must be thoroughly washed again with warm soapy water to remove all traces of the abrasive grit produced during the honing operation. Be sure to run a brush through all oil holes and galleries and flush them with running water. After rinsing, dry the block and apply a coat of light rust preventative oil to all machined surfaces. Wrap the block in a plastic trash bag to keep it clean and set it aside until reassembly.

27 Crankshaft and bearings – inspection

1   Clean the crankshaft with solvent (be sure to clean the oil holes with a stiff brush and flush them with solvent) and dry it thoroughly. Check the main and connecting rod bearing journals for uneven wear, scoring, pitting and cracks. Check the remainder of the crankshaft for cracks and damage.

2   Using a micrometer of the appropriate size, measure the diameter of the main and connecting rod journals and compare the results to the Specifications (photo). By measuring the diameter at a number of points around the journal's circumference, you will be able to determine whether or not the journal is worn out-of-round. Take the measurement at each end of the journal, near the crank throw, to determine whether the journal is tapered.

3   If the crankshaft journals are damaged, tapered, out-of-round or worn beyond the limits given in the Specifications, have the crankshaft reground by a reputable automotive machine shop. Be sure to use the correct undersize bearing inserts if the crankshaft is reconditioned.

4   Even though the main and connecting rod bearings should be replaced with new ones during the engine overhaul, the old bearings should be retained for close examination, as they may reveal valuable information about the condition of the engine.

5   Bearing failure occurs mainly because of lack of lubrication, the

CRATERS OR POCKETS   BRIGHT (POLISHED) SECTIONS

FATIGUE FAILURE   IMPROPER SEATING

SCRATCHES   DIRT IMBEDDED   OVERLAY WIPED OUT
INTO BEARING MATERIAL

SCRATCHED BY DIRT   LACK OF OIL

OVERLAY GONE FROM ENTIRE SURFACE

RADIUS RIDE

TAPERED JOURNAL   RADIUS RIDE

Fig. 2.35 Typical indications of bearing failure (Sec 27)

presence of dirt or other foreign particles, overloading the engine and/or corrosion. Regardless of the cause of bearing failure, it must be corrected before the engine is reassembled to prevent it from happening again.

6   When examining the bearings, remove them from the engine block, the main bearing caps, the connecting rods and the rod caps and lay them out on a clean surface in the same general position as their location in the engine. This will enable you to match any noted bearing problems with the corresponding crankshaft journal.

7   Dirt and other foreign particles get into the engine in a variety of ways. Dirt may be left in the engine during reassembly, or it may pass through filters or breathers. It may get into the oil, and from there into the bearings. Metal chips from machining operations and normal engine wear are often present. Abrasives are sometimes left in engine components after reconditioning, especially when parts are not thoroughly cleaned using the proper cleaning methods. Whatever the source, these foreign objects often end up embedded in the soft bearing material and are easily recognized. Large particles will not embed in the bearing and will score or gouge the bearing and shaft. The best prevention for this cause of bearing failure is to clean all parts

thoroughly and keep everything spotlessly clean during engine assembly. Frequent and regular changes of engine oil, and oil filter, are also recommended.

8 Lack of lubrication (or lubrication breakdown) has a number of interrelated causes. Excessive heat (which thins the oil), overloading (which squeezes the oil from the bearing face) and oil leakage or throw-off (from excessive bearing clearances, worn oil pump or high engine speeds) all contribute to lubrication breakdown. Blocked oil passages, which usually are the result of misaligned oil holes in a bearing shell, will also oil-starve a bearing and destroy it. When lack of lubrication is the cause of bearing failure, the bearing material is wiped or extruded from the steel backing of the bearing. Temperatures may increase to the point where the steel backing turns blue from overheating.

9 Driving habits can have a definite effect on bearing life. Full-throttle low-rpm operation (or 'lugging' the engine) puts very high loads on bearings, which tends to squeeze out the oil film. These loads cause the bearings to flex, which produces fine cracks in the bearing face (fatigue failure). Eventually the bearing material will loosen in pieces and tear away from the steel backing. Short-trip driving leads to corrosion of bearings, as insufficient engine heat is produced to drive off the condensed water and corrosive gases produced. These products collect in the engine oil, forming acid and sludge. As the oil is carried to the engine bearings the acid attacks and corrodes the bearing material.

10 Incorrect bearing installation during engine assembly will lead to bearing failure as well. Tight-fitting bearings, which leave insufficient bearing oil clearance, result in oil starvation. Dirt or foreign particles trapped behind a bearing insert result in high spots on the bearing which lead to failure.

28 Piston/connecting rod assembly – inspection

1 Before the inspection process can be carried out, the piston/connecting rod assemblies must be cleaned and the old piston rings removed from the pistons.

2 Using a piston ring installation tool, carefully remove the rings from the pistons (photo). Do not nick or gouge the pistons in the process.

3 Scrape all traces of carbon from the top (or crown) of the piston. A hand-held wire brush or a piece of fine emery cloth can be used once the majority of the deposits have been scraped away. Do not, under any circumstances, use a wire brush mounted in a drill motor to remove deposits from the pistons. The piston material is soft and will be eroded away by the wire brush.

4 Use a piston ring groove cleaning tool to remove any carbon deposits from the ring grooves (photo). If a tool is not available, a piece broken off the old ring will do the job. Be very careful to remove only the carbon deposits. Do not remove any metal and do not nick or scratch the sides of the ring grooves.

5 Once the deposits have been removed, clean the piston/rod assemblies with solvent and dry them thoroughly. Make sure that the oil hole in the big end of the connecting rod and the oil return holes in the back side of the ring groove are clear.

6 If the pistons are not damaged or worn excessively, and if the engine block is not rebored, new pistons will not be necessary. Normal

piston wear appears as even vertical wear on the piston thrust surfaces and slight looseness of the top ring in its groove. New piston rings, on the other hand, should always be used when an engine is rebuilt.

7 Carefully inspect each piston for cracks around the skirt, at the pin bosses and at the ring lands.

8 Look for scoring and scuffing (on the thrust faces of the skirt), holes (in the piston crown) and burned areas (at the edge of the crown). If the skirt is scored or scuffed, the engine may have been suffering from overheating and/or abnormal combustion, which caused excessively high operating temperatures. The cooling and lubrication systems should be checked thoroughly. A hole in the piston crown, an extreme to be sure, is an indication that abnormal combustion (preignition) was occurring. Burned areas at the edge of the piston crown are usually evidence of spark knock (detonation). If any of the above problems exist, the causes must be corrected or the damage will occur again.

9 Corrosion of the piston (evidenced by pitting) indicates that coolant is leaking into the combustion chamber and/or the crankcase. Again, the cause must be corrected or the problem may persist in the rebuilt engine.

10 Measure the piston ring side clearance by laying a new piston ring in the ring groove and slipping a feeler gauge in beside it. Check the clearance at three or four locations around the groove. Be sure to use the correct ring for each groove; they are different. If the side clearance is greater than specified, new pistons will have to be used and the block rebored to accept them.

11 Check the piston-to-bore clearance by measuring the bore and the piston diameter. Make sure that the pistons and bores are correctly matched. Measure the piston on the thrust faces (at a 90° angle to the piston pin) at the piston pin centerline (photo). Subtract the piston diameter from the bore diameter to obtain the clearance. If it is greater than specified, the block will have to be rebored and new pistons and rings installed. Check the piston pin-to-rod clearance by twisting the piston and rod in opposite directions. Any noticeable play indicates that there is excessive wear, which must be corrected. The piston/connecting rod assemblies should be taken to an automotive machine shop to have the new piston pins installed and the pistons and connecting rods rebored. While they are there, it would be convenient to have the connecting rods checked for bend and twist, as automotive machine shops have special equipment for this purpose.

12 Check the connecting rods for cracks and other damage. Temporarily remove the rod caps, lift out the old bearing inserts, wipe the rod and cap bearing surfaces clean and inspect them for nicks, grooves and scratches. After checking the rods, replace the old bearings, slip the caps in place and tighten the nuts finger tight. Unless new pistons or connecting rods must be installed, do not disassemble the pistons from the connecting rods.

29 Main and rod bearings – checking clearances

1 **Note:** *There are three precautions to observe when working with Plastigage. These are:*

a) Plastigage is soluble in oil, so all oil and grease should be removed from the crankshaft and bearing surfaces before the check is done

28.2 Removing the piston rings (note the special tool)

28.4 Cleaning the piston ring grooves with a piston ring groove cleaning tool

28.11 Measuring the piston diameter with a micrometer

   b)   Do not rotate the crankshaft while the Plastigage is installed, as this may cause damage to the crankshaft or bearing surfaces

   c)   Remove all traces of the Plastigage when the check is complete. Be very careful not to damage the crankshaft or bearing surfaces as the Plastigage is removed. Do not use sharp tools or abrasive cleaners. Instead, remove the used Plastigage with your fingernail or a blunt wood stick

2   Whenever an engine is overhauled, the bearing clearances should be checked. This should be done for reused bearings as well as for new bearings.

3   The procedure is basically the same for both the main bearings and the connecting rod bearings.

4   Remove all oil, grime and foreign matter from the crankshaft and bearing surfaces.

5   With the upper half of the main bearings set into the block, place the crankshaft in the block and install the bearings in the main bearing caps.

6   Place a piece of Plastigage (available at most auto supply shops) along the length of each main bearing journal on the crankshaft.

7   Install each main bearing cap and tighten the attaching bolts to the specified torque. The arrow on each cap should face toward the front of the engine.

8   Now remove each bearing cap and measure the width of the Plastigage strip, which will have flattened out when the caps were tightened (photo). A scale is provided on the Plastigage envelope for measuring the width of the Plastigage strip, and thus, bearing clearance.

9   If the Plastigage is flattened more at the ends than in the middle, or vice versa, this is an indication of journal taper which can be checked in the Specifications section.

10 To test for an out-of-round condition, remove all traces of the Plastigage (be careful not to damage the crankshaft or bearing surfaces) and rotate the crankshaft 90 degrees. With the crankshaft rotated to this point, use the Plastigage to check the clearances again. Compare these measurements with those taken previously to arrive at eccentricity or out-of-round.

11 To check connecting rod bearing clearances, install each piston/rod assembly and use the Plastigage as described above.

12 Connecting rod side clearance can be checked with the piston/rod assemblies temporarily installed for bearing clearance checking.

13 With the piston/rod assemblies installed and the bearing caps tightened to the specified torque, use feeler gauges to check the clearance between the sides of the connecting rods and the crankshaft throws (photo).

14 If the clearance at this point is below the minimum tolerance, the rod may be machined for more clearance at this area.

15 If the clearance is excessive, a new rod must be used or the crankshaft must be replaced with a new one.

16 If the bearings have shown to be within all tolerances, they may be installed following the steps outlined in the appropriate Sections.

17 If not within Specifications, the bearings should be replaced with the correctly sized bearings. Upper and lower bearings should always be replaced as an assembly.

30 Crankshaft oil seals – replacement

Front crankshaft seal

Note: *The following operation requires a special tool for proper seal installation.*

1   Drain the cooling system and crankcase.

2   Remove the radiator.

3   Remove the crankshaft pulley and the timing cover (see Section 19).

4   Drive out the oil seal with a pin punch.

5   Clean out the recess in the cover.

6   Coat the outer edge of the new seal with grease and install it using the special tool designed for this operation. As an alternative, a large piece of pipe can be used to push the new seal in. However, use extreme caution as the seal can be damaged easily with this method. Drive in the seal until it is fully seated in the recess. Make sure that the spring is properly positioned within the seal.

7   Installation is the reverse of the removal procedure.

Rear crankshaft seal

Note: *If rear crankshaft oil seal replacement is the only operation being performed, it can be accomplished with the engine in the vehicle. If, however, the oil seal is being replaced along with the rear main bearing, the engine must be removed.*

8   Disconnect the negative battery cable from the battery, then remove the starter.

9   Remove the transmission (Chapter 7).

10 On manual transmission equipped vehicles, remove the pressure plate, disc and clutch assembly. On automatic transmission equipped vehicles, remove the flexplate.

11 Remove the flywheel attaching bolts and remove the flywheel and engine rear cover plate.

12 Use an awl to punch two holes in the crankshaft rear oil seal.

13 Punch the holes on opposite sides of the crankshaft, just above the bearing cap-to-engine block junction.

14 Thread a sheet metal screw into each punched hole.

15 Use two large screwdrivers or small pry bars and pry against both screws at the same time to remove the crankshaft rear oil seal. A block or blocks of wood placed against the engine will provide additional leverage.

16 Be very careful when performing this operation that you do not damage the crankshaft oil seal contact surfaces.

17 Clean the oil recess in the rear of the engine block and the main bearing cap surface of the crankshaft.

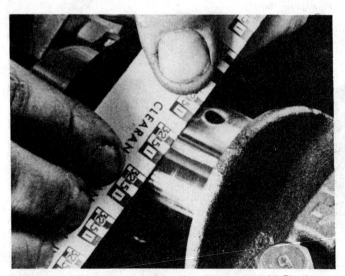

29.8 Determining the crankshaft bearing oil clearance with Plastigage

29.13 Using a feeler gauge to determine the connecting rod end play

18 Inspect, clean and polish the oil seal contact surfaces of the crankshaft.
19 Coat the new oil seal with a light film of engine oil.
20 Coat the crankshaft with a light film of engine oil.
21 Start the seal into the cavity in the back of the engine with the seal lip facing forward and install it with the special drive tool. Make sure that the tool stays in alignment with the crankshaft until the tool contacts the block. See Step 6 for seal installation alternatives.
22 Make sure that the seal has been installed correctly after removing the tool.
23 Install the engine rear cover plate.
24 Attach the flywheel (or flexplate) to the crankshaft.
25 Install the clutch assembly.
26 Install the transmission as described in Chapter 7.
27 Install the starter and hook up the battery cable.

31 Crankshaft and main bearings – installation

1   Crankshaft installation is generally one of the first steps in engine reassembly; it is assumed at this point that the engine block and crankshaft have been cleaned and inspected and repaired or reconditioned.
2   Position the engine block so that the bottom is facing up.
3   Remove the main bearing cap bolts and lift out the caps. Lay them out in the proper order to help ensure that they are installed correctly.
4   If they are still in place, remove the old bearing inserts from the block and the main bearing caps. Wipe the main bearing surfaces of the block and caps with a clean, lint-free cloth (they must be kept spotlessly clean).
5   Clean the back side of the new main bearing inserts and lay one bearing half in each main bearing saddle (in the block) and the other bearing half from each bearing set in the corresponding main bearing cap. Make sure that the tang on the bearing insert fits into the notch in the block or cap. Also, the oil holes in the block and cap must line up with the oil holes in the bearing insert. Do not hammer the bearing into place and do not nick or gouge the bearing faces.
6   The flanged thrust bearing must be installed in the number five cap and saddle.
7   Clean the faces of the bearings in the block and the crankshaft main bearing journals with a clean, lint-free cloth. Check or clean the oil holes in the crankshaft, as any dirt here can only go one way – straight through the new bearings.
8   Once you are certain that the crankshaft is clean, lubricate the main bearings in the block with clean engine oil and carefully lay the crankshaft in position (an assistant would be very helpful here) in the main bearings.
9   Lubricate the bearings in the caps with clean engine oil, then install the caps in their respective positions in the block. **Note:** *Do not*

install the thrust bearing cap (number five) at this time.
10 Install the bolts and tighten them to the specified torque. Work up to the final torque in three steps.
11 Rotate the crankshaft a number of times by hand and check for any obvious binding.
12 Now install the thrust bearing cap and bolts and tighten the bolts finger tight.
13 Using a large screwdriver, pry the crankshaft forward against the thrust surface of the upper bearing half.
14 Hold the crankshaft in this position and pry the thrust bearing cap to the rear. This will align the thrust surfaces of both halves of the bearing.
15 While holding the crankshaft forward, tighten the thrust bearing cap bolts to the specified torque. Again, work up to the final torque in three steps.
16 Check the crankshaft endplay with a dial indicator setup. To do this, mount the indicator so the stem rests against the crankshaft flange, parallel to the crankshaft. Pry the crankshaft as far as possible to the rear, then zero the dial indicator. Pry the crankshaft forward and note the indicator reading (which represents the endplay). If it is less than the minimum allowed, check the thrust bearing faces for scratches, nicks and dirt. If the bearing is not damaged or dirty, make sure it is the correct bearing for your engine and reinstall it by following Steps 12 through 15. Recheck the endplay after it is installed.

32 Piston rings – installation

1   Before installing the new piston rings, the ring end gaps must be checked.
2   Lay out the piston/connecting rod assemblies and the new ring sets so the rings will be matched with the same piston and cylinder during the end gap measurement and engine assembly.
3   Insert the top (number one) ring into the first cylinder and square it up with the cylinder walls by pushing it in with the top of the piston. The ring should be at the bottom of the cylinder, just below the lower limit of the ring travel. To measure the end gap, slip a feeler gauge between the ends of the ring (photo). Compare the measurement to the Specifications.
4   If the gap is larger or smaller than specified, double-check to make sure that you have the correct rings before proceeding.
5   If the gap is too small, it must be enlarged or the ring ends may come in contact with each other during engine operation, which can cause serious damage to the engine. The end gap can be increased by filing the ring ends very carefully with a fine file. Mount the file in a vise equipped with soft jaws, slip the ring over the file so that the ends contact the file face and slowly move the ring to remove material from the ends. When performing this operation, file only from the outside in.

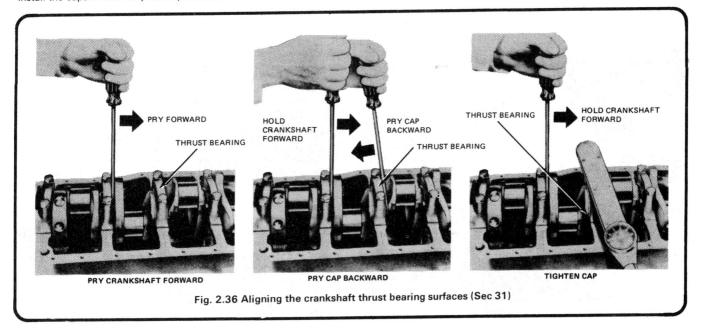

Fig. 2.36 Aligning the crankshaft thrust bearing surfaces (Sec 31)

32.3 Measuring the piston ring end gap with a feeler gauge

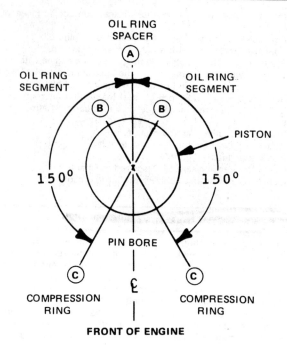
Fig. 2.37 Correct piston ring spacing on the piston (Sec 33)

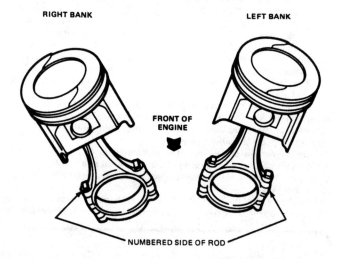
Fig. 2.38 Correct piston and rod positioning when installing in a V8 engine (Sec 33)

6 Excess end gap is not critical unless it is greater than 0.040 in. Again, double-check to make sure you have the correct rings for your engine.
7 Repeat the procedure for each ring that will be installed in the first cylinder and for each ring in the remaining cylinder. Remember to keep rings, pistons and cylinders matched up.
8 Once the ring end gaps have been checked/corrected, the rings can be installed on the pistons.
9 The oil control ring (lowest one on the piston) is installed first. It is composed of three separate components. Slip the spacer expander into the groove then install the upper side rail. Do not use a piston ring installation tool on the oil ring side rails, as they may be damaged. Instead, place one end of the side rail into the groove between the spacer expander and the ring land, hold it firmly in place and slide a finger around the piston while pushing the rail into the groove. Next, install the lower side rail in the same manner.
10 After the three oil ring components have been installed, check to make sure that both the upper and lower side rails can be turned smoothly in the ring groove.
11 The number two (middle) ring is installed next. Use a piston ring installation tool and fit the ring into the middle groove on the piston. Do not expand the ring any more than is necessary to slide it over the piston.
12 Finally, install the number one (top) ring in the same manner.
13 Repeat the procedure for the remaining pistons and rings.

33 Piston/connecting rod assembly – installation

1 Before installing the piston/connecting rod assemblies, the cylinder walls must be perfectly clean, the top edge of each cylinder must be chamfered, and the crankshaft must be in place.
2 Remove the connecting rod cap from the end of the number one connecting rod. Remove the old bearing inserts and wipe the bearing surfaces of the connecting rod and cap with a clean, lint-free cloth (they must be spotlessly clean).
3 Clean the back side of the new upper bearing half, then lay it in place in the connecting rod. Make sure the tang on the bearing fits into the notch in the rod. Also, the oil holes in the rod and bearing insert must line up. Do not hammer the bearing insert into place, and be very careful not to nick or gouge the bearing face. Do not lubricate the bearing at this time.
4 Clean the back side of the other bearing insert half and install it in the rod cap. Again, make sure the tang on the bearing fits into the notch in the cap, and do not apply any lubricant. It is critically important to ensure that the mating surfaces of the old bearing and connecting rod are perfectly clean and oil-free when they are assembled together.
5 Position the piston ring gaps as shown in the accompanying illustration, then slip a section of plastic or rubber hose over each connecting rod cap bolt.
6 Lubricate the piston and rings with clean engine oil and install a piston ring compressor on the piston. Leave the skirt protruding about ¼ in to guide the piston into the cylinder. The rings must be compressed as far as possible.
7 Rotate the crankshaft until the number one connecting rod journal is as far from the number one cylinder as possible (bottom dead center), and apply a uniform coat of engine oil to the number one cylinder walls.
8 With the notch on top of the piston pointing to the front of the engine, gently place the piston/connecting rod assembly into the number one cylinder bore and rest the bottom edge of the ring compressor on the engine block. Tap the top edge of the ring compressor to make sure it is contacting the block around its entire circumference.
9 Clean the number one connecting rod journal on the crankshaft and the bearing faces in the rod.
10 Carefully tap on the top of the piston with the end of a wooden

33.10 Tapping the piston into the cylinder with a hammer handle

hammer handle while guiding the end of the connecting rod into place on the crankshaft journal (photo). The piston rings may try to pop out of the ring compressor just before entering the cylinder bore, so keep some downward pressure on the ring compressor. Work slowly, and if any resistance is felt as the piston enters the cylinder, stop immediately, find out what is hanging up and fix it before proceeding. Do not, for any reason, force the piston into the cylinder, as you will break a ring and/or the piston.

11 Once the piston/connecting rod assembly is installed, the connecting rod bearing oil clearance must be checked before the rod cap is permanently bolted in place. Use Plastigage to check the clearance as described in Section 29. If the clearance is not correct, service bearings are available in 0.001 and 0.002 inch under sizes. Try using one-half of an undersize bearing set as this will often be sufficient to bring connecting rod bearing clearance up to Specifications. Under no circumstances should you use shims or shave any material from a bearing insert. Once the proper clearance has been achieved, proceed to the next step.

12 Carefully scrape all traces of the Plastigage material off the rod journal and/or bearing face (be very careful not to scratch the bearing). Make sure the bearing faces are perfectly clean, then apply a uniform layer of clean, high quality multi-purpose grease (or engine assembly lube) to both of them. You will have to push the piston into the cylinder to expose the face of the bearing insert in the connecting rod; be sure to slip the protective hoses over the rod bolts first.

13 Slide the connecting rod back into place on the journal, remove the protective hoses from the rod cap bolts, install the rod cap and

tighten the nuts to the specified torque. Again, work up to the torque in three steps.

14 Follow the above procedure for the remaining cylinders. Keep the back sides of the bearing inserts and the inside of the connecting rod and cap perfectly clean when assembling them. Make sure you have the correct piston for the cylinder and that the arrow on the piston points to the front of the engine when the piston is installed. Remember, use plenty of oil to lubricate the piston before installing the ring compressor, and be sure to match up the mating marks on the connecting rod and rod cap. Also, when installing the rod caps for the final time, be sure to lubricate the bearing faces adequately.

15 After all the piston/connecting rod assemblies have been properly installed, rotate the crankshaft a number of times by hand and check for any obvious binding.

16 As a final step, the connecting rod big end side clearance must be checked (Section 29).

34 Engine – final assembly and pre-oiling after overhaul

1 After the crankshaft, piston/rod assemblies and the various associated bearings have been installed in the engine block, the remainder of the components (cylinder head, oil pump, camshaft, etc.) can be installed following the installation procedures located in the various Sections of this Chapter.

2 Follow the engine disassembly sequence in the reverse order, using new gaskets where necessary.

3 Adjust the valve lash as described in Chapter 2A.

4 After a major overhaul it is a good idea to pre-oil the engine before it is installed and initially started. This will tell you if there are any faults in the oiling system at a time when corrections can be made easily and without damage. Pre-oiling the engine will also allow the parts to be lubricated thoroughly in a normal fashion, but without heavy loads placed upon them.

5 The engine should be assembled completely with the exception of the distributor and the rocker arm cover.

6 A modified distributor will be needed for this job. This pre-oil tool is a distributor body with the bottom gear ground off and the counterweight assembly removed from the top of the shaft.

7 Place the pre-oiler into the distributor shaft access hole on the left side of the block and make sure the bottom of the shaft mates with the oil pump. Clamp the modified distributor into place just as you would an ordinary distributor. Now attach an electric drill motor to the top of the shaft.

8 With the oil filter installed, all oil galleries plugged (oil pressure sending unit installed) and the crankcase full of oil as shown on the dipstick, rotate the pre-oiler with the drill. Make sure the rotation is clockwise. Soon, oil should start to flow from the rocker arms, signifying that the oil pump and oiling system is functioning properly. It may take two or three minutes for the oil to flow to each rocker arm. Allow the oil to circulate throughout the engine for a few minutes.

9 Check for oil leaks at all locations and correct as necessary.

10 Remove the pre-oiler and install the normal distributor and rocker arm cover.

2B

Chapter 2 Part C V8 engines

Refer to Chapter 13 for Specifications and information on 1984 and later models

Contents

Specifications

255, 302 and 351W engines

General

Bore and stroke	
255	3.68 x 3.00 in
302	4.00 x 3.00 in
351W	4.00 x 3.50 in
Compression pressure	Lowest cylinder must be at least 75% of highest cylinder
Oil pressure (at 2000 rpm, normal operating temperature)	
255 and 302 engines	40 to 60 psi
351W engine	40 to 65 psi

Engine block

Cylinder bore	
Diameter	
255	3.6800 to 3.6835 in
302 on	4.0004 to 4.0052 in
351W	4.0000 to 4.0048 in
Taper limit	0.0010 in
Out-of-round limit	0.005 in
Deck warpage limit	0.003 in per 6 in or 0.006 in overall

Pistons and rings

Piston	
Diameter	
255 coded red	3.6784 to 3.6790 in
255 coded blue	3.6798 to 3.6804 in
302 coded red	3.9984 to 3.9990 in
302 coded blue	3.9960 to 4.000 in
351W coded red	3.9978 to 3.9984 in
351W coded blue	3.9990 to 3.9996 in
Oversizes available	0.003 in
Piston-to-bore clearance – selective fit	0.0018 to 0.0026 in
Piston ring-to-groove clearance	
Top compression	0.0019 to 0.0036 in
Bottom compression	0.002 to 0.004 in
Oil	Snug fit in groove
Service limit	0.002 in max increase in clearance
Piston ring end gap	
Top compression	0.010 to 0.020 in
Bottom compression	0.010 to 0.020 in
Oil	0.010 to 0.035 in
Piston pin diameter (standard)	0.9119 to 0.9124 in

Piston pin-to-piston clearance
    255 and 302 .... 0.0002 to 0.0004 in
    351W .... 0.0003 to 0.0005 in
Piston pin-to-connecting rod bushing clearance .... Interference fit

Crankshaft and flywheel
Main journal
    Diameter
        255 and 302 .... 2.2482 to 2.2490 in
        351W .... 2.9994 to 3.0002 in
    Taper limit – max per inch .... 0.0006 in
    Out-of-round limit .... 0.0006 in
    Runout limit .... 0.002 in TIR
    Service limit .... 0.005 in
Main bearing oil clearance
    Standard
        255 and 302 – No. 1 bearing .... 0.0001 to 0.0015 in
        255 and 302 – all others .... 0.0005 to 0.0015 in
        351W .... 0.0008 to 0.0015 in
    Service limit
        255 and 302 – No. 1 bearing .... 0.0001 to 0.0020 in
        255 and 302 – all others .... 0.0005 to 0.0024 in
        351W .... 0.0008 to 0.0026 in
Connecting rod journal
    Diameter
        255 and 302 .... 2.1228 to 2.1236 in
        351W .... 2.3103 to 2.3111 in
    Taper limit – max per inch .... 0.0006 in
    Out-of-round limit .... 0.0006 in
Connecting rod bearing oil clearance
    Standard .... 0.0008 to 0.0015 in
    Service limit
        255 .... 0.0008 to 0.0024 in
        302 .... 0.0007 to 0.0024 in
        351W .... 0.0008 to 0.0025 in
Connecting rod side clearance
    Standard .... 0.010 to 0.020 in
    Service limit .... 0.023 in
Crankshaft endplay
    Standard .... 0.004 to 0.008 in
    Service limit .... 0.012 in
Flywheel clutch face runout limit .... 0.010 in

2C

Camshaft
Bearing journal diameter
    No. 1 .... 2.0805 to 2.0815 in
    No. 2 .... 2.0655 to 2.0665 in
    No. 3 .... 2.0505 to 2.0515 in
    No. 4 .... 2.0355 to 2.0365 in
    No. 5 .... 2.0205 to 2.0215 in
Bearing oil clearance
    Standard .... 0.001 to 0.003 in
    Service limit .... 0.006 in
Front bearing location .... 0.005 to 0.020 in (distance that front edge of the bearing is located below the front face of the cylinder block)

Lobe lift
    Intake
        355 and 302 .... 0.2375 in
        351W .... 0.2600 in
    Exhaust
        255 1981 .... 0.2375 in
            1982 .... 0.2474 in
        302 1980 and 1981 .... 0.2470 in
            1982 and 1983 .... 0.2474 in
        351W .... 0.2600 in
Maximum allowable lift loss .... 0.005 in
Endplay
    Standard .... 0.001 to 0.007 in
    Service limit .... 0.009 in
Timing chain deflection limit .... 0.500 in

Cylinder heads and valve train
Head warpage limit .... 0.003 in per 6 in or 0.006 in total
Valve seat angle .... 45°
Valve seat width .... 0.060 to 0.080 in
Valve seat runout limit .... 0.0015 in TIR

Valve face angle	44°
Valve face runout limit	0.002 in
Valve margin width	$\frac{1}{32}$ in min
Valve stem diameter	
Intake	0.3416 to 0.3423 in
Exhaust	0.3411 to 0.3418 in
Valve guide diameter	0.3433 to 0.3443 in
Valve stem-to-guide clearance	
Intake	
Standard	0.0010 to 0.0027 in
Service limit	0.0055 in
Exhaust	
Standard	0.0015 to 0.0032 in
Service limit	0.0055 in
Valve spring free length	
Intake	2.04 in
Exhaust	1.85 in
Valve spring pressure (lbs @ specified length)	
Intake (1st check)	74 to 82 @ 1.78 in
Intake (2nd check)	
255	190 to 212 @ 1.36 in
302	196 to 212 @ 1.36 in
351W	190 to 210 @ 1.36 in
Exhaust (1st check)	76 to 84 @ 1.60 in
Exhaust (2nd check)	190 to 219 @ 1.20 in
Service limit	10% loss of pressure
Valve spring installed height	
Intake	
255 and 302	$1\frac{43}{64}$ to $1\frac{45}{64}$ in
351W	$1\frac{49}{64}$ to $1\frac{51}{64}$ in
Exhaust	$1\frac{37}{64}$ to $1\frac{39}{64}$ in
Valve spring out-of-square limit	$\frac{5}{64}$ (0.078) in
Collapsed lifter gap clearance	See Chapter 2A Specifications
Lifter diameter	0.8740 to 0.8745 in
Lifter bore diameter	0.8752 to 0.8767 in
Lifter-to-bore clearance	
Standard	0.0007 to 0.0027 in
Service limit	0.005 in
Pushrod runout limit	0.015 in TIR

Oil pump

Outer race-to-housing clearance	
255 and 302	0.001 to 0.013 in
351W	0.001 to 0.003 in
Rotor assembly end clearance	0.004 in max
Driveshaft-to-housing clearance	0.0015 to 0.0030 in
Relief spring tension (lbs @ specified length)	
255 and 302	10.6 to 12.2 lbs @ 1.74 in
351W	18.2 to 20.2 @ 2.49 in

Torque specifications

	Ft-lb
Camshaft sprocket gear-to-camshaft	40 to 45
Camshaft thrust plate-to-cylinder block	9 to 12
Connecting rod nut	
255 and 302	19 to 24
351W	40 to 45
Timing cover bolts	12 to 18
Cylinder head bolts	
255 and 302	
1st step	55 to 65
2nd step	65 to 72
351W	
1st step	85
2nd step	95
3rd step	105 to 112
Damper-to-crankshaft	70 to 90
EGR valve-to-carburetor spacer or intake manifold	12 to 18
Fuel pump-to-cylinder block or timing cover	19 to 27
Flywheel-to-crankshaft	75 to 85
Main bearing caps	
255 and 302	60 to 70
351W	95 to 105
Intake manifold-to-cylinder head	23 to 25
Exhaust manifold-to-cylinder head	18 to 24

Intake manifold vacuum fittings	Ft-lb
Aluminum	6 to 10
Cast iron	23 to 28
Intake manifold pipe fittings	
Aluminum	12 to 18
Cast iron	23 to 28
Oil inlet tube-to-main bearing cap	22 to 32
Thermactor pump bracket-to-cylinder block	30 to 45
Carburetor mounting stud	5 to 10
Distributor clamp down bolt	17 to 25
Oil filter insert-to-cylinder block adapter	20 to 30
Oil filter-to-adapter or cylinder block	$\frac{1}{2}$ turn after oiled gasket contacts sealing surface
Oil pump inlet tube	10 to 15
Oil pan drain plug	15 to 25
Oil pan-to-cylinder block	9 to 11
Oil pump-to-cylinder block	22 to 32
Pulley-to-damper bolt	35 to 50
Rocker arm stud/bolt-to-cylinder head	18 to 25
Spark plug-to-cylinder head	10 to 15
Valve rocker arm cover	3 to 5
Water outlet housing	9 to 12
Water pump-to-block/timing cover	12 to 18
Alternator bracket-to-cylinder block bolt	12 to 18
Alternator adjusting arm-to-alternator bolt	14 to 40
Thermactor pump pivot bolt	22 to 32
Thermactor pump adjusting arm-to-pump	22 to 32
Thermactor pump pulley-to-pump hub	150 to 22 in-lbs
Fuel filter-to-carburetor	80 to 100 in-lbs
Carburetor attaching nuts	12 to 15

351M and 400 engines

General
Bore and stroke	
351M	4.00 x 3.50 in
400	4.00 x 4.00 in
Compression pressure	Lowest cylinder must be at least 75% of highest cylinder
Oil pressure (at 2000 rpm, normal operating temperature)	50 to 75 psi

Engine block
Cylinder bore	
Diameter	4.0000 to 4.0048 in
Taper limit	0.010 in
Out-of-round limit	0.005 in
Deck warpage limit	0.003 in per 6 in or 0.006 in overall

Pistons and rings
Piston	
Diameter	
Coded red	3.9982 to 3.9998 in
Coded blue	3.9994 to 4.0000 in
Oversizes available	0.003 in
Piston-to-cylinder bore clearance — selective fit	0.0014 to 0.0022 in
Piston ring-to-groove clearance	
Top compression	0.0019 to 0.0036 in
Bottom compression	0.002 to 0.004 in
Oil	Snug fit in groove
Service limit	0.002 in max increase in clearance
Piston ring end gap	
Top compression	0.010 to 0.020 in
Bottom compression	0.010 to 0.020 in
Oil	0.010 to 0.035 in
Piston pin diameter (standard)	0.9749 to 0.9754
Piston pin-to-piston clearance	0.0003 to 0.0005 in
Piston pin-to-connecting rod bushing clearance	Interference fit

Crankshaft and flywheel
Main journal	
Diameter	2.9994 to 3.0002 in
Taper limit — max per inch	0.0005 in
Out-of-round limit	0.0006 in
Runout limit	
TIR maximum	0.002 in
Service limit	0.005 in

2C

Main bearing oil clearance
    Desired .... 0.0008 to 0.0015 in
    Allowable .... 0.0008 to 0.0026 in
Connecting rod journal
    Diameter .... 2.3103 to 2.3111 in
    Taper limit – max per inch .... 0.0006 in
    Out-of-round limit .... 0.0006 in
Connecting rod bearing oil clearance
    Desired .... 0.0008 to 0.0015 in
    Allowable .... 0.0008 to 0.0025 in
Connecting rod side clearance
    Standard .... 0.010 to 0.020 in
    Service limit .... 0.023 in
Crankshaft endplay
    Standard .... 0.004 to 0.008 in
    Service limit .... 0.012 in

Camshaft
Bearing journal diameter
    No. 1 .... 2.1238 to 2.1248 in
    No. 2 .... 2.0655 to 2.0665 in
    No. 3 .... 2.0505 to 2.0515 in
    No. 4 .... 2.0355 to 2.0365 in
    No. 5 .... 2.0205 to 2.0215 in
Bearing oil clearance
    Standard .... 0.001 to 0.003 in
    Service limit .... 0.006 in
Front bearing location .... 0.040 to 0.060 (distance that front edge of the bearing is located from the front face of the cylinder block)
Lobe lift
    Intake .... 0.250 in
    Exhaust .... 0.250 in
    Maximum allowable lift loss .... 0.005 in
Endplay
    Standard .... 0.001 to 0.006 in
    Service limit .... 0.009 in
Timing chain defection limit .... 0.500 in

Cylinder heads and valve train
Head warpage limit .... 0.003 in per 6 in or 0.006 in overall
Valve seat angle .... 45°
Valve seat width
    Intake .... 0.060 to 0.080 in
    Exhaust .... 0.070 to 0.090 in
Valve seat runout limit .... 0.002 in TIR
Valve face angle .... 44°
Valve face runout limit .... 0.002 in TIR
Valve margin width .... 1/32 in min
Valve stem diameter
    Intake .... 0.3416 to 0.3423 in
    Exhaust .... 0.3411 to 0.3418 in
Valve guide diameter .... 0.3433 to 0.3443 in
Valve stem-to-guide clearance
    Intake
        Standard .... 0.0010 to 0.0027 in
        Service limit .... 0.005 in max
    Exhaust
        Standard .... 0.0015 to 0.0032 in
        Service limit .... 0.005 in max
Valve spring free length
    Intake .... 2.06 in
    Exhaust .... 1.93 in
Valve spring pressure (lbs @ specified length)
    Intake
        1st check .... 76 to 84 @ 1.82 in
        2nd check .... 215 to 237 @ 1.39 in
    Exhaust
        1st check .... 79 to 87 @ 1.68 in
        2nd check .... 215 to 237 @ 1.39 in
    Service limit .... 10% loss of pressure
Valve spring installed height
    Intake .... $1\frac{13}{16}$ to $1\frac{27}{32}$ in
    Exhaust .... $1\frac{11}{16}$ to $1\frac{23}{32}$ in
Valve spring out-of-square limit .... $\frac{5}{64}$ (0.078) in

Collapsed lifter gap clearance
    Allowable .... 0.100 to 0.200 in
    Desired .... 0.125 to 0.175 in
Lifter diameter .... 0.8740 to 0.8745 in
Lifter bore diameter .... 0.8752 to 0.8767 in
Lifter-to-bore clearance
    Standard .... 0.007 to 0.027 in
    Service limit .... 0.005 in
Pushrod runout limit .... 0.015 TIR

Oil pump
Outer race-to-housing clearance .... 0.001 to 0.003 in
Rotor assembly end clearance .... 0.004 in max
Driveshaft-to-housing clearance .... 0.0015 to 0.0030 in
Relief spring tension (lbs @ desired length) .... 20.6 to 22.6 @ 2.49 in

Torque specifications
                                                                             Ft-lb (unless otherwise noted)
Camshaft sprocket gear-to-camshaft .... 40 to 45
Camshaft thrust plate-to-cylinder block .... 9 to 12
Connecting rod nut .... 40 to 45
Timing cover .... 12 to 18
Cylinder head bolts
    1st step 75
    2nd step .... 95 to 105
Damper-to-crankshaft .... 70 to 90
EGR valve-to-carburetor spacer or intake manifold .... 12 to 18
Fuel pump-to-cylinder block or timing cover
    Nut .... 14 to 20
    Bolt .... 10 to 15
Flywheel-to-crankshaft .... 75 to 85
Main bearing cap bolts .... 95 to 105
Intake manifold-to-cylinder head
    $\frac{3}{8}$ in .... 22 to 32
    $\frac{5}{16}$ in .... 19 to 25
Exhaust manifold-to-cylinder head .... 18 to 24
Oil filter insert-to-cylinder block/adapter .... 20 to 30
Oil filter-to-adapter or cylinder block .... $\frac{1}{2}$ turn after oiled gasket contacts sealing surface
Oil inlet-to-main bearing .... 22 to 32
Thermactor pump bracket-to-cylinder block .... 30 to 45
Carburetor-to-mounting stud .... 5 to 10
Distributor clamp down bolt .... 17 to 25
Intake manifold vacuum fittings .... 6 to 10
Oil pan drain plug .... 15 to 25
Oil pump-to-cylinder block .... 22 to 32
Oil pan-to-cylinder block .... 7 to 9
Pulley-to-damper bolt .... 35 to 50
Rocker arm stud/bolt-to-cylinder head .... 18 to 25
Spark plug-to-cylinder head .... 10 to 15
Valve rocker arm cover .... 3 to 5
Water outlet housing .... 12 to 18
Water pump-to-block/timing cover .... 12 to 18
Alternator bracket-to-cylinder block bolt .... 15 to 20
Alternator adjusting arm-to-cylinder block bolt .... 15 to 20
Alternator adjusting arm-to-alternator bolt .... 24 to 40
Thermactor pump pivot bolt .... 35 to 45
Thermactor pump pivot bolt .... 35 to 45
Thermactor pump adjusting arm-to-pump .... 22 to 32
Thermactor pump pulley-to-pump hub .... 150 to 220 in-lb
Fuel filter-to-carburetor .... 80 to 100 in-lb
Carburetor attaching nuts .... 12 to 15

460 engine

General
Bore and stroke .... 4.36 x 3.85
Compression pressure .... Lowest cylinder must be at least 75% of highest cylinder
Oil pressure (at 2000 rpm, normal operating temperature) .... 40 to 65 psi

Engine block
Cylinder bore .... 4.3600 to 4.3636 in
Diameter .... 4.3600 to 4.3636 in
Taper limit .... 0.10 in
Out-of-round
    Maximum .... 0.0015 in
    Service limit .... 0.010 in
Deck warpage limit .... 0.003 in per 6 in or 0.006 in overall

2C

Pistons and rings

Piston
    Diameter
        Coded red .... 4.3585 to 4.3591 in
        Coded blue .... 4.3597 to 4.3603 in
Oversizes available .... 0.003 in
Piston to bore clearance — selective fit .... 0.0022 to 0.0030 in
Piston ring-to-groove clearance
    Compression — top and bottom .... 0.0025 to 0.0045
    Oil .... Snug fit in groove
    Service limit .... 0.002 in max increase in clearance
Piston ring end gap
    Compression — top and bottom .... 0.010 to 0.020 in
    Oil .... 0.010 to 0.035 in
Piston pin diameter (standard) .... 1.0398 to 1.0403 in
Piston pin-to-piston clearance .... 0.0002 to 0.0004 in
Piston pin-to-connecting rod bushing clearance .... Interference fit

Crankshaft and flywheel

Main journal
    Diameter .... 2.9994 to 3.0002 in
    Taper limit — max per inch .... 0.0005 in
    Out of round limit .... 0.0006 in
    Runout limit
        TIR maximum .... 0.002 in
        Service limit .... 0.005 in
Main bearing oil clearance
    Standard .... 0.0008 to 0.0015 in
    Service limit .... 0.0008 to 0.0026 in
Connecting rod journal
    Diameter .... 2.4992 to 2.5000 in
    Taper limit— max per inch .... 0.0006 in
    Out-of-round limit .... 0.0006 in
Connecting rod bearing oil clearance
    Desired .... 0.0008 to 0.0015 in
    Allowable .... 0.0008 to 0.0025 in
Connecting rod side clearance
    Standard .... 0.010 to 0.020 in
    Service limit .... 0.023 in
Crankshaft endplay
    Standard .... 0.004 to 0.008 in
    Service limit .... 0.012 in

Camshaft

Bearing journal diameter (all) .... 2.1238 to 2.1248 in
Bearing oil clearance
    Standard .... 0.001 to 0.003 in
    Service limit .... 0.006 in
Front bearing location .... 0.040 to 0.060 (distance that front edge of the bearing is located from the front face of the cylinder block)
Lobe lift
    Intake .... 0.252 in
    Exhaust .... 0.278 in
Maximum allowable lift loss .... 0.005 in
Endplay
    Standard .... 0.001 to 0.006 in
    Service limit .... 0.009 in
Timing chain deflection limit .... 0.500 in

Cylinder heads and valve train

Head warpage limit .... 0.003 in per 6 in or 0.006 in overall
Valve seat angle .... 45°
Valve seat width .... 0.060 to 0.080 in
Valve seat runout limit .... 0.002 in TIR
Valve face angle .... 44°
Valve face runout limit .... 0.002 in TIR
Valve margin width .... $\frac{1}{32}$ in min
Valve stem diameter .... 0.3416 to 0.3423 in
Valve guide diameter .... 0.3433 to 0.3443 in
Valve stem-to-guide clearance
    Standard .... 0.0010 to 0.0027 in
    Service limit .... 0.0055 in
Valve spring free length .... 2.06 in
Valve spring pressure (lbs @ specified length)
    1st check .... 76 to 84 @ 1.81 in
    2nd check .... 218 to 240 @ 1.33 in
    Service limit .... 10% loss of pressure

Valve spring installed height .... $1\frac{51}{64}$ to $1\frac{53}{64}$ in
Valve spring out-of-square limit .... $\frac{5}{64}$ (0.078) in
Collapsed lifter gap clearance
    Allowable .... 0.075 to 0.175 in
    Desired .... 0.100 to 0.150 in
Lifter diameter .... 0.8740 to 0.8745 in
Lifter bore diameter .... 0.8752 to 0.8767 in
Lifter-to-bore clearance
    Standard .... 0.0007 to 0.0027 in
    Service limit .... 0.005 in
Pushrod runout limit .... 0.015 in TIR

Oil pump
Outer race-to-housing clearance .... 0.001 to 0.013 in
Rotor assembly end clearance .... 0.004 in max
Driveshaft-to-housing clearance .... 0.0015 to 0.0030 in
Relief spring tension (lbs @ specified length) .... 20.6 to 22.6 @ 2.49 in

Torque specifications
Ft-lb (unless otherwise specified)
Camshaft sprocket gear-to-camshaft .... 40 to 45
Camshaft thrustplate-to-cylinder block .... 9 to 12
Connecting rod nut
    Through 1990 .... 45 to 50
    1991 .... 41 to 45
Timing cover ($\frac{5}{16}$ in bolt) .... 15 to 21
Cylinder head bolts
    1st step 80
    2nd step 110
    3rd step .... 130 to 140
Damper-to-crankshaft .... 70 to 90
EGR valve-to-carburetor spacer or intake manifold .... 12 to 18
Carburetor mounting stud .... 5 to 10
Fuel pump-to-cylinder block or timing cover .... 19 to 27
Flywheel-to-crankshaft .... 75 to 85
Main bearing cap bolts .... 95 to 105
Intake manifold-to-cylinder head .... 22 to 32
Intake manifold vacuum fittings .... 6 to 10
Exhaust manifold-to-cylinder head .... 28 to 33
Oil filter insert-to-cylinder block/adapter .... 45 to 55
Oil filter adapter-to-cylinder block .... 40 to 50
Oil filter-to-adapter or cylinder block .... $\frac{1}{2}$ turn after oiled gasket contacts sealing surface
Oil inlet tube-to-pump .... 12 to 18
Oil inlet tube-to-main bearing cap .... 22 to 32
Oil pan drain plug .... 15 to 25
Oil pan-to-cylinder block
    $\frac{1}{4}$ in bolts .... 7 to 9
    $\frac{5}{16}$ in bolts .... 9 to 11
Oil pump-to-cylinder block .... 22 to 32
Pulley-to-damper bolt .... 35 to 50
Rocker arm stud/bolt-to-cylinder head .... 18 to 25
Spark plug to cylinder head .... 5 to 10
Valve rocker arm cover .... 5 to 6
Water outlet housing .... 12 to 18
Water pump-to-cylinder block or timing cover .... 12 to 18
Alternator bracket-to-cylinder block bolt .... 35 to 50
Alternator pivot bolt .... 45 to 57
Alternator adjusting arm-to-cylinder block bolt .... 35 to 50
Alternator adjusting arm-to-alternator bolt .... 24 to 40
Thermactor pump bracket-to-cylinder block .... 35 to 50
Thermactor pump pivot bolt .... 35 to 50
Thermactor pump adjusting arm-to-pump .... 22 to 32
Thermactor pump pulley-to-pump hub .... 150 to 220 in-lb
Carburetor attaching nuts .... 12 to 15
Distributor clamp-down bolt .... 17 to 25

35 General information

Several V8s of various displacements were used in the model years covered by this manual. All are gasoline fueled with overhead valves actuated by hydraulic lifters and have five main bearing-supported crankshafts.

'Family' engine groupings include the 255, 302 and 351W cu in models, the 351M and 400 cu in models; and the 460 cu in model.

The 255 cu in V8 was available as an option in some F100 and F150 models in 1981 and 1982; the 302 cu in V8 was available as an option on some F100, F150, F250 and Bronco models in 1980 through 1983; the 351W V8 was available as an option on F150, F250 and Bronco models in 1981 through 1983.

The 351M was available as an option on F100 Canadian models and some F150, F250, F350 and Bronco 49 state models in 1980 and 1981; the 400 cu in V8 was available on F150 4x4, F250 and Bronco Canadian models and all F350 models in 1980 and 1981.

2C

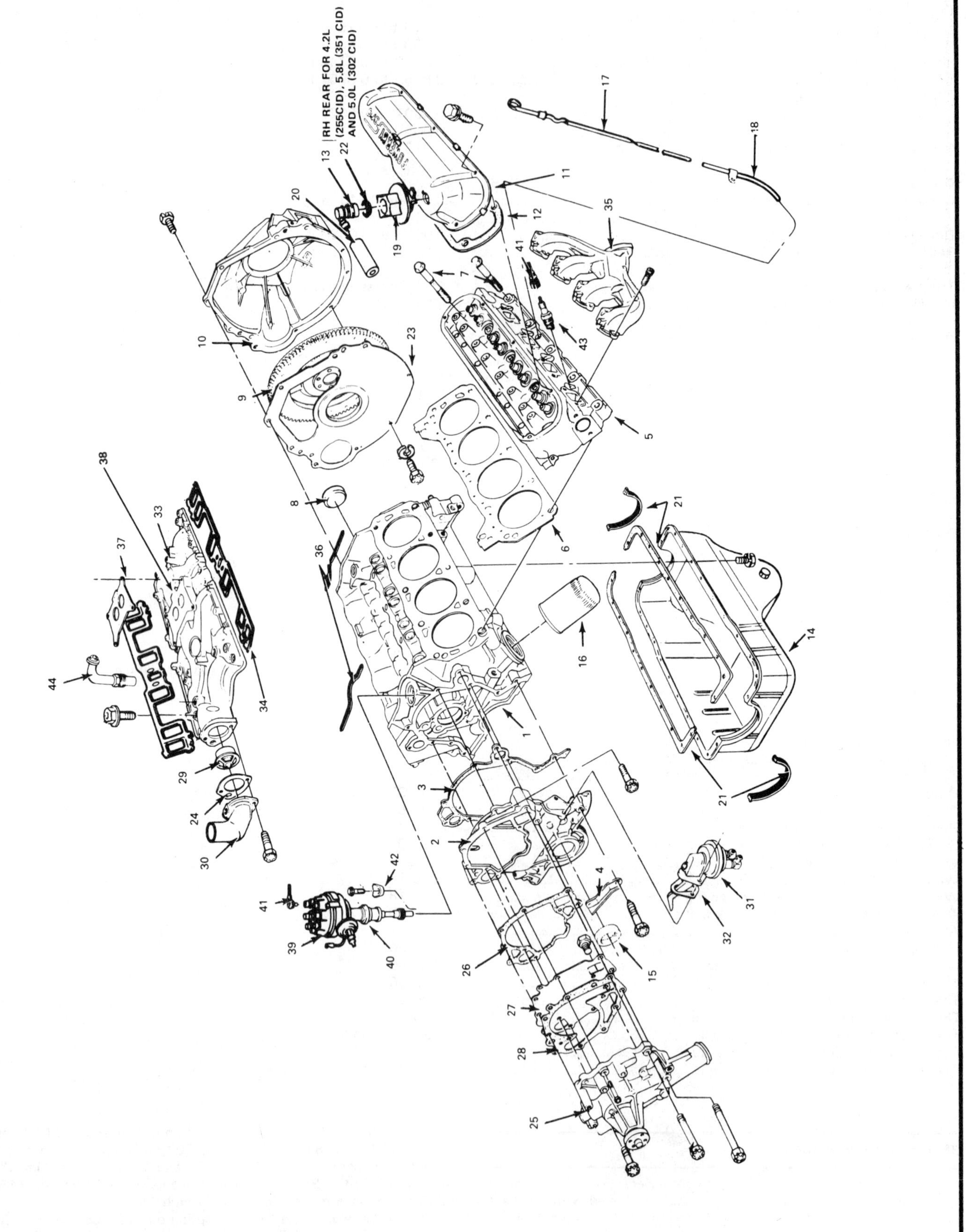

RH REAR FOR 4.2L
(255CID), 5.8L (351 CID)
AND 5.0L (302 CID)
1
2
3
4
5
6
7
8
9
10
11
12
13
14
15
16
17
18
19
20
21
22
23
24
25
26
27
28
29
30
31
32
33
34
35
36
37
38
39
40
41
42
43
44

Fig. 2.39 External components of the 255, 302 and 351W V8 engines – exploded view

1 Cylinder block	12 Rocker arm cover gasket
2 Front cover assembly	13 PCV elbow and valve assembly
3 Front cover gasket	14 Oil pan
4 Timing pointer	15 Front cover seal
5 Cylinder head	16 Oil filter
6 Cylinder head gasket	17 Oil level dipstick
7 Cylinder head bolt	18 Oil level dipstick tube
8 Camshaft rear bearing plug	19 Oil filler cap
9 Flywheel assembly	20 PCV hose
10 Flywheel housing	21 Oil pan gasket set
11 Valve rocker arm cover	22 Crankcase ventilation grommet
	23 Rear engine plate
	24 Water outlet connection gasket
	25 Water pump
	26 Water pump housing gasket
	27 Water pump cover
	28 Water pump cover gasket
29 Thermostat	37 Carburetor gasket
30 Water outlet connection	38 Carburetor mounting flange
31 Fuel pump	39 Distributor cap
32 Fuel pump mounting gasket	40 Distributor assembly
33 Intake manifold	41 Spark plug wire set
34 Intake manifold gasket	42 Distributor holddown clamp
35 Exhaust manifold	43 Spark plug
36 Intake manifold gasket seals	44 Hot water connection elbow

The 460 cu in V8 was available as an option on F250 and F350 models in 1983.

All of these engines are three-point mounted, with two side mounts at the front and one crossmember mount underneath the transmission. The engines can be removed from the vehicle with a normal amount of preparatory work when overhaul or other major operations are necessary.

36 Valve spring, retainer and seal – replacement (on vehicle)

Note: *Broken valve springs, retainers or defective valve stem seals can be replaced without removing the cylinder head involved on engines that have no damage to the valves or valve seats. Two special tools are required for this operation, so read through the instructions carefully and rent or purchase the tools before starting work on the engine.*

1 Remove the air cleaner and related components.
2 Remove the accelerator cable return spring.
3 Remove the accelerator cable linkage at the carburetor.
4 Disconnect the choke cable at the carburetor connecting point.
5 Remove the rocker arm cover (see Section 39).
6 Remove the spark plug from the cylinder which has the bad component.
7 Crank the engine until the piston in the cylinder with the bad component is at top dead center on the compression stroke (refer to Step 4 of Section 9 in Chapter 2A). Note that the distributor should be marked opposite the appropriate terminal; not necessarily number one.
8 Install a special air line adapter which will screw into the spark plug hole and connect to an air source such as a compressor. Remove the rocker arm stud nut, fulcrum seat, rocker arm and pushrod.
9 Apply compressed air to the cylinder in question. If the engine rotates until the cylinder is at bottom dead center, be very careful that you do not drop the valve into the cylinder as it will fall all the way in. Do not release the air pressure or the valve will drop through the guide.
10 Compress the valve spring with a compressor designed to work with the head still on the vehicle.
11 Remove the keepers, spring retainer and valve spring. Remove the valve stem seal. **Note**: *If air pressure fails to hold the valve in the closed position during this operation, there is apparently damage to the seat or the valve. If this condition exists, remove the cylinder head for further repair.*
12 If air pressure has forced the piston to the bottom of the cylinder, wrap a rubber band, tape or string around the top of the valve stem so the valve will not drop through into the combustion chamber. Release the air pressure.
13 Inspect the valve stem for damage. Rotate the valve in its guide and check the valve stem tip for eccentric movement which would indicate a bent valve.
14 Move the valve up and down through its normal travel and make sure that the valve guide and stem do not bind. If the valve stem binds, either the valve is bent and/or the guide is damaged and the head will have to be removed for repair.
15 Reapply air pressure to the cylinder to retain the valve.
16 Lubricate the valve stem with engine oil and install a new valve stem seal.
17 Install the spring in position over the valve. Make sure that the closed coil end of the spring is located next to the cylinder head.
18 Install the valve spring retainer. Compress the valve spring using the valve spring compressor and install the keepers. Remove the compressor tool and make sure that the keepers are installed correctly.
19 Apply engine oil or assembly lube to both ends of the pushrod.
20 Install the pushrod in position.
21 Apply engine oil or assembly lube to the tip of the valve stem.
22 Apply engine oil to the fulcrum seats and socket. Install the rocker arm, fulcrum seat and stud nut. Tighten the stud nut to the specified torque.
23 Remove the air source and the adapter from the spark plug hole.
24 Install the spark plug and connect the spark plug wire to it.
25 Attach a new rocker arm cover gasket to the cover and install the rocker arm cover (see Section 39).
26 Connect the accelerator cable to the carburetor at its connecting point.
27 Install the accelerator cable return spring. Connect the choke cable to the carburetor.
28 Install the air cleaner.
29 Start and run the engine. Make sure that there are no leaks and

2C

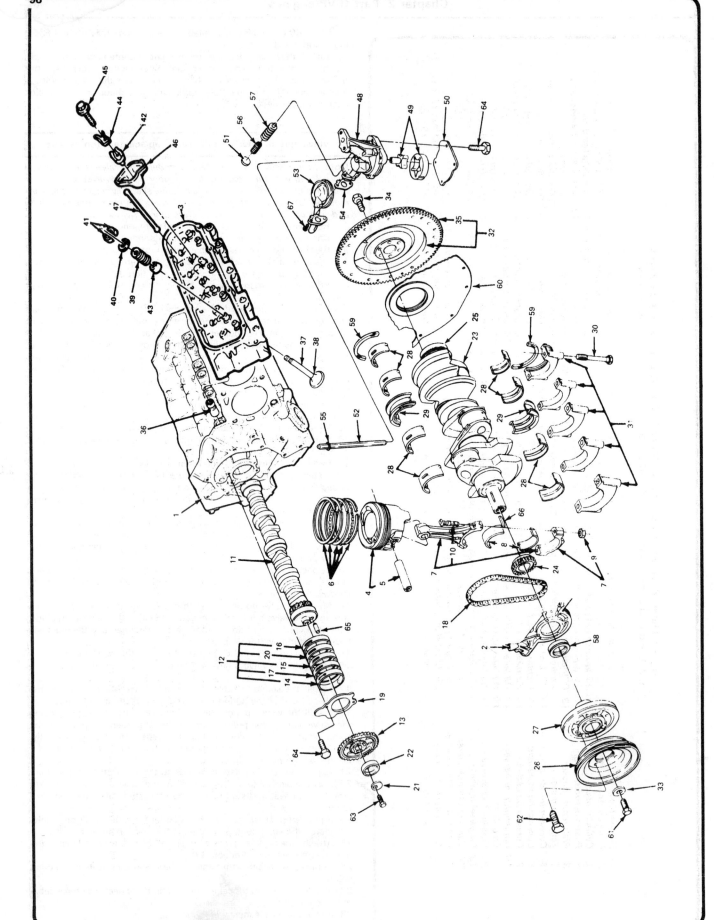

2C

Fig. 2.40 Internal components of the 255, 302 and 351W V8 engines – exploded view

1 Engine block
2 Front cover assembly
3 Cylinder head
4 Piston assembly
5 Piston pin
6 Piston ring set
7 Connecting rod assembly
8 Connecting rod bearing
9 Connecting rod nut
10 Connecting rod bolt
11 Camshaft
12 Camshaft bearing assembly
13 Camshaft sprocket
14 Camshaft front bearing
15 Camshaft center bearing
16 Camshaft rear bearing
17 Camshaft front

intermediate bearing
18 Timing chain
19 Camshaft thrust plate
20 Camshaft rear intermediate
  bearing
21 Camshaft sprocket washer
22 Camshaft fuel pump
  eccentric
23 Crankshaft
24 Crankshaft sprocket
25 Crankshaft-to-flywheel
  mounting flange
26 Crankshaft outer pulley
27 Crankshaft damper
28 Crankshaft main bearing
29 Crankshaft center main
  bearing

30 Crankshaft main bearing
  cap bolt
31 Main bearing cap
32 Flywheel
33 Crankshaft pulley
  retaining washer
34 Flywheel-to-crankshaft
  bolt
35 Flywheel ring gear
36 Hydraulic lifter
37 Exhaust valve
38 Intake valve
39 Valve spring
40 Valve spring retainer
41 Valve spring retainer
  key
42 Valve rocker arm fulcrum

43 Valve stem seal
44 Oil deflector
45 Rocker arm attaching
  bolt
46 Rocker arm
47 Pushrod
48 Oil pump
49 Oil pump rotor and
  shaft assembly
50 Oil pump body plate
51 Oil pump relief valve
  plug
52 Oil pump intermediate
  shaft
53 Oil pump screen, tube
  and cover assembly
54 Oil pump inlet tube

55 Oil pump intermediate
  shaft ring
56 Oil pump relief valve
  spring
57 Oil pump relief valve
  plunger
58 Front cover oil seal
59 Crankshaft rear seal
60 Engine rear plate
61 Bolt ($\frac{5}{8}$-18 x 2)
62 Bolt ($\frac{3}{8}$-16 x 1)
63 Bolt ($\frac{3}{8}$-16 x 1-$\frac{1}{2}$)
64 Bolt ($\frac{1}{4}$-20 x $\frac{5}{8}$)
65 Dowel pin ($\frac{5}{16}$ x 1-$\frac{3}{8}$)
66 Woodruff key (1-$\frac{3}{4}$ x $\frac{7}{32}$ x $\frac{3}{16}$)
67 Bolt ($\frac{5}{16}$-18 x $\frac{7}{8}$)

gasket

Fig. 2.41 External components of the 351M and 400 V8 engines – exploded view (see page 100)

1 Engine block
2 Front cover gasket
3 Timing pointer
4 Cylinder head
5 Cylinder head gasket
6 Cylinder head bolt
7 Front cover plate
8 Camshaft rear bearing
  plug
9 Crankshaft pulley
10 Crankshaft damper
11 Flywheel
12 Flywheel housing
13 Left-hand valve cover
  assembly
13A Right-hand valve cover

assembly
14 Valve cover gasket
15 PCV assembly
16 Oil pan
17 Front cover oil seal
18 Oil pan drain plug
19 Oil filter
20 Drain plug gasket
21 Oil level dipstick
22 Dipstick tube
23 Oil filler cap
24 Crankcase ventilation
  hose
25 Oil pan gasket set
26 Oil filter mounting
  bolt insert

27 PCV grommet
28 Rear engine plate
29 Water outlet connection
  gasket
30 Water pump
31 Water pump housing gasket
32 Bolt ($\frac{7}{16}$-14 x 2-$\frac{9}{16}$)
33 Thermostat
34 Water outlet connection
35 Fuel pump
36 Fuel pump mounting gasket
37 Intake manifold
38 Intake manifold rear seal
39 Intake manifold front seal
40 Exhaust manifold

41 Intake manifold valley
  baffle
42 Carburetor mounting gasket
43 Distributor cap
44 Distributor
45 Spark plug wire set
46 Distributor holddown clamp
47 Spark plug
48 Screw and lockwasher
  ($\frac{5}{16}$-18 x $\frac{3}{4}$)
49 Hex head bolt ($\frac{5}{16}$-18 x 2)
50 Washer head bolt ($\frac{3}{8}$-16 x 2)
51 Bolt ($\frac{5}{16}$-18 x $\frac{7}{8}$)
52 Screw ($\frac{5}{16}$-18 x 1-$\frac{1}{4}$)
53 Screw ($\frac{5}{16}$-18 x 2-$\frac{7}{8}$)

54 Washer head bolt
  ($\frac{5}{16}$-18 x 1-$\frac{7}{8}$)
55 Washer head bolt
  ($\frac{5}{16}$-18 x 2-$\frac{7}{8}$)
56 Bolt ($\frac{3}{8}$-16 x 1)
57 Washer head bolt
  ($\frac{1}{4}$-20 x $\frac{5}{8}$)
58 Bolt ($\frac{5}{16}$-18 x $\frac{3}{4}$)
59 Lock washer ($\frac{5}{16}$ x $\frac{19}{32}$
  x $\frac{5}{64}$)
60 Bolt ($\frac{5}{16}$-18 x $\frac{7}{8}$)
61 Elbow (115° x 0.58 OD)
62 PCV system hose
63 Elbow grommet
64 PCV system tube

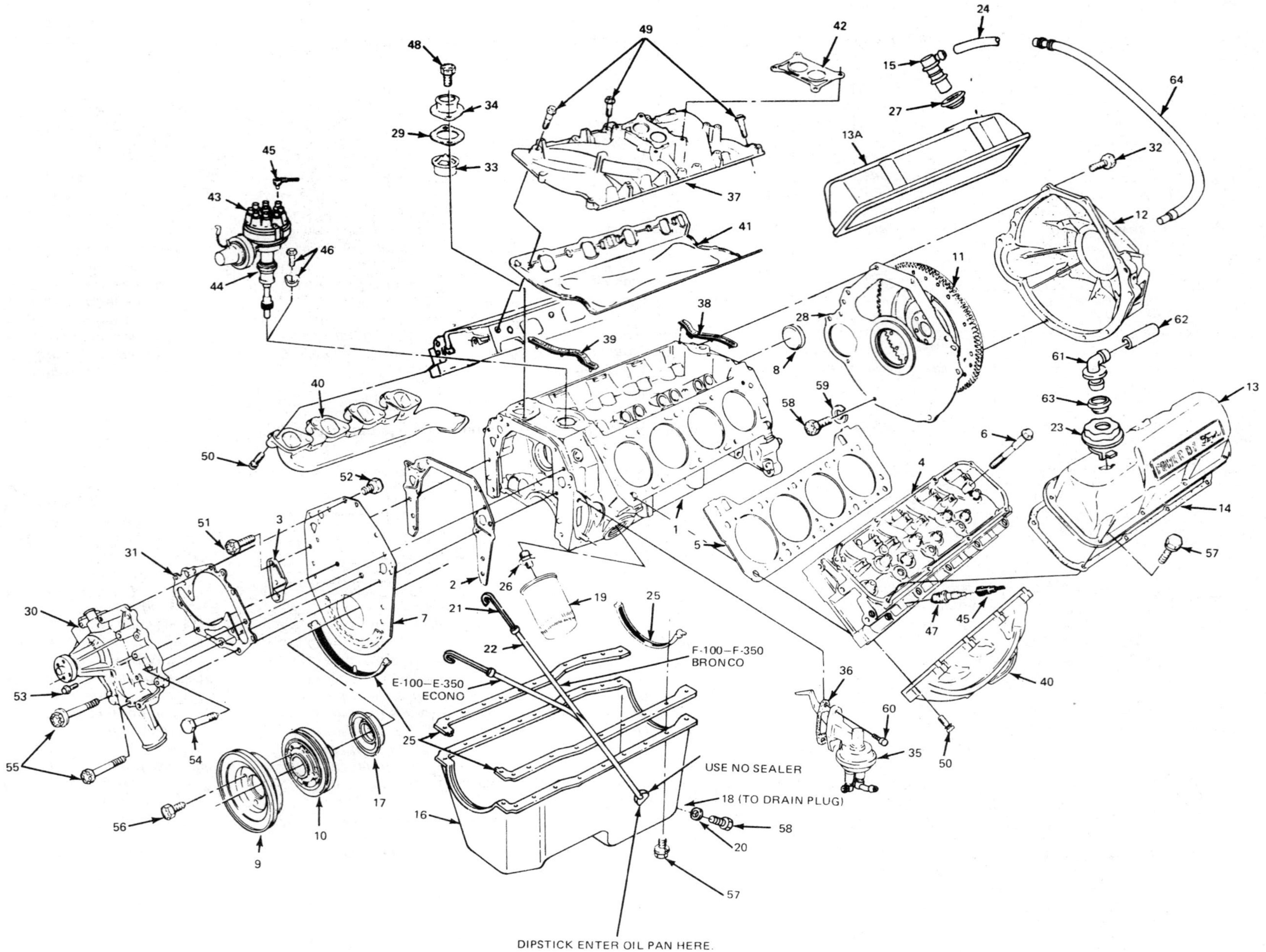

Fig. 2.41 External components of the 351M and 400 V8 engines – exploded view

DIPSTICK ENTER OIL PAN HERE.

F-100–F-350 BRONCO

E-100–E-350 ECONO

USE NO SEALER

18 (TO DRAIN PLUG)

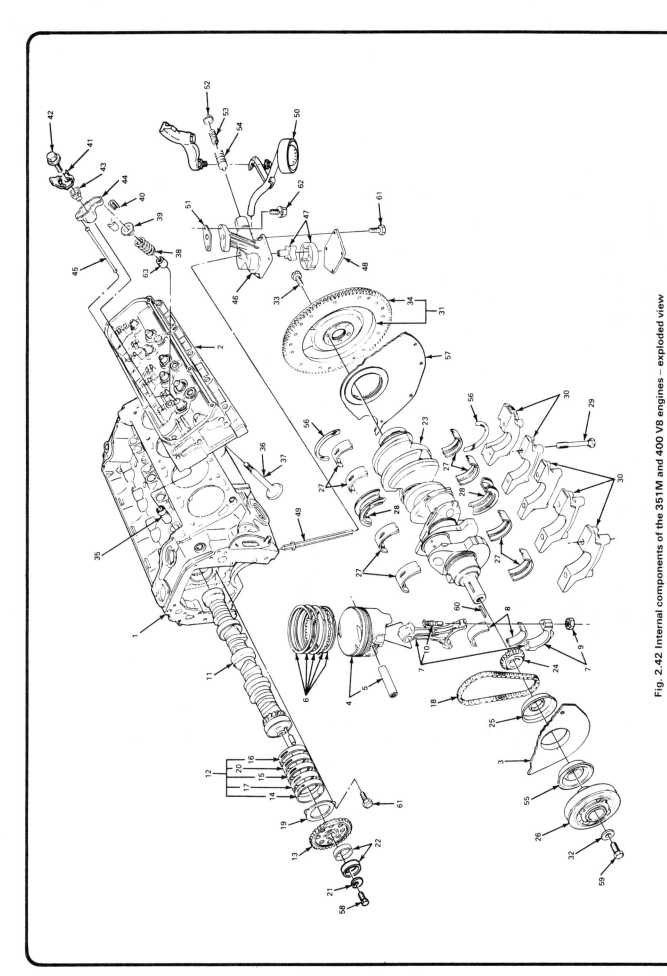

2C

Fig. 2.42 Internal components of the 351M and 400 V8 engines – exploded view

Fig. 2.42 Internal components of the 351M and 400 V8 engines – exploded view (see page 101)

1 Engine block
2 Cylinder head
3 Front engine plate
4 Piston assembly
5 Piston pin
6 Piston ring set
7 Connecting rod assembly
8 Connecting rod bearing
9 Connecting rod nut
10 Connecting rod bolt
11 Camshaft
12 Camshaft bearing assembly
13 Camshaft sprocket
14 Camshaft front bearing
15 Camshaft center bearing
16 Camshaft rear bearing
17 Camshaft front intermediate bearing
18 Timing chain
19 Camshaft thrust plate
20 Camshaft rear intermediate bearing
21 Camshaft sprocket washer
22 Camshaft fuel pump eccentric
23 Crankshaft
24 Crankshaft sprocket
25 Crankshaft oil slinger
26 Crankshaft damper
27 Crankshaft front bearing
28 Crankshaft center bearing
29 Crankshaft main bearing cap bolt
30 Main bearing cap
31 Flywheel
32 Crankshaft pulley retaining washer
33 Flywheel-to-crankshaft bolt
34 Flywheel ring gear
35 Hydraulic tappet
36 Exhaust valve
37 Intake valve
38 Valve spring
39 Valve spring retainer
40 Valve spring retainer key
41 Pushrod oil deflector baffle
42 Rocker arm support bolt
43 Rocker arm fulcrum seat
44 Rocker arm
45 Pushrod
46 Oil pump
47 Oil pump drive rotor and shaft assembly
48 Oil pump body plate
49 Oil pump intermediate shaft
50 Oil pump screen tube and cover assembly
51 Oil pump mounting gasket
52 Oil pump relief valve plug
53 Oil pump relief valve spring
54 Oil pump relief valve plunger
55 Front engine seal
56 Crankshaft rear seal
57 Rear engine plate
58 Slotted head bolt ($\frac{3}{8}$-16 x 1-$\frac{1}{2}$)
59 Bolt ($\frac{3}{4}$ - 16 x $\frac{5}{32}$)
60 Woodruff key (1-$\frac{3}{4}$ x $\frac{7}{32}$ x $\frac{3}{16}$)
61 Bolt ($\frac{1}{4}$-20 x $\frac{5}{8}$)
62 Bolt ($\frac{3}{8}$-16 x 1-$\frac{1}{4}$)
63 Valve stem oil seal

Fig. 2.43 External components of the 460 V8 engine – exploded view

1 Cylinder block
2 Front cover assembly
3 Front cover gasket
4 Timing pointer
5 Cylinder head
6 Cylinder head gasket
7 Cylinder head bolt
8 Camshaft rear bearing plug
9 Flywheel assembly
10 Flywheel housing
11 Valve rocker arm cover
12 Rocker arm cover gasket
13 Oil filler pipe hose
14 Oil pan
15 Front cover seal
16 Oil filter
17 Oil level dipstick
18 Oil level dipstick tube
19 Oil filler cap
20 Oil filler pipe assembly
21 Oil pan gasket set
22 Oil filler adapter
23 Rear engine plate
24 Water outlet connection gasket
25 Water pump
26 Water pump housing gasket
27 Water pump cover
28 Water pump cover gasket
29 Thermostat
30 Water outlet connection
31 Fuel pump
32 Fuel pump mounting gasket
33 Intake manifold
34 Lock washer ($\frac{7}{16}$)
35 Exhaust manifold
36 Intake manifold gasket seals
37 Carburetor gasket
38 Carburetor-to-intake manifold spacer
39 Distributor cap assembly
40 Distributor assembly
41 Spark plug wire set
42 Distributor hold down clamp
43 Spark plug
44 Hot water connection tube
45 Washer head bolt ($\frac{5}{16}$-18 x $\frac{7}{8}$)
46 Bolt ($\frac{5}{16}$ - 18 x $\frac{1}{16}$)
47 Oil filter adapter assembly
48 Intake manifold valley gasket
49 Filler hose-to-carburetor hose

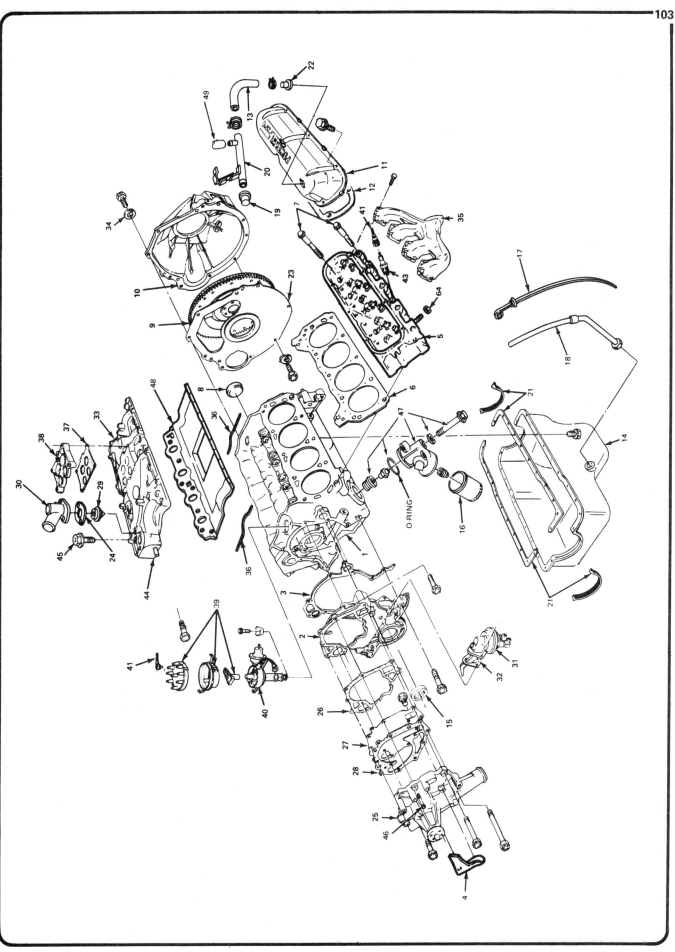

2C

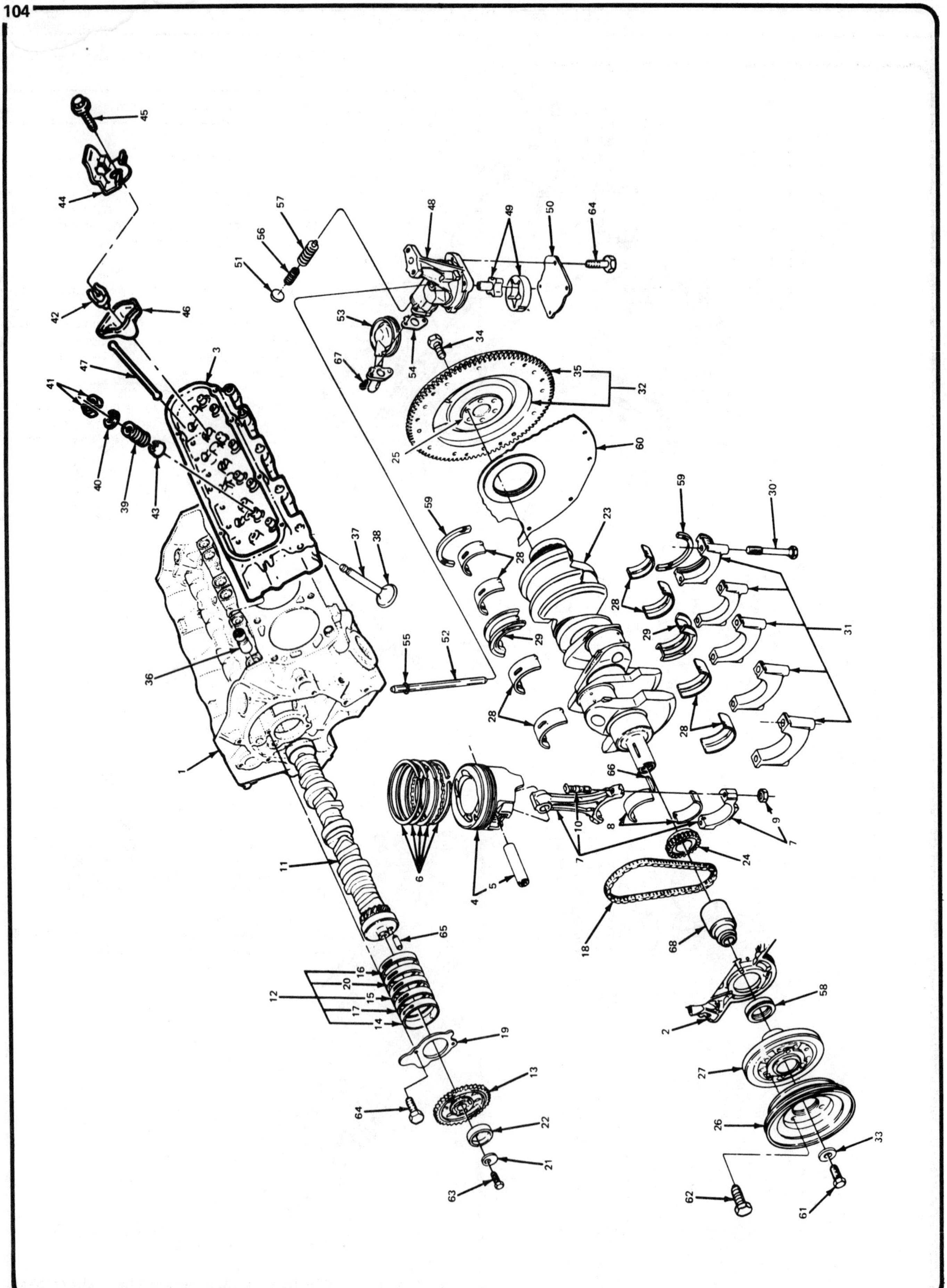
45
44
42
46
47
41
40
39
43
3
57
56
51
53
67
54
48
49
50
64
34
35
32
25
60
37
38
36
59
28
29
23
55
52
30
31
1
66
10
8
9
7
24
6
4
5
11
65
18
68
16
20
15
17
14
12
19
64
13
22
21
63
2
58
27
26
33
62
61

that there are no unusual sounds coming from the valve assembly.

37 Manifolds – removal, disassembly and installation

Intake manifold – removal

Note: *Due to the weight and bulk of the large displacement engine intake manifolds, it is recommended that an engine hoist or puller device coupled with lifting hooks available from hardware stores be used to lift these manifolds from the engine. They can be removed by hand. However, the aid of a helper is suggested to avoid damaging engine components and/or causing personal injury.*

1 Drain the cooling system.
2 Remove the air cleaner and intake duct assemblies.
3 Carefully mark and remove any emissions control connections at the air cleaner.
4 Disconnect the upper radiator hose from the thermostat housing located at the top of the engine. Locate this hose out of the way.
5 Disconnect the heater hose and the water pump by-pass hose at the intake manifold connections.
6 Remove the right rocker arm cover on 460 engines.
7 Disconnect the spark plug wires at the spark plugs. Unclip and remove the distributor cap together with the spark plug wires.
8 Disconnect the primary wiring leads to the coil and mark them so they can be reinstalled correctly.
9 Remove the coil mounting bracket and mounting bolt.
10 Remove the carburetor fuel inlet line from the carburetor and position it out of the way. It may be necessary to disconnect the line or loosen it at the fuel pump in order to perform this operation if the line is constructed of steel.
11 Disconnect the vacuum advance hose(s) from the distributor and mark them for proper installation.
12 Remove the distributor hold down bolt and mark the position of

Fig. 2.44 Internal components of the 460 V8 engines – exploded view

1 Engine block
2 Front cover assembly
3 Cylinder head
4 Piston assembly
5 Piston pin
6 Piston ring set
7 Connecting rod assembly
8 Connecting rod bearing
9 Connecting rod nut
10 Connecting rod bolt
11 Camshaft
12 Camshaft bearing assembly
13 Camshaft sprocket
14 Camshaft front bearing
15 Camshaft center bearing
16 Camshaft rear bearing
17 Camshaft front intermediate bearing
18 Timing chain
19 Camshaft thrust plate
20 Camshaft rear intermediate bearing
21 Camshaft sprocket washer
22 Camshaft fuel pump eccentric
23 Crankshaft
24 Crankshaft sprocket
25 Crankshaft-to-flywheel mounting flange
26 Crankshaft outer pulley
27 Crankshaft damper
28 Crankshaft main bearing
29 Crankshaft center main bearing
30 Crankshaft main bearing
31 Main bearing cap
32 Flywheel
33 Crankshaft pulley retaining washer
34 Flywheel-to-crankshaft bolt
35 Flywheel ring gear
36 Hydraulic tappet
37 Exhaust valve
38 Intake valve
39 Valve spring
40 Valve spring retainer
41 Valve spring retainer key
42 Valve rocker arm fulcrum
43 Valve stem seal
44 Oil deflector
45 Rocker arm attaching bolt
46 Rocker arm
47 Pushrod
48 Oil pump
49 Oil pump rotor and shaft assembly
50 Oil pump body plate
51 Oil pump relief valve plug
52 Oil pump intermediate shaft
53 Oil pump screen, tube and cover assembly
54 Oil pump inlet tube gasket
55 Oil pump intermediate shaft ring
56 Oil pump relief valve spring
57 Oil pump relief valve plunger
58 Front cover oil seal
59 Crankshaft rear packing
60 Engine rear plate
61 Bolt ($\frac{5}{8}$-18 x 2)
62 Bolt ($\frac{3}{8}$-16 x 1)
63 Bolt ($\frac{3}{8}$-16 x 1-$\frac{1}{2}$)
64 Bolt ($\frac{1}{4}$-20 x $\frac{5}{8}$)
65 Dowel pin ($\frac{5}{16}$ x 1-$\frac{3}{8}$)
66 Woodruff key (1-$\frac{1}{4}$ x $\frac{7}{32}$ x $\frac{3}{4}$)
67 Bolt ($\frac{5}{16}$-18 x $\frac{7}{8}$)
68 Crankshaft pulley spacer

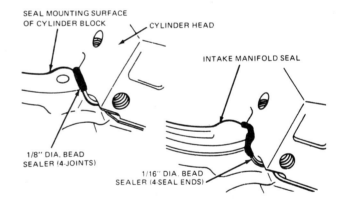

Fig. 2.45 Typical RTV-type sealant application for intake manifold installation on 351M and 400 V8 engines (Sec 37)

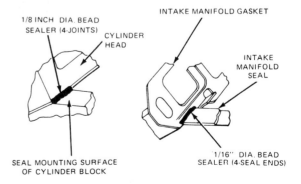

Fig. 2.46 Typical RTV-type sealant application for intake manifold installation on 255, 302 and 351W V8 engines (Sec 37)

2C

the distributor, and the distributor rotor for correct installation. It is a good idea to position the number one piston at top dead center when performing this operation (Section 9, Chapter 2A).
13 Remove the distributor from the engine, taking care that the distributor-to-oil pump driveshaft remains in the engine and connected to the oil pump.
14 Remove the wire from the coolant temperature sender unit.
15 Remove the wire(s) from any sensors mounted in the intake manifold and/or the upper thermostat housing.
16 Remove the throttle cable or linkage connection at the carburetor.
17 Remove the kick-down cable at the carburetor if the vehicle is equipped with an automatic transmission.
18 Remove the pull cable and activating unit from the intake manifold if the vehicle is equipped with a cruise control unit.
19 Remove the vacuum hose leading to the power brake booster from the intake manifold. Secure this hose to the firewall out of the way.
20 Remove the carburetor from the intake manifold if the carburetor is to be serviced separately.
21 Remove any wiring leading to components located on the intake manifold. Locate the wires where they won't be damaged.
22 Disconnect the crankcase vent hose leading from the manifold to the rocker arm cover.
23 Remove the bolts retaining the intake manifold to the cylinder heads.
24 Attach the lifting hooks at opposite corners and lift the intake manifold from the engine. It may be necessary to pry the intake manifold away from the cylinder heads but be careful to avoid damaging the mating surfaces.
25 Clean the mating surfaces of the intake manifold and cylinder heads. Take care not to get any material down into the intake ports.
26 Remove the end gaskets from the top of the engine block.
27 Remove the oil gallery splash pan from the engine (if so equipped).

Intake manifold – disassembly
255, 302, 351 and 400 cu in engines
28 If the vacuum assembly is to be disassembled, identify all vacuum hoses before disconnecting them. Remove the coolant outlet housing gasket and the thermostat. Remove the ignition coil, temperature sending unit, carburetor (if not previously removed), spacer (on EEC engines remove the EGR cooler and related parts), gasket, vacuum fitting, accelerator retracting spring bracket and choke cable bracket.
460 cu in engine
29 If the manifold assembly is to be disassembled, identify all vacuum hoses before disconnecting them. Remove the coolant outlet housing, gasket and thermostat. Remove the automatic choke jet tubes, carburetor (if not previously removed), spacer and gaskets. Remove the thermostatic choke heater tube, the engine temperature sending unit and the EGR valve and gasket. Discard all gaskets.

Intake manifold – installation
30 If the manifold was disassembled, reassemble it by reversing the disassembly procedure. When installing the temperature sending unit, coat the threads with electrical conductive sealer and coat the thermostat gasket with water-resistant sealer.
31 Apply RTV-type gasket sealant to the mating points at the junctions of the cylinder heads and engine block. **Note:** *Do not apply sealer to the waffle section of the end seals on 351W and 400 engines as the sealer will rupture the seals.*
32 Position new seals on the engine block and press the seal locating tabs into the holes in the mating surface. This is a very critical step as correct intake manifold sealing depends on the quality of the installation of these gaskets.
33 Apply RTV-type gasket sealant to the opposite ends of the intake manifold seal. For 351W and 400 engines, see the note in Step 31.
34 Position the intake manifold gasket on the block and cylinder heads with the alignment notches fitting into the dowels on the block. Be sure that all of the holes in the gasket are aligned with the corresponding holes in the cylinder heads.
35 Lower the intake manifold into position using either a lift or two people, being careful not to disturb or dislocate the gaskets. After the manifold is in place, run a finger around the seal area to make sure that the seals are in place. If the seals are not in place, remove the manifold and reposition the seals.
36 Install the intake manifold retaining bolts finger tight. Tighten the

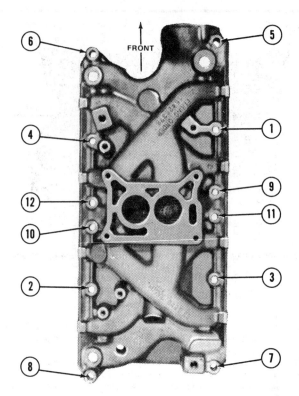

Fig. 2.47 Intake manifold bolt tightening sequence for 255, 302 and 351W V8 engines (Sec 37)

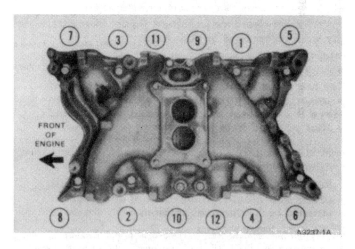

Fig. 2.48 Intake manifold bolt tightening sequence for 351M and 400 V8 engines (Sec 37)

intake manifold bolts in the sequence shown in the accompanying illustrations (note that different engines have different bolt tightening sequences). Work up to the final torque in three steps to avoid warping the manifold.
37 Install the remaining components in the reverse order of removal.
38 Start and run the engine and allow it to reach operating temperature. After it has reached operating temperature, check carefully for leaks.
39 Shut the engine off and retighten the manifolds while the engine is still warm.

Exhaust manifold
40 If the right-hand exhaust manifold is being removed, remove the air cleaner, intake duct and heat stovepipe.
41 If the left-hand exhaust manifold is being removed, remove the

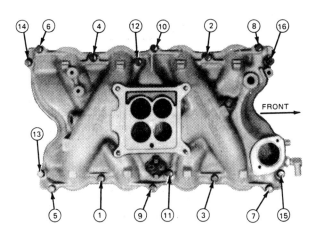

Fig. 2.49 Intake manifold bolt tightening sequence for 460 V8 engines (Sec 37)

engine oil filter on 351M and 400 engine-equipped models. Remove the speed control bracket (if so equipped), and, on all engines except the 460, remove the oil dipstick and tube assembly.

42 On vehicles equipped with a column selector and automatic transmission, disconnect the cross lever shaft for the automatic transmission selector to provide the clearance necessary to remove the manifold.

43 Disconnect the retaining bolts holding the inlet pipe(s) to the exhaust manifold(s).

44 Remove the spark plug heat shields if so equipped.

45 Remove the exhaust manifold retaining bolts.

46 Remove the exhaust manifold.

47 Clean the mating surfaces of the exhaust manifold and the cylinder head.

48 Clean the mounting flange of the exhaust manifold and the inlet pipe.

Exhaust manifold – installation

49 Apply graphite grease to the mating surface of the exhaust manifold.

50 Position the exhaust manifold on the head and install the attaching bolts. Tighten the bolts to the specified torque in three steps, working from the center to the ends.

51 If so equipped, install the spark plug heat shields.

52 Install the gasket or spacer between the inlet pipe and the exhaust manifold outlet.

53 Connect the inlet pipe to the exhaust manifold using new retaining nuts.

54 Tighten the retaining nuts to the proper torque making sure that the exhaust inlet pipe is situated squarely in the exhaust manifold outlet.

55 Install the oil filter if the left exhaust manifold was removed (351M or 400 engine).

56 If removed, install the oil dipstick assembly.

57 Install the automatic transmission selector cross shaft at the chassis and the engine block if the vehicle is equipped with a column shifter.

58 If the right exhaust manifold was replaced, install the air cleaner heat stovepipe, air cleaner and intake duct.

59 Start the engine and check for exhaust leaks.

38 Rocker arm covers – removal and installation

1 Remove the air cleaner and intake duct assembly.

2 Remove the crankcase ventilation hoses and lines where applicable. Make sure that all lines and hoses have been removed from the rocker arm covers and position them out of the way.

3 Remove the PCV valve from the oil filler cap or rocker arm cover.

4 Remove the vacuum line and electric solenoid on 302 unleaded fuel engines (Canadian only).

5 Remove the vacuum solenoid mounted on the left-hand cover (if so equipped).

6 Disconnect the spark plug wires. Mark them so they can be installed in their original locations.

7 Remove the spark plug wires clipped to the rocker arm covers and position them out of the way.

8 Remove the clips retaining the wiring looms running along the left-hand cover.

9 Remove the rocker arm cover retaining bolts.

10 Remove the rocker arm cover(s).

11 Remove all old gasket material and sealant from the rocker arm cover and cylinder head gasket surfaces.

12 Make sure the gasket surfaces of the rocker arm covers are flat and smooth, particularly around the bolt holes. Use a hammer and a block of wood to flatten them out if they are deformed.

13 Attach a new rocker arm cover gasket to the cover. Notice that there are tabs provided in the cover to retain the gasket. It may be necessary to apply RTV-type gasket sealant to the corners of the cover to retain the gasket there.

14 Install the rocker arm cover onto the cylinder head, making sure that the bolt holes are aligned correctly.

15 Install the rocker arm cover retaining bolts finger tight.

16 Working from the center of the rocker arm cover, tighten the retaining bolts to the correct torque. **Caution:** *Do not overtighten the bolts or the valve covers will warp and the gaskets will be pushed out of position, causing leaks.*

17 The remainder of the installation procedure is the reverse of removal.

18 Start the engine and run it until it reaches normal operating temperature, then make sure that there are no leaks.

39 Rocker arms and pushrods – removal, inspection and installation

Removal

1 Remove the rocker arm covers as described in Section 38.

2 Remove the rocker arm fulcrum bolts.

3 Remove the oil deflectors (351M, 400 and 460 engines only), fulcrums, fulcrum guides (255, 302 and 351W engines only) and the rocker arms. If only the pushrods are being removed, loosen the fulcrum retaining bolts and rotate the rocker arms out of the way of the pushrods.

Inspection

4 Inspect the rocker arms for signs of excessive wear, galling or damage.

5 Inspect the hole at the pushrod end of the rocker arm and make sure that it is open.

6 Inspect the rocker arm fulcrum face for galling or checking. If any of these conditions exist, replace the rocker arm and fulcrum as an assembly with new parts.

7 Inspect the pushrods for bending, excessive wear at either end or cracking. If any of these conditions exist, replace the pushrods with new ones.

Installation

8 Apply engine oil or assembly lube to the top of the valve stem and the pushrod guide in the cylinder head.

9 Apply engine oil to the rocker arm fulcrum seat and the fulcrum seat socket in the rocker arm.

10 Install the pushrods in the correct positions, with lubricant applied to both ends.

11 Install the fulcrum guides (255, 302 and 351W engines only), rocker arms, fulcrums, oil deflector (351M and 400 engines only) and fulcrum bolts.

12 Tighten the fulcrum bolts to the specified torque.

13 Replace the rocker arm covers and gaskets as described in Section 38.

14 Start the engine and check for roughness and/or noise. Refer to Section 9 of Chapter 2A for any corrections that may have to be made for either a rough running or excessively noisy engine.

2C

40 Cylinder heads – removal, inspection and installation

Removal

1   Remove the intake manifold and carburetor as an assembly as described previously.
2   Remove the rocker arm cover(s) by referring to the appropriate Section.
3   If the left cylinder head is being removed on a vehicle equipped with factory air conditioning, remove the compressor and support it securely to the side of the engine compartment. **Caution:** *Do not disconnect the air conditioning hoses, as serious injury or damage to the system will result.*
4   If the left cylinder head is being removed and the vehicle is equipped with power steering, remove the power steering bracket retaining bolt from the left cylinder head.
5   Position the power steering pump out of the way so it will not leak fluid.
6   If the right cylinder head is being removed, remove the alternator mounting bracket through-bolt.
7   Remove the air cleaner inlet tube (if so equipped) from the right cylinder head.
8   Remove the ground wire connected to the rear of the cylinder head.
9   Disconnect the exhaust manifold retaining bolts from the exhaust manifolds.
10 Remove the rocker arms or rocker arm assemblies as described previously. Remove the pushrods. Be sure to mark them, as they will need to be reinstalled in their original locations.
11 Loosen the cylinder head retaining bolts by reversing the order shown in the tightening sequence diagram, then remove the bolts from the heads. Keep them in order so they can be installed in their original locations.
12 Using a hoist (or two people), carefully remove the cylinder head from the block, using care to avoid damaging the gasket mating surfaces.

Inspection

13 Refer to Chapter 2B, Secton 18, Step 19 for cylinder head disassembly and inspection procedures.

Installation

14 Make sure that the cylinder head and engine block mating surfaces are clean, flat and prepared properly for the new cylinder head gasket.
15 Position the head gasket over the dowel pins on the block. Make sure that the head gasket is facing the right direction and that the correct surface is exposed. Gaskets are sometimes marked 'front' and 'top' to help clarify their installation position.
16 Using a hoist (or two people), carefully lower the cylinder head(s) into place on the block in the correct position. Take care not to move the head sideways or scrape it across the block as it can dislodge the gasket and/or damage the gasket surfaces.
17 Coat the cylinder head retaining bolts with light engine oil and thread the bolts into the engine block through the head.
18 Tighten the bolts finger tight.
19 Tighten the bolts in the sequence shown in the accompanying illustration. Work up gradually in three steps to the final torque, going through the pattern completely on each step.

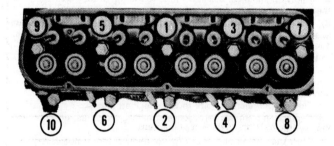

Fig. 2.50 Head bolt tightening sequence for V8 engines (Sec 40)

20 Apply engine oil to the rocker arm fulcrum seat and sockets or the rocker arm assemblies.
21 Install the pushrods as described earlier.
22 Install the rocker arm covers.
23 The remainder of the installation procedure is the reverse of removal.
24 Start and run the engine and check it carefully for leaks and unusual noises.

41 Timing chain and cover – removal and installation

Removal

1   Drain the cooling system.
2   Remove the screws attaching the radiator shroud to the radiator.
3   Remove the bolts attaching the fan to the water pump shaft.
4   Remove the fan and the radiator shroud.
5   Disconnect the upper radiator hose at the thermostat housing.
6   Disconnect the lower radiator hose at the water pump outlet.
7   Disconnect the transmission oil cooler lines at the radiator (if so equipped).
8   Loosen the alternator mounting and adjusting bolts to relieve the tension on the drivebelt. If the vehicle is equipped with air conditioning, loosen the air conditioning idler pulley.
9   Remove the air pump.
10 Remove the drivebelts and the water pump pulley.
11 Remove the bolt attaching the air conditioning compressor support, water pump and compressor. Remove the compressor support. **Caution:** *Do not loosen or remove the air conditioning hoses, as serious personal injury or damage to the system could result.*
12 Remove the bolts and washers retaining the crankshaft pulley to the vibration damper. Remove the crankshaft pulley.
13 Remove the large bolt and washer retaining the vibration damper to the crankshaft.
14 Remove the vibration damper with a puller.
15 Remove the crankshaft pulley spacer.
16 Remove the bypass hose from the top of the water pump.
17 Disconnect the heater return hose or tube at the water pump.
18 Remove and plug the fuel inlet line at the fuel pump.
19 Disconnect the fuel line at the carburetor. Remove the fuel feed line from the fuel pump.
20 Remove the fuel pump.
21 Remove the retaining bolts holding the timing cover to the engine block.
22 Use a thin bladed knife or similar tool to cut the oil pan seal flush with the engine block mating surface.
23 Remove the timing cover and water pump as an assembly.
24 Remove the timing cover gasket and oil pan seal.
25 Remove the water pump from the timing cover if the cover is being replaced with a new one.
26 Check the timing chain deflection by rotating the crankshaft in a counterclockwise direction to take up the slack on the left side of the chain (as you view the engine from the front).
27 Establish a reference point on the block and use a ruler to check the distance from the reference point to the left side of the chain.
28 Rotate the crankshaft in the opposite direction to take up the slack on the opposite (or right) side of the chain.
29 Force the left side of the chain out and measure the distance between the reference point and the chain. This will give you the deflection. If the deflection exceeds the Specifications, the timing chain and sprockets will need replacement with new parts.
30 If the timing chain and sprockets are being removed, turn the engine until the timing marks are aligned as shown in the accompanying illustration.
31 Remove the camshaft sprocket retaining bolt, washer, fuel pump eccentric (two-piece on 460 engines) and front oil slinger (if present) from the crankshaft.
32 Slide the timing chain and sprockets forward and off of the camshaft and crankshaft as an assembly.

Installation

33 Assemble the timing chain and sprockets so the timing marks are in alignment.
34 Install the chain and sprockets onto the camshaft and crankshaft as an assembly. Make sure that the timing marks remain in proper alignment during the installation procedure (photo).

41.34 Correct alignment of the crankshaft and camshaft sprocket timing marks (arrows) during installation on a typical V8 engine

35 Install the oil slinger (if so equipped) over the nose of the crankshaft.
36 Install the fuel pump eccentric, camshaft sprocket retaining bolt and washer. Tighten the retaining bolt to the proper torque. Lubricate the timing chain and gears with engine oil.
37 Clean the old gasket material from the gasket mating surface on the oil pan.
38 Coat the gasket surface of the oil pan with RTV-type gasket sealant. Cut and position the required sections of new front cover-to-oil pan seal on the oil pan.
39 Apply sealant at the corners of the mating surfaces.
40 Coat the gasket surfaces of the cover with sealant and install a new gasket. Coat the mating surface on the block with sealant.
41 Position the timing cover on the block after installing a new front crankshaft seal as described in Section 43.
42 Use care when installing the cover to avoid damaging the front crankshaft seal.
43 Install the cover alignment tool to position the cover properly. If no alignment tool is available, you will have to use the crankshaft pulley to position the seal. It may be necessary to force the cover down slightly to compress the oil pan seal. This can be done by inserting a punch in the retaining bolt holes.
44 Coat the threads of the retaining bolts with RTV-type sealant and install the retaining bolts.
45 While holding the cover in alignment, tighten the oil pan-to-front cover retaining bolts.
46 Remove the alignment punch.
47 Tighten the retaining bolts holding the cover to the engine block.
48 Apply a thin coat of grease to the vibration damper seal contact surface.
49 Install the crankshaft spacer.
50 Install the Woodruff key onto the crankshaft and slide the vibration damper into position.
51 Install the vibration damper retaining bolt and washer.
52 This bolt may be used to push the damper onto the crankshaft if the proper installation tool is not available.
53 Attach the crankshaft pulley to the damper and install the pulley retaining bolts.
54 Attach a new fuel pump gasket to the fuel pump and install the fuel pump.
55 Connect the fuel lines to the fuel pump.
56 The remainder of the installation procedure is the reverse of removal. Make sure that all bolts are tightened securely.
57 If any coolant entered the oil pan when separating the timing chain cover from the block, the crankcase oil should be drained and the oil filter removed. Install a new oil filter and refill the crankcase with the proper grade and amount of oil.
58 Start and run the engine at a fast idle and check for coolant and oil leaks.
59 Check the engine idle speed and ignition timing.

42 Camshaft and lifters – removal, inspection and installation

Removal
1 After marking the hoses for ease of installation and disconnecting them, remove the air cleaner.
2 Remove the intake manifold (see Section 37).
3 Remove the rocker arm covers (see Section 38)
4 Loosen the rocker arm nuts and rotate the rocker arms to the side.
5 Mark the pushrods if they are to be reused and remove them from the engine.
6 Remove the valve lifters from the engine using a special tool designed for this purpose. Sometimes they can be removed with a magnet if there is no varnish build up or wear on them. If they are stuck in their bores, you will have to obtain a special tool designed for grasping lifters internally and work them out.
7 Remove the timing cover, chain and gears.
8 Remove the grille if the engine is in the vehicle.
9 Remove the radiator if the engine is still in the vehicle (see Chapter 3).
10 Remove the retaining bolts securing the camshaft and thrust plate to the engine block.
11 Slowly withdraw the camshaft from the engine, being careful not to damage the bearings with the cam lobes.

Inspection
12 Visually inspect the hydraulic valve lifters for cupping on the camshaft mating face and for signs of excessive wear, galling, or cracking.
13 The hydraulic valve lifters must be tested using special equipment. This procedure must be handled by a suitably equipped automotive machine shop.
14 If you suspect that a lifter is defective, replace it with a new one. It is not necessary to test a new lifter before installation.
15 Check the camshaft lobe lift on a special V-block cradle with a dial indicator. Again, this is a procedure which should be handled by a suitably equipped automotive machine shop.
16 Visually check the camshaft bearing surfaces for any signs of galling or excessive wear. If any of these conditions are present, or if there is a question about the camshaft (and you have no access to testing or measurement equipment), replace it with a new one.

Installation
17 Lubricate the camshaft journals with engine oil and apply engine assembly lube to the cam lobes.
18 Slide the camshaft into position, being careful not to scrape or nick the bearings.
19 Install the camshaft thrust plate. Tighten the thrust plate retaining bolts to the proper torque.
20 Check the camshaft endplay by pushing it toward the rear of the engine.
21 Install a dial indicator so that the stem is on the camshaft sprocket attaching bolt. Zero the dial indicator.
22 Position a large screwdriver between the camshaft gear and the block. Note: *Do not pry against aluminum or nylon camshaft sprockets when any type of valve train load is on the camshaft, as damage to the sprocket can result.*
23 Pull the camshaft forward with the screwdriver and release it.
24 Compare the dial indicator reading to the Specifications.
25 If the endplay is excessive, check the spacer for correct installation before it is removed. If the spacer is installed correctly, replace the thrust plate. Notice that the thrust plate has a groove on it; it should face in on all engines.
26 Check the timing chain deflection as described in Section 41.
27 Install the hydraulic valve lifters in their original bores if the old ones are being used. Make sure they are coated with engine assembly lube. Never use old lifters with a new camshaft.
28 The remainder of the installation procedure is the reverse of removal.

43 Crankshaft oil seals – replacement

Front seal
1 Remove the timing chain cover (see Section 41).

2C

2   On all engines except 351M and 400, tap the front crankshaft seal out using a drive tool. **Note:** *The front oil seal should be replaced with a new one whenever the cover is removed or leakage is apparent.*
3   Clean the grooves in the front cover.
4   Install the new front oil seal using a special drive tool (or a large drift if the drive tool is not available). If you are using a large drift, be very careful not to damage the front seal. Make sure that the spring remains positioned inside the front seal.
5   On 351M-400 engines, remove the front seal using the special puller as shown in the accompanying illustration.
6   Clean the groove which the crankshaft front seal sits in.
7   Install the new seal using the special drive tool.

Rear Seal – two-piece

8   The crankshaft rear seal can be replaced with the engine in the vehicle. The oil pan and oil pump must be removed to gain access to the seal. Refer to Chapter 2B for these procedures.
9   Loosen the main bearing cap bolts slightly to allow the crankshaft to drop no more than $\frac{1}{32}$ inch.
10 Remove the rear main bearing cap and detach the oil seal from the cap. To remove the portion of the rear main seal housed in the block, install a small sheet metal screw in one end of the seal and pull on the screw to rotate the seal out of the groove. Exercise extreme caution

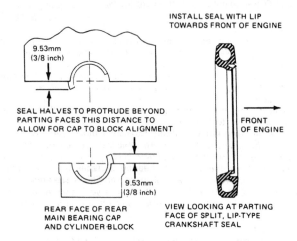

Fig. 2.51a   Correct installation of the crankshaft rear oil seal (Sec 43)

during this procedure to prevent scratching or damaging the crankshaft seal surfaces.
11 Carefully clean the seal grooves in the cap and block with a brush dipped in solvent.
12 Dip both new seal halves in clean engine oil.
13 Carefully install the upper seal (engine block) into the groove with the lip of the seal toward the front of the engine.
14 It will be necessary to rotate it into the seal seat if the crankshaft is still in the engine. Make sure that $\frac{3}{8}$ inch of the seal protrudes on one side below the parting surface of the bearing cap.
15 Remove the oil seal retaining pin from the bearing cap, if so equipped. The pin is not used with the split-lip seal. Install the remaining half of the crackshaft seal in the main bearing cap. Make sure that $\frac{3}{8}$ in protrudes on the opposite side of the main bearing cap parting surface. Make sure that no rubber has been shaved from the outside diameter of the seal by the groove in the block or the crankshaft main bearing cap.
16 Tighten all but the rear main bearing cap bolts to the specified torque.
17 Install the rear main bearing cap and make sure that the parting surfaces of the seals meet each other as shown in the accompanying illustration.
18 Apply a thin coat of RTV-type gasket sealant to the rear main bearing cap at the top of the mating surface and to the block surface (refer to the accompanying illustration). Make sure that no sealer is permitted to get on the inside of the split lip seal.
19 Tighten the cap bolts to the specified torque, making sure that no sealant has worked its way forward of the seal side groove.
20 Install the oil pan and oil pump.
21 The remainder of the installation procedure is the reverse of removal.

Rear Seal – one-piece

22 On models with a one piece rear seal, the transmission and flywheel or flexplate must be removed to gain access to the seal. Refers to Chapters 7 and 2B for these procedures.
23 Using a sharp awl, punch a hole into the seal metal surface between the seal lip and the engine block. Screw in the threaded end of a slide hammer, dent puller, or equivalent tool. Using the puller remove the seal. **Caution:** *Do not scratch or damage the crankshaft or oil sealing surface.*
24 Clean the crankshaft and oil seal recess in the cylinder block and main bearing cap. Inspect the crankshaft to seal contact surface for scratches or nicks that could damage the new seal lip and cause oil leaks.
25 Coat the new seal and the crankshaft with a light coat of engine oil.
26 Start the new seal into the recess with the seal lip facing inward and install with an appropriate tool. Either Ford tool number T65P-6701-A or

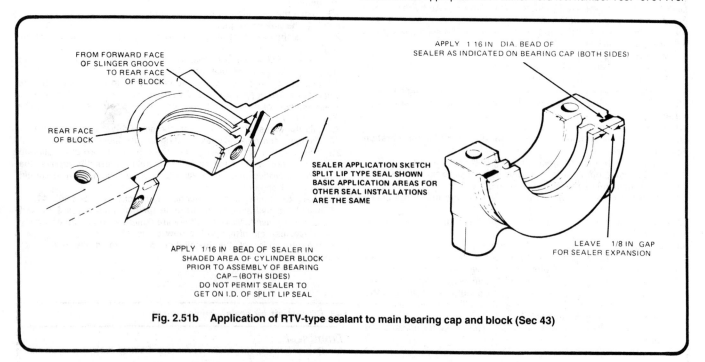

Fig. 2.51b   Application of RTV-type sealant to main bearing cap and block (Sec 43)

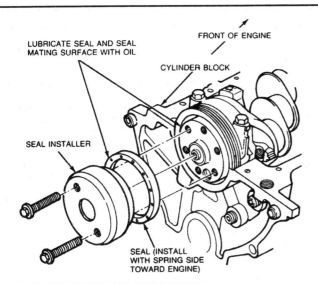

LUBRICATE SEAL AND SEAL MATING SURFACE WITH OIL

FRONT OF ENGINE

CYLINDER BLOCK

SEAL INSTALLER

SEAL (INSTALL WITH SPRING SIDE TOWARD ENGINE)

NOTE: REAR FACE OF SEAL MUST BE WITHIN 0.127mm (0.005-INCH) OF THE REAR FACE OF THE BLOCK

Fig. 2.52   One piece rear seal installation (Sec 43)

T82L-6701-A may be used or you may be able to fashion your own tool from a large section of plastic or metal pipe. Press the seal squarely into the recess bore until the tool contacts the engine block surface. Remove the tool and inspect the seal to ensure it was not damaged during installation.

27   Install the flywheel and transmission (refer to Chapters 7 and 2B).

44   Crankshaft and main bearings – installation

1   Thoroughly clean the groove in the cylinder block and the rear main bearing cap that houses the rear main oil seal.
2   Make sure that the inside surfaces of the main bearing caps are clean and free of burrs, scratches or nicks which could prevent the bearing inserts from seating correctly.
3   Install new crankshaft main bearing upper inserts. Be certain that the inserts installed are the correct size. If the crankshaft has been ground undersize, then corresponding, correct size bearing inserts

should be supplied for proper clearance at the crankshaft journal. Refer to Chapter 2B, Section 29 for bearing oil clearance checking procedures.
4   Make sure that the crankshaft bearing upper inserts fit into the alignment slot provided, and that the groove and hole line up correctly in the main bearing saddle.
5   If so equipped, make sure that the pin which located the rear oil seal on the rear main bearing saddle groove is removed. The new split lip-type seal does not require this pin.
6   Dip the lip-type seal halves in clean engine oil. Install the upper engine oil seal in the bearing cap with the undercut side of the seal facing the front of the engine as shown in the accompanying illustration. Also note that the upper half of the bearing cap seal is allowed to protrude $\frac{3}{8}$ inch on one side to mate with the corresponding upper main bearing cap oil seal.
7   Carefully lower the crankshaft into place making sure that no bearing surfaces are allowed to touch either the block or connecting rods (if they are still installed in the block).
8   Check the clearance of each main bearing using Plastigage as described in Chapter 2B, Section 29.
9   Apply RTV-type sealant to each side of the rear main bearing cap and apply sealant to the block as shown in the accompanying illustration.
10   Apply engine oil to the crankshaft journals and bearings.
11   Install all of the bearing caps except the thrust bearing cap. Make sure that the main bearing caps are all installed in their original positions, as numbered during disassembly.
12   Tighten the main bearing cap bolts to the proper torque.
13   Install the thrust bearing cap with the bolts finger tight.
14   Pry the crankshaft forward against the thrust surface of the upper half of the thrust bearing (see illustrations in Chapter 2B).
15   While holding the crankshaft forward, pry the thrust bearing cap to the rear. This procedure aligns the thrust surfaces of both halves of the thrust bearing in relationship to the crankshaft.
16   Keep applying forward pressure on the crankshaft and tighten the thrust bearing cap bolts to the proper torque.
17   Check the crankshaft endplay with a dial indicator setup. To do this, mount the dial indicator so that the stem rests against the crankshaft flange, parallel to the crankshaft. Force the crankshaft as far as possible to the rear, then zero the dial indicator. Push the crankshaft forward and note the indicator reading (the reading represents crankshaft endplay). If the play is greater than specified, install a new thrust bearing. If it is less than the minimum allowed, check the thrust bearing faces for scratches, nicks and dirt. If the faces are not damaged or dirty, reinstall the bearing by following the alignment procedure in Steps 11 through 16. Recheck the endplay.

2C

Chapter 2 Part D V6 engine

Contents

Specifications

General

Bore and stroke	3.81 x 3.39 in
Oil pressure (hot @ 2500 rpm)	54 to 59 psi

Engine block

Cylinder bore

Diameter	3.81 in
Taper service limit	0.002 in
Out-of-round service limit	0.002 in
Deck warpage limit	0.003 in per 6 in

Pistons and rings

Piston

Diameter

Coded red	3.8095 to 3.8101 in
Coded blue	3.8107 to 3.8113 in
Oversizes available	0.004 in
Piston-to-cylinder bore clearance	0.0014 to 0.0022 in

Piston ring-to-groove clearance

Top compression	0.0016 to 0.0037 in
Bottom compression	0.0016 to 0.0037 in
Oil ring	Snug fit in groove

Piston ring end gap

Top compression	0.01 to 0.02 in
Bottom compression	0.01 to 0.02 in
Oil ring	0.0150 to 0.0583 in
Piston pin diameter	0.9119 to 0.914 in
Piston pin-to-piston clearance	0.0002 to 0.0005 in
Piston pin-to-connecting rod clearance	Press fit at 1800 lbs

Crankshaft and flywheel

Main journal

Diameter	2.5190 to 2.5198 in
Taper limit	0.0003 in per 1 in
Out-of-round limit	0.0003 in per 45° or 0.0006 in total
Journal runout limit	0.002 in*

Main bearing oil clearance

Desired	0.0010 to 0.0014 in
Allowable	0.0005 to 0.0023 in

Connecting rod journal
  Diameter ....   2.3103 to 2.3111 in
  Taper limit ....   0.0003 in per 1 in
  Out-of-round limit ....   0.0003 in per 45° or 0.0006 in total
Connecting rod bearing oil clearance
  Desired ....   0.0010 to 0.0014 in
  Allowable ....   0.0008 to 0.0027 in
Connecting rod side clearance
  Standard ....   0.0047 to 0.0114 in
  Service limit ....   0.014 in max
Crankshaft endplay ....   0.004 to 0.008 in
Flywheel clutch face runout limit ....   0.005 in TIR
Flywheel ring gear lateral runout
  Standard transmission ....   0.025 in TIR
  Automatic transmission ....   0.070 in TIR

Camshaft
Bearing journal diameter ....   2.0505 to 2.0515 in
Bearing oil clearance ....   0.001 to 0.003 in
Lobe lift
  Intake ....   0.240 in
  Exhaust ....   0.241 in
  Allowable lobe lift loss ....   0.005 in
Runout limit ....   0.020 in (runout of no. 2 or no. 3 relative to no. 1 and no. 4)
Endplay ....   (No endplay — camshaft is restrained by spring)
Camshaft drive — assembled gear face runout
  Crankshaft ....   0.002 in
  Camshaft ....   0.018 in

Cylinder heads and valve train
Head warpage limit ....   0.007 in
Valve seat angle ....   45°
Valve seat width (intake and exhaust) ....   0.06 to 0.08 in
Valve seat runout limit ....   0.003 in TIR
Valve face angle ....   44°
Valve face runout limit ....   0.002 in
Valve margin width .... $\frac{1}{32}$ in min
Valve stem diameter (standard)
  Intake ....   0.3416 to 0.3423 in
  Exhaust ....   0.3411 to 0.3418 in
Valve guide diameter (intake and exhaust) ....   0.3433 to 0.3443 in
Valve stem-to-guide clearance
  Intake ....   0.0010 to 0.0027 in
  Exhaust ....   0.0015 to 0.0032 in
Valve spring free length ....   1.70 to 1.78 in
Valve spring pressure (lbs @ specified length)
  Loaded (without damper) ....   215 @ 1.40 in
  Unloaded (without damper) ....   75 @ 1.70 in
  Service limit ....   10% loss of pressure
Collapsed lifter gap ....   See Chapter 2A Specifications
Lifter diameter ....   0.874 in
Lifter bore diameter ....   0.8752 to 0.8767 in
Lifter-to-bore clearance
  Standard ....   0.0007 to 0.0027 in
  Service limit ....   0.005 in

Oil pump
Relief valve spring tension (force @ length) ....   15.2 to 17.1 lbs @ 1.20 in
Relief valve-to-bore clearance ....   0.0017 to 0.0029 in
Oil pump gear backlash ....   0.008 to 0.012 in
Oil pump gear radial clearance (idler and driver) ....   0.0020 to 0.0055 in
Oil pump gear and height (extends beyond housing) ....   0.0005 to 0.0055 in
Idler shaft-to-idler gear clearance ....   0.0005 to 0.0017 in
Driver shaft-to-housing clearance ....   0.0015 to 0.0030 in

Runout of journal numbers 2 and 3 to journal numbers 1 and 4, and runout of adjacent journals to each other.

Torque specifications
	Ft-lb (unless otherwise noted)
Main bearing cap bolts	65 to 81
Camshaft sprocket-to-camshaft bolts	15 to 22
Connecting rod nuts	31 to 36
Front cover-to-cylinder block bolts	15 to 22
Water pump-to-front cover bolts	15 to 22
Oil inlet tube-to-main bearing cap nuts	30 to 40
Oil inlet tube-to-cylinder block bolts	15 to 22
Oil pan-to-cylinder block bolts	80 to 106 in-lb
Oil filter adapter-to-front cover bolts	18 to 22

2D

Oil filter-to-oil filter adapter .... $\frac{1}{2}$ turn after gasket contacts sealing surface
Cylinder head bolts
    Step 1 47
    Step 2 55
    Step 3 63
    Step 4 74
    Step 5 .... Back off all bolts 2 to 3 turns
    Step 6 .... Repeat Steps 1 through 4
Rocker arm fulcrum-to-cylinder head bolt
    Step 1 .... 5 to 11
    Step 2 .... 18 to 26
Fuel pump-to-front cover bolts .... 15 to 22
Intake manifold-to-cylinder head bolts
    Step 1 5
    Step 2 10
    Step 3 18
Rocker arm cover-to-cylinder head screws .... 36 to 61 in-lb
Spark plug-to-cylinder head .... 17 to 22
Flywheel-to-crankshaft bolts .... 54 to 64
Distributor hold-down bolt .... 20 to 29
Crankshaft pulley-to-damper bolts .... 20 to 28
Crankshaft damper-to-crankshaft bolts .... 93 to 121
Spark knock sensor-to-adapter .... 14 to 17
Spark knock sensor adapter-to-intake manifold .... 26 to 33
Vacuum fittings-to-intake manifold .... 26 to 33
Thermostat housing-to-intake manifold bolts .... 15 to 22
Heater tube-to-intake manifold stud bolt .... 15 to 22
Clutch plate-to-flywheel bolts .... 15 to 19
Carburetor hold-down stud-to-intake manifold .... 70 in-lb
Carburetor hold-down nuts .... 107 to 132 in-lb
EGR spacer-to-intake manifold bolts .... 71 to 106 in-lb
EGR spacer stud .... 36 to 70 in-lb
EGR adapter-to-EGR spacer nuts .... 15 to 22
EGR adapter stud .... 27 to 88 in-lb
EGR valve-to-EGR adapter nuts .... 15 to 22
EGR tube end nuts .... 31 to 39
Thermactor check valve-to-intake manifold bolts .... 98 to 132 in-lb
Vacuum tree-to-intake manifold .... 71 to 123 ib-lb
Clutch housing-to-cylinder block bolts .... 40 to 50
Alternator bracket-to-cylinder head bolts .... 30 to 40
Fuel flow sensor bracket-to-sensor nuts .... 45 to 61 in-lb
Fuel flow sensor bracket-to-front cover nuts .... 30 to 40
Exhaust manifold-to-cylinder head bolts .... 15 to 22
Engine damper bracket-to-exhaust manifold nuts .... 15 to 22
Oil dipstick tube-to-exhaust manifold nut .... 15 to 22
Coolant switch-to-intake manifold .... 13 to 18
PVS-to-intake manifold .... 71 to 115 in-lb
Oil pan drain plug-to-pan .... 15 to 25
Thermactor pump pulley-to-pump hub bolts .... 150 to 220 in-lb
EGO sensor-to-exhaust manifold .... 27 to 33
Fan/clutch assembly-to-water pump bolts .... 12 to 18
Accelerator cable bracket-to-intake manifold bolt .... 20 to 30
Exhaust inlet pipe-to-exhaust manifold nuts .... 16 to 24
Starter motor-to-engine bolts .... 15 to 20
Flex plate-to-torque converter bolts .... 20 to 34
Transmission-to-engine bolts .... 41 to 51
Engine mount-to-crossmember bolts .... 25 to 35
Idler bracket-to-alternator top attaching flange bolt .... 24 to 34
Alternator pivot bolt .... 45 to 57
Air pump pivot bolt .... 30 to 40
Air pump-to-support bracket bolt .... 30 to 40
Idler pulley adjustment bolts .... 30 to 40
Idler bracket top bolt .... 30 to 40
Idler bracket lower front attaching bolt .... 30 to 40
Idler bracket upper front attaching bolt .... 52 to 70
Air conditioning lower mounting bracket-to-engine nuts .... 30 to 45
Air conditioning brace-to-engine nuts .... 15 to 22
Air conditioning front brace-to-engine brace bolt .... 30 to 45
Air conditioning compressor support-to-mounting bracket
    assembly bolts .... 30 to 45
Air conditioning compressor mounting bolts .... 30 to 45
Air conditioning compressor front plate-to-mounting bracket bolts .... 30 to 45
Air conditioning compressor front plate-to-engine stud nuts .... 30 to 45
Air conditioning front brace-to-engine stud nuts .... 15 to 22
Lower joint damper-to-no. 2 crossmember bracket bolts .... 30 to 50
Upper joint damper-to-engine bracket bolts .... 60 to 80

	Ft-lb
Engine bracket reinforcement brace-to-engine bracket nuts	60 to 80
Engine bracket reinforcement brace-to-engine bracket bolts	35 to 50
Power steering without air conditioning	
Power steering brace bolts	30 to 45
Power steering front bracket bolts	30 to 45
Power steering with air conditioning	
Power steering upper brace bolt	30 to 45
Power steering lower brace bolt	18 to 24
Power steering front bracket bolts	30 to 35
Power steering front bracket-to-air conditioning bracket bolts	30 to 35
Front bracket-to-power steering pump bolts	30 to 35

45 General information

The 232 cu in V6 is similar to the V8s in construction and components used. However, important differences do exist. In the following paragraphs, similarities and differences between the V6 and V8 will be noted.

Fuel is delivered by a mechanical fuel pump mounted on the right side of the front (timing) cover assembly. The carburetor is mounted on an aluminum manifold which is in turn bolted to aluminum alloy cylinder heads. Service procedures related to these components remain similar to those for the V8. However, a spark plug thread service procedure is provided in the event damage should occur to these threads (see Section 49).

The crankshaft is supported by four main bearings, with the number three bearing designated as the thrust bearing. The crankpins are positioned to provide a power impulse every 120 degrees of crankshaft rotation. This spacing, along with the necessary changes to camshaft lobe and distributor timing, provides smoothness of operation and quietness comparable to a V8.

The camshaft is also supported by four bearings. Thrust loads and endplay are limited by a thrust button and spring installed in the front of the camshaft. The spring-loaded button bears against the inside surface of the front cover with lubrication supplied by oil splash from the timing chain. Immediately behind the thrust button bore are the distributor drivegear and the fuel pump actuating eccentric. These are not separate components installed on the cam, but, like the lobes, are part of the camshaft casting.

The configuration of the valve train is identical to that employed in the V8 and service procedures are the same.

The rotary gear type oil pump, which develops the oil pressure necessary to force-feed the lubrication system, is located in the front cover assembly. The pump driven gear is rotated by the distributor shaft through an intermediate shaft.

Many of the component mating surfaces which are seated with a gasket in V8 engines are sealed in the V6 with silicone rubber. The surfaces sealed in this manner in the V6 include the oil pan sides and front where they mate to the cylinder block and front cover; the thermostat housing-to-the intake manifold; the rocker arm covers-to-the cylinder head; both ends of the intake manifold-to-the cylinder block; along the rear main bearing cap and cylinder block parting line; and the thermactor air injection secondary cover-to-the intake manifold. When applying this sealant, always use the bead size specified and join the components within 15 minutes of application. After that time, the sealant begins to 'set-up' and its sealing effectiveness may be reduced.

Because this engine is equipped with aluminium cylinder heads, a special corrosion inhibited coolant formulation is required to avoid radiator damage (see Chapter 3).

Accessories mounted on the front of the engine are driven by a single, serpentine drivebelt. It is routed over each accessory pulley and is driven by a pulley bolted to the crankshaft damper. The belt is held tight against the drive pulleys by a spring-loaded tensioner mounted on the upper right corner of the engine (see Chapter 1 for service procedures, including tensioning).

46 Manifolds – removal and installation

Intake manifold
1 Drain the cooling system and disconnect the cable from the negative battery terminal.
2 Remove the air cleaner assembly including the air intake duct and heat tube.

3 Disconnect the accelerator cable at the carburetor.
4 If so equipped, disconnect the transmission linkage at the carburetor.
5 Remove the attaching bolts from the accelerator cable mounting bracket and position the cable so it will not interfere with manifold removal.
6 If equipped with a speed control, disconnect the chain at the carburetor and remove the servo bracket assembly attaching nuts. Position the assembly so it will not interfere with manifold removal.
7 Disconnect the carburetor bowl vent hose at the carburetor.
8 Disconnect the thermactor air supply hose at the check valve located at the back of the intake manifold.
9 Disconnect the upper radiator hose at the thermostat housing.
10 Disconnect the fuel inlet line at the carburetor.
11 Disconnect the coolant bypass hose at the manifold.
12 Disconnect the heater tube at the intake manifold and remove the tube support bracket attaching nut.
13 Label and disconnect the vacuum lines at the carburetor and intake manifold.
14 Disconnect the necessary electrical connectors.
15 If equipped with air conditioning, remove the air compressor support bracket attached to the left front intake manifold attaching bolt.
16 Remove the EGR tube.
17 Disconnect the PCV line at the carburetor.
18 Unbolt and remove the carburetor and gasket.
19 Remove the three EGR spacer attaching screws from the manifold.
20 With the EGR adapter and valve attached, work the EGR spacer loose from the manifold and remove the spacer and gasket.
21 Remove the PCV line.
22 Remove the intake manifold attaching bolts in the reverse order shown in Fig. 2.54.
23 Remove the intake manifold. **Note:** *The manifold is sealed at each end with RTV-type sealer. To break the seal, it may be necessary to pry on the front of the manifold with a screwdriver blade. If so, use care to prevent damage to the machined surfaces.*
24 Remove the manifold side gaskets.
25 If the manifold is to be disassembled, remove the thermostat housing and thermostat, water temperature sending unit, thermactor check valve and all vacuum fittings.
26 The heater outlet and water bypass tubes are pressed in and are not serviceable. If they are damaged, replace the manifold with a new one.
27 If the intake manifold was disassembled, apply a coat of pipe sealant to the temperature sending unit, all vacuum fittings, the spark knock sensor/adapter (if so equipped) and the electric PVS (if so equipped) and install them in the manifold.
28 Install the thermostat in the manifold with the outlet side up.
29 Apply a $\frac{1}{16}$ in bead of RTV-type sealer to the thermostat housing and tighten it to the specified torque.
30 Position and install the thermactor check valve and a new gasket in the manifold, tightening the attaching bolts to the specified torque.
31 Apply a bead of contact adhesive to each cylinder head mating surface as shown in Fig. 2.55 and press new intake manifold gaskets into place, using the locating pins.
32 Apply a $\frac{1}{8}$ in bead of RTV-type sealer at each corner where the cylinder head joins the cylinder block and a $\frac{3}{4}$ bead of the same sealer at each end of the cylinder block where the manifold seats against the block.
33 Carefully lower the manifold into position on the cylinder block and cylinder heads. Use the locating pins to prevent smearing the sealant and causing gasket voids.

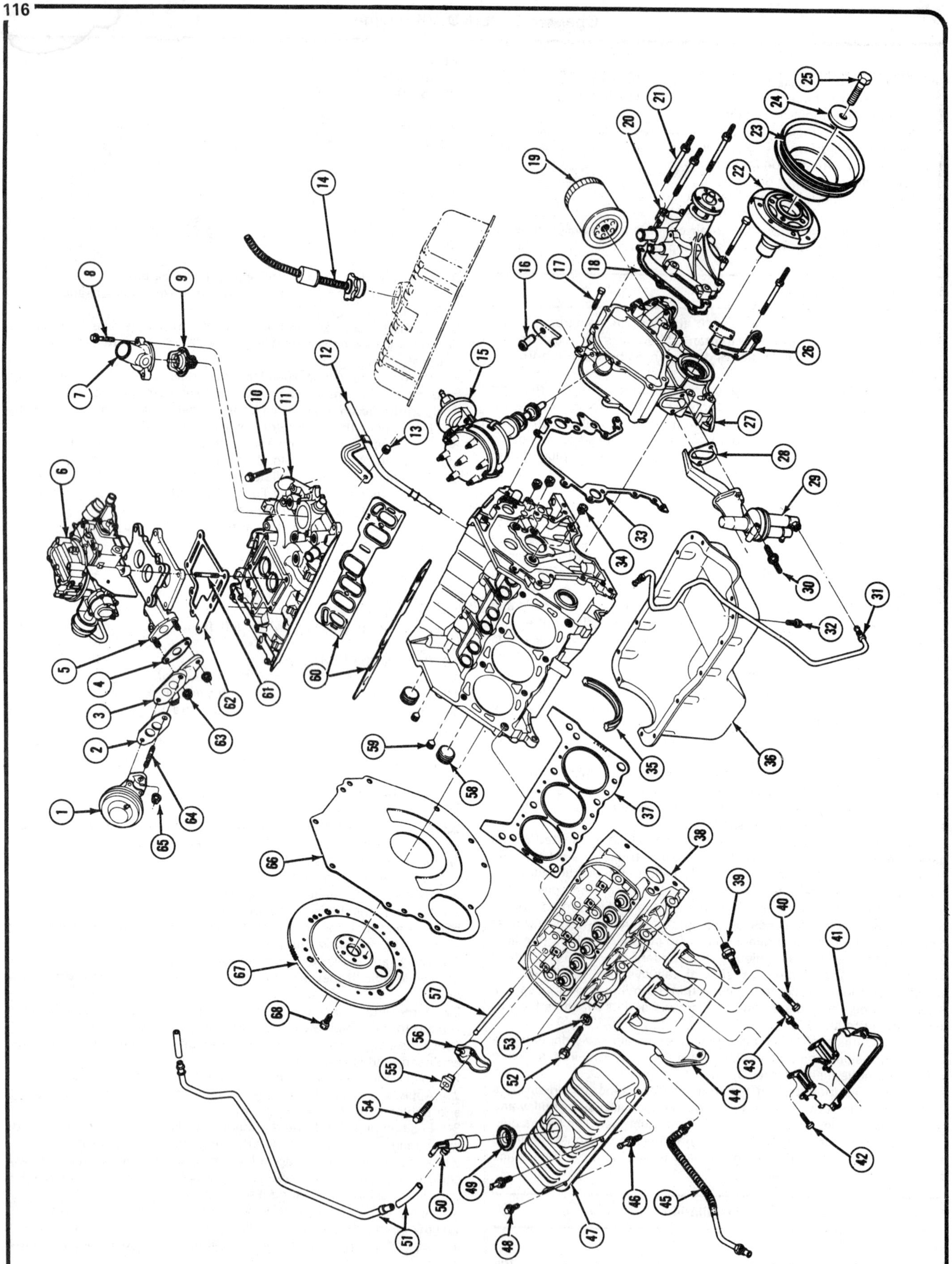
1
2
3
4
5
6
7
8
9
10
11
12
13
14
15
16
17
18
19
20
21
22
23
24
25
26
27
28
29
30
31
32
33
34
35
36
37
38
39
40
41
42
43
44
45
46
47
48
49
50
51
52
53
54
55
56
57
58
59
60
61
62
63
64
65
66
67
68

Fig. 2.53 External components of the 232 V6 engine – exploded view

1	EGR valve	
2	EGR valve adapter gasket	
3	EGR valve adapter	
4	EGR valve adapter-to-carburetor spacer gasket	
5	Carburetor spacer	
6	Carburetor	
7	Thermostat housing	
8	Thermostat housing attaching bolt	
9	Thermostat	
10	Manifold attaching bolt	
11	Intake manifold	
12	Oil level dipstick tube	
13	Tube attaching nut	
14	Oil filler cap, tube	
15	Distributor	
16	Distributor hold down clamp and bolt	
17	Front cover attaching bolt	
18	Water pump gasket	
19	Oil filter and filter assembly	
20	Water pump	
21	Water pump attaching bolts	
22	Crankshaft damper	
23	Crankshaft pulley	
24	Damper bolt washer	
25	Damper attaching bolt	
26	Ignition timing indicator	
27	Engine front cover	
28	Fuel pump gasket	
29	Fuel pump	
30	Fuel pump attaching stud	
31	Fuel pump-to-carburetor fuel line	
32	Oil pan attaching bolt	
33	Front cover gasket	
34	Oil gallery plug	
35	Oil pan rear seal	
36	Oil pan	
37	Cylinder head gasket	
38	Cylinder head	
39	Spark plug	
40	Exhaust manifold attaching bolt	
41	Hot air intake shroud	
42	Shroud and manifold attaching bolt	
43	Shroud and manifold	
44	Exhaust manifold	
45	EGR tube	
46	Valve cover attaching stud	
47	Valve cover	
48	Valve cover attaching bolt	
49	PCV valve grommet	
50	PCV valve	
51	PCV valve hose and tube	
52	Cylinder head attaching bolt	
53	Cylinder head bolt washer	
54	Rocker arm fulcrum attaching bolt	
55	Rocker arm fulcrum	
56	Rocker arm	
57	Pushrod	
58	Water jacket plug	
59	Rear oil gallery plug	
60	Intake manifold gasket	
61	Carburetor attaching stud	
62	Carburetor gasket	
63	Carburetor adapter attaching nut	
64	EGR valve attaching stud	
65	EGR valve attaching nut	
66	Rear engine plate	
67	Driveplate/flywheel	
68	Driveplate/flywheel attaching bolt	

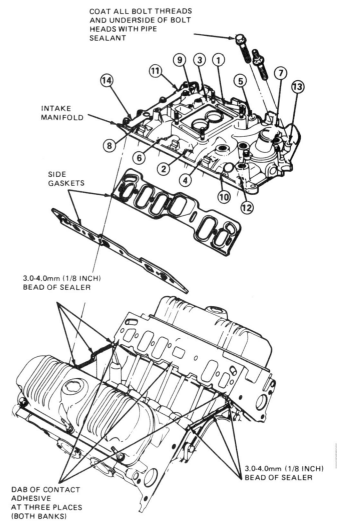

Fig. 2.54 Details of intake manifold installation procedures for the 232 V6 engine (Sec 46)

2D

34 Apply a thin coat of pipe sealant to the manifold attaching bolt threads and to the underside of the bolt heads.

35 Install the 12 bolts and two stud bolts and tighten them in the numerical sequence shown in Fig. 2.54. The bolts should be tightened in three steps (5.10 and 18 ft-lb).

36 Install the remaining components in the reverse order of removal.

37 Fill the cooling system with the specified coolant (see Chapter 3).

38 Start and run the engine and allow it to reach operating temperature, checking carefully for leaks.

39 Shut the engine off and retighten the manifold bolts while the engine is still warm.

Exhaust manifold – left

40 Remove the oil level dipstick tube support bracket.

41 If equipped with a speed control, reposition the air cleaner assembly and disconnect the servo chain at the carburetor.

42 Remove the servo bracket attaching bolts and nuts and position the servo/bracket assembly out of the way.

43 If so equipped, disconnect the EGO sensor at the wiring connector.

44 Disconnect the spark plug wires.

45 Raise the front of the vehicle and place it securely on jackstands.

46 Remove the manifold-to-exhaust pipe attaching nuts.

47 Remove the jackstands and lower the vehicle.

48 Remove the exhaust manifold attaching bolts and the manifold.

49 Installation is the reverse of removal. **Note:** *When installing the*

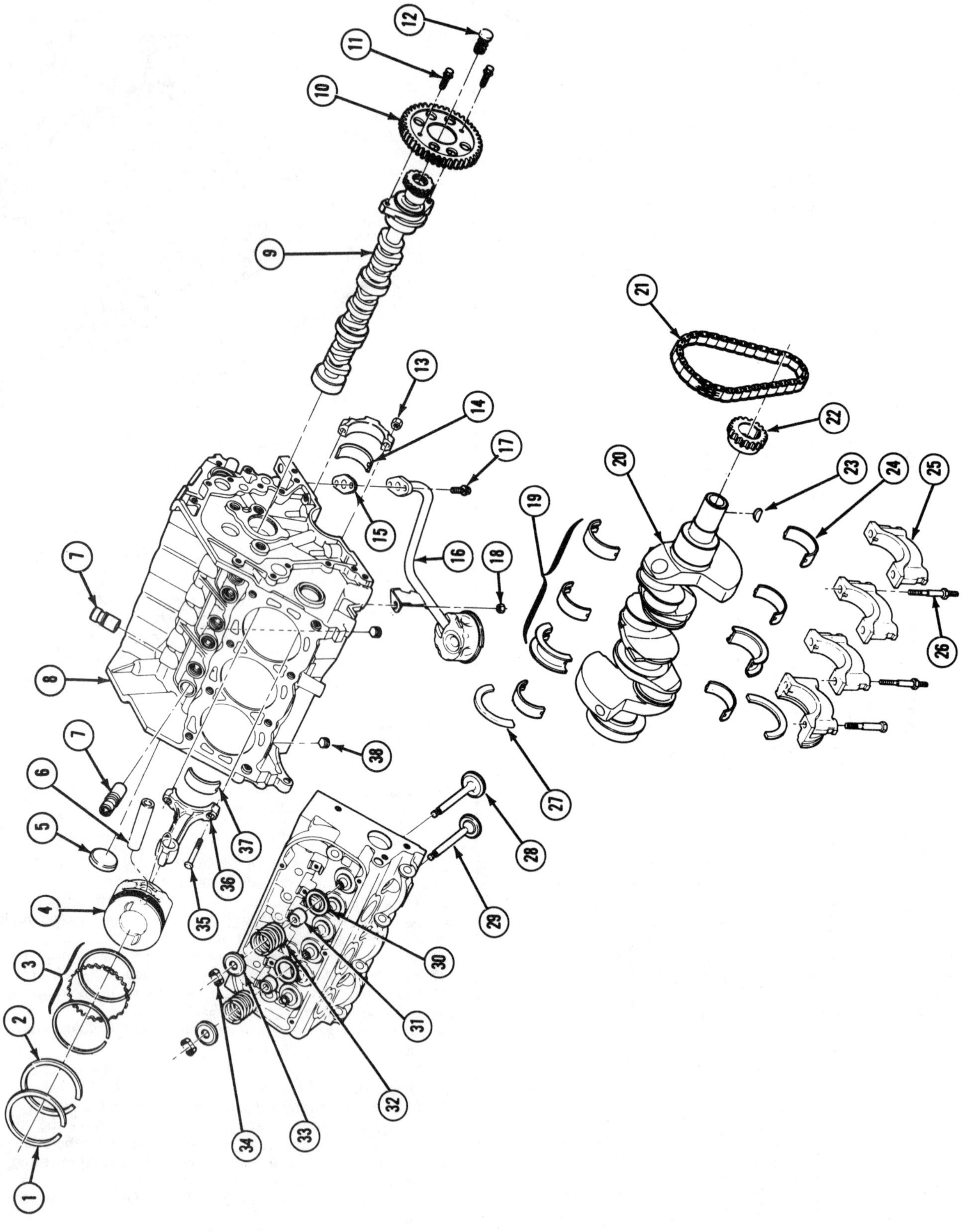
1
2
3
4
5
6
7
7
8
9
10
11
12
13
14
15
16
17
18
19
20
21
22
23
24
25
26
27
28
29
30
31
32
33
34
35
36
37
38

Fig. 2.55 Internal components of the 232 V6 engine – exploded view

1   Top piston compression ring
2   Bottom piston compression ring
3   Piston oil ring
4   Piston
5   Camshaft bore plug
6   Piston pin
7   Hydraulic lifter
8   Engine block
9   Camshaft
10 Camshaft sprocket
11 Camshaft sprocket attaching bolt
12 Camshaft thrust button and spring
13 Connecting rod cap attaching nut
14 Connecting rod bearing (lower)
15 Oil pickup tube and screen assembly gasket
16 Oil pickup tube and screen assembly
17 Oil pickup tube attaching bolt
18 Oil pickup tube bracket attaching bolt
19 Main bearing (upper)
20 Crankshaft
21 Timing chain
22 Crankshaft sprocket
23 Crankshaft Woodruff key
24 Main bearing (lower)
25 Main bearing cap
26 Main bearing cap attaching bolt
27 Crankshaft rear seal
28 Intake valve
29 Exhaust valve
30 Valve spring washer
31 Valve stem oil seal
32 Valve spring
33 Valve spring retainer
34 Valve spring retainer keys
35 Connecting rod attaching bolt
36 Connecting rod
37 Connecting rod bearing (upper)
38 Engine coolant drain plug

attaching bolts, install the pilot bolt (lower front bolt on no. 5 cylinder) first.

50 A slight warpage in the exhaust manifold may cause a misalignment between the bolt holes in the head and manifold. If so, elongate the holes in the exhaust manifold as necessary to correct the misalignment, but do not elongate the pilot hole.

Exhaust manifold – right

51 Remove the air cleaner assembly and heat tube.
52 Disconnect the thermactor hose from the downstream air tube check valve.
53 Remove the downstream air tube bracket attaching bolt at the rear of the right cylinder head.
54 Disconnect the coil secondary wire from the coil and the wires from the spark plugs.
55 Remove the spark plugs and the outer heat shroud.
56 Raise the front of the vehicle and place it securely on jackstands.
57 Remove the transmission dipstick tube, if so equipped.
58 Remove the manifold-to-exhaust pipe attaching nuts.
59 Remove the jackstands and lower the vehicle.
60 Remove the exhaust manifold attaching bolts, then remove the manifold, inner heat shroud and EGR tube as an assembly.
61 Installation is the reverse of removal. If bolt holes are misaligned, see Step 50, but do not elongate the pilot hole (lower rear bolt hole on no. 2 cylinder).

47 Rocker arm covers – removal and installation

1   Disconnect the spark plug wires.
2   Remove the spark plug wire routing clips from the rocker arm cover attaching studs.
3   If the left rocker arm cover is being removed, remove the oil filler cap. If equipped with a speed control, reposition the air cleaner assembly and disconnect the servo chain at the carburetor. Remove the servo bracket attaching bolts and nuts, and position the servo/bracket assembly aside.
4   If the right rocker arm cover is being removed, reposition the air cleaner assembly and heat tube, remove the PCV valve, then disconnect and remove the thermactor diverter valve and hose assembly at the bypass valve downstream air tube and the engine-mounted check valve.
5   Remove the valve cover attaching screws.
6   Loosen the silicone rubber gasketing material by inserting a putty knife under the cover flange. Work the cover loose and remove it. **Note:** *Pry carefully, as the plastic valve covers will break if excessive force is applied.*
7   Installation is the reverse of removal. Apply a $\frac{1}{8}$ to $\frac{3}{16}$ in bead of RTV-type sealer to the rocker arm cover before placing it on the head. Make sure the sealer fills the channel in the cover flange and make sure the installation is made within 15 minutes of the sealer application.

48 Cylinder heads – removal, inspection and installation

1   Drain the coolant into a suitable container.
2   Connect the cable from the negative battery terminal.
3   Remove the air cleaner assembly, including the air intake duct and heat tube.
4   Loosen the accessory drivebelt idler, then remove the drivebelt (see Chapter 3 if necessary).
5   If the left cylinder head is being removed, refer to Steps 6 through 9 and Steps 17 through 30.
6   If equipped with power steering, remove the pump mounting bracket attaching bolts.
7   Leaving the hoses connected, place the pump/bracket assembly aside, making sure that it is in a position to prevent the fluid from leaking out.
8   If equipped with air conditioning, remove the mounting bracket attaching bolts.
9   Leaving the hoses connected, position the compressor aside. **Note:** *Under no circumstances should the air conditioning hoses be disconnected except by an authorized air conditioning service technician, as personal injury and equipment damage may result.*
10 If the right cylinder head is being removed, refer to Steps 11 through 30.

2D

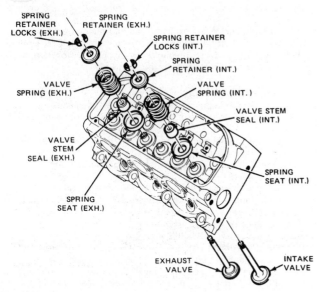

Fig. 2.56 Details of the 232 V6 cylinder head components (Sec 48)

11 Disconnect the thermactor diverter valve and hose assembly at the bypass valve and downstream air tube, then remove the assembly.
12 Remove the accessory drive idler.
13 Remove the alternator.
14 Remove the thermactor pump pulley and pump.
15 Remove the alternator bracket.
16 Remove the PCV valve.
17 Remove the intake manifold (see Section 46).
18 Remove the rocker arm cover(s) (see Section 47).
19 Remove the exhaust manifold(s) (see Section 46).
20 Remove the pushrods (see Chapter 2C, Section 39), making sure to note the position of each rod to facilitate installation.
21 Remove the cylinder head attaching bolts, then remove the cylinder head(s).
22 Remove and discard the old cylinder head gasket(s) and discard the cylinder head bolts.
23 Refer to Chapter 2B, Section 18, Step 19 for cylinder head disassembly and inspection procedures.
24 Position new head gasket(s) on the cylinder block using the dowels for alignment.
25 Position the heads on the block (refer to Fig. 2.57).
26 Apply a thin coat of pipe sealant to the threads of the short

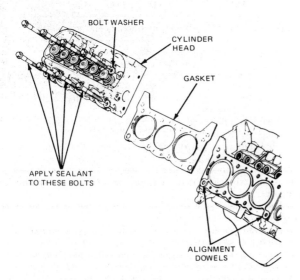

Fig. 2.57 Installing a V6 cylinder head (Sec 48)

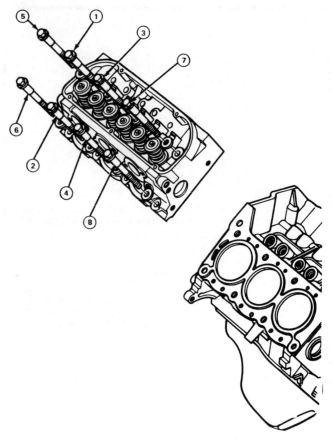

Fig. 2.58 Cylinder head bolt tightening sequence for the V6 engine (Sec 48)

cylinder head bolts (nearest to the exhaust manifold). Do not apply sealant to the long bolts.
27 Lightly oil the cylinder head bolt flat washers and install the flat washers and cylinder head bolts. **Note:** *Always use new cylinder head bolts.*
28 Tighten the attaching bolts in the sequence shown in Fig. 2.58 and in the torque steps listed in the Specifications.
29 When the cylinder head bolts have been tightened in the specified steps, it is not necessary to retighten the head bolts after extended engine operation. However, the bolts may be checked for tightness if desired.
30 The remaining installation steps are the reverse of those for removal. Make sure to use the proper coolant (see Chapter 3) when refilling the cooling system.

49 Spark plug thread service

Note: *This procedure is used to repair damaged threads in the V6s aluminum heads. A special kit, the Ford Tapersert Installation Kit 08-0001 or its equivalent is required for the procedure and the cylinder head with the damaged threads must be removed from the engine, as the procedure involves the cutting of new threads, a process which produces metal chips. Performing this procedure with the cylinder head on the engine will cause metal chips to fall into the cylinder, resulting in damage to the cylinder wall when the engine is started.*

1 Remove the damaged cylinder head (see Section 48).
2 Thoroughly clean the spark plug counterbore, seat and threads of all dirt and foreign matter.
3 Using the tap from the tapersert kit, start the tap into the spark plug hole, being careful to keep it properly aligned.
4 As the tap begins to cut new threads, apply aluminum cutting fluid to the tap.

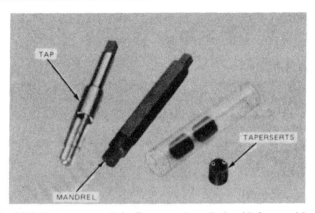

Fig. 2.59 Components of the Tapersert installation kit for repairing damaged threads in the V6 aluminum cylinder heads (Sec 49)

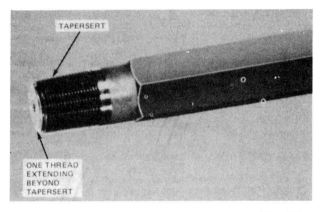

Fig. 2.60 Threading a Tapersert onto the mandrel (Sec 49)

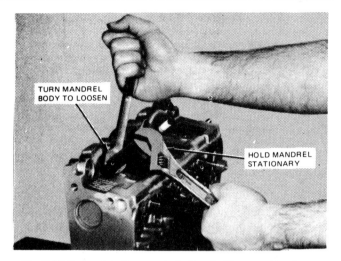

Fig. 2.61 Removing the mandrel after the Tapersert has been installed (Sec 49)

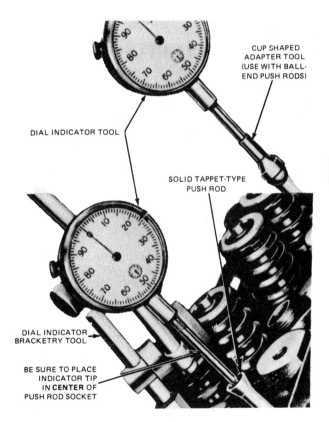

Fig. 2.62 Installing a dial indicator on a pushrod to check timing chain deflection (Sec 50)

5   Continue cutting threads and applying oil until the stop ring on the tap bottoms against the spark plug seat.
6   Remove the tap.
7   Remove all metal chips from the cylinder head, using compressed air if it is available.
8   Using the mandrel from the kit, coat the mandrel threads with cutting oil.
9   Taking one of the taperserts from the kit, thread the tapersert into the mandrel until one thread of the mandrel extends beyond the tapersert (see Fig. 2.60).
10 Thread the tapersert into the tappet spark plug hole using a torque wrench. Continue tightening the mandrel until the torque wrench indicates 45 ft-lbs.
11 To loosen the mandrel for removal, hold the mandrel stationary and turn the mandrel body approximately ½ turn, then remove the mandrel (see Fig. 2.61).
12 Install the cylinder head (see Section 48).

50 Timing chain deflection – checking

1   Remove the right rocker arm cover (refer to Section 47).
2   Loosen the no. 3 exhaust rocker arm and rotate it to one side. (The no. 3 cylinder is the rear cylinder on the right hand side.)
3   Install a dial indicator on the end of the pushrod (see Fig. 2.62).
4   Turn the crankshaft clockwise until the no. 1 piston is at TDC. The damper timing mark should point to TDC on the timing degree indicator (refer to Fig. 2.63). This will also take up the slack in the right side of the chain.
5   Zero the dial indicator.
6   Slowly turn the crankshaft counterclockwise until the slightest movement is seen on the dial indicator. Stop and observe the damper timing mark for the number of degrees of travel from TDC (refer to Fig. 2.64).
7   If the reading on the timing chain degree indicator exceeds 6°, replace the timing chain and sprockets (refer to Section 51).

51 Front cover assembly and timing chain – removal and installation

Removal
1   Disconnect the cable from the negative battery terminal.
2   Drain the cooling system.
3   Remove the air cleaner assembly and air intake duct.
4   Remove the fan shroud attaching screws.
5   Remove the fan/clutch assembly attaching bolts.
6   Remove the fan/clutch assembly and shroud.

2D

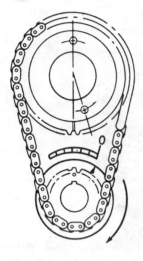
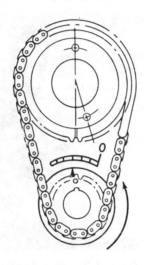

Fig. 2.63 Checking the timing chain deflection (note damper timing mark at TDC) (Sec 50)

Fig. 2.64 Measuring the number of degrees (from TDC) of timing chain deflection (Sec 50)

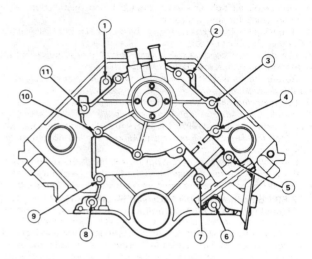

Fig. 2.65 Correct bolt tightening sequence for the front engine cover on the V6 engine (Sec 51)

7   Loosen the accessory drivebelt idler (see Chapter 3 if necessary).

8   Remove the drivebelt.

9   Unbolt and remove the water pump pulley.

10   If equipped with power steering, remove the pump mounting bracket attaching bolts.

11   Leaving the hoses connected, place the pump bracket assembly aside, making sure that it is in a position that prevents the fluid from leaking out.

12   If equipped with air conditioning, remove the compressor front support bracket, leaving the compressor in place. *Do not attempt to disconnect the air conditioning hoses, as personal injury and/or equipment damage may result.*

13   Disconnect the engine coolant bypass hose at the water pump.

14   Disconnect the heater hose at the water pump.

15   Disconnect the radiator upper hose at the thermostat housing.

16   Disconnect the coil wire from the distributor cap, then remove the cap with the spark plug wires attached.

17   Remove the distributor hold-down clamp and lift the distributor out of the front cover.

18   Raise the vehicle and place it securely on jackstands.

19   Remove the crankshaft damper using a suitable puller.

20   Remove the fuel pump crash shield, if so equipped.

21   Disconnect the fuel pump-to-carburetor fuel line at the fuel pump.

22   Remove the fuel pump attaching bolts, pull the pump out of the front cover and lay the pump aside with the flexible line attached.

23   Remove the oil filter.

24   Disconnect the radiator lower hose at the water pump.

25   Remove the oil pan (refer to Section 53). **Note:** *The front cover cannot be removed without lowering the oil pan.*

26   Remove the jackstands and lower the vehicle.

27   Remove the front cover attaching bolts (see Fig. 2.65 for bolt locations). It is not necessary to remove the water pump. **Note:** *Do not overlook the cover attaching bolt located behind the oil filter adapter. The front cover will break if pried upon and all attaching bolts have not been removed.*

28   Remove the ignition timing indicator from the front cover.

29   Remove the front cover and water pump as an assembly.

30   Remove the camshaft thrust button and spring from the end of the camshaft.

31   Remove the camshaft sprocket attaching bolts.

32   Remove the camshaft sprocket, crankshaft sprocket and timing chain. If the crankshaft sprocket is difficult to remove, pry the sprocket off the shaft using a pair of large screwdrivers positioned on the sides of the sprocket.

33   The front cover contains the oil pump and oil pump intermediate shaft. If a new front cover is being installed, remove the water pump, oil pump, oil filter adapter and the oil pump intermediate shaft from the old cover. Refer to Section 52 for procedures involving the oil pump assembly. Refer to Chapter 3 for procedures involving the water pump.

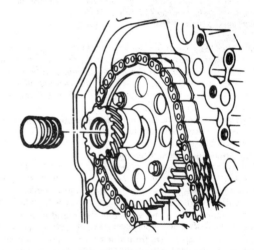

Fig. 2.66 Removing the camshaft thrust button and spring from the end of the camshaft in the V6 engine (Sec 51)

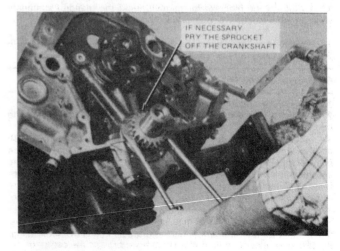

Fig. 2.67 Using two screwdrivers to pry the sprocket off the crankshaft of the V6 engine (Sec 51)

Installation

34 Lightly oil all bolt and stud threads before installation, except those specified for special sealant.

35 If reusing the front cover, replace the crankshaft front oil seal (refer to Chapter 2A, Section 43).

36 If a new front cover is being used, install the oil pump, oil filter adapter, oil pump intermediate shaft and the water pump.

37 Rotate the crankshaft as necessary to position piston no. 1 at TDC and the crankshaft keyway at the 12 o'clock position.

38 Lubricate the timing chain with clean engine oil.

39 Install the camshaft sprocket, crankshaft sprocket and timing chain, making sure the timing marks are exactly opposite each other.

40 Install the camshaft sprocket attaching bolts and tighten them to the specified torque.

41 Lubricate the camshaft thrust button with polyethylene grease and install the thrust button and spring in the front of the camshaft. **Note:** *The thrust button and spring must be bottomed in the camshaft seat. Make sure that the thrust button and spring do not fall out during the installation of the front cover.*

42 Lubricate the crankshaft front oil seal with clean engine oil.

43 Position a new cover gasket on the cylinder block and install the front cover/water pump assembly, using the dowels for proper alignment. Contact adhesive may be used to hold the gasket in position while the front cover is installed.

44 Attach the ignition timing indicator to the front cover.

45 Coat the front cover attaching bolts with pipe sealant and install the front cover, tightening the bolts to the specified torque.

46 Raise the vehicle and position it securely on jackstands.

47 Install the oil pan (refer to Section 53).

48 Connect the lower radiator hose and tighten the clamp securely.

49 Install the oil filter.

50 Turn the crankshaft clockwise 180° to position the fuel pump eccentric away from the fuel pump actuating arm. **Note:** *Failure to turn the crankshaft can result in the threads being stripped out of the front cover when the fuel pump attaching bolts are installed.*

51 Position a new gasket on the fuel pump and install the pump.

52 Connect the fuel line to the fuel pump.

53 Coat the crankshaft damper sealing surface with clean engine oil.

54 Position the crankshaft pulley key in the crankshaft keyway.

55 Using a suitable seal/damper tool (Ford tool T82L-6316-A or equivalent), install the crankshaft damper.

56 Install the damper washer and attaching bolt and tighten to the specified torque. **Note:** *This bolt may be used to push the damper onto the crankshaft if the proper installation tool is unavailable.*

57 Install the crankshaft pulley and tighten the attaching bolts to the specified torque.

58 Turn the crankshaft 180° counterclockwise to bring piston no. 1 back to TDC.

59 Remove the jackstands and lower the vehicle.

60 The remaining installation procedures are the reverse of those for removal. When installing the distributor, make sure the rotor is pointing at the no. 1 distributor cap tower (refer to Chapter 1).

61 Start the engine and check for coolant, oil or fuel leaks.

62 Check the ignition timing and idle speed and adjust as required (refer to Chapters 1 and 4, respectively).

52 Oil pump assembly – removal, inspection and installation

1 Remove the front cover assembly (refer to Section 51).

2 Remove the oil pump cover attaching bolts, the remove the cover.

3 Lift the pump gears out of the pocket in the front cover.

4 Refer to Chapter 2B, Section 24 for the oil pump inspection procedures.

5 To assemble the oil pump, lightly pack the gear pocket with petroleum jelly or heavy oil. **Note:** *Do not use chassis lubricants.*

6 Install the gears in the cover pocket, making sure that the petroleum jelly fills all the voids between the gears and the pocket. **Note:** *Failure to properly coat the oil pump gears may result in failure of the pump to prime when the engine is started, leading to severe engine damage.*

7 Position the cover gasket and install the pump cover.

8 Tighten the pump cover attaching bolts to the specified torque.

9 Using an electric drill, drill a small hole through the center of the relief valve plug.

10 Remove the plug with a sheet metal screw and slide hammer or

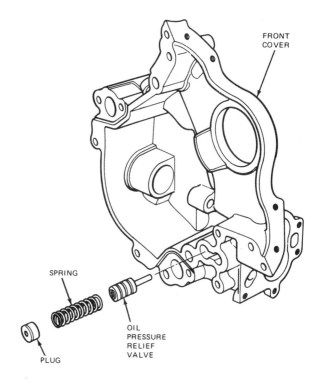

Fig. 2.68 Removing the spring and oil pressure relief valve from the bore of the V6 front engine cover (Sec 52)

by prying it out with an ice pick or similar tool.

11 Remove the spring and valve from the bore.

12 Thoroughly clean the valve bore and valve to remove any metal chips which may have entered the bore as a result of drilling the plug.

13 Refer to Chapter 2B, Section 24 for further relief valve inspection procedures.

14 Lubricate the relief valve with engine oil and install it in its bore.

15 Position the spring in the bore.

16 Tap a new plug into the bore using a soft-faced hammer. Make sure the plug is flush with the machined surface.

17 Remove the clip from the intermediate shaft and slide the shaft out of the cover (refer to Fig. 2.69).

2D

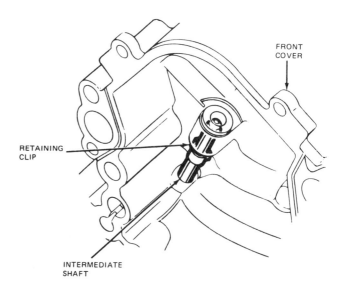

Fig. 2.69 Removing the oil pump drive intermediate shaft from the V6 front engine cover (Sec 52)

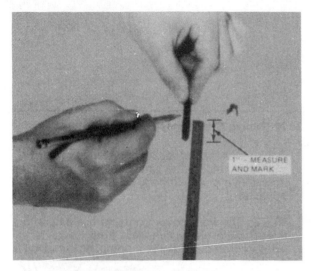

Fig. 2.70 Measuring and marking the intermediate shaft prior to installation in the V6 engine cover (Sec 52)

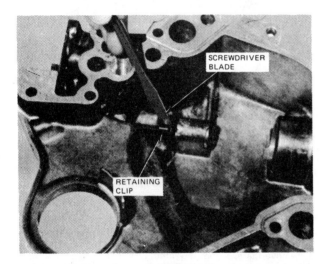

Fig. 2.71 Installing the retaining clip on the intermediate shaft (Sec 52)

18 Before installing the shaft, measure and mark the shaft one inch from the end (refer to Fig. 2.70).
19 Position the shaft in the cover, making sure that it is seated in the oil pump drive gear.
20 Install the clip on the shaft so the top of the clip is just below the mark made in Step 18. Use a screwdriver blade to snap the clip onto the shaft.
21 Install the front cover assembly (refer to Section 51).

53 Oil pan – removal, inspection and installation

Note: *This procedure is intended for removal of the oil pan with the engine in the vehicle. If the engine has been removed from the vehicle, perform only Steps 13 through 14 and 17 through 21.*
1 Disconnect the cable from the negative battery terminal.
2 Remove the air cleaner assembly.
3 Remove the bolts attaching the fan shroud to the radiator and position the shroud over the fan.
4 Remove the engine oil dipstick.
5 Raise the vehicle and place it securely on jackstands.
6 Remove the oil filter.
7 Disconnect the muffler inlet pipes from the exhaust manifolds.
8 Remove the clamp attaching the inlet pipe to the converter pipe

and remove the inlet pipe from the vehicle.
9 Disconnect the transmission shift linkage at the transmission (see Chapter 7, if necessary).
10 If so equipped, disconnect the transmission cooler lines at the radiator.
11 Remove the nuts attaching the engine supports to the chassis brackets (see Chapter 2A, if necessary).
12 Using a jack with a block of wood placed on top of the lifting pad, lift the engine and place wood blocks between the engine supports and the chassis brackets, then remove the jack.
13 Remove the oil pan attaching bolts and drop the oil pan. Unbolt the oil pickup and tube assembly and let them lay in the pan, then remove the pan from the vehicle. Remove the old gaskets and rear pan seal.
14 Clean the oil pan and sealing surfaces. Inspect the gasket sealing surfaces for damage and distortion due to overtightening of the bolts. Repair and straighten as required.
15 Trial fit the pan to the cylinder block. Make sure enough clearance exists to allow the pan to be installed without the sealant scraping off when the pan is positioned for final installation.
16 Lower the oil pan and let it rest on the frame crossmember.
17 Using a new gasket, install the oil pickup and tube assembly. Make sure that the support bracket engages the stud on the no. 2 main bearing cap attaching bolt.
18 Tighten the pickup and tube assembly attaching nuts and bolts to the specified torque.
19 Install a new rear pan seal in the seal groove in the rear main cap, working it into place with a small screwdriver.
20 Apply a $\frac{1}{8}$ in bead of RTV-type sealant to the seam where the front cover and cylinder block join, to each end of the rear seal where the rear main cap and cylinder block join, and along the oil pan rails on the cylinder block. Where the bead crosses the front cover, increase the bead width to $\frac{1}{4}$ in.
21 Position the oil pan on the bottom of the engine and attach it with the retaining bolts. Tighten the bolts to the specified torque.
22 Raise the engine and remove the wood blocks.
23 The remaining installation procedures are the reverse of those for removal.

54 Camshaft and lifters – removal, inspection and installation

Removal
Note: *If the engine is in the vehicle and it is equipped with air conditioning, the condenser must be removed. This requires discharging of the air conditioning system by an authorized air conditioning system technician. Under no circumstances should the home mechanic attempt to discharge the system or disconnect any of the air conditioning system lines while they are still pressurized, as this can cause serious personal injury as well as damage to the air conditioning system.*
1 Disconnect the cable from the negative battery terminal.
2 Drain the coolant into a suitable container.
3 Remove the radiator if the engine is in the vehicle (refer to Chapter 3).
4 If equipped with air conditioning, see note at the beginning of this Section.
5 Remove the grille if the engine is in the vehicle (see Chapter 12).
6 Remove the intake manifold (refer to Section 46).
7 Remove the rocker arm covers (refer to Section 47).
8 Loosen the rocker arm nuts and rotate the rocker arms to the side.
9 Mark the pushrods if they are to be reused and remove them from the engine.
10 Remove the valve lifters from the engine using a special tool designed for this purpose. Sometimes they can be removed with a magnet if there is no varnish build-up or wear on them. If they are stuck in their bores, you will have to obtain a special tool designed for grasping lifters internally and work them out.
11 Remove the timing cover, chain and gears (refer to Section 51).
12 Remove the oil pan (refer to Section 53).
13 Remove the camshaft from the front of the engine by slowly withdrawing it, being careful not to damage the bearings with the cam lobes.

Inspection
14 Visually inspect the hydraulic valve lifters for cupping on the

camshaft mating face and for signs of excessive wear, galling, or cracking.

15 The hydraulic valve lifters must be tested using special equipment. This procedure must be handled by a suitably equipped automotive machine shop.

16 If you suspect that a lifter is defective, replace it with a new one. It is not necessary to test a new lifter before installation.

17 Check the camshaft lobe lift on a special V-block cradle with a dial indicator. Again, this is a procedure which should be handled by a suitably equipped automotive machine shop.

18 Visually check the camshaft bearing surfaces for any signs of galling or excessive wear. If any of these conditions are present, or if there is a question about the camshaft (and you have no access to testing or measuring equipment), replace it with a new one.

Installation

19 Lubricate the cam lobes and bearing surfaces with heavy duty engine oil.

20 The remaining installation procedures are the reverse of those for removal.

55 Piston/connecting rod assemblies – removal

1   Remove the intake manifold (refer to Section 46).
2   Remove the cylinder heads (refer to Section 48).
3   Remove the oil pan (refer to Section 53).
4   Refer to Chapter 2A, Section 24 and perform Steps 2 through 5 to complete the removal procedure.

56 Crankshaft – removal

Note: *The crankshaft may be removed only after then engine has been removed from the vehicle.*

1   Mount the engine in a suitable workstand.
2   Disconnect the spark plug wires at the spark plugs if not previously done.
3   Remove the distributor cap and wires as an assembly.
4   Remove the spark plugs from the cylinder heads.
5   Remove the oil pan and oil pickup tube (refer to Section 53).
6   Remove the front cover and water pump as an assembly (refer to Section 51).
7   Remove the crankshaft sprocket, camshaft sprocket and timing chain (refer to Section 51).
8   Remove the flywheel and rear cover plate (refer to Chapter 2B, Section 14).
9   Refer to Chapter 2B, Section 25 and perform Steps 10 through 18 to complete the crankshaft removal procedures.

57 Crankshaft oil seals – replacement

Front seal

1   Disconnect the cable from the negative battery terminal.
2   Remove the fan shroud attaching screws.
3   Remove the fan/clutch assembly attaching bolts.
4   Remove the fan/clutch assembly and shroud.
5   Loosen the accessory drivebelt idler.
6   Raise the vehicle and place it securely on jackstands.
7   Disengage the accessory drivebelt and remove the crankshaft pulley.
8   Using a suitable puller, remove the crankshaft damper.
9   Remove the seal from the front cover using a suitably sized screwdriver. Be careful not to damage the front cover and crankshaft.
10 Inspect the front cover and crankshaft damper for nicks, burrs or other roughness which may cause the seal to fail. If defects are found, replace the damaged components with new ones.
11 Lubricate the new seal lip with engine oil and install the seal using a suitable seal/damper installing tool.
12 Lubricate the damper seal nose with engine oil and install the damper using a suitable seal/damper installation tool.
13 Install the damper attaching bolt and tighten it to the specified torque.
14 Position the crankshaft pulley and tighten the attaching bolts to

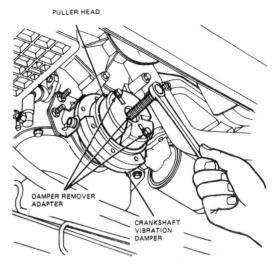

Fig. 2.72 Removing the crankshaft damper from the V6 engine (Sec 57)

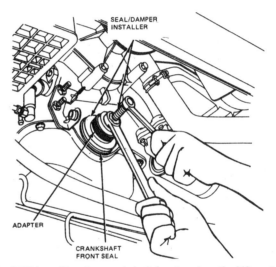

Fig. 2.73 Installing the crankshaft front seal on the V6 engine (Sec 57)

2D

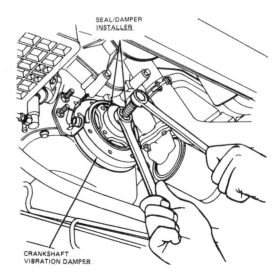

Fig. 2.74 Installing the crankshaft damper on the V6 engine (Sec 57)

the specified torque.

15 Position the accessory drivebelt over the crankshaft pulley.

16 Remove the jackstands and lower the vehicle.

17 The remaining installation procedures are the reverse of those for removal.

18 Adjust the drivebelt tension (refer to Chapter 3).

19 Start the engine and check for oil leaks.

Rear seal

20 The crankshaft rear seal can be replaced with the engine in the vehicle. To gain access to the rear seal, remove the oil pan (refer to Section 53). **Note:** *The oil pump does not have to be removed on this engine.*

21 Refer to Chapter 2C, Section 43 and perform Steps 9 through 21 to complete the procedure.

Chapter 3
Cooling, heating and air conditioning systems

Refer to Chapter 13 for Specifications and information on 1984 and later models

Contents

Specifications

Radiator type .... Vertical flow with integral side tanks

Water pump
Type .... Centrifugal, impeller type
Drivebelt tension .... See Chapter 1, Specifications

Thermostat
Type .... Wax pellet
Opening temperature
    Starts to open .... 170°F
    Fully open .... 210°F

Torque specifications   **Ft-lb**
Coolant outlet housing .... See appropriate engine Chapter
Fan-to-water pump .... 12 to 18
Shroud-to-radiator .... 5 to 8
Transmission oil line fitting-to-radiator .... 18 to 23
Transmission oil line nut-to-fitting on radiator .... 12 to 18

1 General information

Ford light duty pick-up trucks and Broncos produced during the years covered by this manual have a cooling system consisting of a horizontal flow radiator, a thermostat for temperature control and an impeller-type water pump driven by a belt from the crankshaft pulley.

The radiator cooling fan is mounted on the front of the water pump. Certain vehicles with extra heavy-duty cooling systems incorporate an automatic clutch which disengages the fan at high speeds or when the outside temperature is sufficient to maintain a low radiator temperature. On some models, a fan shroud is mounted to the rear face of the radiator to increase cooling efficiency.

The cooling system is pressurized by means of a spring-loaded radiator filler cap. Cooling efficiency is improved by raising the boiling point of the coolant through increased cooling system pressure. If the coolant temperature rises above the boiling point, the extra pressure in the system forces the radiator cap internal spring-loaded valve off its seat and exposes the overflow pipe or the coolant recovery bottle connecting tube to allow the displaced coolant a path of escape.

The cooling system functions as follows: cold water from the radiator circulates up the lower radiator hose to the water pump where it is pumped into the cylinder block and around the water passages to cool the engine. The coolant then travels up into the cylinder head(s), around the combustion areas of the cylinders and valve seats, absorbing heat before it finally passes out through the thermostat. When the engine is running at its correct temperature, the water flow from the cylinder head(s) diverges to flow through the intake manifold, vehicle interior heater (when activated) and the radiator.

When the engine is cool (below its normal operating temperature),

the thermostat valve is closed, thus preventing the coolant from flowing into the radiator and restricting the flow to the engine. The restriction in the flow of coolant enables the engine to quickly warm to its correct operating temperature.

The coolant temperature is monitored by a sender mounted in either the cylinder head or the intake manifold. The sender, together with the gauge on the instrument panel, gives a continuous indication of coolant temperature to the driver.

Normal maintenance consists of checking the level of fluid in the radiator at regular intervals, inspecting the hoses and connections for signs of leakage or material deterioration, and checking the cooling fan drivebelt tension and condition (refer to Chapter 1 for details).

The water pump is located on the front of the engine and is crankshaft-driven by means of an accessory belt.

The heating system utilizes heat produced by the engine to warm the interior of the vehicle, via the flow of coolant through hoses attached to the heater and engine block. The system is manually controlled through dash-mounted levers and switches inside the vehicle.

Air conditioning is an optional accessory, with all components contained in the engine compartment with the exception of the controls, which are also dash-mounted inside the vehicle. This system, like the water pump, is crankshaft-driven by means of an accessory belt.

2 Coolant – general information

1 It is recommended that the cooling system contain a coolant solution of water and ethylene glycol-based antifreeze which will give

protection down to at least −20°F at all times. This provides protection against corrosion and increases the coolant boiling point. When handling antifreeze, take care that it is not spilled on the vehicle paint, since it will invariably cause damage if not removed immediately.

2   It is very important that the antifreeze used in the 232 cu in V6 engine be of a type recommended for engines with aluminum components, as the cylinder heads on this engine are made of aluminum. Use of other types of antifreeze in these engines may lead to rapid deterioration of the aluminum components.

3   The cooling system should be drained, flushed and refilled at least twice a year. The use of coolant solutions for longer than the specified intervals can cause damage and encourage the formation of rust and scale due to the corrosion inhibitors gradually losing their efficiency.

4   Before adding antifreeze to the system, check all hose connections and check for signs of leakage around the thermostat and water pump.

5   The exact mixture of antifreeze-to-water which you should use depends upon the relative weather conditions. Consult the information provided by the antifreeze manufacturer on the container label. A good general guide is water and antifreeze mixed in a 50/50 ratio.

6   To prevent damage to the cooling system when ambient temperatures are below freezing, when adding water or antifreeze to the supply tank, always operate the engine at fast idle for 30 minutes before letting the vehicle stand with the engine off for prolonged periods. This will allow a uniform mixture throughout the cooling system and prevent damage by freezing, providing that sufficient antifreeze is used.

---

3   Thermostat – removal, inspection and installation

Removal

1   Drain the radiator so that the coolant level is below the thermostat.

In-line 6-cylinder engine

2   **Note:** *Refer to Fig. 3.1 to locate and identify components.* Remove the coolant outlet elbow attaching bolts, then pull the elbow away from the cylinder head sufficiently to provide access to the thermostat.

3   Remove the thermostat and gasket, noting the top and bottom to assure proper installation.

V6 and V8 engines

4   **Note:** *Refer to Fig. 3.2 to locate and identify components.* Disconnect the bypass hoses at the water pump and intake manifold.

5   Remove the bypass tube, then remove the water outlet housing attaching bolts.

6   Bend the radiator upper hose upward and remove the thermostat and gasket, taking note of the top and bottom to assure proper installation.

Inspection

7   Due to the minimal cost of a replacement thermostat, it is usually better to purchase a new unit rather than attempt a test. However, the following procedure can be used to detect a faulty thermostat.

8   Heat a pan of water over the kitchen stove until the temperature nears those listed at the front of this Chapter. A thermometer used in the making of candy can be used to monitor the temperature.

9   Using wire, suspend the thermostat into the hot water. The valve should open approximately $\frac{1}{4}$ inch at the specified temperature.

10   If the thermostat does not react to temperature variations as stated above, or if there are any visible defects (corrosion, cracks, etc.), the thermostat should be replaced with a new one.

Installation

In-line 6-cylinder engine

11   After cleaning the coolant outlet elbow and cylinder head gasket surfaces, coat a new gasket with water-resistant sealer and position the gasket on the cylinder head opening. **Note:** *The gasket must be positioned on the cylinder head before the thermostat is installed.*

12   The coolant elbow contains a locking recess into which the thermostat is turned and locked. Install the thermostat with the bridge section in the outlet elbow.

13   Turn the thermostat clockwise to lock it in position on the flats cast into the elbow.

14   Position the elbow against the cylinder head and tighten the attaching bolts to the specified torque (see the Torque specifications in Chapter 2 for your particular engine).

V6 and V8 engines

15   After cleaning the water outlet gasket surfaces, coat a new water outlet gasket with water-resistant sealer.

16   Position the gasket on the intake manifold opening.

17   Install the thermostat in the intake manifold with the copper element toward the engine and the thermostat flange positioned in the recess.

18   Position the water outlet housing against the intake manifold and install and tighten the attaching bolts to the specified torque (see the Torque specifications in Chapter 2 for your particular engine).

19   Install the water bypass line and tighten the hose connections.

All engines

20   Fill the cooling system with the proper amount and type of coolant.

21   Start and run the engine until it reaches normal operating temperature, then check the coolant level and look for leaks.

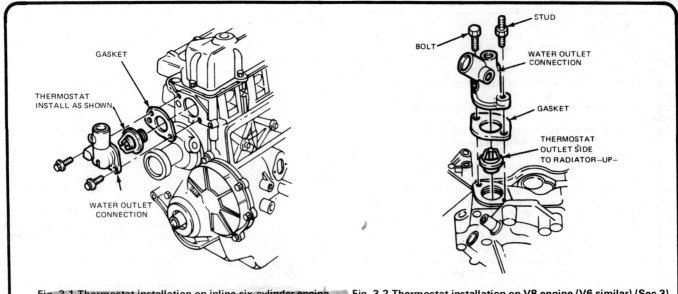

Fig. 3.1 Thermostat installation on inline six-cylinder engine (Sec 3)   Fig. 3.2 Thermostat installation on V8 engine (V6 similar) (Sec 3)

4 Radiator – removal, inspection and installation

Note: *Refer to Chapter 1 for preliminary checks of the cooling system. Refer to Figs. 3.4 and 3.5 to locate and identify components.*

Removal

1   Drain the radiator using the draincock located near the bottom of the radiator. See the information given in Chapter 1 pertaining to this.
2   Remove the lower radiator hose and clamp from the radiator. Be careful not to put excess pressure on the outlet tube, as it can easily break away.
3   Remove the upper radiator hose and clamp from the radiator top tank.
4   If equipped with an automatic transmission, remove the transmission cooler lines from the bottom of the radiator, taking care not to twist the lines or damage the fittings. It is best to use a fitting wrench for this particular job. Plug the ends of the disconnected lines to prevent leakage and stop dirt from entering the system.
5   Remove the bolts which attach the fan shroud to the radiator support. Place the shroud over the fan, allowing space for radiator removal. In some cases the fan itself will have to be removed. Once the fan is out of the way, the shroud and radiator can be lifted straight up together and out of the engine compartment.

Inspection

6   Inspect the radiator for signs of leakage, deterioration and/or rust. Inspect the cooling fins for distortion and/or damage. In most cases a reputable radiator repair shop should be consulted for repairs.

Installation

7   Installation is the reverse of removal. Take care to install the

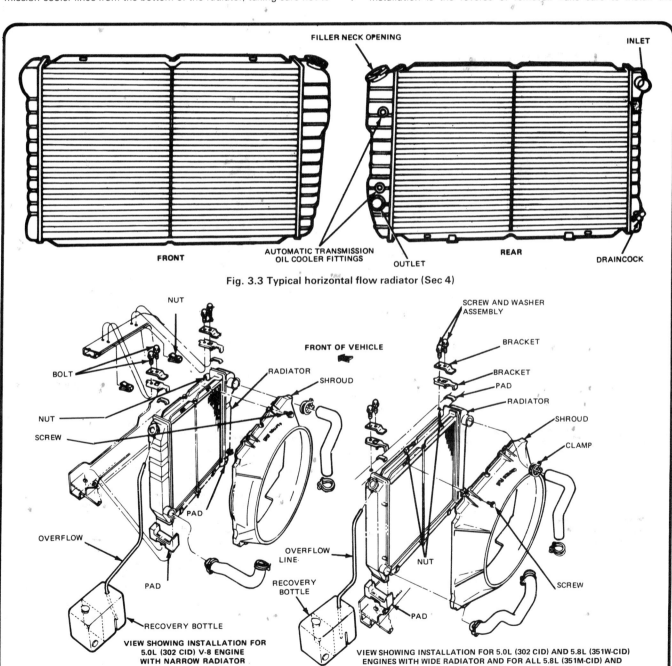

Fig. 3.3 Typical horizontal flow radiator (Sec 4)

Fig. 3.4 Radiator installation details for V8 engines (Sec 4)

3

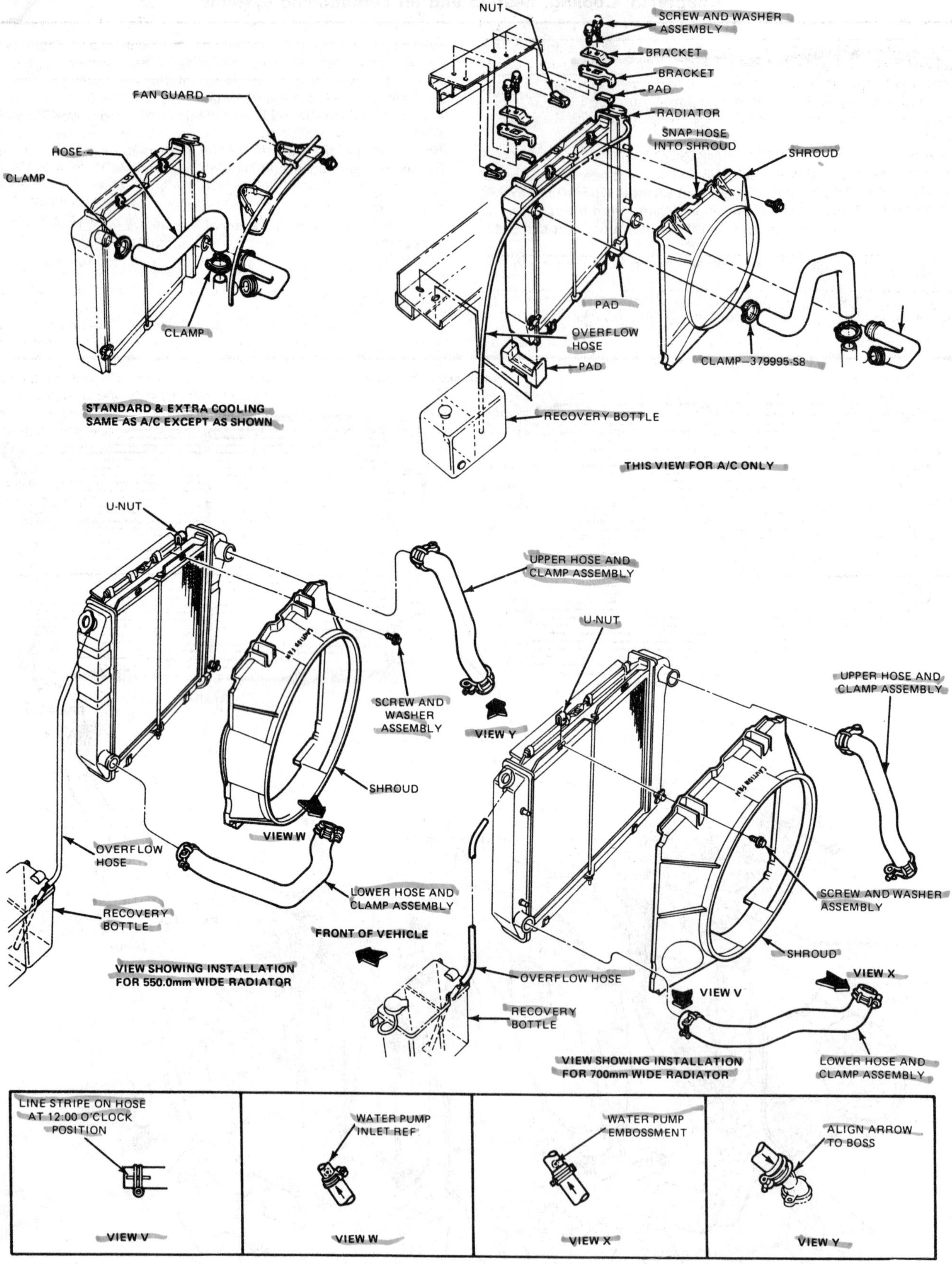

FAN GUARD

HOSE

CLAMP

CLAMP

**STANDARD & EXTRA COOLING
SAME AS A/C EXCEPT AS SHOWN**

NUT

SCREW AND WASHER
ASSEMBLY

BRACKET

BRACKET

PAD

RADIATOR

SNAP HOSE
INTO SHROUD

SHROUD

PAD

OVERFLOW
HOSE

PAD

CLAMP—379995-S8

RECOVERY BOTTLE

THIS VIEW FOR A/C ONLY

U-NUT

UPPER HOSE AND
CLAMP ASSEMBLY

U-NUT

UPPER HOSE AND
CLAMP ASSEMBLY

SCREW AND
WASHER
ASSEMBLY

VIEW Y

SHROUD

OVERFLOW
HOSE

RECOVERY
BOTTLE

VIEW W

LOWER HOSE AND
CLAMP ASSEMBLY

FRONT OF VEHICLE

**VIEW SHOWING INSTALLATION
FOR 550.0mm WIDE RADIATOR**

SCREW AND WASHER
ASSEMBLY

SHROUD

VIEW X

VIEW V

OVERFLOW HOSE

RECOVERY
BOTTLE

**VIEW SHOWING INSTALLATION
FOR 700mm WIDE RADIATOR**

LOWER HOSE AND
CLAMP ASSEMBLY

LINE STRIPE ON HOSE AT 12:00 O'CLOCK POSITION	WATER PUMP INLET REF	WATER PUMP EMBOSSMENT	ALIGN ARROW TO BOSS
VIEW V	VIEW W	VIEW X	VIEW Y

Fig. 3.5 Radiator installation details for inline six-cylinder and V6 engines (Sec 4)

radiator into the vehicle with caution as the cooling fins along with the radiator itself are fragile and can be damaged easily by mishandling or contact with the fan or radiator support. Make sure that the radiator is mounted securely with the proper retaining bolts and that all hoses and clamps are in good condition before you connect them to the radiator.

8 After remounting all components related to the radiator, fill it with the proper type and amount of coolant.

9 Start the engine and allow it to reach normal operating temperature, then check for leaks.

5 Water pump – checking

1 A water pump that is in need of replacement will usually give indications through noise from the bearing and/or leakage.

2 Visually check the water pump for leakage. Pay special attention to the area around the front pump seal at the outlet of the driveshaft and at the drain hole.

3 The front bearing in the water pump can be checked for roughness or excessive looseness by first removing the drivebelt and grasping the fan by hand to check for movement. Attempt to move the fan up and down as well as circularly to test for a loose bearing.

4 Visually check the sealing surfaces where the water pump mates to the front cover (or to the cylinder block on inline 6-cylinder engines) for signs of leakage.

5 If any of the above indications are present, the water pump will have to be removed for further checking and/or replacement.

6 Water pump – removal and installation

1 With the engine cold, drain the cooling system.

2 On V6-equipped vehicles, remove the air cleaner assembly and air intake duct.

3 Remove the fan shroud retaining bolts.

4 Remove the fan/clutch retaining bolts from the nose of the water pump and remove the shroud, fan/clutch and spacer (if so equipped).

5 On V6-equipped vehicles, loosen the accessory drivebelt idler and remove the drivebelt and water pump pulley. **Note:** *In the Steps which follow, further references to drivebelt removal should be ignored if your vehicle is V6-equipped.*

6 If equipped, loosen the power steering pump attaching bolt(s). Loosen the power steering pump drivebelt by releasing the adjustment bolt and allowing the power steering pump to move toward the engine. If the power steering pump bracket is retained at the water pump, the power steering pump should be completely removed and laid to one side to facilitate removal of the bracket.

7 If equipped with air conditioning, **do not** disconnect any of the hoses or lines. The following procedures can be performed by moving, not disconnecting, the a/c compressor. Loosen the air conditioning compressor top bracket retaining bolts. Remove the bracket on engines that have it secured to the pump. Remove the air conditioner idler arm and assembly.

8 Remove the air compressor and power steering pump drivebelt.

9 If equipped, remove the air pump pulley hub bolts and remove the bolt and pulley. Remove the air pump pivot bolt, bypass hose and air pump.

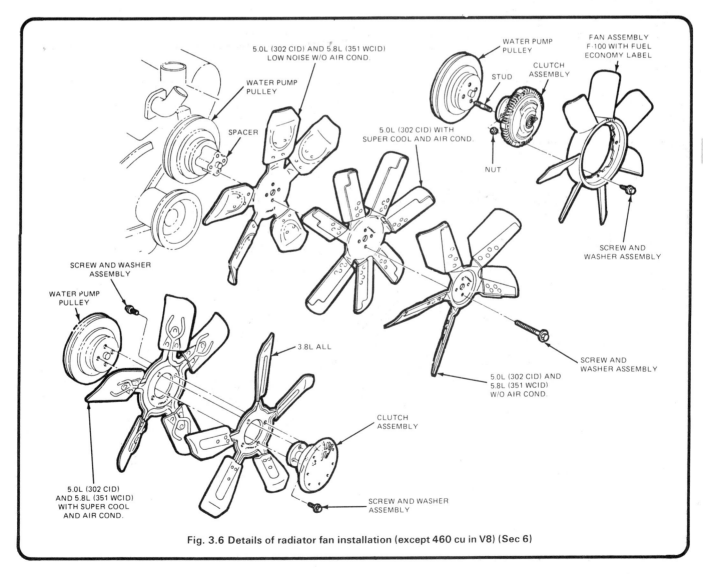

Fig. 3.6 Details of radiator fan installation (except 460 cu in V8) (Sec 6)

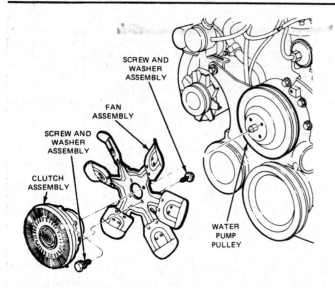

Fig. 3.7 Details of radiator fan installation for 460 cu in V8 (Sec 6)

10 Loosen the alternator pivot bolt.
11 Remove the retaining bolt and spacer for the alternator.
12 Remove the adjustment arm bolt, pivot bolt and alternator drivebelt.
13 Remove the alternator bracket if it is retained at the water pump.
14 Disconnect the lower radiator hose from the water pump inlet.
15 Disconnect the heater hose from the water pump.
16 Disconnect the bypass hose from the water pump.
17 Remove the water pump retaining bolts and remove the water pump from the cylinder front cover or the engine block (depending on engine type). Take note of the installed positions of the various-sized bolts.

18 Remove the separator plate from the water pump (460 engine only).
19 Remove the gaskets from the mating faces of the water pump and from the cylinder front cover or cylinder block.
20 Before installation, remove and clean all gasket material from the water pump, cylinder front cover, separator plate mating surfaces and/or cylinder block.
21 Position new gaskets onto the water pump and coat them on both sides with water resistant sealer.
22 Carefully install the water pump onto the cylinder front cover (or cylinder block).
23 Install the retaining bolts finger-tight and make sure that all gaskets are in place and that the hoses line up in the correct position. It may be necessary to transfer some hose ports and/or fittings from the old pump if you are replacing it with a new pump.
24 Tighten the retaining bolts to the proper torque (see the Torque Specifications in Chapter 2 for your particular engine).
25 Connect the radiator lower hose and clamp.
26 Connect the heater return hose and clamp.
27 Connect the bypass hose to the water pump.
28 If equipped, install the top air conditioning compressor bracket and idler pulley assembly.
29 Attach the remaining components to the water pump and engine in the reverse order of removal.
30 Adjust all of the belts for the alternator, air pump, power steering, air conditioning compressor and other drive accessories (if equipped).
31 Fill the cooling system with the proper coolant mixture.
32 Start the engine and make sure there are no leaks. Check the level frequently during the first few weeks of operation to ensure there are no leaks and that the level in the system is stable.

7 Water temperature sender – checking and replacement

Checking

1 The water temperature indicating system consists of a sending unit which is screwed into the cylinder head or manifold and a corresponding temperature gauge mounted in the instrument panel. When the coolant temperature of the engine is low the resistance of

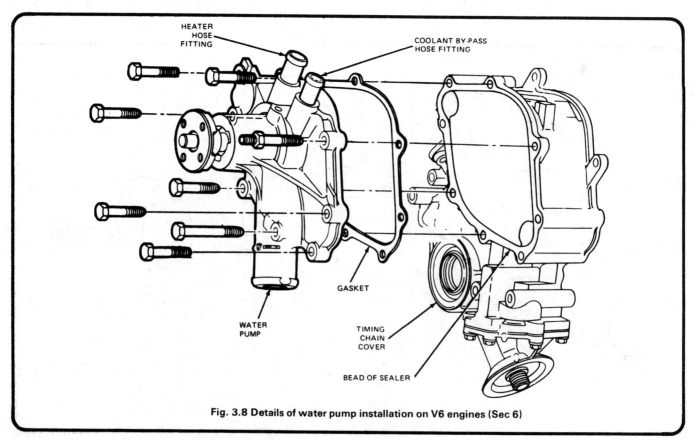

Fig. 3.8 Details of water pump installation on V6 engines (Sec 6)

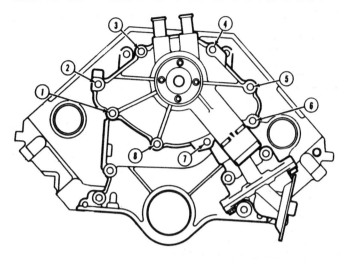

Fig. 3.9 Water pump bolt tightening sequence for V6 engines
(Sec 6)

6   Connect the other test lead to an engine ground.
7   With the ignition switch set to the On or Accessory position, a
flashing light or fluctuating voltage should indicate that the instrument
voltage regulator is operating and the gauge circuit is not grounded.
8   If the light stays on or the voltage reading is steady, the instrument
voltage regulator is bad. If no voltage is indicated by the voltmeter or
test light, check for an open circuit in the system.
9   If all of the above readings check out correctly yet the gauge does
not work properly, the gauge sender needs replacement.

Replacement
10   Disconnect the cable from the negative battery terminal.
11   Disconnect the temperature sending unit wire at the sending unit.
12   Remove the temperature sending unit from the cylinder head by
using the proper socket.
13   Prepare the new temperature sending unit for installation by
applying electrically-conductive thread sealing tape or sealer such as
spray-on copper sealer to the threads.
14   Install the temperature sending unit into the cylinder head or
intake manifold.
15   Connect the wire to the temperature gauge sending unit.
16   Connect the cable at the negative battery terminal.
17   Start the engine and check that the temperature sending unit is
operating correctly.

the sending unit is high and thus sends a restrictive flow of current to
the gauge. This causes the pointer to move only a short distance. As
the temperature of the engine increases, the resistance at the sending
unit decreases and thus causes an increased flow of current and
movement at the gauge. **Note**: *Do not apply 12 volt current directly
to the temperature sender terminal at any time, as the voltage will
damage the unit.*
2   Start the engine and allow it to run with a thermometer placed in
the radiator neck until a minimum temperature of 180°F is read.
3   The gauge in the instrument panel should indicate within the
normal band of the reading scale.
4   If the gauge does not indicate correctly, disconnect the gauge lead
from the terminal at the sender unit.
5   Connect the lead of a 12 volt test light or the positive lead of a
voltmeter to the gauge lead that was disconnected.

8   Heater blower assembly – removal and installation

Note: *If the heater blower motor fails to operate, it should be checked
by an automotive electrical technician. If removal of the heater blower
and/or wheel is indicated, this operation may be performed by the
home mechanic by referring to and performing the steps which follow.*
1   Disconnect the cable from the negative battery terminal.
2   Working in the engine compartment, disconnect the wires or
wiring harness connector from the rear of the blower motor.
3   Remove the screws retaining the blower motor and wheel to the
heater case.
4   Remove the blower motor and wheel from the heater case.
5   Remove the blower wheel hub clamp spring and tab lock washer
from the motor shaft, then pull the blower wheel from the motor shaft.
6   Installation is the reverse of the removal procedures.

3

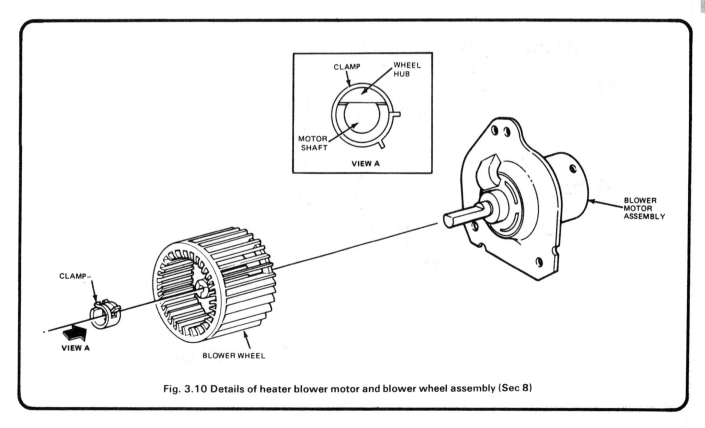

Fig. 3.10 Details of heater blower motor and blower wheel assembly (Sec 8)

9   Heater case and core – removal and installation

Removal
1   Disconnect the cable from the negative battery terminal.

2   Disconnect the temperature control cable from the temperature blend door and the mounting bracket from the top of the heater case.
3   Disconnect the wires from the blower motor resistor and the blower motor.
4   Drain the coolant from the radiator into a suitable container.

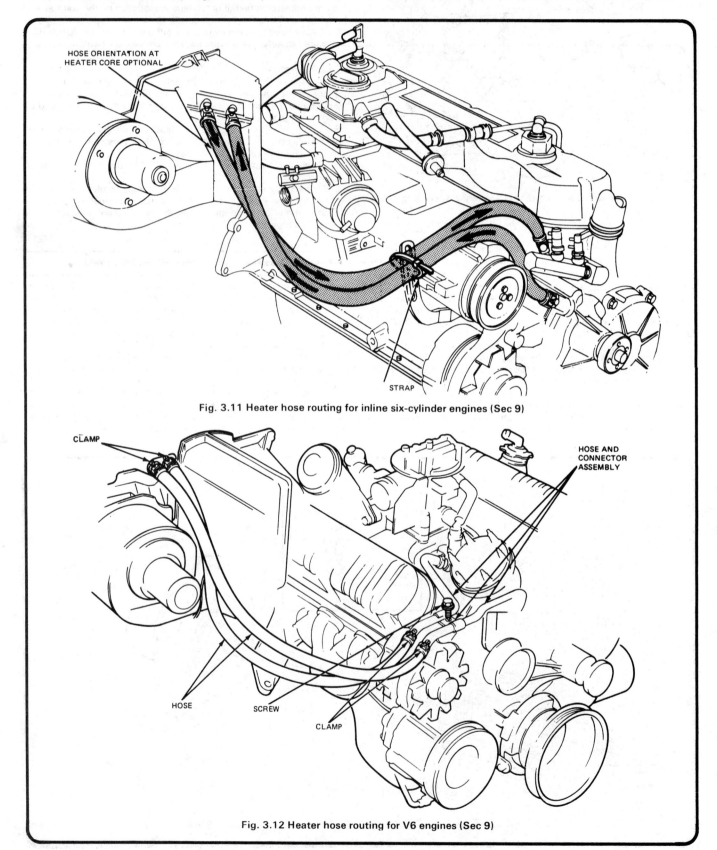

Fig. 3.11 Heater hose routing for inline six-cylinder engines (Sec 9)

Fig. 3.12 Heater hose routing for V6 engines (Sec 9)

5   Disconnect the heater hoses from the heater core on the engine side of the firewall.
6   Working in the passenger compartment, remove the nuts retaining the left end of the heater case and the right end of the plenum to the dash panel.
7   Working in the engine compartment, remove the screw retaining the top center of the heater case to the dash panel.

8   Remove the screws retaining the right end of the heater case to the dash panel and remove the heater case assembly from the vehicle.
9   Remove the screws, nuts and bolts retaining the heater housing plate to the heater case, then remove the heater housing plate.
10 If so equipped, remove the screws attaching the heater core frame to the heater case and remove the frame.
11 Remove the heater core and seal from the heater case.

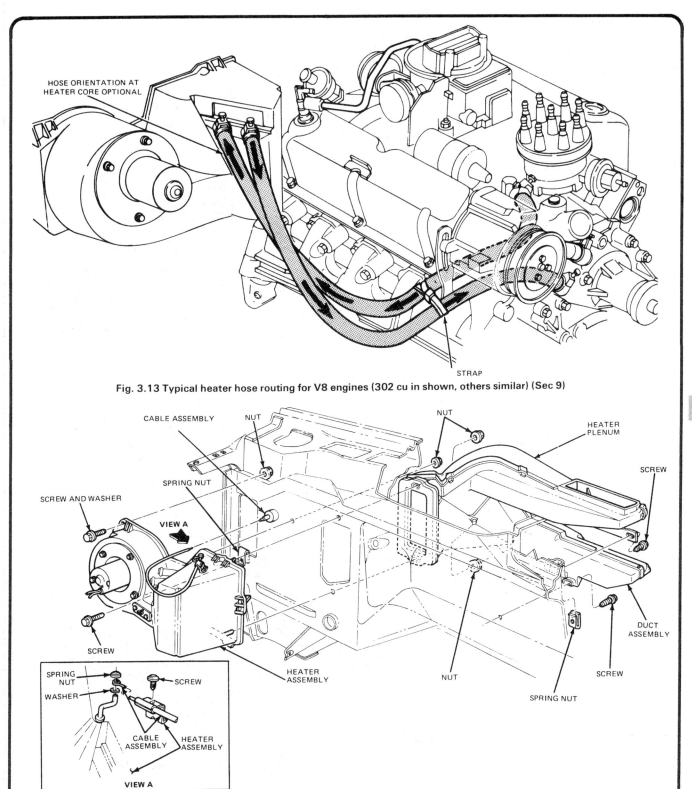

Fig. 3.13 Typical heater hose routing for V8 engines (302 cu in shown, others similar) (Sec 9)

Fig. 3.14 Heater case and plenum assemblies – exploded view (Sec 9)

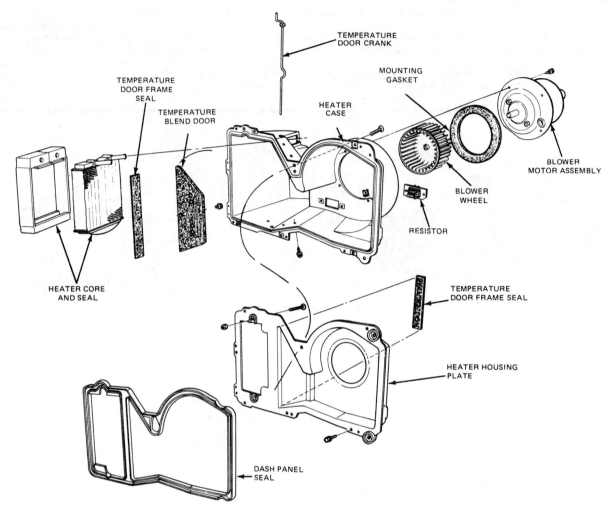

Fig. 3.15 Details of heater case assembly (Sec 9)

Installation

12 Position the heater core and seal in the heater case.
13 If so equipped, install the heater core frame to the heater case.
14 Position the heater housing plate on the heater case and install the retaining screws, nuts and bolts.
15 Position the heater case in the dash panel and install all retaining screws.
16 Working in the passenger compartment, install the nuts retaining the heater case and the right end of the plenum to the dash panel.
17 Connect the heater hoses to the heater core and tighten the clamps.
18 Connect the wires to the blower motor and blower motor resistor.
19 Slide the self-adjusting clip on the temperature control cable to a position approximately one inch from the cable end loop.
20 Snap the temperature control cable onto the cable mounting bracket of the heater case, then position the self-adjusting clip on the temperature blend door crank arm.
21 Adjust the temperature control cable (refer to Section 11).
22 Fill the radiator with the proper type and amount of coolant.
23 Attach the cable to the negative battery terminal.
24 Start the engine and check for leaks.

10 Heater control assembly – removal and installation

Note: *Refer to Figs. 3.18 and 3.19 to locate pertinent components.*

Removal

1 Disconnect the cable from the negative battery terminal.
2 If so equipped, pull the control knobs off the radio shafts.

3 Remove the screws retaining the top of the instrument panel center finish panel to the instrument panel pad and remove the finish panel.
4 Remove the knobs from the control assembly by placing a small screwdriver between the knob and the control assembly face plate. While applying pressure to the spring retainer behind the knob, pull the knob off. Repeat for each knob.
5 Remove the ashtray and the ashtray bracket.
6 Remove the four instrument panel-to-control assembly retaining screws.
7 Disconnect the wiring harness connectors from the blower switch, the panel illumination light and the auxiliary fuel tank switch or rear window switch (if so equipped).
8 On 1980 through 1982 vehicles, remove the screw retaining each control cable (function and temperature) to the control assembly.
9 On 1983 vehicles, remove the function and temperature control cables from the control assembly by disengaging the cable end retainer tab with a screwdriver while pulling on the cable (refer to Fig. 3.20).
10 Remove the spring nut retaining each control cable pigtail to the control lever arms, then remove the control assembly.

Installation

11 If a new control assembly is being installed, transfer the panel illumination light socket and bulb, the blower switch and the rear window switch or auxiliary fuel tank switch (if so equipped) to the new control panel.
12 Install the control cables to the control lever arms (open coil of each pigtail away from the control lever) and install new spring nuts.
Note: *The cable with the black flag connects to the temperature*

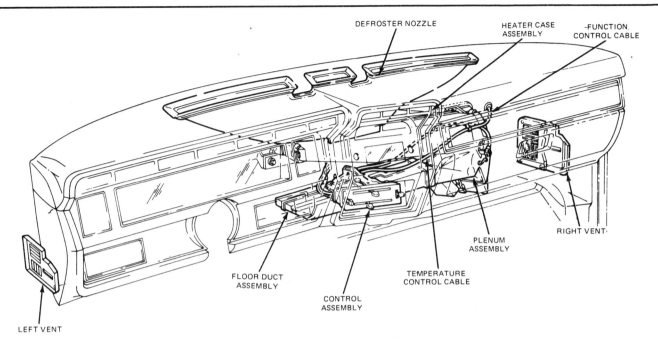

Fig. 3.16 Details of heater system installation (Sec 10)

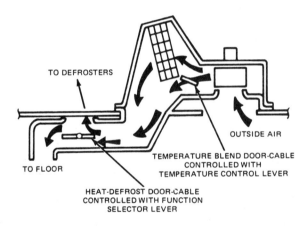

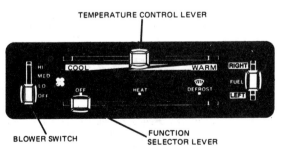

Fig. 3.17 Air flow patterns in typical heater system (top) and details of heater control panel (bottom) (Sec 10)

(upper) lever and the cable with the white flag connects to the function (lower) lever.

13 The remaining installation procedures are the reverse of those for removal.

11 Heater function and temperature control cables – adjustment

1980 and 1981

1 The function and temperature control cables are self-adjusting with the movement of the respective control levers to the right ends of the slots (Warm and Defrost). To prevent kinking of the control cable wires, a pre-set adjustment should be made before attempting to perform the self-adjustment procedure. The pre-set adjustment may be made either with the cables installed in the vehicle or before installation of the cables.

Before installation

2 Insert the blade of a small screwdriver in the end loop of the respective function or temperature cable (refer to Fig. 3.21).

3 Grip the self-adjusting clip with pliers and slide it down the control cable wire until it is approximately one inch away from the end loop.

4 Repeat Steps 2 and 3 for the other cable.

5 Install the cable assembly (refer to Section 9).

6 Move the control levers to the right ends of the slots (function to Defrost, temperature to Warm) to position the self-adjusting clips.

7 Check the system for proper control operation.

After installation

8 Move the control levers to the left ends of the control assembly slots (function to Off, temperature to Cool).

9 Working on one control at a time, hold the crank arm firmly in position, then insert the blade of a small screwdriver into the wire loop (refer to Fig. 3.21) and pull the cable wire through the self-adjusting clip until a space of approximately one inch exists between the clip and the wire end loop.

10 Move the control levers to the right ends of the slots to position the self-adjusting clips.

11 Check the system for proper control operation.

1982 and 1983

Function cable

12 Refer to and perform the appropriate procedures in Steps 2 through 11.

Heater temperature cable

13 The temperature control cable does not normally require adjustment; however, proper cable operation may be checked as follows.

14 Move the temperature control lever all the way to the left and then all the way to the right. When released, the lever should bounce back slightly from both extremes of travel, indicating that the blend door is

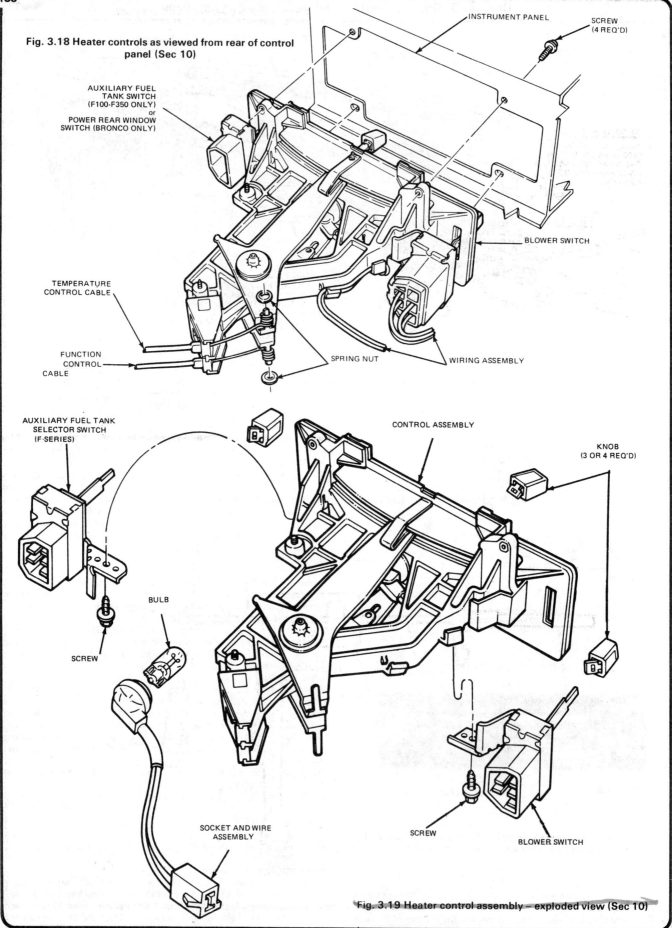

Fig. 3.18 Heater controls as viewed from rear of control panel (Sec 10)

INSTRUMENT PANEL

SCREW (4 REQ'D)

AUXILIARY FUEL TANK SWITCH (F100-F350 ONLY) or POWER REAR WINDOW SWITCH (BRONCO ONLY)

BLOWER SWITCH

TEMPERATURE CONTROL CABLE

FUNCTION CONTROL CABLE

SPRING NUT

WIRING ASSEMBLY

AUXILIARY FUEL TANK SELECTOR SWITCH (F-SERIES)

CONTROL ASSEMBLY

KNOB (3 OR 4 REQ'D)

BULB

SCREW

SCREW

SOCKET AND WIRE ASSEMBLY

BLOWER SWITCH

Fig. 3.19 Heater control assembly – exploded view (Sec 10)

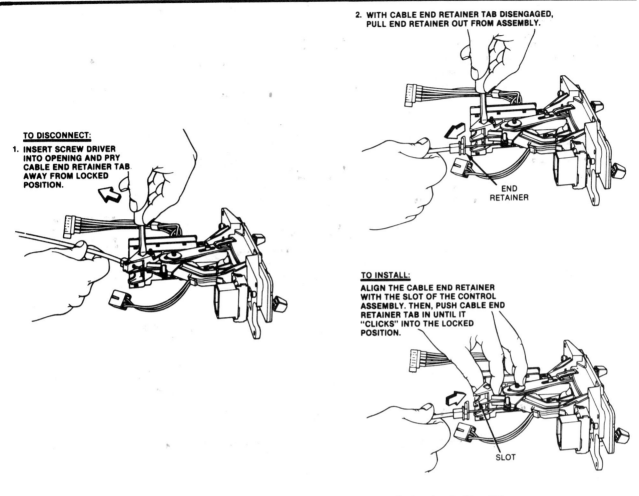

TO DISCONNECT:

1. INSERT SCREW DRIVER INTO OPENING AND PRY CABLE END RETAINER TAB AWAY FROM LOCKED POSITION.

2. WITH CABLE END RETAINER TAB DISENGAGED, PULL END RETAINER OUT FROM ASSEMBLY.

END RETAINER

TO INSTALL:

ALIGN THE CABLE END RETAINER WITH THE SLOT OF THE CONTROL ASSEMBLY. THEN, PUSH CABLE END RETAINER TAB IN UNTIL IT "CLICKS" INTO THE LOCKED POSITION.

SLOT

Fig. 3.20 Heater control cable end removal and installation details (Sec 10)

3

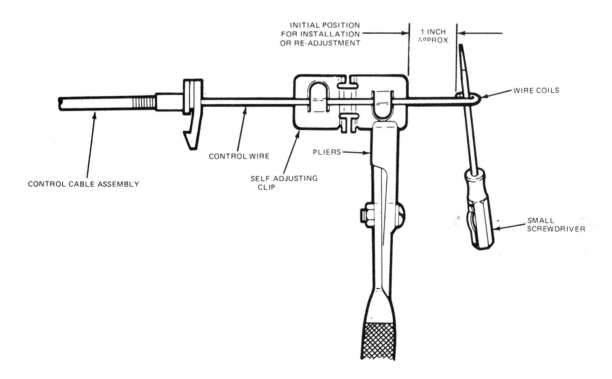

INITIAL POSITION FOR INSTALLATION OR RE-ADJUSTMENT

1 INCH APPROX.

WIRE COILS

CONTROL WIRE

PLIERS

SELF ADJUSTING CLIP

CONTROL CABLE ASSEMBLY

SMALL SCREWDRIVER

Fig. 3.21 Positioning of function and temperature control cable self-adjusting clips on 1980 and 1981 vehicles (Sec 11)

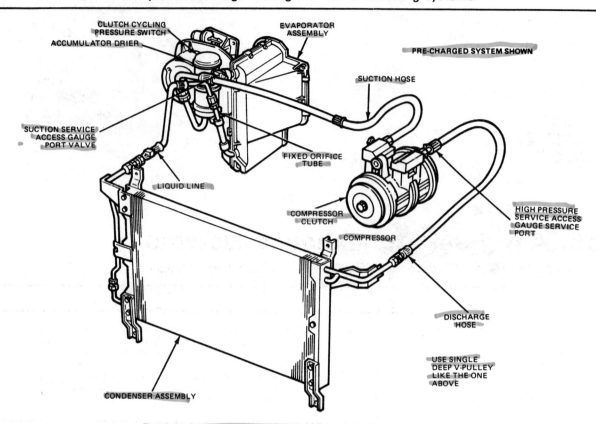

CLUTCH CYCLING
PRESSURE SWITCH

ACCUMULATOR DRIER

EVAPORATOR
ASSEMBLY

PRE-CHARGED SYSTEM SHOWN

SUCTION HOSE

SUCTION SERVICE
ACCESS GAUGE
PORT VALVE

LIQUID LINE

FIXED ORIFICE
TUBE

COMPRESSOR
CLUTCH

COMPRESSOR

HIGH PRESSURE
SERVICE ACCESS
GAUGE SERVICE
PORT

DISCHARGE
HOSE

USE SINGLE
DEEP V-PULLEY
LIKE THE ONE
ABOVE

CONDENSER ASSEMBLY

Fig. 3.22 Basic air conditioning system component layout (Sec 12)

sealing properly.

15 If the temperature control lever moves to either end of the slot without bouncing back, maximum or minimum heat cannot be obtained and the control cable should be adjusted, following Steps 16 through 18 for 1982 vehicles, or Steps 16, 17 and 19 for 1983 vehicles.

16 Remove the screw attaching the cable to the heater case assembly in the engine compartment.

17 Move the instrument panel temperature control lever all the way to the left.

18 On 1982 vehicles, move the heater door crank and cable coil all the way toward the rear of the vehicle, making sure not to move or push on the cable housing or slotted flag while doing this, then tighten the cable mounting screw in the engine compartment.

19 On 1983 vehicles, two drill dimples can be seen on the cable mounting flange. If maximum heat cannot be obtained, drill an 11/64 in hole in the dimple closest to the heater case crank. If minimum heat cannot be obtained, drill the hole in the dimple farthest from the heater case. Install the cable using the newly drilled hole and tighten the cable mounting screw in the engine compartment.

12 Air conditioning system — servicing

Caution: *Before disconnecting any lines or attempting to remove any air conditioning system components, have the system refrigerant evacuated by an air conditioning technician. Do not attempt to do this yourself; the refrigerant used in the system can cause serious injuries and respiratory irritation.*

1 Because of the special tools, equipment and skills required to service air conditioning systems, and the differences between the various systems that may be installed on these vehicles, air conditioner servicing cannot be covered in this manual.

2 Component removal, however, can usually be accomplished without special tools and equipment. The home mechanic may realize a substantial savings in repair costs if he removes components himself, takes them to a professional for repair, and/or replaces them with new ones (see **Caution** above).

3 Problems in the air conditioning system should be diagnosed, and the system refrigerant evacuated by an air conditioning technician before component removal/replacement is attempted.

4 Once the new or reconditioned component has been installed, the system should then be charged and checked by an air conditioning technician.

5 Before indiscriminately removing air conditioning system components, get more than one estimate of repair costs from reputable air conditioning service centers. You may find it to be cheaper and less trouble to let the entire operation be performed by someone else.

Chapter 4 Fuel and exhaust systems

Refer to Chapter 13 for Specifications and information on 1984 and later models

Contents

Specifications

Fuel pump

Type	Mechanical, driven from camshaft
Pressure	
All except in-line six-cylinder engine	6.0 to 8.0 psi
In-line six-cylinder engine	5.0 to 7.0 psi
Volume (at idle rpm)	1 pint in 20 seconds

Torque specifications

	Ft-lb
Fuel system	
Fuel pump retaining bolts	See appropriate Part, Chapter 2
Carburetor retaining nuts	See appropriate Part, Chapter 2
Fuel filter-to-carburetor	See appropriate Part, Chapter 2
Exhaust system	
Inlet pipe-to-exhaust manifold	25 to 38
U-bolt – Managed Thermactor Air (MTA)	5 to 8
U-bolt – catalytic converter-to-outlet pipe, muffler or	
extension pipe	35 to 45
U-bolt – inlet pipe-to-muffler without catalytic converter	
(Bronco and F350 cab chassis with inline 300 cu in six-cylinder	
engine)	35 to 45
Bracket and insulator-to-frame	17 to 24
Bracket or insulator-to-pipe or muffler	17 to 24
General	
$\frac{5}{16}$ in diameter bolt or nut	12 to 17
$\frac{3}{8}$ in diameter bolt or nut	31 to 42
$\frac{7}{16}$ in diameter bolt or nut	50 to 70
$\frac{1}{2}$ in diameter bolt or nut	75 to 105

1 General information

The fuel system on all models consists of a fuel tank (or tanks) mounted in a variety of locations on the chassis, a mechanically-operated fuel pump and a carburetor, equipped with an air cleaner for filtering purposes. A combination of metal and rubber fuel hoses are used to connect these three components and, in the case of some vehicles which have auxiliary tanks, a fuel flow control valve, which is located between the tanks and the fuel pump in the system.

The carburetor is a single, dual or four-venturi, downdraft type, depending on the engine displacement and year of production.

The fuel system (especially the carburetor) is heavily interrelated with the emissions control system on all vehicles produced for sale in the United States. Certain modifying components of the emissions control system are described in Chapter 6.

2 Carburetor – servicing and overhaul

1 A thorough road test and check of carburetor adjustments should

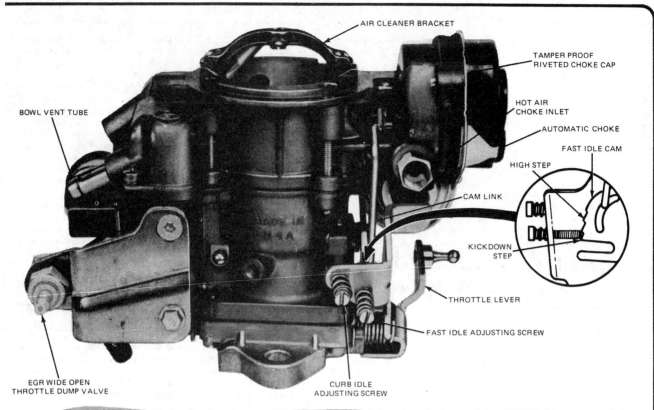

AIR CLEANER BRACKET

TAMPER PROOF RIVETED CHOKE CAP

HOT AIR CHOKE INLET

AUTOMATIC CHOKE

FAST IDLE CAM

HIGH STEP

CAM LINK

KICKDOWN STEP

BOWL VENT TUBE

THROTTLE LEVER

FAST IDLE ADJUSTING SCREW

EGR WIDE OPEN THROTTLE DUMP VALVE

CURB IDLE ADJUSTING SCREW

Fig. 4.1 YFA 1-V non-feedback carburetor, as used on various in-line six-cylinder models – left side (Sec 2)

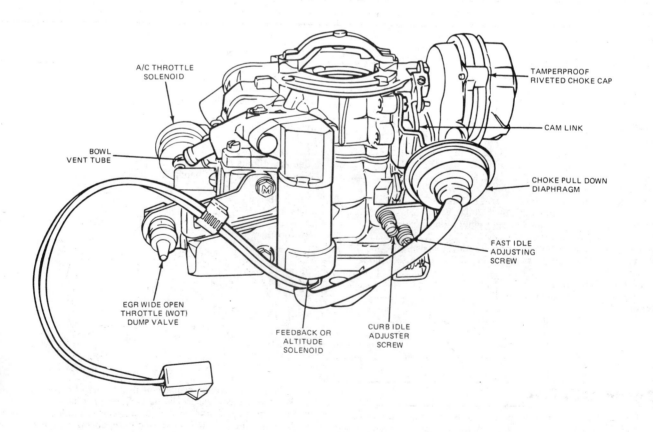

A/C THROTTLE SOLENOID

TAMPERPROOF RIVETED CHOKE CAP

CAM LINK

BOWL VENT TUBE

CHOKE PULL DOWN DIAPHRAGM

FAST IDLE ADJUSTING SCREW

EGR WIDE OPEN THROTTLE (WOT) DUMP VALVE

FEEDBACK OR ALTITUDE SOLENOID

CURB IDLE ADJUSTER SCREW

Fig. 4.2 YFA 1-V feedback model carburetor, as used on various in-line six-cylinder models – left side (Sec 2)

be done before any major carburetor service. Specifications for some adjustments are listed on the Vehicle *Emissions Control Information label* found in the engine compartment.

2   Some performance complaints directed at the carburetor are actually a result of loose, misadjusted or malfunctioning engine or electrical components. Others develop when vacuum hoses leak, are disconnected or are incorrectly routed. The proper approach to analyzing carburetor problems should include a routine check as follows.

   a) Inspect all vacuum hoses and actuators for leaks and proper installation (see Chapter 6, *Emissions control systems).*

   b) Tighten the intake manifold nuts and carburetor mounting nuts evenly and securely.

   c) Perform a cylinder compression test.

   d) Clean or replace the spark plugs as necessary.

   e) Test the resistance of the spark plug wires.

   f) Inspect the ignition primary wires and check the vacuum advance operation. Replace any defective parts.

   g) Check the ignition timing according to the instructions listed on the *Emissions Control Information label.*

   h) Set the carburetor idle mixture.

   i) Check the fuel pump pressure as described in Section 7.

   j) Inspect the heat control valve in the air cleaner for proper operation.

   k) Remove the carburetor air filter element and blow out any dirt with compressed air. If the filter is extremely dirty, replace it with a new one.

   l) Inspect the crankcase ventilation system.

3   Carburetor problems usually show up as flooding, hard starting, stalling, severe backfiring, poor acceleration and lack of response to idle mixture screw adjustments. A carburetor that is leaking fuel and/or covered with wet-looking deposits needs attention.

4   Diagnosing carburetor problems may require that the engine be started and run with the air cleaner removed. While running the engine without the air cleaner it is possible that it could backfire. A backfiring situation is likely to occur if the carburetor is malfunctioning, but removal of the air cleaner alone can lean the air/fuel mixture enough to produce an engine backfire. Perform this type of testing for as short a time as possible and be especially watchful for the potential of backfire and the possibility of starting a fire. Do not position your face or any portions of your body directly over the carburetor during inspection or servicing procedures.

5   Once it is determined that the carburetor is in need of work or an overhaul, several alternatives should be considered. If you are going to attempt to overhaul the carburetor yourself, first obtain a good quality carburetor rebuild kit which will include all necessary gaskets, internal parts, instructions and a parts list. You will also need carburetor cleaning solvent and some means of blowing out the internal passages of the carburetor with air.

6   Due to the many configurations and variations of carburetors offered on the range of vehicles covered in this book, it is not feasible for us to do a step-by-step overhaul of each type. You will find a good, detailed instruction list with any quality carburetor overhaul kit and it will apply in a more specific manner to the carburetor you have.

7   Another alternative is to obtain a new or rebuilt carburetor. These are readily available from dealers and auto parts stores for all engines covered in this manual. The important fact when purchasing one of these units is to make sure the exchange carburetor is identical to the original. Often times a tag is attached to the top plate of your carburetor and will aid the parts man in determining the exact type of carburetor you have. When obtaining a rebuilt carburetor or a rebuild kit, take time to ascertain that the kit or carburetor matches your application exactly. Seemingly insignificant differences can make a considerable difference in the overall running condition of your engine.

8   If you choose to overhaul your own carburetor, allow enough time to disassemble the carburetor carefully, soak the necessary parts in the cleaning solvent (usually for at least one half day or according to the instructions listed on the carburetor cleaner) and reassemble it, which will usually take you much longer than disassembly. When you are disassembling a carburetor, take care to match each part with the illustration in your carburetor kit and lay the parts out in order on a clean work surface to help you reassemble the carburetor. Overhauls by amateurs sometimes result in a vehicle which runs poorly, or not at all, compared to the original condition. To avoid this happening to you, use care and patience when disassembling your carburetor so you can reassemble it correctly.

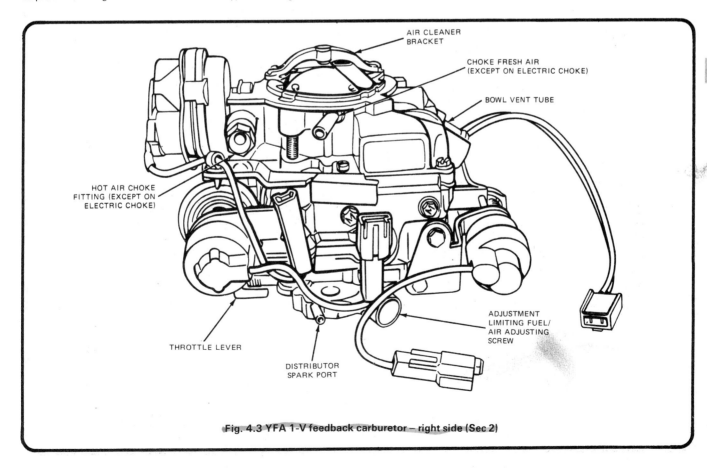

AIR CLEANER BRACKET

CHOKE FRESH AIR (EXCEPT ON ELECTRIC CHOKE)

BOWL VENT TUBE

HOT AIR CHOKE FITTING (EXCEPT ON ELECTRIC CHOKE)

ADJUSTMENT LIMITING FUEL/ AIR ADJUSTING SCREW

THROTTLE LEVER

DISTRIBUTOR SPARK PORT

Fig. 4.3 YFA 1-V feedback carburetor – right side (Sec 2)

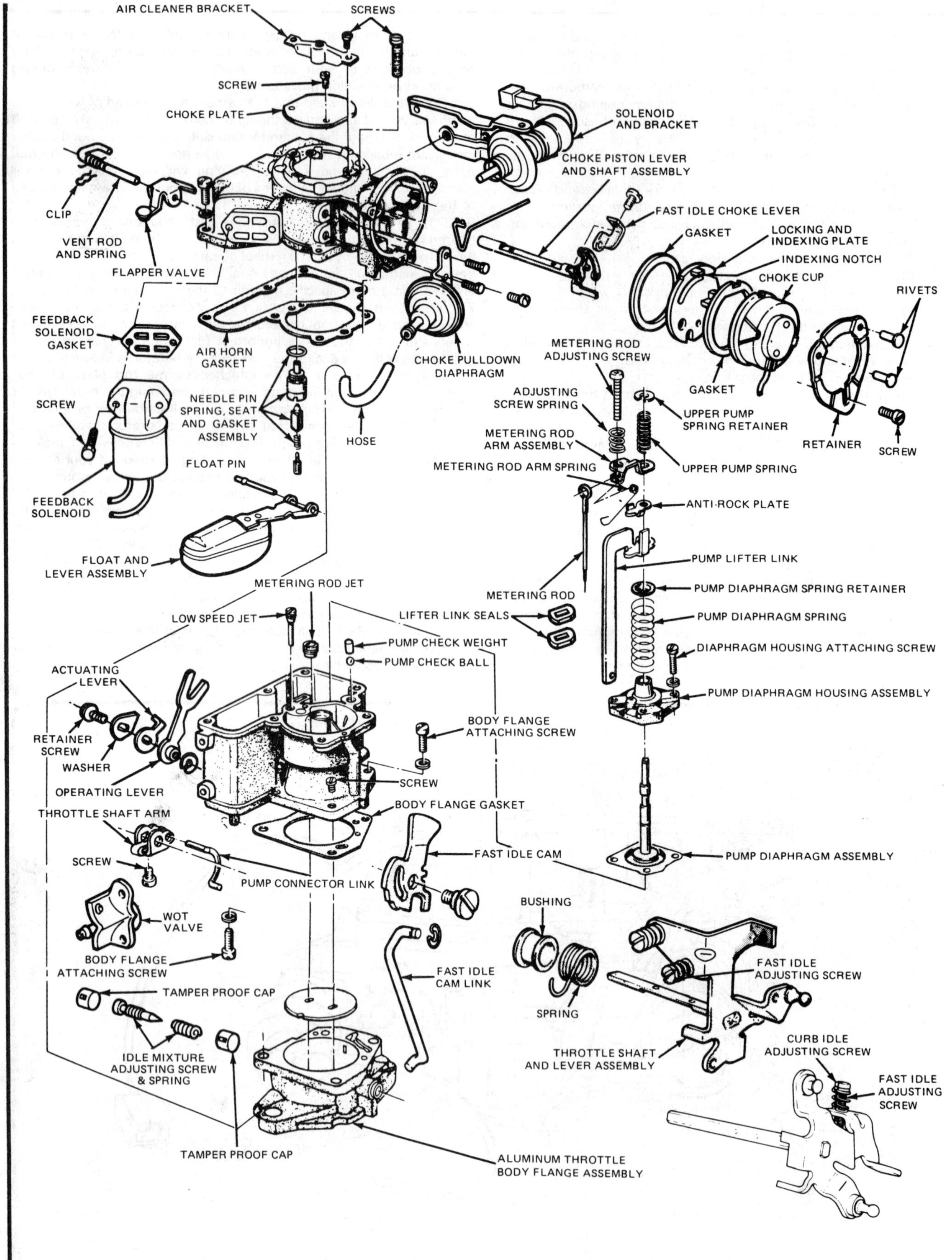

AIR CLEANER BRACKET

SCREWS

SCREW

CHOKE PLATE

SOLENOID AND BRACKET

CHOKE PISTON LEVER AND SHAFT ASSEMBLY

CLIP

VENT ROD AND SPRING

FLAPPER VALVE

FAST IDLE CHOKE LEVER

GASKET

LOCKING AND INDEXING PLATE

INDEXING NOTCH

CHOKE CUP

RIVETS

FEEDBACK SOLENOID GASKET

AIR HORN GASKET

CHOKE PULLDOWN DIAPHRAGM

METERING ROD ADJUSTING SCREW

GASKET

RETAINER

SCREW

SCREW

NEEDLE PIN SPRING, SEAT AND GASKET ASSEMBLY

HOSE

ADJUSTING SCREW SPRING

METERING ROD ARM ASSEMBLY

UPPER PUMP SPRING RETAINER

FLOAT PIN

METERING ROD ARM SPRING

UPPER PUMP SPRING

FEEDBACK SOLENOID

ANTI-ROCK PLATE

FLOAT AND LEVER ASSEMBLY

METERING ROD JET

PUMP LIFTER LINK

LOW SPEED JET

METERING ROD

LIFTER LINK SEALS

PUMP DIAPHRAGM SPRING RETAINER

PUMP CHECK WEIGHT

PUMP DIAPHRAGM SPRING

PUMP CHECK BALL

DIAPHRAGM HOUSING ATTACHING SCREW

ACTUATING LEVER

PUMP DIAPHRAGM HOUSING ASSEMBLY

RETAINER SCREW

BODY FLANGE ATTACHING SCREW

WASHER

SCREW

OPERATING LEVER

BODY FLANGE GASKET

THROTTLE SHAFT ARM

SCREW

PUMP DIAPHRAGM ASSEMBLY

FAST IDLE CAM

PUMP CONNECTOR LINK

WOT VALVE

BUSHING

FAST IDLE ADJUSTING SCREW

BODY FLANGE ATTACHING SCREW

TAMPER PROOF CAP

FAST IDLE CAM LINK

SPRING

CURB IDLE ADJUSTING SCREW

IDLE MIXTURE ADJUSTING SCREW & SPRING

THROTTLE SHAFT AND LEVER ASSEMBLY

FAST IDLE ADJUSTING SCREW

TAMPER PROOF CAP

ALUMINUM THROTTLE BODY FLANGE ASSEMBLY

Fig. 4.4 YFA 1-V feedback carburetor – exploded view (Sec 2)

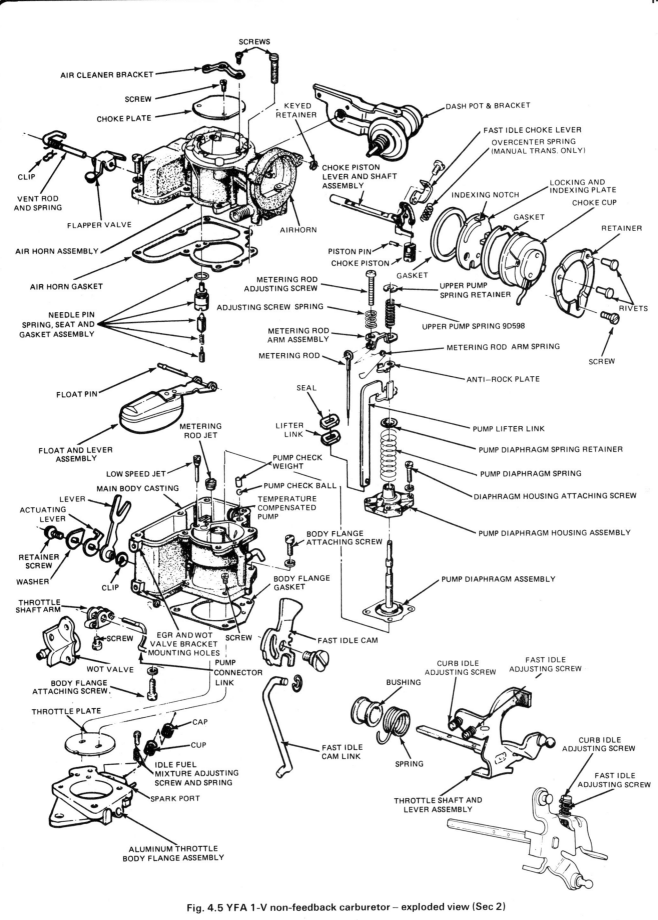

Fig. 4.5 YFA 1-V non-feedback carburetor – exploded view (Sec 2)

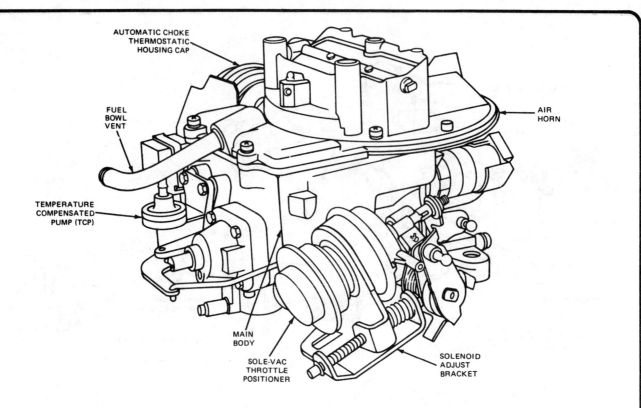

AUTOMATIC CHOKE
THERMOSTATIC
HOUSING CAP

FUEL
BOWL
VENT

AIR
HORN

TEMPERATURE
COMPENSATED
PUMP (TCP)

MAIN
BODY

SOLE-VAC
THROTTLE
POSITIONER

SOLENOID
ADJUST
BRACKET

Fig. 4.6 Model 2150 2-V carburetor, as used on various V6 and V8 engines – left front view (Sec 2)

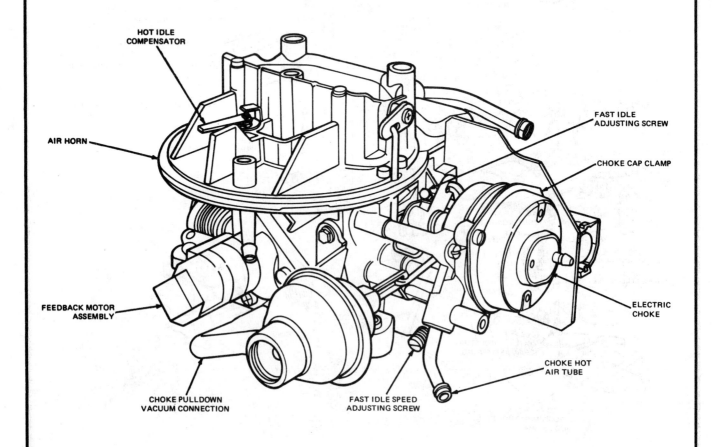

HOT IDLE
COMPENSATOR

FAST IDLE
ADJUSTING SCREW

AIR HORN

CHOKE CAP CLAMP

FEEDBACK MOTOR
ASSEMBLY

ELECTRIC
CHOKE

CHOKE PULLDOWN
VACUUM CONNECTION

FAST IDLE SPEED
ADJUSTING SCREW

CHOKE HOT
AIR TUBE

Fig. 4.7 Model 2150 2-V carburetor, as used on various V6 and V8 engines – right front view (Sec 2)

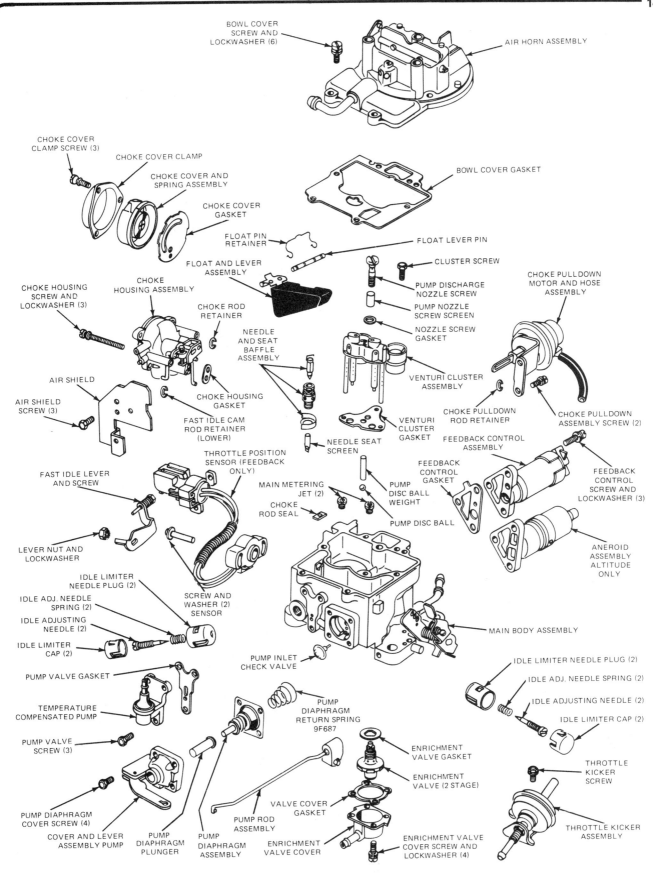

Fig. 4.8 Model 2150A 2-V carburetor, as used on various V6 and V8 engines with feedback and high altitude compensator – exploded view (Sec 2)

4

148

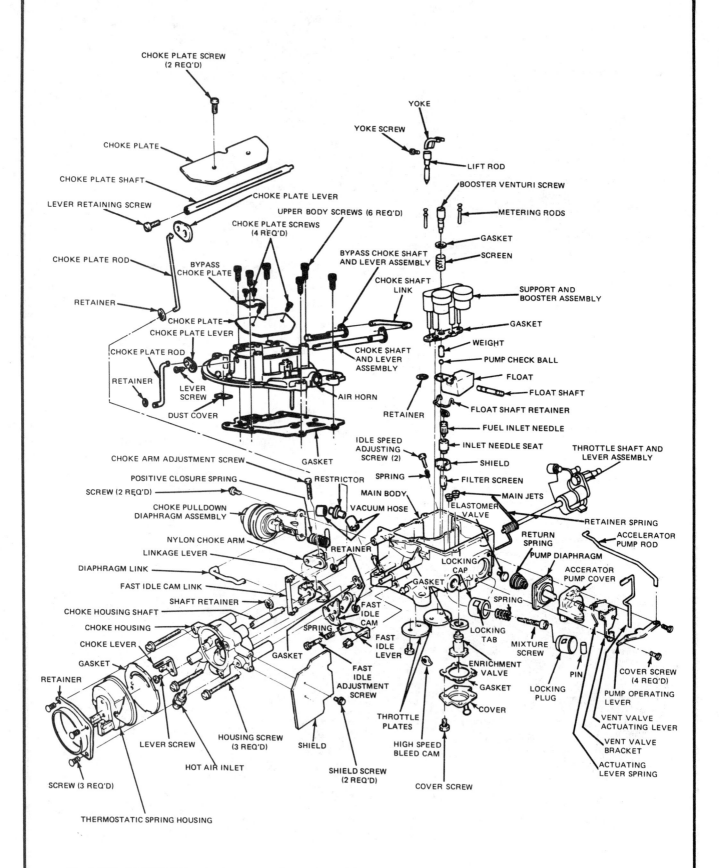

Fig. 4.9 Model 2150 2-V carburetor, as used on various V6 and V8 engines without high altitude compensator – exploded view (Sec 2)

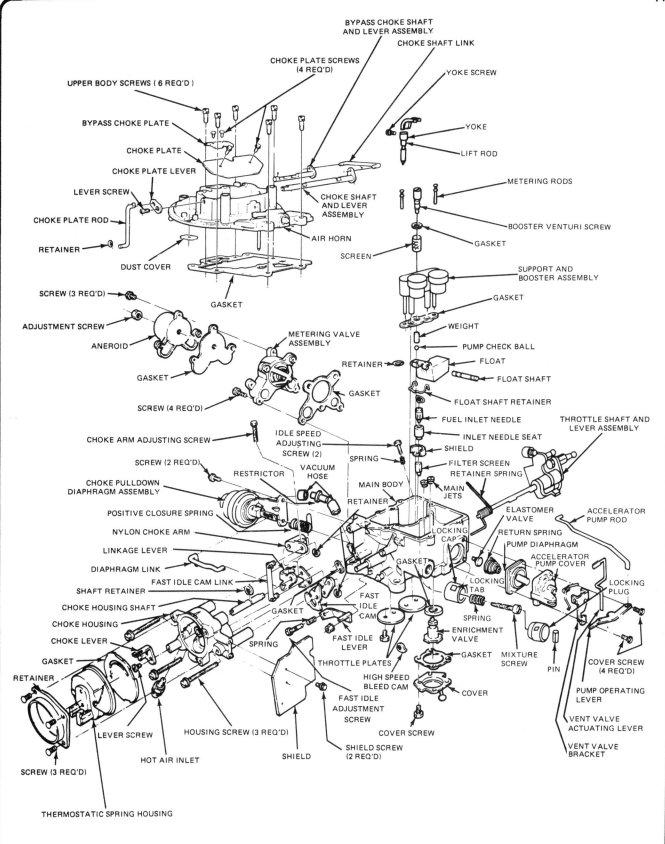

Fig. 4.10 Model 2150 2-V carburetor, as used on various V6 and V8 engines with high altitude compensator – exploded view (Sec 2)

4

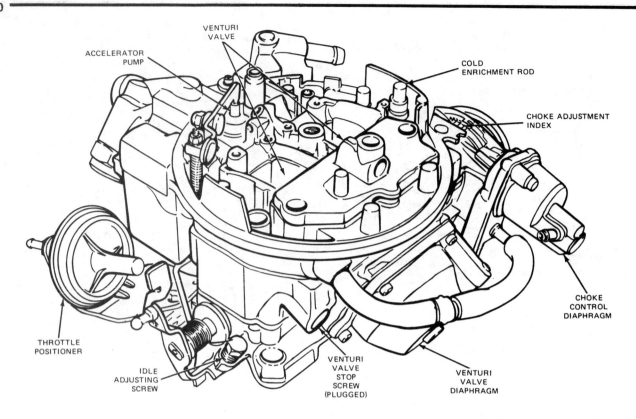

ACCELERATOR PUMP

VENTURI VALVE

COLD ENRICHMENT ROD

CHOKE ADJUSTMENT INDEX

CHOKE CONTROL DIAPHRAGM

THROTTLE POSITIONER

IDLE ADJUSTING SCREW

VENTURI VALVE STOP SCREW (PLUGGED)

VENTURI VALVE DIAPHRAGM

Fig. 4.11 Model 7200 VV (variable venturi) carburetor – left front view (Sec 2)

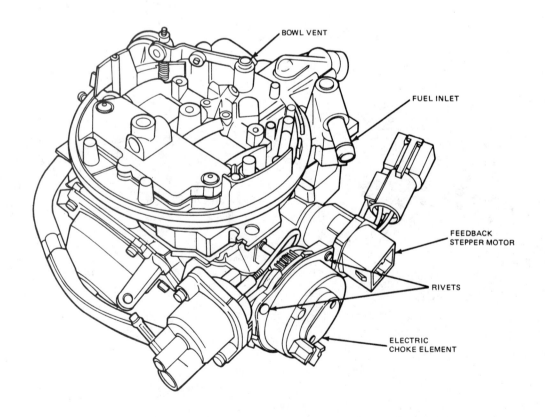

BOWL VENT

FUEL INLET

FEEDBACK STEPPER MOTOR

RIVETS

ELECTRIC CHOKE ELEMENT

Fig. 4.12 Model 7200 VV carburetor – right front view (Sec 2)

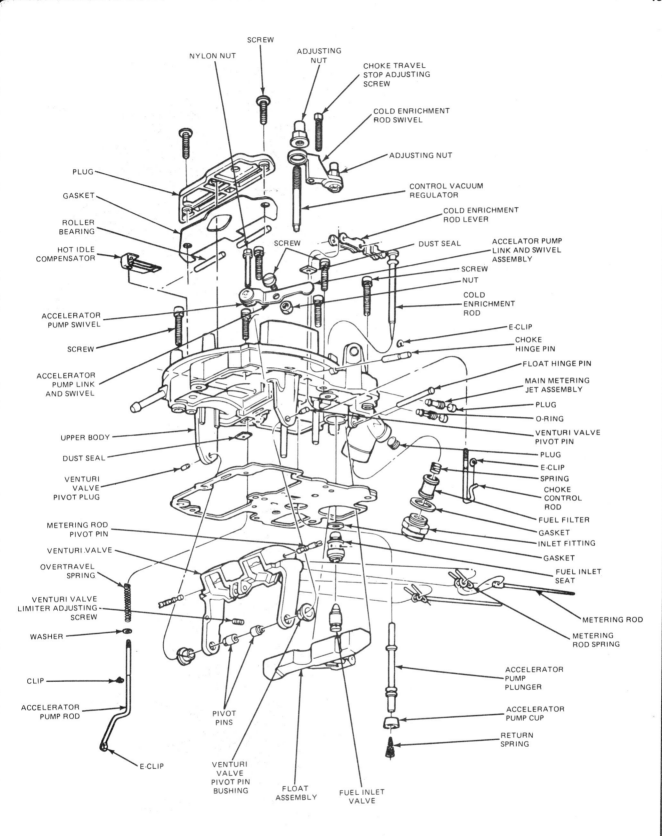

NYLON NUT

SCREW

ADJUSTING NUT

CHOKE TRAVEL STOP ADJUSTING SCREW

COLD ENRICHMENT ROD SWIVEL

ADJUSTING NUT

PLUG

GASKET

ROLLER BEARING

HOT IDLE COMPENSATOR

SCREW

CONTROL VACUUM REGULATOR

COLD ENRICHMENT ROD LEVER

DUST SEAL

ACCELATOR PUMP LINK AND SWIVEL ASSEMBLY

SCREW

NUT

COLD ENRICHMENT ROD

ACCELERATOR PUMP SWIVEL

SCREW

ACCELERATOR PUMP LINK AND SWIVEL

E-CLIP

CHOKE HINGE PIN

FLOAT HINGE PIN

MAIN METERING JET ASSEMBLY

PLUG

O-RING

VENTURI VALVE PIVOT PIN

UPPER BODY

DUST SEAL

VENTURI VALVE PIVOT PLUG

PLUG

E-CLIP

SPRING

CHOKE CONTROL ROD

FUEL FILTER

GASKET

INLET FITTING

GASKET

FUEL INLET SEAT

METERING ROD PIVOT PIN

VENTURI VALVE

OVERTRAVEL SPRING

VENTURI VALVE LIMITER ADJUSTING SCREW

WASHER

CLIP

ACCELERATOR PUMP ROD

E-CLIP

PIVOT PINS

VENTURI VALVE PIVOT PIN BUSHING

FLOAT ASSEMBLY

FUEL INLET VALVE

METERING ROD

METERING ROD SPRING

ACCELERATOR PUMP PLUNGER

ACCELERATOR PUMP CUP

RETURN SPRING

4

Fig. 4.13 Model 7200 VV carburetor air horn assembly – exploded view (Sec 2)

3 Carburetor – removal and installation

Caution: *There are a number of safety precautions to follow when working with gasoline. Refer to 'Safety first' near the front of this manual.*

1 Disconnect the negative battery cable. Remove the hose connections leading to the air cleaner. Mark these with coded pieces of tape to help in reassembly.
2 Remove the air cleaner assembly.
3 Use a small catch-can and disconnect the fuel feed line from the carburetor. Plug the end of this hose to prevent further leakage.
4 Disconnect any electrical leads from the emissions control devices connected to the carburetor. Mark these connections so they can be installed in the proper position.
5 Remove any vacuum lines from the carburetor. Mark them for installation purposes.
6 Disconnect the kick-down lever or cable from the carburetor (if equipped).
7 Disconnect the throttle cable or linkage from the carburetor.
8 Disconnect any under-carburetor heater hoses that may be connected to the carburetor.
9 Disconnect any coolant transfer hoses that may be connected to the choke system.
10 Remove the carburetor retaining nuts from the studs in the intake manifold.
11 Lift off the carburetor, spacer plate (if equipped), and gasket(s). Place a piece of cardboard over the intake manifold surface to prevent debris from falling into the engine while the carburetor is removed.
12 Before installation, carefully clean the mating surfaces of the intake manifold, spacer plate (if equipped), and the base of the carburetor of any old gasket material. These surfaces must be perfectly clean and smooth to prevent vacuum leaks.
13 Install a new gasket(s).
14 Install the carburetor and spacer plate (if equipped) over the studs on the intake manifold.
15 Install the retaining nuts and tighten them to the proper torque. Be careful not to over-torque these retaining nuts as they can warp the base plate of the carburetor.

4 Carburetor – external adjustments

Note: *All carburetors on U.S. vehicles come equipped with adjustment limiters or limiter stops on the carburetor idle mixture screws. All adjustments to these mixture screws are to be made only within the range provided by the limiter devices. In addition, the following procedures are intended for general use only. The information given on the Emissions Control Information label located under the hood is specific for your engine and should be followed.*

The instructions given below should be regarded only as temporary adjustments. The vehicle should be taken to an auto facility equipped with the necessary instruments for adjusting the idle mixture as soon as possible after the vehicle is running. At the same time the idle mixture is set, the idle speed will also be reset, so your carburetor is operating within the range delineated on the Emissions Control Information label.

Note also that all necessary adjustments and/or inspection procedures discussed in Section 2 of this Chapter should be performed before carburetor servicing begins.

Idle speed (preliminary)

1 Set the fuel mixture screws to the full counterclockwise position allowed by the limiter caps.
2 Back off the idle speed adjusting screw until the throttle bore plates are seated in the throttle bore. Some vehicles are equipped with either a dashpot or a solenoid-type idle valve to hold the linkage open. Make sure these devices are not holding the idle up when making this adjustment.
3 Turn the idle adjusting screw inward until it initially contacts the throttle stop. Turn the screw an additional one and one half turns to establish a preliminary idle speed adjustment.

Idle speed (engine running)

4 Set the parking brake and block the wheels to prevent movement. If equipped with an automatic transmission, have an assistant apply the brakes as a further safety precaution during the following procedures.

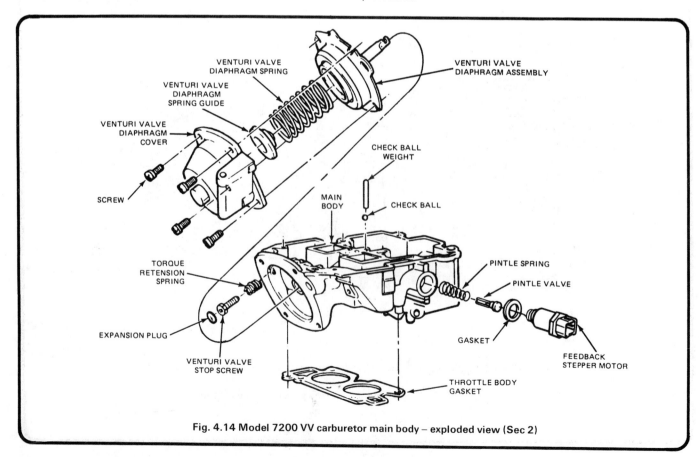

Fig. 4.14 Model 7200 VV carburetor main body – exploded view (Sec 2)

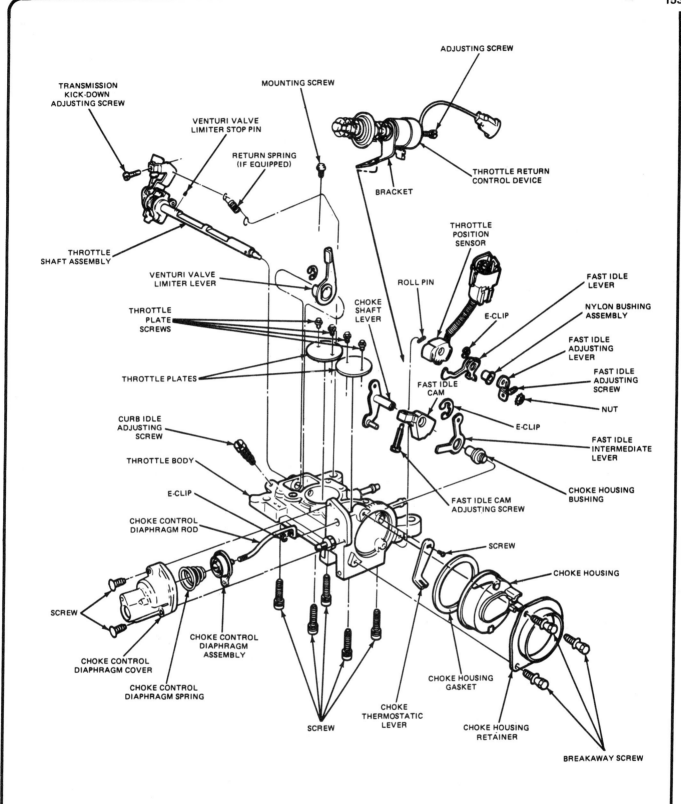

Fig. 4.15 Model 7200 VV carburetor throttle body assembly – exploded view (Sec 2)

4

154

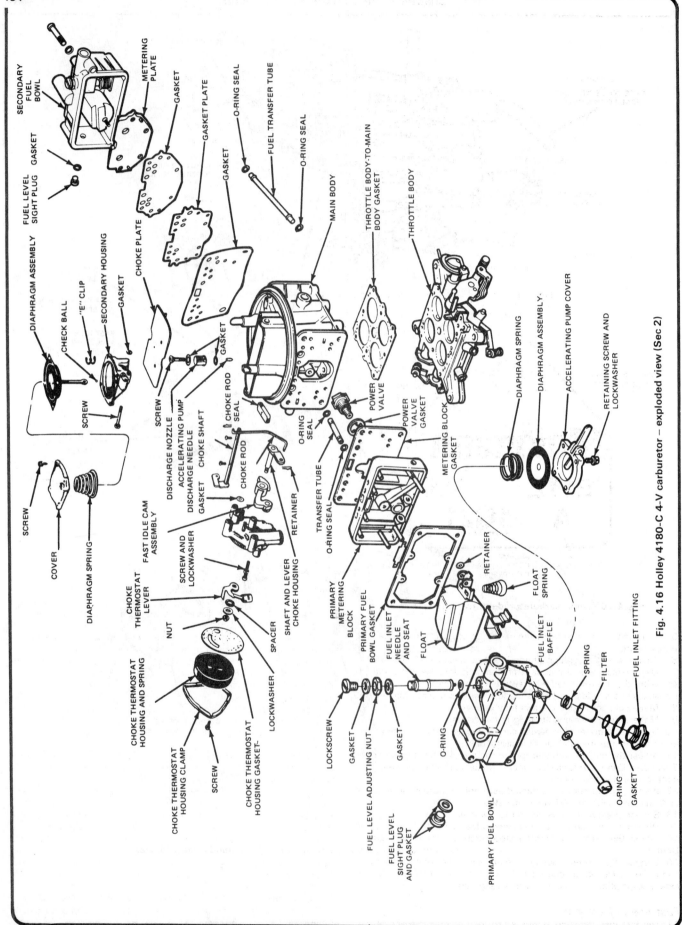

Fig. 4.16 Holley 4180-C 4-V carburetor — exploded view (Sec 2)

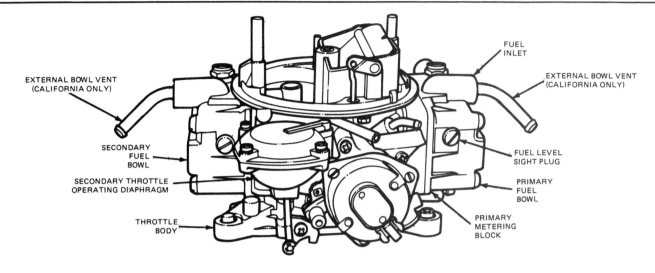

Fig. 4.17 Holley 4180-C 4-V carburetor as used on 460 cu in engines – right side (Sec 2)

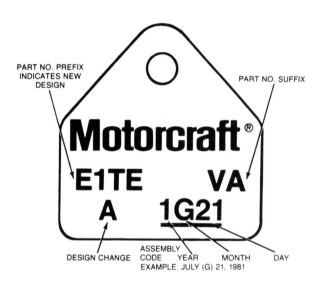

Fig. 4.18 Typical carburetor identification tag (Sec 2)

5   Start the engine and allow the engine to achieve normal operating temperature.
6   Ensure that the ignition timing is set as described in Chapter 1.
7   On a vehicle with a manual shift transmission, the idle should be set with the transmission in Neutral. On vehicles with automatic transmissions, the idle setting is made with the transmission in Drive.
8   Make sure the choke plate is fully opened.
9   Make sure the air conditioning is turned off.
10 Use a tachometer of known accuracy and connect it to the vehicle according to the manufacturer's instructions.
11 Adjust the engine curb idle rpm to the specifications given on the *Emissions Control Information label.* Make sure the air cleaner is installed for this adjustment.
12 If so equipped, turn the solenoid assembly to obtain the specified curb idle rpm with the solenoid activated.
13 Set the automatic transmission to Neutral.
14 Disconnect the power to the solenoid lead wire at the connector.
15 Adjust the carburetor throttle stop screw to obtain 500 rpm in Neutral.
16 Connect the solenoid power wire and open the throttle slightly by hand. The solenoid plunger should hold the throttle lever in the extended position and move the rpm range up.

Fast idle adjustment
17 The fast idle adjusting screw is provided to maintain engine idle

rpm while the choke is operating and the engine has a limited air supply during its cold running cycle. As the choke plate moves through its range of travel from the closed to the open position, the fast idle cam rotates to allow decreasingly slower idle speeds until the normal operating temperature and correct curb idle rpm is reached.
18 Before adjusting the fast idle make sure the curb idle speed is adjusted as previously discussed.
19 With the engine at normal operating temperature and the tachometer attached, manually rotate the fast idle cam until the fast idle adjusting screw rests on the specific step of the cam (see *Emissions Control Information label* for proper step).
20 Turn the fast idle adjusting screw inward or outward to obtain the specified fast idle rpm.

5   Automatic choke – inspection and adjustment

Note: *Choke checking procedures can be found in Chapter 1.*
1   Remove the air cleaner with the engine cold and not running.
2   Rotate the throttle (or have an assistant depress the gas pedal) to the open position and see see if the choke plate shuts tightly in the opening of the upper body air horn. With the accelerator held open, make sure that the choke plate can be moved freely and that it is not hanging up due to deposits of varnish. If the choke plate has excessive deposits of varnish, it will have to be either cleaned with a commercial spray-on carburetor cleaner or the carburetor will need to be dismantled and overhauled or replaced (see Section 2). A spray-on type carburetor cleaner will remove any surface varnish which may be causing sticky or erratic choke plate action. However, care must be used to prevent sediment from entering the throttle venturis.
3   Start the vehicle. If equipped with an electric choke, use a voltmeter to check that the electric assist on the side of the choke thermostat housing has voltage. Voltage should be constantly supplied to the temperature sensing switch as long as the engine is running. If no voltage is present, check the system circuit to determine the problem.
4   Some automatic chokes will come equipped with a thermostatic spring housing which controls the choke action. To adjust this type of housing, loosen the three clamp screws that attach the thermostatic spring housing to the choke housing. The spring housing can now be turned to vary its setting on the choke. Set the spring housing to the specified mark (see *Emissions Control Information label* in the engine compartment) and tighten the retaining screws. Do not try to compensate for poor choke operation by varying the index setting from the specified spot. If the choke is not operating properly, the spring inside the husing may be worn or broken or other problems may exist in the choke system. If this situation exists, the spring housing will need to be replaced.
5   Allow the vehicle to completely cool (at least four hours – preferably overnight) and check for proper operation as described in Chapter 1.

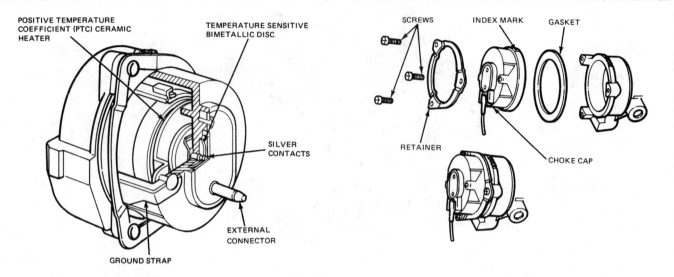

4.19 Typical electric-assisted carburetor choke system (2150 2-V carburetor choke shown) (Sec 5)

Fig. 4.20 Adjustment limiting choke cap on YFA 1-V carburetor for vehicles over 8500 GVW (Sec 5)

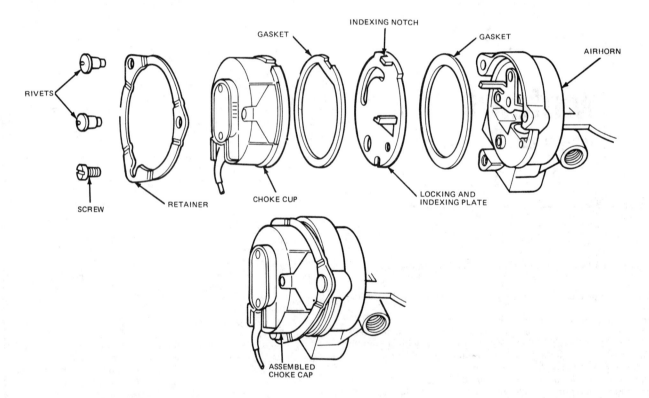

Fig. 4.21 Adjustment limiting choke cap on YFA 1-V carburetor for vehicles under 8500 GVW (Sec 5)

6 Fuel lines and valves – routing and replacement

Caution: *There are a number of safety precautions to follow when working with gasoline. Refer to 'Safety first' near the front of this manual.*

1   The fuel lines of these vehicles are generally made of metal with short lengths of rubber hose connecting critical flex points such as the tank or fuel pump. The metal fuel lines are retained to the body and frame with various clips and brackets. They generally will require no service; however, if they are allowed to come loose from their retaining brackets they can vibrate and eventually be worn through. If a fuel line needs to be replaced, it would be best to leave this service to a dealership or repair shop as it requires special flaring and crimping tools to build the lines.

2   If a short section of fuel line is damaged, rubber fuel hose can be used to replace it if it is no longer than 12 in. Cut a length of fuel quality rubber hose longer than the section to be replaced and use a tubing cutter to remove the damaged portion of the metal line. Install the rubber fuel line using two hose clamps and check to make sure no leaks are present.

3   If new fuel lines are necessary, they must be cut, formed and flared out of fuel system tubing. If you have the equipment to do so, remove the old fuel line from the vehicle and duplicate the bends and length of the removed fuel line.

4   Install the new section of tubing and be careful to install new

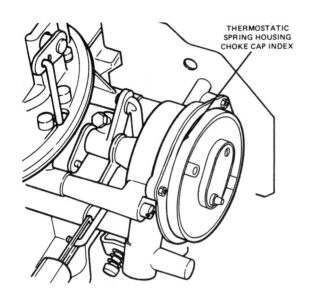

Fig. 4.22 Automatic choke thermostatic spring housing for the 2150 2-V carburetor (Sec 5)

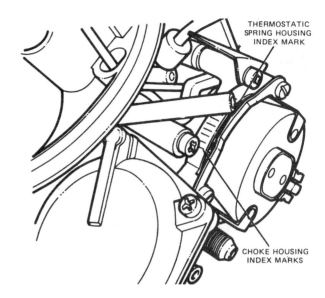

Fig. 4.23 Automatic choke thermostatic spring housing as installed on a Holley-C 4-V carburetor (Sec 5)

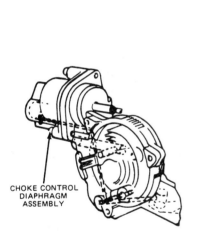

Fig. 4.24 Details of automatic choke control assembly on a Model 7200 VV carburetor (Sec 5)

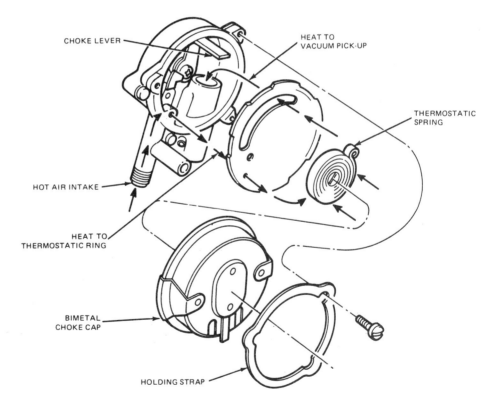

Fig. 4.25 Automatic choke assembly for the 4180-C 4-V carburetor – exploded view (Sec 5)

clamps and/or brackets where needed. Make sure the replacement tubing is of the same diameter, shape and quality as the original one. Make sure all flared ends conform to those on the original fuel line. Make sure fuel lines connected to fuel pumps or other fittings are of the double flare type. Make sure all metal shavings are removed from inside the tubing before installation.

5   Always check rubber hoses for any signs of leakage or deterioration.

6   If a rubber hose needs replacing, it is advisable to also replace the clamp.

7   If the vehicle is equipped with two tanks, it will also have a switching valve somewhere in the system. If a factory auxiliary tank is installed, the switching valve will be located next to the heater controls and will be electrically operated. If this valve is being replaced, double-check that the cable is disconnected from the negative battery terminal before replacement, otherwise sparks could ignite gasoline present when removing the connection to the auxiliary fuel tanks switching valve.

7   Fuel pump – description and testing

Caution: *There are a number of safety precautions to follow when working with gasoline. Refer to 'Safety first' near the front of this manual.*

1   All vehicles are equipped with a single-action mechanical fuel pump.
2   The fuel pump on inline six cylinder engines is located on the lower left portion of the cylinder block, midway between the front of the block and the distributor. The V6 fuel pump is located on the right side of the front cover.
3   The fuel pump on V8 engines is mounted on the left side of the front cylinder cover.
4   All fuel pumps are of the permanently-sealed design and are non-serviceable or rebuildable.
5   All fuel pumps are actuated mechanically by a rocker arm on the fuel pump, operating off an eccentric lobe on the nose of the camshaft.

Testing (preliminary)

6   Before suspecting the fuel pump, check all fuel hoses and lines and the fuel filter (Chapter 1).
7   Disconnect the fuel pipe at the carburetor inlet union and the high tension lead to the ignition coil (to prevent the engine from actually starting).
8   Place a container at the end of the disconnected pipe and have an assistant crank the engine over the driver's seat. A good spurt of gasoline should emerge from the end of the pipe every second revolution.

Testing (pressure)

9   Remove the air cleaner assembly.
10   Disconnect the fuel line at the carburetor or at the fuel filter.
11   Connect a pressure gauge with a flexible hose between the fuel delivery line and the carburetor. Make sure the inside diameter of the hose is no smaller than the diameter of the pressure hose.
12   Connect a T-fitting into the pressure hose so the fuel line can be connected to the carburetor and the pressure gauge.
13   Make sure that the engine has been run and brought to normal operating temperature and that the idle is as specified on the *Emissions Control Information label.*
14   Start and run the engine. Observe the fuel pressure on the gauge. It should be within the Specifications listed at the front of this Chapter.

Testing (volume)

15   To check the fuel pump for volume, a T-fitting must be inserted in the fuel line with a flexible hose leading to a graduated fuel container.

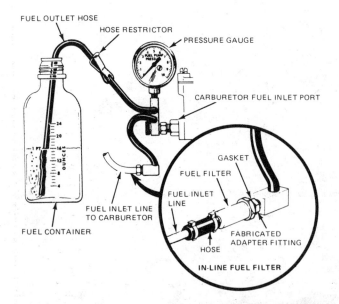

Fig. 4.26 Testing a fuel pump for correct pressure and capacity (Sec 7)

Graduated volume marks should show clearly on the container you use.
16   Install a hose restrictor, valve or other control device on the outlet line to allow the fuel to be shut off to the test container.
17   Start and run the engine with the fuel restrictor or valve shut.
18   Open the restrictor and allow the fuel to run into the container. At the end of the specified test time, close the restrictor and measure the volume of fuel in the container. Compare the volume and time with that given in the Specifications at the front of this Chapter.
19   If the volume is below the specified amount, install a new auxiliary fuel supply onto the inlet side of the fuel pump. A small gas can with a hose fitted tightly into the cap can be used as an auxiliary fuel supply. This will eliminate the possibility of a clogged tank and/or a delivery line. Repeat the test and check the volume. If the volume has changed or now reaches specification, the fuel lines and/or tank(s) are clogged. If the volume is still low, the fuel pump must be replaced with a new one.

8   Fuel pump – removal and installation

Caution: *Use extreme caution when working around the fuel pump as the lines leading to and from the pump will be full of gasoline under pressure. It is a good idea to keep wet rags and a catch-can available to try and keep the amounts of residual gasoline and spray to a minimum. Never smoke or use any type of electrical equipment around the fuel pump when removing or installing it. Use caution not to remove or install the fuel pump in an enclosed area and especially where an open flame is present such as around a water heater. Further safety precautions can be found in 'Safety first' near the front of this manual.*

1   Disconnect the negative battery cable and then remove the inlet line at the fuel pump.
2   Plug the end of the line to prevent further leakage and possible contamination from dirt.
3   Remove the outlet pipe at the fuel pump and allow it to drain into the catch-can.
4   Remove the two bolts and washers securing the fuel pump to the timing cover or cylinder block.
5   Remove the fuel pump and gasket (on some models a spacer plate may be positoned for heat insulation properties).
6   Clean the mating surfaces of the fuel pump, timing cover or cylinder block, and spacer (if so equipped). The mating surfaces must be perfectly smooth for a good gasket seal upon reinstallation.
7   Install a new gasket on the fuel pump mating surface using an oil-resistant sealer.
8   After cleaning the surfaces and applying the gasket, apply oil-resistant sealer to the other side of the gasket and to the threads on the retaining bolts.
9   After installing the pump on the engine block, make sure the rocker arm of the fuel pump is positioned correctly on the camshaft eccentric. It may be necessary to rotate the engine until the eccentric is at its low position to facilitate easier fuel pump installation.
10   Holding the fuel pump tightly against its mounting surface, install the retaining bolts and new lock washers.
11   Tighten the retaining bolts to the proper torque.
12   Remove the plug from the inlet line and connect the inlet line to the fuel pump.
13   Connect the outlet line to the fuel pump.
14   Connect the cable to the negative battery terminal.
15   Start the engine and check it for fuel and/or oil leaks.

9   Fuel tank – description and repair warning

Note: *When working with fuel tanks, observe all precautions listed previously in this Chapter and in 'Safety first' near the front of this manual. Metal fuel tank repairs requiring an open flame (welding, soldering, etc.) should never be performed by a home mechanic.*

1   The fuel tank(s) on these vehicles is made of either metal or plastic. The main tank may be located either midships, between the driveline and frame rail, or aft, between the frame rails and behind the rear axle.
2   An auxiliary tank is offered as an option on most models, usually located in the alternative midship/aft axle position. On Bronco models, an optional tank of larger capacity is available. Both Bronco tanks are

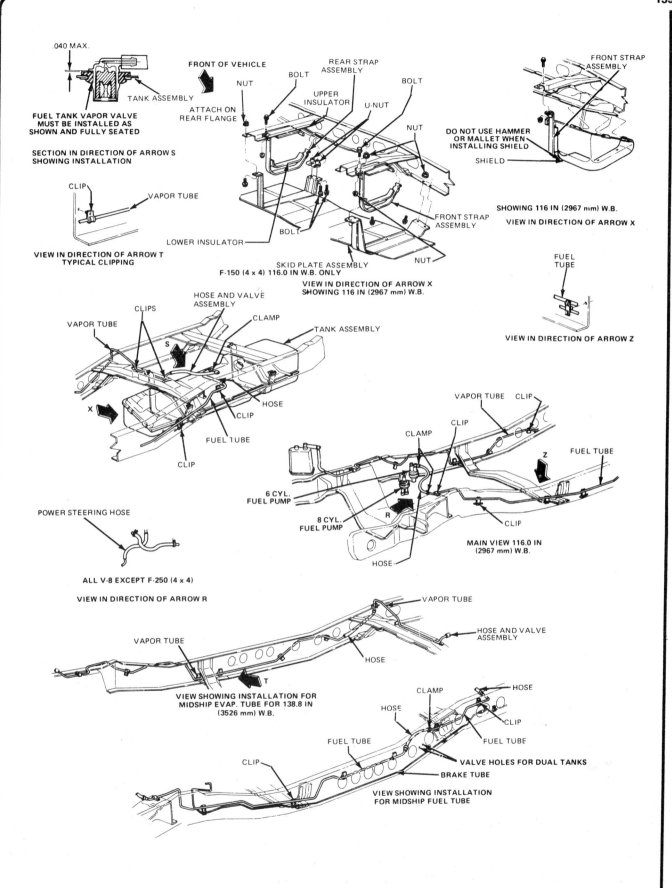

Fig. 4.27 Typical standard capacity midship-located fuel tank installation (Sec 10)

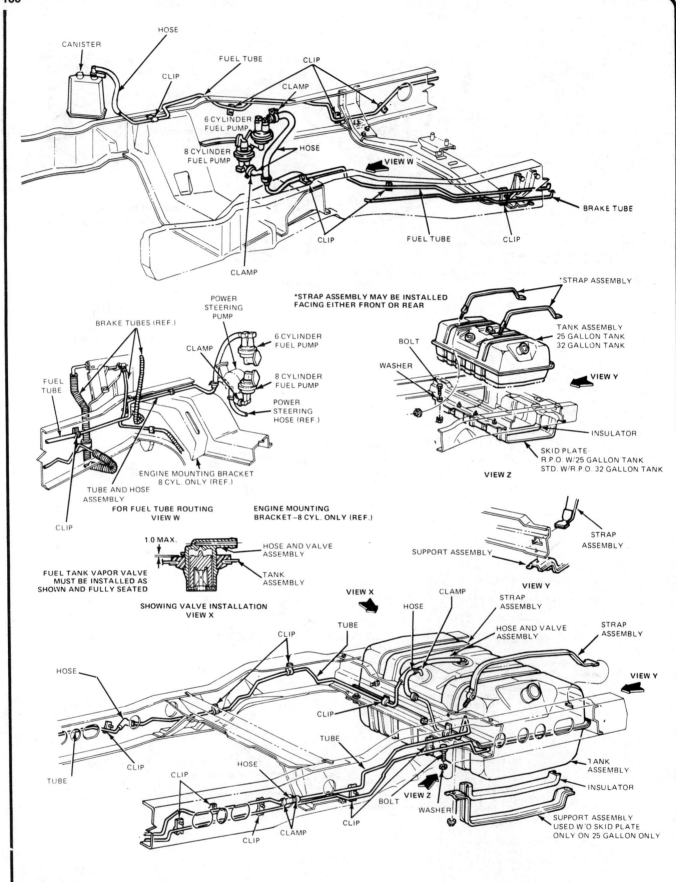

Fig. 4.28 Typical aft axle fuel tank installation (Bronco shown, others similar) (Sec 10)

located in the same position, aft of the axle.

3 If an auxiliary tank is installed on the vehicle, a switching valve assembly, to switch the fuel flow and gauge reading level from one tank to another, is also included.

4 A plastic tank is usually non-repairable and, if damaged, should be replaced with a new one.

10 Fuel tank – removal and installation

Note: *See the previous Section and all precautions given in this Chapter and in 'Safety first' near the front of this manual.*

Midship tanks

1 Disconnect the cable from the negative battery terminal.

2 Drain the fuel into a suitable container by siphoning through the fuel hose at the fuel pump-to-fuel tube connection.

3 On vehicles with dual tanks, disconnect the ground wire after draining both tanks.

4 Remove the clamps and hoses attached to the fuel tank, labeling the hoses for ease of installation.

5 On vehicles with an EVAP system, disconnect the vapor line from the emissions control valve.

6 Remove the nuts and bolts from the tank restraining straps and remove the tank from the vehicle.

7 If the tank is being replaced with a new one, remove the fuel gauge sending unit and vapor control valve by turning their respective retaining rings counterclockwise and pulling the units from the tank.

8 If the tank is to be reused, scrape away the old gasket material from the gauge and valve mounting surfaces on the tank.

9 Installation is the reverse of the removal procedures. Refer to Fig. 4.29 and make careful note of the proper installation method for fuel and vapor hose connections.

Aft axle tanks

10 Disconnect the cable from the negative battery terminal.

11 Raise the rear of the vehicle and place it securely on jackstands.

12 Disconnect the fuel gauge sending unit wire at the fuel tank.

13 Drain the fuel into a suitable container by siphoning through the fuel hose at the fuel pump-to-fuel line connection.

14 On vehicles with dual tanks, disconnect the ground wire after draining both tanks.

15 Loosen the fuel line hose clamps, slide the clamps forward and disconnect the fuel line at the fuel gauge sending unit.

16 If the fuel gauge sending unit is to be removed, turn the unit retaining ring counterclockwise and remove the sending unit, retaining ring and gasket.

17 Loosen the clamps on the fuel filler pipe and disconnect the filler pipe hose and vent hose from the tank. If it is not possible to completely remove the filler pipe and filler pipe vent hose in this position, refer to Step 20 or 24 after performing Steps 18 and 19 or Steps 22 and 23, as appropriate.

18 If removing the metal type tank, support the tank with a floor jack and wood block and remove the bolts attaching the tank supports to the frame.

19 Carefully lower the tank and disconnect the vent tube from the vapor emissions control valve in the top of the tank.

20 Finish removing the filler pipe and filler pipe vent hose if this was not possible in Step 17.

21 Remove the tank from under the vehicle.

22 If removing the plastic type tank, support the tank and remove the bolts attaching the combination skid plate and tank support to the frame.

23 Carefully lower the tank and disconnect the vent tube from the vapor emissions control valve in the top of the tank.

24 Finish removing the filler pipe and filler pipe vent hose if this was not possible in Step 17.

25 Remove the skid plate and tank from under the vehicle, then disassemble the skid plate from the tank.

26 If the fuel tank is being replaced with a new one, remove the vapor emissions control valve by turning its retaining ring counterclockwise and pulling the unit from the tank.

27 Before installing the fuel tank, careful note should be made of the proper installation method for fuel and vapor hose connections (refer to Fig. 4.29).

28 Install the vapor emissions control valve in the tank.

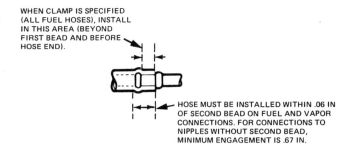

WHEN CLAMP IS SPECIFIED (ALL FUEL HOSES), INSTALL IN THIS AREA (BEYOND FIRST BEAD AND BEFORE HOSE END).

HOSE MUST BE INSTALLED WITHIN .06 IN OF SECOND BEAD ON FUEL AND VAPOR CONNECTIONS. FOR CONNECTIONS TO NIPPLES WITHOUT SECOND BEAD, MINIMUM ENGAGEMENT IS .67 IN.

Fig. 4.29 Proper installation method for fuel and vapor hose connections in the fuel system (Sec 10)

29 Install new support strap insulation as required.

30 If installing the plastic type tank, preassemble the skid plate and support straps to the tank (refer to Fig. 4.28).

31 Raise the tank skid plate and support assembly and attach the vent hose to the vapor emissions control valve.

32 Start the tank neck into the hose.

33 Position the tank assembly against the top straps or frame and install the retaining nuts and bolts.

34 The remaining installation procedures are the reverse of those for removal.

Bronco

35 Disconnect the cable from the negative battery terminal.

36 Drain the fuel into a suitable container by siphoning through the fuel hose at the fuel pump-to-fuel line connection.

37 Raise the rear of the vehicle and place it securely on jackstands.

38 Loosen the clamp on the fuel filler pipe hose at the filler pipe and disconnect the hose from the pipe.

39 Loosen the hose clamps, slide the clamps forward and disconnect the fuel line at the fuel gauge sending unit.

40 Support the tank with a floor jack and wood block and remove the lower support bracket bolts or skid plate bolts (if equipped).

41 Remove the support assembly or skid plate (if equipped) attaching nut at each tank mounting strap, lower the support assemblies, and lower the tank enough to gain access to the tank vent hose.

42 Disconnect the fuel gauge sending wire at the fuel tank.

43 Disconnect the fuel tank vent hose at the top of the tank.

44 Disconnect the fuel tank-to-fuel separator lines at the fuel tank, then remove the fuel tank from under the vehicle.

45 If the fuel gauge sending unit is to be removed, turn the unit retaining ring counterclockwise and remove the sending unit, retaining ring and gasket.

46 Installation is the reverse of the removal procedure.

11 Fuel tank – cleaning and repair

1 If a fuel tank has a build-up of sediment or rust in the bottom it must be removed and cleaned.

2 When the tank is removed it should be flushed out with hot water and detergent or, preferably, sent to a radiator shop for chemical flushing.

3 **Caution:** *Never attempt to weld, solder or make any type of repairs on an empty fuel tank. Leave this work to an authorized repair shop.*

4 The use of a chemical type sealer for on-vehicle repairs is advised only in case of emergency; the tank should be removed and sent to a shop for more permanent repairs as soon as possible.

5 Never store a gas tank in an enclosed area where gas fumes could build up and cause an explosion and/or fire.

12 Exhaust system – general information

1 The exhaust systems employed on the vehicles covered in this manual vary according to the engine, wheelbase, gross vehicle weight and emissions systems incorporated. Most vehicles employ a catalytic

converter in their emissions control system (refer to Chapter 6), and all vehicles employ a single muffler and tailpipe.

2   Retention and alignment of the exhaust system is maintained through a series of metal and rubber clamps and metal brackets and some systems, those in which excessive exhaust temperatures are created as a result of the insulation of emissions control equipment, are equipped with heat shields.

3   Due to the high temperatures inherent in exhaust system operation, any attempt to inspect or repair it should be done only after the entire system has cooled, a process which may take several hours to accomplish.

13 Exhaust system – parts replacement

1   Refer to and perform the operations outlined in Chapter 1, *Exhaust system – inspection.*

2   If your inspection reveals the exhaust system, or portions of it need to be replaced, first secure the proper parts needed to repair the system. The components of the exhaust system can generally be split at their major divisions such as the inlet pipe from the muffler or the muffler from the tailpipe. However, if corrosion is the cause for replacement, it will probably be necessary to replace the entire exhaust system, as follows.

3   Raise the vehicle and support it securely on jackstands.

4   Make sure the exhaust system is cool.

5   Apply some rust penetrant to the retainer bolts for the exhaust inlet pipe flange.

6   Remove the exhaust inlet pipe flange retaining nuts.

7   Remove the shields from the catalytic converter, if equipped.

8   Remove the clamps retaining the muffler or converter to the inlet pipe(s).

9   Remove the hanger supporting the muffer and/or catalytic converter from the vehicle.

10   Remove the clamps retaining the rear of the muffler to the tailpipe.

11   Remove the section(s) necessary for replacement. It may be necessary to allow the axle to hang free from the rear frame in order to get the curved section of the tailpipe over the rear axle housing. Be sure to support the vehicle's frame securely before removing the support from the axle.

12   Installation is the reverse of removal. Always use new gaskets and retaining nuts whenever the system is being replaced. It is also a good idea to use new hangers and/or retaining brackets when replacing the exhaust system.

13   Start the vehicle and check for exhaust leaks and/or rattles caused by misalignment.

Chapter 5 Engine electrical systems

Refer to Chapter 13 for information on 1984 and later models

Contents

Specifications

Ignition system

Distributor type	
1980	Breakerless, Duraspark II
1981 through 1983	Breakerless, Duraspark II or Duraspark III, depending on engine calibration
Automatic advance	
Duraspark II	Vacuum and centrifugal
Duraspark III	Electronic
Distributor direction of rotation	
Six-cylinder in-line engines	Clockwise
V6 engines	Counterclockwise
V8 engines	Counterclockwise
Firing order	
Six-cylinder in-line engines	1-5-3-6-2-4
V6 engines	1-4-2-5-3-6
255, 302 and 460 cu in V8 engines	1-5-4-2-6-3-7-8
351 and 400 cu in V8 engines	1-3-7-2-6-5-4-8
Spark plug gap and type	See Emissions Control Information label in the engine compartment
Spark plug wire resistance	Less than 5000 ohms per inch
Ignition timing	See Emissions Control Information label in the engine compartment
Ignition coil	12 volt

Charging system

Alternator brush length	
New	$\frac{1}{2}$ in
Wear limit	$\frac{1}{4}$ in

Starting system

Starter brush length	
New	$\frac{1}{2}$ in
Wear limit	$\frac{1}{4}$ in

Torque specifications

Distributor hold-down bolt	17 to 25 in-lb
Distributor adapter-to-distributor base	18 to 23 in-lb
Stator assembly lower plate assembly-to-distributor base	15 in-lb minimum
Diaphragm assembly-to-distributor base	15 in-lb minimum
Spark plug	See Chapter 1
Starter motor through bolts	55 to 75 in-lb
Starter motor mounting bolts	15 to 20 ft-lb

1 General information

The engine electrical systems include the ignition, charging and starting components. They are considered separately from the rest of the electrical system (lighting, etc) because of their proximity and importance to the engine and its prime function in the vehicle.

Exercise caution when working around any of these components for several reasons. The components are easily damaged if tested, connected or stressed incorrectly. The alternator is driven by an engine drivebelt which could cause serious bodily harm if your fingers or hands become entangled in it with the engine running. Both the starter and alternator are sources of direct battery voltage which could arc or even cause a fire if overloaded or shorted.

Never leave the ignition switch on for long periods of time with the engine not running. Do not disconnect the battery cable(s) while the engine is running. Be especially careful not to cross-connect battery cables from another source such as another vehicle when jump-starting.

Don't ground either of the ignition coil terminals, even momentarily. When hooking up a test tachometer/dwell meter to the terminal(s) of the coil, make sure it is compatible with the type of ignition system on the vehicle.

Additional safety-related information on the engine electrical system can be found in *Safety first* near the front of this manual. It should be referred to before beginning any operation included in this Chapter.

2 Ignition system – description and operation

Description

The ignition system on all vehicles covered in this manual will be either a Duraspark II or Duraspark III system, depending upon engine calibration. Both systems are all-electronic and function in conjunction with one of three ignition modules, also dependent upon engine calibration. Testing of these ignition modules should be done by a Ford dealer service department. If it is determined that the module requires replacement, make sure that you replace it with an exact duplicate of the original.

The Duraspark II system incorporates normal centrifugal and vacuum advance mechanisms in the distributor body, while the spark advance function in the Duraspark III system is dependent upon an Electronic Engine Control (EEC) system. The EEC controls spark advance in response to various engine sensors. On all Duraspark III systems except the Duraspark III unit for the 232 cu in V6 engine, this includes a crankshaft position sensor which replaces the stator assembly and armature normally located within the distributor body. On all Duraspark III systems except the one for the V6, the distributor, therefore, serves only to distribute the high voltage generated by the ignition coil.

The relationship of the distributor rotor to the cap is of special importance for proper high voltage distribution in the Duraspark III system incorporated on all engines except the V6. For this reason, the distributor is secured to the engine and the distributor rotor, rather than the distributor body, is adjustable (refer to Section 6 for this procedure).

The distributor assembly used for the Duraspark III application on

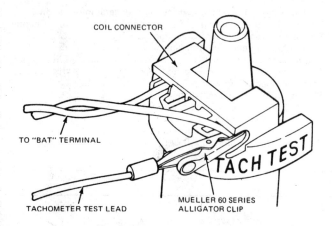

Fig. 5.1 Correct tachometer hook-up (Sec 1)

Labels: COIL CONNECTOR; TO "BAT" TERMINAL; TACHOMETER TEST LEAD; MUELLER 60 SERIES ALLIGATOR CLIP; TACH TEST

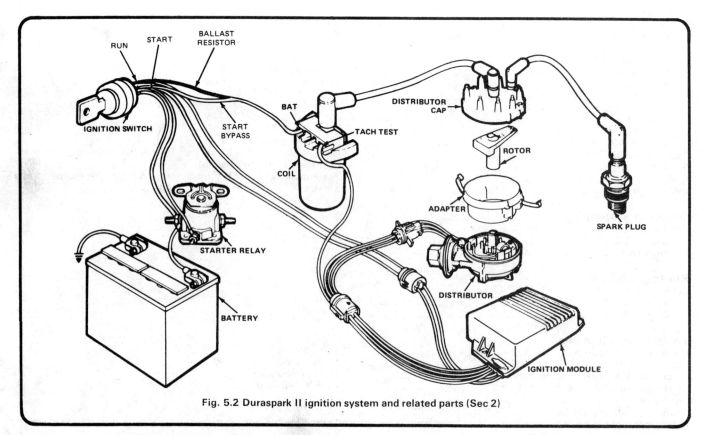

Fig. 5.2 Duraspark II ignition system and related parts (Sec 2)

Labels: RUN; START; BALLAST RESISTOR; IGNITION SWITCH; START BYPASS; BAT; TACH TEST; DISTRIBUTOR CAP; ROTOR; COIL; ADAPTER; SPARK PLUG; STARTER RELAY; BATTERY; DISTRIBUTOR; IGNITION MODULE

the V6 with EEC is a modified Duraspark II assembly. The centrifugal weights have been removed and very strong centrifugal springs are used to keep the sleeve and plate assembly stationary with respect to the distributor shaft. The diaphragm assembly has been replaced by a special clip that prevents movement of the stator assembly. Rotor alignment is not adjustable on this distributor and the only serviceable parts are the cap, rotor and adapter. If the distributor assembly is found to be inoperative, the distributor housing and stator assembly must be replaced as a single unit.

The coil, coil high tension lead, distributor cap and spark plug wires are of standard design.

Operation

The Duraspark II ignition system consists of a primary and a secondary circuit. Included in the primary circuit are the battery, ignition switch, ballast resistor, coil primary winding, ignition module and distributor stator assembly. The secondary circuit consists of the coil secondary winding, distributor rotor, distributor cap, ignition wires and spark plugs.

When the ignition switch is in the Run position, primary circuit

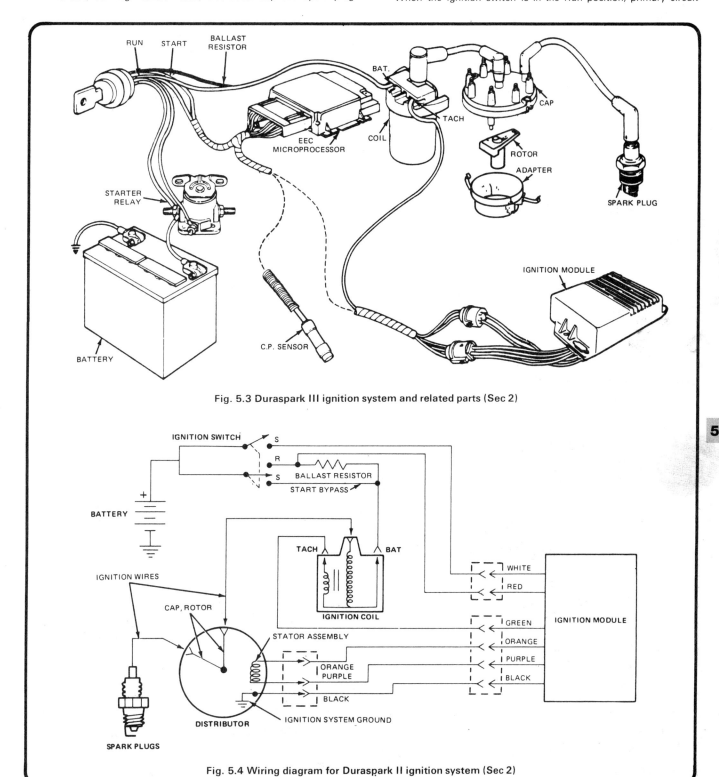

Fig. 5.3 Duraspark III ignition system and related parts (Sec 2)

Fig. 5.4 Wiring diagram for Duraspark II ignition system (Sec 2)

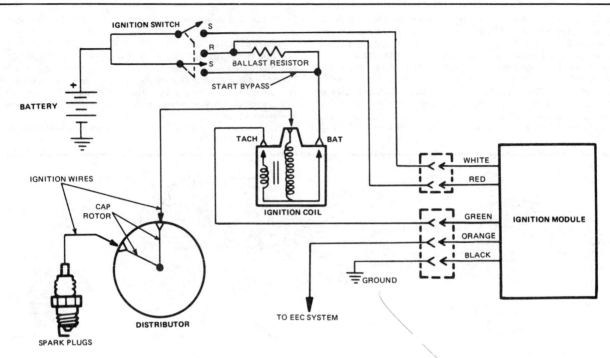

Fig. 5.5 Wiring diagram for Duraspark III ignition system (Sec 2)

current flows from the battery, through the ignition switch, the coil primary, the ignition module and back to the battery through the ignition system ground in the distributor. This current flow causes a magnetic field to be built up in the ignition coil. When the poles on the armature and stator assembly align, the ignition module turns the primary current off, collapsing the magnetic field in the ignition coil. The collapsing field induces a high voltage in the coil secondary winding and the coil wire conducts the high voltage to the distributor, where the cap and rotor distribute it to the appropriate spark plug. A timing circuit in the ignition module turns the primary current back on after a short time. High voltage is produced each time the magnetic field is built up and collapsed.

The red ignition module wire provides operating voltage for the ignition module's electronic components in the Run mode. The white wire provides voltage for the ignition module during the Start mode, while the bypass provides increased voltage for the coil during the Start mode.

The Duraspark III system operates very similarly to the Duraspark II system. The only operational difference is that in the Duraspark III system for all engines except the V6, instead of the distributor stator assembly causing the ignition module to interrupt primary circuit current, a signal from the EEC microprocessor does this. In the Duraspark III for the V6, the stator assembly and armature act to send a signal to the EEC, which, in turn, signals the ignition module *when* and *how* to operate. In all other respects, system operation of the Duraspark II and III is the same.

The ballast resistor is actually a specific length of special wire, used to limit the primary ignition circuit current in the Run mode. It is part of the vehicle wiring harness inside the passenger compartment and under no circumstances should it be cut, spliced or replaced by any other type of non-resistance wire.

3 Ignition system inspection and testing – general information

Note: *Initial checking procedures for many ignition components can be found in Chapter 1.*

Secondary ignition system problems and diagnosis are best handled through the use of an automotive electronic oscilloscope. An experienced operator and an electronic oscilloscope can pinpoint such problems as worn spark plugs, high-resistance spark plug wires, a damaged or cracked distributor cap and/or rotor, leakage between spark plug wires and other similar problems.

Primary system ignition problems can also be determined through the use of an oscilloscope. However, the main components sometimes require special test apparatus, procedures and operations.

A preliminary diagnosis of an ignition system can reveal such things as poor or disconnected wires and/or current leakage from the coil or the distributor.

With electronic ignition, the complexity of the design and testing procedures prevents in-field diagnosis of many of the system's components by the home mechanic. If a preliminary overall visual check reveals no obvious problems such as disconnected, broken or cracked components, the vehicle will have to be taken to an authorized service center to have the components diagnosed. Replacement of components diagnosed as defective may be made either by the service facility or the home mechanic, depending upon the ability of the home mechanic. Replacement parts are available from aftermarket manufacturers as well as from Ford dealers.

4 Spark plugs – general information

Properly functioning spark plugs are necessary if the engine is to perform properly. At the intervals specified in Chapter 1 of your owner's manual, the spark plugs should be replaced with new ones. Removal and installation information can be found in Chapter 1.

It is important to replace spark plugs with new ones of the same heat range and type. A series of numbers and letters are included on the spark plug to help identify each variation.

The spark plug gap is very important. If it is too large or too small, the size of the spark and its efficiency will be seriously impaired. To set it, measure the gap with a feeler gauge, and then bend the outer plug electrode until the correct gap is achieved. The center electrode should never be bent as this may crack the insulation and cause plug failure.

The condition and appearance of the spark plugs will tell much about the condition and state of tune of the engine. If the insulator nose of the spark plug is clean and white with no deposits, this is indicative of a weak mixture, or too hot a plug (a hot plug transfers heat away from the electrode slowly – a cold plug transfers it away quickly).

If the tip and insulator nose are covered with hard black-looking deposits, this is indicative that the mixture is too rich. Should the plug be black and oily, it is likely the engine is fairly worn, as well as the mixture being too rich.

If the insulator nose is covered with light tan to greyish brown deposits, the mixture is correct and it is likely the engine is in good condition.

If there are any traces of long brown tapered stains on the outside of the white portion of the plug, the plug will have to be replaced with a new one, as this indicates a faulty joint between the plug body and the insulator, and compression is being allowed to leak away.

Always tighten a spark plug to the specified torque – no tighter.

5 Ignition coil – checking and replacement

Checking
1 The ignition coil cannot be satisfactorily tested without the proper electronic diagnostic equipment. If a fault is suspected in the coil, have it checked by a dealer or repair shop specializing in electrical repairs. The coil can be replaced with a new one using the following procedure.

Replacement
2 Disconnect the negative battery cable from the battery.
3 Using coded strips of tape, mark each of the wires at the coil to help return the wires to their original positions during reinstallation.
4 Remove the coil-to-distributor high-tension lead.
5 Remove the connections at the coil. On electronic ignitions, these connections may be of the push-lock connector type. Separate them from the coil by releasing the tab at the bottom of the connector.
6 Remove the retaining bolt(s) holding the coil bracket to the cylinder head or intake manifold.
7 Remove the coil from the coil bracket by loosening the clamp bolt.
8 Installation is the reverse of removal. Apply a thin layer of silicone grease to the inside of the coil-to-distributor high-tension lead boot (see Section 1 for more information).

6 Duraspark III – rotor alignment (except V6 engine)

Note: *Refer to Fig. 5.6 to locate and identify pertinent components.*
1 Disconnect the spring clips retaining the distributor cap to the adapter and position the cap and wires to one side.
2 Remove the rotor from the sleeve assembly.

3 Rotate the engine until the number 1 piston is on the compression stroke (refer to Chapter 2A, Sec 9).
4 Slowly rotate the engine until a rotor alignment tool (Ford no. T79P-12200-A) can be inserted in the alignment slots in the sleeve assembly and adapter.
5 Read the timing mark on the crankshaft damper indicated by the timing pointer.
6 If the timing mark reading is 0°, plus or minus 4°, alignment is acceptable.
7 If the timing mark reading is beyond the acceptable limit stated in Step 6, make sure the number 1 piston is on the compression stroke.
8 Slowly rotate the engine until the timing pointer aligns with the 0° timing mark on the crankshaft damper.
9 Loosen the two sleeve assembly adjustment screws and insert the rotor alignment tool into the alignment slots in the sleeve assembly and adapter.
10 Tighten the sleeve assembly adjustment screws and remove the alignment tool.
11 Attach the rotor to the sleeve assembly.
12 Install the distributor cap and ignition wires, making sure that the ignition wires are securely connected to the cap and to the spark plugs. Refer to the information in Chapter 1 regarding the use of silicone grease when installing high-tension wires.

7 Stator assembly (Duraspark II only) – removal and installation

V8 engines
Removal
1 Remove the cable from the negative battery terminal.
2 Disconnect the spring clips retaining the distributor cap to the adapter and place the cap and wires aside.
3 Remove the rotor from the distributor shaft.
4 Disconnect the distributor connector from the wiring harness.
5 Disconnect the spring clips retaining the distributor cap adapter to the distributor body and remove the cap adjuster.

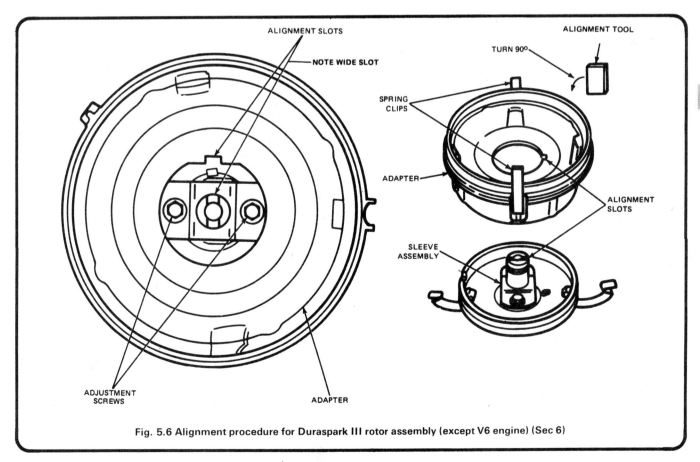

Fig. 5.6 Alignment procedure for Duraspark III rotor assembly (except V6 engine) (Sec 6)

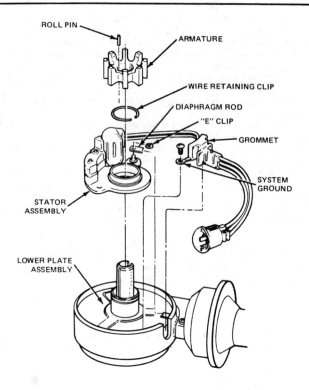

Fig. 5.7 Duraspark II stator assembly and related parts for V8 engines – exploded view (Sec 7)

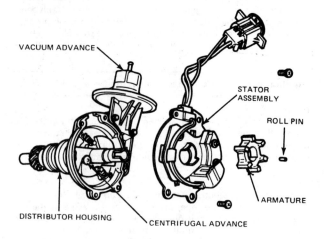

Fig. 5.8 Duraspark II stator assembly and related parts for six-cylinder engines – exploded view (Sec 7)

6   Using a small gear puller or two screwdrivers, remove the armature from the sleeve and plate assembly.
7   Remove the E-clip retaining the diaphragm rod to the stator assembly, then lift the diaphragm rod off the stator assembly pin.
8   Remove the screw retaining the ground strap at the stator assembly grommet.
9   Remove the wire retaining clip securing the stator assembly to the lower plate assembly.
10 Remove the grommet from the distributor base and lift the stator assembly off the lower plate assembly.

Installation
11 If the lower plate assembly is to be reused, clean the bushing to remove any accumulated dirt and grease.
12 Install the stator assembly by reversing the removal procedure. Note when installing the armature that there are two locating notches in it. Install the armature on the sleeve and plate assembly employing the unused notch and a *new* roll pin.
13 Check the initial timing (refer to Chapter 1).

Six-cylinder engines
Removal
14 Disconnect the cable from the negative battery terminal.
15 Disconnect the spring clips retaining the distributor cap and place the cap and wires aside.
16 Remove the rotor from the distributor shaft.
17 Disconnect the distributor connector from the wiring harness.
18 Using a small gear puller or two screwdrivers as levers, remove the armature sleeve and plate assembly.
19 Remove the two screws retaining the lower plate assembly and stator assembly to the distributor base, noting that there are two different size screws employed.
20 Remove the lower plate assembly and stator assembly from the distributor.
21 Remove the E-clip, flat washer and wave washer securing the stator assembly to the lower plate assembly, then separate the stator assembly from the lower plate assembly. Note the installation of the wave washer.
Installation
22 Before installing the stator, remove any accumulated dirt or grease from parts that are to be reused.

23 Place the stator assembly on the lower plate assembly and install the wave washer (outer edges up), flat washer and E-clip.
24 Install the stator assembly/lower plate assembly on the distributor base, making sure to engage the pin on the stator assembly in the diaphragm rod.
25 Attach the lower plate assembly and stator assembly to the distributor base, making sure to install the different size screws in their proper locations.
26 When installing the armature, note that there are two notches in it. Install the armature on the sleeve and plate assembly employing the unused notch and a new roll pin.
27 Connect the distributor connector to the wiring harness.
28 Reinstall the rotor and distributor cap, making sure that the ignition wires are securely connected to the cap and spark plugs. Refer to Section 27 in Chapter 1 regarding the use of silicone grease when installing plug wires.
29 Connect the cable to the negative battery terminal.
30 Check the initial timing (refer to Chapter 1).

8   Distributor – removal and installation

Duraspark II and Duraspark III for V6
Removal
1   Disconnect the spring clips retaining the distributor cap to the adapter and position the cap and wires to one side.
2   Disconnect and plug the diaphragm assembly hose(s), if so equipped.
3   Disconnect the distributor connector from the wiring harness.
4   Rotate the engine to align the stator assembly pole and any armature pole.
5   Scribe a mark on the distributor body and engine block or intake manifold to indicate the position of the distributor in the engine and the position of the rotor in the distributor.
6   Remove the distributor hold-down bolt and clamp.
7   Pull the distributor out of the engine. **Note:** *The engine should not be rotated while the distributor is out of the engine; however, if the engine is rotated, make sure you refer to the appropriate installation procedure below.*
Installation *(if engine was rotated while distributor was removed)*
8   Rotate the engine until the number 1 piston is on the compression stroke (refer to Chapter 2A, Section 9).
9   Align the timing marks for the correct initial timing, determined by referring to the Emissions Control Information label in the engine compartment.
10 Install the distributor in the engine with the rotor pointing at the number 1 cylinder terminal position on the cap and with the armature and stator assembly poles aligned.
11 Make sure the oil pump intermediate shaft properly engages the distributor shaft.

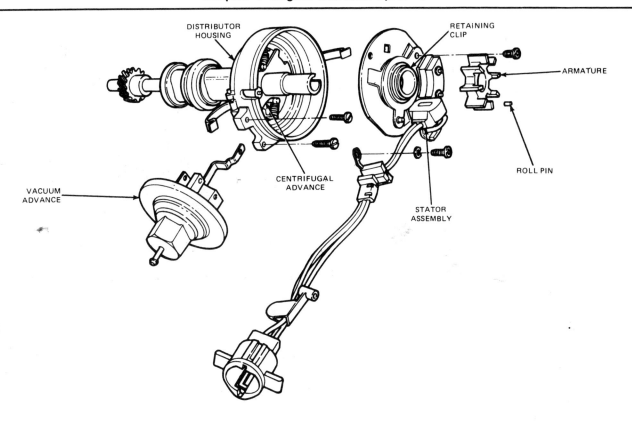

DISTRIBUTOR HOUSING

RETAINING CLIP

ARMATURE

VACUUM ADVANCE

CENTRIFUGAL ADVANCE

STATOR ASSEMBLY

ROLL PIN

Fig. 5.9 Duraspark II distributor assembly for V8 engines – exploded view (Sec 8)

12 If the distributor will not seat properly in the block/manifold, it may be necessary to crank the engine after the distributor gear is partially engaged in order to properly mesh the distributor shaft with the oil pump intermediate shaft, fully seating the distributor.

13 If it was necessary to crank the engine, again rotate the engine until the number 1 piston is on the compression stroke and align the timing marks for correct initial timing.

14 Rotate the distributor in the engine to align the armature and stator assembly poles and verify that the rotor is pointing at the number 1 cylinder cap terminal.

15 Install the distributor hold-down clamp and bolt, but do not tighten.

Installation *(if engine was not rotated while distributor was removed and original distributor is being reinstalled)*

16 Install the distributor in the engine with the rotor and distributor aligned with the previously scribed marks. The armature and stator assembly poles should also align when the distributor is fully seated in the engine and properly installed.

17 If the distributor will not properly seat in the engine, crank the engine until the distributor shaft and oil pump intermediate shaft are properly meshed and the distributor is properly seated.

18 Install the distributor hold-down clamp and bolt, but do not tighten.

Installation *(if the engine was not rotated while the distributor was removed and a new distributor is being installed)*

19 Install the distributor in the engine with the rotor aligned with the previously scribed mark on the block/manifold.

20 If necessary, crank the engine to fully seat the distributor.

21 Rotate the engine until the timing marks for the correct initial timing (determined by referring to the Emissions Control Information label in the engine compartment) are aligned and the rotor is pointing at the number 1 cylinder cap terminal.

22 Rotate the distributor in the block to align the armature and stator assembly poles.

23 Install the distributor hold-down clamp and bolt, but do not tighten.

24 If, in Steps 10, 14, 16 or 22 above, the armature and stator assembly poles cannot be aligned by rotating the distributor in the engine, pull the distributor out of the engine enough to disengage the distributor gear and rotate the distributor shaft to engage a different

gear tooth, then reinstall the distributor and repeat the Steps in the appropriate installation procedure as necessary.

25 Connect the distributor connector to the wiring harness.

26 Install the distributor cap and ignition wires, making sure that the wires are securely connected to the distributor cap and spark plugs. Refer to information in Section 1 regarding use of silicone grease when installing high-tension wires.

27 Set the initial timing according to the Emissions Control Information label located in the engine compartment.

28 Tighten the distributor hold-down bolt to the specified torque.

29 Recheck the initial timing and adjust as necessary.

30 Connect the diaphragm assembly hose(s), if so equipped.

Duraspark III for all engines except V6
Removal

31 Disconnect the spring clips retaining the distributor cap to the distributor cap adapter and position the cap and spark plug wires to one side.

32 Remove the rotor from the distributor shaft.

33 Rotate the engine until the number 1 piston is on the compression stroke (refer to Chapter 2A, Section 9), and the sleeve and adapter alignment slots are in line.

34 Remove the distributor hold-down clamp and bolt. **Note:** *Do not rotate the engine with the distributor removed.*

Installation

35 Position the distributor in the engine so that the slot in the distributor base mounting flange is aligned with the hold-down bolt hole and the sleeve/adapter alignment slots are in line when the distributor is fully seated in the engine.

36 If the sleeve/adapter slots cannot be aligned, pull the distributor out of the engine enough to disengage the distributor gear and rotate the shaft to engage a different distributor gear tooth with the cam gear, then reinstall the distributor.

37 Install the distributor clamp and hold-down bolt and tighten the bolt to the specified torque.

38 Check the rotor alignment (refer to Section 6).

39 Install the distributor cap and wires, making sure that the wires are securely connected to the cap and spark plugs. Refer to the information in Section 1 regarding use of silicone grease when installing high-tension wires.

5

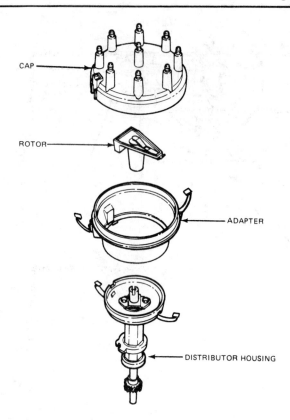

Fig. 5.10 Duraspark III distributor assembly for V8 engines – exploded view (Sec 8)

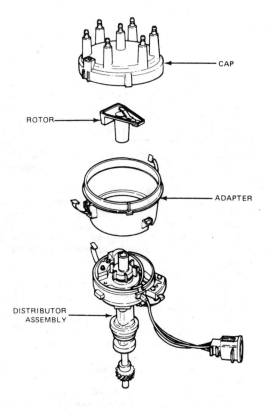

Fig. 5.11 Duraspark III distributor assembly for V6 engines with EEC – exploded view (Sec 8)

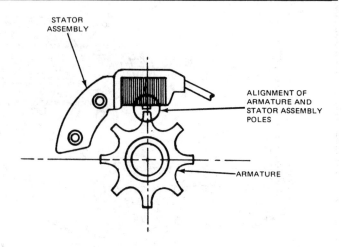

Fig. 5.12 Correct alignment of the distributor armature and stator assemblies (Sec 8)

9 Charging system – general information

The charging system is employed to replenish the battery voltage that is drained through the use of accessories and the running requirements of the engine's ignition system. An alternator provides electrical power and is driven by a V-belt and pulley drive system. It is generally located on the right side of the engine in varying positions depending on vehicle accessories.

Maintenance of the drivebelt tension, along with battery terminal service are the two primary maintenance items in the charging system. Details are provided in Chapter 1. The charging output is regulated by an external regulator mounted on the fender well or radiator support. The regulator is connected to the alternator through the use of a wiring loom utilizing quick-release connectors. The system is protected from circuit over-loading through the use of fusible links and the alternator is connected to the system with heavy gauge wire. A charge indicator light or gauge is provided. Circuit diagrams for the charging system are provided at the end of Chapter 10.

10 Charging system – checking

1   As mentioned in the previous Section, the main components of the charging system are the alternator, voltage regulator and battery.
2   Little maintenance is required for this system to operate properly. A periodic check of the battery cables and connections (Chapter 1), alternator drivebelt tension (Chapter 1) and the various wiring and connectors is all that is necessary.
3   If a fault develops which is traced to this system, the first checks should be those listed above. In many cases a fault is the result of a loose or corroded wire, loose drivebelt or other simple-to-fix problem. If, after all visual checks have been performed, the system is still not operating correctly, the vehicle will have to be inspected by a dealer or automotive electrical shop with the special diagnostic equipment necessary to check the system further.
4   If these diagnostic tests indicate a faulty alternator, you can either replace it with a rebuilt unit as described in Section 11 or check and replace the brushes yourself as described in Section 12. Voltage regulators and batteries are not rebuildable and must be replaced with new units.

11 Alternator – removal and installation

1   Disconnect the negative battery cable.
2   Carefully note the terminal connections at the rear or side of the alternator and disconnect them. Most connections will have a retaining nut and washer on them, however some connections may have a plastic snap-fit connector with a retaining clip. If a terminal is covered by a slip-on plastic cover, be careful when pulling the cover back so as not to damage the terminal or connector.

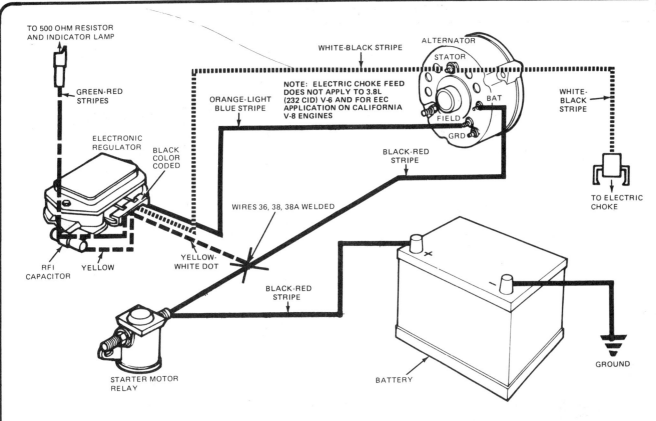

Fig. 5.13 Charging system with electronic regulator and warning light indicator (Sec 9)

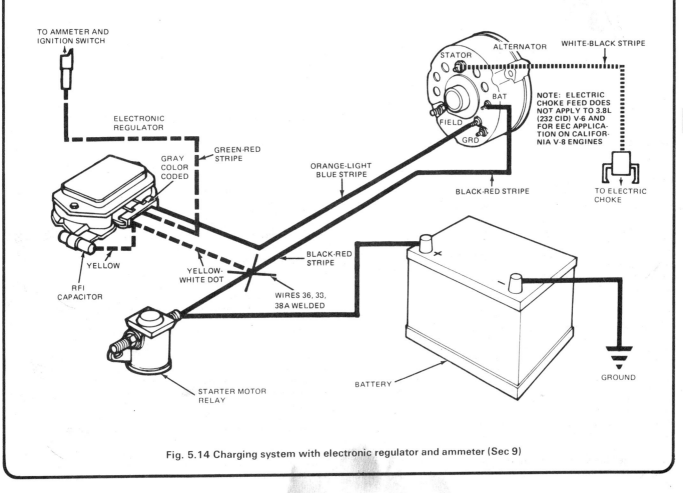

5

Fig. 5.14 Charging system with electronic regulator and ammeter (Sec 9)

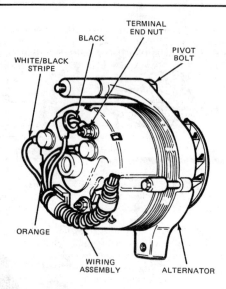

Fig. 5.15 Typical rear terminal alternator wire harness connections (Sec 11)

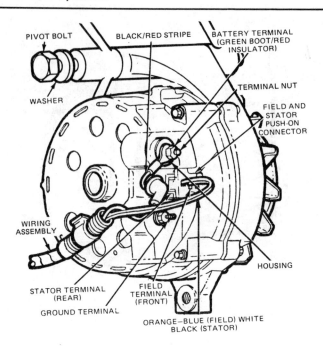

Fig. 5.16 Typical side terminal alternator wire harness connections (Sec 11)

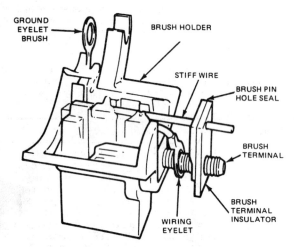

Fig. 5.17 Method of retracting brushes prior to installing brush holder on rear terminal alternator (Sec 12)

3   Loosen the alternator adjustment arm bolt.
4   Loosen the alternator pivot bolt.
5   Pivot the alternator to allow the drivebelt to be removed from the pulleys.
6   Remove the belt(s) from the pulley.
7   Remove the adjustment arm bolt and pivot the arm out of the way.
8   Remove the pivot bolt and spacer and carefully lift the alternator up and out of the engine compartment. Be careful not to drop or jar the alternator as it can be damaged. Note: *If purchasing a new or rebuilt alternator, take the original one with you to the dealer or parts store so the two can be compared side-by-side.*
9   Installation is the reverse of removal. Be careful when connecting all terminals at the rear or side of the alternator. Make sure they are clean and tight and that all terminal ends are tight on the wires. If you find any loose terminal ends, make sure you install new ones, as any arcing or shorting at the wires or terminals can damage the alternator.

12 Alternator brush – replacement

Note: *Internal replacement parts for alternators may not be readily available in your area. Check into availability before proceeding.*

Rear terminal type alternator
1   Remove the alternator as described in Section 11.

2   Scribe a line across the length of the alternator housing to ensure correct reassembly.
3   Remove the housing through-bolts and the nuts and insulators from the rear housing. Make a careful note of all insulator locations.
4   Withdraw the rear housing section from the stator, rotor and front housing assembly.
5   Remove the brushes and springs from the brush holder assembly which is located inside the rear housing.
6   Check the length of the brushes against the wear dimensions given in Specifications at the beginning of the Chapter and replace the brushes with new ones if necessary.
7   Install the springs and brushes in the holder assembly and retain them in place by inserting a piece of stiff wire through the rear housing and brush terminal insulator. Make sure enough wire protrudes through the rear housing so it can be withdrawn at a later stage.
8   Attach the rear housing rotor and front housing assembly to the stator, making sure the scribed marks are aligned.
9   Install the housing through-bolts and rear end insulators and nuts but do not tighten the nuts at this time.
10   Carefully extract the piece of wire from the rear housing and make sure that the brushes are seated on the slip ring. Tighten the through-bolts and rear housing nuts.
11   Install the alternator as described in Section 11.

Side terminal type alternator
12   Remove the alternator as described in Section 11 and scribe a mark on both end housings and the stator for ease of reassembly.
13   Remove the through-bolts and separate the front housing and rotor from the rear housing and stator. Be careful that you do not separate the rear housing and stator.
14   Use a soldering iron to unsolder and disengage the brush holder from the rear housing. Remove the brushes and springs from the brush holders.
15   Remove the two brush holder attaching screws and lift the brush holder from the rear housing.
16   Remove any sealing compound from the brush holder and rear housing.
17   Inspect the brushes for damage and check their dimensions against the Specifications. If they are worn out, replace them with new ones.
18   To reassemble, install the springs and brushes in the brush holders, inserting a piece of stiff wire to hold them in place.
19   Place the brush holder in position in the rear housing, using the

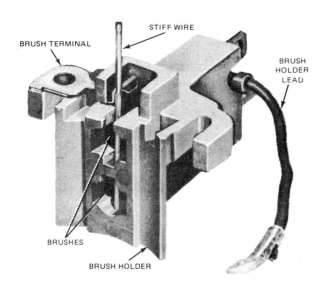

BRUSH TERMINAL

STIFF WIRE

BRUSH HOLDER LEAD

BRUSHES

BRUSH HOLDER

Fig. 5.18 Method of retracting brushes prior to installing brush holder on side terminal alternator (Sec 12)

wire to retract the brushes through the hole in the rear housing.
20 Install the brush holder attaching screws and push the holder toward the shaft opening as you tighten the screws. **Caution:** *The rectifier can be overheated and damaged if the soldering is not done quickly.* Press the brush holder lead onto the rectifier lead and solder them in place.
21 Place the rotor and front housing in position in the stator and rear housing. After aligning the scribe marks, install the through-bolts.
22 Turn the fan and pulley to check for binding in the alternator.
23 Withdraw the wire which is retracting the brushes and seal the hole with waterproof cement. **Note:** *Do not use RTV-type sealer on the hole.*

13 Regulator – removal and installation

1 Remove the negative battery cable from the battery.
2 Locate the voltage regulator. It will usually be positioned on the radiator wall or the fender well near the front of the vehicle.
3 Push the two tabs on either side of the quick-release clip retaining the wiring loom to the regulator. Pull the quick-release clip straight out from the side of the regulator.
4 Remove the two regulator retaining screws. Notice that one screw will locate the ground wire terminal.
5 Remove the regulator.
6 Installation is the reverse of removal. Make sure you get the wiring clip positioned firmly onto the regulator terminals and that both clips click into place.

14 Starting system – general information

The starting system consists of an electric starter motor with an integral positive engagement drive, the battery, a starter switch located in the cab of the vehicle, a Neutral start switch (automatic transmission equipped vehicles only) a starter solenoid and wiring looms connecting these components.

When the ignition switch is turned to the Start position, the starter solenoid is energized through the starter control circuit. The solenoid then connects battery voltage to the starter motor.

Vehicles with an automatic transmission have a Neutral start switch in the starter control circuit which prevents operation of the starter if the selector lever is not in the N or P position.

When the starter is energized by the battery, current flows to the grounded field coil and operates the magnetic switch which drives the starter drive plunger forward to engage the flywheel ring gear.

When the drive plunger reaches its travel, the field coil grounding contacts open and the starter motor contacts engage, allowing the

starter to turn.

A special holding coil is used to maintain the starter drive shoe in its fully-seated position while the starter is turning the engine.

When the battery voltage is released from the starter, a retracting spring withdraws the starter drive pinion from the flywheel and the motor contact is broken.

15 Starter – checking in vehicle

If the starter motor does not rotate when the starter switch is activated, check that the transmission selector lever is in N or P (automatic transmission vehicles only).

Check that the battery is well-charged and that all cables at the battery, starter solenoid and starter are tight and free of corrosion.

If the motor spins but the engine is not cranking, the starter drive is defective and the starter motor will have to be removed for drive replacement.

If the switch does not operate the starter at all but the drive can be heard engaging the flywheel with a loud "click", then the fault lies in the motor activating contacts within the motor itself. The motor will have to be removed and replaced or overhauled.

If the starter motor cranks the engine at an abnormally slow speed, make sure the battery is fully charged and that all terminal connections are tight. It is also necessary to verify that the engine oil viscosity is not too thick and the resistance is not due to a mechanical problem within the engine.

A voltmeter connected to the starter motor terminal of the solenoid (positive) and to the ground (negative) will show the voltage being sent to the starter. If the voltage is adequate and the starter still turns slowly, the resistance is in the starter and the starter should be replaced or overhauled.

If a fault has been definitely traced to the starter, the original unit can be simply replaced by a rebuilt or new starter (Section 16) or the original starter brushes can be checked and replaced (Section 17).

16 Starter – removal and installation

1 Disconnect the negative battery cable from the battery.
2 Disconnect the wire connecting the starter solenoid to the starter motor.
3 Remove the retaining bolts securing the starter to the bellhousing.
4 Pull the starter out of the bellhousing and lower it from the vehicle.
5 Installation is the reverse of removal. When inserting the starter into its opening of the bellhousing, make sure it is situated squarely and the mating faces are flush. Tighten the retaining bolts to the proper torque.

17 Starter brush – replacement

Note: *The starter must be removed from the vehicle before the brushes can be replaced. Before attempting to replace the brushes in the starter make sure the problem you are having is related to the brushes. Often, loose connections, poor battery condition or wiring problems are a more likely cause of no start or poor starting conditions. Check on the availability of internal replacement parts before proceeding.*
1 Remove the starter from the vehicle (Section 16).
2 Remove the two through-bolts from the starter frame.
3 Pull the brush endplate along with the brush springs and brushes from the holder.
4 Remove the ground brush retaining screws from the frame. Remove the brushes from the frame.
5 Cut the insulated brush leads from the field coils as close to the field connection point as possible.
6 Inspect the plastic brush holder for any signs of cracks or broken mounting pads. If these conditions exist, replace the plastic brush holder.
7 Place the new insulated field brush lead onto the field coil connection.
8 Crimp the clip provided with the brushes to hold the brush lead to the connection.
9 Using a low-heat soldering gun (300 watts), solder the lead, the clip and the connection together using rosin-core solder.

5

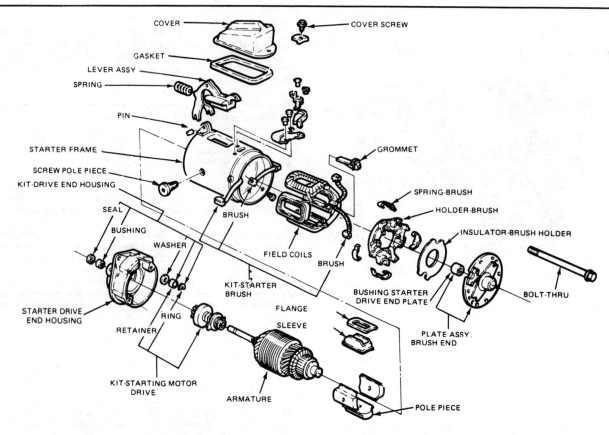

Fig. 5.19 Typical starter assembly – exploded view (Sec 17)

10 Install the ground brush leads to the frame with the retaining screws.

11 Install the brush holder and insert the brushes into the holder.

12 Install the brush springs. Notice that the positive brush leads are positioned in their respective slots in the brush holder to prevent any chance of grounding the brushes.

13 Install the brush endplate in place. Make sure the endplate insulator is positioned correctly on the endplate.

14 Install the through-bolt in the starter frame and tighten it to the correct torque.

15 A battery can be used to check the starter by connecting a heavy cable such as jumper cables to the positive and negative battery posts.

16 Connect the ground lead to the starter.

17 Secure the starter in soft jaws of a vise or other similar clamping device.

18 Momentarily contact the starter connection with the positive cable from the battery.

19 The starter should spin and the solenoid drive should engage the gear in a forward position when this connection is completed.

20 If the starter operates correctly, install the starter in the vehicle as described in the previous Section.

18 Starter solenoid – removal and installation

1 Disconnect the negative battery cable, followed by the positive cable, from the battery.

2 Disconnect the positive battery cable and feed cable from the terminal on the starter solenoid. Mark them to prevent mix-ups during installation.

3 Disconnect the starter feed wire from the opposite terminal on the starter solenoid. Mark the feed wire as above.

4 Disconnect the two starter solenoid triggering wires from the top posts on the solenoid. Make sure you mark or indicate the position of these wires as they can be cross-connected and damage the electrical system.

5 Remove the two starter solenoid-to-fender well retaining bolts.

6 Remove the starter solenoid.

7 Before installing the new or replacement solenoid, use a wire brush to carefully clean the mounting surface on the fender well for better grounding capability.

8 Attach the starter solenoid to the fender well using the retaining bolts and tighten them securely. **Note:** *Use care when tightening these bolts as they are self-threading and can easily be stripped in the mounting hole.*

9 Reconnect all wires to their original positions.

Chapter 6 Emissions control systems

Refer to Chapter 13 for information on 1984 and later models

Contents

1 General information

In order to meet U.S. federal anti-pollution laws, vehicles are equipped with a variety of emissions control systems, depending on the models and the states in which they are sold.

Since the emissions systems control so many of the engine's functions, driveability and fuel consumption, as well as conformance to the law, can be affected should any problems develop. Therefore, it is very important that the emissions systems be kept operating at peak efficiency.

The information in this Chapter describes the sub-systems within the overall emissions control system and the maintenance operations for these sub-systems that are within the reach of the home mechanic. In addition, the Emissions Control Information label, located in the engine compartment, contains information required to properly maintain the emissions control systems as well as for keeping the vehicle correctly tuned.

Due to the complexity of the sub-systems, especially those under the control of electronic devices that require sophisticated electronic analysis, it is suggested that professional technical assistance at a properly equipped facility be sought when you run into an emissions problem that cannot be readily diagnosed and/or repaired.

Note: *Although the information in this Chapter covers all truck models through the 1982 model year, complete information on 1983 emissions systems was not available at the time of publication of this manual. Most 1983 systems were expected to remain the same as those installed in the previous model year, but should any questions arise specific to 1983 truck models, a check with your Ford dealer is advised.*

2 Positive Crankcase Ventilation (PCV) system

General description

1   The positive crankcase ventilation system is a closed recirculating system which is designed to prevent engine crankcase fumes from escaping into the atmosphere through the engine oil filler cap. The crankcase control system regulates these blow-by vapors by circulating them back into the intake manifold where they are burned with the incoming fuel and air mixture.

2   The system consists of a replaceable PCV valve, a crankcase ventilation filter in the air cleaner and connecting hoses and gaskets.

3   The air source for the crankcase ventilation system is in the carburetor air cleaner. Air passes through a filter located in the air cleaner to a hose connecting the air cleaner to the oil filler cap (photo). The oil filler cap is sealed at the opening to prevent the entrance of outside air. From the oil filler cap the air flows into the rocker arm chamber, down past the pushrods and into the crankcase. The air then circulates from the crankcase up into another section of the rocker arm chamber. The air and crankcase gasses then enter a spring-loaded regulator valve (PCV valve) that controls the amount of flow as operating conditions vary. Some engines have a fixed orifice PCV valve that meters a steady flow of gas mixture regardless of the extent of

2.3 PCV system inlet hose connects to the oil filler cap and the air cleaner (V8 engine shown, others similar)

engine blow-by gasses. In either case, the air and gas mixture is routed to the intake manifold through the crankcase vent hose tube and fittings. This process goes on continuously while the engine is running.

Checking

4   The checking procedures for the PCV system are described in Chapter 1, Section 13.

Component replacement

5   The replacement procedures for the PCV system components are described in Chapter 1, Section 13.

3 Fuel evaporative emissions control system

General description

1   This system is designed to limit fuel vapors released to the atmosphere by trapping and storing fuel that evaporates from the fuel tank (and in some cases, from the carburetor) which would normally enter the atmosphere, contributing to hydrocarbon (HC) emissions.

2   The home mechanic-serviceable parts of the system include a charcoal-filled canister, connection lines to the fuel tank and carburetor and the fuel tank filler cap.

3   Fuel vapors are vented from the fuel tank (and in some cases, also from the carburetor) for temporary storage in the canister, which is mounted on the right side frame rail in the engine compartment. The canister outlet is connected to the carburetor air cleaner so the stored vapors will be drawn into the engine and burned. The fuel tank f ller

6

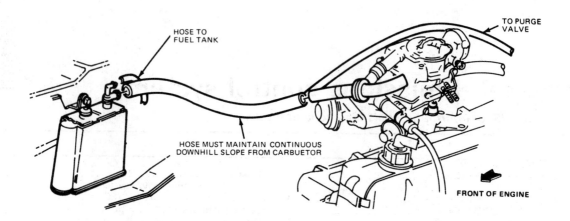

Fig. 6.1 Typical fuel evaporative canister venting system showing connections to other components (six-cylinder shown, others similar) (Sec 3)

cap is of a special design that vents air into the tank to replace the fuel being used, but does not vent fuel vapors to the outside air under normal conditions (unless tank pressure builds up to more than approximately two psi above normal atmospheric pressure).

Checking

4   The checking procedures for the fuel evaporative emissions control system are described in Chapter 1, Section 18.

Component replacement

5   The replacement procedures for the fuel evaporative emissions control system are described in Chapter 1, Section 18.

4   Exhaust Gas Recirculation (EGR) system

General description

1   The EGR system is designed to reintroduce small amounts of exhaust gas into the combustion cycle, thus reducing the generation of nitrous oxide (NOX) emissions. The amount of exhaust gas reintroduced and the timing of the cycle is controlled by various factors such as engine speed, altitude, engine vacuum, exhaust system back pressure, coolant temperatures and throttle angle depending on the engine calibration. All EGR valves are vacuum actuated and the vacuum diagram for your particular vehicle is shown on the Emissions Control Information label in the engine compartment.
2   For the vehicles covered by this manual, there are three basic types of EGR valves: the ported valve, the integral back pressure transducer valve and the electronic sonic valve.

Ported valve
3   Two passages in the base connecting the exhaust system with the intake manifold are blocked by the ported EGR valve, which is opened by vacuum and closed by spring pressure. The valve may be of the poppet or tapered stem design and may have a base entry or side entry, the function being the same.

Integral back pressure transducer valve
4   This poppet-type or tapered (pintle) valve cannot be opened by vacuum until the bleed hole is closed by exhaust back pressure. Once the valve opens, it seeks a level dependent upon the exhaust back pressure flowing through the orifice, and in so doing oscillates at that level. The higher the signal vacuum and exhaust back pressure, the more the valve opens. The valve body may be base entry or side entry.

Electronic sonic valve assembly
5   On vehicles equipped with an electronic engine control system, exhaust gas recirculation is controlled by the EEC through a system of engine sensors. The EGR valve in this system resembles and is operated in the same manner as a conventional ported design valve; however, it uses a tapered pintle valve for more exact control of the flow rate, which is very closely proportional to the valve stem position. A sensor on top of the valve tells how far the EGR valve is open, sends

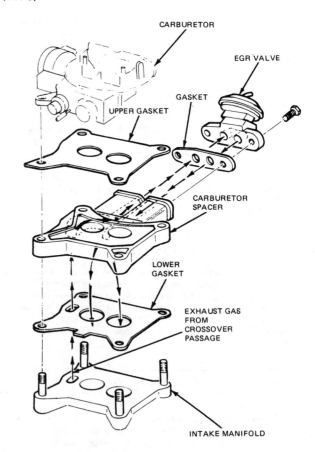

Fig. 6.2 Typical EGR valve installation (V8 shown, others similar) (Sec 4)

an electrical signal to the EEC, which is also receiving several other signals such as temperature, rpm and throttle opening, simultaneously. The EEC then signals the EGR control solenoids to maintain or alter the flow as required by the engine operating conditions. Source vacuum from the manifold is then either bled off or applied to the diaphragm, depending on what the EEC commands. A cooler is used to reduce the temperature of the exhaust gasses, helping the gasses to flow better, reducing the tendency of the engine to detonate and making the valve more durable.
6   The EGR valve operates only in the part-throttle mode; thereafter, it must remain closed in the cranking mode, the closed throttle mode and the wide open throttle mode.

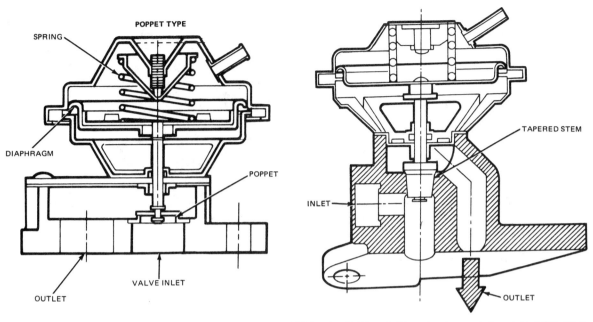

Fig. 6.3 Cross-sectional views of a base entry, poppet-type EGR valve (left) and side entry, tapered stem type EGR valve (right) (Sec 4)

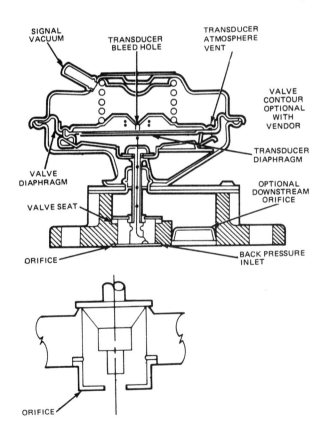

Fig. 6.4 Cross-sectional view of an integral backpressure transducer type EGR valve (Sec 4)

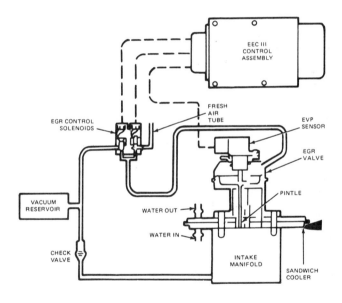

Fig. 6.5 Schematic of a typical EGR system used with an EEC III system and incorporating an electronic sonic valve (Sec 4)

9 Using finger pressure, press in on the diaphragm on the bottom of the valve. If the valve sticks open or closed or does not operate smoothly, clean the valve or replace it with a new one.

Electronic sonic valve assembly

10 If a malfunction is suspected in the electronic sonic valve or the EVP sensor to which it is attached, have the system checked at a Ford dealer service department.

Component replacement

11 When replacing any vacuum hoses, remove only one hose at a time and make sure that the replacement hose is of the same quality and size as the hose being replaced.

12 When replacing the EGR valve, label each hose as it is disconnected from the valve to ensure proper connection to the replacement valve.

13 The valve is easily removed from the intake manifold after

Checking

Ported valve and integral back pressure transducer valve

7 Check that all vacuum lines are properly routed, all connections are secure and that the hoses are not crimped, cracked or broken. If deteriorated hoses are encountered, replace them with new ones.

8 Visually inspect the valve for rust or corrosion. If rust or corrosion is encountered, clean the valve or replace it with a new one.

disconnecting and labeling the attached hoses. Be sure to use a new gasket when installing the valve and check for leaks when the job is complete. Torque specifications can be found in Chapter 2. Refer to the appropriate Part for your particular engine.

5   Spark control system

Note: *The information in this Section is applicable only to vehicles equipped with the Duraspark II ignition system. Because spark advance and retard functions on vehicles equipped with Duraspark III ignition systems are controlled by the EEC microprocessor, checks and tests involving the spark control system on these vehicles must be performed by a Ford dealer service department.*

General description
1   The spark control system is designed to reduce hydrocarbon and oxides of nitrogen (NOX) emissions by advancing the ignition timing only when the engine is cold.
2   These systems are fairly complex and have many valves, relays, amplifiers and other components built into them. Each vehicle will have a system peculiar to the model year, geographic region and gross vehicle weight rating. A schematic diagram located on the underside of the hood will detail the exact components and vacuum line routing of the particular system on your vehicle.
3   Depending on engine coolant temperature, altitude and the position of the throttle, vacuum is applied to either one or both of the diaphragms in the distributor vacuum unit and the ignition timing is changed to reduce emissions and improve cold engine driveability.

Checking
4   Visually check all vacuum hoses for cracks, splits or hardening. Next, remove the distributor cap and rotor. Apply a vacuum to the distributor advance port (and retard port, if so equipped) and see if the breaker or relay plate inside of the distributor moves. The plate should move opposite the distributor direction of rotation when vacuum is applied to the advance port and should move in the direction of rotation if vacuum is applied to the retard port (if so equipped).
5   Checking of the temperature relays, delay valves or other modifiers of the spark timing system is beyond the scope of the average home mechanic. Consult an expert if you suspect that you have other problems within the spark advance system.

Component replacement
6   When replacing any vacuum hoses, remove only one hose at a time and make sure that the replacement hose is of the same quality and size as the hose being replaced.
7   If it is determined that a malfunction in the spark control system is due to a faulty distributor, refer to Chapter 5 for the replacement procedure.

6   Thermactor systems

General description
1   Thermactor systems are employed to reduce carbon monoxide and hydrocarbon emissions. Two types are found on Ford trucks covered by this manual, a conventional thermactor air injection system and a managed air thermactor system.
2   The conventional thermactor air injection system consists of an air supply pump (photo), an air bypass valve, a check valve, an air manifold and connecting hoses. The managed air thermactor system adds a second check valve and an air control valve to the system. The air control valve may be incorporated with the air bypass valve into a single air/bypass control valve in some applications.
3   The thermactor air injection system functions by continuing combustion of unburned gasses after they leave the combustion chamber by injecting fresh air into the hot exhaust system leaving the exhaust ports. At this point, the fresh air mixes with hot exhaust gas to promote further oxidation of both hydrocarbons and carbon monoxide, thereby reducing their concentration and converting some of them into harmless carbon dioxide and water. During some modes of operation, such as extended idle, the thermactor air is dumped into the atmosphere by the bypass valve to prevent overheating of the exhaust system.

6.2 Location of the Thermactor system air pump (V8 engine shown, others similar)

4   The managed air thermactor system serves the same function as the thermactor air injection system, but, through the addition of the air control valve, diverts thermactor air either upstream to the exhaust manifold check valve, or downstream to the added, rear section check valve and on to the dual catalytic converter. The air is utilized in the converter to maintain feed gas oxygen contents at a high level. This system is configured in both electronic and non-electronic controlled versions.

Checking
Air supply pump
5   Check and adjust the drivebelt tension (refer to Chapter 1).
6   Disconnect the air supply hose at the air bypass valve inlet.
7   The pump is operating satisfactorily if air flow is felt at the pump outlet with the engine running at idle, increasing as the engine speed is increased.
8   If the air pump does not successfully pass the above tests, replace it with a new or rebuilt unit.
Air bypass valve
9   With the engine running at idle, disconnect the hose from the outlet valve.
10 Remove the vacuum line from the vacuum nipple and remove or bypass any restrictors or delay valves in the vacuum line.
11 Verify that vacuum is present in the vacuum line by putting your finger over its end.
12 Reconnect the vacuum line to the vacuum nipple.
13 With the engine running at 1500 rpm, air pump supply air should be felt or heard at the air bypass valve outlet.
14 With engine still running at 1500 rpm, disconnect the vacuum line. Air at the valve outlet should be decreased or shut off and air pump supply air should be felt or heard at the silencer ports.
15 Reconnect all disconnected hoses.
16 If the normally closed air bypass valve does not successfully pass the above tests, check the air pump (refer to Steps 5 through 7).
17 If the air pump is operating satisfactorily, replace the air bypass valve with a new one.
Air supply control valve
18 With the engine running at 1500 rpm, disconnect the hose at the air supply control valve inlet and verify the presence of air flow through the hose.
19 Reconnect the hose to the valve inlet.
20 Disconnect the hoses at the vacuum nipple and at outlets A and B (refer to the accompanying illustration).
21 With the engine running at 1500 rpm, air flow should be felt at outlet B with little or no air flow at outlet A.
22 With the engine running at 1500 rpm, connect a line from any manifold vacuum fitting to the vacuum nipple.

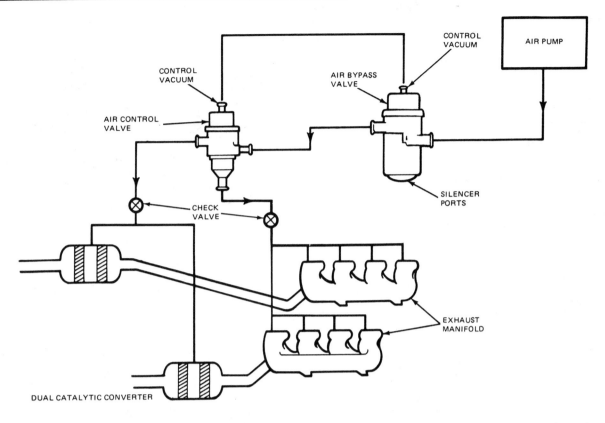

Fig. 6.6 Schematic of a typical managed air thermactor system with separate air control and air bypass valves (Sec 6)

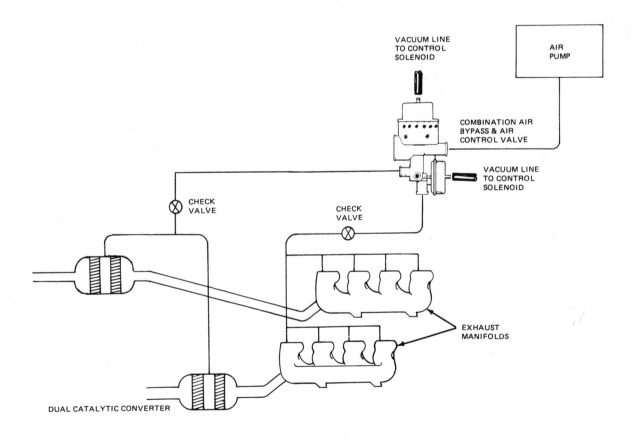

6

Fig. 6.7 Schematic of a typical managed air thermactor system with a combined bypass/control valve (Sec 6)

23 Air flow should be present at outlet A with little or no air flow at outlet B.
24 Restore all connections.
25 If all conditions above are not met, replace the air control valve with a new one.

Combination air bypass/air control valve

26 Disconnect the hoses from outlets A and B (refer to the accompanying illustration).
27 Disconnect the vacuum line at port D and plug the line.
28 With the engine running at 1500 rpm, verify that air flows from the bypass vents.
29 Unplug and reconnect the vacuum line to port D, then disconnect and plug the line attached to port S.
30 Verify that vacuum is present in the line to vacuum port D by momentarily disconnecting it.
31 Reconnect the vacuum line to port D.
32 With the engine running at 1500 rpm, verify that air is flowing out of outlet B with no air flow present at outlet A.
33 Attach a length of hose to port S.
34 With the engine running at 1500 rpm, apply vacuum by mouth to the hose and verify that air is flowing out of outlet A.

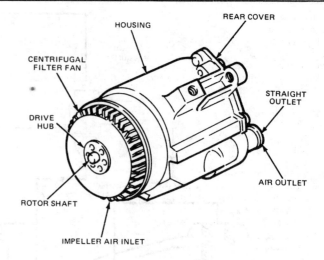

Fig. 6.8 Typical air supply pump for the thermactor system (Sec 6)

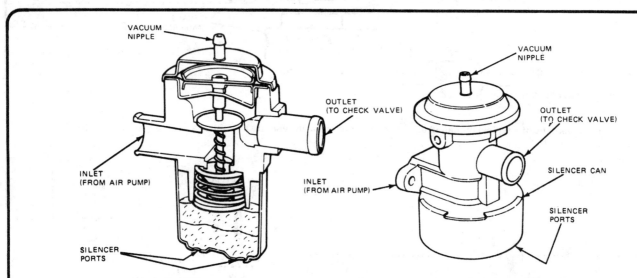

Fig. 6.9 Two styles of normally closed air bypass valves used in thermactor systems – remote mounted (left) and air pump mounted (right) (Sec 6)

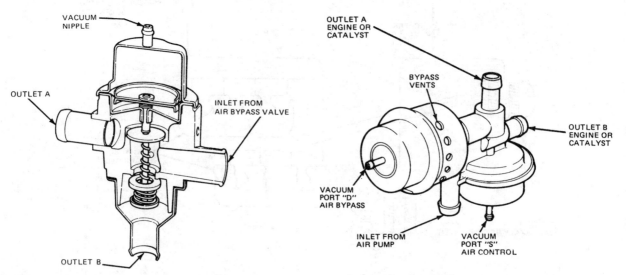

Fig. 6.10 Cross-sectional view of a typical standard air control valve (Sec 6)

Fig. 6.11 Details of a typical combined air bypass/air control valve (Sec 6)

35 Reconnect all hoses. Be sure to unplug the line to Port S before reconnecting it.
36 If all conditions above are not met, replace the combination valve with a new one.

Check valve
37 Disconnect the hoses from both ends of the check valve.
38 Blow through both ends of the check valve, verifying that air flows in one direction only.
39 If air flows in both directions or not at all, replace the check valve with a new one.
40 When reconnecting the valve, make sure it is installed in the proper direction.

Component replacement
41 The air bypass valve, air supply control valve, check valve and combination air bypass/air control valves may be replaced by disconnecting the hoses leading to them (be sure to label the hoses as they are disconnected to facilitate reconnection), replacing the faulty element with a new one and reconnecting the hoses to the proper ports. Make sure that the hoses are in good condition; if not, replace them with new ones.
42 To replace the air supply pump, first loosen the appropriate engine drivebelt(s) (refer to Chapter 1, Section 6 for procedural assistance), then remove the faulty pump from its bracket mounting, labeling all wires and hoses as they are removed to facilitate installation of the new unit.
43 After the new pump is installed, adjust the drivebelt(s) to the specified tension (refer to Chapter 1, Specifications).
44 Torque specifications for thermactor component installation will be found in Chapter 2. Refer to the appropriate Part for your particular engine.

7   Choke control system

General description
1 This system is installed to control emissions by precisely matching fuel supply to engine needs at all temperatures.
2 Choke system modifiers include a full electric choke or electrically assisted heating coil, and pull-down and pull-off assemblies. In addition, various control units which monitor engine temperature and choke position are mounted, along with their linkages, providing

appropriate choke action relative to the engine's ability to run on lean fuel mixtures as it warms up.
3 All of the systems combine to modify choke opening by lessening the time the choke plate is closed, thus lessening the amount of unburned hydrocarbons produced.

Checking
4 Information on the Emissions Control Information label located in the engine compartment and instructions in carburetor rebuild kits applicable to your particular carburetor can be used to service and rebuild these choke modifying devices. Also, refer to the Chapter 1 and Chapter 4 carburetor and choke inspection and adjustment procedures.

Component replacement
5 Due to the variety of carburetors used on Ford trucks covered in this manual and the variance in the choke control system components employed, it is not practical to list all the component replacement procedures. As is the case with general carburetor overhauls, the instructions accompanying the rebuild kit for your particular carburetor will fully explain these procedures.

8   Inlet air temperature control system

General description
1 The air cleaner temperature control system is used to keep the air entering the carburetor at a warm and consistent temperature. The carburetor can then be calibrated much leaner for emissions reduction, improved warm-up and better driveability.
2 Two air flow circuits are used. They are controlled by various intake manifold vacuum and temperature sensing valves. A vacuum motor, which operates a heat duct valve in the air cleaner, is activated by these two previously mentioned circuits.
3 When the under-hood temperature is cold, air is drawn through the shroud which fits over the exhaust manifold, up through the heat riser tube and into the air cleaner. This provides warm air for the carburetor, resulting in better driveability and faster warm-up. As the under-hood temperature rises, the duct valve will be closed by the vacuum motor and the air that enters the air cleaner will be drawn through the cold air snorkel or duct. This provides a consistent intake air temperature.

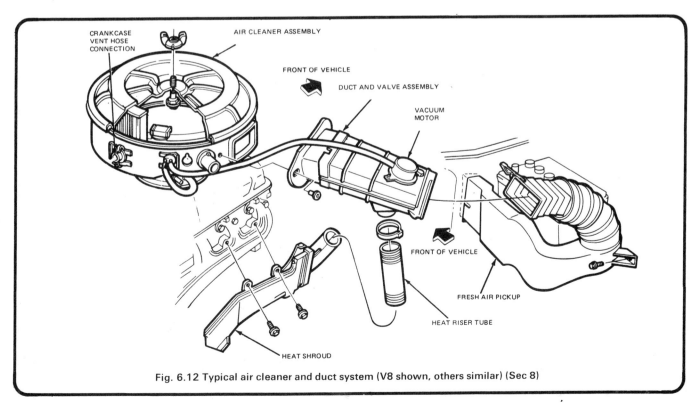

Fig. 6.12 Typical air cleaner and duct system (V8 shown, others similar) (Sec 8)

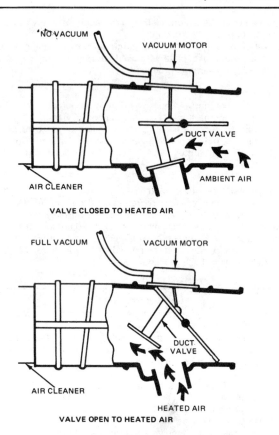

Fig. 6.13 Operation of the vacuum-operated duct valve in the air inlet temperature control system (Sec 8)

Checking

General

4   Checking of this system should be done while the engine is cold.

5   Remove the clamp retaining the air hose to the rear of the metal duct and valve assembly. Start the engine and, looking through the rear of the duct and valve assembly, observe that the duct valve (heat control door) rotates to allow hot air from the heat riser tube to enter the air cleaner. As the engine warms up, the vacuum motor should pull the valve open, closing off the heat riser tube and allowing ambient air to enter the duct.

Duct valve

6   If the duct valve does not perform as indicated, check that it is not rusted in an open or closed position by attempting to move it by hand. If it is rusted, it can usually be freed by cleaning and oiling it, otherwise replace it with a new unit.

Vacuum motor

7   If the vacuum motor fails to perform as indicated, check carefully for a leak in the hose leading to it. If no leak is found, replace the vacuum motor with a new one.

Component replacement

8   Replacement of the valve assembly and vacuum motor is straightforward and is accomplished by unbolting the faulty component, removing the vacuum lines leading to it (where appropriate) and installing the new component.

9   Deceleration throttle control system

General description

1   This system reduces the hydrocarbon and carbon monoxide content of exhaust gasses by opening the throttle slightly during deceleration.

2   The system consists of a throttle positioner, a vacuum solenoid valve, a vacuum sensing switch and electrical linkups to an electronic speed sensor/governor module, although not all components are included in all systems.

3   On those models without a vacuum sensing switch, when the engine speed is higher than a predetermined rpm, a signal is sent to the solenoid, which allows manifold vacuum to activate the throttle positioner.

4   On those models with a vacuum sensing switch, when the engine speed is higher than a predetermined rpm and manifold vacuum is at a certain value, the signal from the vacuum switch sends a signal to the module, then to the solenoid, allowing manifold vacuum to activate the throttle positioner.

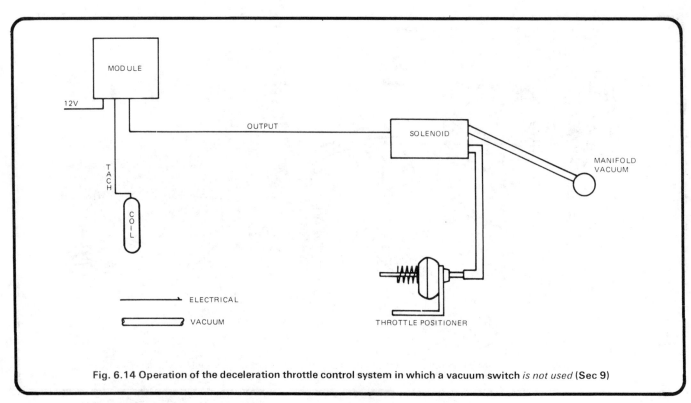

Fig. 6.14 Operation of the deceleration throttle control system in which a vacuum switch _is not used_ (Sec 9)

Checking
General
5   All of the following checks are to be made with the engine at full operating temperature and with all accessories off unless otherwise noted.
6   With the engine at idle, accelerate to 2000 rpm or more, then let the engine fall back to idle while watching to see if the vacuum diaphragm plunger extends and retracts. If the plunger performs as indicated, the system is functioning normally. If not, check the throttle positioner.

Throttle positioner
7   Remove the hose from the throttle positioner and using, a hand-operated vacuum pump, apply a 19 in Hg vacuum to the diaphragm and trap it, If the diaphragm does not respond or will not hold vacuum, replace the throttle positioner with a new one.
8   Remove the vacuum pump from the diaphragm and see if the diaphragm returns within five seconds. If not, replace the throttle positioner with a new one.

Vacuum solenoid valve
9   With the engine at idle, disconnect the vacuum supply hose from the solenoid valve and verify that the hose is supplying vacuum.
10 Disconnect the wires from the solenoid and apply battery voltage to both terminals, verifying that there is no increase in engine speed.
11 With battery voltage supplied to one terminal, ground the other terminal and verify that engine speed increases.
12 Remove the ground and verify that the engine returns to idle rpm.
13 If the solenoid fails to pass any of the above tests, replace it with a new one.

Vacuum sensing switch (if so equipped)
14 Disconnect the hose from the vacuum fitting on the switch.
15 Hook up a hand-operated vacuum pump to the fitting.
16 Using an ohmmeter, verify that the switch is open (no continuity) while applying 19.4 in Hg vacuum or less to the switch.
17 Increase the vacuum to 20.6 in Hg or more and verify that the switch is closed (continuity).
18 If the switch fails to pass either of the above tests, replace it with a new one.

Electronic speed sensor/governor module (if so equipped)
19 If a fault is suspected in the module, it must be checked by a Ford dealer service department.

Component replacement
20 Replacement of the throttle positioner, solenoid valve and/or sensing switch is straightforward, accomplished by disconnecting the attached wires and/or hoses, removing the faulty component and replacing it with a new one.

---

10 Exhaust control system

General description
1   This system is employed to eliminate any condensation of fuel on the cold surfaces of the intake system during cold engine operation and to provide better evaporation and distribution of the air/fuel mixture. The result is better driveability, faster warm-up and a reduction in the release of hydrocarbons to the atmosphere.
2   The component of this system is the exhaust heat control valve, which is controlled by either a thermostat or a vacuum. It is mounted between the exhaust manifold and one branch of the exhaust pipe.
3   The valve operates by remaining closed when the engine is cold and routes hot exhaust gasses to the intake manifold area through the heat riser tube, then slowly opening as the engine temperature increases.

Checking
Bimetal thermostat valve
4   With the engine cold, manually rotate the valve shaft. It must move freely and return to the closed position as long as the engine is cold.
5   Start the engine and, as it warms up, make sure that the valve shaft rotates to the open position.
6   If the valve fails to operate as described, replace it with a new one.
Vacuum operated valve
7   Perform Step 4 above.
8   Warm up the engine to normal operating temperature.

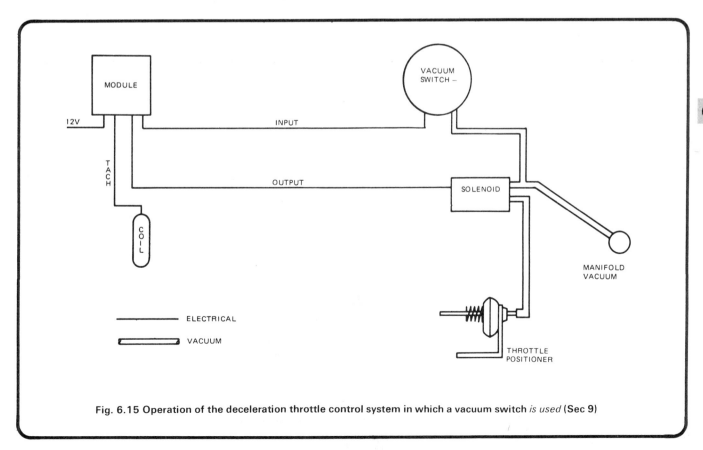

Fig. 6.15 Operation of the deceleration throttle control system in which a vacuum switch *is used* **(Sec 9)**

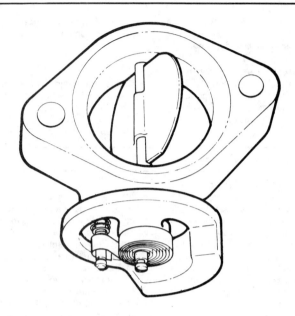

Fig. 6.16 Typical temperature controlled exhaust heat control valve (Sec 10)

9   Disconnect the vacuum line at the valve and verify that there is vacuum at the line. If not, check the vacuum line and vacuum source.
10 If the valve fails to operate as described, replace it with a new one.

Component replacement

11 The replacement of the exhaust heat control valve is straightforward, accomplished by unbolting the faulty valve from its location, cleaning the mating surfaces on the exhaust manifold and head pipe and installing a new valve.

---

11 Catalytic converter

General description

1   The catalytic converter is designed to reduce hydrocarbon (HC) and carbon monoxide (CO) pollutants in the exhaust. The converter oxidizes these components and converts them to water and carbon dioxide.
2   The converter is located in the exhaust system and closely resembles a muffler. Some models have two converters, a light-off catalyst type, mounted just past the exhaust manifold pipe, and a conventional oxidation catalyst or three-way catalyst type mounted farther downstream.
3   **Note**: *If large amounts of unburned gasoline enter the catalyst, it may overheat and cause a fire. Always observe the following precautions:*

> *Use only unleaded gasoline*
> *Avoid prolonged idling*
> *Do not prolong engine compression checks*
> *Do not run the engine with a nearly empty fuel tank*
> *Avoid coasting with the ignition turned Off*
> *Do not dispose of a used catalytic converter along with oily or gasoline soaked parts*

Checking

4   The catalytic converter requires little if any maintenance and servicing at regular intervals. However, the system should be inspected whenever the vehicle is raised on a lift or if the exhaust system is checked or serviced.
5   Check all connections in the exhaust pipe assembly for looseness or damage. Also check all the clamps for damage, cracks, or missing fasteners. Check the rubber hangers for cracks.
6   The converter itself should be checked for damage or dents (maximum $\frac{3}{4}$ in deep) which could affect its performance and/or be hazardous to your health. At the same time the converter is inspected, check the metal protector plate under it as well as the heat insulator above it for damage or loose fasteners.

Component replacement

7   Do not attempt to remove the catalytic converter until the complete exhaust system is cool. Raise the vehicle and support it securely on jackstands. Apply some penetrating oil to the clamp bolts and allow it to soak in.
8   Remove the bolts and the rubber hangers, then separate the converter from the exhaust pipes. Remove the old gaskets if they are stuck to the pipes.
9   Installation of the converter is the reverse of removal. Use new exhaust pipe gaskets and tighten the clamp bolts to the specified torque (refer to Chapter 4, Specifications). Replace the rubber hangers with new ones if the originals are deteriorated. Start the engine and check carefully for exhaust leaks.

Chapter 7 Part A Clutch and flywheel

Refer to Chapter 13 for information on 1984 and later models

Contents

Specifications

Torque specifications

	Ft-lb
Pressure plate-to-flywheel bolts	15 to 20

1 Clutch – general information

The clutch assembly consists of a single, dry pressure plate, a single friction disc and a bearing which pushes on the fingers of the pressure plate to release the clutch.

The pressure plate contains several springs which provide continuous surface pressure on the plate face for clutch engagement.

The clutch disc is splined and slides freely along the input shaft of the transmission. Friction lining material is riveted to the clutch disc. It has a spring-cushioned hub to absorb driveline shocks and provide smooth engagement.

The clutch is operated by a series of levers and cranks known as the linkage. This linkage transfers motion at the clutch pedal into movement at the throwout bearing arm. When the clutch pedal is depressed, the throwout bearing pushes on the arms of the pressure plate assembly, which in turn pulls the pressure plate friction disc away from the lining material of the disc.

When the clutch pedal is released, the pressure plate springs force the pressure plate into contact with the lining on the clutch disc. Simultaneously, the clutch disc is pushed a fraction of an inch forward on the transmission splines by the pressure of the plate, which engages the disc with the flywheel. The clutch disc becomes firmly sandwiched between the pressure plate and the engine flywheel and engine power is transferred to the transmission.

2 Clutch – inspection (in vehicle)

1 Some vehicles are equipped with a removable inspection plate on the bottom of the clutch housing, observable from under the vehicle. If your vehicle is so equipped, be sure to raise the vehicle and place it securely on jackstands before attempting to remove the plate.

2 Remove the bolts retaining the plate to the housing, then remove the plate.

3 Inspect the clutch assembly from the bottom of the housing. Look for any broken, loose or worn parts. If no apparent defect is revealed, compare the thickness of the clutch disc (sandwiched between the pressure plate and the flywheel) to a new disc. This comparison will give you some idea of the clutch disc life left in your vehicle and the need for replacement.

4 Reinstall the plates and bolts.

5 Remove the jackstands and lower the vehicle.

3 Clutch assembly – removal, inspection and installation

Note: *Refer to Figs. 7.1, 7.2 and 7.3*

Removal

1 Remove the transmission (and transfer case if 4x4) as described in Chapter 7B.

2 Disconnect the clutch throwout bearing lever retracting spring and pushrod from the lever.

3 Remove the starter.

4 If the clutch housing is not provided with a dust cover, the housing must be removed. Remove the clutch housing retaining bolts and remove the housing, then remove the release lever and the hub-to-release bearing assembly from the housing.

5 If the clutch housing is provided with a dust cover, remove it from the housing, then remove the release lever and the hub-and-release bearing assembly from the clutch housing.

6 Scribe an indexing mark on the flywheel and pressure plate assembly if the pressure plate is to be reinstalled. This ensures that the two components are installed in the same position relative to each other.

7 Working in a pattern around the circumference of the pressure plate assembly, loosen the retaining bolts a little at a time. This procedure is necessary to prevent warpage of the pressure plate.

8 Remove the pressure plate and disc from the flywheel. These parts can be removed through the opening in the bottom of the clutch housing on models equipped with a dust cover.

Inspection

9 Closely check the clutch disc for glazing, cracking, warpage, the presence of oil or grease, broken hub springs or wear close to the rivets of the bonded facing. If any of these conditions exist, replace the clutch disc with a new one. Always replace the disc if a new pressure plate is being installed.

10 Check the pressure plate for any scoring, cracks, weak springs or heat marks (blue streaks on the friction surface). If any of these conditions exist, replace the pressure plate with a new one. If the clutch was chattering or rough in engagement while in operation, the clutch pressure plate and disc should be replaced.

11 Check the flywheel surface for any indications of scoring, cracks or heat marks. If these conditions exist, replace or resurface the flywheel (Section 4). Also check the pilot bearing at this time.

186

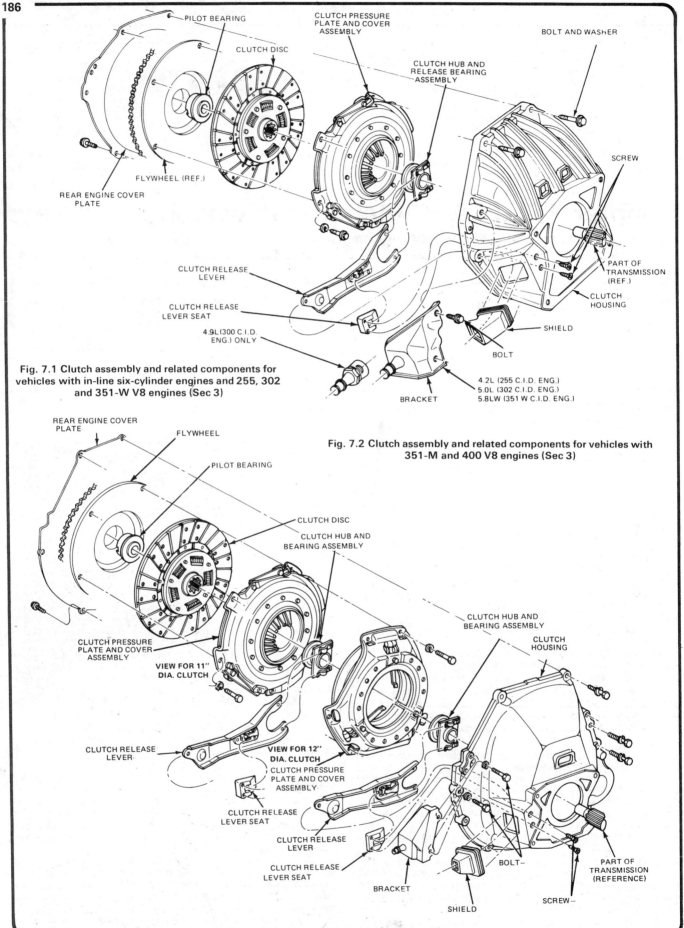

PILOT BEARING

CLUTCH PRESSURE PLATE AND COVER ASSEMBLY

BOLT AND WASHER

CLUTCH DISC

CLUTCH HUB AND RELEASE BEARING ASSEMBLY

SCREW

PART OF TRANSMISSION (REF.)

CLUTCH HOUSING

REAR ENGINE COVER PLATE

FLYWHEEL (REF.)

CLUTCH RELEASE LEVER

CLUTCH RELEASE LEVER SEAT

4.9L (300 C.I.D. ENG.) ONLY

SHIELD

BOLT

BRACKET

4.2L (255 C.I.D. ENG.)
5.0L (302 C.I.D. ENG.)
5.8LW (351 W C.I.D. ENG.)

Fig. 7.1 Clutch assembly and related components for vehicles with in-line six-cylinder engines and 255, 302 and 351-W V8 engines (Sec 3)

REAR ENGINE COVER PLATE

FLYWHEEL

Fig. 7.2 Clutch assembly and related components for vehicles with 351-M and 400 V8 engines (Sec 3)

PILOT BEARING

CLUTCH DISC

CLUTCH HUB AND BEARING ASSEMBLY

CLUTCH HUB AND BEARING ASSEMBLY

CLUTCH HOUSING

CLUTCH PRESSURE PLATE AND COVER ASSEMBLY

VIEW FOR 11" DIA. CLUTCH

CLUTCH RELEASE LEVER

VIEW FOR 12" DIA. CLUTCH

CLUTCH PRESSURE PLATE AND COVER ASSEMBLY

CLUTCH RELEASE LEVER SEAT

CLUTCH RELEASE LEVER

CLUTCH RELEASE LEVER SEAT

BRACKET

SHIELD

BOLT

PART OF TRANSMISSION (REFERENCE)

SCREW

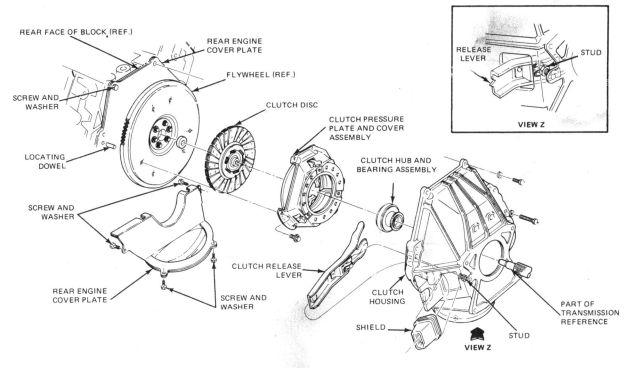

Fig. 7.3 Clutch assembly and related components for vehicles with 460 V8 engines (Sec 3)

12 Check the clutch release bearing for roughness and excessive wear (where the surface pushes on the clutch pressure plate fingers). If any of these conditions exist, replace the release bearing assembly. It is usually a good idea to replace the release bearing any time the clutch is being serviced, as the cost is relatively small compared to the labor required to gain access to it.

Installation
13 Place the clutch disc on the flywheel with the correct side facing the flywheel. Make sure the disc is clean and free of any grease, oil or contaminants. Clean it off with an evaporative clutch and brake cleaner. Make sure the flywheel surface is clean and undamaged.
14 Position the clutch pressure plate over the disc and use an alignment tool to hold the clutch disc in correct alignment with the crankshaft axis.
15 Start the retaining bolts into the pressure plate and tighten them finger tight. Slowly begin to tighten these bolts, a little at a time, working around the circumference of the pressure plate. Tighten the bolts to the proper torque. Remove the clutch alignment tool.
16 The remainder of the installation procedure is the reverse of removal. Be sure to tighten all bolts securely.

4 Flywheel and pilot bearing – inspection and replacement

Inspection
1   Prior to inspecting the flywheel and pilot bearing, the transfer case (if 4x4), transmission, clutch housing and clutch assembly must be removed.
2   Visually inspect the flywheel for any signs of cracking, warpage, scoring or heat checking. If any of these conditions exist, the flywheel must be removed and replaced, or resurfaced at an automotive machine shop.
3   If the flywheel appears to be warped or has excessive runout (indicated by high spots on the friction surface), install a dial indicator on the rear of the engine block. Hold the crankshaft forward (to take up any clearance in the crankshaft thrust bearing) and slowly turn the engine through one revolution by hand. Observe the reading on the dial indicator. If the runout exceeds the Specification (refer to Chapter 2B), replace the flywheel.
4   Carefully insert your finger into the inner race of the pilot bearing located in the center of the crankshaft flange. Check for any burrs or

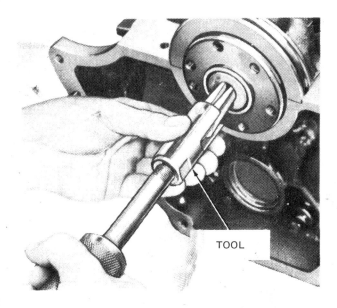

Fig. 7.4 Removing the clutch pilot needle bearing assembly (Sec 4)

scoring. Rotate the bearing and feel for roughness or excessive play. If any of these conditions exist, replace the pilot bearing.

Replacement
5   Remove the pilot bearing with a special inside puller designed for this purpose. You can purchase one from an auto parts store or they are often available from rental yards.
6   Replace the bearing using a suitable pusher tool. Always replace the bearing with the single-piece, bronze, oil-impregnated bearing. If the bearing has been in stock for a long period of time, it would be a good idea to soak the bearing in 20W engine oil prior to installing it. Installation can be made easier by chilling the bearing in a freezer to shrink it enough to fit easily into the crankshaft.
7   If the flywheel is to be replaced, refer to Chapter 2B.

7A

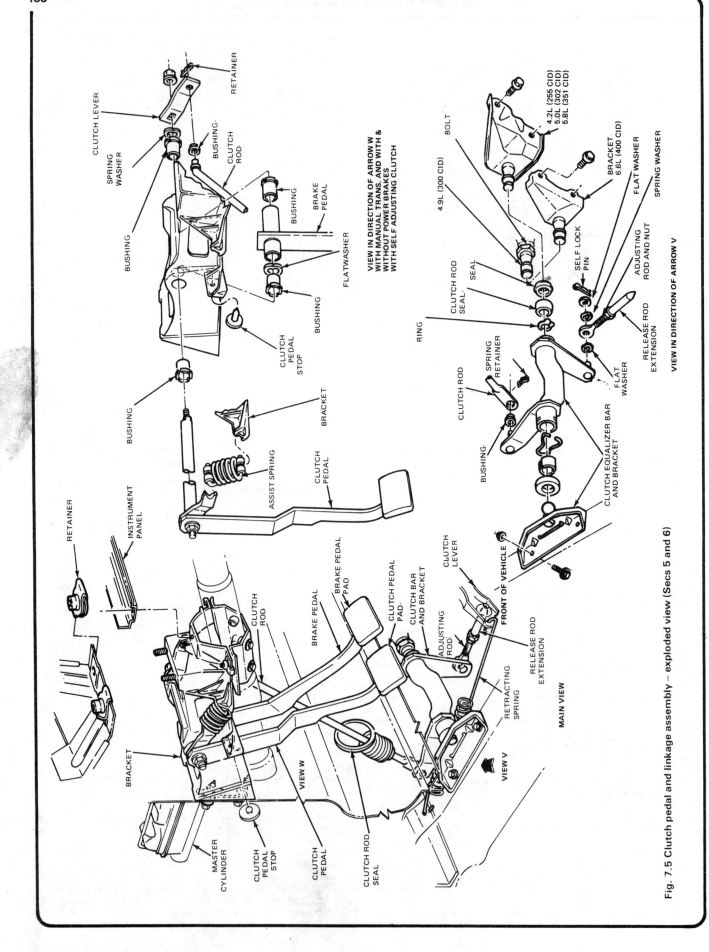

Fig. 7.5 Clutch pedal and linkage assembly — exploded view (Secs 5 and 6)

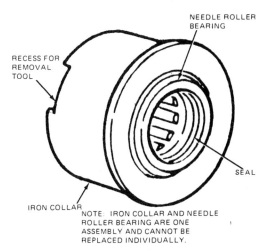

RECESS FOR REMOVAL TOOL

NEEDLE ROLLER BEARING

SEAL

IRON COLLAR
NOTE: IRON COLLAR AND NEEDLE ROLLER BEARING ARE ONE ASSEMBLY AND CANNOT BE REPLACED INDIVIDUALLY.

Fig. 7.6 Clutch pilot needle bearing assembly (Sec 4)

5   Clutch linkage – removal and installation

Note: *Refer to Fig. 7.6.*
1   The most likely source of wear in the clutch linkage is the equalizer bar bushings.
2   To replace the bushings, first jack up the front of the vehicle and place it on jackstands.
3   Disconnect the clutch release lever retracting spring.
4   Remove the retainer spring clip and disconnect the clutch pedal-to-equalizer bar rod and bushing from the equalizer outer arm.
5   Remove the clutch adjuster assembly from the equalizer bar swivel.
6   Remove the bolts attaching the outer equalizer bar pivot bracket to the chassis and remove the bracket and equalizer bar.
7   Remove the snap-rings holding the equalizer bar bushings to the inner and outer pivot brackets and remove the bushings and washers.
8   Installation is the reverse of the removal procedure. Lubricate all bushings and pivot points with multi-purpose grease. When installing the equalizer bar assembly, it should be parallel to the dash panel and the ground, and perpendicular to the engine crankshaft centerline.

6   Clutch pedal – removal and installation

Note: *Refer to Fig. 12.16 or 7.5*
1   Remove the retracting spring from the clutch release lever.
2   Working under the dash, with the assist spring (if so equipped) in place, temporarily wire the spring coil to prevent it from expanding beyond its normal installed length.
3   Remove the clutch rod retainer clip and disconnect the clutch-pedal-to-equalizer bar rod.
4   To remove the assist spring (if so equipped) when it has been wired as in Step 2, carefully push the clutch pedal to the floor and remove the spring.
5   If a new assist spring is to be installed, clip and remove the coil retaining wire installed in Step 2.
6   Remove the locknut attaching the clutch lever to the clutch pedal assembly shaft and remove the lever.
7   Loosen the locknut attaching the clutch pedal to the clutch pedal shaft.
8   Remove the shoulder bolt bushing and locknut retaining the brake pedal to the master cylinder pushrod.
9   Pull the clutch pedal and shaft out until the brake pedal and bushing can be removed.
10   Remove the locknut retaining the clutch pedal to the clutch shaft.
11   Installation is basically the reverse of the removal procedure. Lubricate all bushings and pivot points with multi-purpose grease.
12   When installing a new assist spring, first compress and temporarily wire the spring to maintain a compressed length of $2\frac{1}{2}$ in across the end rollers. Do not compress the spring solid as spring damage will occur and clutch pedal effort will be increased.
13   Reinstall the lower fastener on the assist spring bracket and tighten the lower and upper bracket fasteners.
14   Push the pedal to the floor and place the assist spring into its brackets.
15   Clip and remove the coil retaining wires installed in Step 12.
16   Pull the pedal up until it hits the stop.
17   When the installation is complete, check the pedal free travel and adjust as necessary (refer to Chapter 1).

7A

Chapter 7 Part B Transmission

Refer to Chapter 13 for information on 1988 and later models

Contents

Specifications

Torque specifications

Ft-lb (unless otherwise noted)

Manual transmission

Gearshift linkage adjusting nuts

3.03 3-speed	12 to 18
4-speed overdrive	15 to 20

Transmission-to-flywheel housing bolts

3.03 3-speed	42 to 50
T-18 4-speed	35 to 50
T-19B 4-speed	37 to 42
New process 435 4-speed	70 to 110
Single rail 4-speed overdrive	35 to 45
4-speed overdrive	35 to 45

Automatic transmission

Shift rod adjusting nuts	12 to 18
Neutral start switch-to-case	6.5 to 8
Intermediate and reverse band adjusting locknut (refer to text for procedure)	40
Converter-to-driveplate	20 to 30
Oil pan-to-transmission case	12 to 16
Converter housing-to-transmission case	28 to 40

Converter cover-to-converter housing

Except 460 engine	12 to 16
460 engine	30 to 60 in-lb

Transmission-to-engine

C4	40 to 50
C5	
232 cu in V6 engine	28 to 38
255 cu in V8 engine	40 to 50
C6	40 to 50
AOD	40 to 50

7 Manual transmission – general information

Manually shifted transmissions available in vehicles covered by this manual include the Ford 3.03 3-speed, the Warner T-18 4-speed, the Warner T-19 4-speed, the New Process 435 4-speed, the single-rail 4-speed overdrive (SROD) and the 4-speed overdrive.

All transmissions are fully synchronized with all gears, except the reverse sliding gear, in constant mesh.

Application of the transmissions depends on the year, engine and model of the vehicle in which it is installed. If you are in doubt as to which transmission is in your particular vehicle, check with your local Ford dealer or automotive transmission facility.

Due to the complexity of transmissions and because of the special tools and expertise required to perform an overhaul, it is not advised that it be undertaken by the home mechanic. Therefore, the procedures in this Chapter are limited to routine adjustments, and removal and installation procedures.

Depending upon the expense involved in having a faulty transmission overhauled, it may be of advantage to consider replacing the unit with either a new or rebuilt one. Your local dealer or transmission specialty shop should be able to supply you with information concerning these units as to their cost, availability and exchange policy. Regardless of how you decide to remedy a faulty transmission problem, however, you can still save considerable expense by removing it and installing it yourself.

8 Manual transmission – linkage adjustment

Note: *Refer to Figs 7.7 and 7.8 to locate components.*
1 The Ford 3.03 3-speed and the 4-speed overdrive transmissions have provisions for adjustment of the shifting linkage. The other transmissions applicable to vehicles covered by this manual are of the direct-shifting, non-adjustable type.

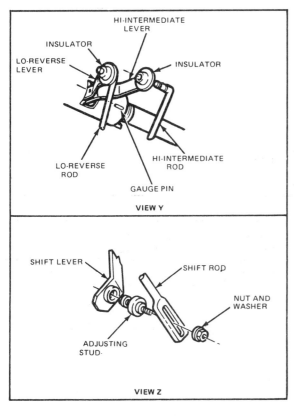

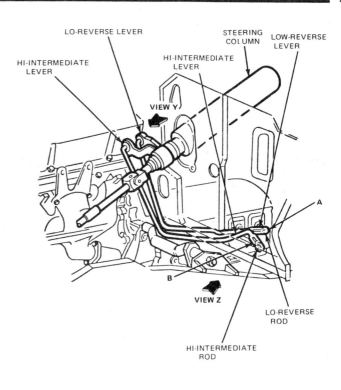

Fig. 7.7 Shift linkage details for the Ford 3.03 column shift transmission (Sec 8)

7B

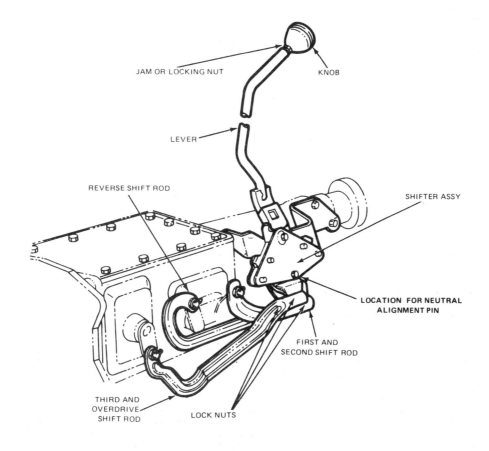

Fig. 7.8 Shift linkage details for the 4-speed overdrive transmission (Sec 8)

Ford 3.03

2   Install a steel pin of $\frac{3}{16}$ in diameter through the locating hole and plastic spacer in the steering column shift levers with the levers in Neutral.

3   Loosen nuts A and B and position the transmission shift levers in the Neutral detent positions.

4   Tighten nuts A and B, using care to prevent movement between the studs and rods as the nuts are tightened.

5   Remove the gauge pin from the steering column shift levers.

6   Check the linkage operation.

7   **Note**: *Always use new retaining rings and insulators when making linkage adjustments.*

4-speed overdrive

8   Disconnect the three shift rods from the shifter assembly by removing the locknuts.

9   Make sure the levers are in the Neutral position and insert a $\frac{1}{4}$ in diameter steel pin through the alignment hole at the bottom of the shifter assembly.

10   Align the three transmission levers as follows: forward lever (3rd-4th) in the mid-position (Neutral); rear lever (1st-2nd) in the mid-position (Neutral); and the middle lever (Reverse) rotated counter-clockwise to the Neutral position.

11   Carefully jack up the rear of the vehicle and place it securely on jackstands.

12   Rotate the driveshaft manually to assure that the transmission is in Neutral.

13   Shift the Reverse lever clockwise to the Reverse position. This causes the interlock system to align the 1-2 and 3-4 rails in their precise Neutral position.

14   Reattach the 1-2 and 3-4 shift rods to their corresponding transmission levers and tighten the locknuts.

15   Rotate the Reverse lever counterclockwise back to the Neutral position and install the Reverse shift rod and locknut.

16   Remove the alignment pin from the shifter assembly.

17   Check the linkage operation.

18   Remove the jackstands and lower the vehicle.

9   Manual transmission – removal and installation

Removal

1   Drain the transmission lubricant into a suitable container. On vehicles equipped with direct-shifting (no external linkage arms) type 4-speed transmissions, remove the rubber boot, floor mat and floor pad (if so equipped). On some vehicles it may be necessary to remove the seat and the transmission floor pan cover plate for clearance purposes.

2   Raise the vehicle and support it securely.

3   Disconnect the back-up light switch located on the rear of the transmission.

4   Remove the speedometer cable retaining bolt and remove the speedometer cable and gear assembly. Position the cable out of the way to avoid damage or contamination.

5   Disconnect the parking brake lever from its linkage and remove the cable from the crossmember.

6   Disconnect and remove the driveshaft or coupling shaft.

7   If the vehicle is a 4x4, remove the transfer case as described in Section 16.

8   Support the transmission with a transmission jack. Make sure the transmission is securely clamped to the jack.

9   Remove the shift linkage arms and assembly on 4-speed overdrive transmission equipped vehicles. Remove the gearshift housing on direct-shifting (no external linkage arms) type transmission equipped vehicles. Remove the shift arms from vehicles equipped with a 3-speed transmission.

10   Remove the transmission rear mount retaining bolt(s) and remove the rear support crossmember (4x2 vehicles only). It may be necessary to raise the transmission slightly to allow the crossmember to clear the rear mount.

11   Remove the transmission retaining bolts from the rear of the clutch housing.

12   Slowly withdraw the transmission from the clutch housing, making sure not to put unnecessary pressure on the transmission input shaft. Once the input shaft has cleared the clutch housing, lower the transmission and remove it from beneath the vehicle.

Installation

13   Apply a light coating of Ford C1AZ-19590-B lubricant or its equivalent to the clutch release lever fulcrum and fork. Apply this lubricant sparingly, as any excess will contaminate the clutch disc.

14   Secure the transmission to the transmission jack and raise it up to the level of the clutch housing face. Make sure the clutch is aligned with an alignment tool if it was removed and replaced. Make sure the clutch throwout bearing and hub are properly positioned on the release lever fork.

15   Install guide studs in the retaining holes of the clutch housing. These studs can be purchased or made from bolts (with the correct thread) about two to three inches long. Cut the head off the bolts and grind off any burrs. A slot cut into the end of the bolt will enable you to thread it in and out with a screwdriver.

16   Raise the transmission and start the holes of the transmission face onto the guide studs. Slide the transmission forward on the studs until the input shaft engages the clutch splines. Continue to slide the transmission forward until the face of the case mates with the clutch housing face.

17   Remove the guide studs and install the retaining bolts.

18   The remaining steps are basically the reverse of removal.

10   Automatic transmission – general information

Due to the complexity of automatic transmissions, if performance is not up to par and overhaul is necessary, the job should be performed by a dealership or other shop with the qualified personnel and special equipment necessary. The Sections which follow in this Chapter are designed to provide the home mechanic with service information and instructions for operations that he may perform without specialized

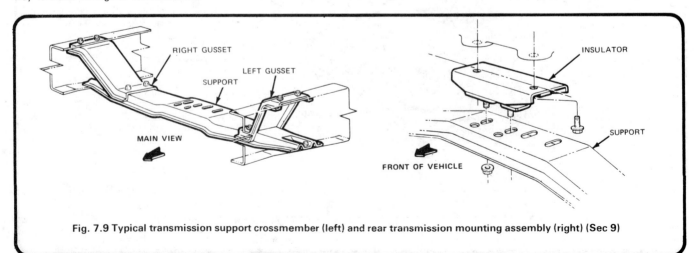

Fig. 7.9 Typical transmission support crossmember (left) and rear transmission mounting assembly (right) (Sec 9)

Fig. 7.10 Bottom view of automatic transmission (C6 shown) and transfer case (Borg-Warner 1345 shown)

1 Front heat shield
2 Rear transmission mount-
to crossmember insulator
3 Rear transmission support
bracket bolt
4 Transmission oil pan
5 Neutral safety switch
6 Transmission shift
linkage
7 Front driveshaft
8 Crossmember
9 Transfer case
10 Rear driveshaft
universal joint
11 Rear heat shield

7B

equipment and training.

Vehicles covered by this manual and equipped with an automatic transmission may contain wether the C4, C5, C6 or automatic overdrive transmission (AOD) unit, depending on year, model and engine.

The AOD unit is different from conventional 3-speed automatic transmissions, like the C4, C5, and C6, in that the planetary gear set operates in fourth (overdrive) gear. Also, unlike the 3-speed automatics, the AOD has no selection position for Second gear, thus starts in Second are not possible. The overdrive may be locked out by placing the selector in the D position, providing increased acceleration and engine braking performance as conditions and terrain demand. The transmission may be shift from **Ⓓ** (overdrive) to D, or the opposite, at any speed.

Note: *All automatic transmissions supplied as original equipment on vehicles covered by this manual are equipped with high-temperature-resistant seals. This includes those seals used on the manual and kickdown levers, the O-rings and oil pan gasket. Under no circumstances should older design seals be used on the transmission, except for the regular service replacement oil pan gasket (which is of special leak prevention design and should still be used).*

11 Automatic transmission – removal and installation

Note: *If the transmission being removed is in a 4x4 vehicle, the transfer case must be removed prior to removal of the transmission (refer to Section 16 in Chapter 7C).*

1   If possible, raise the vehicle on a hoist or place it over an inspection pit. Alternatively, raise the vehicle to obtain the maximum possible amount of working room underneath. Support it securely.

2   Place a large drain pan beneath the transmission oil pan. Then, working from the rear, loosen the attaching bolts and allow the fluid to drain. Remove all the bolts except the two front ones to drain as much fluid as possible, then temporarily install two bolts at the rear to hold it in place.

3   Remove the torque converter drain plug access cover and adapter plate bolts from the lower end of the converter housing.

4   Remove the driveplate-to-converter attaching nuts, turning the engine as necessary to gain access by means of a socket on the crankshaft pulley attaching bolt. **Caution:** *Do not rotate the engine backward.*

5   Rotate the engine until the converter drain plug is accessible, then remove the plug, catching the fluid in the drain pan. Install and tighten the drain plug afterward.

6   Remove the driveshaft by referring to Chapter 8. Place a polyethylene bag over the end of the transmission to prevent dirt from entering.

7   Detach the speedometer cable from the extension housing by removing the hold-down bolt and withdrawing the cable and gear.

8   Disconnect the shift rod at the transmission manual lever and the kickdown rod at the transmission downshift lever. Remove the two bolts securing the bellcrank bracket to the coverter housing (photo).

9   Remove the three bolts retaining the starter to the engine and position the starter out of the way.

10   Disconnect the Neutral safety switch leads or wire connector.

11   Disconnect the vacuum lines from the vacuum modulator (C4 and C6 only).

12   Position a transmission jack beneath the transmission and raise it so that it *just begins* to lift the transmission weight.

13   Remove the nuts and bolts securing the rear mount and insulators to the crossmember (photo).

14   If right and left gussets are installed between the crossmember and frame rails, remove the gusset attaching nuts and bolts and remove the gussets.

15   Remove the nuts and bolts securing the crossmember to the frame rails, raise the transmission slightly and remove the crossmember.

16   Disconnect the inlet pipe flange(s) from the exhaust manifold(s).

17   Support the rear of the engine using a jack or suitable blocks of wood.

18   Disconnect the oil cooler lines at the transmission and plug them to prevent dirt from entering. Use a flare nut wrench to avoid rounding off the nuts.

19   Remove the lower converter housing-to-engine bolts and the transmission filler tube.

20   Make sure that the transmission is securely mounted on the jack, then remove the two upper converter housing-to-engine bolts.

21   Carefully move the transmission to the rear and down and away from the vehicle.

22   Installing the transmission is essentially the reverse of the removal procedure, but the following points should be noted:

a)   Rotate the converter to align the bolt drive lugs and drain plug with their holes in the driveplate.

b)   Do not allow the transmission to take a 'nose-down' attitude as the converter will move forward and disengage from the pump gear.

c)   When installing the driveplate-to-converter bolts, position the driveplate so the pilot hole is in the six o'clock position. First, install one bolt through the pilot hole and torque tighten it, followed by the remaining bolts. Do not attempt to install it in any other way.

d)   Adjust the kickdown rod and selector linkage as necessary.

e)   When the vehicle has been lowered to the ground, add sufficient fluid to bring the level up to the Max mark on the dipstick with the engine not running. Having done this, check and top-up the fluid level as described in Chapter 1.

12 Automatic transmission – linkage adjustment

Note: *Refer to Figs. 7.12 and 7.13 to locate components.*

1   With the engine off and the parking brake applied, place the transmission selector lever at the steering column in the D (C4, C5, C6) or **Ⓓ** (AOD) position and hold it against the stop by tying an eight (8) pound weight to the selector lever knob.

2   Loosen the shift rod adjusting nut at point A.

3   Shift the manual lever at the transmission into the Drive position by moving the lever all the way to the rear, then forward two (2) detents.

4   With the selector lever and transmission manual lever both in the Drive position, tighten the nut at point A to the specified torque, using

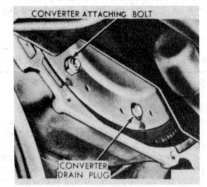

Fig. 7.11 Typical automatic transmission converter attaching bolt and converter drain plug locations (Sec 11)

11.8 View from under the vehicle of the automatic transmission manual shift linkage and kickdown rod

11.13 View from under the vehicle of a rear transmission mount-to-crossmember insulator set

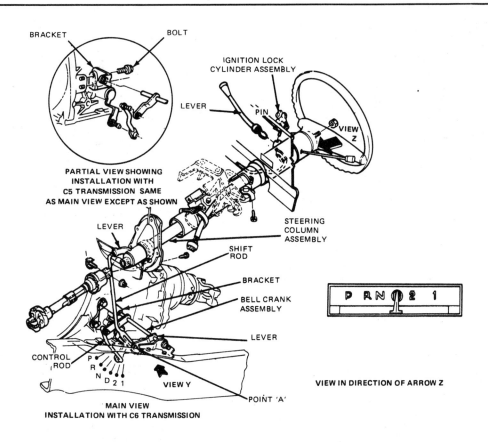

Fig. 7.12 Shift linkage assembly for C4, C5 and C6 automatic transmissions – exploded view (Sec 12)

care to prevent movement between the stud and rod.
5   Remove the weight from the shift lever knob and check the operation of the shift lever in all positions to make certain the manual lever at the transmission is in full detent in all gear ranges. Readjust the linkage as required.

13 Neutral start switch – adjustment (C4, C5, C6 only)

Note: *Refer to Fig. 7.14 to locate components.*
1   With the automatic transmisison linkage properly adjusted (refer to Section 12), loosen the two Neutral start switch retaining bolts.
2   Place the transmission selector lever in Neutral.
3   Rotate the switch and insert a No. 43 drill bit (shank end) into the gauge pin holes of the switch. **Note**: *The drill shank must be inserted a full 31/64 in, through all three holes of the switch.*
4   Tighten the two switch retaining bolts to the specified torque and remove the gauge pin from the switch.
5   Check the operation of the switch. The back-up lights should come on when the transmission is in Reverse and the engine should start only with the transmission lever in Park and Neutral.

14 Automatic transmission – band adjustment (C4, C5, C6 only)

Note: *Refer to Figs. 7.15 and 7.16 to locate components.*

Intermediate band (C4, C5, C6)
1   The intermediate or front band is used to hold the sun gear stationary to produce Second gear. If it is not correctly adjusted, there will be noticeable slip during the First-to-Second gear shift or on the downshift from the High to Second gear. The first symptoms of these problems will be very sluggish shifts instead of the usual crisp action.
2   To adjust the intermediate band, loosen, remove and discard the locknut on the band adjustment screw (located on the left-hand side of the case). Tighten the adjusting screw to 10 ft-lb, then loosen it exactly $1\frac{3}{4}$ turns (C4), $4\frac{1}{4}$ turns (C5) or $1\frac{1}{2}$ turns (C6). Install a new

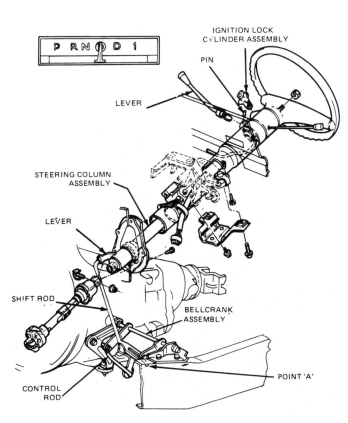

Fig. 7.13 Shift linkage assembly for the automatic overdrive transmission – exploded view (Sec 12)

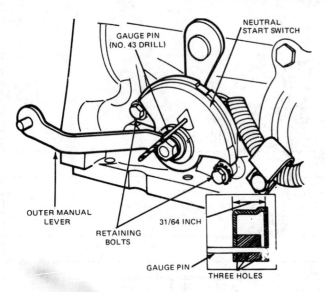

Fig. 7.14 Adjusting the Neutral start switch as found on C4, C5 and C6 automatic transmissions (Sec 13)

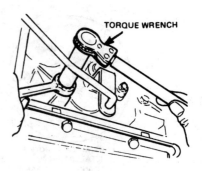

Fig. 7.15 Adjusting the intermediate band on C4, C5 and C6 automatic transmissions (Sec 14)

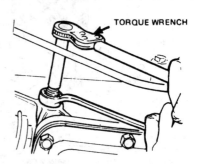

Fig. 7.16 Adjusting the Low-and-Reverse band on C4 and C5 automatic transmissions (Sec 14)

locknut and tighten it to the specified torque while holding the adjustment screw to keep it from turning.

Low and reverse band (C4, C5)

3   The low and reverse band is operational when the selector lever is placed in the Low or Reverse positions. If it is not correctly adjusted, there will be no drive with the selector lever in Reverse (also associated with no engine braking with the selector lever in Low).

4   To adjust this band, remove the adjusting screw locknut from the screw (located on the right-hand side of the case) and discard it. Tighten the adjusting screw to 10 ft-lb, then loosen it exactly three turns. Install a new locknut and tighten it to the specified torque while holding the adjusting screw to keep it from turning.

Chapter 7 Part C Transfer case

Refer to Chapter 13 for information on 1988 and later models

Contents

Specifications

Torque specifications

Ft-lbs (unless otherwise noted)

New Process 208 transfer case

Gear locking plate bolts	26 to 36
Rear bearing retainer bolts	20 to 25
Case-half attaching bolts	20 to 25
4-wheel-drive indicator switch	15 to 20
Poppet ball screw	20 to 25
Drain and filler plugs	30 to 40
Shift levers-to-transfer case	70 to 90
Assembly-to-assembly shift lever mounting bolts (for vehicles equipped with SROD transmission only)	25 to 43
Shift lever assembly-to-control shaft nut	14 to 20
Yoke nuts-to-transfer case	90 to 130
Transfer case-to-transmission adapter	25 to 43
Heat shield-to-transfer case	
Upper bolt	40 to 45
Lower bolt	11 to 16
Skid plate-to-frame	11 to 16

Borg-Warner 1345 transfer case

Shift levers-to-transfer case	70 to 90
Oil pump retaining bolts	36 to 40 in-lb
Case-to-cover attaching bolts	35 to 40 in-lb
4-wheel drive indicator switch	8 to 12
Yoke nuts-to-transfer case	100 to 130
Drain plug	6 to 14
Fill plug	15 to 25
Transfer case-to-transmission adapter	25 to 43
Heat shield-to-transfer case	
Upper bolt	40 to 45
Lower bolt	11 to 16
Skid plate-to-frame	11 to 16

15 Transfer case – general information

Ford vehicles for the years covered by this manual may contain either a New Process 208 or a Borg-Warner 1345 transfer case, depending upon model and configuration. Both types are of two-piece all-aluminium construction.

Due to the time and expense involved in rebuilding a transfer case, it may be a good idea to consider replacing the faulty unit with either a new or rebuilt one. Your dealer or local transmission specialty shop should be able to supply you with information as to the cost, availability and exchange policy concerning these units.

If you decide to do the work yourself, first read through all the procedures which follow to familiarize yourself with the scope and requirements of the job.

One of the biggest problems a beginner will face when dismantling an assembly as complex as a transfer case is trying to remember exactly where each part came from. To help alleviate this problem, it may be helpful to draw your own simple diagram or take instant photos during the disassembly process. Laying each part out in the order in which it was removed and tagging parts may also be useful.

Try to anticipate which parts may have to be replaced and have them available before beginning. Regardless of broken or badly worn components, there are certain items which must be replaced as a matter of course when the transfer case is reassembled. These include gaskets, snap-rings, oil seals and sometimes bearings. You will also need some multi-purpose grease and a silicone-type gasket sealer to properly reassemble the transfer case.

Cleanliness is extremely important when working on a precision piece of equipment such as a transfer case. The work area should be kept as clean and free of dirt and dust as possible. Also, adequate space should be available to lay out the various parts as they are removed.

16 Transfer case – removal and installation

1   If possible, raise the vehicle on a lift. If a lift is not available, raise the vehicle on ramps or jackstands, making sure that it is safely supported before beginning work.

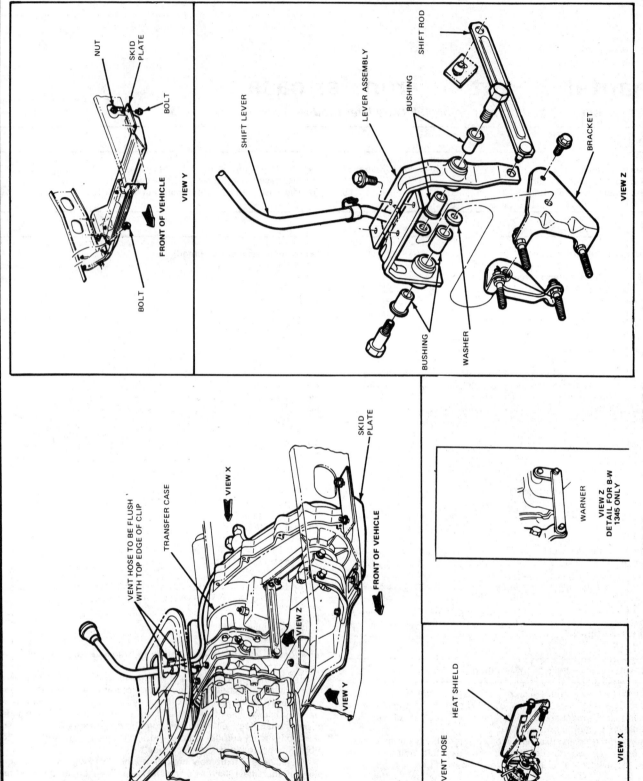

NUT

SKID
PLATE

BOLT

BOLT

FRONT OF VEHICLE

VIEW Y

SHIFT LEVER

LEVER ASSEMBLY

BUSHING

SHIFT ROD

BRACKET

BUSHING

WASHER

VIEW Z

VENT HOSE TO BE FLUSH
WITH TOP EDGE OF CLIP

TRANSFER CASE

VIEW X

SKID
PLATE

VIEW Z

FRONT OF VEHICLE

VIEW Y

WARNER

VIEW Z
DETAIL FOR B-W
1345 ONLY

HEAT SHIELD

VENT HOSE

SPEEDOMETER
DRIVE GEAR

VIEW X

Fig. 7.17 Typical transfer case installation (SROD transmission and NP 208 transfer case shown; except as noted, other installations
similar) (Sec 16)

2   Drain the transfer case oil into a suitable container.
3   Disconnect the 4x4 drive indicator switch wire connector at the transfer case.
4   Disconnect the speedometer driven gear from the transfer case rear bearing retainer.
5   Disconnect the vent hose from the transfer case.
6   From inside the vehicle, remove the floor pan cover.
7   Disconnect the transfer case shift rod from the shift lever.
8   On vehicles equipped with SROD transmission, remove the two bolts holding the shift lever assemblies together.
9   Remove the bolt retaining the shift lever to the transfer case, then remove the shift lever and bushings.
10   If so equipped, unbolt and remove the skid plate from the frame.
11   Unbolt the heat shield from the transfer case. **Note:** *The catalytic converter is located beside the heat shield. Be careful when working in this area, since the converter generates extremely high temperatures.*
12   Support the transfer case with a transmission jack.
13   Disconnect the front and rear driveshafts and tie them out of the way of the work area. Refer to Chapter 8 for further information.
14   Remove the bolts retaining the transfer case to the transmission adapter, then remove the gasket between the transfer case and adapter.
15   Carefully move the transfer case to the rear, until the input shaft clears the adapter, and lower the assembly from the vehicle.
16   Installation is the reverse of the removal procedure. Be sure to fill the transfer case with the correct grade and quantity of lubricant (refer to Chapter 1).

17 Transfer case (New Process 208) – overhaul

Note: *Refer to Fig. 7.22 to locate components.*

Disassembly
Major assemblies
1   Remove the transfer case from the vehicle (refer to Section 2).
2   Position the transfer case on a workbench.
3   Remove the retaining nuts from the front and rear output yokes, then remove the yokes, oil slinger (front yoke only) and sealing washers.
4   Remove the four bolts retaining the rear bearing retainer to the rear transfer case half and remove the retainer.
5   Remove the snap-ring, speedometer drivegear, nylon oil pump housing and oil pump gear from the rear output shaft.
6   Remove the bolts retaining the transfer case halves.
7   Separate the case halves by inserting a flat blade screwdriver into the pry slots on the case housing and prying.
8   Remove the magnetic chip collector from the bottom of the rear transfer case half.
9   Slide the thick thrust washer, the thrust bearing and the thin thrust washer off the front output shaft assembly.
10   Remove the drive chain by pushing the front output shaft out. Adequate clearance may be obtained by angling the front output gear

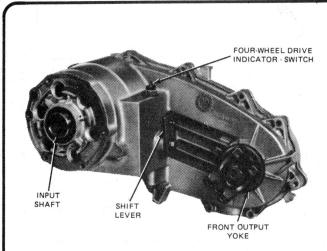

Fig. 7.18 Details of the front case half of the NP 208 transfer case (Sec 17)

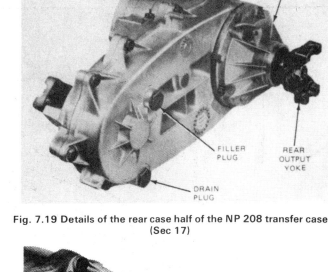

Fig. 7.19 Details of the rear case half of the NP 208 transfer case (Sec 17)

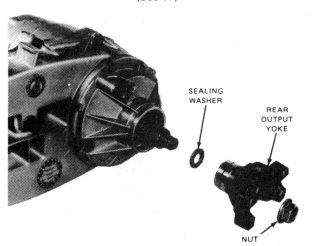

Fig. 7.20 Details of the NP 208 transfer case rear yoke (Sec 17)

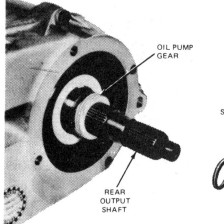
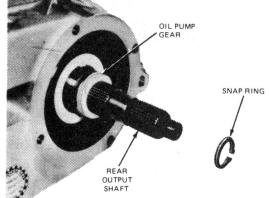

Fig. 7.21 Removing the oil pump gear from the rear output shaft of the NP 208 transfer case (Sec 17)

7C

Fig. 7.22 NP 208 transfer case – exploded view (Sec 17)

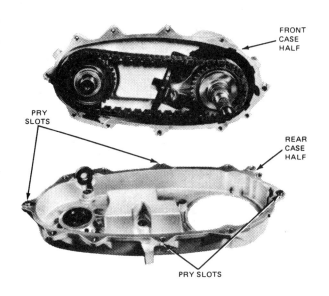

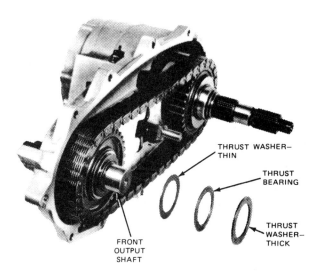

Fig. 7.23 Location of the pry slots utilized to separate the case halves of the NP 208 transfer case (Sec 17)

Fig. 7.24 Removing the front output shaft washers from the NP 208 front case (Sec 17)

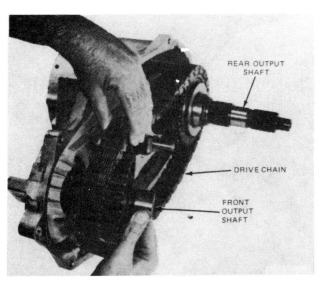

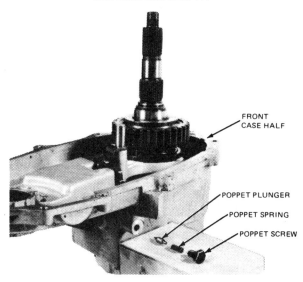

Fig. 7.25 Removing the drive chain from the NP 208 transfer case (Sec 17)

Fig. 7.26 Removing the poppet assembly from the NP 208 transfer case (Sec 17)

slightly as the output shaft is moved.

11 Remove the output shaft from the front case half assembly and slide the thick thrust washer, thrust bearing and thin thrust washer off the output side of the front output shaft.

12 Remove the screw, poppet spring and poppet plunger from the bottom of the front case half.

13 Remove the 4x4 indicator switch and washer from the top of the front case half.

14 Position the front case half on the workbench with the rear output shaft assembly pointing straight up.

15 Lift out the rear output shaft, sliding clutch, clutch shift fork and clutch shift spring.

16 With a piece of cloth wrapped around the shift rail, clamp vise-grip pliers onto the shift rail.

17 Remove the shift rail by prying up on the vise-grip pliers with a pry bar.

18 Remove the snap-ring and thrust washer from the planetary gear set assembly in the front case half.

19 Remove the annulus gear assembly and shift fork from the case.

20 Lift the planetary gear assembly and thrust washer from the front case half.

21 In order, remove the thrust bearing, sun (input) gear, second thrust bearing and the thrust washer from the front case half.

22 Remove the six bolts retaining the gear locking plate to the front case half and remove the plate.

23 Remove the nut retaining the external shift lever and washer.

24 Press the shift control shaft in and remove the shift selector plate and washer from the inside of the case.

25 Remove the snap-ring and thrust washer retaining the rear output shaft drivegear (sprocket) to the rear output shaft, then slide the sprocket from the sprocket carrier gear.

26 Remove the retaining ring from the sprocket carrier gear.

27 Carefully slide the sprocket carrier gear from the rear output shaft and remove the two rows of 60 needle bearings (120 bearings total).

28 Remove the three separator rings and thrust washer from the rear output shaft.

Front output shaft

29 Using snap-ring pliers, remove the snap-ring retaining the drive gear to the front output shaft.

30 Slide the drivegear and thrust bearings from the output shaft.

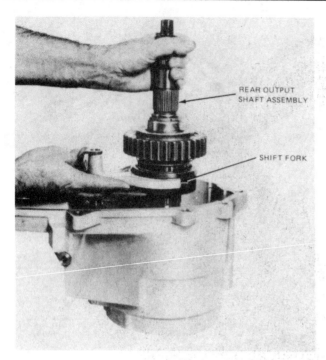

Fig. 7.27 Removing the rear output shaft assembly from the NP 208 transfer case (Sec 17)

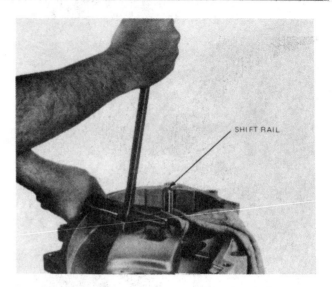

Fig. 7.28 Removing the shift rail from the NP 208 transfer case (Sec 17)

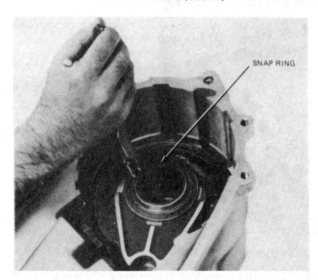

Fig. 7.29 Removing the planetary gear set snap-ring from the NP 208 transfer case (Sec 17)

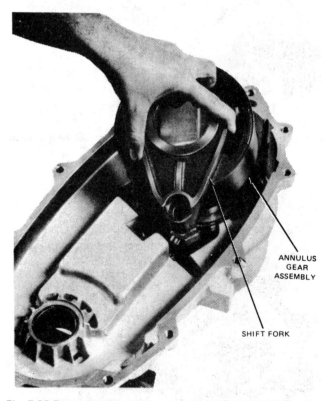

Fig. 7.30 Removing the annulus gear assembly and shift fork from the NP 208 transfer case (Sec 17)

Rear bearing retainer

31 Cut the output shaft oil seal in three evenly spaced spots, 120° apart. The slits should be made in the recessed area between the seal lip and the seal outside diameter.

32 Install a seal remover tool (Ford no. 1175-AC or equivalent) through the slits in the seal and expand the remover tool. Attach a slide hammer (Ford no. T50T-100-A or equivalent) to the remover tool and remove the seal from the case. **Note:** *Take care not to nick the aluminum case while removing the seal.*

33 From inside the case, remove the ball bearing retainer snap-ring with snap-ring pliers.

34 Support the inner face of the output shaft bore in the rear bearing retainer and press the ball bearing assembly from the bore. **Note:** *The ball bearing assembly can only be removed by pressing it in. A lip on the output shaft bore prevents its removal to the outside.*

Rear case half

35 Using the appropriate tool from a blind hole puller set (Ford no. D80L-100-A or equivalent), install it on the needle bearing assembly and attach a slide hammer (Ford no. T50T-100-A or equivalent), then pull the bearing from the bore.

36 If the rear case half is to be replaced, remove the drain and fill plugs from the rear case half.

Front case half

37 Cut the two input shaft oil seals in three evenly spaced spots, 120° apart. The slits should be made in the recessed area between the seal lip and the seal outside diameter.

38 Install a seal remover tool (Ford no. 1175-AC or equivalent)

Fig. 7.31 Removing the planetary gear set and thrust washer from the NP 208 transfer case (Sec 17)

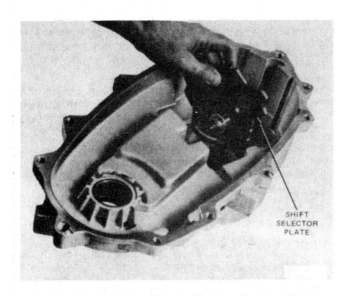

Fig. 7.33 Removing the shift selector plate from the NP 208 transfer case (Sec 17)

Fig. 7.32 Removing the sun gear and thrust washer from the NP 208 transfer case (Sec 17)

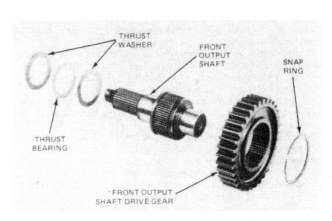

Fig. 7.34 Details of the NP 208 transfer case front output shaft assembly (Sec 17)

7C

needle bearing from the input shaft bore.

41 Remove the O-ring retainer and O-ring from the shift control shaft bore.

42 Remove the oil seal from the front output shaft bore.

43 Using the collet and actuator pin listed in Step 39, remove the needle bearing from the front output shaft bore.

Cleaning and inspection

44 Discard all old gaskets and seals.

45 Carefully inspect all bearings and rollers for evidence of pitting, chipping, cracking or worn spots.

46 Inspect all shaft splines and gears for chipped teeth or excessive wear.

47 Replace worn or damaged components, as necessary, with new ones.

Reassembly

Front case half

48 Press the needle bearing into the front output shaft bore while

through the slits in the double lip seal and expand the remover tool. Attach a slide hammer (Ford no. T50T-100-A or equivalent) to the remover tool and remove the seal from the case. **Note**; *Take care not to nick the aluminum case while removing the seal.*

39 Using a collet (Ford no. D80L-100-U or equivalent) and actuator pin (Ford no. D80L-100-H or equivalent) from the blind hole puller set, remove the first needle bearing in the front input shaft bore.

40 Using a bridge assembly (Ford no. D80L-100-W or equivalent) and actuator pin (D80L-100-H or equivalent), remove the second

supporting the front case half.

49 Press the oil seal into the front output shaft bore.
50 Install the shift control O-ring seal and retainer into the case bore.
51 Press the inner needle bearing into the input shaft bore.
52 Press the outer needle bearing into the input shaft bore.
53 Press the two oil seals into the input shaft bore.

Rear case half
54 Using a bearing replacer (Ford no. T80T-4000-R or equivalent), press the needle bearing into the rear case half.
55 If the rear case half is being replaced, install the drain and fill plugs.

Rear bearing retainer
56 Press the ball bearing assembly into its seat. The ball bearings should be visible from inside the case.
57 Using snap-ring pliers, install the ball bearing retainer snap-ring.
58 Turn the case over and press the seal into the bore, making sure the new seal has the side marked 'outside' showing.

Front output shaft
59 Slide the drive gear onto the front output shaft.
60 Using snap-ring pliers, install the snap-ring.

Major assemblies
61 Slide the thrust washer against the gear on the rear output shaft.
62 Place the three spacer rings in position on the rear output shaft.
63 Liberally coat the output shaft with petroleum jelly and install the 120 needle bearings in two rows of 60 each in position on the rear output shaft.
64 Taking care not to dislodge any of the needle bearings, carefully slide the sprocket carrier gear over the output shaft.
65 Using retainer ring pliers, install the retaining ring on the sprocket carrier gear.
66 Slide the rear output shaft drivegear (sprocket) onto the sprocket carrier gear.
67 Install the thrust washer and snap-ring on the rear output shaft.
68 From the internal side of the front case half, install the shift selector plate and washer through the case half.
69 Place the shift lever assembly on the shift control shaft, install the retaining nut and tighten it to the specified torque.
70 Install the gear locking plate in the front case half and tighten its six retaining bolts to the specified torque.
71 Place the thrust bearing and washer over the input shaft of the sun (input) gear, then insert the input shaft through the front case half from the inside and insert the thrust bearing.
72 Install the planetary gear assembly so the fixed plate and planetary gears engage the sun (input) gear.
73 Slide the annulus gear and clutch assembly, with the shift fork assembly engaged, over the hub of the planetary gear assembly. The shift fork pin must engage the slot in the shift selector plate. Install the thrust washer and snap-ring.
74 Position the shift rail through the shift fork hub in the front case half.
75 Tap the rail lightly with a soft-faced hammer to seat the rail in the hole.
76 Place the sliding clutch shift fork on the shift rail and place the sliding clutch and clutch shift spring into the front case half.
77 Slide the rear output shaft into the case.
78 On the output side of the front output shaft, assemble the thin thrust washer, the thrust bearing and the thick thrust washer, then partially insert the front output shaft into the case.
79 Place the drive chain on the rear output shaft drivegear.
80 Insert the rear output shaft into the front case half and engage the drive chain on the front output shaft drive gear, angling the gear slightly as the chain is installed.
81 Push the front output shaft into place in the case.
82 Install the thin thrust washer at the rear thrust bearing and the thick thrust washer at the front output shaft drivegear.
83 Place the magnetic clip collector into the slot in the rear case half.
84 Apply a bead of RTV-type sealant completely around the face of the front case half.
85 Carefully assemble the case halves, making sure that the shift rail and front output shaft are properly retained.
86 Install the bolts retaining the case halves and tighten them alternately to the specified torque.

87 Slide the oil pump gear over the output shaft and into position.
88 Install the speedometer drivegear into the rear output shaft and install the snap-ring.
89 Use petroleum jelly to hold the nylon oil pump housing in position to the rear bearing retainer.
90 Apply a bead of RTV-type sealant around the mounting surface of the rear bearing retainer and carefully position it over the output shaft and onto the rear case half. The retainer must be installed so the vent fitting is vertical when the transfer case is installed in the vehicle.
91 Install the four retainer assembly bolts and tighten them to the specified torque.
92 Place a sealing washer under each yoke and attach them to their respective output shafts, making sure to place the oil slinger under the front output shaft.
93 Install the yoke retaining nuts and tighten them to the specified torque after coating the faces of the nuts with thread lock and sealer (Ford no. EOAZ-19554-A or equivalent).
94 Install the poppet plunger, spring and screw in the front case half and tighten the retaining screw to the specified torque.
95 Install the 4x4 drive indicator switch and washer in the top of the front case half.
96 Remove the fill plug and add seven pints of the specified lubricant (see Chapter 1).
97 Install the fill plug.
98 Install the transfer case (refer to Section 2).
99 Make sure the sealant used to join the case halves has had at least an hour to cure before operating the vehicle.

18 Transfer case (Borg-Warner 1345) – overhaul

Note: *Refer to Fig. 7.36 to locate components.*

Disassembly
Major assemblies
1 Remove the transfer case from the vehicle (refer to Section 2).
2 Position the transfer case on a workbench.
3 Remove the retaining nuts and washers from the front and rear output yokes, press off the oil slinger (front yokes only) and remove the sealing washers from both yokes.
4 Remove the 4x4 indicator switch from the cover.
5 Separate the cover from the case by removing the attaching bolts and prying the case and cover apart with a flat-blade screwdriver or pry bar.
6 Remove the magnetic chip collector from the boss in the bottom of the case half.
7 Slide the shift collar hub off the rear output shaft.
8 Using a screwdriver, compress the shift fork spring and remove the upper and lower spring retainers from the shift rail.
9 As an assembly, lift the 4-wheel-drive lockup fork and lockup shift collar out of the case. Be careful not to lose the nylon wear pads on the lockup fork. Note the location holes on the nylon wear pads and lockup fork to facilitate reassembly.
10 Using snap-ring pliers, remove the snap-ring from the front output

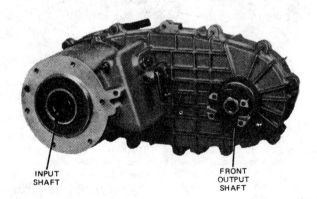

Fig. 7.35 Details of the front case half of the B-W 1345 transfer case (Sec 18)

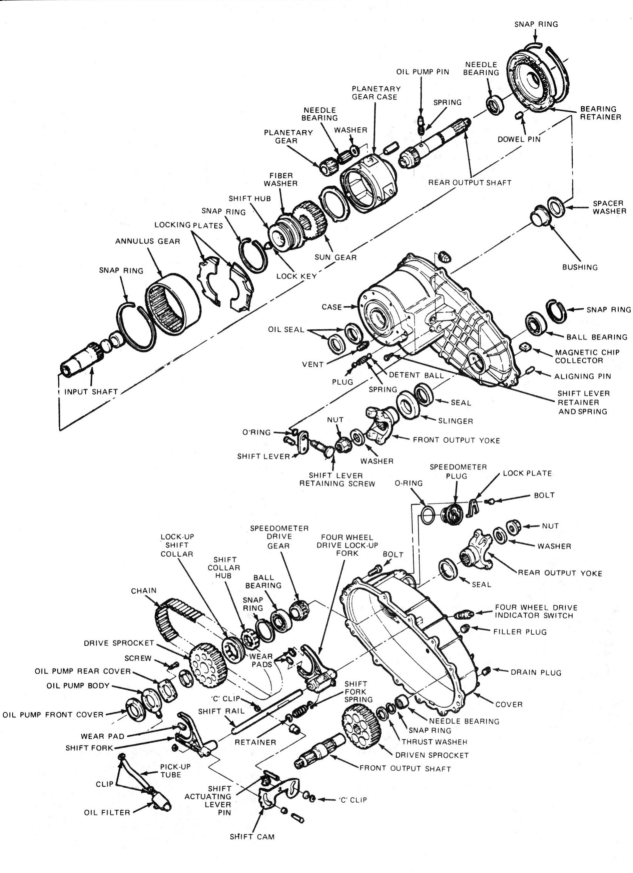

Fig. 7.36 B-W 1345 transfer case – exploded view (Sec 18)

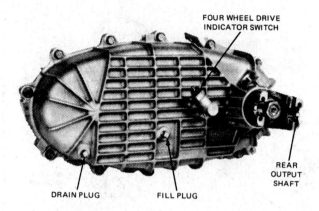

Fig. 7.37 Details of the rear cover half of the B-W 1345 transfer case (Sec 18)

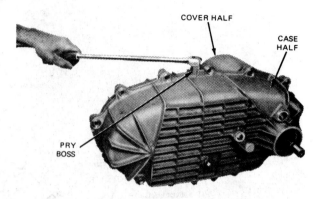

Fig. 7.38 Separating the case half from the cover half of the B-W 1345 transfer case (Sec 18)

Fig. 7.39 Removing the shift collar hub of the B-W 1345 transfer case (Sec 18)

Fig. 7.41 Removing the lockup fork and shift collar from the B-W 1345 transfer case (Sec 18)

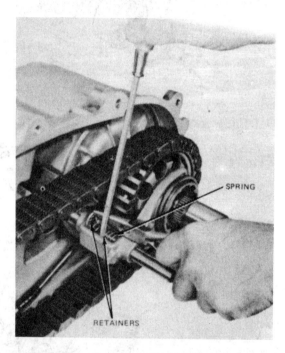

Fig. 7.40 Removing the spring retainers from the shift rail of the B-W 1345 transfer case (Sec 18)

16 From the rear output shaft, remove the oil pump rear cover, pick-up tube, filter and pump body, two pump pins, pump spring and oil pump front cover.

17 Disconnect the oil pick-up tube from the pump body by removing the two retaining clips.

18 Using snap-ring pliers, remove the snap-ring retaining the rear output shaft bearing retainer inside the case.

19 Pull up on the nose of the rear output shaft while tapping on the bearing retainer with a soft-faced hammer.

20 When the bearing retainer breaks loose, lift the rear output shaft and retainer out of the case.

21 Retrieve the two dowel pins that will fall into the case when the retainer is removed.

22 Remove the rear output shaft from the bearing retainer, tapping the nose of the shaft with a plastic hammer if necessary. If the bearing is worn, use a press to remove it from the bearing retainer.

23 Remove the C-clip that retains the shift cam to the shift actuating lever inside the case.

24 Remove the shift lever retaining screw and remove the shift lever from the case. Note: *When removing the lever, the shift cam will disengage from the shift lever shaft and may release the detent ball*

shaft, then remove the thrust washer.

11 Support the case on the workbench with the output shafts pointing up.

12 Grip the chain and both sprockets and lift straight up to remove them from the output shafts.

13 Remove the thrust washer from the rear output shaft.

14 Lift the front output shaft from the case.

15 Remove the four oil pump retaining bolts.

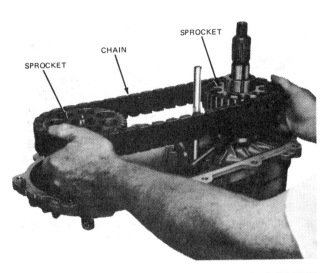

Fig. 7.42 Removing the sprockets and chain from the B-W 1345 transfer case (Sec 18)

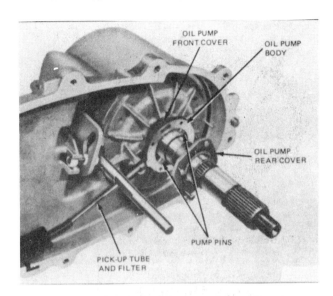

Fig. 7.43 Removing the oil pump assembly from the B-W 1345 transfer case (Sec 18)

Fig. 7.44 Removing the rear output shaft from the B-W 1345 transfer case (Sec 18)

Fig. 7.45 Removing the C-clip from the shift cam of the B-W 1345 transfer case (Sec 18)

7C

and spring from the case.

25 As an assembly, remove the planetary gear set, shift rail, shift cam, input shaft and shift fork from the case. Be careful not to lose the two nylon wear pads on the shift fork.

26 Remove the spacer washer and bushing from the bottom of the case.

27 If not previously removed, remove the detent ball and spring from the case, using a magnet if necessary.

28 Using a drift and hammer, drive the plug out of the detent spring bore.

Planetary gear set

29 Slide the input shaft to the rear, out of the planetary gear set.

30 Using snap-ring pliers, remove the snap-ring from the annular gear, then remove the shift hub and planetary gear assembly from the annular gear.

31 Unlock the two locking plates from the hub.

32 Using snap-ring pliers, remove the shift hub snap-ring and T-shaped lock key.

33 Lift the shift hub from the planetary gear assembly.

34 Remove the outer fiber washer and sun gear from the assembly.

35 Rotate the inner fiber washer slightly, allowing the positioning tabs to clear the planetary gears, and remove it from the assembly.

36 Discard the fiber washers.

Cover

37 Using snap-ring pliers, remove the snap-ring retaining the rear output shaft ball bearing assembly to the cover.

38 Turn the cover over and install a seal remover tool (Ford no. 1175-AC or equivalent) to the rear output shaft seal.

39 Attach a slide hammer (Ford no. T50T-100-A or equivalent) to the seal remover tool and remove the seal.

40 Remove the speedometer drivegear from the cover.

41 Using a press and collar, press the rear output shaft ball bearing out of the cover.

42 Unbolt the lock plate retaining the speedometer plug and remove the plate, speedometer plug and O-ring from the cover.

43 Install a collet (from Ford no. D80L-100-A, blind hole puller set, or equivalent) to the front output shaft inner needle bearing.

44 Attach a slide hammer (Ford no. T50T-100-A or equivalent) to the collet and remove the needle bearing.

Case

45 Using snap-ring pliers, remove the snap-ring retaining the front

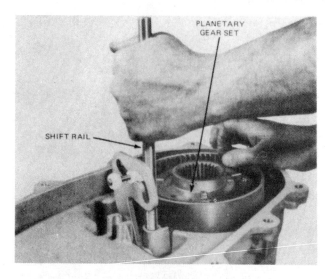

Fig. 7.46 Removing the shift rail from the B-W 1345 transfer case
(Sec 18)

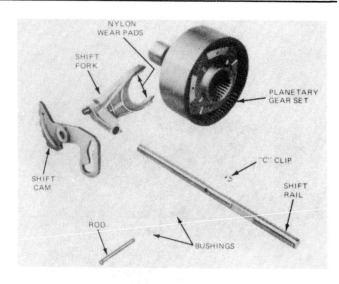

Fig. 7.47 Details of the shifter assemblies of the B-W 1345
transfer case (Sec 18)

Fig. 7.48 Removing the detent ball plug from the case half of the
B-W 1345 transfer case (Sec 18)

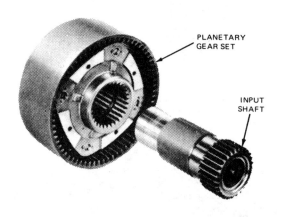

Fig. 7.49 Separating the input shaft from the planetary gear set of
the B-W 1345 transfer case (Sec 18)

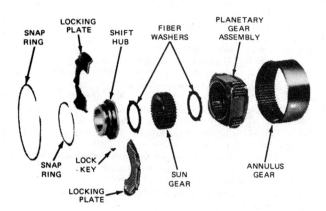

Fig. 7.50 Planetary gear set of the B-W 1345 transfer case –
exploded view (Sec 18)

output shaft ball bearing assembly to the case.
46 Remove the front output shaft seal and both input shaft seals from
the case using a seal removal tool and slide hammer.
47 Using a press and collar, press the front output shaft bearing and
input shaft bushing from the case.

Cleaning and inspection
48 Discard all old gaskets and seals.
49 Carefully inspect all bearings and rollers for evidence of pitting,
chipping, cracking or worn spots.
50 Inspect all shaft splines and gears for chipped teeth or excessive
wear.
51 Replace worn or damaged components as necessary with new
ones.

Reassembly
Note: *Before assembling the transfer case components, lubricate all
parts with automatic transmission fluid (Dexron II or equivalent).*
Case
52 Using a press and collar, press the input shaft bushing into the
case, making sure the lug is facing down.
53 Install the output shaft ball bearing and snap-ring.
54 Press both input shaft seals into the case.
55 Press the front output shaft seal into the case.

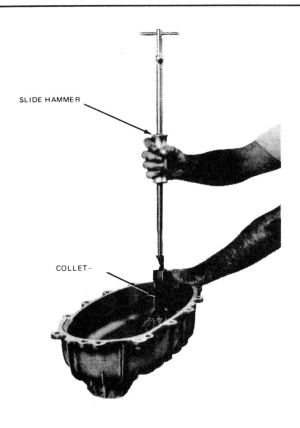

Fig. 7.51 Removing the needle bearing from the cover of the B-W 1345 transfer case (Sec 18)

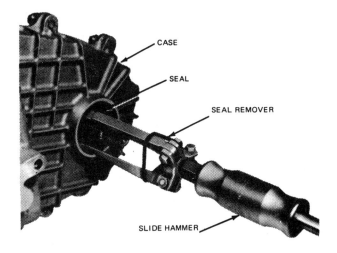

Fig. 7.52 Removing the front output shaft seal from the case half of the B-W 1345 transfer case (Sec 18)

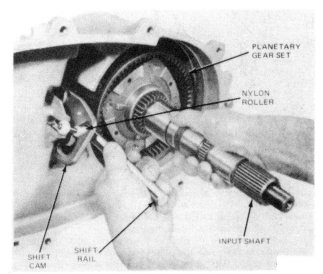

Fig. 7.53 Installing the planetary gear set and shifter assembly in the B-W 1345 transfer case (Sec 18)

Cover

56 Using a bearing replacer (Ford no. T80T-7127-B or equivalent), press the front output shaft inner needle bearing into the cover.

57 Press the rear output shaft ball bearing into the cover and install the snap-ring.

58 Turn the cover over and install the speedometer drivegear.

59 Install the rear output shaft seal in position in the cover.

60 Install the speedometer plug O-ring, speedometer plug, lock plate and bolt in the cover.

Planetary gear set

61 Place the inner fiber washer into the planetary gear housing, turning it slightly to position the tabs.

62 Install the sun gear into the planetary gear cage.

63 Coat the outer fiber washer with petroleum jelly and install the washer on the shift hub.

64 Place the hub in the planetary gear cage and install the T-shaped lock key and snap-ring.

65 Install the locking plates on the shift hub with the dished side toward the planetary gear set.

66 Lower the planetary assembly into the annulus gear, making sure the tabs on the locking plates engage the annulus gear teeth, then install the snap-ring.

Major assemblies

67 Assemble the planetary gear set, shift rail, shift cam, input shaft and shift fork together as a unit, making sure the boss on the shift cam is installed toward the case.

68 Install the spacer washer on the input shaft.

69 Install the rear output shaft in the planetary gear set, making sure the shift cam engages the shift fork actuating pin.

70 Lay the case on its side.

71 Insert the rear output shaft and planetary gear set into the case, making sure the spacer remains on the input shaft.

72 Install the shift rail into its hole in the case and install the outer roller bushing into the guide in the case.

73 Remove the rear output shaft and position the shift fork in Neutral as illustrated in the accompanying diagram.

74 Place the shift control lever shaft through the cam and install the C-clip. To ensure that the shift control lever is in Neutral, make sure it is pointed down, parallel with the front face of the case.

75 Check that the shift fork and planetary gear engage freely, without any binding.

76 If the needle bearing was removed from the bearing retainer during disassembly, press a new bearing into the retainer using a bearing replacer (Ford no. T80T-7127-C or equivalent).

77 Install the rear output shaft through the bearing retainer from the bottom.

78 Insert the rear output shaft pilot into the rear bushing of the input shaft.

79 Align the dowel holes and lower the bearing retainer into position in the case.

80 Install the dowel pins into the retainer and install the snap-ring that retains the bearing retainer to the case.

81 Insert the detent ball and spring into the detent bore in the case.

82 Coat the seal plug with RTV-type sealant and drive the plug into the case with a soft-faced hammer.

83 Use a drift and hammer to drive the lip of the plug $\frac{1}{32}$ in below the surface of the case.

84 Using a ball-pein hammer, pein the case metal over the plug in two places to secure it.

85 Install the oil pump front cover over the rear output shaft with the flanged side down (the word 'top' must be facing the top of the

7C

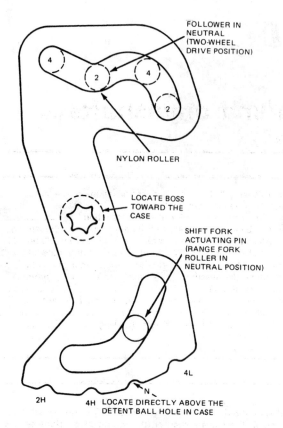

Fig. 7.54 Correct shift cam engagement of the shift fork actuating pin (Sec 18)

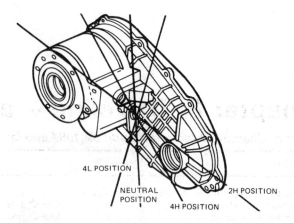

Fig. 7.55 Correct positioning of the shift control lever in the Neutral position during assembly of the B-W 1345 transfer case (Sec 18)

transfer case when the case is installed in the vehicle).

86 Attach the oil pump pick-up tube to the oil filter and install the retaining clips.

87 Install the oil pump spring and the two pump pins into the rear output shaft, with the flat sides of the pins out.

88 Depress the pins and install the oil pump body, pick-up tube and filter. The 'rear' markings on the pump body must face up.

89 Prime the pump with automatic transmission fluid (Dexron II or equivalent).

90 Install the oil pump rear cover on the rear output shaft with the flanged side down (the words 'top rear' must face the top of the transfer case when the case is installed in the vehicle).

91 Apply Loctite or equivalent to the oil pump retaining bolts and install them.

92 Tighten the oil pump retaining bolts to the specified torque, rotating the pump with the rear output shaft while tightening. **Note:** *When the oil pump is correctly installed, it will rotate freely on the output shaft.*

93 Install the thrust washer on the rear output shaft, next to the oil pump.

94 Install the front output shaft into the case.

95 Install the chain on the drive and driven sprockets.

96 Lower the chain and sprockets into position in the case. The driven sprocket is installed over the front output shaft and the drive sprocket is placed on the rear output shaft.

97 Install the washer and snap-ring behind the driven sprocket.

98 Engage the 4-wheel-drive lockup fork on the lockup collar.

99 Slide the lockup fork over the shift rail and the collar over the rear output shaft.

100 Make sure the nylon wear pads are installed on the fork tips with the location holes correctly aligned and that the necked down portion of the collar is facing to the rear.

101 Using a screwdriver, press the fork spring down and install the upper spring retainer, then press the spring up and install the lower retainer.

102 Install the shift collar hub on the rear output shaft.

103 Install the magnetic chip collector in the boss in the bottom of the case.

104 Apply a bead of RTV-type sealant to the case mounting surface.

105 Lower the cover over the rear output shaft and align the shift rail with the blind hole in the cover. Make sure that the front output shaft is fully seated in its support bearing.

106 Install the case-to-cover retaining bolts and tighten them to the specified torque.

107 Install the 4-wheel-drive indicator switch in the cover and tighten it to the specified torque.

108 Press the oil slinger onto the front output shaft yoke and install the seal.

109 Attach the seal to the rear output shaft yoke.

110 Attach the yokes to the shafts, then install the washers.

111 Coat the faces of the yoke nuts with thread lock and sealer (Ford no. EOAZ-19554-A or equivalent), install the nuts and tighten them to the specified torque.

112 If previously removed, install the transfer case drain plug.

113 Fill the transfer case with 6.5 pints of the specified lubricant (refer to Chapter 1) and install the fill plug.

114 Install the transfer case in the vehicle (refer to Section 16).

115 Make sure the sealant used when joining the case and cover of the transfer case has had at least an hour to cure before operating the vehicle.

Chapter 8 Driveline – axles and driveshafts

Refer to Chapter 13 for information on 1987 and later models

Contents

Specifications

Rear axle

Type	Ford semi-floating with integral carrier (8.8 in ring gear); Ford semi-floating with removable carrier (9.0 in ring gear); Dana semi-floating and full-floating with integral carrier
Ratio	Varies; ratio is stamped on metal tag attached to rear cover bolt
Endplay (full-floating)	0.001 to 0.010 in

Front axle

Type	Dana standard and heavy-duty
Ratio	Varies; ratio is stamped on metal tag attached to rear cover bolt
Endplay	
Bronco and F150 with Dana 44-IFS/44-IFS-HD	0.000 to 0.006 in
F250 and F350 with Dana 50-IFS	0.001 to 0.009 in

Driveshaft

Type	One-piece or two-piece depending on wheelbase of vehicle (refer to Section 16)

Torque specifications

Ft-lb (unless otherwise noted)

Rear axle

Dana

Pinion shaft nut	250 to 270
Pinion mate shaft lockpin	20 to 25
Differential bearing cap bolts	80 to 90
Ring gear attaching bolts	100 to 120
Cover-to-housing bolts	30 to 40
Spring and shock absorber nuts and bolts	Refer to Chapter 11
Axleshaft retaining bolts (full-floating models)	40 to 50
Wheel bearing adjusting nut (full-floating models only)	120 to 140 (back off $\frac{1}{8}$ to $\frac{3}{8}$ turn)
Universal joint bolts	15 to 20
Lubricant fill plug	20 to 30

Ford (integral carrier axle)

Differential bearing cap bolt	70 to 85
Pinion mate shaft lock bolt (using Loctite or equivalent)	15 to 30
Ring gear attaching bolts (using Loctite or equivalent)	70 to 85
Rear cover screw	25 to 35
Driveshaft-to-axle companion flange bolts	7 to 15
Lubricant fill plug	15 to 30
Spring and shock absorber nuts and bolts	Refer to Chapter 11

Ford (removable carrier axle)

Pinion retainer-to-carrier bolts	30 to 45
Ring gear attaching bolts	70 to 85
Bearing cap, bolts	70 to 85

8

	Ft-lb (unless otherwise noted)
Carrier-to-housing nuts	25 to 40
Adjusting nut lock bolts	12 to 25
Axleshaft bearing retainer nuts (bearing retainer plate)	20 to 40
Driveshaft-to-rear axle U-bolt nuts	8 to 15
Spring and shock absorber nuts and bolts	Refer to Chapter 11
Lubricant fill plug	15 to 30
Front axle	
Vehicles with coil springs	
Drive axle-to-crossmember pivot bolt	120 to 150
Axle arm-to-radius arm bolts	180 to 240
Coil spring-to-lower spring seat retaining nut	30 to 70
Upper coil spring retainer screw	13 to 18
Vehicles with leaf springs	
Shock absorber mounting plate-to-leaf spring and axle assembly U-bolts	85 to 120
Drive axle-to-crossmember pivot bolt	120 to 150
All vehicles	
Spindle-to-knuckle stud retaining nuts	
Bronco, F150-F250	20 to 30
F350	50 to 60
Front wheel bearing adjusting nuts (4x4 only)*	
1980 (F150/350 Bronco)	
Inner bearing	50 (back off $\frac{1}{4}$ turn)
Outer bearing	50
1981 (F150/250 and Bronco)	
Inner bearing	50 (back off $\frac{1}{8}$ turn)
Outer bearing	50
1981 (F350)	
Inner bearing	50 (back off $\frac{3}{8}$ turn)
Outer bearing	65
1982 (F150/250 and Bronco)	
Inner bearing	50 (back off $\frac{1}{8}$ turn)
Outer bearing	150
1982 (F350)	
Inner bearing	50 (back off $\frac{3}{8}$ turn)
Outer bearing	65
1983 (F150 and Bronco)	50
Inner bearing	50 (back off $\frac{1}{8}$ turn)
Outer bearing	150
1983 (F250/350)	
Inner bearing	50 (back off $\frac{3}{8}$ turn)
Outer bearing	65
Manual locking hub capscrews	35 to 55 in-lb
Automatic locking hub capscrews	40 to 50 in-lb
Driveshafts	
Single snap-ring type U-joint	
Coupling shaft center bearing bracket-to-support	37 to 54
Driveshaft U-joint-to-rear yoke bolt	90 to 110
U-joint adapter-to-rear axle bolt and nut	60 to 70
Double cardan type U-joint	
Driveshaft-to-transfer case bolts	20 to 28
Driveshaft-to-front and rear axle U-bolts	8 to 15

*See text in this Chapter for details of the procedure

1 Rear axle – general information

The rear axle assembly consists of a straight, hollow housing enclosing a differential assembly and axleshafts. These assemblies support the vehicle's 'sprung' weight components through leaf or coil springs attached between the axle housings and the vehicle's frame rails.

The axle assemblies employed on vehicles covered by this manual are of two designs: those with semi-floating axleshafts and those with full-floating axleshafts. As a general rule, trucks with Gross Vehicle Weight (GVW) below 7000 pounds employ semi-floating axleshafts while those trucks with ratings above 7000 GVW employ a full-floating design axleshaft. Full-floating axleshafts do not themselves bear any of the vehicle's weight and can be removed independent of the tapered roller wheel bearings. Both types of rear end designs use

hypoid gears with the ring gear centerline below the axleshaft centerline.

Due to the need for special tools and equipment, it is recommended that operations on these models be limited to those described in this Chapter. Where repair or overhaul is required, remove the axle assembly and take it to a rebuilder, or exchange it for a new or reconditioned unit. It is becoming increasingly rare to find individual axle components for local repair work as it is generally recognized that dismantling and rebuilding this unit is an 'in plant' job requiring special equipment and techniques.

Always make sure that an axle unit is changed for one of identical type and gear ratio.

Routine maintenance and minor repair procedures can be performed without removing the differential assembly from the axle housing or the rear axle assembly from the vehicle. The following components can be serviced as described above: axleshafts, wheel hubs, wheel hub bearings, wheel hub grease seals, wheel hub lugs.

2 Rear axleshaft oil seal (semi-floating type) – replacement

Note: *The following procedure is for oil seal replacement on axles with ball bearings. Tapered roller bearings are used on certain semi-floating axles and require bearing removal for oil seal replacement (See Section 3.*

1   Remove the axleshaft as described in Section 5.
2   The axleshaft seal must be pulled out of the housing with a special slide hammer type puller.
3   Inspect the inner surface of the housing for any conditions that would prevent the new seal from fitting into its seat correctly. Remedy any problems of this type such as burrs, galling or rust before attempting to install the seal.
4   Smear a small amount of oil-resistant sealer on the outer edge of the seal. Do not allow the sealer to touch the sealing lip.
5   Drive the new seal into its bore. The seal must receive even pressure around its circumference, thus a tubular drift, large socket or special tool should be used for this. Push the seal into the housing until it seats.
6   Install the axleshaft.

3 Rear axle bearings and seal (full-floating type) – replacement

Note: *Refer to Fig. 8.1 to locate and identify pertinent components.*
1   Raise the rear of the vehicle and place it securely on jackstands.
2   Remove the rear wheels, then remove the axleshafts as described in Section 6.
3   Remove the locking wedge from the adjusting nut keyway slot with a screwdriver. **Note:** This must be done before the adjusting nut is removed or even turned.
4   Remove the wheel bearing adjusting nut using the correct size large socket.
5   Pull the brake drum and hub off the spindle. If the brake drum won't come off easily, it may be necessary to loosen the brake shoes slightly (Chapter 9).
6   Remove the outer bearing assembly from inside the hub.
7   Use a brass drift to drive the inner bearing cone and inner seal out

of the wheel hub.
8   Clean the inside of the wheel hub to remove all axle lubricant and grease. Clean the spindle.
9   Inspect the bearing assemblies for signs of wear, pitting, galling and other damage. Replace the bearings if any of these conditions exist. Inspect the bearing races for signs of erratic wear, galling and other damage. Drive out the bearing races with a brass drift if they need replacement. Install the new races with a suitable tool designed for this purpose. Never use a drift or punch for this operation as these races must be seated correctly and can be damaged easily.
10 Prior to installation, pack the inner and outer wheel bearing assemblies with the correct type of wheel bearing grease. If you do not have access to a bearing packer, pack each assembly carefully by hand and make sure the entire assembly is penetrated with lubricant.
11 Install the newly packed inner wheel bearing into the brake drum hub. Install a new hub inner seal with a suitable drive tool (tubular drift, large socket, special tool) being careful not to damage the seal.
12 Wrap the spindle around the end and threaded area with electrician's tape to prevent damage to the inner wheel bearing seal during installation.
13 Carefully slide the hub and drum assembly over the spindle, being very careful to keep it straight so as not to contact the spindle with the seal (which would damage it). Remove the electrician's tape.
14 Install the newly packed outer wheel bearing. Install the wheel bearing adjusting nut by hand.
15 While rotating the hub/drum assembly, tighten the adjusting nut to 120 to 140 ft-lb. Back off the nut enough to get 0.001 to 0.010 in end play. This should require about $\frac{1}{8}$ to $\frac{3}{8}$ of a turn.
16 Position the locking wedge in the keyway and hammer it into position. **Note:** *It must be bottomed against the shoulder of the adjusting nut when fully installed.* The locking wedge and adjusting nut can be used over, providing the locking wedge cuts a new groove in the nylon retainer material within $\frac{1}{8}$ to $\frac{3}{8}$ of a turn. The wedge must be pressed into a previously cut groove. If it is not possible to back the nut off within the $\frac{1}{8}$ to $\frac{3}{8}$ turn limit, obtain the proper end play and align uncut nylon in which to press the locking wedge, discard the nut and wedge and replace them with new ones. Also discard the nut and/or wedge if there is any evidence of damage.
17 Install the axleshaft with a new axle flange gasket, lock washers

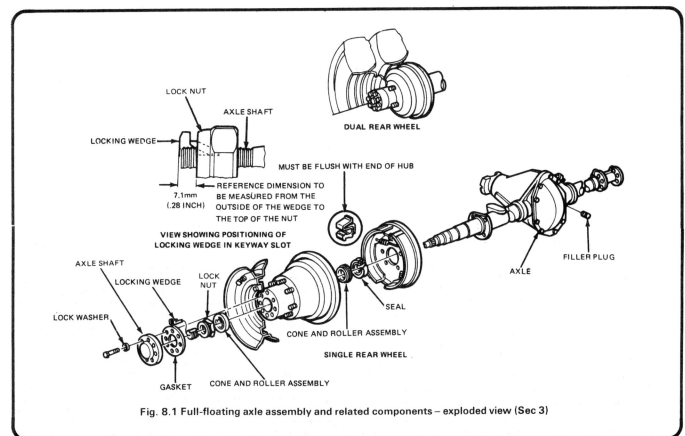

Fig. 8.1 Full-floating axle assembly and related components – exploded view (Sec 3)

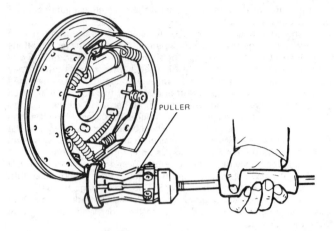

Fig. 8.2 Removing the rear wheel bearing cup from the axleshaft housing of a semi-floating-type rear axle (Sec 4)

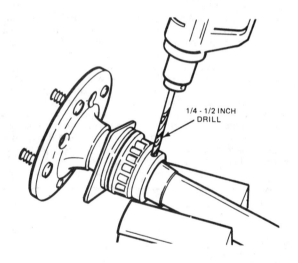

Fig. 8.3 Drilling a hole in the inner retainer ring (do not exceed a depth of $\frac{3}{4}$ in) (Sec 4)

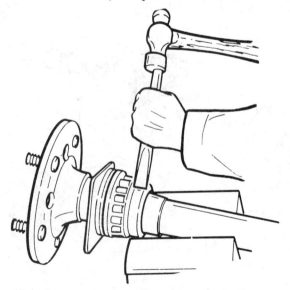

Fig. 8.4 Using a chisel and hammer to remove the retainer ring after a hole has been drilled (Sec 4)

and new axleshaft retaining bolts, tightening the bolts to the specified torque.
18 Adjust the brakes if they were loosened for removal purposes.
19 Install the wheel, remove the jackstands and lower the vehicle.

4 Rear wheel bearing (semi-floating type) – replacement

1 Remove the axleshaft as described in Section 5.
2 When it is determined that the wheel bearing is to be replaced, the bearing cup, which normally remains in the axle housing when the axleshaft is removed, must also be replaced. Use a slide hammer-type puller to remove it from the housing.
3 Before the wheel bearing and/or seal can be replaced, the inner retainer ring must first be removed. Never use heat to remove the ring as this would damage the axleshaft. Use the procedure which follows.
4 Using a drill of $\frac{1}{4}$ to $\frac{1}{2}$ in diameter, drill a hole in the outside diameter of the inner retainer approximating $\frac{3}{4}$ of the thickness of the retainer ring. Do not drill all the way through the retainer ring, as the drill would damage the axleshaft.
5 After drilling the hole in the retainer ring, use a chisel positioned across the drilled hole and strike it sharply to split the retainer ring.
6 Due to the need for a hydraulic press and various adapters to remove the wheel bearing, you must take the axleshaft(s) to an automotive machine shop or parts store with the equipment required for the work. On vehicles with tapered roller wheel bearings, the axleshaft seal should be replaced at the same time.
7 After the new bearing has been pressed onto the axleshaft, install it as described in Section 5.

5 Rear axleshaft (semi-floating type) – removal and installation

Ford 8.8 in and Dana
Note: *Refer to Figs. 8.6 and 8.7 to identify components.*
1 Jack up the rear of the vehicle and place it securely on jackstands.
2 Remove the wheel(s).
3 Release the parking brake and remove the brake drum(s) (refer to Chapter 9 if necessary).
4 Drain the rear axle lubricant into a suitable container by removing the rear axle housing cover.
5 If still in place, discard the gasket.
6 Remove the differential pinion mate shaft lockpin and discard it.
Note: *It is possible for some Dana floating axles to be equipped with lockpins coated with Loctite (or equivalent), or with lockpins with torque-prevailing threads. The Loctite-treated lockpins have a $\frac{5}{32}$ in hexagram socket head, and the torque-prevailing lockpin has a 12-point drive head. If the axle is equipped with a Loctite-treated lockpin, it must not be reused under any circumstances. If the lockpin is of the torque-prevailing type, it may be reused up to four times (four removals and installations). When in doubt as to the number of times the torque-prevailing pin has been used, replace it with a new one.*
7 Lift out the differential pinion mate shaft.

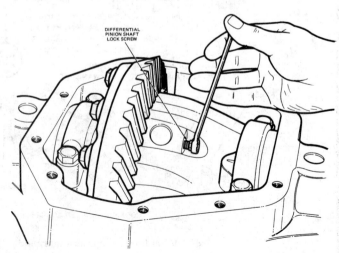

Fig. 8.5 Removing the differential pinion shaft lock screw (Sec 5)

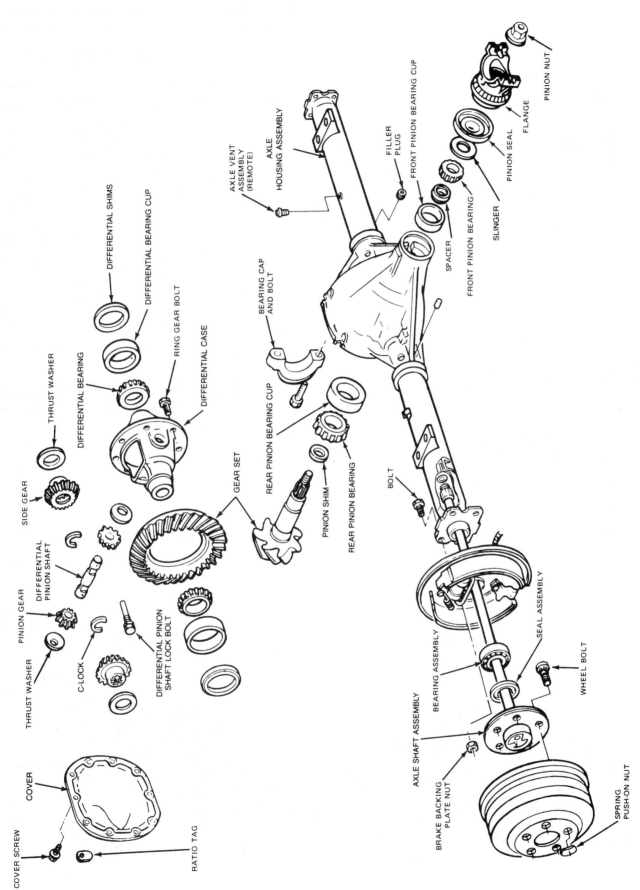

COVER SCREW

COVER

RATIO TAG

THRUST WASHER

PINION GEAR

DIFFERENTIAL
PINION SHAFT

C-LOCK

DIFFERENTIAL PINION
SHAFT LOCK BOLT

SIDE GEAR

DIFFERENTIAL
PINION SHAFT

GEAR SET

REAR PINION BEARING CUP

PINION SHIM

REAR PINION BEARING

BOLT

THRUST WASHER

DIFFERENTIAL SHIMS

DIFFERENTIAL BEARING CUP

DIFFERENTIAL BEARING

RING GEAR BOLT

DIFFERENTIAL CASE

BEARING CAP
AND BOLT

AXLE VENT
ASSEMBLY
(REMOTE)

AXLE
HOUSING ASSEMBLY

FILLER
PLUG

FRONT PINION BEARING CUP

FRONT PINION BEARING

SPACER

SLINGER

PINION SEAL

FLANGE

PINION NUT

AXLE SHAFT ASSEMBLY

BEARING ASSEMBLY

SEAL ASSEMBLY

BRAKE BACKING
PLATE NUT

WHEEL BOLT

SPRING
PUSH-ON NUT

Fig. 8.6 Ford 8.8 integral carrier rear axle assembly – exploded view (Sec 5)

8

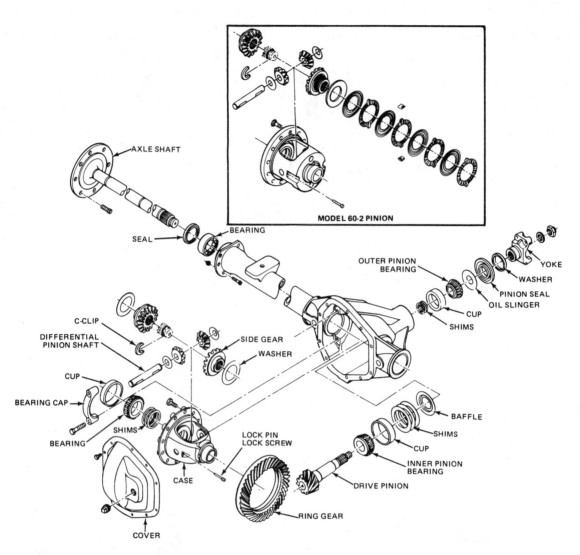

MODEL 60-2 PINION

AXLE SHAFT

SEAL — BEARING

OUTER PINION BEARING — YOKE

WASHER

PINION SEAL

OIL SLINGER

CUP

SHIMS

C-CLIP

DIFFERENTIAL PINION SHAFT

SIDE GEAR

WASHER

CUP

BEARING CAP

SHIMS

BEARING

BAFFLE

SHIMS

CUP

INNER PINION BEARING

LOCK PIN LOCK SCREW

DRIVE PINION

CASE

RING GEAR

COVER

Fig. 8.7 Dana semi-floating rear axle assembly – exploded view (Sec 5)

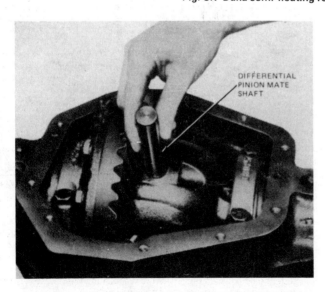

DIFFERENTIAL PINION MATE SHAFT

Fig. 8.8 Removing the differential pinion mate shaft (Sec 5)

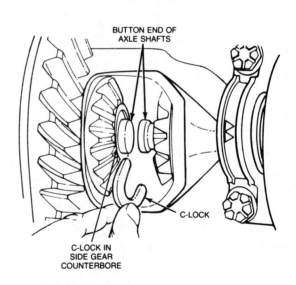

BUTTON END OF AXLE SHAFTS

C-LOCK

C-LOCK IN SIDE GEAR COUNTERBORE

Fig. 8.9 Removing the C-clip from the axleshaft (Sec 5)

8   Push the flanged end of the axleshaft toward the center of the vehicle and remove the C-clip from the button end of the shaft. **Note:** *Make sure not to lose or damage the rubber O-ring which is in the axleshaft groove under the C-clip.*

9   Pull the axleshaft from the housing, making sure not to damage the oil seals.

10   Installation is basically the reverse of the removal procedure. Make sure not to damage the axle seal when reinstalling the axleshaft (the splines on the end of the shaft are sharp). Tighten the pinion mate shaft lockpin to the specified torque.

11   Most axle housing covers are sealed with silicone rubber sealant rather than a gasket. Before applying this sealant (Ford no. D6AZ-19562-B or equivalent), make sure the machined surfaces on both cover and carrier are clean and free of oil. When cleaning the surfaces, cover the inside of the axle with a clean lint-free cloth to prevent contamination. Apply a continuous bead of the sealant to the carrier casting face, inside the cover bolt holes. Install the cover within 15 minutes of the application of the sealant and tighten the bolts in a crisscross pattern to the specified torque. Tighten the wheel assembly lug bolts to the specified torque.

Ford 9.0 in axle assembly

12   Refer to and perform Steps 1 through 3 of this Section.

13   Loosen the axle retaining nuts by inserting a socket and extension through the hole provided in the axle flange. Rotate the axle to allow access to all four nuts. Remove the nuts.

14   Remove the axleshaft by pulling on the flange. If the axle is stuck it can sometimes be removed by reinstalling the wheel assembly and using the greater leverage of the wheel to pull it out. When pulling out the axle, be careful not to damage the seal if you are reusing it although seals should always be replaced whenever an axle is removed. Secure the brake backing plate to the housing with one nut to make sure it doesn't fall off while you are performing other operations on the axleshaft or housing.

15   Installation is the reverse of removal. Install a new gasket between the brake backing plate and the axle housing flange. Be careful not to damage the inner lips of the axle seal when you are inserting the axleshaft into the housing (the splines on the end of the shaft are sharp). Tighten the axleshaft retaining nuts and the wheel lug bolts to the correct torque.

6   Rear axleshaft (full-floating type) – removal and installation

Note: *Refer to Fig. 8.10 to identify components.*

1   Unscrew and remove the bolts which attach the axleshaft flange to the hub. There is no need to remove the tire and wheel or jack up the vehicle.

2   Tap the flange with a soft-faced hammer to loosen the shaft and then grip the rib of the face of the flange with a pair of locking pliers; twist the shaft slightly in both directions and then withdraw it from the axle tube.

3   Installation is the reverse of removal but hold the axleshaft level in order to engage the splines at its inner end with those in the differential side gear. Always use a new gasket on the flange and keep both the flange and hub mating surfaces free of grease and oil.

7   Rear differential assembly (removable carrier type) – removal and installation

Note: *Refer to Fig. 8.11 to identify components.*

1   The differential assembly used in the light-duty axle housing is of the removable type. This unit must be removed for service operations including pinion seal replacement and gear lash preload to correct for noise or wear. This type of differential is used in conjunction with semi-floating axles.

2   Raise the vehicle and support the rear axle housing or frame securely.

3   Drain the rear axle housing using the plug under the center section.

4   Remove the axleshafts (Sec 5). It is not necessary to remove them totally but pull them out about ten inches to clear the differential side gears.

5   Remove the driveshaft.

6   Remove the carrier housing retaining nuts and washers around the entire circumference of the housing. Be careful not to lose the identification tag retained by one of these nuts as it contains valuable information about the differential assembly.

7   Clean the area around the mating surfaces of the differential carrier housing.

8   Support the unit (a transmission jack is ideal) and remove the differential assembly.

9   Clean the mating surface on the carrier housing and remove any old gasket material from the housing or the carrier assembly. Installation is the reverse of removal. Make sure you use a new gasket and that the mating faces of the housing and the carrier assembly are clean. Fill the differential with the correct type and grade of lubricant (Chapter 1).

8   Rear axle assembly – removal and installation

Note: *On vehicles with rear anti-lock brakes (RABS), be sure to un-plug the brake sensor wire harness connectors before removing the rear axle assembly.*

1   Chock the front wheels, jack up the rear of the vehicle and support it on jackstands placed under the rear frame member.

2   Remove the wheels, brake drums and axleshafts as described in Section 5 or 6.

3   Remove the driveshaft.

4   Disconnect the lower end of the shock absorbers from the axle housing and disconnect the rear stabilizer bar (if so equipped).

5   Remove the brake vent tube (if equipped) from the brake pipe junction and retaining clamp.

6   Remove the brake pipes from the clips that retain them to the axle but do not disconnect any of the pipe unions.

7   Remove the brake linings and brake back plates and support them with wire to avoid straining the hydraulic brake lines which are still attached (See Chapter 9).

8   Support the weight of the axle on a jack and remove the nuts from the spring retaining U-bolts. Remove the bottom clamping plates.

9   Lower the axle assembly on the jack and withdraw it from the rear of the vehicle.

10   The axle assembly is installed by reversing the removal procedure. Tighten the U-bolt and shock absorber nuts to the correct torque.

9   Front drive axle assembly (4x4) – general information

Note: *Refer to Fig. 8.13 to identify and locate components pertinent to 4x4 vehicle front-drive axles and related assemblies.*

Three types of Dana front-drive axles are available for Ford 4x4 light-duty truck application. The Dana 44-IFS (independent front suspension) is available on Bronco and F150 4x4s. The Dana 44-IFS-HD (heavy duty) is available on F250 4x4s. The Dana 50-IFS was available on F350 4x4s in 1980 and on F250 and F350 4x4s from 1981 through 1983.

All axles are basically alike with only minor differences among the three. The 44-IFS is on vehicles equipped with coil front springs. The 44-IFS-HD and 50-IFS are on vehicles equipped with leaf front springs.

Manual locking hubs are standard on all three axles, with automatic locking hubs optionally available on 44-IFS and 44-IFS-HD models only.

10   Manual locking hubs – removal and installation

Note: *Refer to Fig. 8.14 to identify components.*

1   Remove the six socket head capscrews attaching the cap assembly to the body assembly.

2   Remove the cap assembly.

3   Using retainer ring pliers, remove the retainer ring from the end of the axleshaft.

4   Using needle-nose pliers, remove the lock ring seated in the groove of the wheel hub.

5   Slide the body assembly out of the wheel hub. If necessary, use an appropriate puller to remove the body assembly.

6   Installation is the reverse of the removal procedure. Tighten the socket head capscrews to the specified torque.

8

218

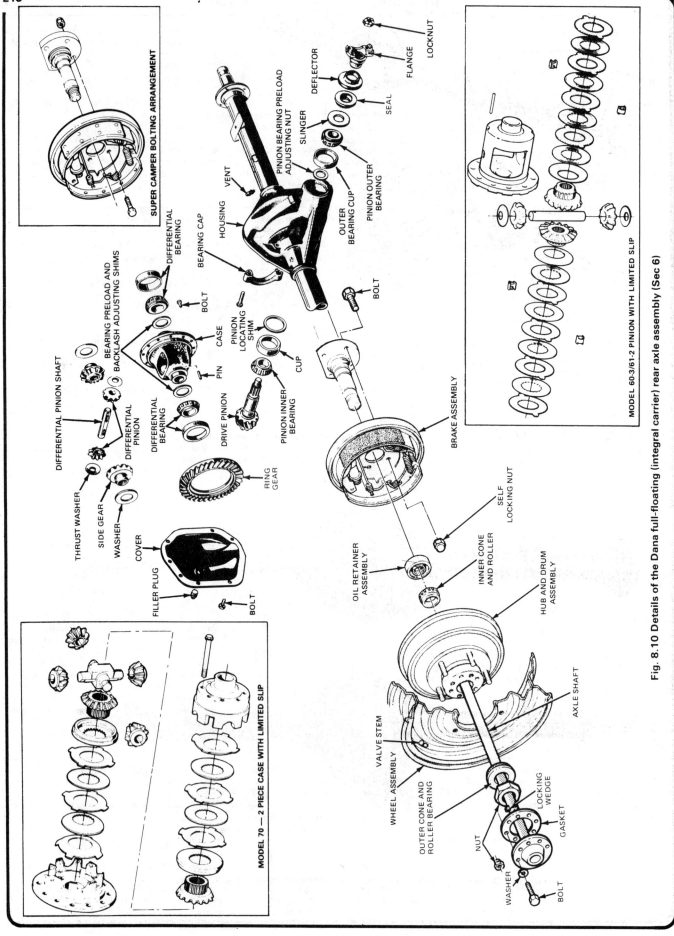

SUPER CAMPER BOLTING ARRANGEMENT

MODEL 60-3/61-2 PINION WITH LIMITED SLIP

MODEL 70 — 2 PIECE CASE WITH LIMITED SLIP

DIFFERENTIAL BEARING
BEARING CAP
HOUSING
VENT
DIFFERENTIAL BEARING
BEARING PRELOAD AND BACKLASH ADJUSTING SHIMS
BOLT
CASE
PIN
PINION LOCATING SHIM
CUP
DIFFERENTIAL PINION SHAFT
DIFFERENTIAL PINION
DIFFERENTIAL PINION
DIFFERENTIAL BEARING
DRIVE PINION
PINION INNER BEARING
THRUST WASHER
SIDE GEAR
WASHER
COVER
FILLER PLUG
BOLT
RING GEAR

LOCKNUT
FLANGE
DEFLECTOR
SLINGER
SEAL
PINION BEARING PRELOAD ADJUSTING NUT
OUTER BEARING CUP
PINION OUTER BEARING
BOLT
BOLT

BRAKE ASSEMBLY
SELF LOCKING NUT
OIL RETAINER ASSEMBLY
INNER CONE AND ROLLER
HUB AND DRUM ASSEMBLY
VALVE STEM
WHEEL ASSEMBLY
OUTER CONE AND ROLLER BEARING
NUT
WASHER
BOLT
LOCKING WEDGE
GASKET
AXLE SHAFT

Fig. 8.10 Details of the Dana full-floating (integral carrier) rear axle assembly (Sec 6)

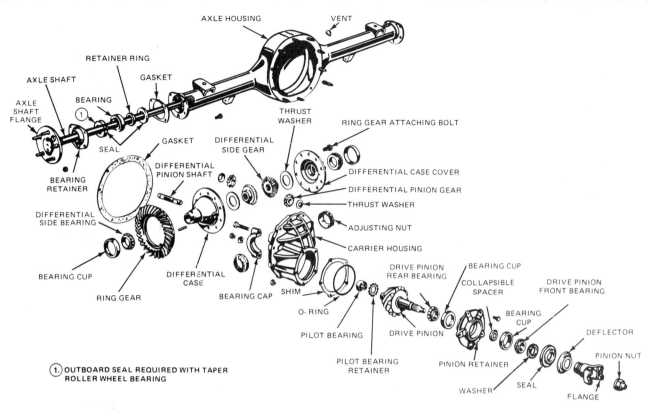

AXLE HOUSING
VENT
RETAINER RING
GASKET
AXLE SHAFT
BEARING
AXLE SHAFT FLANGE
SEAL
THRUST WASHER
RING GEAR ATTACHING BOLT
BEARING RETAINER
GASKET
DIFFERENTIAL PINION SHAFT
DIFFERENTIAL SIDE GEAR
DIFFERENTIAL CASE COVER
DIFFERENTIAL PINION GEAR
THRUST WASHER
DIFFERENTIAL SIDE BEARING
ADJUSTING NUT
CARRIER HOUSING
BEARING CUP
RING GEAR
DIFFERENTIAL CASE
BEARING CAP
SHIM
O-RING
PILOT BEARING
DRIVE PINION
DRIVE PINION REAR BEARING
BEARING CUP
COLLAPSIBLE SPACER
DRIVE PINION FRONT BEARING
BEARING CUP
DEFLECTOR
PINION NUT
PILOT BEARING RETAINER
PINION RETAINER
WASHER
SEAL
FLANGE

1. OUTBOARD SEAL REQUIRED WITH TAPER ROLLER WHEEL BEARING

Fig. 8.11 Details of the Ford 9.0 semi-floating (removable carrier) rear axle assembly (Sec 7)

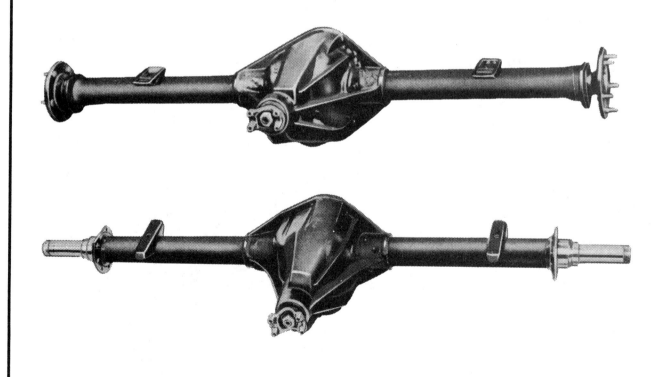

8

Fig. 8.12 Dana semi-floating (top) and full-floating (bottom) rear axle models (Sec 8)

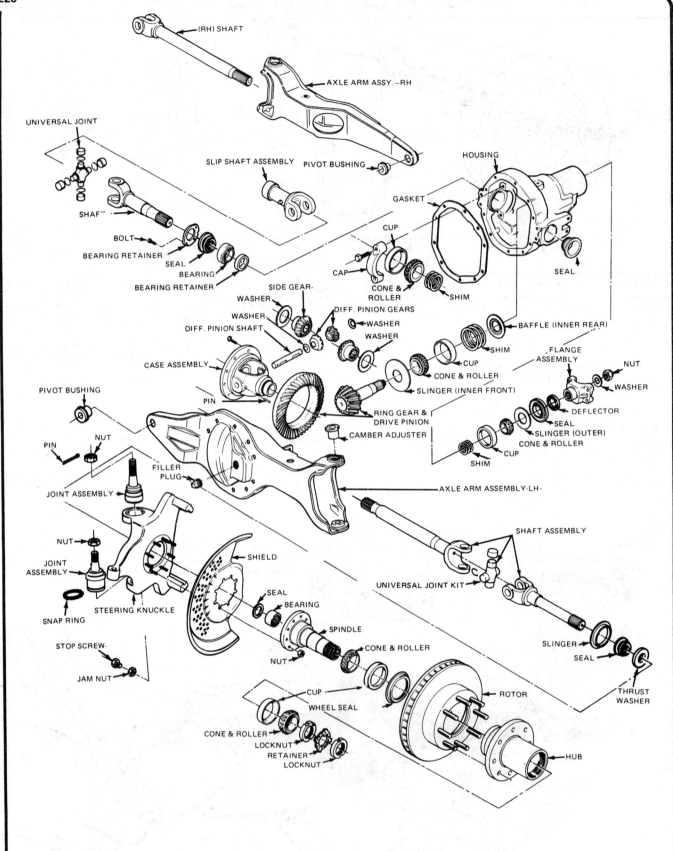

Fig. 8.13 Dana full-floating front drive axle assembly (Model 44-IFS-HD shown, others similar) (Sec 9)

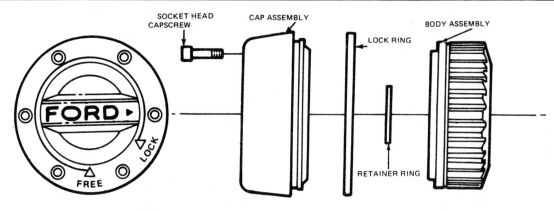

Fig. 8.14 Manual locking hub assembly – exploded view (Sec 10)

11 Automatic locking hubs – removal and installation

Note: *Refer to Fig. 8.15 to identify components.*
1   Remove the five capscrews attaching the cap assembly to the body assembly.
2   Remove the cap, making sure not to drop the ball bearing, bearing race or spring.
3   Remove the sealing ring.
4   Remove the seal bridge retainer (small metal stamping) from the retainer ring.
5   Remove the retainer ring by closing the ends with needle-nose pliers while pulling the hub lock from the wheel hub.
6   If the wheel hub and spindle are to be removed, follow Steps 7 through 9.
7   Remove the C-washer from the stub shaft groove.
8   Remove the splined spacer from the shaft.
9   Remove the wheel bearing locknuts and lock washer.
10 If the wheel bearing and lock washer were removed, refer to Section 13 for the proper installation procedures, then install the splined spacer and C-washer on the axleshaft.
11 Remove any excessive grease from the hub lock and hub splines.
12 Start the hub lock assembly into the hub, making sure the large tangs are lined up with the lock washer and that the outside-diameter

and inside-diameter splines are in line with the hub and axleshaft splines.
13 Install the retainer ring by closing the ends with needle-nose pliers and at the same time push the hub lock assembly into the hub.
14 The remaining installation steps are the reverse of the removal procedures. Tighten the five capscrews to the specified torque.

12 Front wheel grease seal and bearing (4x4) – replacement and repacking

Note: *Before disassembling your vehicle, purchase or rent the tool necessary to remove the locknut and adjusting nut from the spindle. Also obtain the parts necessary to replace the inner bearing seal as it should always be replaced whenever the entire front hub assembly is dismantled. If you cannot obtain the special tool necessary for the locknut and adjusting nut, this operation would be best handled by a dealership or shop specializing in this type of work.*
1   Raise the front of the vehicle and place it securely on jackstands.
2   Remove the manual or automatic locking hubs as described in Sections 10 and 11.
3   Remove the wheel bearing locknut, lock ring and adjusting nut using the special tool.
4   Pull the hub and disc assembly off the spindle. The outer wheel-bearing cone and roller assembly will slide out as the hub is removed.
5   Remove the spindle retaining nuts, then carefully remove the

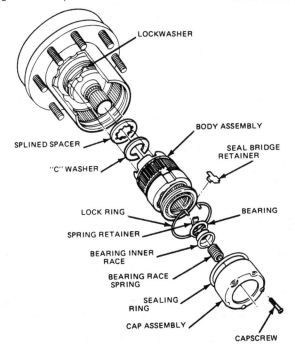

Fig. 8.15 Automatic locking hub assembly – exploded view (Sec 11)

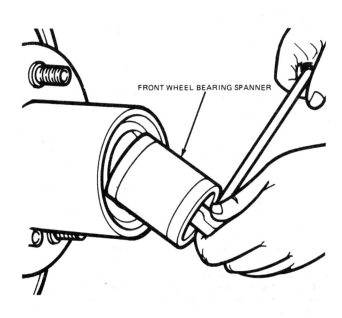

Fig. 8.16 Removing the adjusting nut from the front wheel assembly of a 4x4 vehicle (note special tool) (Sec 12)

8

spindle from the knuckle studs and axleshaft.

6   Using solvent, clean all old grease from the bearings and spindle bore seal. Blow the bearings dry with compressed air but do not 'dry spin' the bearings.

7   Inspect the above parts and replace them with new ones if signs of excessive wear are noted.

8   Using multi-purpose lubricant (Ford no. C1AZ-19590-B or equivalent), thoroughly lubricate the needle bearing and pack the spindle face that mates with the spindle bore seal.

9   Install the spindle over the axleshaft onto the knuckle studs. Tighten the retaining nuts to the specified torque.

10   Remove the inner bearing cone, grease seal and bearing cups from the hub using an appropriate puller and slide hammer.

11   Inspect the bearing cups for pits or cracks. If necessary, remove them with a drift, then drive in new cups with a tubular drift or large socket, taking care not to damage them. If new cups are installed, also install new cone and roller assemblies.

12   Lubricate the bearings with multi-purpose lubricant. If a bearing packer is not available, work as much lubricant as possible between the rollers and cages.

13   Clean all old grease from the hub.

14   Position the inner bearing cone and roller in the inner cup and install the grease seal.

15   Carefully position the hub and disc assembly on the spindle.

16   Install the outer bearing cone and roller and the adjusting nut.

17   Adjust the wheel bearing (refer to Section 13).

18   Install the locking hubs (refer to Section 10 or 11).

19   Adjust the brake if necessary (refer to Chapter 9).

20   Remove the jackstands and lower the vehicle.

13   Front wheel bearing (4x4) – adjustment

Note: *A special tool is required for tightening and loosening the bearing adjusting nut and locknut.*

1   Raise the vehicle and place it securely on jackstands.

2   Remove the hub lock assembly (refer to Section 10 or 11).

Bronco and F150 vehicles with Dana 44-IFS/44-IFS-HD driving axle

3   Using a bearing spanner (Ford no. T59T-1197-B or equivalent) and a torque wrench, tighten the inner bearing adjusting nut to 50 ft-lb while rotating the wheel back-and-forth to seat the bearing.

4   Back off the adjusting nut approximately 45 degrees.

5   Assemble the lock washer by turning the inner locknut to the nearest hole in the lock washer. To lock it, install the outer locknut and tighten to 150 ft-lb.

6   Grab the top of the tire with one hand and the bottom of the tire with the other. Move the tire in and out on the spindle. End play should be less than 0.006 in.

7   Install the hub lock assembly (refer to Section 10 or 11).

8   Remove the jackstands and lower the vehicle.

F250 and F350 vehicles with Dana 50-IFS driving axle

9   Using a bearing spanner (Ford no. D78T-1197-A or equivalent) and a torque wrench, tighten the inner locknut to 50 ft-lb to seat the bearing.

10   Back off the inner locknut and retighten it to 31 to 39 ft-lb.

11   While rotating the hub, back off the locknut 135° to 150°.

12   Assemble the outer lock washer and locknut and tighten to 65 ft-lb.

13   Bend one ear of the lock washer over the inner nut and the other ear of the lock washer over the outer nut.

14   Check the end play as described in Step 6. End play should be 0.001 to 0.009 in.

15   Install the hub lock assembly (refer to Section 10 or 11).

16   Remove the jackstands and lower the vehicle.

14   Front axleshaft (4x4) – removal and installation

1   Jack up the front of the vehicle and place it on jackstands, then remove the wheel and tire assemblies.

2   Remove the front axle bearings and seals and the spindle assembly (refer to Section 12).

3   Pull the axleshaft assembly from the axle housing, being very cautious as you pull the universal joint through the knuckle bore.

4   At this point the axle assembly can be serviced (universal joints, spindle bore seals, deflectors and spindle bore needle bearings).

5   Make sure all components mentioned in Step 4 are in good, serviceable condition. If not, replace them with new ones.

6   To install the axleshaft, carefully insert it through the knuckle bore, being careful not to damage the axle or seals. Engage the axle spline with the side gears of the differential and push the axle into its correct position.

7   The remaining installation steps are the reverse of the removal procedure. Tighten all fasteners to the specified torque.

15   Front drive axle assembly (4x4) – removal and installation

Vehicles with coil springs

Note: *Refer to Fig. 8.17 to identify components.*

1   Raise the front of the vehicle and support it by placing jackstands under the radius arm brackets.

2   Remove the wheel and tire assemblies.

3   Remove the brake calipers (refer to Chapter 9). **Note:** *Position the brake calipers on the frame after removal in a manner that will prevent suspending the caliper from the hose at any time during the axle removal and installation procedures. These precautions are necessary to prevent damage to the tube portion of the caliper hose assembly.*

4   Position a jack under the axle arm assembly and remove the bolt retaining the upper spring retainer to the spring and shock bracket, then remove the upper spring retainer.

5   Lower the jack and remove the nut from inside the coil that retains the lower spring retainer, insulator and lower spring seat.

6   Remove the coil spring, retainer, insulator and seat.

7   Repeat Steps 4 through 6 for the other coil spring.

8   Disconnect the bolts retaining the shock absorbers at the radius arm brackets and spring and shock brackets, then remove the shock absorbers.

9   On each side, remove the stud retaining the radius arm to the top of the axle arm by turning it out of the boss in the axle arm. Remove the bolt retaining the radius arm to the bottom of the axle arm.

10   Disconnect the vent tube at the differential housing and discard the hose clamps.

11   Remove the vent fitting and install a $\frac{1}{8}$ in pipe plug to prevent contamination.

12   Disconnect the front driveshaft at the flange and suspend it out of the way. Secure the universal joint caps so that they do not fall off.

13   Remove the pivot bolt securing the right-hand axle arm assembly to the crossmember, then remove the right-hand drive axle assembly and pull the axleshaft from the slip yoke.

14   Position a jack under the differential housing.

15   Remove the bolt securing the left-hand axle assembly to the crossmember and remove the left-hand drive axle assembly from under the vehicle.

16   Installation is basically the reverse of the removal procedure, except that the springs are installed before the shock absorbers. Use new studs and bolts when attaching the radius arms to the axle assemblies. Be sure to tighten all nuts and bolts to the specified torque.

17   After work on the front axle assembly has been completed, the caster and camber should be checked by an alignment technician.

Vehicles with leaf springs

Note: *Refer to Fig. 8.18 to identify components.*

18   Raise the vehicle and support it by placing jackstands under the frame members.

19   Remove the wheel and tire assemblies.

20   Remove the brake calipers (refer to Chapter 9). **Note:** *Position the brake calipers on the frame after removal in a manner that will prevent suspending the caliper from the hose at any time during the axle removal and installation procedures. These precautions are necessary to prevent damage to the tube portion of the caliper hose assembly.*

21   Position a jack under the right-hand axle assembly.

22   Remove the two U-bolts securing the shock absorber mounting plate and leaf spring to the tube and yoke assembly.

23   Disconnect the vent tube at the differential housing and discard the hose clamps.

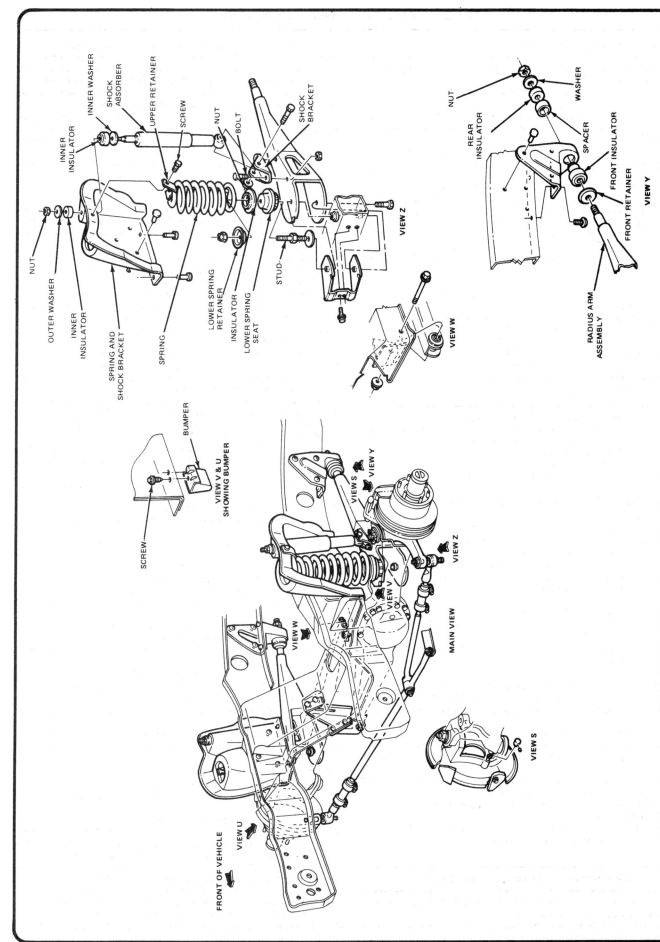

Fig. 8.17 Front drive axle assembly with coil springs – exploded view (Sec 15)

8

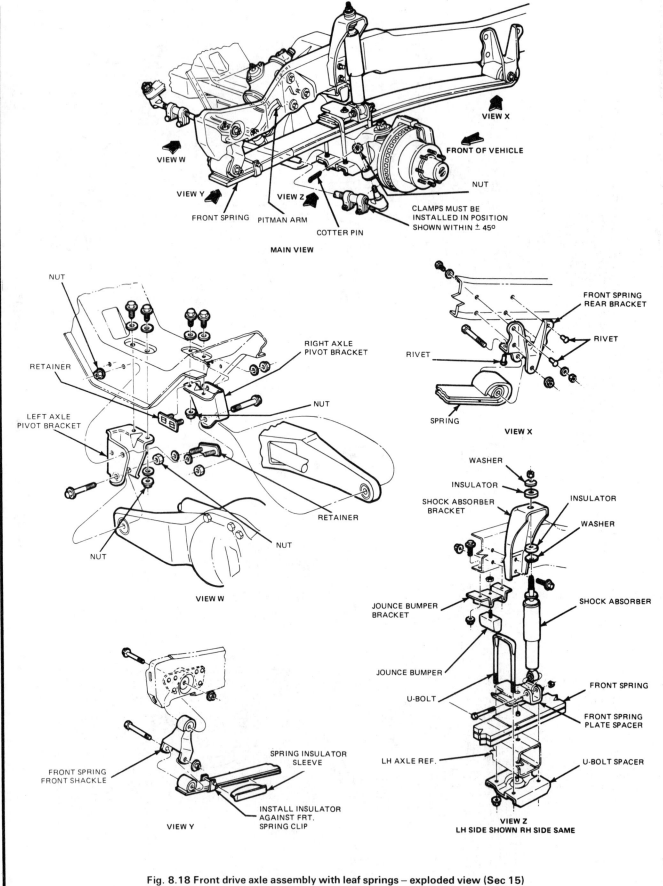

MAIN VIEW

VIEW X

FRONT OF VEHICLE

VIEW W

NUT

VIEW Y   VIEW Z

FRONT SPRING   PITMAN ARM   COTTER PIN

CLAMPS MUST BE
INSTALLED IN POSITION
SHOWN WITHIN ± 45°

NUT

RETAINER

LEFT AXLE
PIVOT BRACKET

RIGHT AXLE
PIVOT BRACKET

NUT

RETAINER

NUT

NUT

VIEW W

FRONT SPRING
REAR BRACKET

RIVET

RIVET

SPRING

VIEW X

WASHER

INSULATOR

INSULATOR

SHOCK ABSORBER
BRACKET

WASHER

SHOCK ABSORBER

JOUNCE BUMPER
BRACKET

JOUNCE BUMPER

U-BOLT

LH AXLE REF.

FRONT SPRING

FRONT SPRING
PLATE SPACER

U-BOLT SPACER

**VIEW Z
LH SIDE SHOWN RH SIDE SAME**

FRONT SPRING
FRONT SHACKLE

SPRING INSULATOR
SLEEVE

INSTALL INSULATOR
AGAINST FRT.
SPRING CLIP

VIEW Y

Fig. 8.18 Front drive axle assembly with leaf springs – exploded view (Sec 15)

24 Remove the vent fitting and install a $\frac{1}{8}$ in pipe plug to prevent contamination.

25 Disconnect the front driveshaft at the flange and suspend it out of the way. Secure the universal joint caps so that they do not fall off.

26 Remove the pivot bolt securing the right-hand axle arm assembly to the crossmember, then remove the right-hand drive axle assembly and pull the axleshaft from the slip yoke.

27 Position the jack under the left-hand axle assembly.

28 Remove the two U-bolts securing the shock absorber mounting plate and leaf spring to the tube and yoke assembly.

29 Position the jack under the differential housing.

30 Remove the bolt securing the left-hand drive axle assembly to the crossmember and remove the left-hand drive axle assembly from under the vehicle.

31 Installation is the reverse of the removal procedure. After work on the front axle is complete, the caster, camber and toe-in should be checked by an alignment technician.

16 Driveshaft(s) – general information

The driveshaft is of tubular construction and may be of a one or two-section type according to the wheelbase of the vehicle.

On 4-wheel-drive vehicles, the rear wheel driveline is very similar to that described above, but in order to drive the front wheels a driveshaft is incorporated between the transfer case and the front axle. This shaft is basically similar to the shafts used to drive the rear axle.

All driveshafts used to drive the rear wheels have needle bearing type universal joints. Single-section shafts have a splined sliding sleeve at the front end connecting to the output shaft of the transmission, while two-section shafts have a central slip joint. The purpose of these devices is to accommodate, by retraction or extension, the varying shaft length caused by the movement of the rear axle as the rear suspension deflects. On some 4-wheel-drive models, due to the extent of the front driveshaft angle, a constant velocity joint is used at the transfer case end of the driveshaft.

Where a two-section shaft is used, the shaft is supported near its forward end on a ball bearing which is flexibly mounted in a bracket attached to the frame crossmember.

The attachment of the rear end of the driveshaft to the rear axle pinion flange (or the attachment of the front driveshaft to the front axle pinion flange) may be by U-bolt or bolted strap, according to the date of production and model.

The driveshaft is finely balanced during manufacture and it is recommended that care be used when universal joints are replaced to help maintain this balance. It is sometimes better to have the universal joints replaced by a dealership or shop specializing in this type of work. If you replace the joints yourself, mark each individual yoke in relation to the one opposite in order to maintain the balance. Do not drop the assembly during servicing operations.

17 Driveshaft(s) – balancing

1 Vibration of the driveshaft at certain speeds may be caused by any of the following:

Undercoating or mud on the shaft
Loose rear strap attachment bolts
Worn universal joints
Bent or dented driveshaft

2 Vibrations which are thought to be emanating from the driveshaft are sometimes caused by improper tire balance. This should be one of your first checks.

3 If the shaft is in a good, clean, undamaged condition, it is worth disconnecting the rear end attachment straps and turning the shaft 180 degrees to see if an improvement is noticed. Be sure to mark the original position of each component before disassembly so the shaft can be returned to the same location.

4 If the vibration persists after checking for obvious causes and changing the position of the shaft, the entire assembly should be checked out by a professional shop or replaced.

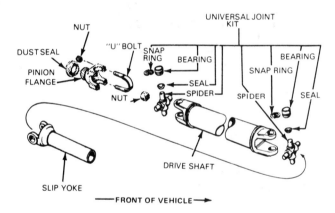

Fig. 8.19 One-piece driveshaft as used on most 4x2, short-wheelbase trucks (Sec 16)

18 Driveshaft(s) – removal and installation

Note: *Where two-piece driveshafts are involved, the rear shaft must be removed before the front shaft.*

1 Raise the vehicle and support it securely on jackstands.

2 Use chalk or a scribe to 'index' the relationship of the driveshaft(s) to the mating flange. This ensures correct alignment when the driveshaft is reinstalled.

3 Remove the nuts or bolts securing the universal joint clamps to the flange. If the driveshaft has a spline on one end (either to the transmission or the center carrier bearing) be sure to place marks on the mating flange or shaft to retain proper alignment during reinstallation.

4 Remove the nuts or bolts retaining the straps or universal joint to the flange on the opposite end of the driveshaft (if so equipped).

5 Pry the universal joint away from its mating flange and remove the shaft from the flange. Be careful not to let the caps fall off of the universal joint (which would cause contamination and loss of the needle bearings).

6 Repeat this process for the opposite end if it is equipped with a universal joint coupled to a flange.

7 If the opposite end is equipped with a sliding joint (spline), simply slide the yoke off the splined shaft.

8 If the shaft being removed is the front shaft of a two-piece unit, the rear is released by unbolting the two bolts securing the center bearing assembly. Again, make sure both ends of the shaft have been marked for installation purposes.

9 Installation is the reverse of removal. If the shaft cannot be lined up due to the components of the differential or transmission having been rotated, put the vehicle in Neutral or rotate one wheel to allow the original alignment to be achieved. Always tighten the retaining

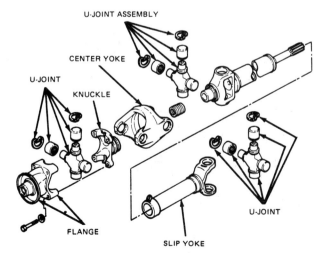

Fig. 8.20 Double Cardan-type driveshaft used on Bronco models (Sec 16)

8

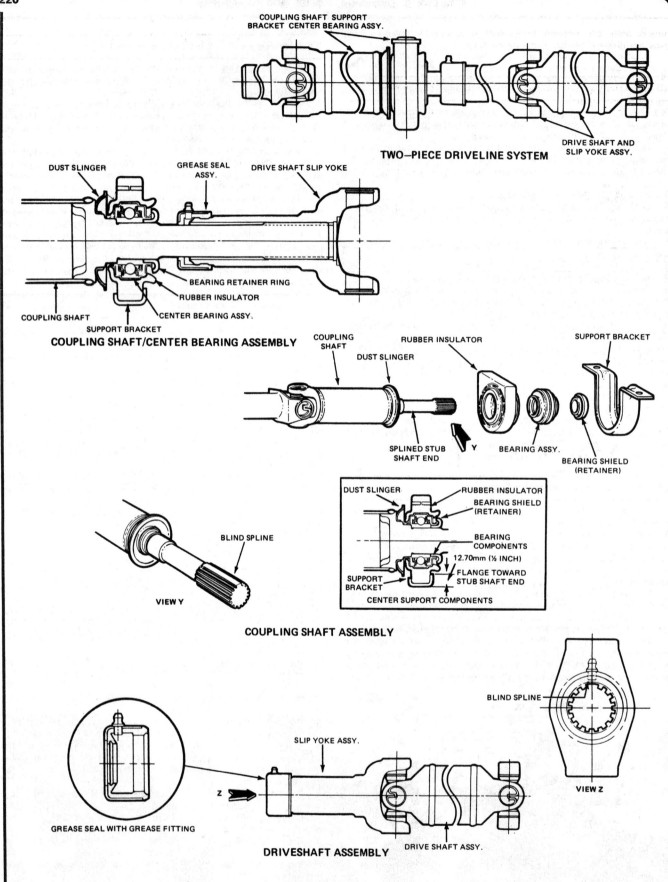

COUPLING SHAFT SUPPORT
BRACKET CENTER BEARING ASSY.

TWO—PIECE DRIVELINE SYSTEM

DRIVE SHAFT AND
SLIP YOKE ASSY.

DUST SLINGER

GREASE SEAL
ASSY.

DRIVE SHAFT SLIP YOKE

BEARING RETAINER RING

RUBBER INSULATOR

CENTER BEARING ASSY.

COUPLING SHAFT

SUPPORT BRACKET

COUPLING SHAFT/CENTER BEARING ASSEMBLY

COUPLING
SHAFT

DUST SLINGER

RUBBER INSULATOR

SUPPORT BRACKET

SPLINED STUB
SHAFT END

Y

BEARING ASSY.

BEARING SHIELD
(RETAINER)

BLIND SPLINE

VIEW Y

DUST SLINGER

RUBBER INSULATOR

BEARING SHIELD
(RETAINER)

BEARING
COMPONENTS

12.70mm (½ INCH)

SUPPORT
BRACKET

FLANGE TOWARD
STUB SHAFT END

CENTER SUPPORT COMPONENTS

COUPLING SHAFT ASSEMBLY

BLIND SPLINE

VIEW Z

GREASE SEAL WITH GREASE FITTING

SLIP YOKE ASSY.

Z

DRIVE SHAFT ASSY.

DRIVESHAFT ASSEMBLY

Fig. 8.21 Two-piece driveshaft with U-bolt or slip-yoke attachment to the transmission (Secs 16 and 18)

nuts or bolts to the correct torque and make sure the universal joint caps are properly placed in the flange seat.

19 Driveshaft carrier bearing – checking and replacement

1 The carrier bearing can be checked in a similar manner as the universal joints are examined. Check for looseness or deterioration of the flexible rubber mounting.
2 Further examination of the carrier bearing can be made by running the vehicle in gear with the rear wheels raised in the air. However, this should be done only by an authorized dealer who can perform the tests safely.
3 Remove the driveshaft assembly.
4 With the driveshaft removed from the vehicle and the shaft sections separated at the center bearing, remove the bearing dust shield.
5 Remove the strap which retains the rubber cushion to the bearing support bracket.
6 Separate the cushion, bracket and bearing.
7 Pull the bearing assembly from the driveshaft.
8 Replace any worn components with new ones and reassemble. If the inner deflector was removed, install it to the shaft and stake it at two opposite points to ensure that it is a tight fit.
9 Pack the space between the inner dust deflector and the bearing with lithium-base grease.
10 Carefully tap the bearing and slinger assembly onto the driveshaft journal until the components are tight against the shoulder on the shaft. Use a suitable piece of tubing to do this, taking care not to damage the shaft splines.
11 Install the dust shield (small diameter first) and press it up against the outer slinger.
12 Install the bearing rubber cushion, bracket and strap.
13 Reconnect the driveshafts, making sure the previously made marks are aligned.

20 Universal joints – general information

Universal joints are mechanical couplings which connect two rotating components that meet each other at different angles.

These joints are composed of a yoke on each side connected by a crosspiece called a trunnion. Cups at each end of the trunnion contain needle bearings which provide smooth transfer of the torque load. Snap-rings, either inside or outside of the bearing cups, hold the assembly together.

Two main types of universal joints are used in Ford trucks with small differences in retention providing further variation.

The first type of universal joint is constructed with a single joint retained to its yoke with either internal or external snap-rings.

The second type referred to as a 'double cardan', has two universal joints, a centering socket yoke and a center yoke. This type of coupling must be used in 4x4 vehicles where high torque loads and steep drive-line angles are encountered (Broncos and some pick-ups).

21 Universal joints – lubrication and checking

1 Refer to Chapter 1, Section 19 for details on universal joint lubrication. Also see the routine maintenance schedule at the beginning of Chapter 1.
2 Wear in the needle roller bearings is characterized by vibration in the transmission, noise during acceleration, and in extreme cases of lack of lubrication, metallic squeaking and ultimately grating and shrieking sounds as the bearings disintegrate.
3 It is easy to check if the needle bearings are worn with the driveshaft in position, by trying to turn the shaft with one hand, the other hand holding the rear axle flange when the rear universal joint is being checked, and the front half coupling when the front universal joint is being checked. Any movement between the driveshaft and the front half couplings, and around the rear half couplings, is indicative of considerable wear. Another method of checking for universal joint wear is to use a pry bar inserted into the gap between the universal joint and the driveshaft or flange. Leave the vehicle in gear and try to pry the joint both radially and axially. Any looseness should be apparent with this method. A final test for wear is to attempt to lift the shaft and note any movement between the yokes of the joints.
4 If any of the above conditions exist, replace the universal joints with new ones.

22 Universal joints – overhaul

Outer snap-ring type
1 With the driveshaft removed, mark the location of the joint yokes in relation to each other.
2 Extract the snap-rings from the ends of the bearing cups (photo).
3 Using sockets or pieces of pipe of suitable diameter, use a vise to press on the end of one cup and to displace the opposite one into the larger socket wrench or pipe. The bearing cup will not be fully ejected and it should be gripped with pliers and twisted completely out of the yoke (photos).
4 Remove the first bearing cup by pressing the trunnion in the opposite direction, then repeat the operations on the other two cups.
5 Clean the yoke and inspect for damage or cracks.
6 Obtain the appropriate repair kit which will include trunnion, cups, needle rollers, seals, washers and snap-rings.
7 Before beginning reassembly, pack the reservoirs in the ends of the trunnion with grease and work some into the needle bearings taking care not to displace them from their location around the inside of the bearing cups.
8 Position the trunnion in the yoke, partially install one cup into the yoke and insert the trunnion a little way into it. Partially install the opposite cup, center the trunnion, then, using the vise, press both cups into position using sockets of diameter slightly less than that of the bearing cups. Make sure that the needle bearings are not displaced and trapped during this operation.
9 Install the snap-rings.
10 Align the shaft yokes and install the other bearing cups in the same way.

22.2 Removing a snap-ring from a bearing cup

22.3A Removing the bearing cups from the yoke, using different size sockets either side of the cup

22.3B Pliers are used to twist the cup completely out of the yoke

8

Injected plastic (inner snap-ring) type

11 This type of universal joint may be found on some vehicles covered in this manual. Repair can be carried out after destroying the production line plastic retainers and fitting conventional snap-ring type repair kits.

12 Support the joint yoke in a press so that, using a suitable forked pressing tool, pressure can be applied to two 'eyes' of the yoke to eject a bearing cup partially into a socket wrench of adequate diameter.

13 Repeat on all the cups and then twist the cups out of the yokes with a vise.

14 Clean away all trace of the plastic bearing cup retainers. This can be facilitated by probing through the plastic injection holes.

15 Obtain the appropriate repair kit which will include one prelubricated trunnion assembly, bearing cups, seals and other components.

16 Assemble the universal joint as described in paragraphs 8, 9 and 10 of this Section. Note that the snap-rings are installed on the inside of the yokes on this type of joint.

17 When reassembly is complete, and the joint is stiff to move, apply some hammer blows to the yoke which will free the bearing cups from the snap-rings.

Double cardan type constant velocity joint

18 An inspection kit containing two bearing cups and two retainers is available to permit the joint to be dismantled to the stage where the joint can be inspected. Before any dismantling is started, mark the flange yoke and coupling yoke to permit reassembly in the same position, then follow the procedure given previously for the snap-ring or injected plastic type, as applicable.

19 Disengage the flange yoke and trunnion from the centering ball. Pry the seal from the ball socket and remove the washers, spring and the three ball seats.

20 Clean the ball seat insert bushing and inspect for wear. If evident, the flange yoke and trunnion assembly must be replaced.

21 Clean the seal, ball seats, spring and washers and inspect for wear. If excessive wear is evident or parts are broken, a repair kit must be used.

22 Remove all plastic material from the groove of the coupling yoke (if applicable).

23 Inspect the centering ball, if damaged it must be replaced with a new one.

24 Withdraw the centering ball from the stud using a suitable extractor.

25 Press a new ball onto the stud until it seats firmly on the stud shoulder. It is extremely important that no damage to the ball occurs during this stage.

26 Using the grease provided in the repair kit, lubricate all the parts and insert them into the ball seat cavity in the following order: spring washer (small o.d.), three ball seats (largest opening outward to receive the ball), washer (large o.d.) and the seal.

27 Lubricate the seal lips and press it (lip in) into the cavity. Fill the cavity with the grease provided.

28 Install the flange yoke to the centering ball, ensuring that the alignment marks are correctly positioned.

29 Install the trunnion caps as described previously for the snap-ring or injected plastic types.

Chapter 9 Brakes

Refer to Chapter 13 for information on 1988 and later models

Contents

Specifications

General
Brake fluid type .... DOT type 3 heavy duty

Drum brakes
Drum wear limit .... Specified on drum
Lining wear limit .... $\frac{1}{32}$ in above rivet head or metal shoe

Disc brakes
Rotor minimum thickness
    F100 with power brakes and 4650 to 4900 GVWR ...... 0.81 in
    Bronco and F150 (4x4) .... 1.12 in
    F250 (4x4) .... 1.18 in
    F100/F150/F250 with 6200 to 6900 GVWR and light-duty
      integral hub and rotor .... 1.12 in
    F100/F150/F250 with 6200 to 6900 GVWR and heavy-duty
      integral hub and rotor .... 1.18 in
    Two-piece hub and rotor .... 1.18 in
Rotor runout
    Integral hub and rotor .... 0.003 in
    Two-piece hub and rotor .... 0.010 in
Pad lining wear limit .... $\frac{1}{32}$ in above rivet head or metal backing plate

Torque specifications
	Ft-lb
Drum brake adjustable anchor pin nut	80 to 100
Master cylinder-to-firewall or vacuum booster nuts	13 to 25
Vacuum booster mounting bracket-to-firewall nuts	13 to 25
Key retaining screw (light duty)	12 to 20
Key retaining screw (heavy duty)	14 to 22
Anchor plate-to-spindle	74 to 102
Brake hose-to-caliper attaching bolt	17 to 25
Hydraulic tube nuts	
$\frac{3}{8}$ x 24	10 to 15
$\frac{7}{16}$ x 24	10 to 15
$\frac{1}{2}$ x 20	10 to 17
$\frac{9}{16}$ x 18	10 to 17

1 General information

Ford pick-up truck and Bronco models cover in this manual are equipped with hydraulically activated front disc brakes and rear drum brakes.

The hydraulic system has a dual master cylinder and separate front and rear brake line circuits. The master cylinder contains two hydraulic pistons (primary and secondary) fed by separate fluid reservoirs. A pressure differential valve and warning switch are incorporated into the hydraulic system. This valve provides a higher percentage of braking force to the front wheels to compensate for weight transfer when the brakes are applied. The warning switch indicates to the vehicle's operator when a failure has occurred in one of the braking circuits. If a failure in one of the circuits occurs, the other one will continue to operate the brakes, although total braking efficiency will be half or less of normal.

On some vehicles, the hydraulic brake system may be assisted by a vacuum booster installed as either standard or optional equipment. The booster unit for all but F350 vehicles is a single-diaphragm, dash-mounted model. The F350 unit is similar but operates through a tandem diaphragm.

A parking brake system is provided and operates independently of the normal hydraulic brake system. A pedal on the driver's side of the cab operates a system of cables to activate the rear brake shoes only.

2 Drum brakes (light duty) – replacement

1   The brakes on F100, F150 and F250 (standard) vehicles are considered light duty. In addition, the above models equipped with 4-wheel drive and Bronco models are classed as light duty.
2   Raise the vehicle and support it securely with jackstands. Remove the wheel(s) and brake drum(s). If difficulty is encountered, see Step 3.
Note: *It is advisable to service the brakes on one side of the vehicle at a time, leaving the other side fully assembled for reference if necessary.*
3   If the drum will not come off after removing the proper retaining components, the brake adjustment needs to be released. Start this procedure by removing the rubber cover from the slot provided in the brake backing plate. Insert a small screwdriver through the slot and hold the brake adjusting lever away from the adjusting screw. Use a brake adjustment tool to retract the automatic adjuster by turning the

adjustment wheel downward with the tool. Once the shoes are retracted sufficiently, the brake drum can be removed. Be careful not to damage the brake adjustment wheel while performing this operation.
4   Install a brake cylinder clamp over the ends of the wheel cylinder cups. Be careful not to tear or damage the wheel cylinder boots. This will push in the ends of the wheel cylinder to relieve pressure on the brake system.
5   Release the adjusting lever from the adjusting screw by pivoting it backward. Retract the adjusting screw as far as possible.
6   Move the outboard side of the adjusting screw back and up off the pivot nut as far as possible. It will now be possible to pivot the hook assembly down and to the rear far enough to unhook the pivot from the rear brake shoe.
7   Remove the automatic adjusting spring and adjusting lever. Keep these parts together on the side of the vehicle you are working on as they are not designed to interchange from one side to the other.
8   Remove the secondary shoe retracting spring from the upper anchor with a brake tool designed for this purpose. Be careful, it is under a great deal of pressure.
9   Remove the primary shoe retracting spring from the upper anchor with the same special tool.
10 Remove the self-adjuster cable hook and the anchor pin plate (if so equipped) from the anchor pin.
11 Remove the self-adjuster cable guide from the rear shoe.
12 Remove the brake shoe hold-down caps, springs and pins from each shoe. This is done by depressing the spring, and then turning the pin until the head of the pin aligns with the slot in the cap. Keep these parts separate as they are often different for each shoe.
13 Remove each brake shoe. As you remove the shoes, the adjusting screw, pivot nut and pivot socket will fall free from the bottom of the shoes. Keep these parts together.
14 The parking brake link and spring will be released from the top of the shoes as they are pulled free. Note which direction they fit and keep these parts together.
15 Pull the parking brake cable spring forward on the cable which will enable you to release the cable end from the hook on the parking brake lever. The parking brake lever can be removed from the secondary

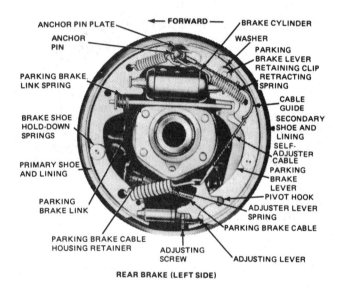

Fig. 9.1 Typical drum brake assembly as employed on rear wheels of Bronco and light-duty truck models (Sec 2)

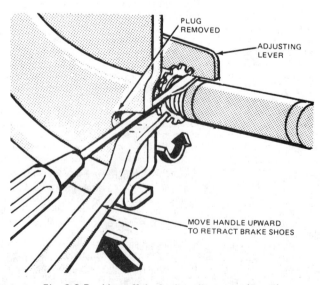

Fig. 9.2 Backing off the brake adjustment (Sec 2)

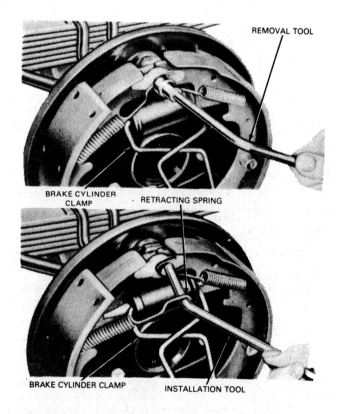

Fig. 9.3 Removing (top) and installing (bottom) the retracting springs (note use of special tool) (Sec 2)

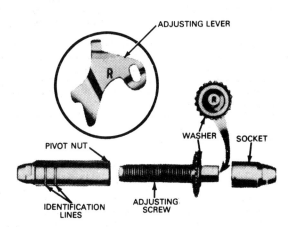

Fig. 9.4 Adjusting screw and lever assemblies for light-duty (bottom) and heavy-duty (top) vehicles (Secs 2 and 3)

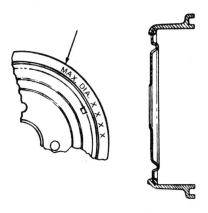

Fig. 9.5 Location of the maximum inside diameter marking on a typical brake drum (Sec 2)

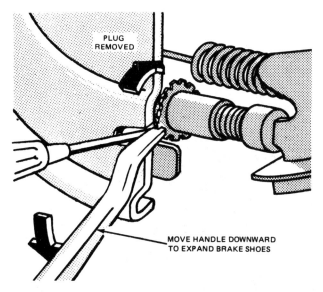

Fig. 9.6 Expanding the brake shoes after installation (Sec 2)

brake shoe by releasing the C-clip and then removing the lever and spring. Keep these parts together.

16 Clean all of the parts with brake cleaning solvent or rubbing alcohol. Do not use any other types of petroleum solvents or gasoline.

17 Clean the backing plate and other components with a vacuum cleaner. Do not use compressed air to blow the dust out because the flying asbestos brake particles are very hazardous to breathe and can irritate the skin. With the brake assembly dismantled to this point, now is the time to determine if wheel cylinder overhaul and brake drum servicing is required. If the wheel cylinder (brake cylinder) shows any signs of fluid leakage or if the rubber boots are damaged, it would be wise to overhaul the cylinder at this point (see Section 4). Inspect the inside of the brake drum for cracks, scores, deep scratches or 'hard spots' which will appear as small discolorations. If fine emery cloth will not bring the drum back to a smooth, even finish, the drums should be resurfaced at an automotive repair shop. Many mechanics have this done routinely as a part of the brake job — the cost is minimal. Also measure the brake drum's inside diameter and check it with the maximum diameter figure that will be found stamped on the outer edge of the drum. Replace the drum with a new one if the measurement exceeds the maximum allowable diameter.

18 Lubricate the brake shoe contact points (on the backing plate) with brake lube.

19 Assemble the parking brake lever to the rear brake shoe along with the spring. Use a new C-clip to retain the lever.

20 Place the primary brake shoe onto the backing plate and install the hold-down pin, spring and clip. Repeat the process for the rear brake shoe after hooking the cable to the parking brake lever. Install the parking brake link, spring and washer.

21 Install the anchor pin plate (if so equipped). Install the self-adjuster cable end over the anchor pin with the crimped side facing inward.

22 Install the primary shoe retracting spring with the special brake spring tool. Crimp the end of the spring closer together after it is installed over the anchor pin if it has sprung open.

23 Install the flanged hole of the cable guide into the proper hole in the rear brake shoe web. Thread the cable around the groove in the cable guide.

24 Install the long rear shoe return spring with the brake tool. Again, crimp the end if the hook has opened up (don't crimp the spring end any tighter than a U shape). Recheck the adjuster cable end to make sure it isn't cocked or binding. It should sit squarely on the anchor pin and pivot freely behind the return springs.

25 Remove the brake cylinder clamp after making sure the pins are correctly positioned between the wheel cylinder and the brake shoes.

26 Apply brake lubricant to the threads and socket end of the adjusting screw. Retract the adjusting screw to its minimum size and back it out $\frac{1}{2}$-turn. Notice that the socket end of the screw is stamped with an R or an L. This letter should correspond to the side of the vehicle you are working on (L on the left or driver's side or R on the right or passenger's side).

27 Assemble the adjusting socket to the adjustment screw and pivot nut and install this assembly between the brake shoes with the screw end closest to the secondary (rear) shoe.

28 Install the hooked end of the adjusting cable into the pivot hook from the backing plate side. Make sure you are using the correct adjusting lever as they also are stamped L or R.

29 Place the hooked end of the adjuster spring into the large hole in the primary shoe web; then connect the loop end of the spring to the adjustment lever hole. Make sure that the adjustment cable is properly routed through the cable guide and is not caught on any springs or other brake components.

30 Pull the combination assembly (adjustment lever, cable end and spring) down toward the rear and engage the hook end of the pivot into the large hole of the secondary shoe web.

31 Check the operation of the self-adjusting mechanism by pulling the cable and cable pivot back far enough for the engagement tang on the pivot to ride up past one tooth on the adjusting screw and catch the tooth immediately above the original position. The spring action of the adjusting lever should pivot the adjusting screw as it springs back

9

to its normal position. If this action checks out correctly, install the drum (and hub) assembly.

32 If the self-adjuster mechanism does not operate correctly, check the components for proper installation position and condition. Often, a stretched cable is the culprit in a non-operating system. Replace any components in questionable condition with new ones.

33 Manually adjust the brakes (by turning the adjustment screw) until there is a slight drag on the brake drum as it is slipped into place over the brake assembly.

34 Complete the assembly by installing the wheels and lowering the vehicle to the ground. Check the operation of the brakes before attempting to drive the vehicle. In some cases it will be necessary to adjust the brakes (Chapter 1) before road testing the vehicle.

3 Drum brakes (heavy duty) – replacement

1 Heavy duty drum brakes are found on F250 models with higher Gross Vehicle Weight ratings and on F350 series vehicles. Before beginning, observe the notes and cautions in Section 2.

2 Remove the wheel(s) from the vehicle after raising and supporting it securely. Refer to the appropriate Sections in Chapter 8 for hub and drum assembly removal instructions.

3 If the drum will not come off after removing the proper retaining components, refer to Section 2, Step 3 of this Chapter for brake releasing instructions.

4 Remove the spring clip retainer holding the adjusting cable anchor fitting to the brake spring anchor pin (front brakes only).

5 Remove the parking brake lever assembly retaining nut from the rear of the backing plate. Remove the parking brake lever assembly.

6 Remove the adjusting cable assembly from the anchor pin. Unthread it from the cable guide and disconnect the other end from the adjusting lever.

7 Remove the brake shoe retracting springs from both the primary and secondary brake shoes. Use the brake service tool for this operation.

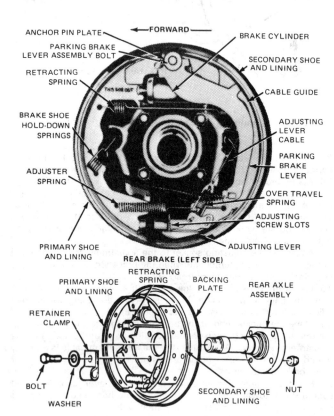

Fig. 9.7 Typical drum brake assembly as employed on rear wheels of heavy-duty truck models (Sec 3)

8 Remove the brake shoe hold-down springs from both the primary and secondary brake shoes.

9 Remove the brake shoes. The adjusting screw assembly will fall loose at this time. Keep all parts of this assembly together.

10 Clean all of the springs and adjusting components with brake cleaner or rubbing alcohol. **Caution:** *Never use any petroleum solvents and never blow the parts clean with compressed air as fine asbestos dust is a serious health hazard if inhaled.*

11 Clean the brake backing plate and hub components left on the vehicle. If the six ledge pads on the backing plate are corroded or rusty, sand them lightly to bare metal.

12 Apply a light coat of brake lube to the ledge pads. Apply a coating of lube to the retracting and hold-down spring contact points on the brake shoes and backing plate.

13 Dismantle and clean the pivot nut, adjusting screw, washer and socket. Take care not to mix these adjusting components from side-to-side as they are built for left- or right-side installation only. If these components become mixed, the adjusting lever and the socket end of the adjusting screw are stamped with the letter L or R. Carefully inspect the brake cylinder (wheel cylinder) and drum at this time. See Section 2 for further instructions.

14 Lubricate the threads of the adjustment components with brake lube and retract the adjustment to the smallest dimension.

15 Install the upper brake retracting spring between the two brake shoes and make sure you have the shoes positioned correctly.

16 Place the shoes and spring assembly into position on the backing plate and position the wheel cylinder pushrods into their proper slots on the brake shoe webbing.

17 Install both brake shoe hold-down springs.

18 Position the brake shoe adjustment screw assembly into place between the bottom of the brake shoes with the slot in the head of the adjusting screw pointed toward the primary shoe.

19 Install the lower brake shoe retracting spring.

20 Install the adjusting lever spring and the cable assembly to the adjusting lever. Position the adjusting lever onto the proper pin of the secondary shoe.

21 Place the adjusting lever cable into its proper position around the cable guide and hook the cable end to the anchor pin.

22 Install the spring clip retainer over the anchor pin and cable end on front brakes. Install the parking brake lever and retaining nut.

23 Manually adjust the brakes (by turning the adjustment screw) until there is a slight drag on the brake drum as it is slipped into place over the brake assembly.

24 Install the brake drum and hub assembly. Adjust the bearings as described in Chapter 8. Install the wheels. Lower the vehicle from the stands or supports.

25 Check the brakes by applying them several times before attempting to drive the vehicle. Make sure they are adjusted by backing up and applying the brakes several times. Test drive the vehicle by making several light-effort, slow-speed stops to seat the brake linings. Avoid any high-speed or panic stops during the first brake applications.

4 Drum brake wheel cylinders – removal, overhaul and installation

Removal

1 The type of wheel cylinder and the method of removal is basically the same for all models. **Note:** *Obtain a wheel cylinder repair kit which will have all the necessary replacement parts.*

2 Refer to Section 2 or 3 as appropriate and remove the brake shoes.

3 Unscrew the brake pipe union from the rear of the wheel cylinder. Do not pull the metal tube from the cylinder as it will bend, making installation difficult.

4 Remove the two bolts securing the wheel cylinder to the brake backplate assembly.

5 Remove the wheel cylinder assembly.

6 Plug the end of the hydraulic pipe to stop the loss of too much hydraulic fluid and/or the entry of dirt.

Overhaul

7 Remove the rubber boots from the ends of the wheel cylinder.

8 Remove the pistons, cups and piston return spring. Remove the

BOOT
CUP
CYLINDER
BOOT
CUP
PISTON
BLEEDER
SCREW –
RETURN SPRING AND
CUP EXPANDER ASSY.
PISTON

Fig. 9.8 Typical double servo brake cylinder – exploded view (Sec 4)

piston expander assembly from the cylinder.

9   Remove the bleeder screw from the cylinder.

10 Inspect the interior bore of the cylinder for scoring, corrosion or other damage. A very light film or accumulation can be cleaned out with a brake cylinder hone. However, if any question about the cylinder condition exists, it is best to replace it with a new one.

11 Clean the cylinder thoroughly with brake cleaning fluid.

12 Using brake assembly lubricant, coat all of the parts in the repair kit.

13 Install the piston return spring and a piston expander assembly between the two cups. Make sure the cups face wide-side in. Install a piston into each end of the bore. Install the boot and link over each end of the cylinder. Clamp the pistons together with a brake clamp if necessary.

Installation

14 Place the completed brake cylinder onto the backing plate and install the retaining bolts and lock washers.

15 Install a new gasket on the brake line fitting and connect the line to the cylinder. Install the bleeder screw.

16 Refer to Section 2 or 3 and install the brake shoes and hardware.

17 Bleed the hydraulic system as described in Section 13.

5   Disc brake pads (light duty) – replacement

Note: *Always replace disc brake pad sets in pairs. Never install pads on one wheel only. It is advisable to disassemble one side at a time, leaving the other side fully assembled for use as reference if necessary. Refer to Figs. 9.9 and 9.10 to locate and identify pertinent components.*

1   To avoid fluid overflow when the caliper piston is pressed into the caliper cylinder bore, siphon or dip part of the brake fluid out of the larger master cylinder reservoir (connected to the front disc brakes) and discard the removed fluid.

2   Loosen the lugs on the front wheels.

3   Chock the rear wheels.

4   Set the parking brake.

5   Raise the front of the vehicle and place it securely on jackstands.

6   Remove the lugs and the front wheels.

7   Place a large C-clamp on the caliper and tighten the clamp to bottom the caliper piston in the cylinder bore, then remove the clamp.

8   Remove the retaining screw from the caliper retaining key.

9   Use a hammer and a soft drift to carefully tap the caliper retaining key and spring either in or out of the anchor plate. Use care so as not

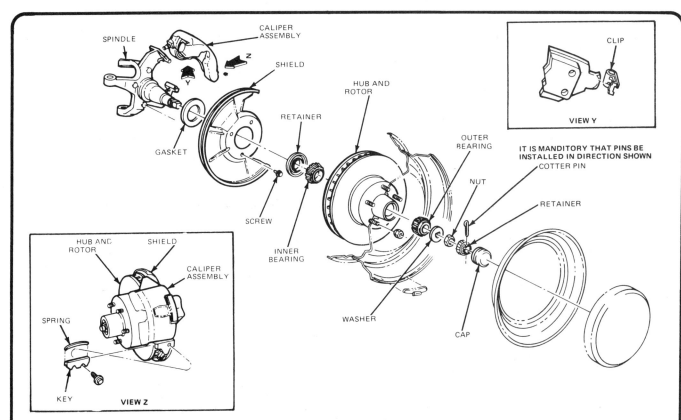

Fig. 9.9 Typical light-duty brake caliper assembly as installed on F150 through F250 (6900 GVW) 4x2 vehicles (Sec 5)

9

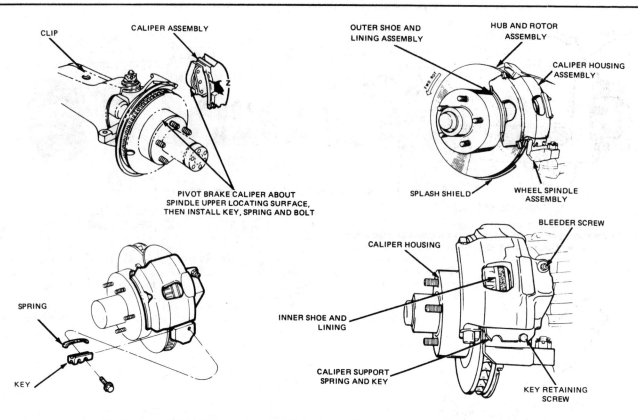

Fig. 9.10 Typical F150 4x4 and Bronco light-duty caliper assembly installation (Sec 5)

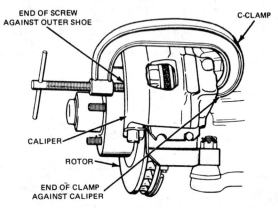

Fig. 9.11 Bottoming the caliper piston in the cylinder bore (light-duty) (Sec 5)

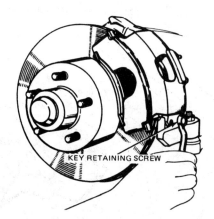

Fig. 9.12 Removing the retaining screw from the caliper retaining key (light-duty) (Sec 5)

to damage the key.

10 Press the caliper assembly in and up against the caliper support springs and pivot the caliper off the rotor. Once the bottom of the caliper has cleared the anchor plate, pull it straight off the plate.

11 Use caution not to stretch or kink the flexible rubber brake hose and use wire to suspend the caliper from an upper suspension component out of the way.

12 If the pads are being reused, mark them for position so they can be installed in their original location.

13 Remove the pads from the anchor plate. The anti-rattle clips will come out with the pads as they are removed.

14 Clean the bracket, caliper and pads (if they are being reused) with brake cleaning solvent. Replace the pads if they measure less than the minimum thickness listed in the Specifications. Have the rotor resurfaced or replace it if it is scored, damaged or cracked.

15 If new pads are being installed, the replacement outer unit differs slightly from the original part. The replacement has tabs on the outer flange at the lower edge of the shoe, and the distance between the upper tabs and lower flange is reduced to provide a slip-on

interference fit. To install a replacement unit, position the outer shoe and lining on the caliper and use your fingers to press the shoe tabs into place. If the shoe cannot be pressed into place by hand, compress it with a C-clamp as shown in the accompanying illustration. Be careful not to damage the lining with the clamp.

16 Install the anti-rattle clips and pads onto the anchor plate. If the old pads are being reinstalled, make sure they are in their original position.

17 Detach the caliper from its supporting wire and position it against the anchor plate with the lower beveled edge on top of the rear caliper support spring. Make sure the pads and clips remain in their correct position.

18 Carefully slide the caliper over the pads with a pivoting motion until the caliper upper beveled edge can be pushed over the forward caliper support spring.

19 Use a large screwdriver or similar tool to hold the caliper over the upper caliper support spring and against the anchor plate.

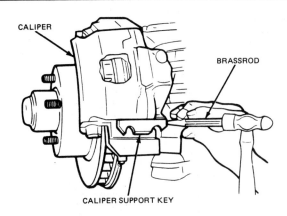

Fig. 9.13 Removing the caliper support spring and key from the anchor plate (light-duty) (Sec 5)

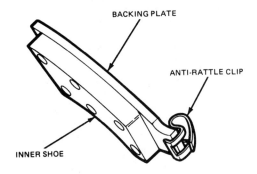

Fig. 9.15 Typical disc brake inner pad assembly (Sec 5)

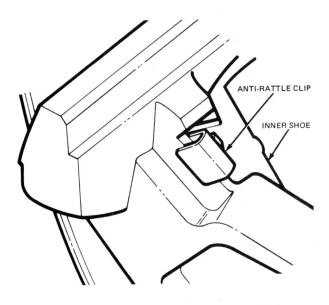

Fig. 9.17 Installing the inner pad assembly (Sec 5)

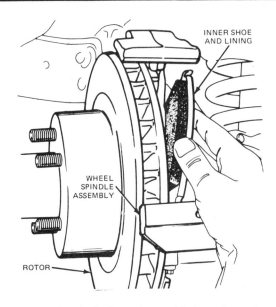

Fig. 9.14 Removing the brake pad assembly from the anchor plate (Sec 5)

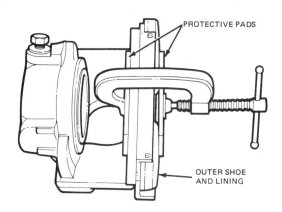

Fig. 9.16 Installing the outer disc brake shoe with a C-clamp (Sec 5)

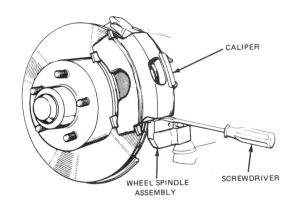

Fig. 9.18 Using a screwdriver to hold the caliper in place during installation (Sec 5)

20 Carefully install the caliper retaining key and spring. Remove the screwdriver and carefully tap the caliper key into its correct position.
21 Install the caliper key retaining screw and tighten it to the correct torque.
22 Install the wheel and tighten the lug nuts. Lower the vehicle to the ground.
23 Press the brake pedal several times before attempting to drive it. It will take several strokes of the brakes to bring the pads into contact with the rotor. If the brake hose was not disconnected, bleeding will

not be necessary.
24 Test drive the vehicle and make the first several stops gentle ones to seat the brake pads.

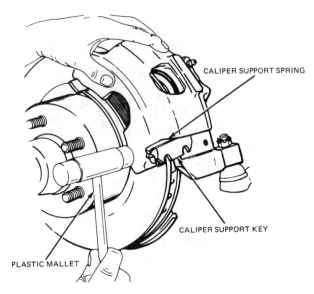

Fig. 9.19 Installing the caliper support spring and key (Sec 5)

6   Disc brake pads (heavy duty) – replacement

Note: *Refer to Fig. 9.20 to locate and identify pertinent components.*
1   Refer to the note at the beginning of Section 5.
2   Loosen the lugs on the front wheels.
3   Chock the rear wheels.
4   Set the parking brake.
5   Raise the front of the vehicle and place it securely on jackstands.

6   Remove the lugs and the front wheels.
7   Remove the retaining screw from the key.
8   Use a soft punch and a light hammer to drive out the key and spring.
9   Rotate the caliper out and away from the rotor by pulling on the key and spring end. Slide the opposite end of the caliper free of the slide in the support until the caliper clears the rotor. Support the caliper assembly with some wire from a suspension member. Be careful not to twist or stretch the flexible rubber brake hose.
10 Remove the large brake shoe anti-rattle spring.
11 Remove the inner and outer brake pads.
12 Clean the caliper and piston facings of dust or accumulated debris. Be especially watchful of the area on the support that the caliper slides on.
13 To avoid fluid overflow when the caliper pistons are pressed into the caliper cylinder bores, siphon or dip part of the brake fluid out of the larger master cylinder reservoir (connected to the front disc brakes) and discard the removed fluid.
14 Position a C-clamp and one of the old disc brake pads into place on the caliper. Tighten the C-clamp to compress the pistons into the bottom of their bore. If both calipers have been removed, block the opposite side pistons to prevent them from popping out during this operation. Remove the clamp and pad.
15 Install the new shoes onto the support. Install the anti-rattle spring.
16 Place the bottom of the caliper assembly onto the support and rotate the assembly up into place over the pads and rotor.
17 Position the spring between the key and the caliper with the spring tangs overlapping the ends of the key. You may need a screwdriver or brake adjusting tool to support the caliper to start these pieces into their proper position.
18 Using the hammer and soft punch, tap the key and spring into place until the notch in the key lines up for the retaining screw.
19 Install the key retaining screw and tighten it to the proper torque.
20 Pump the brake pedal several times to push the pads against the discs. Refill the master cylinder reservoir with new fluid.
21 Install the wheels and lower the vehicle to the ground.

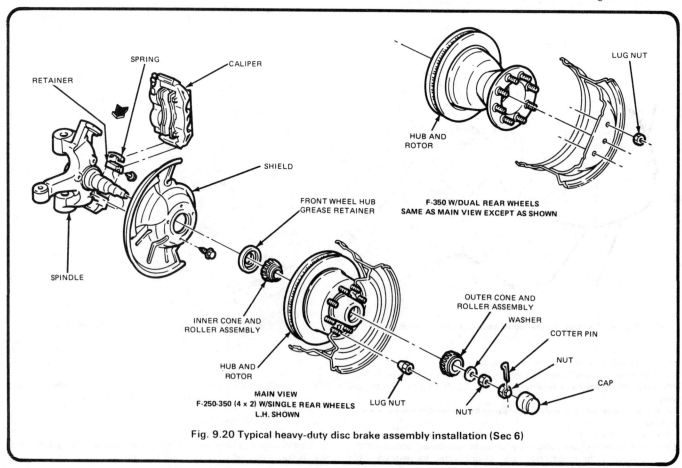

Fig. 9.20 Typical heavy-duty disc brake assembly installation (Sec 6)

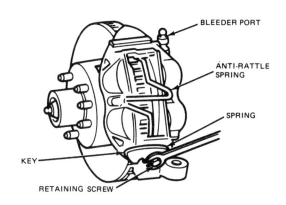

Fig. 9.21 Removing the retaining screw from the caliper retaining key (heavy-duty) (Sec 6)

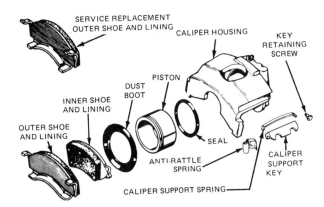

Fig. 9.24 Components of a typical light-duty brake caliper – exploded view (Sec 7)

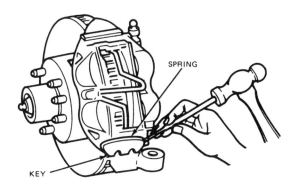

Fig. 9.22 Removing the caliper support spring and key from the anchor plate (heavy-duty) (Sec 6)

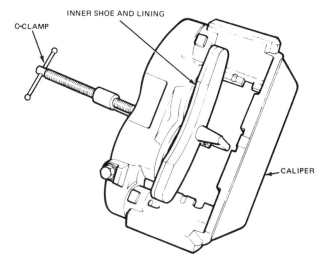

Fig. 9.23 Bottoming the caliper pistons in the cylinder bores (heavy-duty) (Sec 6)

22 Test drive the vehicle and apply the brakes lightly the first few times so that the pads will seat correctly.

7 Disc brake caliper (light duty) – overhaul

Note: Refer to Fig. 9.24 to locate and identify pertinent components.
1   If brake fluid is leaking from the caliper it will be necessary to

install new seals. If brake fluid is found running down the side of the wheel, or if you notice that a pool of fluid forms alongside one wheel or the level in the master cylinder drops excessively, it is also indicative of seal failure. Obtain an overhaul kit which will contain all necessary parts.
2   Refer to Section 5 and remove the caliper. Remove the flexible hose and plug it to prevent fluid loss or contamination.
3   Wrap a cloth around the caliper and, using compressed air at the fluid port, carefully eject the pistons.
4   If the piston has seized in the bore, carefully tap around the piston while applying air pressure. Caution: The piston will come out with force.
5   Remove the rubber dust boot from the caliper assembly.
6   Carefully remove the rubber piston seal from the cylinder bore with a soft wood or plastic tool. Do not use a screwdriver as it could damage the bore.
7   Thoroughly wash all parts in brake cleaning solvent or alcohol. During reassembly, new rubber seals should be installed and they should be well lubricated with clean brake fluid or brake assembly lube.
8   Inspect the piston and bore for signs of wear, score marks or other damage; if evident, a new caliper assembly will be necessary.
9   To reassemble, first place the new caliper piston seal into its groove in the cylinder bore. The seal must not become twisted.
10 Install a new dust boot and ensure that the flange seats correctly in the outer groove of the caliper bore.
11 Carefully insert the piston into the bore. When it is about three-quarters of the way in, spread the dust boot over the piston. Seat the dust boot in the piston groove and push the piston fully into the bore.
12 Reassembly is now complete and the unit is ready for installation on the vehicle as described in Section 5.
13 After installing the caliper and pads in the vehicle, bleed the brakes as described in Section 13.

8 Disc brake caliper (heavy duty) – overhaul

Note: Refer to Fig. 9.25 to locate and identify pertinent components.
1   Refer to Section 6 and remove the brake pads. Disconnect the flexible hose from the caliper.
2   Remove the calipers as described in Section 6. Obtain an overhaul kit which will contain all necessary parts.
3   Drain the brake fluid from the cylinders and secure the caliper assembly in a vise.
4   Place a $1\frac{1}{8}$ in block of wood between the caliper and the cylinders and apply low pressure air to the brake hose inlet, forcing the pistons out against the wooden block.
5   Remove the wood block and pistons, remove the bolts securing the piston housing to the caliper and separate the components.
6   Remove and discard the rubber piston boots and seals and examine the pistons and bores for signs of wear or scoring. Replace any damaged components.
7   Lubricate new piston seals with brake assembly lube and fit them into the grooves in the cylinder bores.

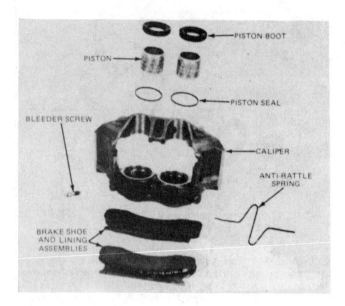

Fig. 9.25 Components of a typical heavy-duty brake caliper –
exploded view (Sec 8)

8   Lubricate the cylinder bores with brake fluid and fit the lips of the
rubber boots into the cylinder bore grooves.
9   Insert the pistons through the rubber boots and push them into the
cylinder bores past the piston seals. Take great care not to damage or
dislodge the piston seals from their groove in the cylinders.
10   Push both pistons all the way in using a block of wood.
11   Reinstall the piston housing to the caliper and tighten the retaining
bolts to the specifications.
12   Install the calipers and pads as described in Section 6.
13   Bleed the brakes as described in Section 13.

9 Disc brake rotor – inspection

1   Refer to Section 5 or 6 and remove the disc brake pads and caliper
assembly.
2   Inspect the rotor for deep scratches, scoring and signs of cracking
or breakage. If any of these conditions exist, the rotor must be
removed for refinishing at a shop equipped for this type of machining
work. If the rotor does not have any of the above-mentioned defects,
measure the runout (especially if any signs of wobble such as a
pulsating pedal exist).
3   Runout is measured with a dial indicator. These are available as
rentals or they can be purchased. Tighten the spindle nut to eliminate
all end play from the bearings, but be sure the hub and rotor can be
turned. Attach the base of the indicator to some part of the suspension
so that the indicator's stylus touches the rotor surface approximately
1 inch from the rotor's outer edge. Starting with the indicator set at
zero, slowly rotate the disc through one revolution. Note the high and
low readings on the dial as the rotor revolves. The difference between
the high and low readings is the total rotor runout. If the rotor exceeds
the maximum specification for runout, it will have to be removed for
machining or replacement.
4   If the rotor has to be removed for machining or replacement,
follow the instructions in Chapter 8 (4x4) or Chapter 11 for hub and
bearing assembly removal.
5   After machining or replacement, install the rotor(s) as described in
Chapter 8 or Chapter 11.
6   Install the brake caliper and brake pads as described in Sections 5
or 6 of this Chapter.
7   **Note**: *Be sure to adjust the spindle nut as described in Chapter 8,
after the runout check.*

10 Master cylinder – removal, overhaul and installation

Note: *Refer to Figs. 9.26 and 9.27 to locate pertinent components.*

Removal
1   Disconnect the cable from the negative battery terminal.
2   If the vehicle is equipped with a power brake booster system, push
the brake pedal down to expel the vacuum.
3   If equipped with manual (not power) brakes, disconnect the wires
from the stoplight switch, located adjacent to the brake pedal. Remove
the nut and shoulder bolt securing the master cylinder pushrod to the
brake pedal.
4   Place newspapers, rags, etc. under the master cylinder to catch
leaking brake fluid. Brake fluid will ruin paint.
5   Unscrew the brake lines from the primary and secondary outlets of
the master cylinder. Plug the ends of the lines to prevent any dirt from
entering.
6   Remove the two screws securing the master cylinder to the
firewall (or servo unit).
7   Pull the master cylinder forward and lift it up and out of the vehicle
(photo). **Caution:** *Do not allow fluid to contact any paint as it will
damage it.*

Overhaul
Note: *It should be noted that new and rebuilt master cylinders are
commonly available for these vehicles. If one of these is purchased,
skip to Step 24 for installation instructions. If it is decided to overhaul
the original unit, obtain an overhaul kit, which will contain all
necessary parts, and then proceed as follows.*
8   Clean the exterior of the master cylinder and wipe dry with a lint-
free rag.
9   Remove the filler cover and diaphragm (sometimes called gasket)
from the top of the reservoir and pour out any remaining brake fluid.
10   Remove the secondary piston stop bolt from the bottom of the
master cylinder body.
11   Remove the bleed screw.
12   Depress the primary piston and remove the snap-ring from the
groove at the rear of the master cylinder bore (photo). Remove the
primary piston assembly.
13   *Do not* remove the screw that retains the primary return spring
retainer, return spring, primary cup and protector on the primary
piston. This is factory set and must not be disturbed.
14   Remove the secondary piston assembly.
15   *Do not* remove the outlet line seats, outlet check valves and outlet
check valve springs from the master cylinder body.
16   Examine the bore of the cylinder carefully for signs of scoring and
damage. If the imperfections are slight, a hone can be used to smooth

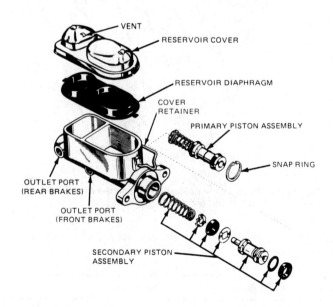

Fig. 9.26 Typical brake master cylinder – exploded view (Sec 10)

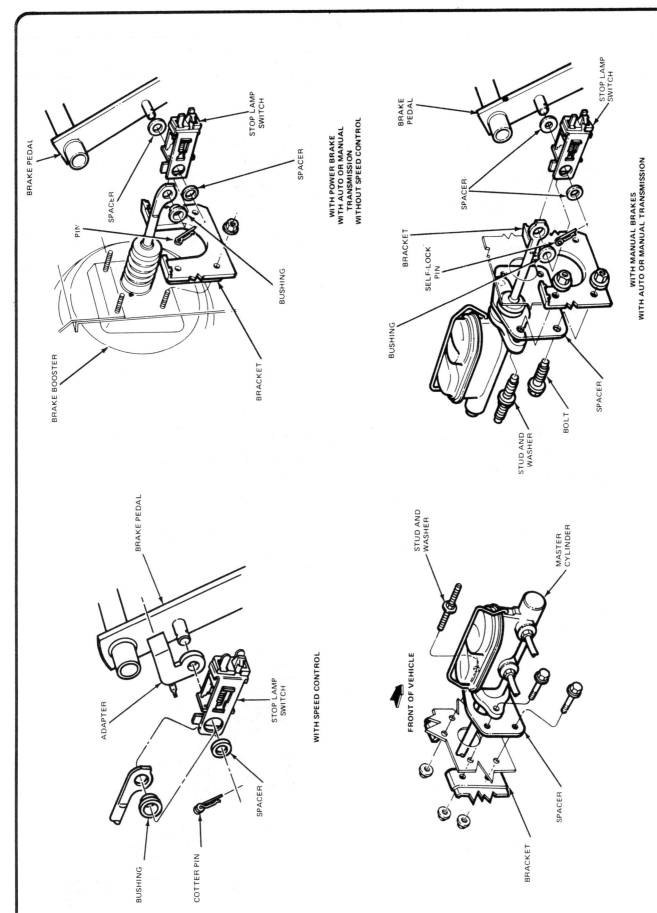

BRAKE PEDAL

SPACER

PIN

BRAKE BOOSTER

STOP LAMP SWITCH

SPACER

BUSHING

BRACKET

WITH POWER BRAKE WITH AUTO OR MANUAL TRANSMISSION WITHOUT SPEED CONTROL

BRAKE PEDAL

STOP LAMP SWITCH

SPACER

BRACKET

SELF-LOCK PIN

BUSHING

STUD AND WASHER

BOLT

SPACER

WITH MANUAL BRAKES WITH AUTO OR MANUAL TRANSMISSION

BRAKE PEDAL

ADAPTER

STOP LAMP SWITCH

BUSHING

COTTER PIN

SPACER

WITH SPEED CONTROL

STUD AND WASHER

MASTER CYLINDER

FRONT OF VEHICLE

BRACKET

SPACER

Fig. 9.27 Details of typical master cylinder installation (Sec 10)

9

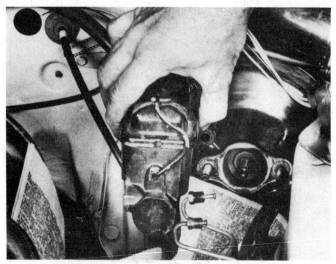

10.7 Removing the master cylinder from the servo unit (note the newspapers placed to catch fluid leakage)

10.12 Removing the snap-ring from the rear of the master cylinder

10.16 Using a hone to smooth the master cylinder bore

10.20 Inserting the assembled secondary piston into the master cylinder

the interior (photo). If damage is extensive, a new cylinder must be used.

17 If the rubber seals are swollen or very loose on the pistons, suspect oil contamination in the system. Oil will swell these rubber seals and if one is found to be swollen it is reasonable to assume that all seals in the brake system need attention.

18 Thoroughly clean all parts with brake cleaner or alcohol. Ensure that the ports are clear.

19 All components should be assembled wet after dipping in brake assembly lube.

20 Carefully insert the complete secondary piston and return spring assembly into the master cylinder bore, easing the seals into the bore, taking care that they do not roll over. Push the assembly all the way in (photo).

21 Insert the primary piston assembly into the master cylinder bore.

22 Push in the primary piston and tighten the secondary piston stop screw in the bottom of the cylinder.

23 Depress the piston again and install the snap-ring.

Installation

24 The master cylinder should be bled before it is installed. Fill the cylinder with fluid. Loosely install plugs in the outlet ports of the cylinder. Pump the primary piston until no air bubbles appear in the reservoir. Tighten the plugs and push on the piston. If the piston

doesn't move, proceed with the installation. If it does move, continue the bleeding process until all of the air is displaced.

25 If equipped with a power brake booster system, check the pushrod-to-mounting-face distance as shown in the accompanying illustration. It may be necessary to turn the adjusting screw to achieve the correct dimension.

26 Installation of the cylinder is the reverse of the removal procedure. After the cylinder is installed, bleed the hydraulic system as described in Section 13.

11 Brake pressure differential valve – resetting and replacement

Resetting

1 If the light for the brake warning system comes on, a leak or problem has arisen in the braking system which must be corrected. Once the leak or problem has been repaired or if the hydraulic system has been opened up for brake cylinder overhaul or a similar repair, the pressure differential valve must be centered. Once the valve is centered, the brake light on the dash will go out.

2 To center the valve, first fill the master cylinder reservoir and make sure the hydraulic system has been bled (Sec 13).

3 Turn the ignition switch to On or Accessory. Slowly press the brake pedal down and the piston will center itself, causing the light to

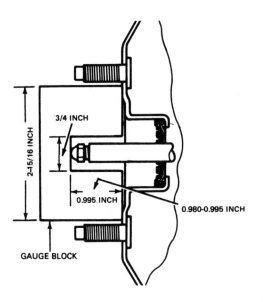

Fig. 9.28 Dimensions of the pushrod-to-booster mounting face measurement (Sec 10)

go out.
4   Check the brake pedal for firmness and correct operation.

Replacement
5   If the pressure differential valve has been determined to be defective or if it is leaking, it must be replaced. It is a non-serviceable unit and no repair operations are possible by the home mechanic.
6   Disconnect the brake warning light connector from the warning light switch.
7   Disconnect the front inlet and rear outlet pipe unions from the valve assembly. Plug the ends of the lines to prevent loss of brake fluid and the entry of dirt.
8   Remove the bolts and nuts securing the valve assembly to the chassis member.
9   Remove the valve assembly and bracket, taking care not to allow any brake fluid to contact the paint as it is highly corrosive.
10   Installation is the reverse of removal.
11   Bleed the system after the replacement valve has been installed.
12   Center the valve as described in Steps 1 through 4 above.

12 Hydraulic lines – inspection and replacement

1   The hydraulic system has a series of flexible rubber lines connecting the disc brake calipers and the rear axle fitting to metal lines running the length of the frame as well as connecting the differential valve and master cylinder. If an inspection (Chapter 1) reveals a problem in either a rubber hose or a metal line, the component must be replaced immediately for continued safe use of the vehicle.
2   Before replacing a line or hose, determine the cause of failure and remedy it or the hose or line will fail again. Often components such as exhaust pipes have come loose and are rubbing the line, causing the break or tear.
3   Replacement steel and flexible brake lines are commonly available from dealer parts departments and auto parts stores. **Caution:** *Do not, under any circumstances, use anything other than genuine steel or approved flexible brake hoses as replacement items.*
4   When removing any brake line or hose flare-nut fitting, always use the proper flare-nut wrenches when loosening and tightening the connections.
5   At the junction where a brake line meets a bracket supporting it and its connection, remove the spring clip with pliers or a vise grip after loosening the connection.
6   Steel brake lines are usually retained along their span with clips. Always remove these clips completely before removing any brake line

that they are supporting. Always replace these clips when replacing a metal brake line, as they provide support and keep the lines from vibrating, which will fatigue and eventually break the line.
7   Once a line has been replaced, the hydraulic system must be bled to rid the system of any air bubbles. Refer to Section 13.

13 Hydraulic system – bleeding

1   When any part of the brake hydraulic system has been removed or disconnected for repair or servicing, the system must be bled to purge it of any air which may have entered.
2   The system must be in good condition with no leaks or loose fittings before any bleeding operation is attempted. If the master cylinder has been overhauled or a new one is being installed, bleed the master cylinder as described at the end of Section 10.
3   The system may be bled with either a pressure bleeder or manually, utilizing two people. Follow the instructions of the pressure bleeder manufacturer if you are using that system. The manual bleeding procedure is as follows:
4   On vehicles with disc brakes, a bleeder rod located on the pressure differential valve must be released to allow fluid to run to the front calipers. On all vehicles except F350 models, the bleeder rod must be pulled out. Construct a tool like the one shown in the accompanying illustration, or use vise grips to maintain the rod during the bleeding procedure. On F350 vehicles, the bleeder rod must be pushed in. **Caution:** *When the bleeding procedure is complete, be sure to restore the rod to its original position.*
5   Fill the master cylinder with fluid to within $\frac{1}{4}$ inch of the top of the reservoirs. Keep the cylinders filled during the bleeding process. Cover the cylinder with a lint-free shop towel to prevent brake fluid from splashing on the painted surfaces and eroding them.
6   It may be necessary to raise the vehicle to gain access to the bleeder screws located at each brake cylinder or caliper. If this is necessary, support it securely before attempting this procedure.
7   If the hydraulic system is equipped with a frame-mounted vacuum booster, bleed the hydraulic section of the booster before bleeding the rest of the system. Bleed the system with the engine off and with no vacuum in the system. If the brake pedal is still spongy after the first bleeding, repeat the bleeding procedure.
8   Bleeding of the hydraulic section of the brake line between the master cylinder and the vacuum booster is accomplished by following Steps 9 through 13. If the system is not equipped with a vacuum booster, proceed to Step 14.
9   Attach a tight-fitting section of rubber tubing over the bleeder screw at the end plate of the booster (the bleeder screw nearest the power chamber). On a master cylinder without bleed screws, loosen the master cylinder-to-hydraulic line nut.

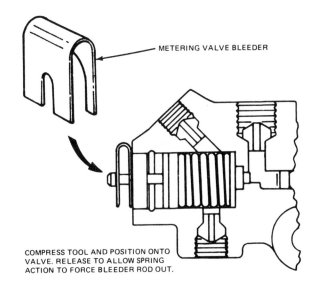

METERING VALVE BLEEDER

COMPRESS TOOL AND POSITION ONTO VALVE. RELEASE TO ALLOW SPRING ACTION TO FORCE BLEEDER ROD OUT.

Fig. 9.29 Installation of a pressure bleeding tool to maintain bleeder rod in the out position during the bleeding procedure (all vehicles except F350) (Sec 13)

10 Wrap a shop towel around the tubing below the fitting to absorb escaping brake fluid, taking care to avoid getting any fluid on painted surfaces.

11 Have an assistant push the brake pedal to the floor by hand, forcing air trapped in the master cylinder to escape at the fitting.

12 While the pedal is held to the floor, tighten the fitting. Be sure the pedal is not released until the fitting is tight or air will re-enter the master cylinder.

13 Repeat Steps 9 through 12 for the other bleeder screw (if so equipped), then bleed the rest of the hydraulic system as follows:

14 Start with the wheel cylinder farthest from the master cylinder (right rear). Wipe the bleeder screw clean and install a tight-fitting section of rubber tubing over the fitting. The other end of the tubing should be placed into a container of new brake fluid. (Glass jars work well for this as they allow the person operating the bleeder to see any air bubbles coming from the hose).

15 Have the person assisting you sit in the driver's seat of the vehicle. Open the bleeder screw using a box-end or flare nut wrench and have the assistant push the brake pedal down. Once the pedal reaches the bottom of its travel, have him hold the pedal down while you close the bleeder valve. Have him release the brake pedal only after you have closed the valve tightly. Continue this sequence until only brake fluid and no air bubbles are being pushed from the hose into the container. It may be necessary to stop and fill the master cylinder reservoir from time to time as it must *not* be allowed to run dry.

16 Repeat this process at the next farthest brake cylinder from the master cylinder (left rear) and so on until you have covered all four wheels. At this time, the 'feel' at the brake pedal should be firm with no sponginess. Top off the master cylinder for the last time and replace the lid.

17 Once you have ascertained that the brake hydraulic system is free of air, release the bleeder rod and lower the vehicle to the ground. Check the brake pedal once again for feel before road testing the vehicle. Make the first few brake applications at low speeds to make certain the system is working properly and all valves and connections are tight.

18 If the brake warning light is on, center the differential valve as described in Section 11.

14 Vacuum booster unit – general information

A servo is installed in the brake hydraulic circuit in series with the master cylinder to provide assistance to the driver when the brake pedal is depressed. This reduces the effort required by the driver to operate the brakes under all braking conditions.

The unit operates by vacuum obtained from the intake manifold and consists of a booster diaphragm and check valve. The servo and hydraulic master cylinder are connected together so the servo piston rod acts as the master cylinder pushrod. The driver's braking effort is transmitted through another pushrod to the servo piston and its built-in control system. The servo piston does not fit tightly into the cylinder, but has a strong diaphragm to keep its edges in constant contact with the cylinder wall, thus assuring an air-tight seal between the two parts. The forward chamber is held under the vacuum conditions created in the intake manifold of the engine, and during periods when the brake pedal is not in use, the controls open a passage to the rear chamber, thus placing it under vacuum conditions as well. When the brake pedal is pressed, the vacuum passage to the rear chamber is cut off and the chamber is opened to the atmospheric pressure. The consequent rush of air pushes the servo piston forward in the vacuum chamber and operates the main pushrod to the master cylinder.

The controls are designed so that assistance is given under all conditions and, when the brakes are not required, vacuum in the rear chamber is established when the brake pedal is released. All air from the atmosphere entering the rear chamber is passed through a small air filter.

Under normal operating conditions the servo will give trouble-free service for a long time. If, however, it is suspected that it is faulty, ie, increase in foot pressure is required to apply the brakes, it must be exchanged for a new servo. No attempt should be made to repair the old servo as it is not a serviceable item.

Note: *If the master cylinder pushrod is removed or accidentally pulled out, make sure that the booster rubber reaction disc is properly installed, as shown in the accompanying illustration. A dislodged disc may cause excessive pedal travel and extreme operation sensitivity.*

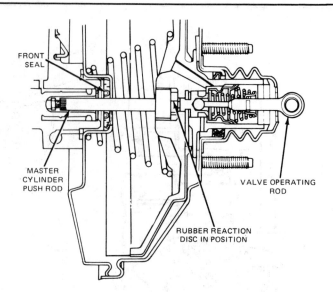

FRONT SEAL

MASTER CYLINDER PUSH ROD

VALVE OPERATING ROD

RUBBER REACTION DISC IN POSITION

Fig. 9.30 Checking the position of the booster reaction disc (Sec 14)

The disc is black in color when compared to the silver-colored valve plunger that will be exposed after the pushrod and front seal are removed. As noted previously, the booster unit is serviced as an assembly and it must be replaced if the reaction disc cannot be properly installed and aligned, or if it cannot be located within the unit itself.

15 Vacuum booster unit – removal and installation

1 Remove the stoplight switch and actuating rod from the brake pedal as described in Section 17.

2 Working under the hood, remove the air cleaner from the carburetor and the vacuum hose from the servo.

3 Remove the master cylinder from the front of the servo and withdraw it sufficiently to allow removal of the servo. **Note:** *It is not necessary to disconnect the hydraulic pipes from the master cylinder, but great care must be taken to avoid bending the pipes excessively.*

4 Remove the bolts securing the servo bracket to the engine compartment and lift the servo out of the vehicle.

5 Reinstall the servo by reversing the removal procedure. If it was necessary to disconnect the hydraulic pipes, the system must be bled as described in Section 13.

16 Parking brake – general information

Truck parking brakes employ a cable system that incorporates a tension limiter. If the parking brake system is in normal operating condition, depressing the parking brake pedal to the floor will automatically set the proper tension and pedal feel. If the parking brake system becomes inoperative, special gauges and equipment are required to measure and adjust parking brake cable tension. For this reason, an inoperative parking brake system should be checked, adjusted and repaired by an authorized service facility with the necessary equipment.

17 Brake pedal assembly – removal and installation

1 On vehicles equipped with a manual transmission, the brake pedal operates on the same shaft as the clutch pedal, and both pedals are removed as described in Chapter 7.

2 On automatic transmission models, disconnect the master cylinder pushrod and loosen the shoulder bolt nut. Slide the shoulder bolt to the right until the brake pedal and pedal bushings can be removed.

3 Replace the bushings if worn and install the pedal and pushrod using the reverse of the removal procedure.

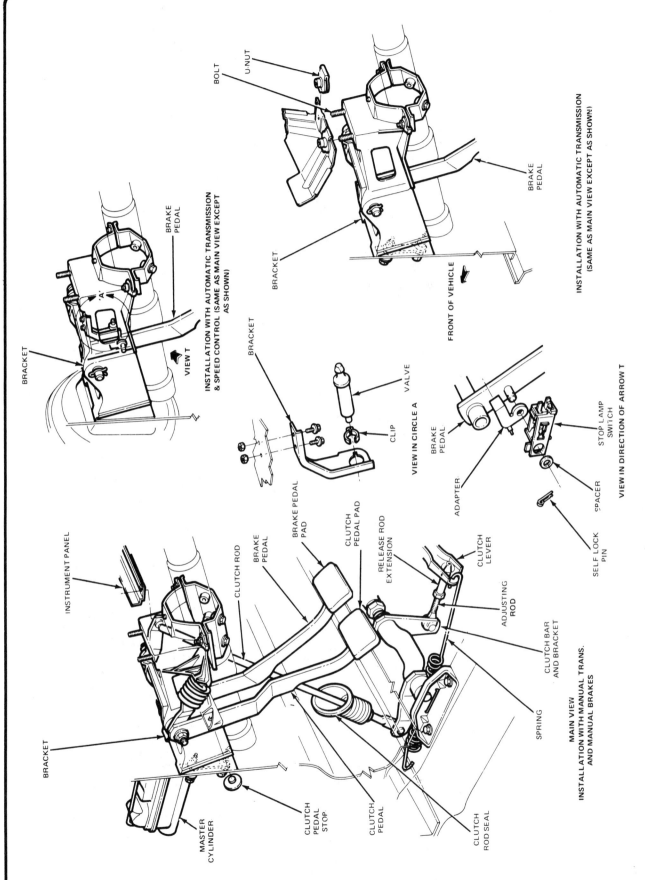

BOLT

U-NUT

BRACKET

BRAKE
PEDAL

INSTALLATION WITH AUTOMATIC TRANSMISSION
& SPEED CONTROL (SAME AS MAIN VIEW EXCEPT
AS SHOWN)

VIEW T

BRACKET

BRAKE
PEDAL

BRACKET

FRONT OF VEHICLE

INSTALLATION WITH AUTOMATIC TRANSMISSION
(SAME AS MAIN VIEW EXCEPT AS SHOWN)

BRACKET

VALVE

CLIP

VIEW IN CIRCLE A

BRAKE
PEDAL

ADAPTER

STOP LAMP
SWITCH

SPACER

SELF LOCK
PIN

VIEW IN DIRECTION OF ARROW T

INSTRUMENT PANEL

CLUTCH ROD

BRAKE PEDAL
PAD

CLUTCH
PEDAL PAD

RELEASE ROD
EXTENSION

CLUTCH
LEVER

ADJUSTING
ROD

BRAKE
PEDAL

CLUTCH BAR
AND BRACKET

SPRING

BRACKET

MASTER
CYLINDER

CLUTCH
PEDAL STOP

CLUTCH
PEDAL

CLUTCH
ROD SEAL

MAIN VIEW
INSTALLATION WITH MANUAL TRANS.
AND MANUAL BRAKES

Fig. 9.31 Typical brake pedal installation (all vehicles except F250 and F350 models with 460 engines) (Sec 17)

9

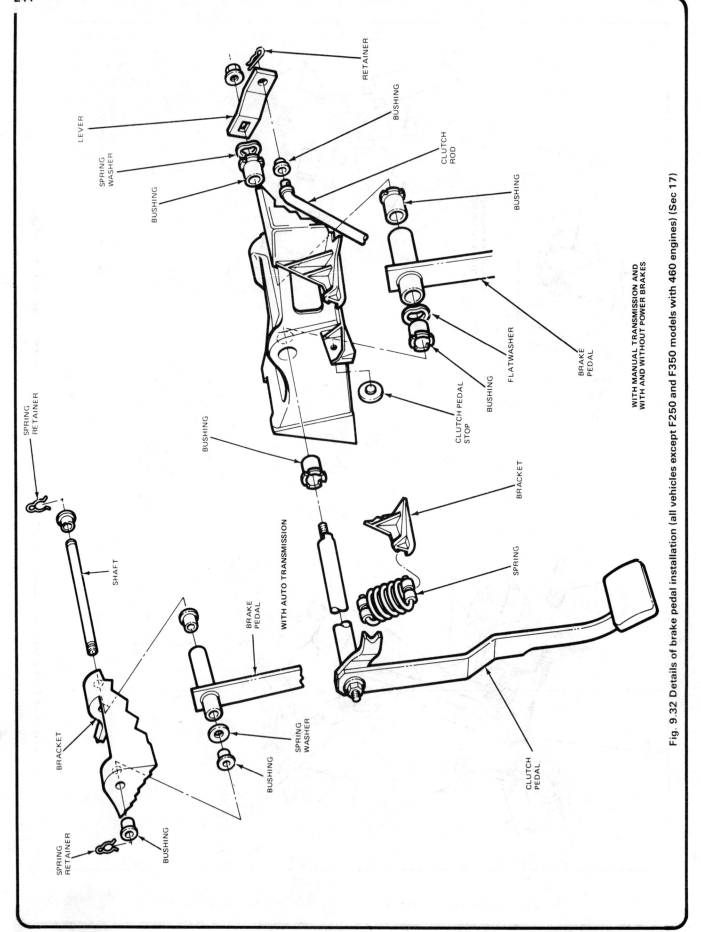

Fig. 9.32 Details of brake pedal installation (all vehicles except F250 and F350 models with 460 engines) (Sec 17)

RETAINER

BUSHING

LEVER

CLUTCH ROD

SPRING WASHER

BUSHING

BUSHING

BUSHING

FLATWASHER

CLUTCH PEDAL STOP

BUSHING

BRAKE PEDAL

WITH MANUAL TRANSMISSION AND WITH AND WITHOUT POWER BRAKES

BUSHING

SPRING RETAINER

BRACKET

SHAFT

BUSHING

BRAKE PEDAL

WITH AUTO TRANSMISSION

SPRING

SPRING WASHER

BRACKET

BUSHING

SPRING RETAINER

BUSHING

CLUTCH PEDAL

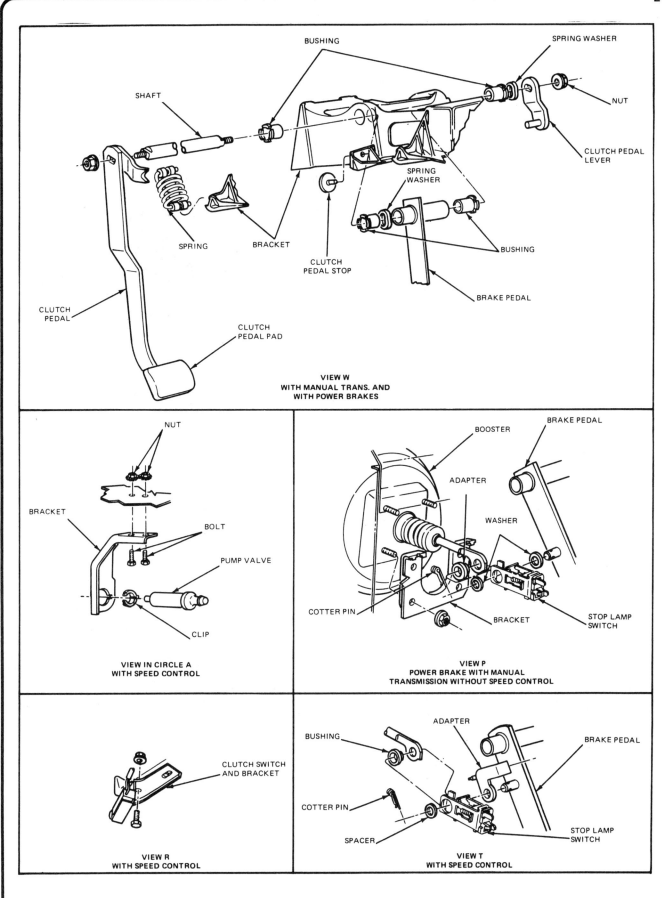

Fig. 9.33 Details of brake pedal installation on F350 vehicles with 460 engines (Sec 17)

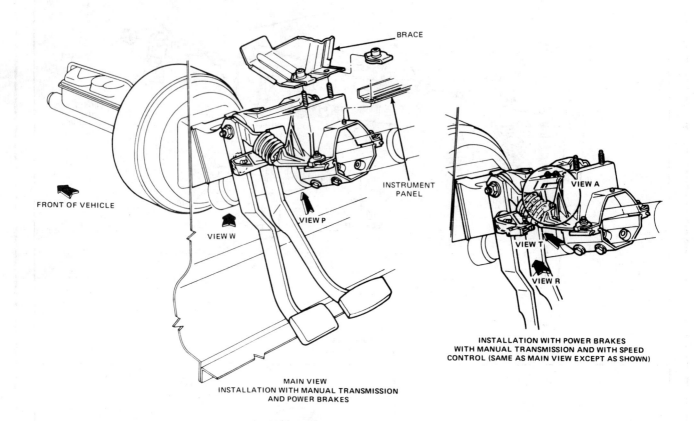

Fig. 9.34 Brake pedal installation on F250 and F350 vehicles with 460 engines (Sec 17)

18 Brake light switch – adjustment

1   The brake light switch is located under the dashboard directly above the brake pedal. It is activated by the pedal traveling away from its bottomed position, which releases the plunger and closes an electrical circuit in the system. The switch is mounted in a metal bracket which can be bent to vary its position.

2   Make sure the switch is fully seated in its bracket. Use an assistant or a mirror to determine when the circuit is activated. A test light connected to the two terminals of the switch would also provide you with this information.

3   The switch should activate the brake circuit within the first $\frac{1}{2}$ inch of brake pedal travel.

4   If the switch does not perform in this manner, bend the mounting bracket up or down to yield this action. Do not bend the bracket down to the point where it is preventing the pedal from returning fully.

5   The factory suggests that a 25-pound or less pull up on the pedal is sufficient to adjust the switch. Again, make sure the switch is seated correctly in its bracket after performing this step.

Chapter 10 Chassis electrical system

Refer to Chapter 13 for information on 1984 and later models

Contents

Specifications

General
Windshield wiper saddle centerline-to-lower molding .... 2.4 to 3.7 in

Torque specifications
	Ft-lb (unless otherwise noted)
Steering wheel retaining nut	30 to 42
Ignition switch retaining nuts	40 to 65 in-lb
Floor opening plate screws	6 to 10
Column support bracket bolts	13 to 27

1 General information

The electrical system is of the 12 volt, negative ground type.

Power for the lighting system and all electrical accessories is supplied by a lead/acid battery which is charged by an alternator.

This Chapter covers repair and service procedures for the various lighting and electrical components not associated with the engine. Information on the battery, alternator, voltage regulator and starter motor can be found in Chapter 5.

It should be noted that whenever portions of the electrical system are worked on, the negative battery cable should be disconnected to prevent electrical shorts and/or fires.

Various types of electrical connectors are employed throughout the vehicle's electrical system. The procedures to be used when disengaging and engaging these components are shown in accompanying illustrations and should be referred to whenever procedures in this Chapter involve the connectors.

2 Fuses and fusible links – replacement

1   The electrical circuits of the vehicle are protected by a combination of fuses, circuit breakers and fusible links.
2   The fuse box in most models is located underneath the dashboard, on the left side of the vehicle (photo). It is easily accessible for fuse inspection or replacement without completely removing the box from its mount.
3   Each of the fuses is designed to protect a specific circuit and the various circuits are identified on the fuse panel itself.
4   If an electrical component has failed, your first check should be the fuse. A fuse which has 'blown' can be readily identified by inspecting the element inside the glass tube. If this metal element is broken, the fuse is faulty and must be replaced with a new one.
5   When removing and installing fuses it is important that metal tools are not used. Plastic fuse pullers are available for this purpose.
6   It is also important that the correct fuse be installed. The different electrical circuits need different amounts of protection, indicated by the amperage rating on the fuse.
7   At no time should the fuse be bypassed by using metal or foil. Serious damage to the electrical system could result.

2.2 Location of the fuse box under the dashboard

8   If the replacement fuse immediately fails, do not replace it until the cause of the problem is isolated and corrected. In most cases this will be a short circuit in the wiring system caused by a broken or deteriorated wire.
9   In addition to fuses, the wiring system incorporates fusible links for overload protection. These links are used in circuits which are not ordinarily fused, such as the ignition circuit.
10   Although the fusible links appear to be of a heavier gauge than the wire they are protecting, this appearance is due to the heavy insulation. All fusible links are several wire gauges smaller than the wire they are incorporated into. They are color coded the same as the circuit they protect.
11   The exact locations of the fusible links used may differ slightly but their protective circuits are the same.
12   The fusible links cannot be repaired, but rather a new link of the

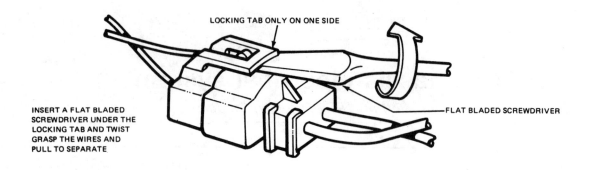

LOCKING TAB ONLY ON ONE SIDE

FLAT BLADED SCREWDRIVER

INSERT A FLAT BLADED SCREWDRIVER UNDER THE LOCKING TAB AND TWIST GRASP THE WIRES AND PULL TO SEPARATE

PLACE A THUMB UNDER THE LOCKING TAB AND PUSH UP. GRASP THE WIRES AND PULL TO SEPARATE.

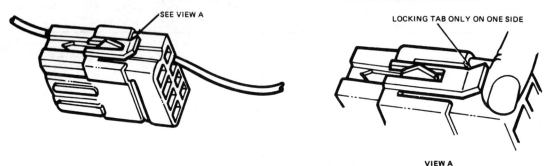

SEE VIEW A

LOCKING TAB ONLY ON ONE SIDE

VIEW A

INSERT A FLAT BLADED SCREWDRIVER UNDER THE LOCKING TAB AND TWIST. GRASP THE WIRES AND PULL UNTIL THE LOCKING TAB IS ON THE RAMP. TURN THE CONNECTOR OVER AND REPEAT THE PROCEDURE ON THE OPPOSITE SIDE OF THE CONNECTOR. THEN GRASP THE WIRES AND PULL APART.

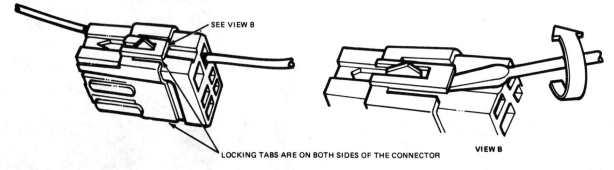

SEE VIEW B

LOCKING TABS ARE ON BOTH SIDES OF THE CONNECTOR

VIEW B

GRASP THE WIRES WITH BOTH HANDS AND PULL THE CONNECTOR APART

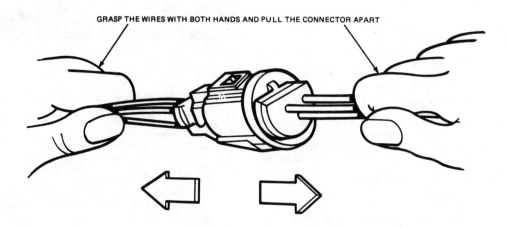

Fig. 10.1 Methods of disengaging various electrical connectors encountered in the chassis electrical system

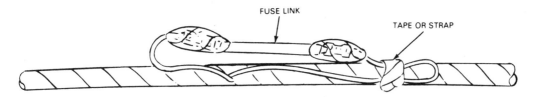

FUSE LINK

TAPE OR STRAP

TYPICAL REPAIR FOR ANY IN-LINE FUSE LINK USING THE SPECIFIED GAUGE FUSE LINK FOR THE SPECIFIC CIRCUIT

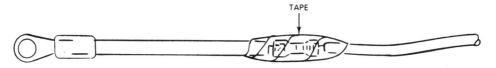

TAPE

TYPICAL REPAIR USING THE EYELET TERMINAL FUSE LINK OF THE SPECIFIED GAUGE FOR ATTACHMENT TO A CIRCUIT WIRE END

Fig. 10.2 Methods of attaching new fusible links in the wiring circuit (Sec 2)

identical wire size and special insulation type can be put in its place. This process is as follows:

13 Disconnect the battery ground cable.

14 Disconnect the fusible link from its electrical source.

15 Cut the damaged fusible link out of the wiring system. Do this just behind the connector. Some links have eyelet connectors and can be unbolted instead of cut.

16 Strip approximately $\frac{1}{2}$ inch of the insulation from the circuit wiring.

17 Position a new connector on the new fusible link and crimp it into place in the wiring circuit.

18 Use rosin core solder at each end of the new link to obtain a good solder joint.

19 Use plenty of electrical tape around the soldered joint. No wiring should be exposed.

20 Reconnect the fusible link at its source. Connect the battery ground cable. Test the circuit for proper operation.

21 **Note**: *Do not mistake a resistor wire for a fusible link. The resistor wire is usually longer and is imprinted, 'Resistor wire — don't cut or splice.' When attaching a single 16, 17, 18 or 20 gauge fusible link to a heavy gauge wire, always double the stripped wire end of the fusible link before inserting it into the butt connector. This assures positive wire retention.*

3 Light bulbs – replacement

Headlight

1 The headlights are replaceable sealed-beam units. The high- and low-beam filaments are contained in the same unit. If one fails, the entire unit must be replaced with a new one.

2 To replace the headlight unit, first remove the screws retaining the headlight door (decorative trim ring surrounding the headlight). Be careful not to disturb the two headlight adjusting screws.

3 Remove the four retaining ring screws if the vehicle is equipped with a rectangular headlight unit (photo). Loosen the retaining ring screws and rotate the ring counterclockwise to release it from the screws (if the vehicle has a round headlight unit).

4 Pull the headlight unit out far enough to allow access to the rear. Disconnect the plug from the unit.

5 Replace the headlight unit with one of the exact same size and type. Attach the plug to the prongs at the back of the unit. Place the bulb into the bucket with the large number embossed on the lens at the top. Make sure the alignment lugs cast into the unit are positioned in the recesses of the bucket.

6 Install the retaining ring (if so equipped) and the trim ring.

Front parking lights

7 From inside the engine compartment, locate the rear of the socket housing the bulb.

8 Turn the socket counterclockwise and pull it out of the housing.

9 Replace the defective bulb with a new one and reinstall the socket in the housing.

HEADLAMP
ELECTRICAL
CONNECTOR   ADJUSTING
RING

BULB ASSEMBLY

RETAINING RING

SCREW

Fig. 10.3 Typical headlight assembly – exploded view (Sec 3)

3.3 Location of the four headlight retaining ring screws

10

Side marker lights

10 Remove the two screws securing the side marker lens.
11 Pull the lens and bulb housing out of the fender.
12 Turn the socket housing the bulb counterclockwise and pull it out of the housing.
13 Replace the defective bulb with a new one and reinstall the assembly by reversing the removal procedure.

Taillights

Styleside pick-up and Bronco
14 Remove the two screws from the face of the taillight lens (photo).
15 With the tailgate down, remove the two screws from the rear of the lens (photo) and pull the lens and light assembly away from the body far enough to gain access to the bulb socket.
16 Turn the socket counterclockwise and pull it out of the light assembly.
17 Replace the defective bulb with a new one and reinstall the assembly by reversing the removal procedure.

Flareside pick-up
18 Remove the four screws retaining the lens.
19 Replace the defective bulb with a new one and reinstall the lens.

License plate light (vehicles with rear bumper)

20 From the rear side of the light assembly, rotate the bulb socket $\frac{1}{4}$ turn and pull the socket out.
21 Remove the defective bulb and replace it with a new one, then reinstall the socket in the light assembly.

License plate light (vehicles without rear bumper)

Styleside pick-up
22 Remove the screws retaining the license plate light cover to the light assembly.

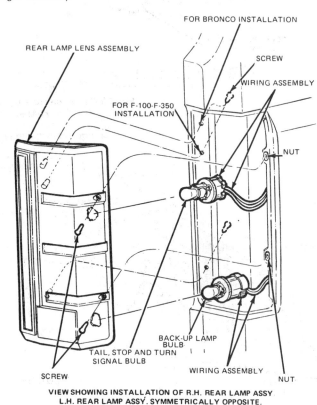

Fig. 10.5 Rear lamp assembly of Bronco and Styleside pick-up — exploded view (Sec 3)

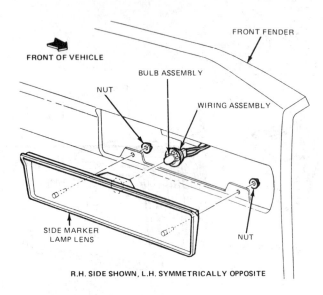

Fig. 10.4 Details of a typical side marker lamp assembly (Sec 3)

3.14 Removing the screws from the face of the taillight lens on a Styleside pick-up

3.15 Removing the screws from the rear of the taillight lens on a Styleside pick-up

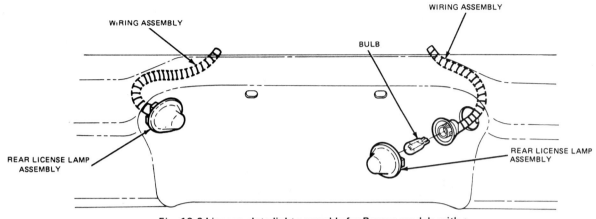

Fig. 10.6 License plate light assembly for Bronco models with a straight rear bumper (Sec 3)

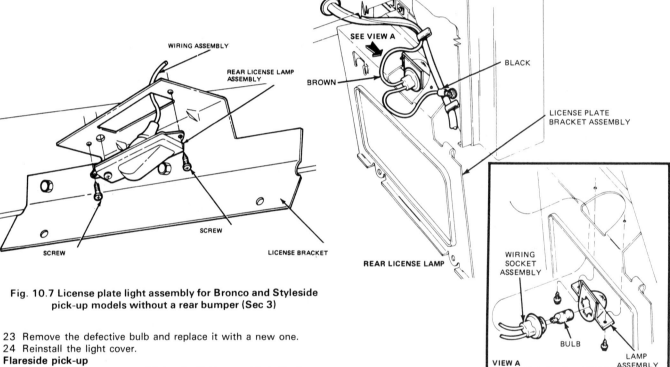

Fig. 10.7 License plate light assembly for Bronco and Styleside pick-up models without a rear bumper (Sec 3)

23 Remove the defective bulb and replace it with a new one.
24 Reinstall the light cover.

Flareside pick-up
25 Remove the two screws retaining the light assembly to the license plate bracket assembly.
26 Rotate the bulb socket $\frac{1}{8}$ turn and pull it out of the light assembly.
27 Remove the defective bulb and replace it with a new one.
28 Install the socket in the light assembly.
29 Install the light assembly.

Dome light
30 Using a screwdriver at the corners of the plastic lens, carefully pry it off the light assembly.
31 Replace the defective bulb with a new one and snap the plastic lens back into place.

Cargo area light
F100-F350
32 Remove the two screws retaining the lens and light assembly to the rear of the cab.
33 Replace the defective bulb with a new one and reinstall the lens and light assembly.
Bronco
34 Using a screwdriver at the corners of the light assembly in the cargo area, carefully pry it from the body.
35 Replace the defective bulb with a new one and snap the light assembly back into place.

Fig. 10.8 License plate light assembly for Flare-Side pick-up models (Sec 3)

Dash lights
36 Most cluster illumination and indicator bulbs can be replaced by reaching under the instrument panel, removing the defective bulb and replacing it with a new one.
37 If the defective bulb cannot be reached from under the panel, access can usually be gained by removing the instrument cluster (refer to Section 7).

Fog lights
38 **Note**: *The fog light assembly utilizes a quartz Halogen bulb. The following procedure must be used for fog light bulb replacement.*
39 Remove the two screws that retain the lens assembly to the housing.
40 Remove the lens and body assembly from the housing.
41 From the rear of the body assembly, release the bulb socket retainer from the locking tab.
42 Remove the light and socket assembly from the body and pull the bulb directly out of the socket. **Caution:** *Do not touch the new bulb with your bare hands or an oily cloth, as this could cause contamination of the quartz and early failure of the bulb. Do not remove the protective plastic sleeve until the light is inserted in the*

10

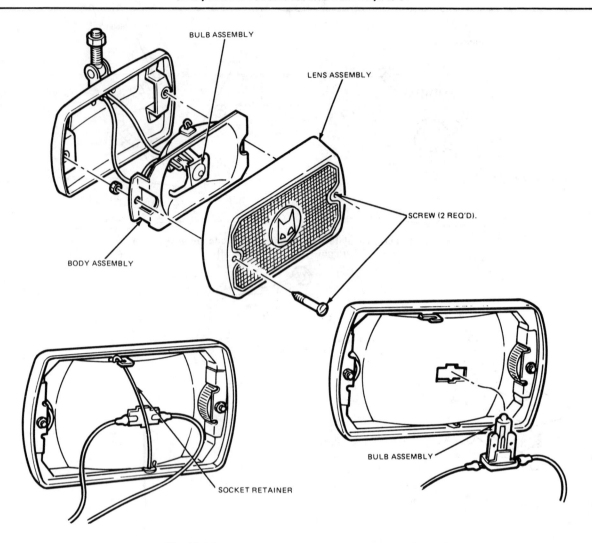

Fig. 10.9 Details of the optional fog light assembly (Sec 3)

socket. Be sure that the circuit is not energized. If the quartz is inadvertently handled, it should be cleaned with a cloth moistened with alcohol before installation.
43 After inserting the bulb into the socket, the remaining installation steps are the reverse of the removal procedure. Be sure the lens is right side up, as indicated on the lens.

Shift indicator light (if so equipped)
44 Disconnect the cable at the negative battery terminal.
45 Remove the instrument trim panel and instrument cluster (refer to Section 7).
46 Locate the shift indicator light assembly at the far left end of the instrument panel.
47 Remove the defective bulb and replace it with a new one.
48 Installation is the reverse of the removal procedure.

4 Headlight switch – removal and installation

1 Disconnect the cable from the negative battery terminal.
2 Remove the knob on each switch in the instrument cluster finish panel by reaching under the dash and pressing the knob lock tab while pulling the knob away from the cluster panel.
3 Remove the steering column shroud.
4 Remove the three screws securing the top of the instrument cluster finish panel to the dash and remove the finish panel.
5 Unscrew the headlight switch mounting nut.
6 Remove the switch from the panel, then disconnect the wiring connector from the switch.

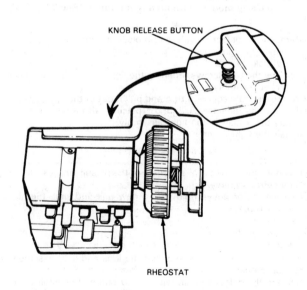

Fig. 10.10 Headlight switch knob release button location (Sec 4)

7 Installation of the headlight switch is the reverse of the removal procedure. It is not necessary to push the knob lock tabs when reinstalling the knobs.

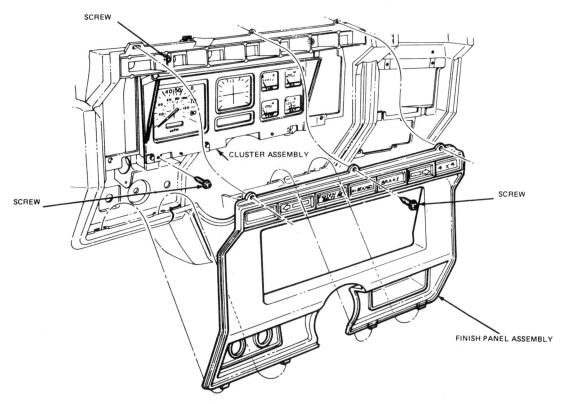

Fig. 10.11 Typical Bronco and pick-up instrument cluster finish panel installation (Sec 4)

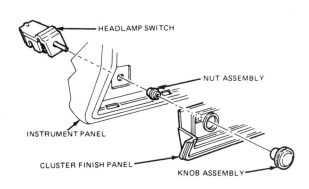

Fig. 10.12 Typical headlight switch installation for Broncos and pick-ups (Sec 4)

5 Turn signal and hazard switch – replacement

Note: *Refer to Fig. 10.13 to locate pertinent components.*
1 Remove the steering wheel (refer to Chapter 11).
2 Disconnect the turn signal indicator switch combination connector by lifting the lock tabs and carefully pulling it apart.
3 Unscrew the turn signal switch lever from the switch. A flat is provided on the shank of the lever to enable a wrench to fit it.
4 Remove the steering column shroud by removing the retaining screws.
5 Remove the screws that retain the switch assembly to the steering column.
6 On vehicles with a fixed steering column, remove the switch assembly from the vehicle by lifting it out of the column and guiding the connector plug through the opening in the shift spocket.
7 On vehicles equipped with tilt steering columns, it is necessary to remove the connector plug prior to removing the switch assembly, as the opening in the shift socket provided for the wiring harness is not

large enough for the connector to pass through. Refer to Steps 8 through 10.
8 Record the color codes and locations of the wires as they lead into the combination connector. Remove each individual wire from the combination connector by releasing the tang on the terminal with a pointed tool.
9 Connect a pull wire to the end of the wiring harness after all of the wires have been removed from the connector.
10 Remove the switch and wires from the top of the steering column. Disconnect the pull wire from the end of the switch harness.
11 Installation is the reverse of removal. Check the operation of the turn signals and hazard flashers after the reassembly process has been completed.

6 Wiper and washer system – description and component replacement

1 The windshield wiper/washer system on Ford trucks covered by this manual consists of a motor with dual speed capabilities (plus optional interval operations), linkages to convert rotary motion of the motor to oscillating movement at the blades and the wiper blades themselves. Windshield wiper blade replacement instructions can be found in Chapter 1. In addition, washer chores are handled by a plastic reservoir equipped with a pump which distributes washing fluid to a nozzle on each side of the windshield. A single control on the instrument panel next to the light switch activates both systems.

Arm and blade assembly
2 Raise the blade end of the arm off the windshield and move the slide latch away from the pivot latch.
3 The wiper arm can now be pulled off the pivot shaft without the aid of any tools.
4 Reinstall the arm and blade assembly by holding the main arm head on the pivot shaft while raising the blade end of the wiper arm and pushing the slide latch into the lock under the pivot head shaft.
Note: *When reinstalling the wiper arms, make sure the motor is in the Parked position by allowing it to run a few cycles, then turning it off.*

10

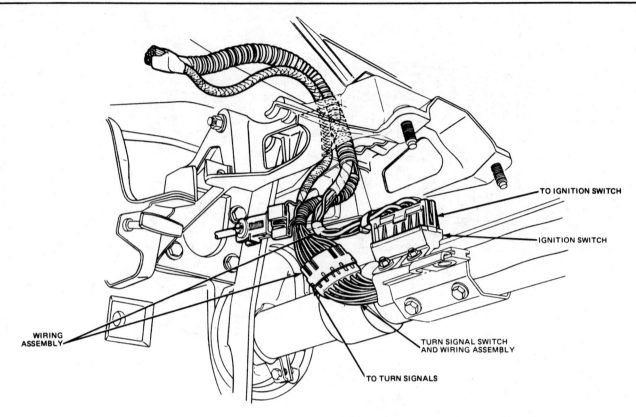

Fig. 10.13 Typical turn signal wiring harness installation for Broncos and pick-ups (Sec 5)

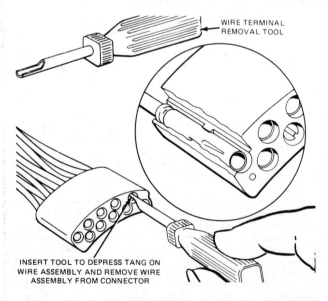

Fig. 10.14 Method of removing wires from the turn signal wire terminal (necessary for removal of turn signal assembly on vehicles equipped with tilt steering wheels only) (Sec 5)

The shafts will then come to rest in the parked position. Install the blades so that the measurement from the centerline of the wiper saddle to the top of the weatherstrip or lower molding is as specified.

Wiper motor

5   Disconnect the cable from the negative battery terminal.
6   Remove both wiper arm and blade assemblies from the pivot shafts.
7   Remove the cowl grille attaching screws and lift the grille slightly.
8   Disconnect the washer nozzle hose and remove the grille assembly.

9   Remove the wiper linkage clip from the motor output arm and disconnect the linkage from the arm.
10 Disconnect the wiper motor wiring connector.
11 Remove the three motor attaching screws and remove the motor (photo).
12 Installation is the reverse of the removal procedure.

Pivot shaft and linkage

13 Refer to and perform Steps 5 through 9.
14 Remove the pivot body to cowl screws, then remove the linkage and pivot shaft assembly. The left and right pivots and linkage are independent and can be serviced separately.
15 Installation is the reverse of the removal procedure. Refer to the Note in Step 4.

Wiper control switch

16 Remove the wiper switch knob with a hooked tool inserted in the rear to release the clip.
17 Remove the bezel nut by unthreading it from the switch. Remove the switch bezel.
18 Pull the switch out from the rear of the instrument panel.
19 Disconnect the plug-in wire connector from the switch and remove the switch.
20 Installation is the reverse of the removal procedure.

Interval governor (if so equipped)

21 Disconnect the two wire connectors from the governor.
22 Remove the two governor attaching screws and remove the governor. **Note:** *On models with an electric rear window, remove the electric device switch assembly to obtain tool clearance for the right-hand governor attaching screw.*
23 Installation is the reverse of the removal procedure.

Washer reservoir and pump

24 The windshield washer reservoir and pump are located on the left inner fender well, inside the engine compartment (photo). If the reservoir or the pump needs replacement, the reservoir may be removed by removing the three retaining screws and pulling the wiring connector out of the motor terminals.

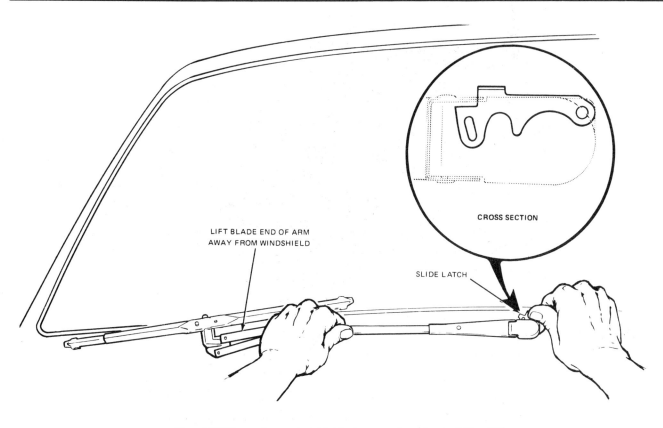

Fig. 10.15 Removing a windshield wiper arm from its pivot (Sec 56)

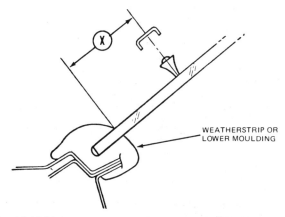

Fig. 10.16 Make measurement for proper windshield wiper arm installation at position X (Sec 6)

25 Using a small screwdriver, pry out the retaining ring.
26 To remove the pump from the reservoir, grasp the wall of the pump near the electrical terminals with pliers and pull the pump out of the reservoir. If the impeller and/or the seal come off of the motor during this operation, they may be reassembled.
27 Installation is basically the reverse of the removal procedure. Lubricate the outside of the pump seal with a dry lubricant such as powdered graphite. Align the tang of the motor end cap with the slot in the reservoir before pushing the motor into the reservoir. Also, use a 1 inch socket (preferably 12 point) to hand press the retaining ring securely against the motor end plate.

7 Instrument cluster – removal and installation

1 Disconnect the cable from the negative battery terminal.

2 Using a hook tool to release each knob lock tab, remove the knobs from the wiper-washer, headlight and fog light (if so equipped) switches.
3 Remove the screws retaining the steering column shrouds. **Note:** *Caution should be taken not to damage the transmission control selector indicator on vehicles equipped with an automatic transmission.*
4 On vehicles with an automatic transmission, remove the loop on the indicator cable assembly from the retainer pin and open the cable retaining clips (two for tilt column-equipped vehicles, one for non-tilt steering). Remove the bracket screw from the cable bracket and slide the bracket out of the slot in the column.
5 Remove the screws retaining the cluster finish panel to the dash and remove the finish panel.
6 Remove the four cluster panel retaining screws and pull the cluster panel out far enough to reach behind it and pry the retaining tab up to release the speedometer cable from the cluster. Disconnect the wire connector from the printed circuit and disconnect the 4x4 indicator light (if so equipped).
7 Remove the instrument cluster.
8 When installing the instrument cluster, reconnect the wire connector, cable and light, then install the cluster retaining screws.
9 On vehicles with an automatic transmission, place the loop on the transmission indicator cable assembly over the retainer on the column.
10 Position the tab on the cable bracket in the slot in the column.
11 Align the pointer and attach the retaining screw.
12 Reposition the cable conduit in the retaining clip(s) and secure it.
13 With the parking brake applied, place the transmission selector at the steering column in the Drive position. Hold the lever against the Drive stop using a weight of approximately eight pounds attached to the selector lever knob.
14 Secure the cable to the column mounting clip(s) and adjust the bracket to position the pointer in the adjustment band as shown in the accompanying illustration.
15 Shift the transmission lever to each gear, checking the pointer position at each transmission shift position.
16 The remainder of the installation steps are the reverse of those for removal.

10

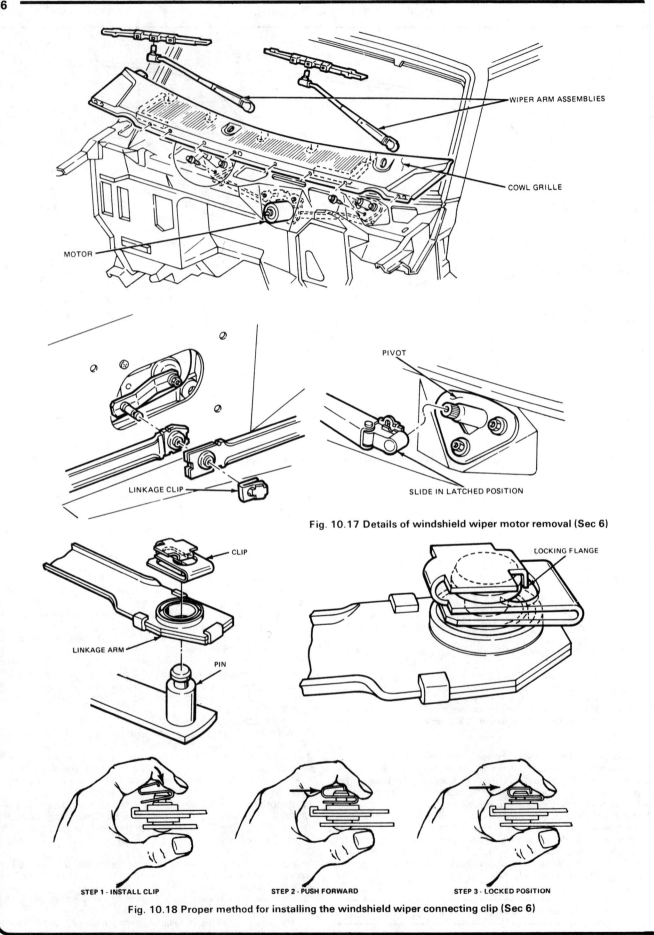

WIPER ARM ASSEMBLIES

COWL GRILLE

MOTOR

PIVOT

LINKAGE CLIP

SLIDE IN LATCHED POSITION

Fig. 10.17 Details of windshield wiper motor removal (Sec 6)

CLIP

LOCKING FLANGE

LINKAGE ARM

PIN

STEP 1 - INSTALL CLIP

STEP 2 - PUSH FORWARD

STEP 3 - LOCKED POSITION

Fig. 10.18 Proper method for installing the windshield wiper connecting clip (Sec 6)

6.11 Location of the windshield wiper motor beneath the cowl in the engine compartment

INTERVAL WIPER SWITCH

STANDARD WIPER SWITCH

NUT

KNOB ASSEMBLY

Fig. 10.19 Typical windshield wiper control switch installation for Broncos and pick-ups (Sec 6)

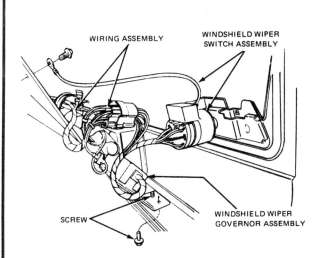

WIRING ASSEMBLY

WINDSHIELD WIPER SWITCH ASSEMBLY

SCREW

WINDSHIELD WIPER GOVERNOR ASSEMBLY

Fig. 10.20 Typical windshield wiper interval governor installation (Sec 6)

6.24 Location of the windshield washer reservoir and pump assembly in the engine compartment

10

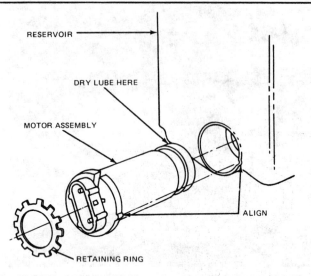

Fig. 10.21 Typical windshield washer motor installation (Sec 6)

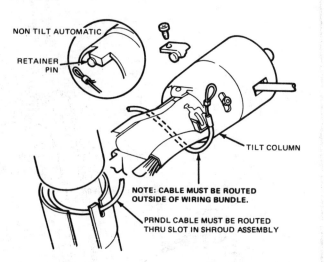

Fig. 10.22 Typical automatic transmission indicator cable installations (Sec 7)

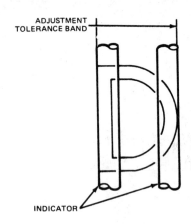

Fig. 10.23 Automatic transmission selector indicator adjustment (Sec 7)

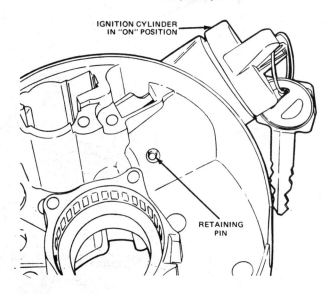

Fig. 10.24 Location of the lock cylinder retaining pin on a non-tilt steering wheel column (Sec 8)

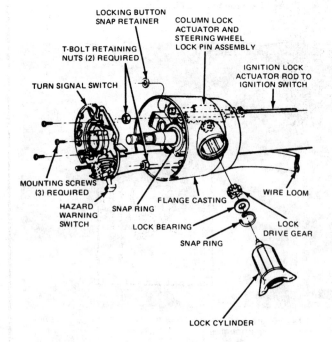

Fig. 10.25 Details of removal of a typical ignition lock cylinder (non-tilt steering column shown) (Sec 8)

8   Ignition lock – removal and installation

1   Remove the steering wheel (refer to Chapter 11).
2   If equipped with an automatic transmission, place the gearshift in Park.
3   With the key, turn the lock cylinder to the On position.
4   Using a small drift or $\frac{1}{8}$ inch diameter drill bit, depress the lock cylinder retaining pin while pulling on the lock cylinder to remove it from the steering column housing. The pin is located inside the column near the base of the lock cylinder on non-tilt steering columns and adjacent to the hazard warning button on tilt wheel steering columns.
5   To install the lock cylinder, first lubricate it with multi-purpose grease.
6   Turn the cylinder to the On position and depress the retaining pin, then insert the cylinder into its housing in the flange casting.
7   Check that the cylinder is fully seated and aligned in the interlocking washer before turning the key to the Off position, permitting the cylinder retaining pin to extend into the cylinder casting housing hole.
8   Using the ignition key, rotate the lock cylinder to ensure correct mechanical operation in all positions.
9   The remaining installation steps are the reverse of removal. When

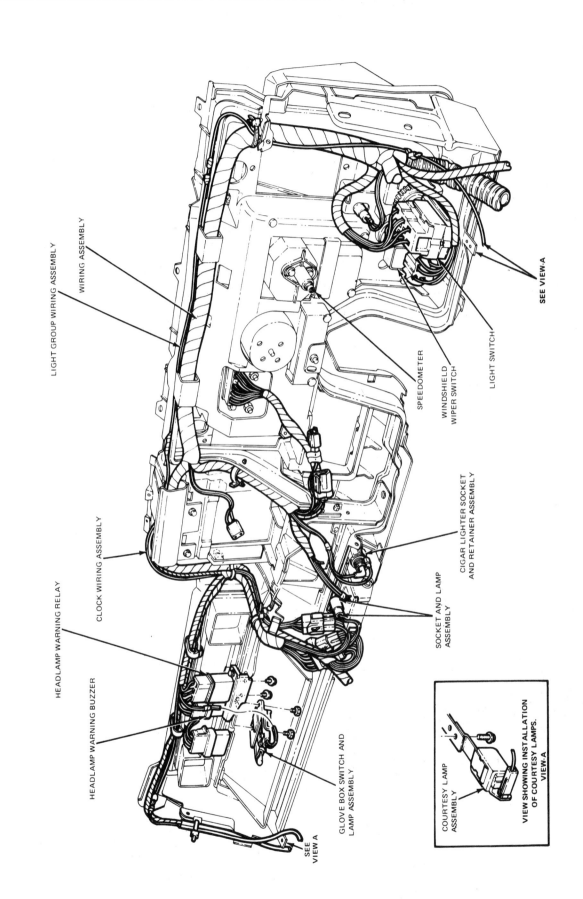

LIGHT GROUP WIRING ASSEMBLY

WIRING ASSEMBLY

SEE VIEW-A

SPEEDOMETER

WINDSHIELD WIPER SWITCH

LIGHT SWITCH

HEADLAMP WARNING RELAY

CLOCK WIRING ASSEMBLY

HEADLAMP WARNING BUZZER

GLOVE BOX SWITCH AND LAMP ASSEMBLY

SEE VIEW A

SOCKET AND LAMP ASSEMBLY

CIGAR LIGHTER SOCKET AND RETAINER ASSEMBLY

COURTESY LAMP ASSEMBLY

VIEW SHOWING INSTALLATION OF COURTESY LAMPS. VIEW-A

Fig. 10.26 Typical instrument cluster for Bronco and pick-ups – rear view (Sec 7)

10

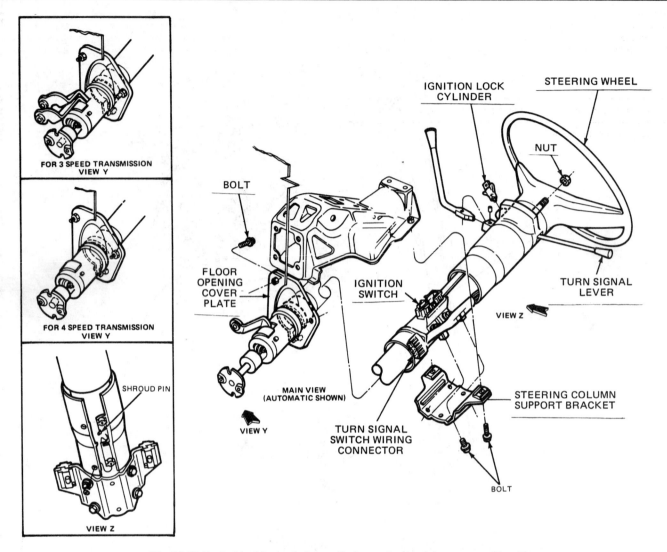

Fig. 10.27 Typical ignition switch installation and related components (Sec 9)

the installation is complete, check for proper start in Park and Neutral, and be sure that the start circuit cannot be actuated in the Drive and Reverse positions (automatic transmission).

9 Ignition switch – removal and installation

Note: *Refer to Fig. 10.27 to locate pertinent components.*
1   Disconnect the cable at the negative battery terminal.
2   Remove the screws retaining the steering column shroud and remove the shroud.
3   To gain working room for access to the ignition switch, lower the steering column by removing the retaining bolts from the column support bracket, the screws from the steering column floor opening plate and the instrument panel steering column opening cover.
4   Disconnect the wiring connector.
5   Remove the two nuts retaining the switch to the steering column.
6   Lift the switch vertically to disengage the actuator rod from the switch and remove the switch.
7   When installing the ignition switch, both the locking mechanism at the top of the column and the switch itself must be in the Lock position for proper operation.
8   To hold the mechanical parts of the column in the Lock position, move the shift lever into Park (automatic transmission) or Reverse (manual transmission), turn the key to Lock and remove the key. **Note:** *New replacement switches, when received, are already pinned in the Lock position by a metal shipping pin inserted in a locking hole on the side of the switch.*

9   Engage the actuator rod in the switch.
10   Position the switch on the column and install the retaining nuts, but do not tighten them at this time.
11   Move the switch up and down along the column to locate the mid-position of rod lash, then tighten the two ignition switch retaining nuts (top nut first to minimize rod binding) to the specified torque.
12   Remove the lock pin (if present), connect the battery cable and make sure that the engine starts (in Park or Neutral with automatic transmission). Also make sure that the engine cannot be started in Drive or Reverse (with automatic transmission).
13   Raise the steering column and secure it, tightening the fasteners to the specified torque.
14   Install the steering column shroud.
15   Confirm that the accessories are deactivated with the ignition switch Off and that the accessories are operable with the switch in the On position.

10 Battery – removal and installation

1   The battery is the heart of the entire electrical system and must be maintained properly. Battery maintenance and charging details can be found in Chapter 1.
2   Removal and installation of the battery is a simple process. Remove both battery cables from the posts of the battery. Use a battery terminal puller and never pry on the posts, as they can be easily damaged. Remove the battery hold-down nuts and retaining bracket.
3   Lift the battery from the battery box with a tool designed for this

task. Do not attempt to lift the battery by hand as it is heavy and often has a thin corrosive film on its surface.

4   Installation is the reverse of removal. Coat the battery hold-down threads with petroleum jelly or a special terminal lubricant to prevent corrosion.

11 Neutral start switch – removal and installation

1   Remove the downshift linkage return spring from the Low/Reverse servo cover.

2   To avoid damaging the inner lever shaft, apply penetrating oil to the outer lever retaining nut. After the penetrating oil has soaked for a sufficient time, remove the downshift outer lever retaining nut. Remove the lever.

3   Remove the two bolts retaining the switch to the transmission. Disconnect the two multiple wiring connectors. Remove the switch from over the shaft.

4   Install the Neutral safety switch over the shift shafts and install the two retaining bolts. Do not tighten the bolts.

5   Refer to Chapter 7, Part B for the proper adjustment procedures.

See page 323 for wiring diagrams

10

Chapter 11 Steering and suspension systems

Refer to Chapter 13 for Specifications and information on 1984 and later models

Contents

Specifications

Front suspension type

2-wheel drive (4x2)	Forged or stamped twin I-beam axles with coil springs and telescoping shock absorbers
4-wheel drive (4x4)	Independent front suspension (IFS) with two-piece front drive axle assembly, leaf or coil springs and telescoping shock absorbers

Rear suspension type (all)

Leaf spring with telescoping shock absorbers

Steering systems

Manual

Type	Recirculating ball
Ratio	24:1
Lock-to-lock turns (not attached to Pitman arm)	6
Worm bearing preload (torque required to rotate input shaft at approximately $1\frac{1}{2}$ turns on either side of center with the gearbox out of the vehicle or the Pitman arm disconnected)	5 to 8 in-lb
Sector shaft backlash (torque required to rotate input shaft and worm assembly past the center high point)	10 to 16 in-lb
Total steering meshload on center	16 in-lb
Power assisted type	Ford integral worm and sector, torsion-bar feedback
Ratio	17:1
Lock-to-lock turns (not attached to Pitman arm)	4
Pump fluid	Type F
Power assisted over-center meshload	10 to 14 in-lb

Torque specifications

Front suspension (4x2)

Ft-lb (unless otherwise noted)

Spring upper retainer-to-spring upper seat	13 to 18
Shock absorber stud-to-spring upper seat	15 to 25
Shock absorber-to-lower bracket	40 to 60
Shock lower bracket-to-radius arm	27 to 37
Spring lower retainer-to-spring lower seat	
Forged axle	30 to 70
Stamped axle	70 to 100
Radius arm-to-front axle and bracket	
Forged axle	240 to 320
Stamped axle	269 to 329
Radius arm-to-bracket	80 to 120
Radius arm bracket-to-frame	77 to 110
Front axle-to-pivot bracket	120 to 150
Stabilizer bar link-to-bracket (stamped axle only)	52 to 74
Stabilizer bar link-to-stabilizer bar (stamped axle only)	52 to 74

	Ft-lb
Stabilizer bar retainer-to-frame crossmember mounting bracket (stamped axle only)	27 to 37
Wheel spindle pin lock pin nut (forged axle only)	38 to 62
Wheel spindle steering arm-to-rod and link assembly	
Forged axle	70 to 100
Stamped axle	52 to 73
Wheel spindle plug (forged axle only)	35 to 50
Stabilizer bar bracket-to-frame (F250 and F350 with stamped axle only	52 to 74
Upper balljoint nut (stamped axle only)	85 to 110
Lower balljoint nut (stamped axle only)	
Ford part no. 388981	140 to 180
Ford part no. 33850	104 to 146
Steering rod and link assembly clamp bolts	30 to 42
Steering rod and link assembly-to-Pitman arm	52 to 73
Spring upper seat-to-frame (stamped axle, left side only)	52 to 73
Front suspension (4x4)	
Coil spring (F150, Bronco)	
Radius arm-to-bracket	80 to 100
Spring retainer-to-upper spring seat	13 to 18
Lower spring retainer-to-radius arm	70 to 100
Front shock-to-shock bracket (lower)	40 to 60
Front shock absorber stud (upper)	25 to 35
Front shock-to-shock bracket (upper)	25 to 35
Radius arm pivot bracket-to-frame	77 to 110
Stabilizer bar link-to-bracket	52 to 74
Stabilizer bar link-to-stabilizer	52 to 74
Stabilizer bar retainer-to-bracket and bracket-to-frame (Sno-Fiter only)	27 to 37
Stabilizer bar bracket-to-bracket (F150 Super Cab only)	27 to 37
Stabilizer bar retainer-to-frame (F150 Super Cab only)	52 to 74
Stabilizer bar retainer-to-crossmember and mounting bracket (F150 Regular Cab only)	27 to 37
Leaf spring (F250/F350)	
Front spring-to-axle U-bolt	85 to 120
Front spring assembly-to-hanger bracket	120 to 150
Front spring shackle-to-shackle bracket	150 to 210
Front spring rear bracket-to-frame	35 to 50
Front spring-to-shackle	120 to 150
Front shock bracket-to-frame	48 to 65
Front shock absorber stud	25 to 35
Front shock-to-front spring plate spacer	52 to 74
Stabilizer bar mounting bracket-to-frame and plate assembly	27 to 37
Stabilizer bar retainer-to-stabilizer bar mounting bracket	27 to 37
Stabilizer link assembly-to-stabilizer bar	15 to 25
Stabilizer link assembly-to-spring seat cap	48 to 65
Rear suspension	
Lower shock mount	40 to 64
Upper shock mount	40 to 64
Spring-to-axle U-bolt	
F100, F150, F250, Bronco	75 to 100
F350	150 to 210
Spring-to-front hanger	
F100, F150 (4x2)	75 to 115
F150 (4x4), F250, F350, Bronco	150 to 200
Spring-to-rear shackle	
All vehicles except 137 and 161 in wheelbase	75 to 115
Vehicles with 137 and 161 in wheelbase	150 to 200
Rear shackle-to-shackle bracket	
All vehicles except 137 and 161 in wheelbase	75 to 115
Vehicles with 137 and 161 in wheelbase	150 to 200
Stabilizer link-to-frame or frame bracket	15 to 25
Stabilizer link-to-stabilizer bar	15 to 25
Stabilizer retainer-to-bracket and frame	
F100, F150, Bronco	40 to 50
F250, F350	35 to 50
Steering	
Steering gearbox-to-frame	54 to 66
Flex coupling-to-worm (input) shaft	25 to 34
Drag link/tie-rod end studs	52 to 74
Linkage adjusting sleeve clamp	29 to 41
Flange and insulator assembly-to-steering gearbox	28 to 35
Flange and insulator assembly-to-coupling shaft	14 to 21
Coupling shaft-to-steering shaft	45 to 59
Steering wheel-to-steering shaft	30 to 42

11

	Ft-lb (unless otherwise stated)
Support bracket-to-steering column	13 to 20
Upper bolts	13 to 27
Lower bolts	8 to 20
Steering column floor opening cover plate-to-floor	6 to 11
Steering column floor opening cover plate clamp	8 to 18
Steering column shroud	10 to 15 in-lb
Ignition switch-to-steering column	40 to 60 in-lb
Sector shaft cover	
Manual steering	30
Power steering	55 to 70
Worm bearing (preload) adjuster locknut	85
Sector shaft backlash adjuster screw locknut	
Manual steering	25
Power steering	35 to 45
Pitman arm-to-sector shaft	
Manual steering	170 to 230
Power steering	190 to 230
Pressure hose-to-gearbox	16 to 25
Return hose-to-gearbox	25 to 34

1 General information

The front suspension system of Ford light duty trucks (4x2) is unusual in design with its patented twin I-beam layout. This design, with its two independent I-beam axles (one for each side) suspended by coil springs, has a number of advantages. The I-beam axles provide high strength and durability while the independent feature allows each side to absorb bumps and provide a smoother ride for passengers and cargo.

Two versions of the twin I-beam layout are employed on 4x2 vehicles covered by this manual: a stamped axle employing balljoints at the spindle on F100 and F150 pick-ups, and a forged axle employing spindle pins, bushings and thrust washers on F250 and F350 pick-ups.

The outer wheel spindle of each axle is located by a radius arm mounted in rubber and damped by a hydraulic telescoping shock absorber. The inner ends of the I-beam are attached to a pivot bracket on the opposite side of the vehicle. This design provides for good suspension compliance and long spring travel.

The Bronco and F150 (4x4) independent front suspension system (IFS) comprises a two-piece front driving axle assembly (refer to Chapter 8), two coil springs and two radius arms. One end of each axle assembly is anchored to the frame, with the other end supported by the coil spring and radius arm.

The F250 and F350 (4x4) IFS employs the same type of two-piece driving axle as the Bronco and F150, but is attached to the frame with two semi-elliptic leaf-type springs. Each spring is clamped to the axle arm assembly with two U-bolts at the spring center. The rear eye of the leaf spring is attached to the frame by a hanger bracket, with the front eye attached via a shackle bracket.

The rear suspension consists of leaf-type springs mounted to the axle with U-bolts. The springs are mounted to the frame by brackets and shackles and telescoping shock absorbers are used for damping.

Several types of manual and power assisted steering gearboxes are used and the steering wheel is connected through a collapsible shaft and flexible coupling. Some models incorporate a hydraulic damper in the steering linkage to reduce road shock at the steering wheel.

Due to the special techniques and tools required, several procedures involving the complicated assemblies such as power steering pumps and the front axle on 4-wheel-drive vehicles are beyond the scope of the home mechanic. Consequently, only tasks which can be accomplished with standard tools and limited experience are described in this Chapter.

2 Front coil spring – removal and installation

Note: *Coil springs should always be replaced in pairs to maintain proper ride height and performance characteristics. As an additional safety precaution, use a chain to secure the spring to the axle during removal and installation. This will prevent the spring from flying out of position during the procedures. Refer to Fig. 11.2 or 11.3 to locate components.*

1   Raise the front of the vehicle and support it securely under the frame. Remove the wheels.

2   Support the bottom of the axle being worked on with a floor jack.

Note: *The axle must be supported on the jack throughout the spring removal and installation, and must not be permitted to hang by the brake hose. If the brake hose is not long enough to provide clearance for removal and installation of the spring, the disc brake caliper must be removed (refer to Chapter 9). After removing the caliper, it must be placed on the frame or otherwise supported to prevent suspending the caliper by the brake hose.*

3   Disconnect the lower end of the shock absorber while using the jack to compress the spring and support the axle.

4   Remove the bolts holding the upper spring retainer to the frame. Remove the upper spring retainer.

5   Carefully lower the axle until the open end of the spring is exposed. Drop the axle/spring assembly slowly as the coil spring could spring out slightly as the axle is moved.

6   Use a socket and several long extensions to unfasten the lower spring retaining nut through the open end of the top of the spring. Remove the nut, washer, chain and spring from the axle.

7   To install, place the spring in position on the lower seat. Position it so that the end of the spring fits correctly into the recess of the upper spring cup. The spring can fit into a number of different positions, but the flat surface of the spring end must fit into the area where it is retained by the upper spring retainer.

8   Install the lower spring retainer washer and nut. Tighten the nut to the correct torque.

9   Raise the spring/axle combination until the spring top fits snugly against the upper spring cup. Work slowly and carefully to ensure that the spring is properly seated.

10   Install the upper spring retainer and retaining bolts. Tighten the retaining bolts to the correct torque.

11   Connect the lower end of the shock absorber.

12   If the brake caliper was removed, reinstall it.

13   Install the wheel. Lower the axle and remove the jack. Lower the vehicle to the ground.

3 Front leaf spring – removal and installation

Note: *Refer to Fig. 11.12 to locate components.*

1   Raise the vehicle frame until the weight is off the affected spring, but the tire is still touching the ground.

2   Place the frame securely on jackstands and support the axle to prevent rotation.

3   Disconnect the lower end of the shock absorber from the front spring plate spacer.

4   Remove the spring U-bolt nuts, U-bolt and spacer.

5   Remove the nut from the hanger bolt retaining the rear of the spring.

6   Drive the hanger bolt out of the spring eye. If the bolt is to be reused, use a soft brass drift so the bolt is not damaged.

7   Remove the nut connecting the front shackle and spring eye.

8   Remove the bolt in the same manner as in Step 6.

9   Remove the spring from under the vehicle.

10   If the spring eye bushings are worn or damaged, they must be

Fig. 11.1 Front suspension and steering components – F250 4x4 (without stabilizer bar) shown

1 Shock absorber
2 Drag link
3 Steering damper
4 Pitman arm
5 Tie-rod
6 Tie-rod ball stud
7 Spring/axle U-bolt
8 Leaf spring
9 Adjusting sleeve
10 Spindle pin
11 Spindle

11

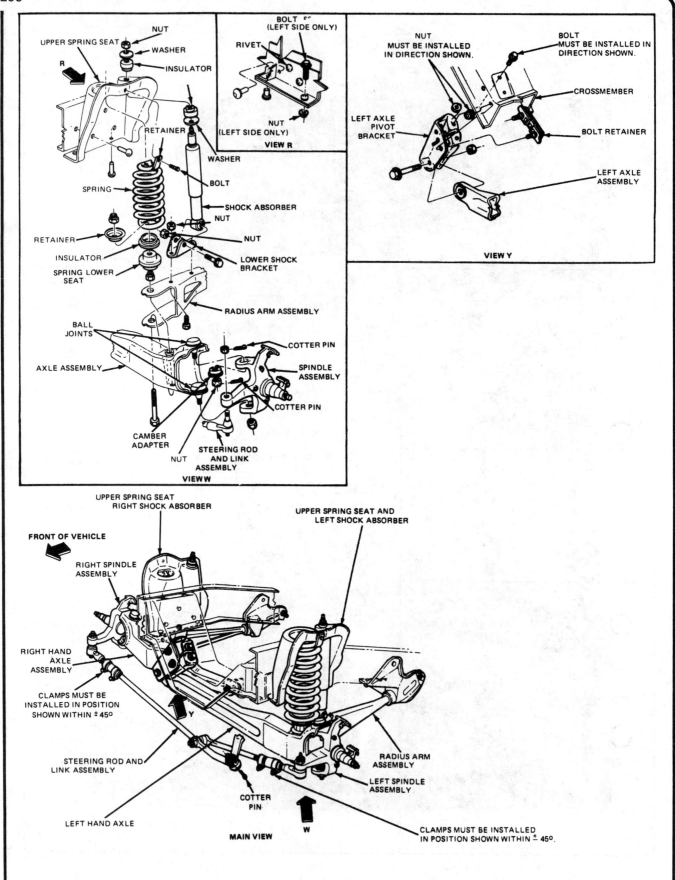

Fig. 11.2 Front suspension components – F100 through F350 4x2 with stamped axle (Secs 2, 4, 6, 8 and 10)

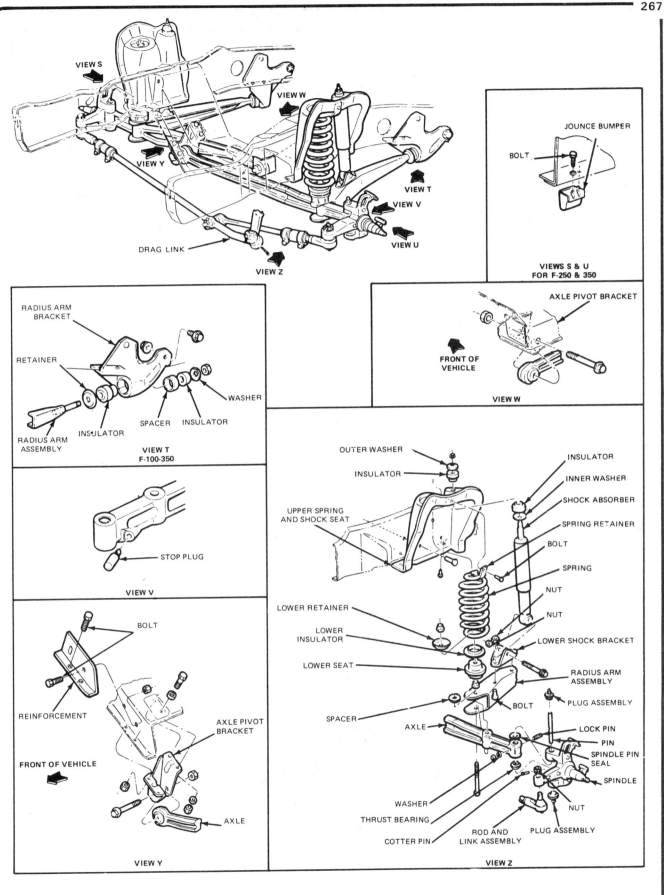

VIEW S

VIEW W

VIEW Y

VIEW T

VIEW V

VIEW U

DRAG LINK

VIEW Z

JOUNCE BUMPER

BOLT

VIEWS S & U
FOR F-250 & 350

RADIUS ARM
BRACKET

RETAINER

INSULATOR

WASHER

SPACER   INSULATOR

RADIUS ARM
ASSEMBLY

VIEW T
F-100-350

AXLE PIVOT BRACKET

FRONT OF
VEHICLE

VIEW W

STOP PLUG

VIEW V

BOLT

REINFORCEMENT

AXLE PIVOT
BRACKET

FRONT OF VEHICLE

AXLE

VIEW Y

OUTER WASHER

INSULATOR

UPPER SPRING
AND SHOCK SEAT

LOWER RETAINER

LOWER
INSULATOR

LOWER SEAT

SPACER

AXLE

WASHER

THRUST BEARING

COTTER PIN

ROD AND
LINK ASSEMBLY

INSULATOR

INNER WASHER

SHOCK ABSORBER

SPRING RETAINER

BOLT

SPRING

NUT

NUT

LOWER SHOCK BRACKET

RADIUS ARM
ASSEMBLY

PLUG ASSEMBLY

BOLT

LOCK PIN

PIN

SPINDLE PIN
SEAL

SPINDLE

NUT

PLUG ASSEMBLY

VIEW Z

Fig. 11.3 Front suspension components – F100 through F350 4x2 with forged axle (Secs 2, 4, 6, 8 and 10)

11

replaced by an automotive repair shop with the necessary hydraulic press and associated tools.

11 To install the spring, position it on the spring seat and install the lower shackle bolt through the shackle and spring. Tighten the nut to the specified torque.

12 Position the rear of the spring and install the hanger bolt through the hanger and spring. Tighten the nut to the specified torque.

13 Install the front spring plate spacer and install the U-bolts through the holes in the U-bolt spacer. Finger tighten the U-bolt nuts.

14 Connect the lower end of the shock absorber to the front spring plate spacer and tighten the nut and bolt to the specified torque.

15 Lower the vehicle to the ground and tighten the U-bolt nuts to the specified torque.

4   Front spindle and bushing (4x2) – removal and installation

Note: *Refer to Fig. 11.2 or Fig. 11.3 to locate components.*

Removal

All vehicles

1 Raise the front of the vehicle and place it securely on jackstands.

2 Remove the wheel and tire.

3 Remove the brake caliper (refer to Chapter 9) and support it out of the way with wire.

4 Remove the dust cap, cotter pin, nut retainer, nut, washer and outer bearing (refer to Chapter 1 if necessary).

5 Remove the rotor from the spindle (refer to Chapter 8 if necessary).

6 Remove the inner bearing cone and seal, and discard the seal.

7 Remove the brake dust shield.

8 Disconnect the steering linkage from the integral spindle and spindle arms by removing the cotter pin and nut.

9 Remove the tie-rod end from the spindle arm with an appropriate tie-rod puller.

Vehicles with forged front I-beam axles

10 Remove the nut and lock washer from the spindle pin lock pin, then remove the lock pin with a brass drift.

11 Remove the upper and lower spindle pin plugs.

12 Drive the spindle pin out of the top of the axle with a brass drift.

13 Remove the spindle from the axle.

14 Remove the spindle pin seal and thrust bearing from the axle.

Vehicles with stamped front I-beam axles

15 Remove the cotter pins from the upper and lower balljoint studs.

16 Remove the nuts from the upper and lower balljoint studs.

17 Using a hammer with a soft head, strike the inside of the spindle at the tapered bosses to pop the balljoints loose from the spindle. If this procedure fails to loosen the balljoints, strike the outside of the upper spindle, as shown in the accompanying illustration. **Note:** *Do not use a 'pickle fork' type tool to separate the balljoint from the spindle as this will damage the seal and the balljoint socket.*

18 Remove the spindle.

Installation

Vehicles with forged front I-beam axles

19 Check the spindle pin hole in the axle for nicks, burrs, corrosion and foreign matter. Clean up the bore as necessary and lightly coat the surface with grease.

20 Install a new spindle pin seal with the metal backing facing up, toward the bushing. Carefully press the seal into position, taking care not to distort the casing.

21 Install a new thrust bearing with the lip flange facing down, toward the lower bushing. Press the bearing until it is firmly seated against the surface of the spindle.

22 Lightly coat the bushing surfaces with grease and position the spindle on the axle.

23 Install the spindle pin with the end stamped with a T toward the top and the notch in the pin aligned with the lock pin hole in the axle.

24 Drive the pin through the bushings and the axle from the top until the spindle pin notch and the axle lock pin hole are aligned.

25 Install the lock pin with the threads pointing forward and the wedge groove facing the spindle pin notch. Drive the lock pin into position and install the lock washer and nut. Tighten the nut to the specified torque.

26 Install the spindle pin plugs in the threads at the top and bottom of the spindle. Tighten the plugs to the specified torque.

27 Using multi-purpose grease, lubricate the spindle pin and bushings

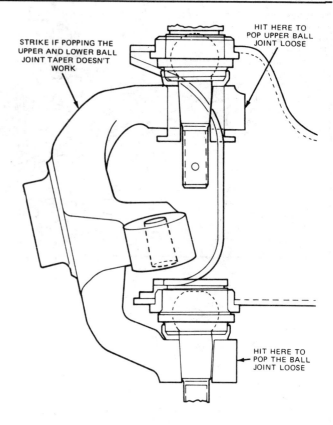

Fig. 11.4 Methods of loosening the upper and lower balljoints (Sec 4)

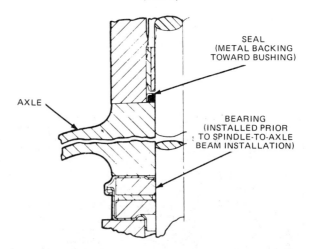

Fig. 11.5 Positioning of the spindle pin seal and thrust bearing (Sec 4)

through both fittings until grease is seen seeping past the upper seal at the top and from the thrust bearing slip joint at the bottom. If grease does not appear, recheck the installation procedure. **Note:** *Lack of proper lubrication will result in rapid failure of the spindle components.*

Vehicles with stamped front I-beam axles

28 Before installing the spindle, make sure the upper and lower balljoint rubber seals are in place.

29 Place the spindle over the balljoints.

30 Install the nut on the lower balljoint stud and partially tighten it to about 30 ft-lb. **Note:** *The lower nut must be installed first.*

31 Install the nut on the upper balljoint and tighten it to the specified torque. Hold the camber adapter with a wrench to keep the ball stud from turning. Continue tightening the castellated nut until the cotter pin can be inserted through the hole in the stud.

32 Tighten the lower nut to the specified torque, then advance the

castellated nut until the cotter pin can be inserted through the hole in the stud.

All vehicles

33 Install the brake dust shield.

34 Pack, install and adjust the front wheel bearing assembly (refer to Chapter 1).

35 Install the brake caliper.

36 Connect the steering linkage to the spindle and tighten the nut to the specified torque, then advance the castellated nut as required for installation of the cotter pin.

37 Install the wheel and tire and lower the vehicle.

5 Upper and lower balljoints – replacement

1 Remove the spindle (refer to Section 4).

2 Remove the snap-ring from both balljoints, using snap-ring pliers.

3 Using a C-clamp and a receiver cup (Ford no. D81T-3010-A or equivalent), install the apparatus over the upper balljoint, as illustrated, and turn the forcing screw on the clamp clockwise until the balljoint is removed from the axle.

4 Assemble the above apparatus on the lower balljoint and remove it in a like manner. **Note:** *Always remove the upper balljoint first.*

5 **Caution:** *Do not heat the balljoint or the axle to aid in removal as it will remove the temper from the axle.*

6 To install the lower balljoint, assemble a C-clamp, a receiver cup (Ford no. D81T-3010-A5 or equivalent), an installation cup (Ford no. D81T-3010-A1 or equivalent) and an inside cup (Ford no. D81T-3010-A4) over the new balljoint, as illustrated. Turn the forcing

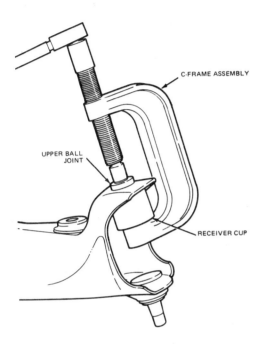

Fig. 11.6 Removing the upper balljoint (Sec 5)

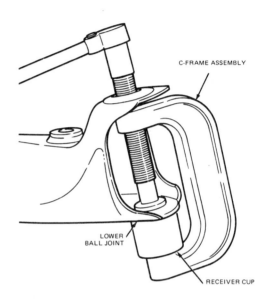

Fig. 11.7 Removing the lower balljoint (Sec 5)

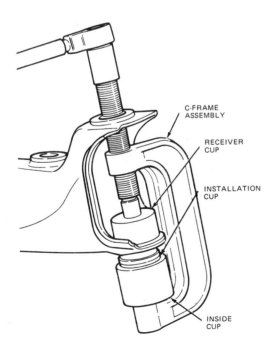

Fig. 11.8 Installing the lower balljoint (Sec 5)

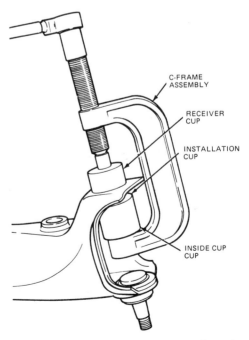

Fig. 11.9 Installing the upper balljoint (Sec 5)

11

screw on the clamp until the balljoint is seated, then install the snap-ring.

7   Assemble the above apparatus on the upper balljoint and install it in a like manner. Install the snap-ring. **Note:** *Always install the lower balljoint first.*

8   **Caution:** *Do not heat the balljoint or axle to aid in installation.*

9   Reinstall the spindle (refer to Section 4).

6 Front shock absorber – removal, inspection and installation

Note: *Refer to Fig. 11.2 or Fig. 11.3 to locate components.*

1   Chock the rear wheels, apply the parking brake, loosen the front wheel nuts, jack up the front of the vehicle and support it securely. Remove the wheel.

2   Remove the nut, washer and bushing from the top end of the shock absorber.

3   Remove the nut and bolt securing the bottom end of the shock absorber to the lower bracket.

4   Examine the shock absorber for signs of damage to the body, distorted piston rod, loose mounting or hydraulic fluid leakage which, if evident, means a new unit should be installed.

5   To test for shock absorber efficiency, hold the unit in a vertical position. Completely extend the piston rod and then invert the unit and completely compress it. Perform this sequence several times to work out any trapped air bubbles. Mount the bottom end of the shock absorber in a soft-jawed vise. Grasp the upper rod of the shock absorber, extend it fully and then contract it fully as rapidly as possible. The resistance should be smooth and uniform throughout the entire stroke in both directions. The resistance should be greater during the extension stroke than during the compression stroke. If there is erratic or notchy resistance during either stroke, or if the resistance is the same (or less) during the extension stroke, the shock absorbers should be replaced. The shock absorbers on each axle should have identical action and shock absorbers should always be replaced in pairs (on the same axle).

6   Installation is the reverse of removal. If old shock absorbers are being reinstalled (after being checked for correct operating action), the bushings should be replaced if there are any signs of deterioration or wear. New shock absorbers always come equipped with new bushings. When installing new bushings, never compress them beyond the diameter of the steel washers retaining them.

7 Steering damper – removal and installation

Note: *Refer to Fig. 11.10 to locate components.*

1   The steering damper is attached to the steering linkage on some 4-wheel-drive models. It is a specially calibrated shock absorber mounted horizontally and fastened to the frame on one end and the steering cross linkage on the other end.

2   The removal and installation procedure is the same as for a shock absorber with the exception of the location. When testing the damper, it should have the same resistance to compression as it does to extension. All other test and inspection procedures are the same as for a normal suspension shock absorber. Replace any worn or deteriorated grommets and tighten all mounting nuts and bolts to the specified torque.

8 Radius arm – replacement

4x2 vehicles

Note: *Refer to Fig. 11.2 or Fig. 11.3 to locate components.*

1   Jack up the front of the vehicle and support it securely.

2   Place a jack beneath the outer end of the axle and remove the wheel.

3   Disconnect the lower end of the shock absorber from the support bracket. Detach the front stabilizer bar (if equipped) at the link.

4   Remove the front spring using the method described in Section 2.

5   Remove the lower spring seat from the radius arm and then remove the nut and bolt securing the front of the radius arm to the axle.

6   Remove the nut, washer and rubber insulator from the rear end of the radius arm.

7   Push the front of the radius arm away from the front axle and withdraw it from the rear support bracket.

8   Remove the front retainer and rubber insulator from the rear of the radius arm and retrieve any shims that may be fitted.

9   Install the radius arm by reversing the procedure, ensuring that the

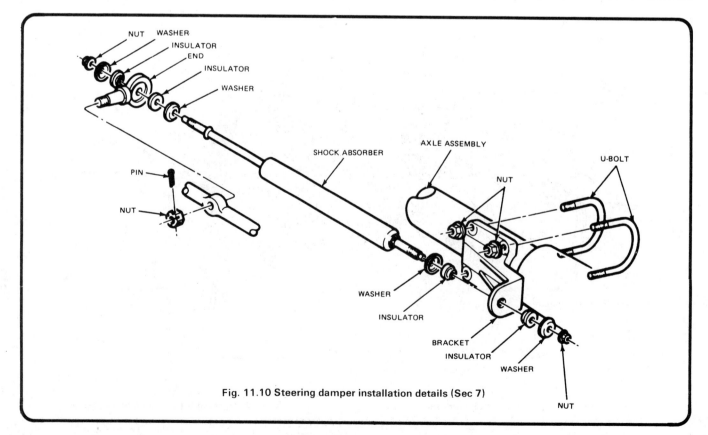

Fig. 11.10 Steering damper installation details (Sec 7)

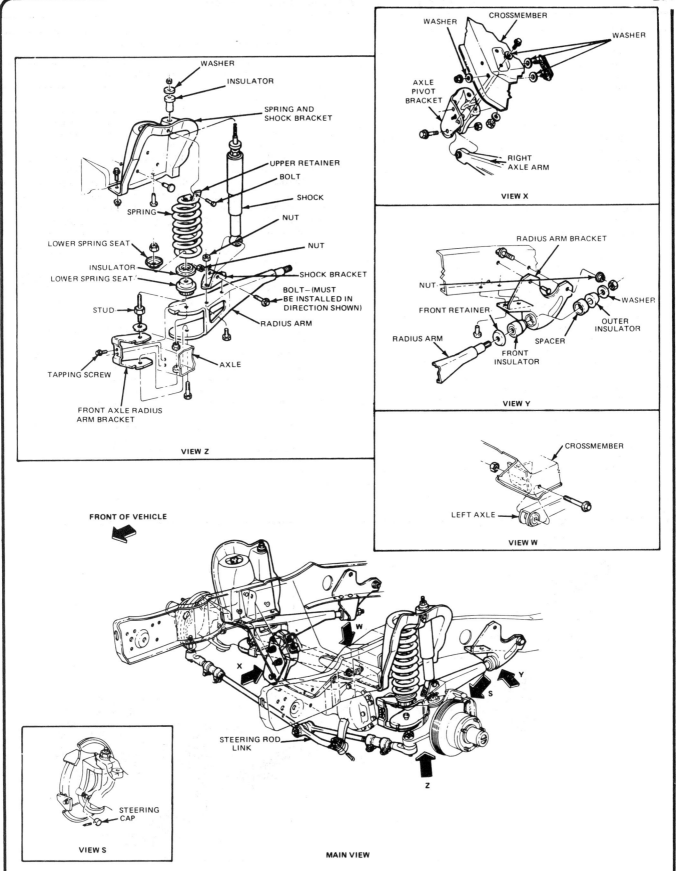

Fig. 11.11 Front suspension as installed on F150 4x4 and Bronco vehicles (Sec 8)

11

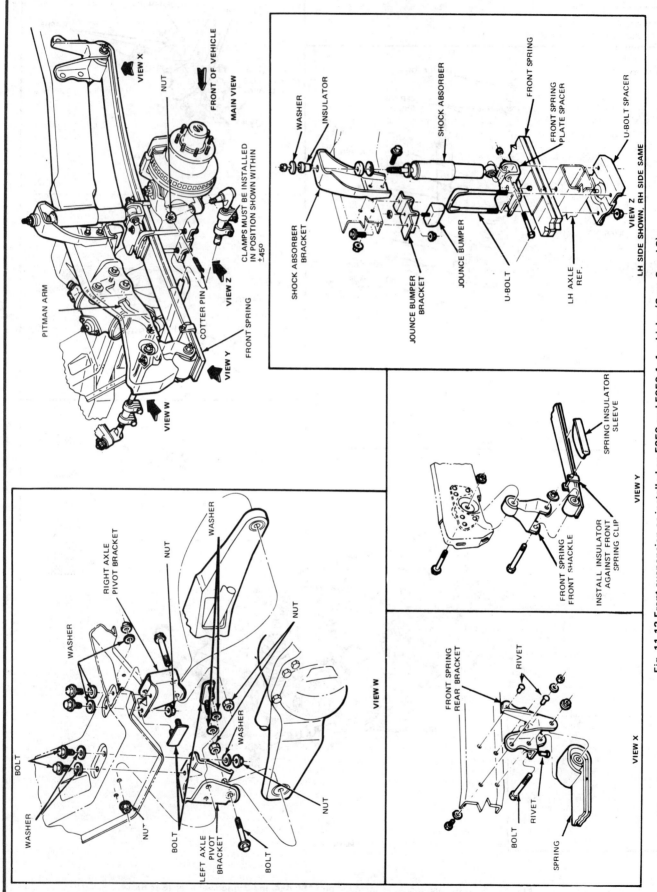

Fig. 11.12 Front suspension as installed on F250 and F350 4x4 vehicles (Secs 3 and 8)

rubber insulators are installed in the correct order. Tighten the radius arm-to-axle bolt to the specified torque and secure it with the cotter pin. Tighten the rear nut to the specified torque.
10 Have the front-end wheel alignment checked by your dealer or a suitably equipped shop.

F150 (4x4) and Bronco
Note: Refer to Fig. 11.11 to locate components.
11 Raise the front of the vehicle and position it on jackstands placed under the frame side rails. Remove the tire.
12 Using a floor jack, support the bottom of the axle to which the radius arm being worked on is attached. Note: The axle must be supported on the jack throughout the radius arm removal and installation procedures. If the brake hose is not long enough to provide clearance for removal and installation of the radius arm, the disc brake caliper must be removed (refer to Chapter 9). After removing the caliper, it must be hung on the frame or otherwise supported to prevent suspending the caliper by the brake hose.
13 Remove the shock absorber-to-lower bracket attaching bolt and nut, then pull the shock absorber off the radius arm. Detach the front stabilizer bar (if equipped) at the link.
14 Remove the spring lower attaching bolt from the inside of the coil spring.
15 Loosen the appropriate axle pivot bolt.
16 Remove the nut retaining the radius arm to the frame bracket, then remove the radius arm rear plastic spacer, the insulator and the washer.
17 Remove the two self-tapping screws that retain the front axle-to-radius arm bracket to the axle tube.
18 Remove the bolt and stud retaining the radius arm to the axle.
19 Move the axle forward by carefully moving the jack supporting the axle, then remove the radius arm from the axle.
20 Remove the rear of the radius arm from the frame bracket then remove the front insulator and retainer.
21 Clean all mating surfaces between the radius arm, axle and bracket prior to installation.
22 To install the arm, place the front insulator and retainer on the rear of the radius arm and insert the arm into the frame bracket.
23 Place the rear spacer, insulator and washer on the radius arm and loosely install the retaining nut.
24 Position the radius arm and front axle-to-radius arm bracket on the axle.
25 Loosely install a new stud and bolt attaching the radius arm to the axle. Note: A new stud and bolt are required because of the adhesive coating on the original parts. If new fasteners are not available, thoroughly clean the old parts and apply Loctite No. 242 (or equivalent) to the threads of the fasteners.
26 The remaining installation steps are the reverse of the removal procedure. Be sure to tighten all nuts and bolts to the specified torque. Note: It is important that the shock absorber-to-lower bracket retaining bolt is installed with the bolt head toward the tire to maximize clearance to the brake system components.
27 Have the front end wheel alignment checked by an alignment shop.

9 Front stabilizer bar – removal and installation

F100 – F350 (4x2) vehicles
Note: Refer to Fig. 11.13 to locate components.
1 Raise the front of the vehicle and place it securely on jackstands.
2 Disconnect the right and left ends of the stabilizer bar from the link assembly attached to the I-beam bracket.
3 Disconnect the retainer bolts and remove the stabilizer bar.
4 Disconnect the stabilizer link assemblies by loosening the right and left locknuts from their respective I-beam brackets.
5 To install the bar, loosely assemble all stabilizer bar components, with both link assemblies outboard of the stabilizer bar. Note: To help identify the left and right link assemblies, an R or L is stamped on the shaft of the link. Force the stabilizer bar to the rear to connect the bar ends to the link assemblies.
6 Tighten the nuts and bolts retaining the link assemblies to the stabilizer bar and axle brackets.
7 Check to be sure the insulators are seated in the retainers and that the stabilizer bar is centered in the assembly.

8 Tighten the stabilizer bar-to-frame retainer nuts and bolts and the frame mounting bracket nuts and bolts to the specified torque.
9 Remove the jackstands and lower the vehicle.

Bronco and F150 (4x4) vehicles
Note: Refer to Fig. 11.14 to locate components.
10 Raise the front of the vehicle and place it securely on jackstands.
11 Remove the nuts, bolts and washers connecting the stabilizer bar to the connecting links.
12 Remove the nuts and bolts attaching the stabilizer bar retainers to the crossmember (and frame bracket if equipped with the Sno-Fiter option).
13 If the upper link mounting bracket is bent or otherwise damaged, the coil spring must be removed as described in Section 2.
14 Remove the lower spring seat after removing the spring. The bracket attaching stud and bracket can now be removed.
15 To install the upper link mounting bracket, locate it so that the locating tang is positioned in the radius arm notch (or quad shock bracket notch, if so equipped).
16 Install a new bracket attaching stud and tighten it to the specified torque. Note: A new stud is required because of the adhesive on the threads. If a new stud is not available, thoroughly clean the old one and apply Loctite no. 242 (or equivalent) to the threads.
17 Install the lower spring seat and install the spring and retainers (refer to Section 2).
18 If the crossmember bracket (to which the stabilizer bar retainer and insulator were bolted) is bent or damaged, remove it by removing the remaining nut and bolt. Replace it with a new one, tightening the retaining nut and bolt to the specified torque.
19 If the vehicle is equipped with the optional Sno-Fiter and the frame bracket (to which a retainer and insulator were attached) is damaged, unbolt the bracket and flange to which it was bolted and replace them with new ones. Tighten the retaining bolts to the specified torque.
20 Inspect all components including the insulators for wear or damage and replace any worn or damaged parts with new ones.
21 To install the stabilizer bar, attach all nuts, bolts and washers loosely to the bar, brackets, retainers and links.
22 With the bar positioned correctly, first tighten the insulator retainer bolts, then tighten the nuts at the link assemblies to the specified torque.
23 Remove the jackstands and lower the vehicle.

F250 and 350 (4x4) vehicles
Note: Refer to Fig. 11.15 to locate components.
24 Raise the front of the vehicle and place it securely on jackstands.
25 Remove the nuts, bolts and washers securing the link assemblies to the spring seat caps on both sides of the vehicle.
26 Remove the nuts and bolts securing the insulator retainers to the stabilizer bar mounting brackets and remove the retainers.
27 Remove the stabilizer bar from the vehicle.
28 Inspect all components for wear and damage and replace any worn or damaged parts with new ones.
29 To install the stabilizer bar, reinstall the components in the reverse order of removal without tightening the fasteners.
30 In order, tighten the nuts connecting the links to the spring seats on both sides, the nuts connecting the links to the stabilizer bar and the nuts and bolts connecting the retainers to the mounting brackets.
31 Remove the jackstands and lower the vehicle.

10 Front I-beam axle – removal and installation

Note: Refer to Fig. 11.2 or Fig. 11.3 to locate components. The following procedure is for 4x2 vehicles. The procedure for 4x4 vehicle front axle removal and installation is described in Chapter 8.
1 Raise the vehicle and support the frame securely on jackstands.
2 Remove the front wheel spindle from the axle using the procedure described in Section 4.
3 Remove the front spring as described in Section 2.
4 Remove the stabilizer bar (if equipped) as described in Section 9.
5 Remove the lower spring seat from the radius arm and remove the nut and bolt securing the front of the radius arm to the axle.
6 Remove the nut and bolt securing the end of the axle to the pivot bracket and withdraw the axle from beneath the vehicle.
7 Examine the bushings and pivot bolt for wear and replace it if

11

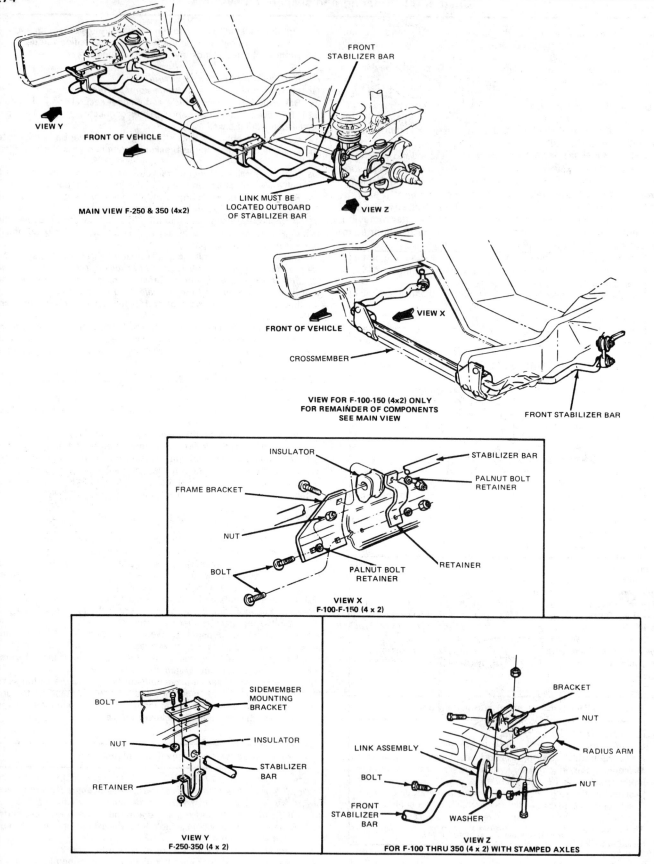

FRONT STABILIZER BAR

VIEW Y

FRONT OF VEHICLE

MAIN VIEW F-250 & 350 (4x2)

LINK MUST BE LOCATED OUTBOARD OF STABILIZER BAR

VIEW Z

FRONT OF VEHICLE

VIEW X

CROSSMEMBER

VIEW FOR F-100-150 (4x2) ONLY FOR REMAINDER OF COMPONENTS SEE MAIN VIEW

FRONT STABILIZER BAR

INSULATOR

STABILIZER BAR

PALNUT BOLT RETAINER

FRAME BRACKET

NUT

BOLT

PALNUT BOLT RETAINER

RETAINER

VIEW X
F-100-F-150 (4 x 2)

BOLT

SIDEMEMBER MOUNTING BRACKET

NUT

INSULATOR

STABILIZER BAR

RETAINER

VIEW Y
F-250-350 (4 x 2)

BRACKET

NUT

RADIUS ARM

LINK ASSEMBLY

BOLT

NUT

FRONT STABILIZER BAR

WASHER

VIEW Z
FOR F-100 THRU 350 (4 x 2) WITH STAMPED AXLES

Fig. 11.13 Front stabilizer bar installation on 4x2 vehicles (Sec 9)

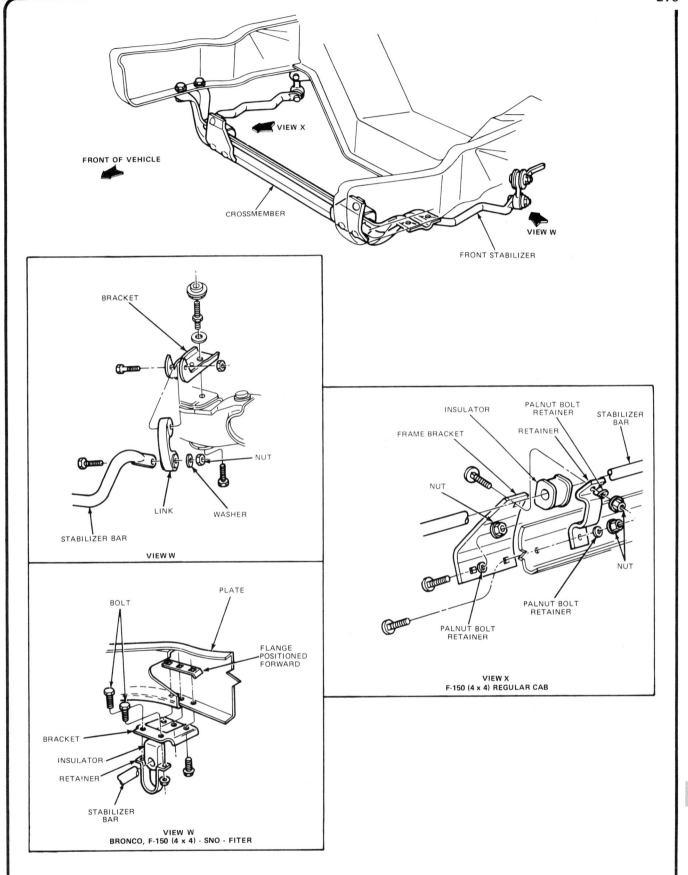

Fig. 11.14 Front stabilizer bar installation on F150 4x4 and Bronco vehicles (Sec 9)

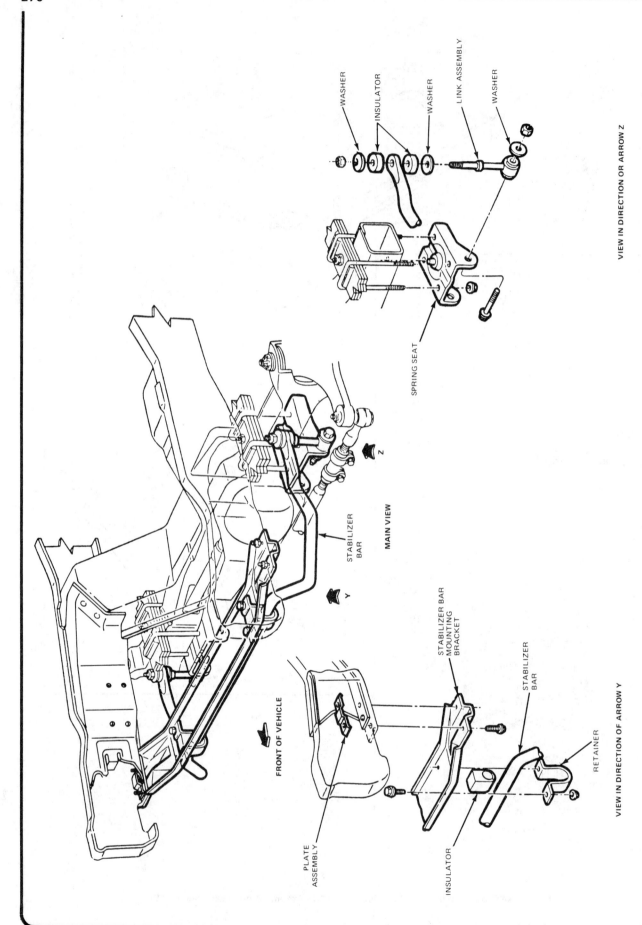

WASHER
INSULATOR
WASHER
LINK ASSEMBLY
WASHER

VIEW IN DIRECTION OR ARROW Z

SPRING SEAT

MAIN VIEW

STABILIZER BAR

Z

Y

FRONT OF VEHICLE

PLATE ASSEMBLY

STABILIZER BAR MOUNTING BRACKET

INSULATOR

STABILIZER BAR

RETAINER

VIEW IN DIRECTION OF ARROW Y

Fig. 11.15 Front stabilizer bar installation on F250 and F350 4x4 vehicles (Sec 9)

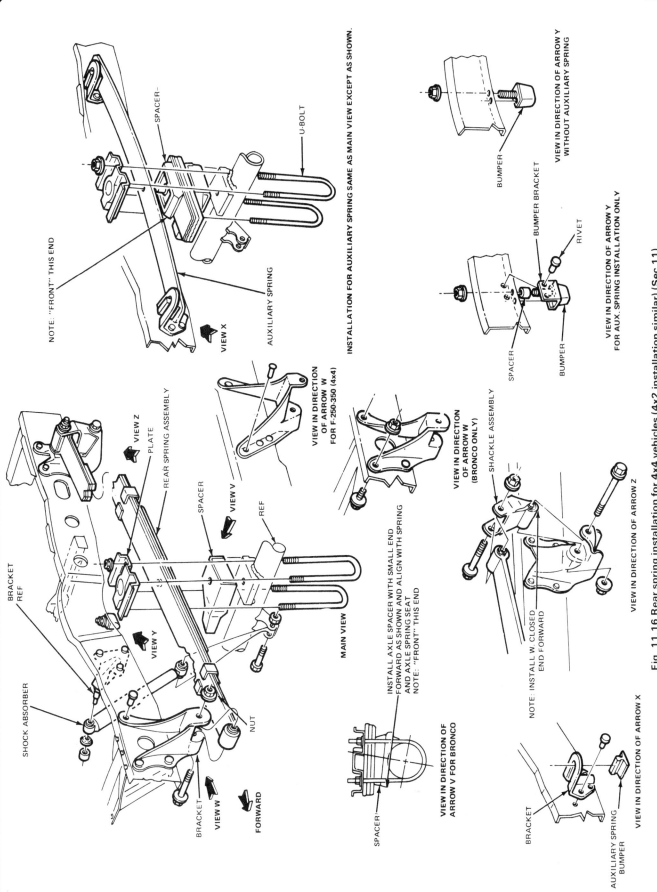

Fig. 11.16 Rear spring installation for 4x4 vehicles (4x2 installation similar) (Sec 11)

11

necessary. If the axle is bent, take it to a Ford dealer or alignment specialist with the necessary equipment for straightening it.
8   Install the axle by reversing the removal procedure. Tighten the nuts to the specified torque.

11   Rear leaf spring – removal and installation

Note: Refer to Fig. 11.16 to locate components.
1   Raise the vehicle until the weight is off the rear spring being worked on, but the tire is still touching the ground.
2   Place the frame securely on jackstands.
3   Remove the nuts from the spring U-bolts and drive the U-bolts from the U-bolt plate.
4   If so equipped, remove the auxiliary spring and spacer.
5   Remove the spring-to-bracket nut at the front of the spring and drive the bolt out of the spring eye bushing. If the bolt is to be reused, use a soft brass drift so that the bolt is not damaged.
6   Remove the spring shackle upper and lower nuts, and remove the bolts in the same manner as in Step 5.
7   Remove the spring and shackle assembly from the rear shackle bracket.
8   Remove the spring from under the vehicle.
9   If the spring eye bushings are worn or damaged, they must be replaced by an automotive repair shop with the necessary hydraulic press and associated tools.
10   To install the spring, position the rear of the spring in the shackle and install the upper shackle-to-spring bolt and nut with the bolt head facing out. Finger tighten the nut.
11   Position the front of the spring in the bracket and install the bolt and nut. Finger tighten the nut.
12   Position the shackle in the rear bracket and install the bolt and nut.
13   Position the spring on top of the axle with the spring tie bolt centered in the hole in the seat.
14   If so equipped, install the auxiliary spring and spacer.
15   Install the spring U-bolts, U-bolt plate and nuts. Finger tighten the nuts.
16   Lower the vehicle to the ground, then, in order, tighten the U-bolt nuts, the front spring nut and bolt and the rear shackle bolts and nuts to the specified torque.

12   Rear shock absorber – removal and installation

1   Chock the front wheels. Raise the rear of the vehicle and support it securely on jackstands.
2   Remove the shock absorber lower attaching nut (photo) and pull it free of the mounting bracket.
3   Remove the securing nut from the upper mounting stud and withdraw the shock absorber from the vehicle.

12.2 Rear shock absorber mounting (F250 4x4 shown, others similar)

4   Examination and testing of the rear shock absorber is similar to that for the front shock absorber. Refer to Section 6.
5   Installation of the rear shock absorber is the reverse of removal, but be sure to tighten the mounting nuts to the specified torque.

13   Rear stabilizer bar – removal and installation

Note: Refer to Fig. 11.17 or Fig. 11.18 to locate components.
1   Raise the rear of the vehicle and place it securely on jackstands.
2   Remove the nut from the lower end of the stabilizer bar link.
3   Remove the outer washer and insulator.
4   Disconnect the stabilizer bar from the link.
5   Remove the inner insulators and washers and disconnect the link from the frame by removing the retaining nuts and bolts.
6   Remove the nuts which attach the retainer and bracket to the U-bolt, then remove the U-bolt and stabilizer bar.
7   Installation is the reverse of the removal procedure. Tighten the nuts and bolts to the specified torque.

14   Steering gear systems – general information

The manual steering gear for all vehicles covered by this manual is a recirculating ball-nut type, with the steering shaft, worm shaft and ball nut all in line.
The steering shaft and worm shaft are separated by a flexible coupling which permits removal of the gearbox assembly or steering shaft (with column) independent of one another.
The mechanical element of the steering gearbox is a low-friction, high-efficiency, recirculating ball system in which steel balls act as a rolling thread between the steering worm and ball nut. The one-piece ball nut is geared to the sector shaft and the lash between the sector shaft and rack of the ball nut is controlled by an adjusting screw through the sector cover which is retained in the end of the sector shaft.
The power steering system installed in all vehicles with which this manual is concerned employs a Ford C-II pump, which is a belt-driven slipper type with a fiberglass nylon reservoir attached to the rear side of the pump housing front plate. The pump body is encased within the housing and reservoir. The pressure hose is attached with a quick-connect fitting, located below the filler neck at the outboard side of the reservoir, which allows the line to swivel. This is normal and does not indicate a loose fitting.
The pump supplies fluid under pressure to an integral power steering gearbox of the torsion-bar feedback type. This gearbox is designed with a one-piece rack piston, with the worm and sector shaft in one housing and the rotary valve assembly in an attached housing. This makes possible internal fluid passages between the valve and the power cylinder, eliminating all external hoses except the pressure and return lines between the pump and the gearbox.
Due to the complexity of the power steering system and the special tools required to work on its components, servicing and adjustments described here are limited to those operations that can readily be performed by the home mechanic. Any other work should be referred to a dealership or other reputable automotive repair shop specializing in this type of work.

15   Steering gearbox – check and adjustment

1   Check the reservoir fluid level (if so equipped).
2   Check the steering linkage for wear if there is looseness present in the steering.
3   If the looseness is traceable to wear in the steering box, check and adjust it as follows:

Manual steering
Note: Refer to Fig. 11.19 to locate components.
4   Remove the Pitman arm from the steering gear sector shaft using an appropriate puller. Caution: Do not hammer on the end of the sector shaft.
5   Lubricate the worm shaft seal with a drop of power steering fluid.
6   Remove the horn pad assembly from the steering wheel.
7   Be sure the steering column is properly aligned, so that no resistance to turning is induced by column binding.

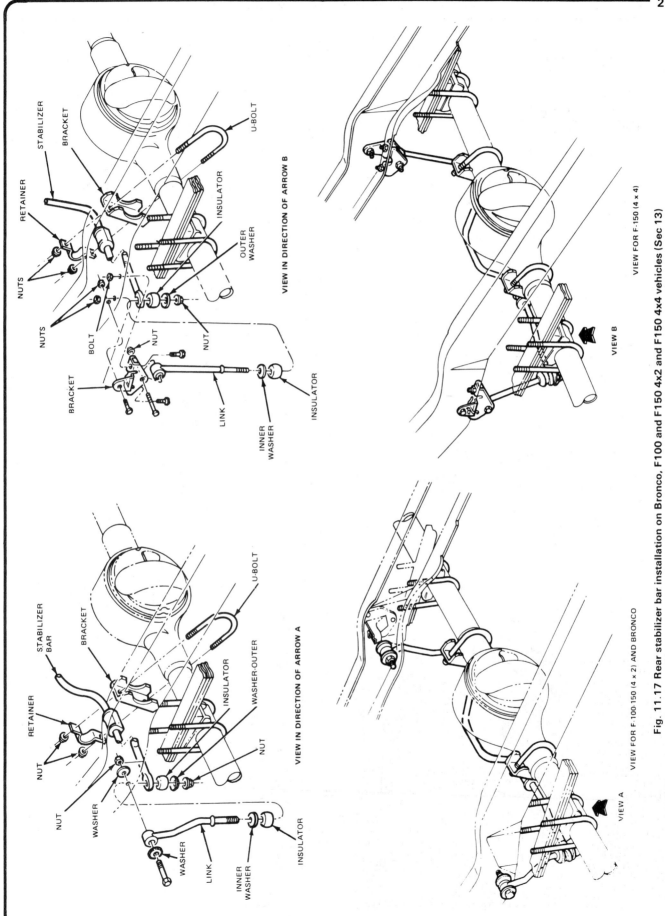

STABILIZER
RETAINER
BRACKET
U-BOLT
NUTS
INSULATOR
OUTER WASHER
NUTS
BOLT
NUT
NUT
BRACKET
LINK
INNER WASHER
INSULATOR
VIEW IN DIRECTION OF ARROW B

VIEW FOR F-150 (4 x 4)

VIEW B

STABILIZER BAR
BRACKET
RETAINER
U-BOLT
NUT
INSULATOR
WASHER-OUTER
NUT
NUT
WASHER
WASHER
LINK
INNER WASHER
INSULATOR
VIEW IN DIRECTION OF ARROW A

VIEW FOR F-100-150 (4 x 2) AND BRONCO

VIEW A

Fig. 11.17 Rear stabilizer bar installation on Bronco, F100 and F150 4x2 and F150 4x4 vehicles (Sec 13)

11

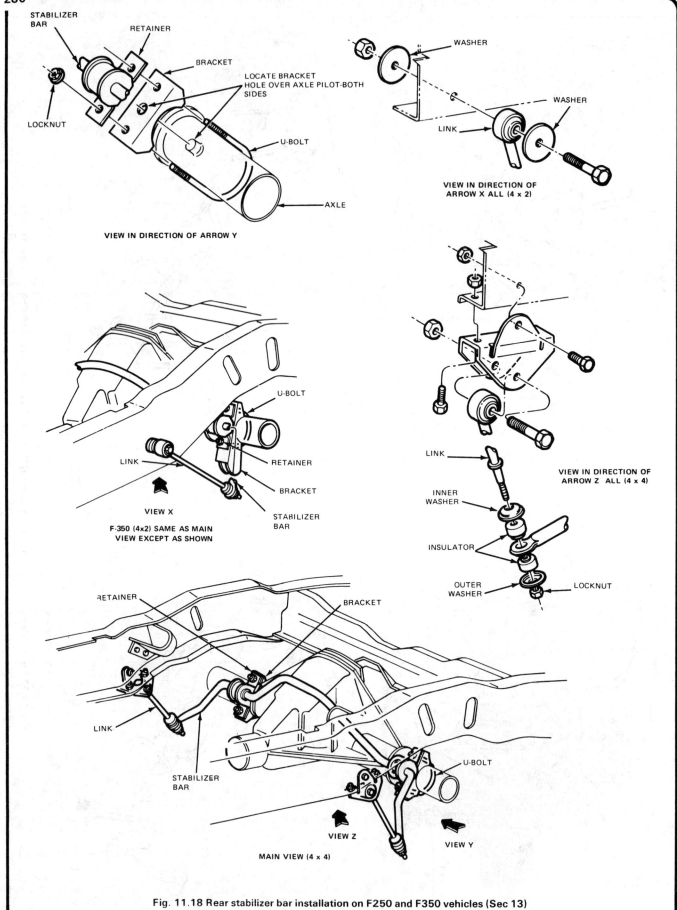

STABILIZER BAR

RETAINER

BRACKET

LOCATE BRACKET HOLE OVER AXLE PILOT-BOTH SIDES

LOCKNUT

U-BOLT

AXLE

VIEW IN DIRECTION OF ARROW Y

WASHER

WASHER

LINK

VIEW IN DIRECTION OF ARROW X ALL (4 x 2)

U-BOLT

LINK

RETAINER

BRACKET

STABILIZER BAR

VIEW X

F-350 (4x2) SAME AS MAIN VIEW EXCEPT AS SHOWN

LINK

INNER WASHER

INSULATOR

OUTER WASHER

LOCKNUT

VIEW IN DIRECTION OF ARROW Z ALL (4 x 4)

RETAINER

BRACKET

LINK

STABILIZER BAR

U-BOLT

VIEW Z

VIEW Y

MAIN VIEW (4 x 4)

Fig. 11.18 Rear stabilizer bar installation on F250 and F350 vehicles (Sec 13)

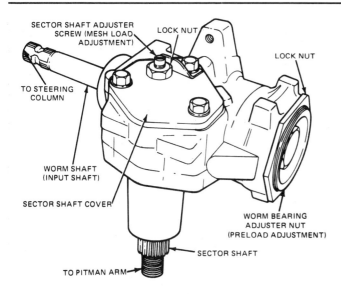

Fig. 11.19 Manual steering gearbox components (Sec 15)

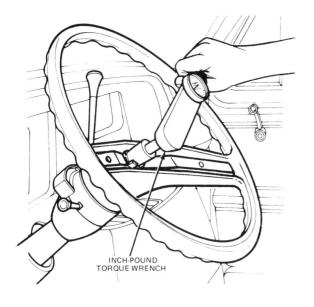

Fig. 11.20 Checking the manual steering gear preload (Sec 15)

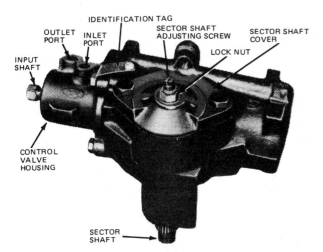

Fig. 11.21 Integral power steering gearbox components (Sec 15)

8   Turn the steering wheel all the way to one side.
9   Place an in-lb torque wrench on the steering wheel nut and measure the lowest torque required to turn the wheel at a constant rate. This is the worm bearing preload.
10 Check that the torque is within the Specifications. If not, remove the steering gear from the vehicle (refer to Section 15).
11 Be sure that the sector cover bolts are tightened to the specified torque.
12 Loosen the preload adjuster locknut and tighten the worm bearing adjuster nut until all end play has been removed.
13 Using an $\frac{11}{16}$-inch, 12-point socket and an in-lb torque wrench, carefully turn the worm shaft all the way to the right and then turn it back about one-half turn.
14 Tighten the adjuster nut until the specified worm bearing preload is obtained.
15 Tighten the adjuster nut locknut to the specified torque.
16 Rotate the worm shaft from stop-to-stop, counting the total number of turns, then turn the shaft back half way, placing the gear on center.
17 Loosen the sector shaft adjuster locknut by turning it in a counterclockwise direction.
18 Turn the sector shaft adjuster screw clockwise to remove all lash between the ball nut and the sector teeth, then tighten the sector shaft locknut to the specified torque.
19 Using an $\frac{11}{16}$-inch, 12-point socket and an in-lb torque wrench, observe the highest reading while the gear is turned through the center position. This is the backlash measurement.
20 Check that the backlash is within the Specifications.
21 If necessary, repeat Steps 17 through 19 until the proper backlash is obtained.
22 Reinstall the steering gear.
23 Reinstall the Pitman arm and tighten the retaining nut to the specified torque.

Power steering
Note: Refer to Fig. 11.21 to locate components.
24 Remove the Pitman arm and the steering wheel hub cover. Disconnect and plug the fluid return line at the reservoir.
25 Place the fluid return line in a suitable container and turn the steering wheel lock-to-lock several times to discharge all of the fluid from the steering gear.
26 Turn the shaft back 45° from the left stop and attach a torque wrench calibrated in inch-pounds to the steering wheel nut.
27 Rotate the steering gear about one-eighth of a turn and then move it back across the center position several times. Loosen the adjuster locknut and turn the adjuster screw until the specified torque reading is reached when the steering gear is rotated through the over-center position.
28 Hold the screw and tighten the nut.
29 Install the Pitman arm and steering wheel center cover. Reconnect the fluid return line and refill the reservoir. Be sure the Pitman arm retaining nut is tightened to the specified torque.

---

16 Steering gearbox – removal and installation

Manual steering
Note: Refer to Fig. 11.22 to locate components.
1   Raise the front of the vehicle and place it securely on jackstands.
2   Disengage the flex coupling shield from the steering gear input shaft shield and slide it up the intermediate shaft.
3   Disconnect the flex coupling from the intermediate steering shaft flange by removing the attaching bolts.
4   Using an appropriate tie-rod end remover, disconnect the drag link from the Pitman arm.
5   Remove the Pitman arm-to-sector shaft attaching nut and washer.
6   Using an appropriate puller, remove the Pitman arm from the steering gear sector shaft. Caution: Do not hammer on the end of the sector shaft or tool.
7   While supporting the steering gear, remove the bolts and washers that attach the steering gear to the frame rail.
8   Lower the steering gear assembly out of the vehicle.
9   Remove the coupling-to-gear attaching bolt from the lower half of the flex coupling and remove the coupling from the assembly.
10 To install the gearbox, position the flex coupling on the input shaft of the steering gear. Note: Be sure to use a new coupling-to-gear

11

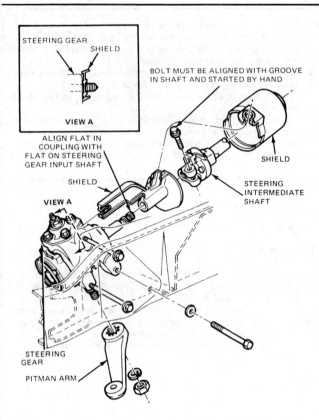

Fig. 11.22 Manual steering gearbox installation (Sec 16)

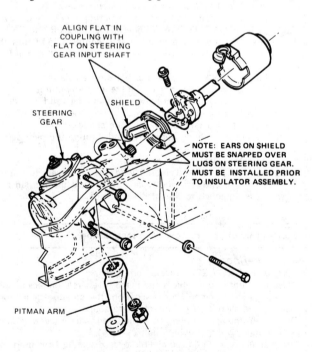

Fig. 11.23 Power steering gearbox installation (Sec 16)

attaching bolt and tighten it to the specified torque.
11 Center the input shaft (the center position is approximately three turns from either stop).
12 Position the steering gear assembly so that the stud bolts on the flex coupling enter the bolt holes in the steering shaft flange and the holes in the mounting bosses of the gearbox match the bolt holes in the frame rail.
13 While supporting the gearbox in the proper position, install the gearbox-to-frame rail attaching bolts and washers and tighten the

bolts to the specified torque. **Note:** *If new bolts and washers are required, be sure that they are Grade 9.*
14 Connect the drag link to the Pitman arm, install the drag link ball stud nut and tighten the nut to the specified torque. Install a new cotter pin.
15 Place the Pitman arm on the sector shaft, pointing down. Install the attaching nut and washer and tighten the nut to the specified torque.
16 Attach the flex coupling to the steering shaft flange with the two attaching nuts and tighten the nuts to the specified torque.
17 Snap the flex coupling shield to the steering gear input shaft shield.
18 Remove the jackstands and lower the vehicle.

Power steering
Note: *Refer to Fig. 11.23 to locate components.*
19 Place a drain pan under the steering gearbox.
20 Disconnect the pressure and return lines from the gearbox and plug the lines and the ports in the gearbox to prevent contamination.
21 Disengage the flex coupling shield from the splash shield.
22 Disconnect the flex coupling at the steering gearbox by removing the retaining bolt.
23 Raise the front of the vehicle and place it securely on jackstands.
24 Using an appropriate tie-rod end remover, disconnect the tie-rod from the Pitman arm.
25 Remove the nut and washer attaching the Pitman arm to the sector shaft.
26 Using an appropriate puller, remove the Pitman arm from the sector shaft. **Caution:** *Be very careful not to damage the seals.*
27 Support the steering gearbox and remove the steering gearbox-to-frame rail attaching bolts.
28 Work the steering gearbox free of the flex coupling and remove steering gearbox from the vehicle.
29 Remove the splash shield from the retaining lugs on the steering gearbox.
30 To install the gearbox, position the splash shield over the gearbox lugs.
31 Turn the steering wheel so that the spokes are in the horizontal position.
32 Slide the flex coupling into position on the steering shaft assembly.
33 Center the steering gear input shaft with the index flat facing down (the center position is approximately three turns from either stop).
34 Slide the steering gear input shaft into the flex coupling and the gearbox into place on the frame rail.
35 Install the flex coupling attaching bolt and tighten it to the specified torque.
36 Install the gearbox-to-frame rail attaching bolts and tighten them to the specified torque.
37 Be sure that the wheels are in the straight ahead position, then install the Pitman arm on the sector shaft.
38 Install the Pitman arm attaching washer and nut and tighten the nut to the specified torque.
39 Attach the drag link to the Pitman arm, install the retaining nut and tighten it to the specified torque. Install a new cotter pin.
40 Remove the jackstands and lower the vehicle.
41 Install and tighten the pressure and return lines. Be sure you have removed the plugs from the lines and ports.
42 Snap the flex coupling shield over the hose fittings and the splash shield.
43 Disconnect the coil wire from the distributor.
44 Fill the power steering fluid reservoir, then turn on the ignition and turn the steering wheel from lock-to-lock to distribute the fluid.
45 Recheck the fluid level and add more if necessary.
46 Connect the coil wire, start the engine and turn the steering wheel from side-to-side.
47 Inspect for leaks.

---

17 Power steering system – bleeding

1 If bubbles are visible in the power steering fluid, the air in the system should be bled off.
2 Fill the reservoir as described in Chapter 1.
3 Run the engine until the fluid reaches normal operating temperature (165° to 175°F or 74° to 79°C).

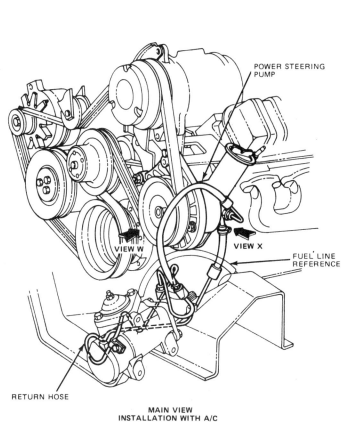

POWER STEERING PUMP

VIEW W

VIEW X

FUEL LINE REFERENCE

RETURN HOSE

MAIN VIEW
INSTALLATION WITH A/C

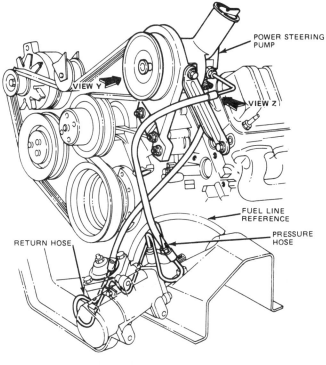

POWER STEERING PUMP

VIEW Y

VIEW Z

FUEL LINE REFERENCE

RETURN HOSE

PRESSURE HOSE

MAIN VIEW
INSTALLATION WITHOUT A/C

PULLEY

POWER STEERING PUMP

BOLT

PRESSURE HOSE

RETURN HOSE

BRACKET

VIEW IN DIRECTION OF ARROW W

BRACKET

A/C BRACKET REFERENCE

SPACER

BRACKET

BOLT

VIEW IN DIRECTION OF ARROW X

POWER STEERING PUMP

PULLEY GROOVE

BRACKET

PRESSURE HOSE

RETURN HOSE

VIEW IN DIRECTION OF ARROW Y

BRACKET

BRACKET

WATER PUMP REFERENCE

VIEW IN DIRECTION OF ARROW Z

11

Fig. 11.24 Power steering pump installation on vehicles equipped with a V6 engine (Sec 18)

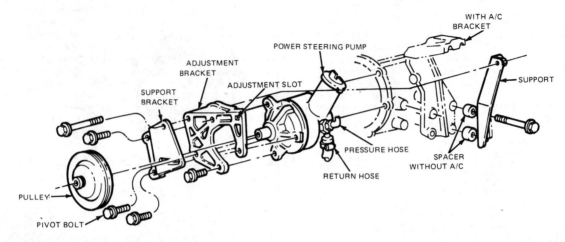

Fig. 11.25 Power steering pump installation on vehicles equipped with an in-line six-cylinder engine (Sec 18)

4   Turn the steering wheel lock-to-lock several times. **Note:** *Do not hold the wheel all the way to the left or right for more than five seconds or you may damage the pump.*
5   Recheck the fluid level and add more as necessary.

18 Power steering pump – removal and installation

Note: *Refer to Figs. 11.24 through 11.27 to locate components.*
1   Remove the power steering fluid from the pump reservoir by disconnecting the fluid return hose at the reservoir and draining the fluid into a suitable container.
2   Disconnect the pressure hose from the pump.
3   Remove the bolts from the pump adjustment bracket.
4   Loosen the pump enough to allow removal of the belt from the pulley.
5   Remove the pump (still attached to the adjustment bracket) from the support bracket and from the vehicle.
6   If the pulley and adjustment bracket are to be removed from the pump, follow Steps 7 through 14.
7   Drain as much fluid as possible from the pump through the filler pipe.
8   Place the pump in a bench vise.
9   Attach a suitable pulley removal tool. On pulleys with a diameter of $1\frac{3}{8}$ inches, use Ford no. T69L-10300-A or equivalent. On pulleys with a diameter of $1\frac{1}{8}$ inches, use Ford no. T75L-3733-A or equivalent.
10 Rotate the tool nut counterclockwise to remove the pulley, then

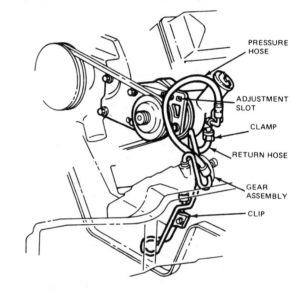

Fig. 11.26 Power steering pump installation on vehicles equipped with a V8 engine (except 460) – typical (Sec 18)

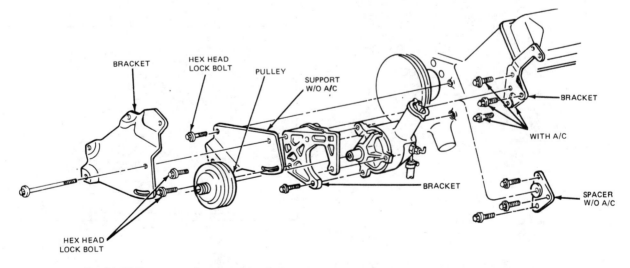

Fig. 11.27 Power steering pump installation on vehicles equipped with a 460 V8 engine (Sec 18)

remove the bolts attaching the adjustment bracket to the pump and remove the bracket.

11 To install the pump, place the adjustment bracket on the pump and install and tighten the retaining bolts to the specified torque.

12 Attach a suitable pulley installation tool. On pulleys with a diameter of $1\frac{3}{8}$ inches, use Ford no. T65P-3A733-C or equivalent. On pulleys with a diameter of $1\frac{1}{8}$ inches, use Ford no. T75L-3733-A or equivalent.

13 Rotate the tool nut clockwise to install the pulley on the shaft. **Caution**: *Do not apply in-and-out pressure on the shaft as such pressure will damage the internal pump components.* When properly installed, the pulley hub face must be flush within plus or minus 0.010 inch of the end of the pump shaft.

14 Place the pump with the attached pulley and adjustment bracket on the support bracket.

15 Install the bolts connecting the support bracket to the adjustment bracket and tighten them securely.

16 Place the belt on the pulley and adjust the belt tension as described in Chapter 1. **Note**: *Do not pry against the reservoir. Pressure on the fiberglass reservoir will cause it to crack.*

17 Attach the pressure hose to the pump fitting.

18 Connect the return hose to the pump and tighten the clamp.

19 Fill the reservoir and bleed the system (refer to Section 17).

20 Check for leaks and recheck the fluid level, adding fluid if necessary.

19 Steering linkage – removal and installation

Note: *Refer to Figs. 11.28 through 11.30 to locate components.*

1 Steering linkages for Ford pick-ups and Broncos come in many configurations and combinations, depending on drive axle, suspension type and load carrying capabilities. They are all of a common type and consist of a connecting link with either two ball-type links on either end or one ball-type link and a male or female thread (photo).

2 If a linkage is bent or if the balljoint end is excessively worn, it must be replaced.

3 Any balljoint end can be removed after the cotter pin and retaining nut are first withdrawn. A 'pickle fork' designed for this job is the quickest and easiest method for removing this type of connection. However, the rubber dust seal is usually damaged with this type of tool

and the seal should be replaced (even if the joint is being reused). A balljoint end can also be removed with a puller. Use the jaws of the puller to grasp the housing of the component (Pitman arm, sector shaft, spindle arm, etc.). Situate the point of the screw on the center of the balljoint bolt. Tighten the puller to put tension on it and lightly tap the housing with a brass hammer to help break the joint free. Be careful not to damage either the joint or the housing.

4 If the threaded end of a linkage component is being removed, first mark the component so that the threads can be reinserted to the same exact depth. The vehicle will still need an alignment, but the setting will be close to original so the vehicle can be driven to the alignment facility.

5 Unscrew the component after releasing the bolts and nuts of the clamps. Install the new component to a depth matching the original part and install a retaining nut and new cotter pin. Tighten the bolts

19.1 Details of drag link installation (F250 4x4 shown, others similar)

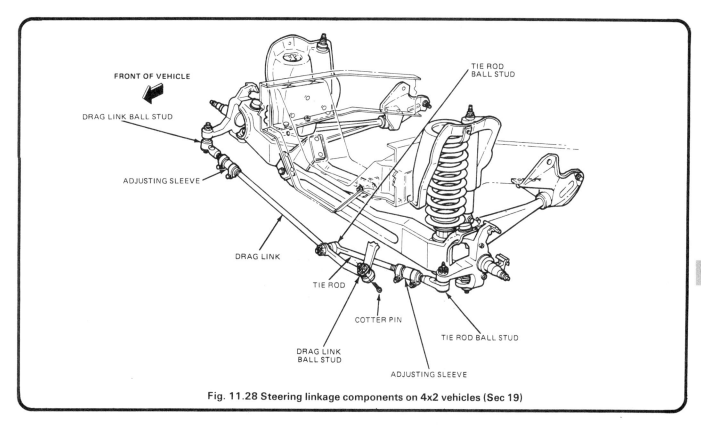

Fig. 11.28 Steering linkage components on 4x2 vehicles (Sec 19)

11

and nuts on any clamps to the prescribed torque and have the vehicle's front end alignment checked.

20 Steering wheel – removal and installation

1　Park the vehicle with the front wheels in the straight ahead position.
2　Disconnect the cable from the negative battery terminal.
3　Remove one screw from the underside of each steering wheel spoke and lift the horn switch assembly (steering wheel pad) off the steering wheel to gain access to the wires beneath. Do not remove the horn assembly at this time.
4　Disconnect the horn switch wires by pulling the spade terminals from the blade connectors.
5　On vehicles without speed control, remove the horn switch assembly.
6　On vehicles with speed control, pinch the J-clip ground wire terminal firmly and pull it out of the hole in the steering wheel. **Note:** *Do not pull the ground terminal out of the threaded hole without*

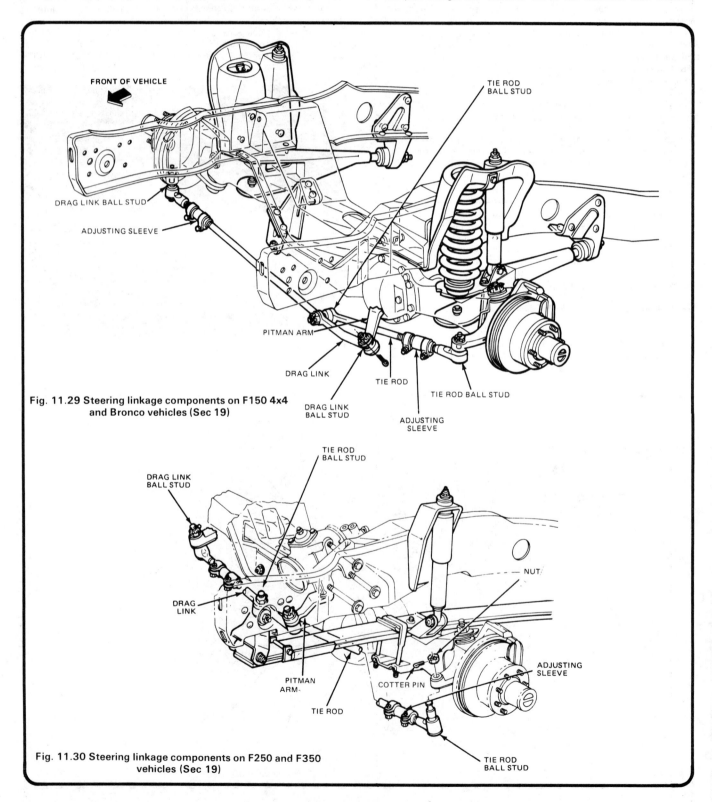

Fig. 11.29 Steering linkage components on F150 4x4 and Bronco vehicles (Sec 19)

Fig. 11.30 Steering linkage components on F250 and F350 vehicles (Sec 19)

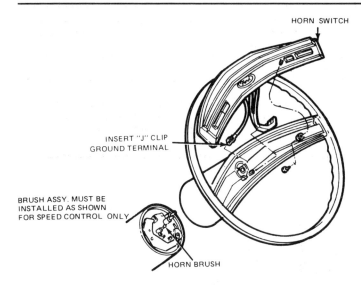

Fig. 11.31 Details of the horn switch assembly on vehicles equipped with speed control (Sec 20)

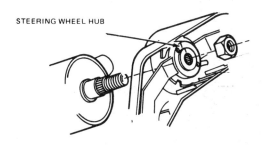

Fig. 11.32 Details of the steering wheel assembly (Sec 20)

pinching the terminal clip to relieve the spring retention of the terminal in the threaded hole. Remove the horn switch assembly.

7   Remove the steering wheel retaining nut.

8   Using a steering wheel puller (Ford no. T67L-3600-A or equivalent), remove the steering wheel. **Note:** *Do not use a hammer on the steering wheel or center shaft, and do not use a knock-off type steering wheel puller, as either procedure will damage the steering column.*

9   The installation is the reverse of the removal procedure. When attaching the steering wheel to the steering column shaft, place it on the shaft so that the mark and the flat on the wheel are in line with the mark and the flat on the shaft. Tighten the steering wheel retaining nut to the specified torque.

21 Steering alignment – check and adjustment

Note: *Since wheel alignment and testing equipment is generally out of the reach of the home mechanic, this section is intended only to familiarize the reader with the basic terms used and procedures followed during a typical wheel alignment job. In the event that your vehicle needs a wheel alignment check or adjustment, we recommend that the work be done by a reputable front-end alignment and repair shop.*

1   The three basic adjustments made when aligning a vehicle's front end are toe-in, caster and camber.

2   Toe-in is the amount the front wheels are angled in relationship to the centerline of the vehicle. For example, in a vehicle with zero toe-in, the distance measured between the front edges of the wheels is the same as the distance measured between the rear edges of the wheels. The wheels are running parallel with the centerline of the vehicle. Toe-in is adjusted by lengthening or shortening the tie-rods. Incorrect toe-in will cause tires to wear improperly by making them 'scrub' against the road surface.

3   Camber and caster are the angles at which the wheel and suspension upright are inclined to the vertical. Camber is the angle of the wheel in the lateral (side-to-side) plane, while caster is the angle of the wheel and upright in the longitudinal (fore-and-aft) plane. Camber angle affects the amount of tire tread which contacts the road and compensates for change in the suspension geometry when the vehicle is traveling around curves or over an undulating surface. Caster angle affects the self-centering action of the steering, which governs straight-line stability.

4   Some vehicles covered in this manual have caster and camber angles designed into the front suspension and no provision is available to change them. On other vehicles, provision is made for camber adjustment, but not for caster adjustment. Still others have provisions for adjustment to both caster and camber. For those vehicles with no provision for these adjustments, in extreme cases, certain components may be bent by a shop with the proper equipment in order to correct the caster and camber. In all cases, however, steering alignment work should always be performed by a facility with the proper equipment and experienced personnel.

11

Chapter 12 Body

Contents

1 General information

Ford pick-ups are built with body-on-separate frame construction. The frame is ladder-type, consisting of two C-section steel side rails joined by a variable number of crossmembers. All crossmembers are riveted, with the exception of the one under the transmission, which is bolted in to facilitate transmission removal and installation. The number of crossmembers in the frame depends on the vehicle wheelbase and load rating.

Pick-up body styles available range from standard cabs to super cabs and crew cab models. All cabs are of single welded unit construction. The cabs are bolted to the frame and use rubber mounts for noise and vibration isolation.

Front fenders, hood, inner fender panels and grilles are bolted to the cab and the radiator support at the front of the vehicle. The radiator support is attached to the front frame rails and insulated with rubber donuts'. Bolts retain the support.

Bumpers are bolted to the frame horns at the front and to the frame rails at the rear via mounting brackets.

Doors, seats, and dashboard are all bolted to the cab and are individually replaceable.

2 Maintenance – body and frame

1 The condition of your vehicle's body is very important, as it is on this that the secondhand value will mainly depend. It is much more difficult to repair a neglected or damaged body than it is to repair mechanical components. The hidden areas of the body, such as the fender wells, the frame, and the engine compartment, are equally important, although obviously not requiring as frequent attention as the rest of the body.

2 Once a year, or every 12 000 miles, it is a good idea to have the underside of the body and the frame steam cleaned. All traces of dirt and oil will be removed and the underside can then be inspected carefully for rust, damaged brake lines, frayed electrical wiring, damaged cables, and other problems. The suspension components should be greased upon completion of this job.

3 At the same time, clean the engine and the engine compartment using either a steam cleaner or a water soluble degreaser.

4 The fender wells should be given extra attention, as undercoating can peel away and stones and dirt thrown up by the tires can cause the paint to chip and flake, allowing rust to set in. If rust is found, clean down to the bare metal and apply an anti-rust paint.

5 The body should be washed once a week (or when dirty). Thoroughly wet the vehicle to soften the dirt, then wash it down with a soft sponge and plenty of clean soapy water. If the surplus dirt is not washed off very carefully, it will in time wear down the paint.

6 Spots of tar or asphalt coating thrown from the road surfaces should be removed with a cloth soaked in solvent.

7 Once every six months, give the body and chrome trim a thorough wax job. If a chrome cleaner is used to remove rust on any of the vehicle's plated parts, remember that the cleaner also removes part of the chrome, so use it sparingly.

3 Maintenance – upholstery and interior

Mats and carpets should be brushed or vacuum cleaned regularly to keep them clean. If they are badly stained, remove them from the vehicle for scrubbing and make sure they are dry before reinstalling them. Seats and interior trim panels can be kept clean by wiping with a damp cloth. If they do become stained (which will be more apparent on light-colored upholstery) use a little liquid detergent and a soft brush to scour the grime out of the grain of the material. Keep the headlining clean in the same way as the upholstery. When using liquid cleaners inside the vehicle, do not apply too much water to surfaces being cleaned. After cleaning, vinyl and plastic surfaces should be treated with a commercially available preservative to prevent drying, cracking and fading. Clear instrument faces can be carefully wiped with a commercially available cleaner designed to remove tiny surface scratches and hazing.

4 Body repair – minor damage

Refer to the accompanying photos which illustrate the following procedures.

Repair of minor scratches

If the scratch is very superficial and does not penetrate to the metal of the body, repair is very simple. Lightly rub the area of the scratch with a fine rubbing compound to remove loose paint from the scratch and to clear the surrounding paint of wax buildup. Rinse the area with clean water.

Apply touch-up paint to the scratch using a small brush. Continue to apply thin layers of paint until the surface of the paint in the scratch is level with the surrounding paint. Allow the new paint at least two weeks to harden, then blend it into the surrounding paint by rubbing with a very fine rubbing compound. Finally, apply a coat of wax to the scratch area.

If the scratch has penetrated the paint and exposed the metal of the body, causing the metal to rust, a different repair technique is required. Remove any loose rust from the bottom of the scratch with a pocket knife, then apply rust inhibiting paint to prevent the formation of rust in the future. Using a rubber or nylon applicator, coat the scratched area with glaze-type filler. If required, this filler can be mixed with thinner to provide a very thin paste which is ideal for filling narrow scratches. Before the glaze filler in the scratch hardens, wrap a piece of smooth cotton cloth around the top of a finger. Dip the cloth in thinner and then quickly wipe it along the surface of the scratch. This will ensure that the surface of the filler is slightly hollowed. The scratch can now be painted over as described earlier in this Section.

Repair of dents

When deep denting of the vehicle's body has taken place, the first task is to pull the dent out until the area nearly attains its original shape. There is little point in trying to restore the original shape completely as the metal in the damaged area will have stretched on impact and cannot be completely restored to its original contours. It is better to bring the level of the dent up to a point which is about $\frac{1}{8}$ inch below the level of the surrounding metal. In cases where the dent is very shallow, it is not worth trying to pull it out at all.

If the underside of the dent is accessible, it can be hammered out gently from behind using a mallet with a wooden or plastic head. While doing this, hold a block of wood firmly against the metal to absorb the hammer blows and prevent large areas of the metal from being stretched out.

If the dent is in a section of the body which has double layers, or some other factor making it inaccessible from behind, a different technique is in order. Drill several small holes through the metal inside the damaged area, particularly in the deeper sections. Screw long self-tapping screws into the holes just enough for them to get a good grip in the metal. Now the dent can be removed by pulling on the protruding heads of the screws with a pair of locking pliers.

The next stage of the repair is the removal of the paint from the damaged area and from an inch or so of the surrounding 'sound' metal. This is easily accomplished by using a wire brush or sanding disc in a drill motor, although it can be done just as effectively by hand with sandpaper. To complete the preparation for filling, score the surface of the bare metal with a screwdriver or the tang of a file (or drill small holes in the affected area). This will provide a really good 'grip' for the filler material. To complete the repair, see the Section on filling and painting.

Repair of rust holes or gashes

Remove all paint from the affected area and from an inch or so of the surrounding 'sound' metal using a sanding disc or wire brush mounted in a drill motor. If these are not available, a few sheets of sandpaper will do the job just as effectively. With the paint removed, you will be able to determine the severity of the corrosion and, therefore, decide whether to replace the whole panel, if possible, or to repair the affected area. New body panels are not as expensive as most people think and it is often quicker and more desirable to install a new panel than to attempt to repair large areas of rust.

Remove all trim pieces from the affected area (except those which will act as a guide to the original shape of the damaged body (ie. headlamp shells, etc.). Then, using metal snips or a hacksaw blade, remove all loose metal and any other metal that is badly affected by rust. Hammer the edges of the hole in to create a slight depression for the filler material.

Wire brush the affected area to remove the powdery rust from the surface of the metal. If the back of the rusted area is accessible, treat it with rust inhibiting paint.

Before filling can be done, it will be necessary to block the hole in some way. This can be accomplished with sheet metal riveted or screwed into place or by stuffing the hole with wire mesh.

Once the hole is blocked off, the affected area can be filled and painted (see the following Section on filling and painting).

Filling and painting

Many types of body fillers are available but generally speaking, body repair kits which contain filler paste and a tube of resin hardener are best for this type of repair work. A wide, flexible plastic or nylon applicator will be necessary for imparting a smooth contoured finish to the surface of the filler material.

Mix up a small amount of filler on a clean piece of wood or cardboard (use the hardener sparingly). Follow the maker's instructions on the package, otherwise the filler will set incorrectly.

Using the applicator, apply the filler paste to the prepared area. Draw the applicator across the surface of the filler to achieve the desired contour and to level the filler surface. As soon as a contour that approximates the correct one is achieved, stop working the paste. If you continue, the paste will begin to stick to the applicator. Continue to add thin layers of filler paste at 20-minute intervals until the level of the filler is just above the surrounding metal.

Once the filler has hardened, excess can be removed using a body

file. From then on, progressively finer grades of sandpaper should be used, starting with a 180-grit paper and finishing with 600-grit wet-or-dry paper. Always wrap the sandpaper around a flat rubber or wooden block, otherwise the surface of the filler will not be completely flat. During the sanding of the filler surface, the wet-or-dry paper should be periodically rinsed in water. This will ensure that a very smooth finish is produced in the final stage.

At this point, the repair area should be surrounded by a ring of bare metal, which in turn should be encircled by the finely feathered edge of the good paint. Rinse the repair area with clean water until all of the dust produced by the sanding operation is gone.

Spray the entire area with a light coat of primer. This will reveal any imperfections in the surface of the filler. Repair these imperfections with fresh filler paste or glaze filler and once more smooth the surface with sandpaper. Repeat this spray-and-repair procedure until you are satisfied that the surface of the filler and the feathered edge of the paint are perfect. Rinse the area with clean water and allow it to dry completely.

The repair area is now ready for painting. Paint spraying must be carried out in a warm, dry, windless and dustfree atmosphere. These conditions can be created if you have access to a large indoor working area but if you are forced to work in the open, you will have to pick your day very carefully. If you are working indoors, dousing the floor in the work area with water will help to settle the dust which would otherwise be in the air. If the repair area is confined to one body panel, mask off the surrounding panels. This will help to minimize the effects of a slight mismatch in paint color. Trim pieces such as chrome strips, door handles, etc., will also need to be masked off or removed. Use masking tape and several thicknesses of newspaper for the masking operations.

Before spraying, shake the paint can thoroughly, then spray a test area until the technique is mastered. Cover the repair area with a thick coat of primer. The thickness should be built up using several thin layers of primer rather than one thick one. Using 600-grit wet-or-dry sandpaper, rub down the surface of the primer until it is very smooth. While doing this, the work area should be thoroughly rinsed with water, and the wet-or-dry sandpaper periodically rinsed as well. Allow the primer to dry before spraying additional coats.

Spray on the top coat, again building up the thickness by using several thin layers of paint. Begin spraying in the center of the repair area and then, using a circular motion, work out until the whole repair area and about two inches of the surrounding original paint is covered. Remove all masking material 10 to 15 minutes after spraying on the final coat of paint. Allow the new paint at least two weeks to harden, then using a very fine rubbing compound, blend the edges of the paint into the existing paint. Finally, apply a coat of wax.

5 Body and frame repairs – major damage

1   Major damage must be repaired by an auto body shop equipped to perform body and frame repairs. These shops have available the welding and hydraulic straightening equipment required to do the job properly.
2   If the damage is extensive, the frame must be checked for proper alignment or the vehicle's handling characteristics may be adversely affected and other components may wear at an accelerated rate.
3   Due to the fact that all of the major body components (cab, hood, bed, fenders etc.) are separate and replaceable units, any seriously damaged components should be replaced rather than repaired. Sometimes these components can be found in a wrecking yard that specializes in used vehicle components (often at a considerable saving over the cost of new parts).

6 Door trim panel – removal and installation

Note: *Refer to Fig. 12.1 to locate components.*
1   Remove the screw retaining the armrest section of the trim panel to the door inner panel and remove the section (photo).
2   Remove the screw retaining the inside door handle and remove the handle.
3   On vehicles with manually operated window cranks, remove the screws retaining the crank, then remove the crank and washer.
4   On vehicles with power windows, remove the power window switch panel by inserting a thin-blade screwdriver between the bezel

12

These photos illustrate a method of repairing simple dents. They are intended to supplement *Body repair - minor damage* in this Chapter and should not be used as the sole instructions for body repair on these vehicles.

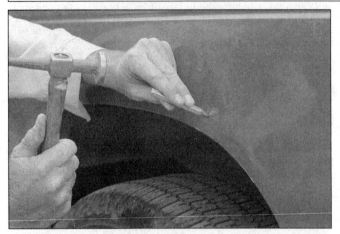

1   If you can't access the backside of the body panel to hammer out the dent, pull it out with a slide-hammer-type dent puller. In the deepest portion of the dent or along the crease line, drill or punch hole(s) at least one inch apart . . .

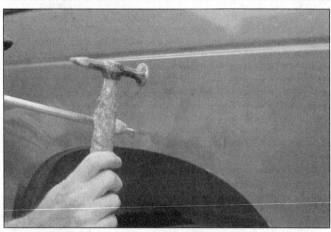

2   . . . then screw the slide-hammer into the hole and operate it. Tap with a hammer near the edge of the dent to help 'pop' the metal back to its original shape. When you're finished, the dent area should be close to its original contour and about 1/8-inch below the surface of the surrounding metal

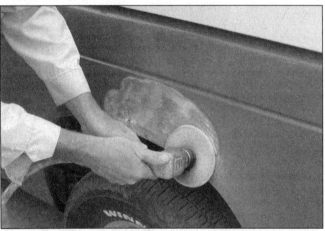

3   Using coarse-grit sandpaper, remove the paint down to the bare metal. Hand sanding works fine, but the disc sander shown here makes the job faster. Use finer (about 320-grit) sandpaper to feather-edge the paint at least one inch around the dent area

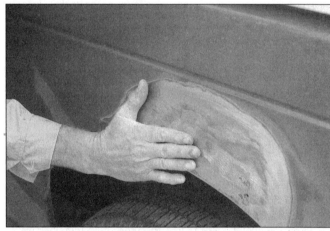

4   When the paint is removed, touch will probably be more helpful than sight for telling if the metal is straight. Hammer down the high spots or raise the low spots as necessary. Clean the repair area with wax/silicone remover

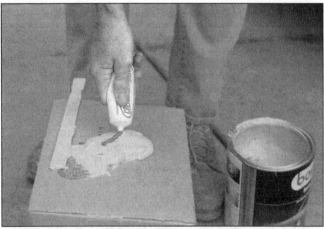

5   Following label instructions, mix up a batch of plastic filler and hardener. The ratio of filler to hardener is critical, and, if you mix it incorrectly, it will either not cure properly or cure too quickly (you won't have time to file and sand it into shape)

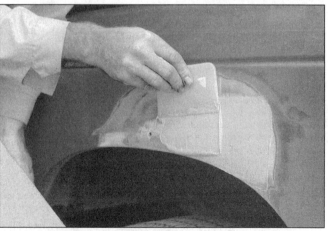

6   Working quickly so the filler doesn't harden, use a plastic applicator to press the body filler firmly into the metal, assuring it bonds completely. Work the filler until it matches the original contour and is slightly above the surrounding metal

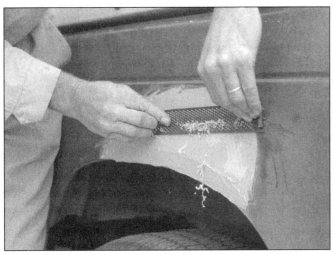

7   Let the filler harden until you can just dent it with your fingernail. Use a body file or Surform tool (shown here) to rough-shape the filler

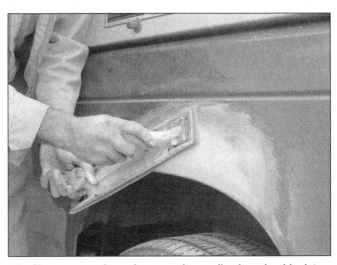

8   Use coarse-grit sandpaper and a sanding board or block to work the filler down until it's smooth and even. Work down to finer grits of sandpaper - always using a board or block - ending up with 360 or 400 grit

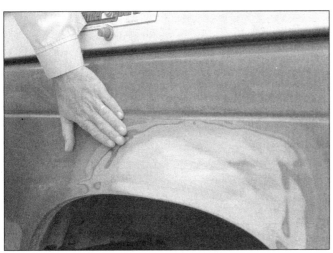

9   You shouldn't be able to feel any ridge at the transition from the filler to the bare metal or from the bare metal to the old paint. As soon as the repair is flat and uniform, remove the dust and mask off the adjacent panels or trim pieces

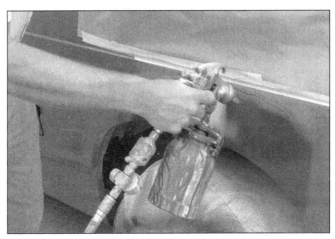

10   Apply several layers of primer to the area. Don't spray the primer on too heavy, so it sags or runs, and make sure each coat is dry before you spray on the next one. A professional-type spray gun is being used here, but aerosol spray primer is available inexpensively from auto parts stores

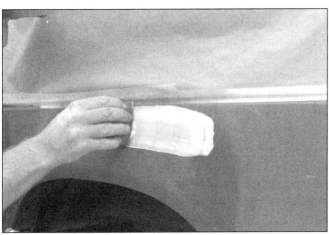

11   The primer will help reveal imperfections or scratches. Fill these with glazing compound. Follow the label instructions and sand it with 360 or 400-grit sandpaper until it's smooth. Repeat the glazing, sanding and respraying until the primer reveals a perfectly smooth surface

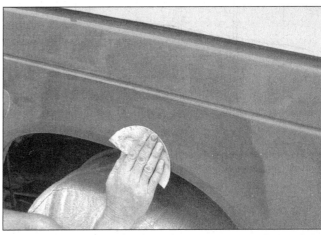

12   Finish sand the primer with very fine sandpaper (400 or 600-grit) to remove the primer overspray. Clean the area with water and allow it to dry. Use a tack rag to remove any dust, then apply the finish coat. Don't attempt to rub out or wax the repair area until the paint has dried completely (at least two weeks)

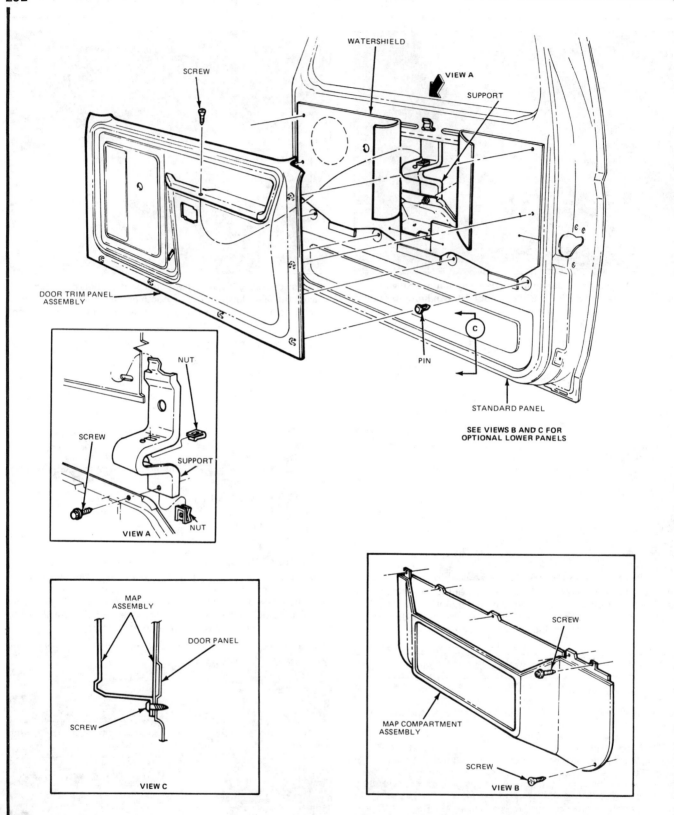

WATERSHIELD

SCREW

VIEW A

SUPPORT

DOOR TRIM PANEL
ASSEMBLY

NUT

SCREW

SUPPORT

NUT

VIEW A

PIN

C

STANDARD PANEL

SEE VIEWS B AND C FOR
OPTIONAL LOWER PANELS

MAP
ASSEMBLY

DOOR PANEL

SCREW

VIEW C

SCREW

MAP COMPARTMENT
ASSEMBLY

SCREW

VIEW B

Fig. 12.1 Typical pick-up and Bronco door trim panel installation (Sec 6)

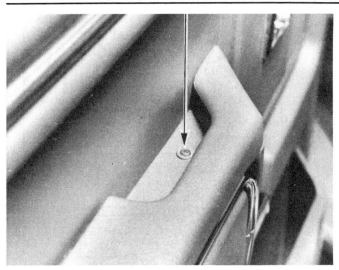

6.1 Location of armrest section removal screw

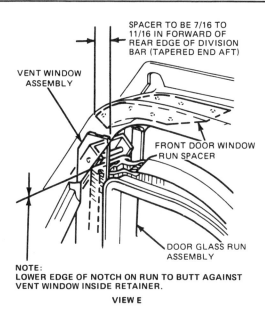

SPACER TO BE 7/16 TO 11/16 IN FORWARD OF REAR EDGE OF DIVISION BAR (TAPERED END AFT)

VENT WINDOW ASSEMBLY

FRONT DOOR WINDOW RUN SPACER

DOOR GLASS RUN ASSEMBLY

NOTE:
LOWER EDGE OF NOTCH ON RUN TO BUTT AGAINST VENT WINDOW INSIDE RETAINER.

VIEW E

Fig. 12.2 Correct positioning of the front door window run spacer when installing the vent window assembly (Sec 7)

and the trim panel, at either side of the bezel, then carefully pry the bezel from the trim panel and the housing assembly will snap out. On the left side door only, remove the two retaining screws from the bottom side of the connector.
5   On models so equipped, remove the door lock control knob.
6   On models with power door locks, remove the switch housing assembly from the panel by inserting a thin-blade screwdriver into the spring tab slot located at the top and bottom of the switch housing, apply pressure and the assembly will pop out. Disconnect the housing from the wiring assembly connector by separating the locking fingers.
7   If equipped with a power outside rear view mirror, remove the switch housing bezel by removing the two retaining bezel nuts and the bezel.
8   Using a thin-blade screwdriver or putty knife, insert it at each of the retaining clip locations and carefully pry the clip from the door.
Note: *Do not use the panel itself to pull the clips from the door, as damage to the panel may occur.*
9   Replace any damaged or missing clips with new ones.
10   Position the trim panel on the inner door panel, locating the clips properly in the countersunk holes and firmly push the trim panel by hand at each clip location to seat the panel. Do not use a hammer or other tool, as damage to the trim panel may occur.
11   The remaining installation steps are the reverse of the removal procedure.

---

7   Vent window assembly – removal and installation

Note: *Refer to Figs. 12.2 and 12.3 to locate components.*
1   Refer to Section 6 and remove the door trim panel.
2   Remove the screw retaining the division bar to the inner door panel.
3   Remove the screws retaining the vent window assembly to the leading edge of the door.
4   Lower the door glass to the bottom of its travel.
5   Pull the glass run out of the upper run retainer next to the vent window division bar. Pull the glass run out just far enough to allow the vent window assembly to be removed.
6   Tilt the vent window and the division bar assembly toward the rear of the door. Carefully guide the assembly up and out of the door.
7   Remove the two upper pivot-to-vent frame screws.
8   Remove the retaining nut and tension spring from the vent window lower pivot.
9   Separate the vent glass retainer and the pivot stops from the vent frame and weatherstripping assembly.
10   Installation is the reverse of the removal procedure. The pivot tension spring should be adjusted so the vent will remain open at highway speeds. Be sure the front door window spacer is in place when installing the vent window and division bar assembly.

---

8   Door glass and window regulator – removal and installation

---

Note: *Refer to Figs. 12.3 and 12.4 to locate components.*
1   Remove the door panel trim (refer to Section 6).
2   Remove the vent window assembly (refer to Section 7).
3   Rotate the front edge of the door glass down, then lift the glass and channel assembly from the door.
4   If the glass is to be replaced, it must be removed and new glass installed in the glass channel by a glass shop with the special tools required for the job.
5   To remove the regulator, remove the center pin from the regulator attaching rivets using a drift punch. Using a $\frac{1}{4}$ inch drill, remove the head from each rivet and remove the rivet. Be careful not to enlarge the sheet metal holes during the drilling procedure.
6   Disengage the regulator arm from the glass bracket and remove the regulator.
7   Installation is the reverse of the removal procedure. When inserting the glass and channel into the door, be sure that the regulator roller arm is positioned correctly in the glass bracket channel.
8   If rivets are not available when installing the regulator, a $\frac{1}{4}$-20 x $\frac{1}{2}$ inch screw and washer assembly, and a $\frac{1}{4}$-20 nut and washer assembly may be used instead.
9   All window regulator rollers, shafts and the entire length of the roller guides should be lubricated with polyethylene grease before installation.

---

9   Door handle (outside) and lock cylinder – removal and installation

---

Door handle
Note: *Refer to Fig. 12.6 to locate components.*
1   Remove the inner door trim panel as described in Section 6. Remove the plastic watershield from the inside of the door.
2   Disconnect the latch actuator rod from the hole on the inside of the door handle assembly.
3   Using a socket and small ratchet, remove the nut and the screw retaining the door handle assembly.
4   Remove the door handle assembly and the pads from the door.
5   If the handle is being replaced, transfer the pads and the actuator rod clip to the new handle assembly.
6   Installation is the reverse of removal. Check the handle assembly for correct operation before installing the inner door watershield and panel.

12

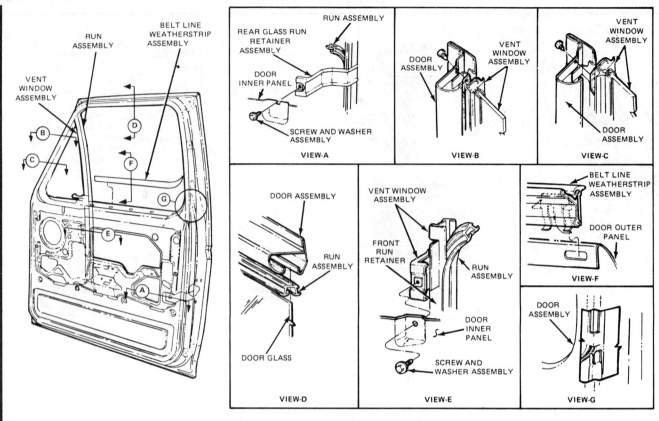

Fig. 12.3 Details of the door glass and vent window assembly installation (Secs 7 and 8)

Fig. 12.4 Details of the window regulator assembly installation (Sec 8)

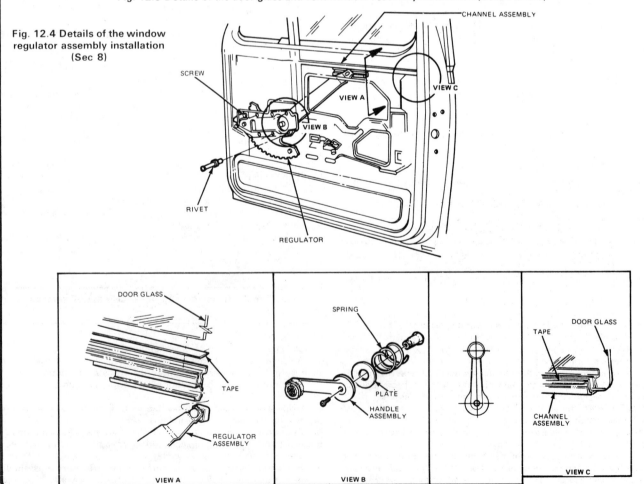

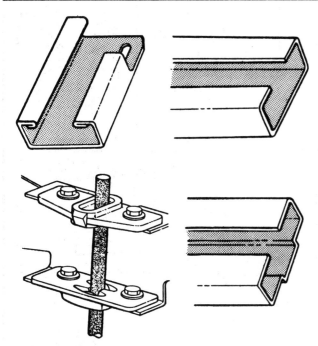

Fig. 12.5 The shaded areas of the roller guides and shafts should be lubricated with polyethylene grease prior to installation (Sec 8)

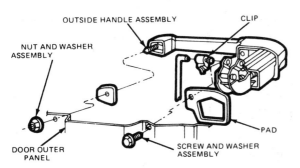

Fig. 12.6 Typical outside door handle assembly – exploded view (Sec 9)

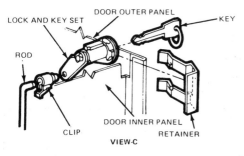

Fig. 12.7 Details of the door lock cylinder assembly (Sec 9)

Lock cylinder
Note: *If a lock cylinder is being replaced, it should be replaced in both doors and the ignition cylinder. These cylinders come in sets and allow the vehicle to be unlocked and driven with one key. Refer to Fig. 12.7 to locate components.*
7   Roll the window all the way up.
8   Remove the inner door trim panel and watershield as described in Section 6.
9   Disconnect the lock actuating rod from the lock control link clip.
10   Slide the lock cylinder retaining clip out of the groove in the lock cylinder. Remove the lock cylinder from the outside of the door.
11   Installation is the reverse of removal. Be careful when reinstalling

the watershield to ensure that it fits tightly to the door and is not torn or deformed in any way. If this shield is not watertight, it can cause an accumulation of water inside of the door and eventual rusting. It is sometimes necessary to reglue the lip of the seal, using contact cement.

10 Windshield – removal and installation

Due to the possibility of glass breakage when installing a new windshield and/or possible damage to the surrounding body panels and paint, it is recommended that a damaged windshield be replaced by a dealership or auto glass shop.

11 Rear window – removal and installation

1   Using a screwdriver from the inside of the cab, pry carefully around the weatherstrip lip forcing the weatherstripping out. Have an assistant pull on the window assembly to remove it, with the weatherstripping attached.
2   On sliding type rear windows, using a screwdriver and pliers, remove the sliding glass stopper from the channel.
3   From the channel track, remove the four screws holding the two fixed frames.
4   With the window assembly standing vertically on its lower edge, place a folded rag near the center of the window frame to protect the channel.
5   Stand on the rag with one foot and gently lift the top edge of the frame and remove the sliding windows and fixed frames.
6   Move the rag toward either end of the channel frame and remove the two non-sliding windows in the same manner.
7   To install the rear window, first transfer the weatherstripping from the non-sliding window(s) being replaced to the new window(s).
8   Apply soapy water to the contact face of the weatherstripping surrounding the glass channel and to the glass channel flange.
9   The remaining assembly steps are the reverse of those for disassembly. It is probable that the old weatherstripping has become weather-hardened and may develop water leaks. Replace the weatherstripping with new material if any such deterioration is indicated.
10   Once the rear window is assembled, apply a working cord along the weatherstripping groove, as shown in the accompanying illustration.
11   Begin the installation in the center of the lower part of the glass.
12   Attach the window assembly to the body by pulling on the cord from the inside while an assistant pushes along the weatherstripping from the outside.
13   Seat the window assembly by tapping around the circumference of the glass with your open hand.

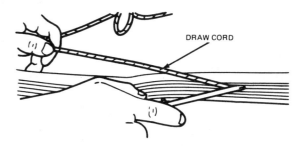

Fig. 12.8 Installation of a draw cord to assist in rear window installation (Sec 11)

12 Hood – removal and installation

Note: *Refer to Fig. 12.11 to locate components.*
1   This procedure must be performed with two people to avoid personal injury and to avoid damage to the hood and surrounding body components.
2   With the hood open, carefully mark the position of the hood in

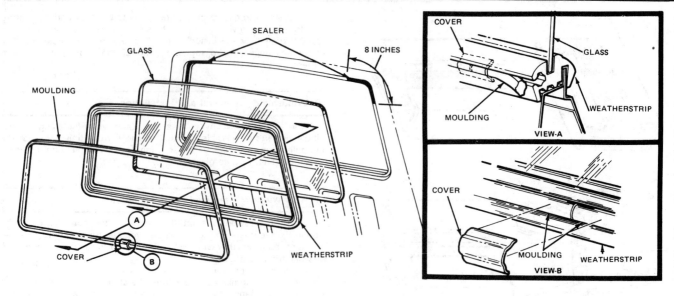

Fig. 12.9 Stationary back window assembly (Sec 11)

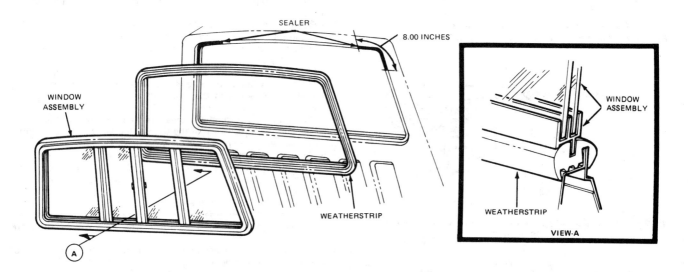

Fig. 12.10 Sliding back window assembly (Sec 11)

relationship to the link assemblies and hinges.

3   If the vehicle is equipped with an underhood light, disconnect it.

4   With one person situated on either side of the hood, loosen and remove the link assembly and hood-to-hinge bolts on both sides.

5   Pivot the nose of the hood down slowly until the assembly is level and remove it toward the front of the vehicle.

6   Installation is the reverse of removal. Be sure to position the hood carefully and align it with the previously made marks. Tighten all bolts securely and check the hood for proper operation.

13 Grille assembly – removal and installation

Note: *Refer to Fig. 12.12 to locate components.*

Radiator grille
1   Remove one screw at the hood latch support brace at the lower center of the grille.

2   Remove two screws at both the left and right sides of the grille where it is attached to the radiator grille support.

3   Remove the three upper grille attaching screws where they are

fastened to the upper grille molding (photo).

4   Remove the grille.

5   Installation is the reverse of the removal procedure.

Upper grille molding
6   Remove the radiator grille (refer to Steps 1 through 4).

7   Remove the right and left-hand headlight door assemblies (refer to Chapter 10, Section 3).

8   Remove the three screws which fasten the upper grille molding to the molding retainer assembly.

9   Remove the molding.

10 Installation is the reverse of the removal procedure.

Lower grille molding
11 **Note:** *It is not necessary to remove the radiator grille in order to remove the lower molding.* Remove the right and left-hand headlight door assemblies (refer to Chapter 10, Section 3).

12 Remove one screw at the hood latch support brace at the center of the lower molding, then remove the screws at the right and left ends of the molding where it attaches to the radiator grille support.

13 Remove the molding.

14 Installation is the reverse of the removal procedure.

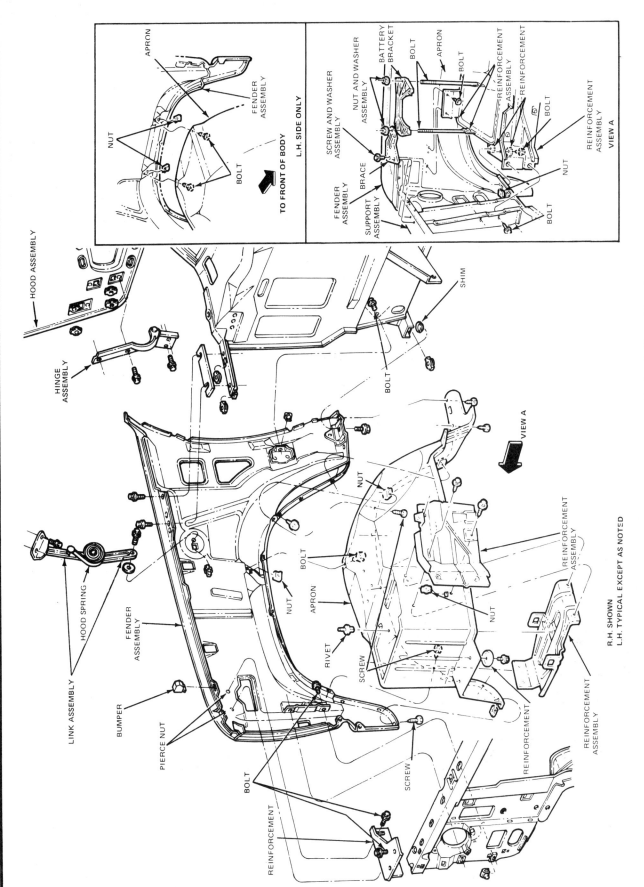

Fig. 12.11 Typical front fender and hood assembly details (Secs 12 and 14)

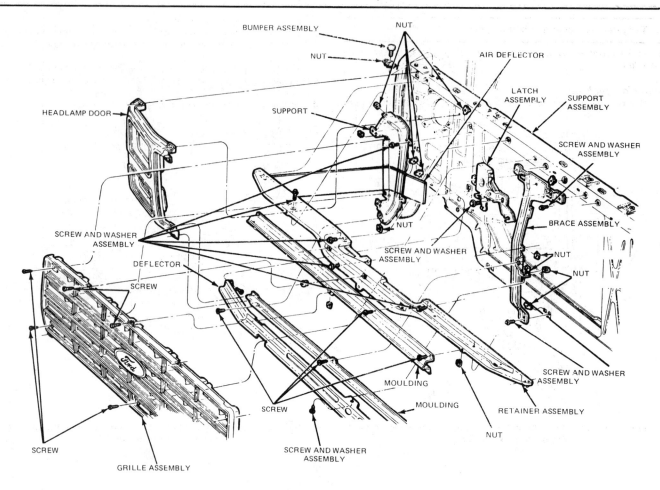

Figs. 12.12 Typical grille assembly details (Sec 13)

13.3 Removing screw retaining grille to upper grille molding

14 Front fender – removal and installation

Note: Refer to Fig. 12.11 to locate components.
1 Remove the hood assembly (refer to Section 12).
2 Remove the grille assembly (refer to Section 13).
3 Clean all dirt from the fender attaching hardware.
4 Remove the headlight assembly (refer to Chapter 10, Section 3).

5 Remove the screws retaining the front of the fender to the radiator support at the upper and lower attaching points.
6 Remove the screw retaining the lower rear end of the fender to the lower corner of the cab.
7 From inside the cab, remove the screw retaining the lower rear end of the fender to the cowl.
8 Remove the screws retaining the top edge of the fender at the rear to the cowl extension.
9 Remove the screws around the wheel opening that attach the fender apron.
10 Remove the fender retaining bolts along the top of the apron.
11 If the right fender is being removed, remove the bolts that retain the battery tray to the fender.
12 If the left fender is being removed, remove the bolts attaching the auxiliary battery tray or tool box (if so equipped).
13 Remove the hood latch cable from the left fender, or the main wiring harness from the right fender.
14 Remove the screws attaching the hood prop spring to the fender.
15 Remove the fender from the vehicle.
16 To install the fender, place it in the correct position with all of the attaching hardware in place.
17 Apply body sealer to the upper edge of the apron.
18 Attach the fender to the apron and install the screws loosely.
19 From inside the cab, loosely install the screw retaining the rear lower end of the fender to the cowl.
20 Loosely install the screw retaining the rear lower end of the fender to the lower corner of the cab.
21 Loosely install the screws retaining the front of the fender to the radiator support.
22 Adjust the fender position until it is aligned and tighten all attaching hardware.
23 Install the hood prop spring to the fender.
24 Install the grille and headlamp assemblies.
25 Install the hood.

15 Tailgate – removal and installation

Note: *To facilitate tailgate removal, a helper should assist in the procedure.*

Styleside pick-up

1   Remove the screws retaining the left and right tailgate support straps at the upper attachment points.
2   Lift the tailgate off at the right-hand lower hinge, then remove the tailgate from the left-hand hinge. Be careful not to lose the hinge inserts.
3   If a new tailgate is being installed, transfer all moldings, latches, hinges, brackets, links, clips and washers from the old tailgate to the new one.
4   Installation is the reverse of the removal procedure.

Flareside pick-up

5   Unhook the tailgate chains from the tailgate.

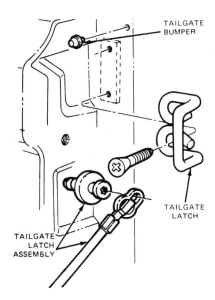

Fig. 12.13 Removing the upper tailgate support straps on a Styleside pick-up (Sec 15)

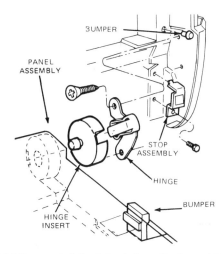

Fig. 12.14 Removal of the tailgate from the lower hinge on a Styleside pick-up (Sec 15)

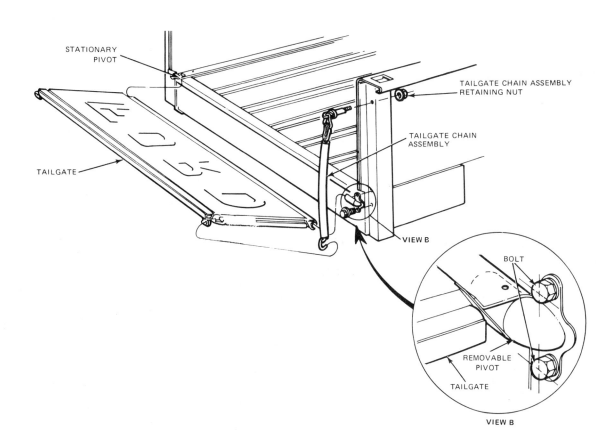

Fig. 12.15 Removal of the tailgate from a Flareside pick-up (Sec 15)

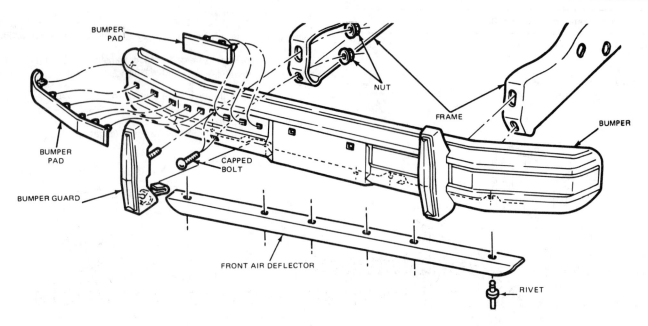

Fig. 12.16 Details of a typical front bumper assembly (Sec 16)

6   Remove the two bolts retaining the removable pivot to the body on the right side, then remove the pivot.

7   Slide the tailgate off the stationary pivot on the left.

8   If a new tailgate is being installed, refer to Step 3.

9   Installation is the reverse of the removal procedure.

16 Bumpers – removal and installation

Front
Note: *Refer to Fig. 12.16 to locate components.*

1   On models with the bumper bolted directly to the frame, remove the two bolts on each side and lift the bumper off the frame.

2   On models with bumper guards, first remove the upper attachment nuts from the bumper guards, then remove the screws retaining the bumper guard brackets to the bumper and remove the bumper guards.

3   Remove the two lower bumper bolts and remove the bumper from the vehicle.

4   Installation is the reverse of the removal procedure.

Rear
5   Remove the bumper bracket-to-frame retaining bolts.

6   Remove the bumper and brackets from the vehicle.

7   If a new bumper and/or brackets are being installed, transfer any undamaged components from the old assembly to the new component.

8   Installation is the reverse of the removal procedure.

Chapter 13 Supplement:
Revisions and information on later models

Contents

1   Introduction

This supplement contains specifications and service procedure changes that apply to 1984 and later Ford pick up trucks (except Super Duty trucks) and full-size Bronco models. Also included is material related to previous models which was not available at the time of the original production of this manual.

Where no differences (or very minor differences) exist between the later models and previous models, no information is given. In such instances, the original material included in Chapters 1 through 12 (pertaining to 1983 models) should be used. Therefore, owners of vehicles manufactured between the above years should refer to this Chapter before using the information in the original Chapters of the manual.

2 Specifications

Tune-up and routine maintenance
Recommended lubricants and fluids

Engine oil type (1986 on)	SAE grade SF
Automatic transmission fluid type (1988 on – C6 and AOD) ..	**MERCON ATF** (Ford part no. XT-2-QDS)
Manual transmission/transfer case lubricant type (1988 on) ..	**MERCON ATF** (Ford part no. XT-2-QDS)

Coolant capacity – 1984 on

300 cu in inline six cylinder	
standard cooling	13 qts
air conditioning and super cooling	14 qts
302 cu in V8	
standard cooling	13 qts
air conditioning and super cooling	14 qts
351 cu in V8	
standard cooling	15 qts
all others	16 qts
460 cu in V8 (all)	18 qts

Manual transmission capacity – 1988 on

Mazda M50D 5-speed	7.6 pts
S5BZF 5-speed	3.5 qts

Automatic transmission capacity – 1984 on

C6 transmission	
4X2	12.0 qts
4X4	13.5 qts
C5 transmission (4X2)	11.0 qts
AOD transmission (all)	12.3 qts

Transfer case capacity – 1984 on

New process 2-speed part-time	9.0 pts
Warner 1345 full-time	6.5 pts

Differential capacity – 1984 on

Rear axle	
Ford 8.8 inch ring gear	5.5 pts
Ford 9.0 inch ring gear	6.5 pts
Ford 10.25 inch ring gear	7.5 pts
Ford 9.0 inch ring gear	6.5 pts
Front axle	
Dana 44-IFS	3.8 pts
Dana 50-IFS	4.1 pts
Dana 60 Monobeam	5.8 pts

Torque specifications

	Ft-lbs
Wheel lug nuts (1987 on)*	
1/2 in nut	100
9/16 in nut (single rear wheels)	140

Retorque after 500 miles each time lug nuts are loosened

Engine
Torque specifications
4.9L (1987 on)

	Ft-lbs (unless otherwise indicated)
Lower intake manifold-to-head	22 to 32

5.0L and 5.8L

Lower intake manifold bolts	23 to 25
Lower intake manifold stud nut	8 to 10

7.5L (1988 on)

Camshaft thrust plate-to-engine block	70 to 105 in-lbs
Exhaust manifold-to-cylinder head	22 to 30
Intake manifold-to-cylinder head	
1st step	8 to 12
2nd step	12 to 22
3rd step	22 to 35
Oil filter insert-to-engine block/adapter	45 to 150
Oil filter adaptor-to-engine block	40 to 65
Rocker arm cover bolts	6 to 9
Water outlet housing bolts	12 to 18

Fuel, exhaust and emission control systems
Fuel pump (EFI only)
Type	Electric
Pressure	35 to 45 psi
Volume	5.6 ounces in 10 seconds minimum

Torque specifications
Ft-lbs *(unless otherwise indicated)*

4.9L engine (1987 on)
Air bypass valve-to-throttle body	71 to 102 in-lbs
Cooling manifold	35 to 50
EGR tube	25 to 35
EGR valve-to-upper intake manifold	13 to 19
Fuel injector manifold-to-fuel charging assembly	12 to 15
Fuel pressure regulator-to-injector manifold	27 to 40 in-lbs
Throttle body-to-upper intake manifold	12 to 18
Throttle position sensor-to-throttle body	14 to 16 in-lbs
Upper intake manifold-to-lower intake manifold bolts	12 to 18

5.0L engine (through 1986)
Upper intake manifold bolts	12 to 18

5.0L and 5.8L engines (1987 on)
Air bypass valve-to-throttle body	71 to 102 in-lbs
EGR tube	25 to 35
EGR valve-to-upper intake manifold	13 to 19
Fuel injector manifold-to-fuel charging assembly	12 to 15
Fuel pressure regulator-to-injector manifold	27 to 40 in-lbs
Throttle position sensor-to-throttle body	14 to 16 in-lbs
Throttle body-to-upper intake manifold	12 to 18
Upper intake manifold-to-lower intake manifold	15 to 22

7.5L engine (1988 on)
Fuel Pressure regulator-to-injector manifold	27 to 40 in-lbs
Fuel injector manifold-to-fuel charging assembly	70 to 105 in-lbs
Air bypass valve-to-lower manifold	70 to 100 in-lbs
Air supply tube clamps	12 to 20 in-lbs
Throttle body-to-upper intake manifold	70 to 100 in-lbs
Throttle position sensor-to-throttle body	11 to 16 in-lbs
Upper intake manifold-to-lower intake manifold bolts	12 to 18
Thermactor pump-to-pump bracket	30 to 40
Thermactor pump pulley-to-pump hub	100 to 130 in-lbs
EGR tube	25 to 35
EGR valve-to-upper intake manifold	70 to 100 in-lbs

Engine electrical systems

TFI–IV ignition coil resistance
Primary	0.3 to 1.0 ohms
Secondary	8000 to 11,500 ohms

Torque specifications (7.5L engine)
Ft-lbs
Alternator bracket-to-water pump bolt	30 to 40
Alternator pivot bolt	40 to 50
Alternator adjusting arm-to-water pump bolt	30 to 40
Alternator adjusting arm-to-alternator bolt	30 to 40

Steering and suspension systems
Torque specifications
Ft-lbs
Upper shock absorber nuts	25 to 35
Lower shock absorber nuts	40 to 60

---

3 Tune-up and routine maintenance

Routine maintenance intervals

Every 5000 miles (8000 Km)
    Check the manual transmission lubricant level
    Check the transfer case lubricant level
Every 30,000 miles (48,000 Km)
    Repack the front wheel bearings (Chapter 1)
    Drain and replace the automatic transmission fluid (Chapter 1)
Every 60,000 miles (96,000 Km)
    Replace the EGR valve (all 1987 and later models with EFI)
    Replace the heated exhaust gas oxygen sensor (all models with EFI)
    Clean the idle speed control bypass valve (all models with EFI)

Fuel filter — removal and installation (EFI engine)

Note: *The fuel filter used on EFI equipped vehicles should be good for the life of the vehicle. The factory does not recommend replacement at time/mileage intervals.*

Caution: *If the fuel filter canister is being serviced with the rear of the vehicle higher than the front, or if the tank is pressurized, fuel leakage or siphoning from the lines could occur. To prevent this condition, maintain the vehicle front end at or above the rear end of the vehicle. Also, relieve tank pressure by loosening the filler cap.*

Warning: *The fuel system pressure must be relieved before loosening the canister when replacing the filter (see Section 6 in this Chapter).*

1   Remove the four screws securing the reservoir heat shield to the

13

frame and remove the shield (Fig. 13.1).
2   Using a strap wrench, unscrew the lower canister and remove it from the frame rail. **Warning:** *The canister will be full of fuel.*
3   Remove the filter cartridge and O-ring from the canister.
4   Install a new filter cartridge.
5   Position a new O-ring on the O-ring grove of the canister.
6   Hold the canister level and position it on the reservoir housing hand tight.
7   Use a strap wrench to tighten the canister one-sixth of a turn past initial O-ring compression.

Manual transmission/transfer case lubricant level check

8   Manual transmissions and transfer cases don't have a dipstick. The oil level is checked by removing a plug from the side of the case (Figs. 13.2 and 13.3). Locate the plug and use a rag to clean the plug and the area around it. If the vehicle is raised to gain access to the plug, be sure to support it safely on jackstands — DO NOT crawl under the vehicle when it's supported only by a jack!
9   With the engine and drivetrain components cold, remove the plug. If lubricant immediately starts leaking out, thread the plug back into the case — the level is correct. If it doesn't, completely remove the plug and reach inside the hole with your little finger. The level should be even with, or very near, the bottom of the plug hole.
10 If the transmission or transfer case needs more lubricant, use a syringe or small pump to add it through the hole.
11 Thread the plug back into the case and tighten it securely. Drive the vehicle then check for leaks around the plug.

EGR valve — replacement

12 Follow the procedure in Section 4 of Chapter 6, but note that the EGR valve used on EFI models has a wire harness that must be disconnected and an EGR tube.

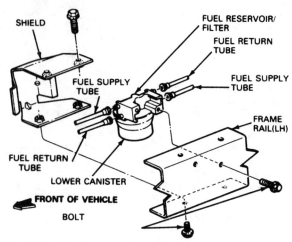

Fig. 13.1   On EFI engines the fuel filter is located in the left rear frame rail (Sec 3)

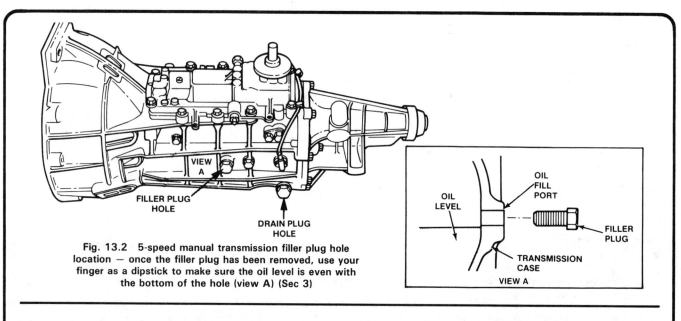

Fig. 13.2   5-speed manual transmission filler plug hole location — once the filler plug has been removed, use your finger as a dipstick to make sure the oil level is even with the bottom of the hole (view A) (Sec 3)

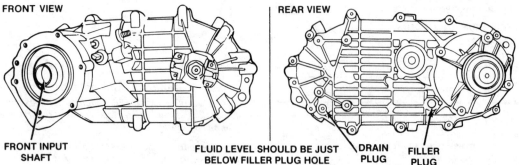

Fig. 13.3   Transfer case filler plug hole location (on some models the filler plug may be located in the lower center of the rear case half) — once the filler plug has been removed, use your finger as a dipstick to make sure the oil level is even with the bottom of the hole (Sec 3)

Heated exhaust gas oxygen sensor — replacement

13 Locate the HEGO sensor between the exhaust manifold and the catalytic converter.
14 Allow the exhaust system to cool completely before removing the oxygen sensor.
15 Follow the sensor wire to the connector, then unplug it — be careful, it's made of plastic and will break if mishandled.
16 Unscrew the sensor. It may be necessary to use a crow-foot wrench on some vehicles.
17 Installation is the reverse of removal.

Idle speed control bypass valve — cleaning

18 Locate the ISC bypass valve on the upper intake manifold or throttle body (see Figs. 13.25 and 13.26). Unplug the wire harness connector (be careful not to break the plastic body of the connector).
19 Remove the bolts and detach the ISC bypass valve from the throttle body or upper intake manifold.
20 Remove the electrical solenoid from the bypass valve.
21 Soak the mechanical portion of the valve in Carburetor and combustion chamber cleaner (Ford part no. D9AZ-19579-B) or equivalent for 2 or 3 minutes maximum. **Warning:** *Do not exceed the 3 minutes soak time and don't use choke cleaner, as the internal O-ring may begin to deteriorate.*
22 While soaking, shake the valve and push the rod in and out. Dry it with compressed air.
23 Clean the gasket surfaces. Be careful not to drop gasket material into the throttle body.
24 Reassemble the bypass valve and install it on the throttle body or upper intake manifold. Use a new gasket and don't overtighten the bolts.

Engine drivebelt(s) – check, adjustment and replacement

All 1989 and later models are equipped with a serpentine drivebelt like the one used on earlier models with a V6 engine (see Section 6 in Chapter 1). On most models, an automatic tensioner maintains the belt tension (as long as the correct length belt is installed). To verify proper tensioner operation, check to see if the belt length indicator mark is between the maximum and minimum marks on the tensioner.

---

4 Engine

Intake manifold — removal and installation (inline six-cylinder EFI engine only)

1 Make sure the ignition is off, then disconnect the negative battery cable from the battery.
2 Remove the fuel filler cap to relieve fuel tank pressure.

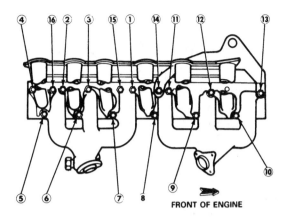

Fig. 13.4 Intake and exhaust manifold bolt tightening sequence — 4.9L inline six-cylinder engine (1987 on) (Sec 4)

3 Disconnect the accelerator cable and remove the cable bracket.
4 Remove the upper intake manifold and throttle body (see Section 6).
5 Move the vacuum harness away from the lower intake manifold.
6 Release the fuel pressure from the fuel system (see Section 6).
7 Remove the injector cooling manifold from the lifting eye attachment.
8 Remove the sixteen bolts that attach both the lower intake and the exhaust manifolds to the cylinder head. Do not remove the bolts that attach only the exhaust manifolds.
9 Remove the lower intake manifold assembly from the cylinder head.
10 Remove all traces of old gasket material with a scraper, then clean the mating surfaces with lacquer thinner or acetone. Check the mating surfaces of the lower intake manifold and the cylinder head for nicks and other damage that could prevent proper sealing.
11 Clean and oil the manifold bolt threads.
12 Position the lower intake manifold and a new gasket on the cylinder head and install the bolts. Tighten the bolts to the specified torque in the sequence shown (see Fig. 13.4).
13 The remaining installation steps are the reverse of removal.

Intake manifold — removal and installation (5.0L and 5.8L EFI engine only)

14 The procedure in Chapter 2, part B, is essentially correct, but note the following points.
15 Remove the upper intake manifold/throttle body assembly (Refer to Section 6 in this Chapter).
16 Disconnect the wires from the engine coolant temperature sensor, the temperature sending unit, the air charge temperature sensor and the knock sensor.

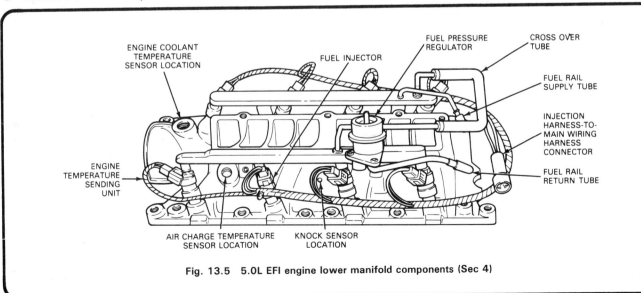

Fig. 13.5 5.0L EFI engine lower manifold components (Sec 4)

13

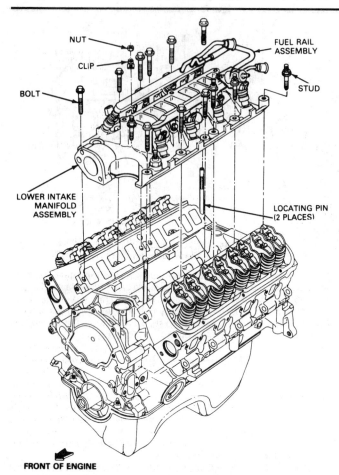

FRONT OF ENGINE

Fig. 13.6   Lower manifold bolts, stud and locking pins (Sec 4)

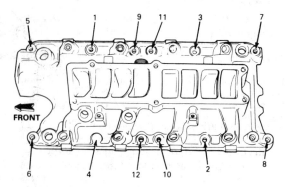

Fig. 13.7   Tighten the manifold bolts in the order shown
(Sec 4)

17 Disconnect the injector wiring harness and remove the EGO ground wire from the intake manifold stud.
18 Disconnect the fuel supply and return lines from the fuel rails (see fuel supply manifold assembly removal and installation in Section 6 of this Chapter).
19 Remove the air cleaner bracket (two nuts on the intake manifold and one nut on the exhaust manifold).
20 When installing the manifold, position the locating pins in opposite corners and make sure the gaskets interlock with the end seal tabs. Tighten the manifold bolts to the specified torque in the sequence shown (see Fig. 13.7). Wait ten minutes, then tighten the bolts a second time to the same torque.
21 The remaining installation steps are the reverse of removal.

Intake manifold — removal and installation (7.5L EFI engine only)

22 The procedure in Chapter 2, Part B, is essentially correct, but note the following points:
23 Remove the fuel filler cap and relieve fuel tank pressure.
24 Remove the upper intake manifold/throttle body assembly (see Section 6).
25 Disconnect the wiring harness from the main wiring harness.
26 Disconnect the fuel lines at the fuel rail and remove the fuel rail (see Section 6).
27 Remove the intake manifold bolts. Note the positions of the stud bolts and different length bolts.
28 Remove the intake manifold. If necessary, pry the manifold away from the cylinder head, but be careful not to damage the gasket sealing surface.
29 After the gasket sealing surfaces have been cleaned, inspect the manifold for cracks, damaged gasket surfaces and anything that would make it unfit for installation.
30 Install the intake manifold bolts and nuts and tighten them to the specified torque in the recommended sequence.
31 The remaining steps are the reverse of removal.

Cylinder heads — removal, inspection and installation (7.5L only)

The procedure in Chapter 2 is correct, but be sure to place the two long cylinder head bolts in the two rear, lower bolt holes in the left-hand cylinder head. Also, place a long cylinder head bolt in the rear, lower bolt hole in the right-hand cylinder head. Use rubber bands to retain the bolts in position, above the head-to-block mating surface, until the cylinder heads are installed.

Rocker arm covers — removal and installation (7.5L only)

Follow the procedure in Chapter 2, but note that the bolts on later models are in the center of the cover, rather than at the edges. A special tightening sequence is recommended by the manufacturer (Fig. 13.8).

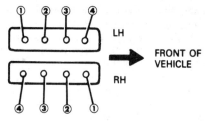

Fig. 13.8   Tightening sequence for 7.5L (460 cu in) V8 engine rocker arm cover bolts (1988 on) (Sec 4)

Oil cooler — removal and installation (7.5L only)

Note: *The oil cooler used on 1990 models is a new design. It's attached to the engine at the water pump inlet and the oil filter/cooler adapter on the block and coolant is routed through it to reduce the oil temperature. To remove it, detach the hose from the water pump inlet and remove the bolt that threads into the engine block to hold the adapter in place. Installation is the reverse of removal. Tighten the hollow oil cooler adapter-to-block bolt to 40 to 65 ft-lbs.*

32 Raise vehicle and support it securely on jackstands.
33 Remove the front grille (refer to Chapter 12).
34 From under the vehicle, disconnect the oil cooler lines at the filter adapter. A back-up wrench on the line fitting must be used when disconnecting this line. **Warning:** *Be prepared for oil to spill from the lines and the adapter.* **Caution:** *Do not attempt to disconnect the lines at the cooler fittings. The fittings or the cooler could be damaged.*
35 Pull the lines out toward the front.
36 Remove the six cooler bolts and lift out the oil cooler.
37 If the oil filter adapter must be removed, remove the through bolt at the center of the adapter.
38 When reinstalling the filter adapter use a new O-ring between the engine block and the adapter.
39 Position the oil cooler on the radiator support and install the six bolts.
40 Install the oil cooler lines in their original positions.
41 Put sealing compound on the threads of the line fittings and reinstall the lines on the filter adapter. Use a back-up wrench on the adapter fittings.

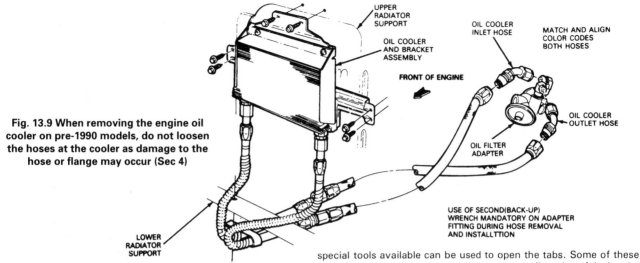

Fig. 13.9 When removing the engine oil cooler on pre-1990 models, do not loosen the hoses at the cooler as damage to the hose or flange may occur (Sec 4)

42 Check the oil level and correct if necessary.
43 Start the engine and check for oil leaks.
44 Remove the vehicle from the jackstands.

Engine — removal and installation (7.5L only)

45 On engine oil cooler equipped vehicles, disconnect the oil cooler lines at the oil filter adapter using a back-up wrench on the line fitting.
46 Before reinstalling the cooler lines, use thread sealer at the fittings.

---

5 Cooling, heating and air conditioning systems

Aluminum core radiator — general information

1 The cross flow fin and tube design radiator used on F-Series and Bronco vehicles is constructed with a vacuum brazed aluminum core and nylon end tanks. The nylon end tanks are attached to the aluminum core by bending tabs on the core over the edge of the nylon tank. An O-ring gasket is placed between the nylon tank and the radiator core to achieve a seal between the tank and the core. The nylon tanks are a molded one-piece design with the mounting brackets part of each tank. It is possible for the home mechanic to replace these tanks or correct a leak between the tank and the core.

Radiator tank — removal and installation

2 When removing a nylon tank, a screwdriver or one of the various special tools available can be used to open the tabs. Some of these tools, including a screwdriver, may cause a small section of the header side to bend with the tabs as they are opened. This slight deformation is permissible, provided the tabs are opened only enough for tank removal. The header sides will usually return to the normal position when the tabs are crimped during tank installation.
3 Procedures are given for tank removal using a screwdriver. Follow the manufacturers' instructions for other radiator tab opening and closing tools.
4 Insert the end of a medium screwdriver between the end of the header tab and the tank (see illustration). Press the screwdriver blade against the tank to bend the tab away from the tank edge. Repeat this procedure for each tab. **Note:** *Bend the tabs only enough for tank removal.*
5 Lift the tank from the core when all of the tabs are bent away from the tank edge.
6 Remove the O-ring gasket from the core. **Note:** *If any header tabs are missing from the aluminum core, the core should be replaced.*
7 Inspect the seal surface of the radiator core to be sure it is clean and free of foreign material or damage.
8 Check the new O-ring to be sure it is not twisted.
9 Dip the new O-ring in glycol or silicone lubricant, and place the gasket in the header groove.
10 If the outlet tank is being replaced and is equipped with an oil cooler, transfer the oil cooler from the replaced tank to the new tank.
11 Position the tank on the core using care not to scratch the tank sealing surfaces with the header tabs.
12 Clamp the tank in position on the core with two clamps as shown in Fig. 13.11. Tighten the header clamps to compress the O-ring gasket.

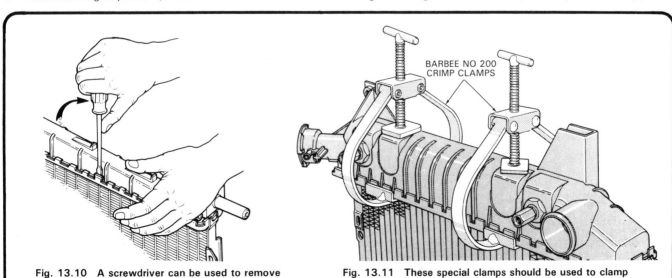

Fig. 13.10   A screwdriver can be used to remove the nylon tanks from the radiator core (Sec 5)

Fig. 13.11   These special clamps should be used to clamp the end tank into position (Sec 5)

13

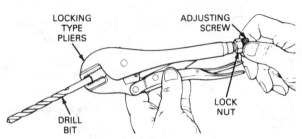

Fig. 13.12   Locking pliers are used to bend the tabs (first install a locking nut on the adjusting shaft and adjust the jaws with a 13/32-inch drill bit) (Sec 5)

13 If locking type pliers are used to squeeze the header tabs against the tank, install a locking nut on the adjusting screw.

14 With the jaws of the pliers closed and locked, turn the adjusting screw to position the jaws against the shank of a 13/32-inch drill bit (see Fig. 13.12). Tighten the nut on the adjusting screw against the handle to lock the adjustment in place.

15 Squeeze the header tabs down against the lip of the tank base with the locking-type pliers while rotating the pliers toward the tank. **Caution:** *It is important that the assembled height of the crimp be 13/32-inch when measured from the bottom of the header to the top of the tab.*

16 Remove the header clamps and squeeze the header tabs down that were behind the clamps.

17 Leak test the radiator at 21 psi. Most minor leaks at the header to tank seal can be corrected by again squeezing the header tabs down against the tank lip in the area of the leak.

Oil cooler — transfer or replacement

18 Remove the outlet tank from the radiator as described in the previous Steps.

19 Remove the nuts and washers from the oil cooler inlet and outlet connections. Lift the oil cooler from the radiator outlet tank (see Fig. 13.14).

20 Remove the rubber gaskets from the oil cooler inlet and outlet connections if the oil cooler is to be reused.

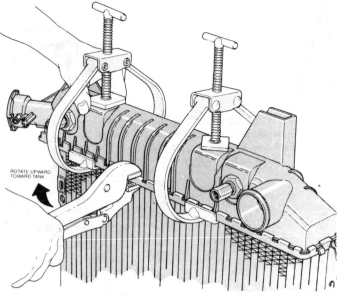

Fig. 13.13   Use a rotating motion as you squeeze the locking pliers closed (Sec 5)

21 Install new rubber gaskets on the oil cooler inlet and outlet connections.

22 Position the oil cooler in the radiator outlet tank and insert the inlet and outlet connections through the holes in the outlet tank.

23 Install the flat washer and nut on each oil cooler connection to retain the oil cooler in the radiator outlet tank.

24 Install the outlet tank on the radiator core header as described in the previous Steps.

Aluminum core radiator — cleaning

External

25 The aluminum core can be cleaned externally with a soft bristle brush, warm water and a mild liquid detergent.

26 If the radiator is equipped with an oil cooler, install plugs in the

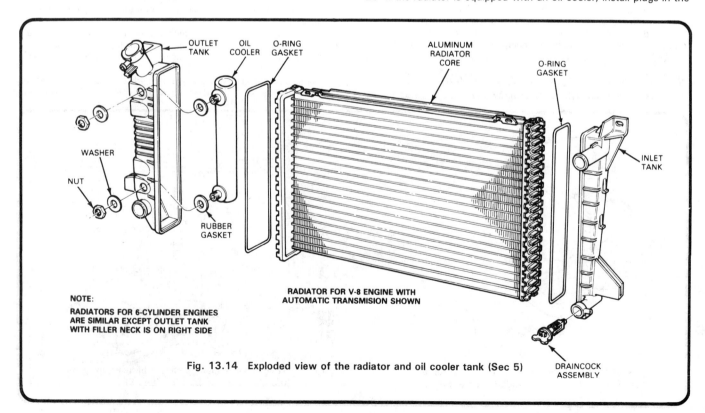

NOTE:

RADIATORS FOR 6-CYLINDER ENGINES ARE SIMILAR EXCEPT OUTLET TANK WITH FILLER NECK IS ON RIGHT SIDE

RADIATOR FOR V-8 ENGINE WITH AUTOMATIC TRANSMISION SHOWN

Fig. 13.14   Exploded view of the radiator and oil cooler tank (Sec 5)

oil cooler fittings before cleaning and keep them installed during the entire service operation.

Internal

Caution: *Do not use caustic cleaning solutions or copper/brass radiator cleaning agents on aluminum radiators.*

27 Internal cleaning of the aluminum tubes can be accomplished with sonic cleaning equipment or by removing one end tank to gain access to tubes.

28 Clean the tubes with a mild liquid detergent. Rinse the core with clean water when completed. Do not use a metal brush to clean an aluminum core. Use only horsehair, bristle or nylon bushes.

Quick disconnect heater hoses — general information

29 Some later models are equipped with quick disconnect heater hoses, which require two special tools to disconnect. When reconnecting the hoses, always use new O-rings (Fig. 13.15).

TO DISCONNECT COUPLING

CAUTION — ENGINE SHOULD BE OFF BEFORE DISCONNECTING COUPLING

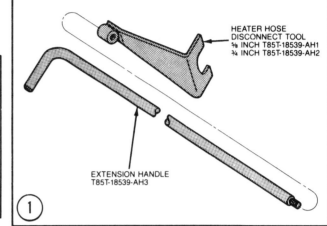

HEATER HOSE
DISCONNECT TOOL
⅜ INCH T85T-18539-AH1
¾ INCH T85T-18539-AH2

EXTENSION HANDLE
T85T-18539-AH3

TO CONNECT COUPLING

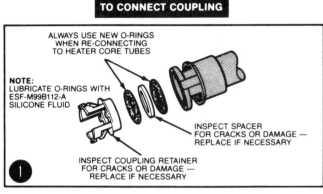

ALWAYS USE NEW O-RINGS
WHEN RE-CONNECTING
TO HEATER CORE TUBES

NOTE:
LUBRICATE O-RINGS WITH
ESF-M99B112-A
SILICONE FLUID

INSPECT SPACER
FOR CRACKS OR DAMAGE —
REPLACE IF NECESSARY

INSPECT COUPLING RETAINER
FOR CRACKS OR DAMAGE —
REPLACE IF NECESSARY

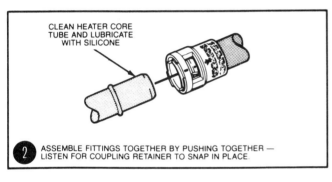

CLEAN HEATER CORE
TUBE AND LUBRICATE
WITH SILICONE

② ASSEMBLE FITTINGS TOGETHER BY PUSHING TOGETHER —
LISTEN FOR COUPLING RETAINER TO SNAP IN PLACE.

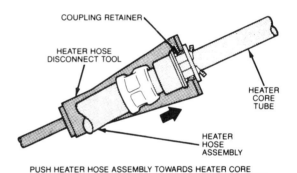

COUPLING RETAINER

HEATER HOSE
DISCONNECT TOOL

HEATER
CORE
TUBE

HEATER
HOSE
ASSEMBLY

PUSH HEATER HOSE ASSEMBLY TOWARDS HEATER CORE
TUBE TO ENSURE LOCKING TABS ARE FULLY EXPOSED, THEN
PUSH TOOL OVER COUPLING RETAINER WINDOWS TO
COMPRESS RETAINER LOCKING TABS — THEN PULL HOSE
ASSEMBLY AWAY FROM HEATER CORE TUBE.
REMOVE TOOL THEN CONTINUE PULLING HOSE ASSEMBLY
AWAY FROM HEATER CORE TUBE.

② NOTE: WHEN COMPRESSING WHITE COUPLING RETAINER,
THE TOOL MUST BE PERPENDICULAR AND ON THE HIGHEST
POINT OF THE COUPLING RETAINER AS SHOWN ABOVE.

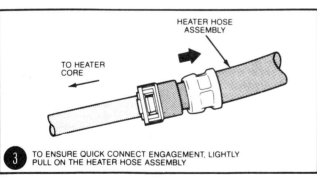

HEATER HOSE
ASSEMBLY

TO HEATER
CORE

③ TO ENSURE QUICK CONNECT ENGAGEMENT, LIGHTLY
PULL ON THE HEATER HOSE ASSEMBLY

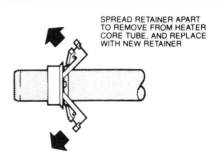

SPREAD RETAINER APART
TO REMOVE FROM HEATER
CORE TUBE, AND REPLACE
WITH NEW RETAINER

③ WHEN THE QUICK CONNECT COUPLING IS DISCONNECTED — THE
WHITE COUPLING RETAINER WILL REMAIN ON THE HEATER CORE TUBE.
INSTALL NEW COUPLING RETAINER, SPACER & NEW LUBRICATED
O-RINGS INTO QUICK CONNECT ASSEMBLY HOUSING BEFORE
RE-INSTALLING HEATER HOSE ASSEMBLY TO HEATER CORE TUBES.

Fig. 13.15 Quick disconnect heater hose details (two special tools are needed to disconnect the hoses — the tools can be purchased from a Ford dealer or parts store); always use new O-rings when reconnecting the hoses (Sec 5)

13

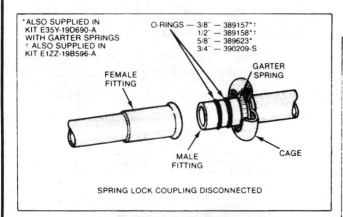

*ALSO SUPPLIED IN
KIT E35Y-19D690-A
WITH GARTER SPRINGS
† ALSO SUPPLIED IN
KIT E1ZZ-19B596-A

O-RINGS — 3/8" — 389157*†
1/2" — 389158*†
5/8" — 389623*
3/4" — 390209-S

FEMALE
FITTING

GARTER
SPRING

MALE
FITTING

CAGE

SPRING LOCK COUPLING DISCONNECTED

TO CONNECT COUPLING

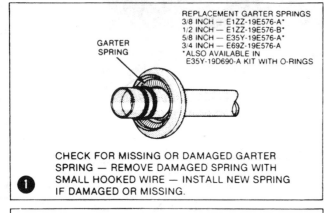

GARTER
SPRING

REPLACEMENT GARTER SPRINGS
3/8 INCH — E1ZZ-19E576-A*
1/2 INCH — E1ZZ-19E576-B*
5/8 INCH — E35Y-19E576-A*
3/4 INCH — E69Z-19E576-A
*ALSO AVAILABLE IN
E35Y-19D690-A KIT WITH O-RINGS

① CHECK FOR MISSING OR DAMAGED GARTER
SPRING — REMOVE DAMAGED SPRING WITH
SMALL HOOKED WIRE — INSTALL NEW SPRING
IF DAMAGED OR MISSING.

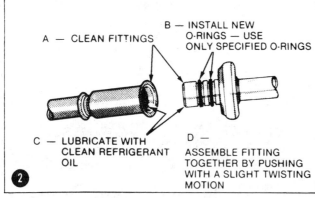

A — CLEAN FITTINGS

B — INSTALL NEW
O-RINGS — USE
ONLY SPECIFIED O-RINGS

C — LUBRICATE WITH
CLEAN REFRIGERANT
OIL

D —
ASSEMBLE FITTING
TOGETHER BY PUSHING
WITH A SLIGHT TWISTING
MOTION

②

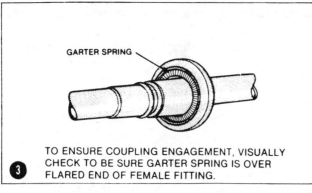

GARTER SPRING

③ TO ENSURE COUPLING ENGAGEMENT, VISUALLY
CHECK TO BE SURE GARTER SPRING IS OVER
FLARED END OF FEMALE FITTING.

TO DISCONNECT COUPLING

CAUTION — DISCHARGE SYSTEM BEFORE DISCONNECTING COUPLING

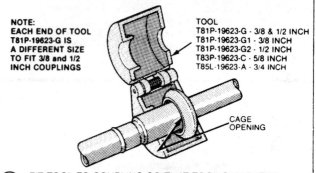

NOTE:
EACH END OF TOOL
T81P-19623-G IS
A DIFFERENT SIZE
TO FIT 3/8 and 1/2
INCH COUPLINGS

TOOL
T81P-19623-G - 3/8 & 1/2 INCH
T81P-19623-G1 - 3/8 INCH
T81P-19623-G2 - 1/2 INCH
T83P-19623-C - 5/8 INCH
T85L-19623-A - 3/4 INCH

CAGE
OPENING

① FIT TOOL TO COUPLING SO THAT TOOL CAN ENTER
CAGE OPENING TO RELEASE THE GARTER SPRING.

PUSH TOOL INTO
CAGE OPENING

② PUSH THE TOOL INTO THE CAGE
OPENING TO RELEASE THE FEMALE FITTING FROM
THE GARTER SPRING.

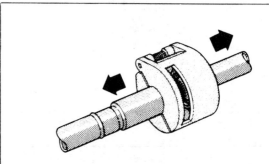

③ PULL THE COUPLING MALE AND FEMALE
FITTINGS APART.

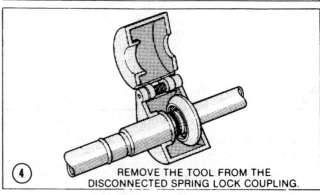

④ REMOVE THE TOOL FROM THE
DISCONNECTED SPRING LOCK COUPLING.

Fig. 13.16 Quick disconnect air conditioning system hose details (make sure the A/C system has been discharged before
disconnecting the hoses — special tools are needed and can be purchased from a Ford dealer or parts store) (Sec 5)

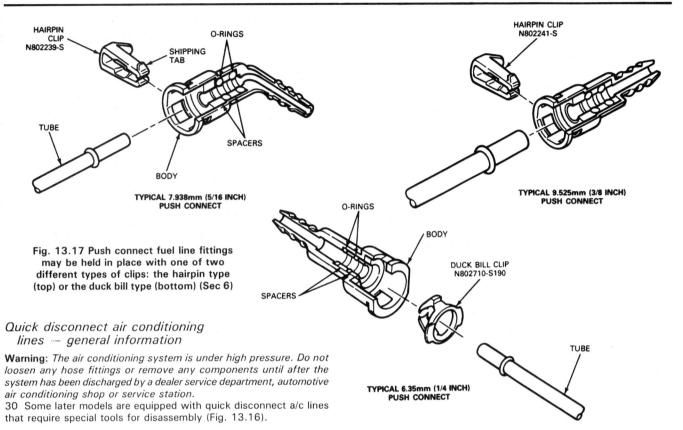

Fig. 13.17 Push connect fuel line fittings may be held in place with one of two different types of clips: the hairpin type (top) or the duck bill type (bottom) (Sec 6)

Quick disconnect air conditioning lines — general information

Warning: *The air conditioning system is under high pressure. Do not loosen any hose fittings or remove any components until after the system has been discharged by a dealer service department, automotive air conditioning shop or service station.*

30 Some later models are equipped with quick disconnect a/c lines that require special tools for disassembly (Fig. 13.16).

6 Fuel and exhaust systems

Plastic fuel lines — general information

1 The plastic fuel lines used on later models can be damaged by torches, welding sparks, grinding and other operations which involve heat and high temperatures. Plastic fuel lines must not be repaired with hoses and hose clamps. Push connect fittings cannot be repaired except to replace the retaining clips. If the plastic lines, push connect fittings or steel tube ends become damaged and leak, only approved service parts should be used for repairs.

Push connect fuel line fittings — general information

2 The push connect fittings used on later model fuel lines are designed with two different retaining clips. The fittings used to connect 3/8-inch and 5/16-inch lines have a "hairpin" clip. The fittings used to connect 1/4-inch diameter lines have a "duck bill" clip and require a special tool for disassembly. Use new clips each time the lines are disconnected (Fig. 13.17).

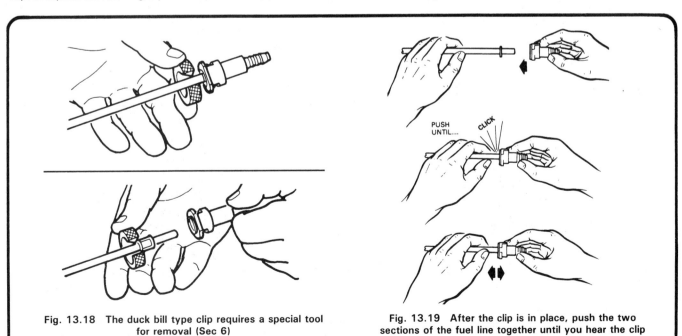

Fig. 13.18   The duck bill type clip requires a special tool for removal (Sec 6)

Fig. 13.19   After the clip is in place, push the two sections of the fuel line together until you hear the clip snap into place, then try to pull them apart (Sec 6)

13

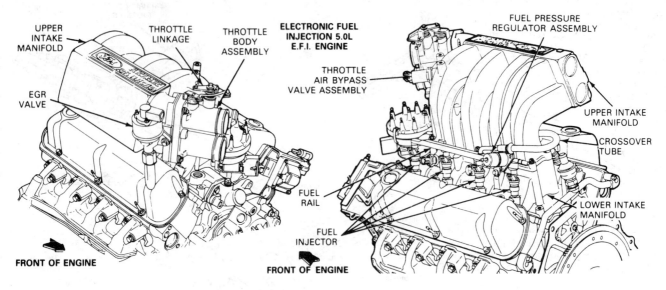

Fig. 13.20   Typical EFI component location (5.0L engine shown) (Sec 6)

Electronic Fuel Injection (EFI) - general information

3   The EFI system is a multipoint, pulse time, mass air flow fuel injection system. Fuel is metered into the intake air stream in accordance with engine demand through eight injectors mounted on an intake manifold. An on-board computer (EEC-IV) accepts information from various engine sensors to determine the required fuel flow rate necessary to maintain a prescribed fuel/air mixture throughout the entire engine operational range. The computer then sends a command to the injectors to meter the required amount of fuel.

4   The fuel delivery sub-system consists of a low pressure in-tank fuel pump, a fuel filter/reservoir and a high pressure, chassis mounted electric fuel pump, which delivers fuel from the tank through a 20 micron filter to the fuel charging manifold assembly. Beginning in 1990, some models use a single high-pressure pump mounted in the fuel tank. The fuel charging manifold incorporates electrically actuated fuel injectors directly above each of the eight intake ports. The injectors, when energized, spray a metered quantity of fuel into the intake air stream.

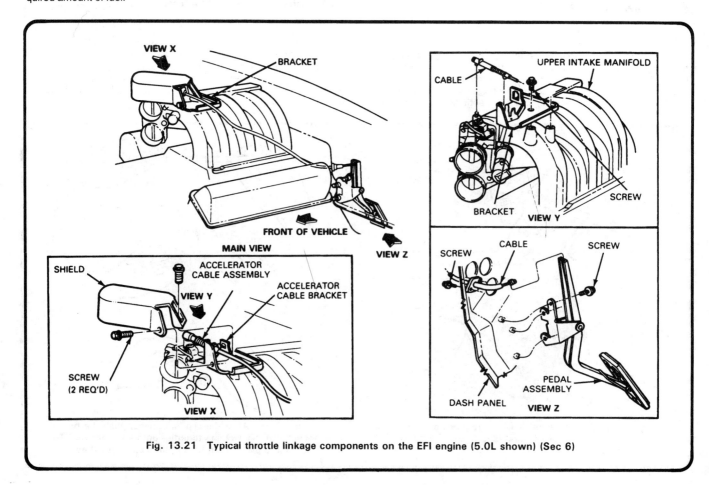

Fig. 13.21   Typical throttle linkage components on the EFI engine (5.0L shown) (Sec 6)

5   A constant fuel pressure drop is maintained across the injector nozzles by a pressure regulator. Excess fuel supplied by the pump, but not required by the engine, passes through the regulator and returns to the tank through a fuel return line.

6   One bank of four injectors is energized simultaneously, once every crankshaft revolution, followed by the second bank of injectors the next crankshaft revolution. The period of time that the injectors are energized is controlled by the computer.

7   Air entering the engine is measured by an air flow meter. The computer receives input from various engine sensors and uses the information to compute the required fuel flow rate necessary to sustain the fuel/air mixture required for any given engine operating condition.

EFI components — removal and installation

Warning: *Fuel supply lines on EFI equipped engines will remain pressurized for a period of time after the engine is shut off. The pressure must be relieved before servicing any component of the fuel system. Remember, gasoline is extremely flammable, so extra precautions must be taken when working on any part of the fuel system. Do not smoke or allow open flames or bare light bulbs near the work area. Also, do not work in a garage if a natural gas appliance equipped with a pilot light is present.*

Fuel system pressure relief

8   Locate and disconnect the wire from either the fuel pump relay, the inertia switch or the in-line high pressure fuel pump. Remove the fuel tank filler cap to relieve pressure from the tank.

9   Crank the engine for approximately ten seconds. The engine may start and run, then stall. If it does, crank it over for an additional five seconds after it stalls.

10 Reconnect the wire that was disconnected.

11 Disconnect the negative battery cable from the battery.

Upper intake manifold and throttle body removal

12 Relieve the fuel system pressure as described above.

13 Remove the fuel filler cap.

14 Disconnect the wires from the air bypass valve, the throttle position sensor and the EGR position sensor (see Fig. 13.20).

15 Detach the throttle linkage from the throttle ball and the AOD transmission linkage from the throttle body (if equipped with an automatic transmission). Remove the two bolts and detach the cables and bracket (see Fig. 13.21).

16 Mark and detach the vacuum hoses from the vacuum tree, the EGR valve and the fuel pressure regulator.

17 Disconnect the PCV system hose from the fitting on the rear of the upper manifold.

18 Detach the air cleaner-to-throttle body tubes from the throttle body.

19 Remove the two canister purge lines from the fittings on the throttle body.

20 Detach the coolant lines from the throttle body. Be prepared for some coolant loss.

21 Remove the flange nut and detach the tube from the EGR valve.

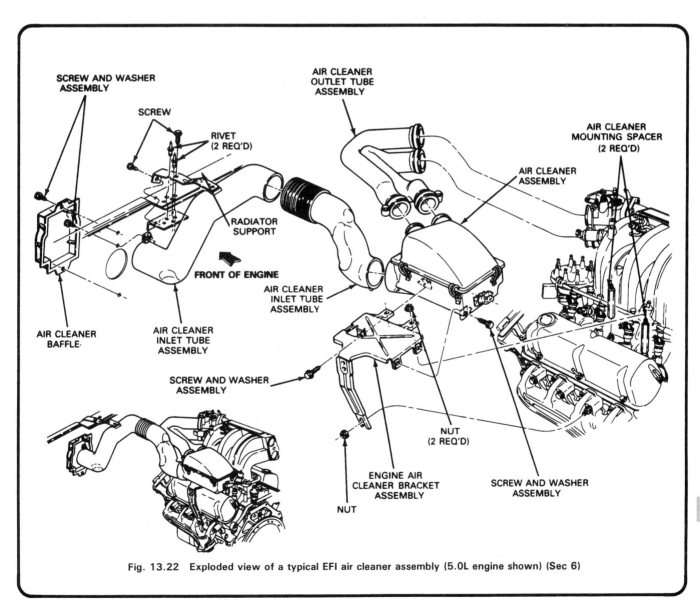

Fig. 13.22   Exploded view of a typical EFI air cleaner assembly (5.0L engine shown) (Sec 6)

13

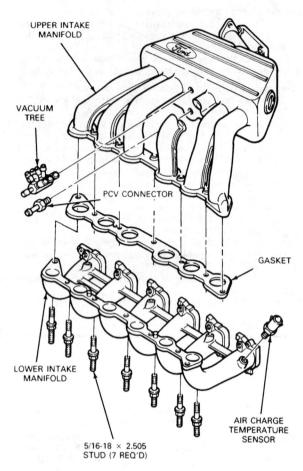

Fig. 13.23 1987 and later inline six-cylinder engine intake manifolds — exploded view (Sec 6)

22 Remove the upper support bracket-to-upper manifold bolt and the upper intake manifold retaining bolts.
23 Carefully separate the upper manifold and throttle body, as an assembly, from the lower manifold.

Upper intake manifold and throttle body installation
24 Clean and check the mounting faces of the intake manifold. Position a new gasket on the lower manifold mounting face.
25 Carefully lower the upper manifold into place. Don't disturb the gasket in the process. Install the upper manifold retaining bolts and tighten them to the specified torque. Install and tighten the support bracket-to-upper manifold bolt.
26 The remaining steps are the reverse of removal. Make sure the vacuum lines and wires are routed and attached correctly.

Throttle body
27 Open the hood and detach the air intake duct, then disconnect the throttle position sensor and air bypass valve wires.
28 Remove the four throttle body bolts and detach the throttle body from the upper intake manifold.
29 Remove and discard the gasket. Make sure the gasket surfaces of the manifold and throttle body are clean and smooth. If scraping is necessary, do not scratch or nick the manifold or throttle body and do not allow material to fall into the intake manifold.
30 Installation is the reverse of removal.

Throttle position sensor
31 Detach the sensor wiring harness, then scribe a reference mark across the edge of the sensor and the throttle body.
32 Remove the screws and detach the sensor.
33 Installation is the reverse of removal. Position the sensor with the wiring harness parallel to the throttle bores, then rotate it clockwise to align the reference marks before installing the screws. The wiring harness should point directly to the air bypass valve. The sensor should be adjusted by a Ford dealer service department.

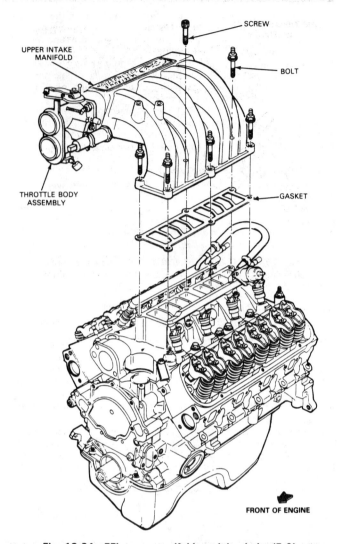

Fig. 13.24 EFI upper manifold retaining bolts (5.0L engine) (Sec 6)

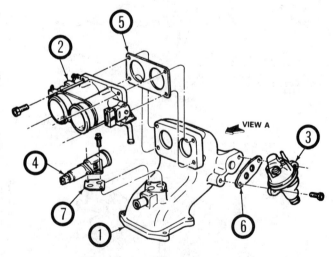

Fig. 13.25 460 cu in (7.5L) engine throttle body and upper intake manifold components (1988 on) (Sec 6)

1 *Upper intake manifold*   5 *Throttle body gasket*
2 *Throttle body*   6 *EGR valve gasket*
3 *EGR valve*   7 *Air bypass valve gasket*
4 *Throttle air bypass valve*

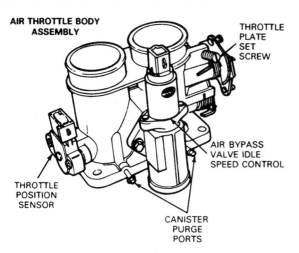

Fig. 13.26 This is a typical throttle body assembly showing the air bypass valve and the throttle position sensor locations (Sec 6)

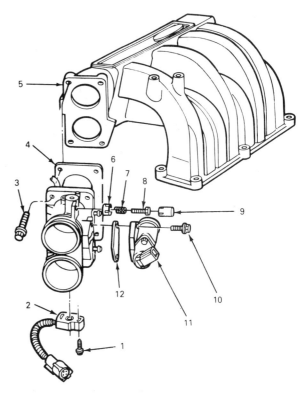

Air bypass valve

34 Disconnect the wiring harness, then remove the air valve mounting bolts.

35 Detach the valve from the throttle body and remove the gasket.

36 Make sure the gasket surfaces of the valve and throttle body are clean and smooth. If scraping is necessary, do not scratch or nick the valve or throttle body and do not allow material to fall into the throttle body.

37 Installation is the reverse of removal. Be sure to use a new gasket.

Fuel supply manifold assembly

38 Remove the upper intake manifold assembly as described previously, then disconnect the crossover fuel hose from the fuel supply manifold. A special tool (number T81P-19623-G or G1), available from Ford dealers, must be used when disconnecting the hose (see Fig. 13.28).

39 Disconnect the fuel supply and return lines at the fuel supply manifold.

40 Remove the four (two per side) retaining bolts. Carefully disengage

Fig. 13.27 Exploded view of the throttle body assembly (5.0L engine shown) (Sec 6)

1 TPS bolt
2 Throttle position sensor
3 Throttle body bolt
4 Throttle body gasket
5 Upper intake manifold
6 Idle screw lock plug
7 Spring
8 Idle screw
9 Idle screw cap
10 Air bypass valve bolt
11 Air bypass valve
12 Air bypass valve gasket

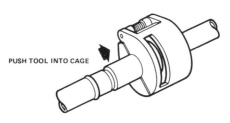

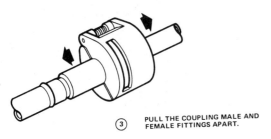

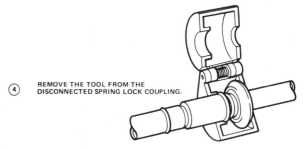

Fig. 13.28 This special tool will be needed to disconnect the fuel lines at the fuel rail (Sec 6)

13

the manifold from the injectors and remove it (see Figs. 13.29 and 13.30).

41 Installation is the reverse of removal. Make sure the injector caps are clean before installing the manifold and that the injectors are seated properly. The fuel lines are connected by pushing the sections together carefully. Make sure they are locked.

Fuel pressure regulator

42 If the supply manifold is in place on the engine, relieve the fuel pressure as described above and remove the fuel tank cap.

43 Detach the vacuum line from the regulator and remove the three retaining screws from the regulator housing.

44 Remove the regulator, gasket and O-ring. Discard the gasket and check the O-ring for cracks and deterioration.

45 Make sure the gasket surfaces are clean and smooth. If scraping is necessary, do not damage the regulator or fuel supply line surfaces.

46 Installation is the reverse of removal. Lubricate the O-ring with light oil, but do not use silicone grease, as the injectors may clog. Turn the ignition switch On and Off several times without starting the engine to check for fuel leaks.

Fuel injectors

47 Remove the upper intake manifold and fuel supply manifold as described previously.

48 Carefully detach the wiring harness from individual injectors (see Fig. 13.31).

49 Grasp the injector body and pull up while gently rocking the injector from side-to-side.

50 Check the injector O-rings (two each) for damage and deterioration (see Fig. 13.32). Replace them with new ones if necessary.

51 Check the plastic hat covering the pintle for damage and deterioration. If it is missing, look for it in the intake manifold.

52 Installation is the reverse of removal. Lubricate the O-rings with light oil, but do not use silicone grease, as the injector will clog.

53 Start engine and check the fuel system for leaks.

Electric fuel pump

General information

54 The electric fuel pump system uses a low pressure in-tank mounted pump and an externally mounted high pressure in-line pump. The fuel tank has an internal sump cavity in which the low pressure fuel pump inlet rests. This design provides for satisfactory pump operation during extreme vehicle maneuvers and steep vehicle attitudes with low tank fill levels.

55 The low pressure electric fuel pump is to provide pressurized fuel to the inlet of the high pressure pump. The inlet of the low pressure fuel pump has a nylon filter on it to prevent dirt and other particulate matter from entering the system. The low pressure pump has an external resistor in the electrical circuit to reduce the operating voltage to 11 volts. **Note:** *Beginning in 1990, some models use a single high-pressure pump mounted in the fuel tank.*

56 The externally mounted fuel pump is a high pressure unit with a working pressure of 39 psi. The pump has an internal relief valve to provide overpressure protection in the event the fuel flow becomes restricted (clogged filter, damaged fuel lines, etc.). The system pressure is controlled by a pressure regulator on the engine. The electrical system has a fuel pump control relay controlled by the electronic engine control (EEC) module, which provides power to the fuel pump.

Diagnosis

57 Electric fuel pump malfunctions will result in a loss or reduction of fuel flow and/or pressure. This diagnosis procedure will concentrate on determining if the electric fuel pump is operating properly.

58 Check the fuel tank for adequate fuel supply. **Note:** *The tank must*

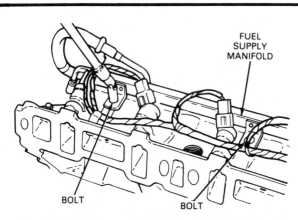

Fig. 13.29 There are four fuel supply manifold retaining bolts — be careful not to bend the fuel lines when removing them (Sec 6)

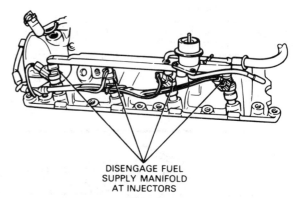

Fig. 13.30 Pull straight up when disengaging the fuel rail from the injectors (Sec 6)

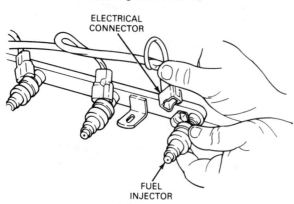

Fig. 13.31 A firm straight pull will disengage the electrical connector from the fuel injector (Sec 6)

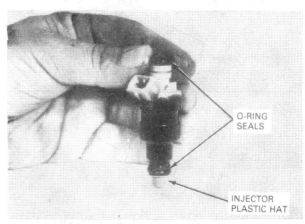

Fig. 13.32 Before reinstalling the fuel injectors check the sealing O-rings for condition (Sec 6)

be at least half full for the following procedures.
59 Check for fuel leakage at all fittings and lines.
60 Check for electrical continuity to the fuel pump by disconnecting the electrical connector at the high pressure pump.
61 Connect a voltmeter to the body wiring harness connector.
62 Turn the key to On while watching the voltmeter.
63 The voltage should rise to battery voltage, then return to zero after approximately one second.
64 If the voltage is not as specified check the inertia switch and electrical system.
65 Connect a continuity tester (ohmmeter) to the pump wiring harness connector. If no continuity is present check continuity directly at the pump terminals.
66 If there is no continuity at the pump terminals, replace the pump. If continuity is present here but not in Step 65, service or replace the wiring harness.
67 Connect the continuity tester across the body wiring harness connector. If continuity is present (about 5 ohms), the low pressure pump circuit is electrically OK.
68 If no continuity is present in Step 67 it will be necessary to remove the fuel tank (refer to Chapter 4) and check for continuity at the fuel pump/pump sender flange terminals. If no continuity at pump flange terminals is present, replace the assembly. If continuity is present at the pump but not in Step 67, service or replace the wiring harness to the low pressure pump.
69 To check electric fuel pump operation, disconnect the return line at the fuel rail. Use care to avoid fuel spillage.
70 Connect a hose from the fuel rail fitting to a calibrated container of at least one quart.
71 Connect pressure gauge T80L-9974-A or equivalent to fuel diagnostic valve on fuel rail.
72 Disconnect the electrical connector to the electric fuel pump located just forward of the pump outlet if not already disconnected from Step 60.
73 Connect an auxiliary wiring harness to the electrical connector.
74 Energize the fuel pump for 10 seconds by connecting the auxiliary wiring harness to a fully charged 12 volt battery. Observe the pressure while energized. If there is no pressure, check the polarity of the wiring harness and also check the terminal connectors at the fuel pump.
75 Allow the fuel to drain from the hose into the container and note the volume.
76 The fuel pump is operating properly if:
  a) The fuel pressure reaches 35 to 40 psi.
  b) Fuel flow is a minimum of 5.6 ounces in 10 seconds.
  c) Fuel pressure remains at a minimum of 30 psi immediately after de-energization.
77 If all three conditions are met the fuel pump is operating normally.
78 If pressure condition is met but flow is not, check for a blocked

filter and fuel supply lines. If flow conditions are still not met replace the fuel pump.
79 If both pressure and flow conditions are met but pressure will not maintain after de-energization, check for a leaking regulator or injectors. If both check OK replace the fuel pump.
80 If no flow or pressure is seen the fuel system should be checked as in Step 78. If no trouble is found replace the fuel pump and drop the fuel tank and replace the fuel filter on the low pressure pump.
81 Check the low pressure in-tank pump as follows:
82 Remove the inlet push connect fitting and the line from the high pressure pump assembly. **Caution:** *Raise the end of the fitting above the level of the fluid in the tank to prevent siphon action.*
83 Connect a hose from the fuel tank to a calibrated container of at least one quart capacity.
84 Place the ignition switch in the Run position until the fuel pump times out (about 1 second).
85 Check the container for presence of some fuel. The amount of fuel should be a minimum of 1.5 ounces for one second of operation.
86 If no fuel is present, repeat Steps 85 and 86 two or three times (recycle key).
87 If no fuel is present, check for a pinched line between the fuel tank and the fitting and then proceed to drop the fuel tank (refer to Chapter 4).
88 Connect a voltmeter to the chassis electrical connector from the fuel pump and turn the key to the On position. Voltage should rise to about battery voltage for one second and then return to zero volts.
89 If voltage is as specified and the electrical connector is OK at the pump, replace the fuel pump assembly and repeat the low pressure pump test.
90 If no voltage is present service the electrical circuit.

High pressure in-line pump assembly — removal and installation
91 Depressurize the fuel system and remove the gas tank cap.
92 Raise the vehicle and support it securely on jackstands.
93 Disconnect the electrical connector from the body harness. Remove the inlet and outlet fuel hoses from the fuel pump.
94 Remove the bolts and detach the pump from the frame (see Fig. 13.33).
95 The electrical wiring harness may be removed from the assembly by inserting a screwdriver or knife between the connector and retaining clip and sliding the connector towards the pump inlet.
96 Installation is basically the reverse of removal noting the following points:
97 Make sure the fittings on the pump have gaskets in place, are properly positioned and that the fittings have been tightened properly (inlet 19 to 22 ft-lbs, outlet 8 to 12 ft-lbs.). Check the wiring harness boots to make sure they are pushed onto the pump terminals far enough to seal and that the wire terminals are pushed onto the pump terminals fully.

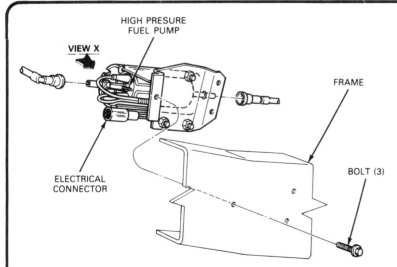
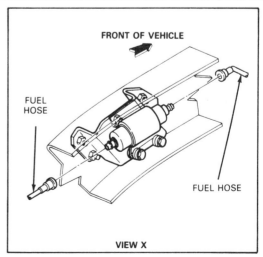

Fig. 13.33 After disconnecting both fuel lines, remove the three bolts holding the high pressure pump to the frame rail (Sec 6)

13

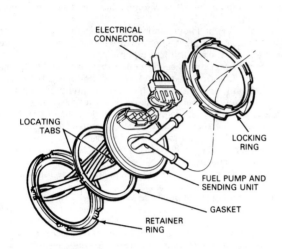

Fig. 13.34   Low pressure fuel pump assembly — exploded view (Sec 6)

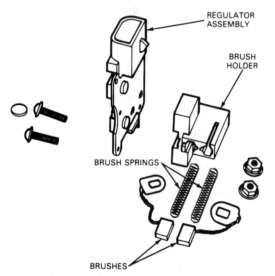

Fig. 13.36   Exploded view of the brush assembly (Sec 7)

98 After wrapping the isolator around the fuel pump, locate the slot in the isolator so it faces the bracket base and push the pump and isolator assembly into the bracket. Make sure the tab of the isolator contacts the tab of the bracket and that the bracket tabs do not contact the pump case.

99 Start the vehicle and check for proper operation of the pump and for leaks.

Low pressure in-tank assembly — removal and installation

100 The low pressure fuel pump is located in the top of the fuel tank and requires removal of the fuel tank for servicing (refer to Chapter 3). The low pressure pump is removed in the same manner as the fuel sender by removing the hoses, fittings and the locking ring and removing the assembly from the tank. **Note:** *The plastic fuel tank on 1989 and later models is equipped with a threaded locking ring. To remove it, turn it counterclockwise.*

Installation

101 Clean the fuel pump mounting flange and the fuel tank mounting surface and seal ring groove.

102 Put a light coating of heavy duty grease on a new seal ring to hold it in place during assembly and install it in the fuel ring groove.

103 Install the fuel pump and bracket assembly carefully to insure that the filter is not damaged. Be sure that the locating keys are in the keyways and that the seal ring remains in the groove.

104 Hold the pump assembly in place and install the locking ring finger

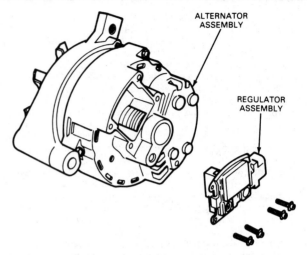

Fig. 13.35   A no. 20 Torx bit will be needed to remove the regulator/brush assembly (Sec 7)

tight, being sure that all the locking tabs are under the tank lock ring tabs.

105 Secure the fuel pump unit with the locking ring by rotating clockwise until the ring stops against stops.

106 Install the electrical connector.

107 Install the fuel line fitting.

108 Install the tank.

109 Turn the ignition key to the On position for 3 seconds. Turn the ignition key Off and On for 3 seconds repeatedly (5 to 10 times) to pressurize the system. Check for leaks at the fittings.

110 Start the engine and recheck for leaks.

---

7   Engine electrical system

Integral regulator alternator — brush replacement

1   Remove the alternator using the procedure in Chapter 5.

2   With the alternator on a workbench, remove the four screws (T20 Torx type head) attaching the regulator to the alternator rear housing (see Fig. 13.35). Remove the regulator, with brush holder attached, from the alternator.

3   Remove the A terminal insulator and two screws attaching the regulator to the brush holder. Separate the regulator, attaching nuts, brushes and brush springs from the brush holder.

4   Install the springs and new brushes in the brush holder.

5   Hold the brushes in place by inserting a 1-3/8 inch long piece of stiff wire into the brush holder pin hole (see Fig. 13.37).

6   Position the two nut and washer assemblies into the retaining slots in the brush holder. Tip the holder back slightly so that the nut and washer assemblies fall to the nut side of the slots. Insert the brush terminals past the washers and into the slots.

7   Wipe the regulator base plate with a clean cloth. Position the regulator against the brush holder and install the regulator to brush holder attaching screws. Tighten the screws to 20 to 30 in-lbs. Loop the brush leads toward the brush end of the brush holder.

8   Install the adhesive backed insulator onto the A terminal screw head.

9   Wipe the regulator mounting surface of the alternator rear housing with a clean cloth. Position the regulator and brush holder assembly onto the alternator rear housing.

10 Install the regulator attaching screws. Tighten the screws to 25 to 35 in-lbs.

11 Remove the wire holding the brushes. **Caution:** *This step is important. Failure to remove the wire will result in a short circuit that will destroy the regulator.*

12 Place a daub of waterproof sealer over the brush pin to prevent water entry. **Note:** *Do not use silicone sealer on the brush pin hole.*

165 amp alternator – general information

A new 165 amp alternator is used on 1990 models. If charging system voltage is above or below 14.2 to 14.3 volts, the regulator can be adjusted as follows: Remove the nylon screw from the regulator on

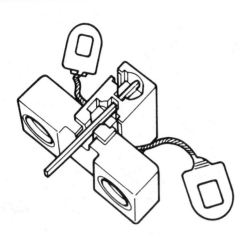

Fig. 13.37   A piece of stiff wire can be used to hold the new brushes in place (Sec 7)

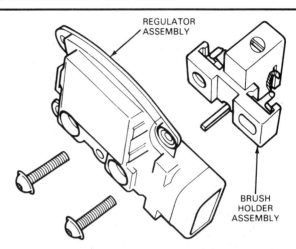

Fig. 13.38   With the wire still holding the brushes in place, assemble the brush holder to the regulator (Sec 7)

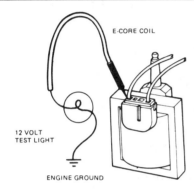

Fig. 13.39   Checking ignition coil primary circuit switching (Sec 7)

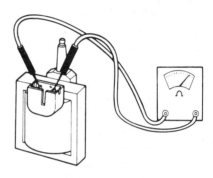

Fig. 13.40   Measuring ignition coil primary resistance (Sec 7)

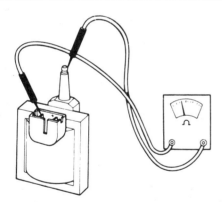

Fig. 13.41   Measuring ignition coil secondary resistance (Sec 7)

the back of the alternator and start the engine. With the engine running at approximately 1000 rpm, carefully turn the adjusting screw (clockwise to raise the output, counterclockwise to lower it.) Don't force the screw beyond the stops or damage will occur. If charging system voltage is to high and adjustment doesn't lower it, the regulator must be replaced with a new one.

TFI-IV ignition system

General information

The TFI-IV ignition system is used on 1984 and later models. It is a solid state electronic design consisting of an ignition module, coil, distributor, spark plug wires and spark plugs. The system has no centrifugal or vacuum advance. Basically, the system functions similarly to the Duraspark ignition system. A Hall Effect vane switch assembly located in the distributor signals the EEC-IV and TFI-IV modules to switch the ignition coil on and off.

Ignition coil and circuits – check

Ignition coil primary circuit

13   Unplug the electrical connector from the ignition module. Inspect it for dirt, corrosion and damage, then plug it back in.
14   Attach a 12-volt DC test light between the coil TACH terminal and a good engine ground (see Fig. 13.39).
15   Crank the engine.
16   If the light flashes, or comes on but doesn't flash, refer to Step 19.
17   If the light stays off or is very dim, take the vehicle to a dealer service department for further testing.
18   Remove the test light.

Ignition coil primary resistance

19   Turn the ignition switch to Off.
20   Unplug the ignition coil wire harness connector. Inspect it for dirt, corrosion and damage.
21   Measure the resistance between the primary terminals of the ignition coil (see Fig. 13.40).
22   If the indicated resistance is within the limits listed in this Chapter's Specifications, proceed to Step 24.
23   If the indicated resistance is less or more than specified, replace the ignition coil.

Ignition coil secondary resistance

24   Measure the resistance from the negative primary terminal to the secondary terminal of the ignition coil (see Fig. 13.41).
25   If the indicated resistance is within the limits listed in this Chapter's Specifications, proceed to Step 28.
26   If the indicated resistance is less or more than the specified resistance, replace the ignition coil.
27   Reconnect the ignition coil wires.

13

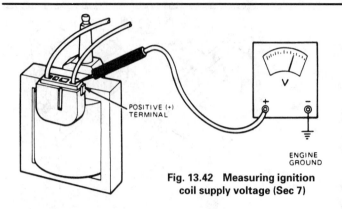

Fig. 13.42   Measuring ignition coil supply voltage (Sec 7)

Fig. 13.43   To replace the ignition coil, detach the cable from the negative terminal of the battery, unplug the coil primary connector (arrow), detach the coil secondary lead and remove both coil bracket bolts (arrows)

Ignition coil supply voltage

28   Unplug the ignition coil wire harness.
29   Attach the negative lead of a VOM to the distributor base.
30   Measure battery voltage.
31   Turn the ignition switch to the Run position.
32   Measure the voltage at the positive terminal of the ignition coil (see Fig. 13.42).
33   If the indicated voltage is 90 percent of battery voltage, inspect the ignition coil connector and terminals for dirt, corrosion and damage. Further checking must be done by a dealer service department.
34   If the indicated voltage is less than 90-percent of battery voltage, inspect and repair the circuit between the ignition coil and the ignition switch (refer to the wiring diagrams at the end of the book). Check the ignition switch for damage and wear (refer to Chapter 12).

Ignition coil – removal and installation

This procedure is essentially the same as the procedure described in Chapter 5. Refer to the accompanying illustration (see Fig. 13.43).

Distributor – removal and installation

This procedure is the same as the procedure described for Duraspark II in Chapter 5. After installing the distributor, set the ignition timing as described below.

Ignition timing – check and adjustment

Ignition timing does not require periodic adjustment. You need to set the timing only when the distributor has been removed or the timing has been changed from its original setting.
Follow the procedure in Chapter 1, except, before checking the timing, unplug the single wire connector located immediately above the harness connector for the module. Plug in the connector after the timing has been checked.

Ignition module – check and replacement

Caution: *The ignition module is a delicate and relatively expensive electronic component. The following tests must be done with the right equipment by someone who knows how to use it properly. Failure to follow the step-by-step procedures could result in damage to the module and/or other electronic devices, including the EEC-IV microprocessor itself.*
Note: *All devices under computer control are protected by a Federally mandated extended warranty. Check with your dealer before attempting to diagnose them yourself.*

Check
EEC-IV/TFI-IV circuits
35   Unplug the electrical connector from the ignition module. Inspect it for dirt, corrosion and/or damage, then plug it back in.
36   Unplug the single wire connector located immediately above the ignition module connector.
37   Using a calibrated spark tester (available at auto parts stores), check for spark.
38   If there is no spark, proceed to the distributor/TFI-IV module check (Step 41).

39   If there is spark, but the ignition system is malfunctioning, the problem lies either with the inferred mileage sensor (IMS) or within the EEC-IV electronic control module (ECM). Diagnosis of these items is beyond the scope of the home mechanic. Take the vehicle to a dealer service department.
40   Remove the spark tester and reconnect the single wire connector.

Distributor/TFI-IV module
Note: *You must purchase a new ignition module before performing the following check. Since the check can result in only one of two possibilities (you will need a new module, or you won't), the odds are 50/50 that you'll be buying a new module that you may not need. Electronic components can't be returned once they're purchased, so if you're unwilling to invest in a new module that you may need now or you may not use until later, stop here. Take the vehicle to a dealer and have the module checked out.*
41   If the module is mounted on the distributor and access to the module is blocked, remove the distributor (see Chapter 5).
42   Install a new module (see Step 45 or 50 below). Connect the body harness to the module. If the distributor is removed, make sure the unit is grounded with a jumper lead from the distributor to the engine. If the distributor is removed, rotate the distributor shaft by hand. If it's not removed, have an assistant crank the engine with the ignition key. **Warning:** *Stay clear of rotating engine components as the engine's being cranked. Check for spark at the secondary coil wire with the ignition tester.*
43   If there is spark, the old module has failed. Leave the new module in place and install the distributor, if removed.
44   If there is no spark, the module is Okay, but there are other problems in the ignition system. Check the ignition coil and circuits, as described above. If they're okay, take the vehicle to a dealer service department for further diagnosis.

Replacement
Module mounted on distributor
45   If access to the module is blocked, remove the distributor from the engine (see Chapter 5).
46   Remove the two module mounting screws with a 1/4-inch drive 7/32-inch deep socket (see Fig. 13.44).
47   Pull straight down on the module to disconnect the spade connectors from the stator connector (see Fig 13.45).
48   Whether you are installing the old module or a new one, wipe the back side of the module clean with a soft, clean rag and apply a film of silicone dielectric grease to the back side of the module (see Fig 13.46).
49   Installation is the reverse of removal. When plugging in the module, make sure that the three terminals are inserted all the way into the stator connector.

Fig. 13.44   To remove the ignition module from the distributor base, remove the two screws (arrows), (Sec 7) . . .

Fig. 13.45   . . . then pull the module straight down to detach the spade terminals from the stator connector (Sec 7)

Fig. 13.46   Be sure to wipe the back side of the module clean and apply a film of dielectric grease (essential for cool operation of the module) – DO NOT use any other type of grease! (Sec 7)

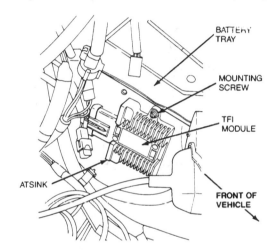

Fig. 13.47   Fender-mounted module and heat sink details (Sec 7)

Module mounted on left fender apron

50   Remove the two screws mounting the module/heatsink to the fender apron (see Fig 13.47).

51   Disconnect the electrical connector from the module and re-move the module/heatsink from the vehicle.

52   Remove the two screws securing the heatsink to the module. Re-move the module.

53   Whether you are installing the old module or a new one, wipe the back side of the module clean with a soft, clean rag and apply a film of silicone dielectric grease to the back side of the module.

54   Installation is the reverse of removal.

Distributor stator assembly – replacement

Note: *The factory doesn't specify a check for the TFI-IV system stator (sensor). If you suspect a problem with the stator, have it checked out by a dealer service department before deciding to replace the stator.*

55   Remove the distributor cap and position it out of the way with the wires attached.

56   Unplug the wire harness from the TFI-IV module.

57   Remove the distributor (see Chapter 5).

58   Remove the rotor (see Chapter 1 if necessary).

59   Although not absolutely necessary, it's a good idea to remove the ignition module from the distributor (see above) to prevent pos-sible damage to the module while the distributor is being disas-sembled.

60   Clamp the lower end of the distributor housing in a vise. Place a shop rag in the vise jaws to prevent damage to the distributor and don't overtighten the vise.

Fig. 13.48   With the distributor mounted securely in a vise lined with several shop rags to prevent damage to the housing, drive out the roll pin with a 5/32-inch pin punch (Sec 7)

61   Before removing the drive gear, note that the roll pin is slightly offset. When the distributor is reassembled, the roll pin cannot be re-installed through the drive gear and distributor shaft holes unless the holes are perfectly lined up.

62   With an assistant holding the distributor steady in the vise, use a 5/32-inch diameter pin punch to hammer the roll pin out of the shaft (see Fig. 13.48).

63   Loosen the vise and reposition the distributor with the drive gear facing up.

13

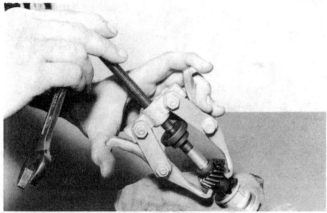

Fig. 13.49   With the distributor shaft pointing up like this, use a small puller to separate the drive gear from the shaft (Sec 7)

Fig. 13.50   Inspect the distributor shaft for burrs and residue buildup like this in the vicinity of the hole for the drive gear roll pin – remove it with emery cloth to prevent damage to the distributor shaft bushing when removing and installing the shaft (Sec 7)

Fig. 13.51   As soon as you remove the distributor shaft, note how the washer is installed before removing it (it could easily fall out and get lost) (Sec 7)

Fig. 13.52   To detach the octane rod from the distributor, remove the bolt – note the condition of the small square rubber grommet that seals the octane rod hole when you pull the rod out (it seals the interior of the distributor to prevent moisture from damaging the electronics) (Sec 7)

64   Remove the drive gear with a small puller (see Fig. 13.49).
65   Before removing it from the distributor, check the shaft for burrs and built up residue, particularly around the drive gear roll pin hole (see Fig. 13.50). If burrs or residue are evident, polish the shaft with emery paper and wipe it clean to prevent damage to the lip seal and bushing in the distributor base.
66   After removing any burrs/residue, remove the shaft assembly by gently pulling on the plate. Note the relationship of the spacer washer to the distributor base before removing the washer (see Fig. 13.51).
67   Remove the octane rod mounting bolt (see Fig. 13.52).
68   Lift the inner end of the rod off the stator retaining post (see Fig. 13.53) and pull the octane rod from the distributor base. **Note:** *Don't lose the grommet installed in the octane rod hole. The grommet protects the electronic components of the distributor from moisture.*
69   Remove the two stator screws (see Fig 13.53).
70   Gently lift it straight up and remove the stator assembly from the distributor.
71   Check the shaft bushing in the distributor base for wear or signs of excessive heat buildup. If signs of wear and/or damage are evident, replace the complete distributor assembly.
72   Inspect the O-ring at the base of the distributor. If it's damaged or worn, remove it and install a new one (see Fig. 13.54).
73   Inspect the housing casting for cracks and wear. If any damage is evident, replace the distributor assembly.
74   Place the stator assembly in position over the shaft bushing and press it down onto the distributor base until it's completely seated on the posts.
75   Install the stator screws and tighten them securely.
76   Insert the octane rod through the hole in the distributor base and push the inner end of the rod onto the post. **Note:** *Make sure that the octane rod hole is properly sealed by the grommet.*
77   Reinstall the octane rod bolt and tighten it securely.

78   Apply a light coat of engine oil to the distributor shaft and insert the shaft through the bushing.
79   Mount the distributor in the vise with the lower end up. Be sure to line the vise jaws with a few clean shop rags to protect the distributor base. Place a block of wood under the distributor shaft to support it and prevent it from falling out while the drive gear is being installed.
80   Using a deep socket and hammer, carefully tap the drive gear back onto the distributor shaft (see Fig. 13.55). Make sure the hole in the drive gear and the hole in the shaft are lined up. Because the holes were drilled off center by the factory, they must be perfectly aligned or the roll pin cannot be installed (see Fig. 13.56).
81   Once the drive gear is seated and the holes are lined up, turn the distributor sideways in the vise and, with an assistant steadying it, drive a new roll pin into the drive gear with a 5/32-inch pin punch. Make sure that neither end of the roll pin protrudes from the drive gear.
82   Check the distributor shaft for smooth rotation, then remove the distributor assembly from the vise.
83   Install the TFI-IV module (see above).
84   Install the rotor (refer to Chapter 1 if necessary).
85   Install the distributor.

8   Emission control systems

Fuel evaporative emissions control system

1   A new system has been installed on 5.0L EFI engines.
2   The system is serviced the same as previous systems with the exception of different vacuum hose routing (see Fig. 13.57).

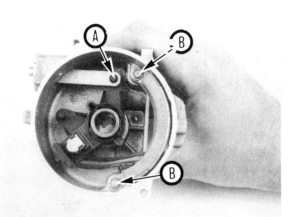

Fig. 13.53   To remove the octane rod, lift the inner end of the rod off the stator assembly post (A) – to remove the stator assembly, remove both mounting screws (B) and lift the stator straight up off the posts (Sec 7)

Fig. 13.55   After securing the distributor assembly upside down in a vise, "eyeball" the roll pin holes in the drive gear and the shaft, then tap the drive gear onto the shaft with a deep socket and hammer (Sec 7)

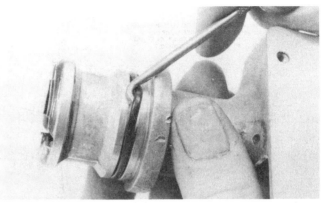

Fig. 13.54   If the O-ring at the base of the distributor is worn or damaged, replace it with a new one (Sec 7)

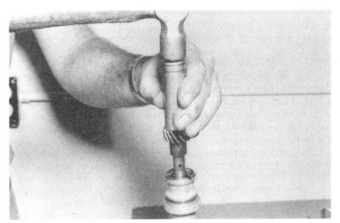

Fig 13.56   If the drive gear and shaft roll pin holes are misaligned, the roll pin cannot be driven through the drive gear and shaft holes – it must now be pulled off the shaft and realigned (Sec 7)

Check engine warning light (EFI models)

3   On all vehicles the check engine warning light is used to indicate malfunctions in the electronic engine control system. If the system is functioning properly, the indicator light will come on when the ignition key is turned to the On position prior to engine cranking and go out when the engine starts.

4   If the indicator light fails to come on when the ignition key is turned on, or comes on and remains on while driving, contact a dealer for service as soon as possible.

5   If the indicator light comes on and later goes out while driving, it is an indication that a temporary condition has corrected itself. Under such circumstances, it is not necessary to take the vehicle to a dealer. However, if the frequency of the intermittent problem becomes troublesome, a Ford dealer service department or repair shop can identify and correct the cause.

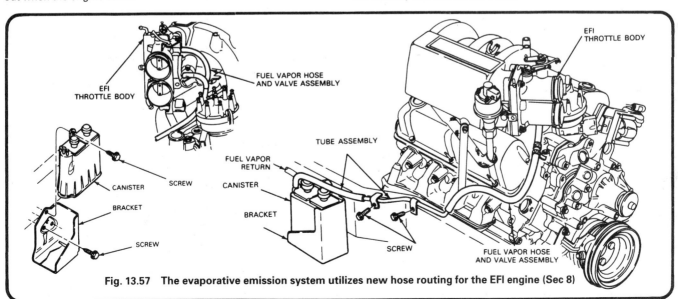

Fig. 13.57   The evaporative emission system utilizes new hose routing for the EFI engine (Sec 8)

13

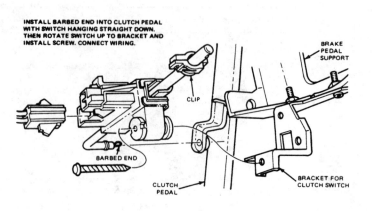

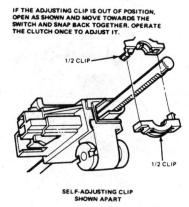

Fig. 13.58   Typical self-adjusting clutch/starter interlock switch (Sec 9)

9   Clutch and flywheel

Description and operation

1   The hydraulic clutch control system consists of a combination clutch fluid reservoir and master cylinder assembly, a slave cylinder and connecting lines. **Note:** *Beginning with the 1990 model year, a concentric slave cylinder, mounted inside the bellhousing, is used. A special disconnect tool is required to detach the hydraulic line from the bellhousing coupling.*

2   The combination clutch reservoir and master cylinder is located to the left of the brake vacuum booster. Fluid level is checked at the reservoir. The clutch slave cylinder is mounted on the bellhousing.

3   The hydraulic clutch system provides automatic clutch adjustment. No adjustment of clutch linkage or pedal position is required.

Clutch/starter interlock switch
Description

4   Starting in 1984 all manual transmission vehicles are equipped with a starter clutch interlock system which requires the clutch pedal to be depressed all the way to the floor in order to start the engine. The system operates by means of a switch located on the brake and clutch pedal support bracket. The switch plunger is attached to the clutch pedal and extends as the clutch pedal is depressed to actuate the switch. The switch is electrically connected across the ignition switch and the starter motor relay coil to maintain an open starter circuit with the clutch engaged (pedal up) position. The switch is designed with a self adjusting feature which provides for the switch to be set automatically with the first flooring of the clutch pedal.

Testing

5   Disconnect the connector at the switch by flexing the retaining tab on the switch housing and withdraw the connector.

6   Using a test light or continuity tester, check the electrical continuity of the switch. The switch contacts should be open with the clutch pedal up (clutch engaged) and the contacts should be closed when the clutch pedal is depressed to the floor (clutch disengaged).

7   If the switch does not operate as described in Step 6, check if the self adjusting clip is out of position on the rod. If so, remove the clip and reposition the clip closer to the switch.

8   Reset the switch by depressing the clutch pedal to the floor.

9   If the switch still does not operate, replace the switch.

Adjustments

10   If the adjusting clip is out of position on the rod, remove both halves of the clip. Position both halves of the clip closer to the switch and snap the clips together on the rod. Depress the clutch pedal to the floor to adjust.

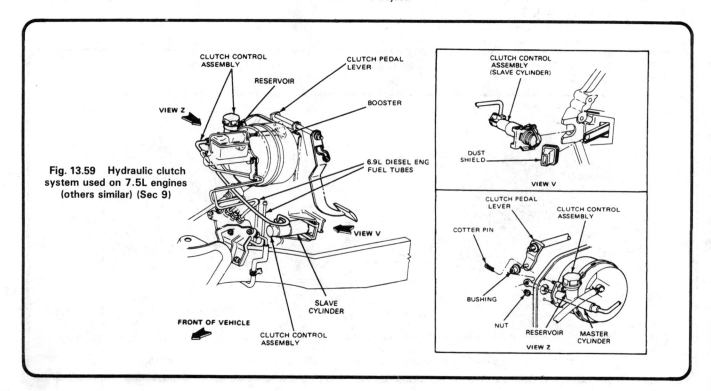

Fig. 13.59   Hydraulic clutch system used on 7.5L engines (others similar) (Sec 9)

Clutch hydraulic system — removal and installation

Caution: *Prior to any vehicle service that requires removal of the slave cylinder such as transmission and clutch housing removal), the master cylinder push rod must be disconnected from the clutch pedal. If not disconnected, permanent damage to the slave cylinder will occur if the clutch pedal is depressed while the slave cylinder is disconnected.*

11 From the inside of the cab, remove the cotter pin retaining the clutch master cylinder push rod to the clutch pedal lever. Disconnect the push rod and remove the bushing.

12 Remove the two nuts retaining the clutch reservoir and master cylinder assembly to the firewall.

13 From the engine compartment, remove the clutch reservoir and master cylinder assembly from the firewall. Note the clutch tubing routing to the slave cylinder.

14 On 7.5L engine equipped vehicles, use a screwdriver or a similar tool and lift the two retaining tabs of the slave cylinder retaining bracket. Disengage the tabs from the bellhousing lugs and slide outward to remove. On 4.9/5.0/5.8L engine equipped vehicles, remove the C-clip from the slave cylinder. Disengage the push rod from the release lever as the slave cylinder is removed.

15 Remove the clutch hydraulic system from the vehicle.

16 Position the clutch fluid reservoir and master cylinder assembly on the firewall, and from inside the cab install the two nuts and tighten.

17 Route the clutch tubing and slave cylinder to the bellhousing. **Note:** *Care must be taken during routing of the nylon line to keep it away from engine exhaust system components.*

18 Install the slave cylinder by pushing the slave cylinder push rod into the cylinder. On 7.5L engine equipped vehicles, engage the push rod into the release lever and slide the slave cylinder into the bellhousing lugs. Seat the cylinder into the recess in the lugs. For 4.9/5.0/5.8L engine equipped vehicles, attach the C-clip after the slave cylinder is installed. **Note:** *When installing a new hydraulic system, the slave cylinder contains a shipping strap that prepositions the push rod for installation and also provides a bearing insert. Following installation of the new slave cylinder, the first actuation of the clutch pedal will break the shipping strap and give normal system operation.*

19 Clean and apply a light film of engine oil to the master cylinder push rod bushing.

20 From inside the cab, install the bushing on the clutch lever pedal. Connect the clutch master cylinder push rod to the clutch pedal lever and install the cotter pin.

21 Check the clutch reservoir and add fluid if required. Depress the clutch pedal at least ten times to verify smooth operation and proper release. **Note:** *The proper fluid level is indicated by a step on the reservoir. Do not overfill. The upper portion of the reservoir must accept fluid that is displaced from the slave cylinder as the clutch wears.*

10 Manual transmission

General information

1 Later models may be equipped with one of two new 5-speed transmissions — the Mazda M50D or the S5-42-ZF.

2 The Mazda M50D, introduced in 1988, is a top shift, fully synchronized, manual transmission equipped with an overdrive fifth gear ratio. The transmission main case, top cover and extension housing are constructed of aluminum alloy.

3 The S5-42-ZF 5-speed transmission features an aluminum case with an integral clutch housing.

11 Transfer case

General information

1 Later model 4-wheel drive vehicles are equipped with a Borg-Warner 13-56 transfer case. The Borg-Warner 13-56 electronic shift transfer case is used on Bronco (4x4) vehicles with an automatic transmission only.

2 The Borg-Warner 13-56, transfer case is a three piece all magnesium design (except for the manual shift unit equipped with a power take off, which will have a magnesium case half and an aluminum case half). The unit is lubricated by a positive displacement oil pump that channels oil flow through drilled holes in the rear output shaft. The pump turns with the rear output shaft and allows towing of the vehicle without disconnecting the rear driveshaft.

Removal and installation

3 Removal and installation is basically the same as outlined in Chapter 7, Part C, for the earlier type transfer case, but note that electronic shift units have a wire harness that must be disconnected.

Overhaul

4 Overhauling a transfer case is a difficult job for the do-it-yourselfer. It involves the disassembly and reassembly of many small parts. Numerous clearances must be precisely measured and, if necessary, changed with select fit spacers and snap-rings. As a result, if transfer case problems arise, it can be removed and installed by a competent do-it-yourselfer, but overhaul should be left to a transmission repair shop. Rebuilt cases may be available — check with your dealer parts department and auto parts stores. At any rate, the time and money involved in an overhaul is almost sure to exceed the cost of a rebuilt

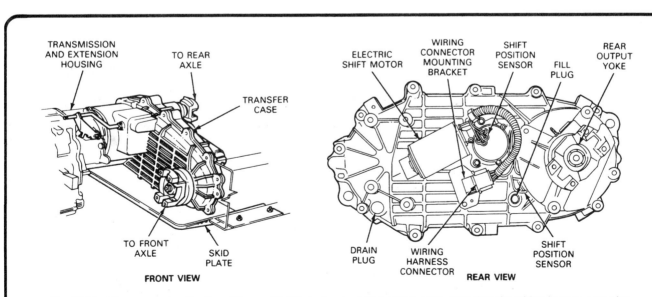

Fig. 13.60 When removing the Borg-Warner 13-56 electronic shift transfer case, note that the wiring harness must be disconnected (Sec 11)

13

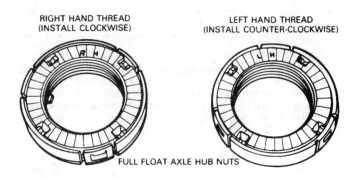

Fig. 13.61 On 1987 and later models, the hub nuts look like these – the nut on the right side of the vehicle has right-hand threads and the nut on the left has left-hand threads (they are marked LH and RH so you don't mix them up) (Sec 12)

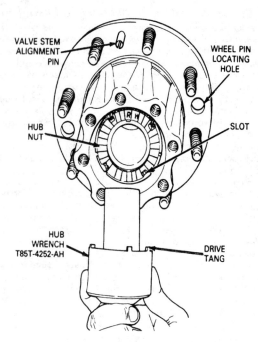

Fig. 13.62 A special hub wrench is required to loosen and tighten the hub nut – the drive tangs on the tool must fit into the slots on the nut (Sec 12)

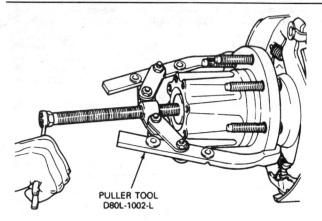

Fig. 13.63 A puller may be required to remove the hub – the number shown is a Ford tool number, but any common puller with the right jaw size should work (Sec 12)

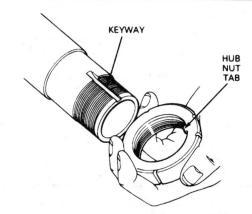

Fig. 13.64 When installing the hub nut, be sure to engage the hub nut tab with the keyway before you begin threading on the nut (Sec 12)

unit.
5   Nevertheless, it's not impossible for an inexperienced mechanic to rebuild a transfer case if the special tools are available and the job is done in a deliberate step-by-step manner so nothing is overlooked.
6   The tools necessary for an overhaul include internal and external snap-ring pliers, a bearing puller, a slide hammer, a set of pin punches, a dial indicator and possibly a hydraulic press. In addition, a large, sturdy workbench and a vise or stand will be required.
7   During disassembly of the transfer case, make careful notes of how each piece comes off, where it fits in relation to other pieces and what holds it in place.
8   Before taking the transfer case apart for repair, it will help if you have some idea what area is malfunctioning. Certain problems can be closely tied to specific areas, which can make component examination and replacement easier.

12 Driveline – axles and driveshafts

Rear axle bearings and seal (full-floating type) – replacement

Beginning in 1987, a new type of hub bearing adjustment nut is used (see Fig. 13.61). Also, the brake drum can be removed separately from the hub. The axle bearing and seal replacement procedure is basically the same as that described in Chapter 8; however, keep the following points in mind:
1   You can separate the brake drum from the hub immediately after removing the wheel. It should pull off easily; however, if you have difficulty, the brake shoes may need to be backed off (see Chapter 9) or the drum may be rusted to the hub. If it's rusted, try spraying some penetrating oil into the hub-to-drum joint and tapping the drum with a hammer.
2   A special tool is required to remove the hub nut (see Fig. 13.62).
3   If the hub assembly won't pull off easily, a puller may be required (see Fig. 13.63).
4   Before installing the hub, clean the spindle with a rag and apply axle lubricant to the spindle.
5   When installing the hub nut, make sure the tab is located in the keyway (see Fig. 13.64).
6   Install the hub with the outer bearing in place – the bearing acts as a pilot, making installation easier.
7   After installation, tighten the hub nut to 55 to 65 ft-lbs, rotating the hub while tightening. Then back off the hub nut, listening for clicking from the hub nut. For new bearings, back off the nut five clicks. For used bearings, back off the nut 8 clicks.

Front wheel bearing (4x4) – adjustment

Beginning in 1989, Broncos and F-150's and F-250's with Dana 441FS driving axles and manual locking hubs have a different front wheel bearing adjustment procedure.

8 Raise the vehicle and place it securely on jackstands.
9 Remove the hub lock assembly (see Chapter 8).
10 Using a torque wrench and spanner locknut wrench (Ford tool T86T-1197-A or equivalent), apply inward pressure to unlock the adjusting nut locking splines and turn the nut clockwise to tighten the nut to 70 ft-lbs. while rotating the wheel back and forth to seat the bearing.
11 Apply inward pressure on the spanner locknut wrench to disengage the adjusting nut locking splines and back off the adjusting nut approximately 90-degrees.
12 Retighten the adjusting nut to 15 to 20 ft-lbs. Remove the tool and torque wrench.
13 Check that the hub and rotor assembly has no endplay.
14 Check that the torque required to rotate the hub and rotor assembly does not exceed 20 in-lbs.
15 Install the hub lock assembly
16 Lower the vehicle.

13 Brakes

Disc brake pads – replacement (1986 on)

Warning: *Disc brake pads must be replaced on both wheels at the same time – never replace the pads on only one wheel. Also, brake system dust may contain asbestos, which is harmful to your health. Never blow it out with compressed air and don't inhale any of it. Do not, under any circumstances, use petroleum-based solvents to clean brake parts. Use brake cleaner or denatured alcohol only.*

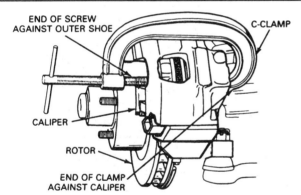

Fig. 13.65 A large C-clamp can be used to compress the piston into the caliper bore to provide room for the new, thicker brake pads (Sec 13)

1 Block the rear wheels, apply the parking brake, loosen the front wheel lug nuts, raise the front of the vehicle and support it on jackstands. Remove the wheels.
2 Before the caliper is removed, use a large C-clamp to push the piston into the bore (do not use a screwdriver to pry the piston away from the rotor). Position the screw end against the outer pad (sometimes called a shoe) and the frame end against the caliper body, then slowly and carefully tighten the clamp screw. The piston should move into the bore and provide room for the new, thicker pads (see Fig. 13.65). If resistance is encountered, the piston may be seized – do not apply excess force or the caliper may be damaged. Check the brake fluid level in the master cylinder as this is done. Fluid may have to be siphoned out to prevent overflow at the reservoir.

Single piston caliper (light duty)
3 The caliper is held in place by two pin rails, one at the top and one at the bottom of the caliper. Use a wire brush to remove any dirt from the pin rail tabs (located at the ends of the pins).
4 Using a punch and hammer, tap the upper pin rail in until it contacts the anchor plate on the spindle. Insert a screwdriver blade into the slot behind each tab on the inner end of the rail. At the same time, compress the outer end of the pin rail with needle-nose pliers and pull on it until the tabs slip into the grooves (see Fig. 13.66).
5 Pull the rail out with the pliers or tap it out with a hammer and punch. Repeat the procedure for the lower pin rail.
6 Push the caliper down and rotate the upper end up and out to detach it from the anchor plate. The inner brake pad will remain in the anchor plate, while the outer pad will stay in the caliper.
7 Suspend the caliper assembly from a chassis member with a piece of wire. **Warning:** *Do not stretch or twist the rubber brake hose.*
8 If the pads are going to be reused, mark them so they can be reinstalled in their original locations. They must not be interchanged.
9 The pad can now be removed from the anchor plate. The anti-rattle clips will probably come out when the pad is removed (see Fig. 13.67). Note how the anti-rattle clips are installed – they must be repositioned in the exact same manner during installation.
10 Clean the caliper, spindle anchor plate and disc (rotor), then check for fluid leaks, wear and damage. The area on the anchor plate that mates with the caliper must be clean and smooth so the caliper can slide freely without binding. Measure the thickness of the pad lining. If the lining is less than 1/16-inch thick, the pads must be replaced with new ones. The replacement outer pad is slightly different than the original. It has tabs on the flange at the lower edge of the pad and the distance between the upper tabs and lower flange is reduced to provide a slip-fit.
11 Position a new anti-rattle clip on the lower end of the inner pad (see Fig. 13.67). Be sure the tab on the clip is positioned correctly and

Fig. 13.66 Remove the pin rail by directing the tabs into the grooves with a screwdriver and pulling on the rail with needle-nose pliers (Sec 13)

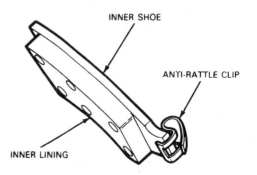

Fig. 13.67 Don't overlook the anti-rattle clip attached to the inner pad (Sec 13)

13

the clip is seated completely. The loop-type spring on the clip must face away from the rotor. The installation directions that come with the new pads should contain detailed drawings showing the correct position of the anti-rattle clip(s).

12   If the old pads are being reused, they must be installed in their original locations. Place the inner pad and anti-rattle clip in the anchor plate with the clip tab against the abutment (see Fig. 13.68). Compress the clip and slide the upper end of the pad into position.

13   Position the outer pad in the caliper and press the tabs into place. If necessary, use a C-clamp to seat the pad, but be careful not to damage the lining material (place a small piece of wood between the clamp and pad surface).

14   Detach the caliper from the wire.

15   Apply high-temperature disc brake grease (ESA-M1C72-A or equivalent) to the caliper and anchor plate grooves, then install the caliper and position the pin rails with the tabs adjacent to the grooves (see Fig. 13.69). Tap the pins into place until the retention tabs on the inner end snap out of the groove and bear against the flanks of the spindle anchor plate. Do not tap the pin rails in too far or the outer retention tabs may enter the grooves (the tabs on each end of the rail must be free to contact the spindle anchor plate flanks) (see Fig. 13.70).

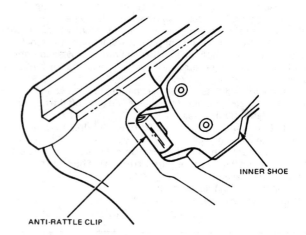

Fig. 13.68 The anti-rattle clip engages in the anchor plate (Sec 13)

Dual piston caliper (heavy duty)

16   The heavy duty caliper is mounted just like the light duty caliper – follow the procedure in Steps 3 through 5 above.

17   Remove the caliper and suspend it with wire from a suspension member. **Warning:** *Do not twist or stretch the rubber brake hose.*

18   After making careful note of how it's installed, remove the large brake shoe anti-rattle spring.

19   Remove the inner and outer brake pads from the caliper.

20   Clean the caliper and piston faces to remove dust and accumulated debris. The area on the anchor plate that mates with the caliper must be clean and smooth so the caliper can slide freely without binding.

21   To avoid brake fluid overflow when the caliper pistons are pressed into the bores, siphon or dip part of the brake fluid out of the large master cylinder reservoir (connected to the front brakes) and discard the fluid.

22   Use a C-clamp to compress the pistons into the bores (see Fig. 13.65). **Caution:** *If both calipers have been removed, block the opposite side pistons to prevent them from popping out during this operation.*

23   Install the new pads and the anti-rattle spring.

24   Install the caliper assembly on the anchor plate and over the rotor.

25   Follow the procedure in Step 15 above.

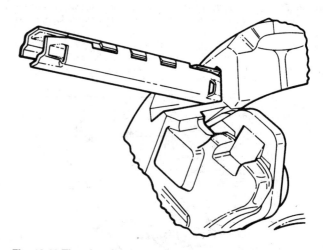

Fig. 13.69 The pin rail tabs must enter the anchor plate groove as shown here (Sec 13)

All calipers

26   Repeat the procedure for the remaining caliper. Depress the brake pedal several times to seat the pads and center the calipers, then check the brake fluid level as described in Chapter 1.

27   Install the wheels, lower the vehicle and check the operation of the brakes before driving the vehicle in traffic. Try to avoid heavy braking until after the brakes have been applied lightly several times to seat the pads.

Anti-lock brakes – general information

Rear anti-lock brakes (RABS) became standard equipment in 1988 on all F–150/250/350 truck and Bronco models. If there is a fault with the RABS, a rear anti-lock light will illuminate on the instrument panel. Due to the complex nature of RABS, the do-it-yourself mechanic should take the vehicle to a Ford dealer service department or a repair shop that can service RABS.

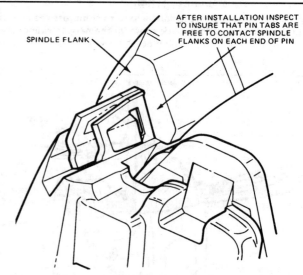

Fig. 13.70 The tabs on each end of the pin rail must contact the spindle anchor plate flanks to prevent the rail from sliding out of place (Sec 13)

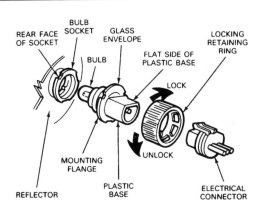

**Fig. 13.71   Halogen headlight bulb and related components –
exploded view (Sec 14)**

14   Chassis electrical system

Halogen headlight bulbs – removal and installation

Warning: *The halogen headlight bulb contains gas under pressure.
The bulb may shatter if the glass envelope is scratched or the bulb is
dropped. Grasp the bulb only by the plastic base and avoid touching
the glass envelope. Keep the bulb out of the reach of children. Energize the bulb only when installed in the headlight. A burned out bulb
should not be removed from the headlight reflector until just before a
replacement bulb is installed. The removal of a bulb for an extended
period of time may allow contaminants (dust, moisture, smoke, etc.)
to enter the headlight body and affect the performance of the bulb.*

1   Check and make sure the headlight switch is off.
2   Remove the electrical connector from the bulb by grasping the
wires firmly and snapping the connector to the rear.
3   Remove the bulb retaining ring by rotating it counterclockwise
(when viewed from the rear) about 1/8–turn, then slide it off the plastic base. Keep the ring as it can be used again.
4   Carefully remove the bulb from the socket in the reflector by
gently pulling it straight back out of the socket. Do not rotate the bulb
during removal.
5   With the flat side of the plastic base facing up, insert the glass envelope of the new bulb into the socket. Turn the base slightly to the
left or right, if necessary, to align the grooves in the forward part of
the plastic base with the corresponding locating tabs inside the socket. When the grooves are aligned, push the bulb firmly into the socket
until the mounting flange on the base contacts the rear face of the
socket.
6   Slip the bulb retaining ring over the rear of the plastic base
against the mounting flange. Lock the ring into the socket by rotating
the ring clockwise. A stop will be felt when the retaining ring is fully
engaged.
7   Push the electrical connector into the rear of the plastic base until
it snaps and locks into position.
8   Turn the headlights on and check for proper operation.

Wiring diagrams

Note that wiring diagrams for later model vehicles have been included at the end of this Chapter. Due to space limitations, we are not

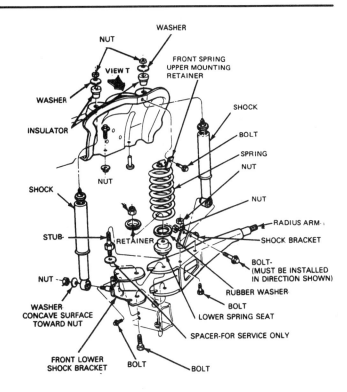

Fig. 13.72   Exploded view of the quad shock suspension (Sec 15)

able to provide every diagram for all years. However, the diagrams
included are typical of later models.

15   Steering and suspension systems

Quad front shock absorbers – removal and installation

1   Raise the vehicle and support it securely on jackstands.
2   Remove the wheel from the side to be replaced.
3   For removal and installation of shock absorbers, insert a wrench
to hold the upper shock absorber retaining nut. Loosen the stud by
turning the hex provided on the exposed (lower) part of the stud and
remove the nut and washer.
4   Disconnect the lower end of the shock absorber by removing the
bolt and nut on the rear one and the nut and washer on the forward
shock.
5   Compress the shock absorber and lift it from the vehicle.
6   Cut out the insulators from the upper spring seat.
7   Insert the new one-piece insulators into the top surface of the upper spring seat (a soap and water solution will help).
8   Insert the new shock absorber stud through the insulator.
9   Replace the steel washer and hand start the nut.
10   While holding the nut as in Step 1, tighten by turning the hex provided on the stud.
11   Reinstall the lower shock mounts and wheels.

13

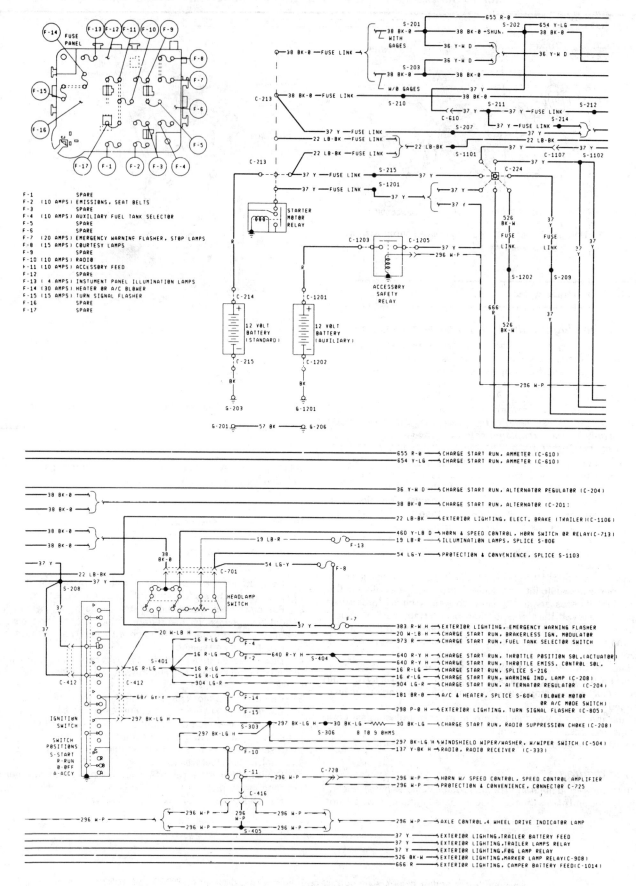

Power distribution wiring diagram for 1980 and 1981

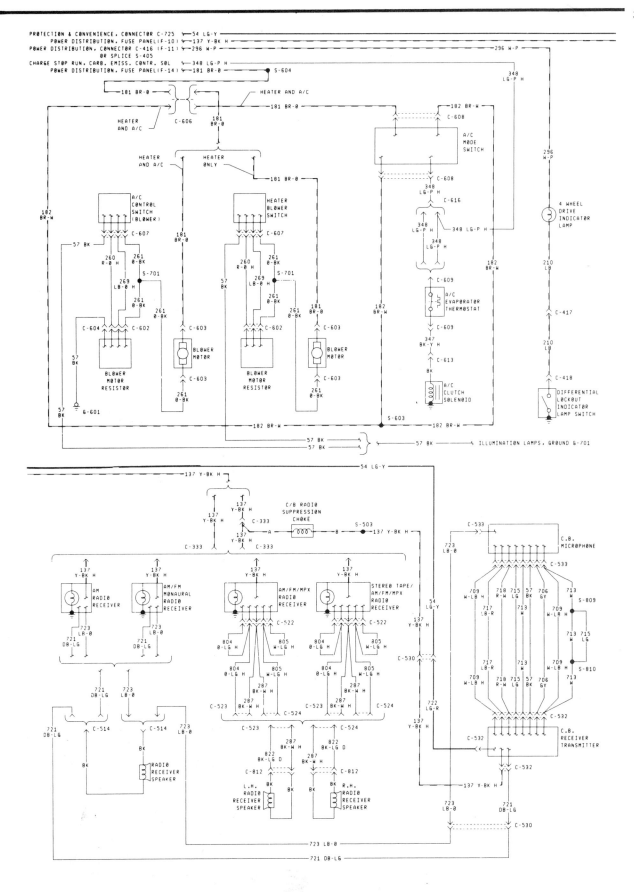

Air conditioner and/or heater, axle control and radio wiring diagram for 1980 and 1981

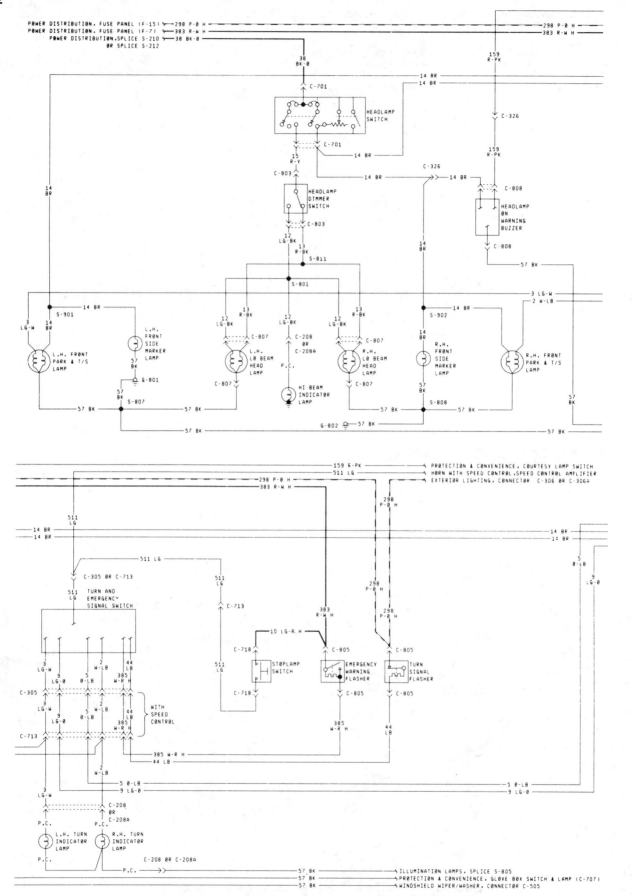

Exterior lighting wiring diagram for 1980 and 1981 (1 of 3)

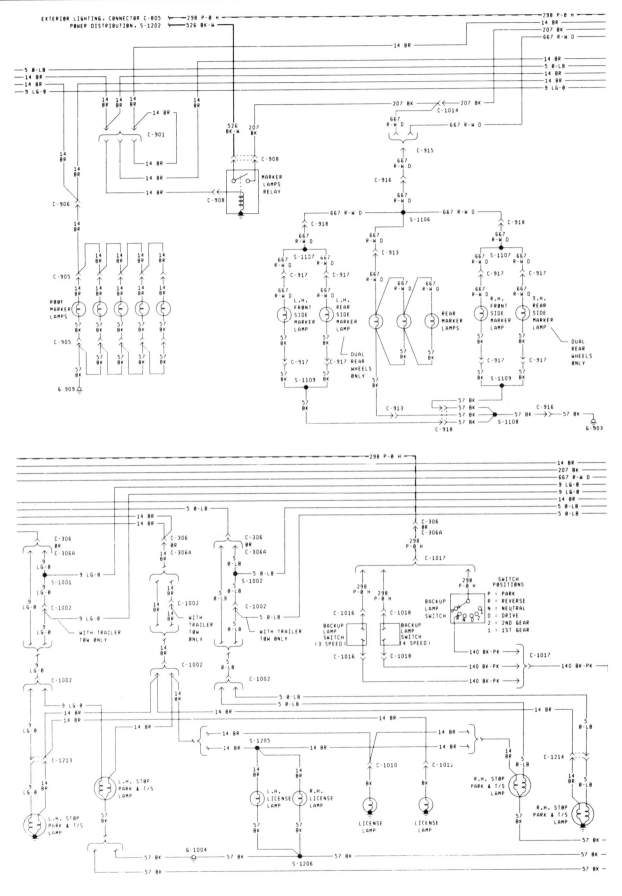

Exterior lighting wiring diagram for 1980 and 1981 (2 of 3)

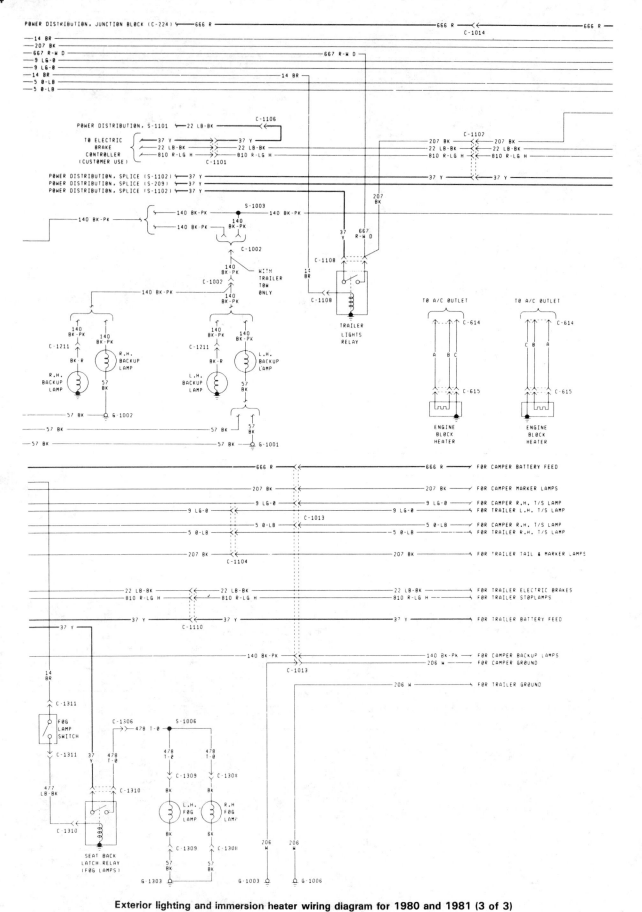

Exterior lighting and immersion heater wiring diagram for 1980 and 1981 (3 of 3)

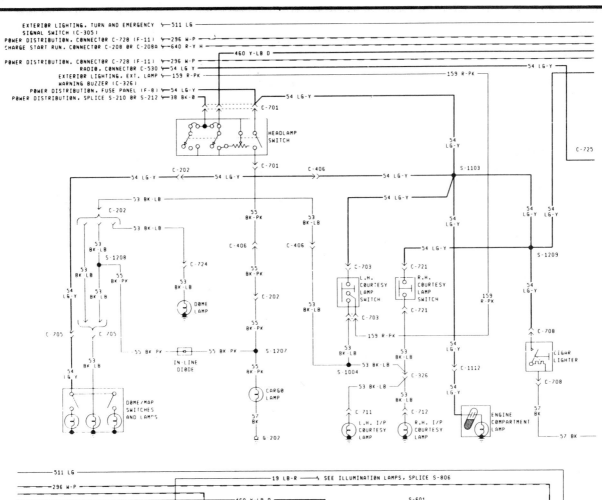

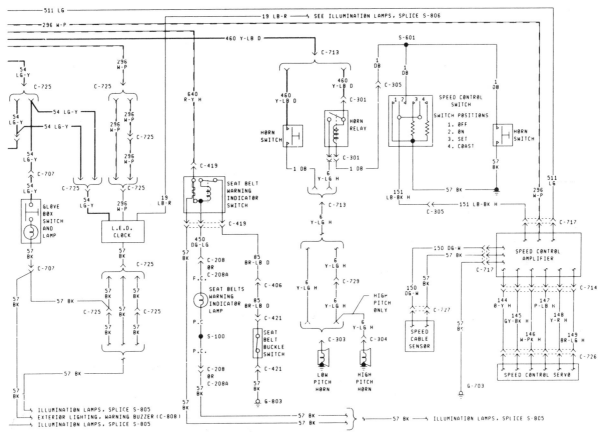

Horn/speed control, and protection and convenience wiring diagram for 1980 and 1981

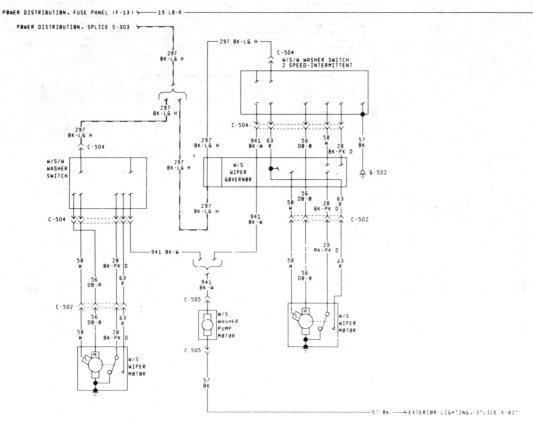

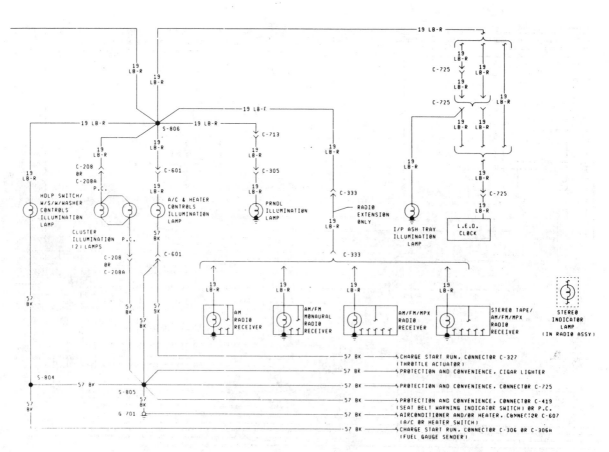

Windshield wiper/washer and illumination lamps wiring diagram for 1980 and 1981

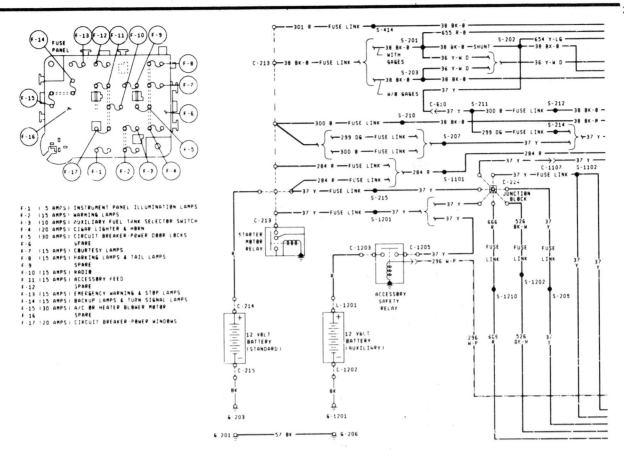

F-1 (5 AMPS) INSTRUMENT PANEL ILLUMINATION LAMPS
F-2 (15 AMPS) WARNING LAMPS
F-3 (10 AMPS) AUXILIARY FUEL TANK SELECTOR SWITCH
F-4 (20 AMPS) CIGAR LIGHTER & HORN
F-5 (30 AMPS) CIRCUIT BREAKER-POWER DOOR LOCKS
F-6   SPARE
F-7 (15 AMPS) COURTESY LAMPS
F-8 (15 AMPS) PARKING LAMPS & TAIL LAMPS
F-9   SPARE
F-10 (15 AMPS) RADIO
F-11 (15 AMPS) ACCESSORY FEED
F-12   SPARE
F-13 (15 AMPS) EMERGENCY WARNING & STOP LAMPS
F-14 (15 AMPS) BACKUP LAMPS & TURN SIGNAL LAMPS
F-15 (30 AMPS) A/C OR HEATER BLOWER MOTOR
F-16   SPARE
F-17 (20 AMPS) CIRCUIT BREAKER-POWER WINDOWS

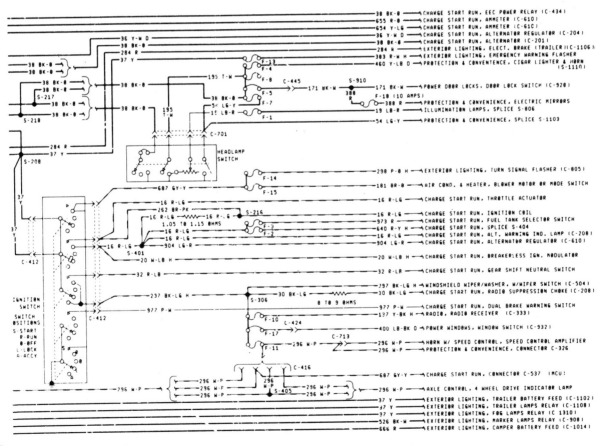

Power distribution wiring diagram for 1982 and 1983

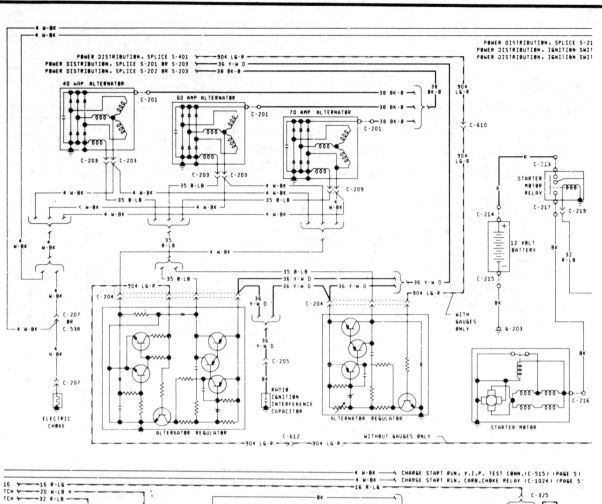

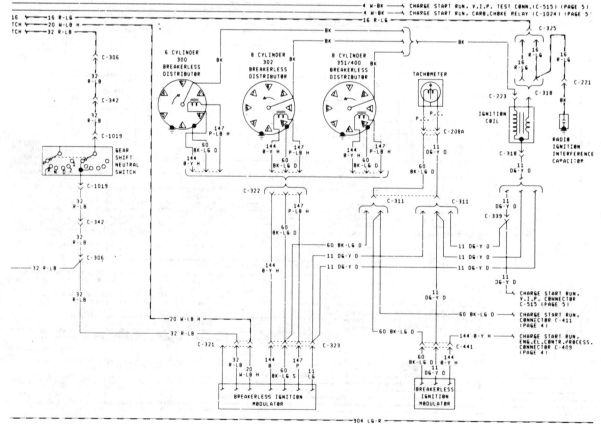

Charge, start and run wiring diagram for 1982 and 1983 (1 of 4)

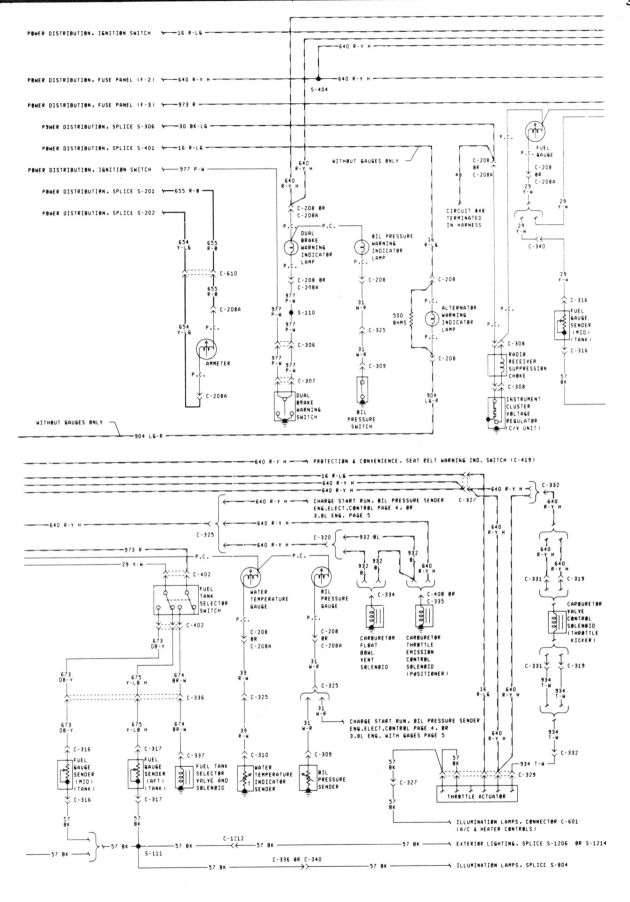

Charge, start and run wiring diagram for 1982 and 1983 (2 of 4)

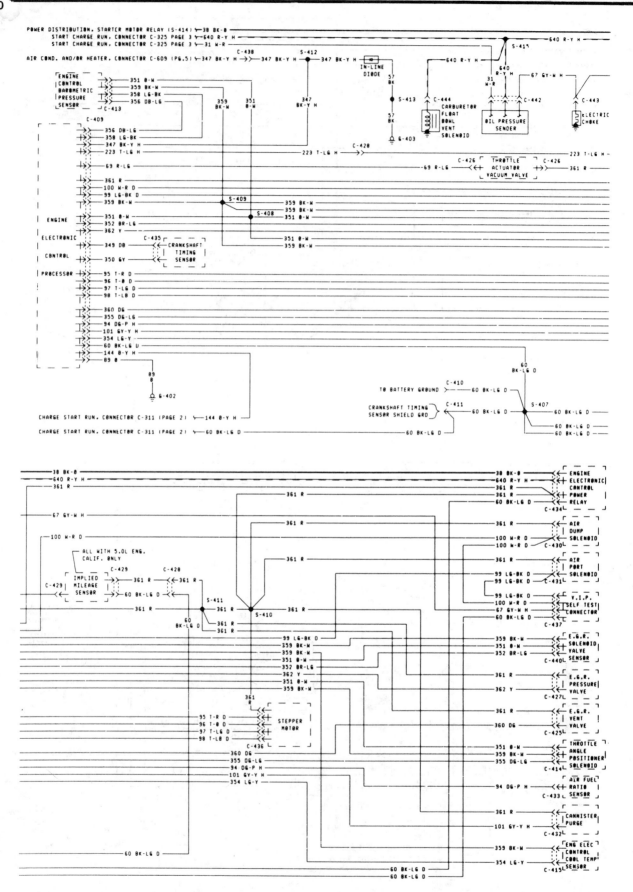

Charge, start and run wiring diagram for 1982 and 1983 (3 of 4)

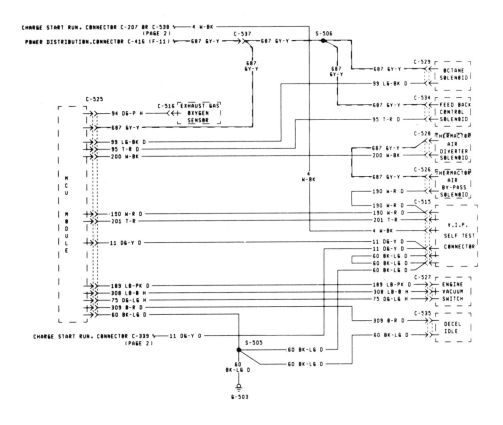

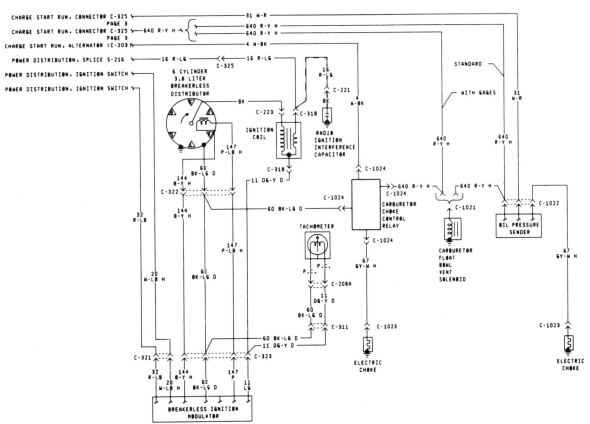

Charge, start and run wiring diagram for 1982 and 1983 (4 of 4)

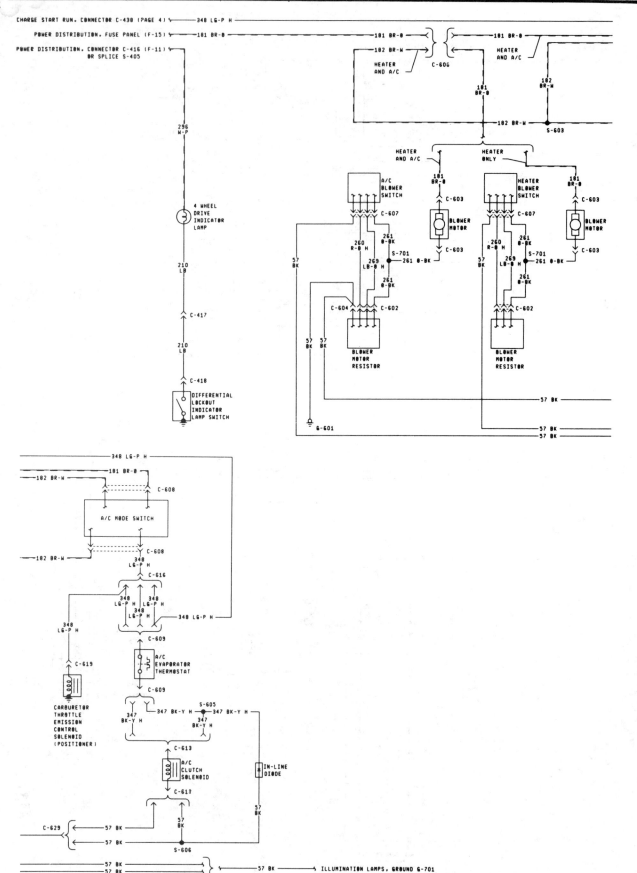

Air conditioner and/or heater, and axle control wiring diagram for 1982 and 1983

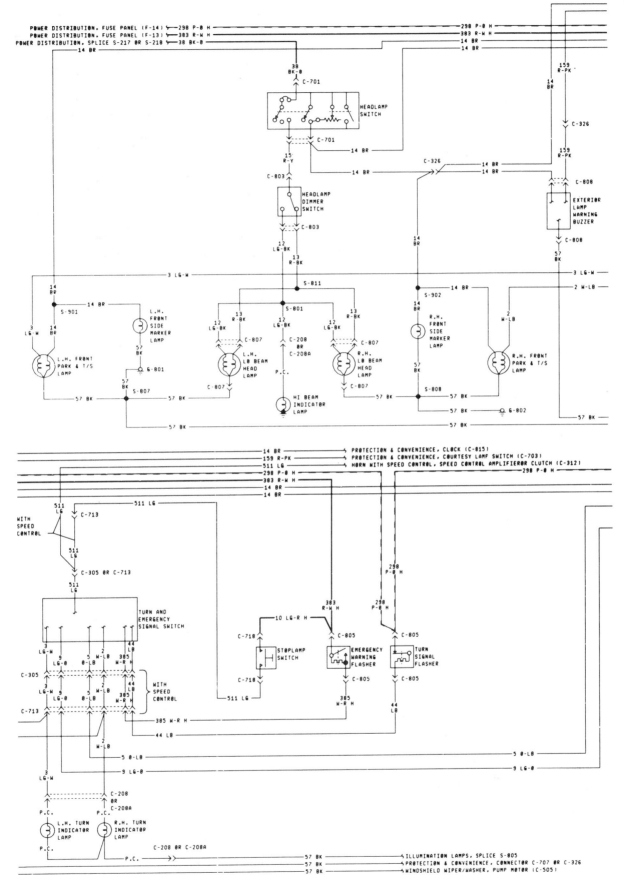

Exterior lighting wiring diagram for 1982 and 1983 (1 of 3)

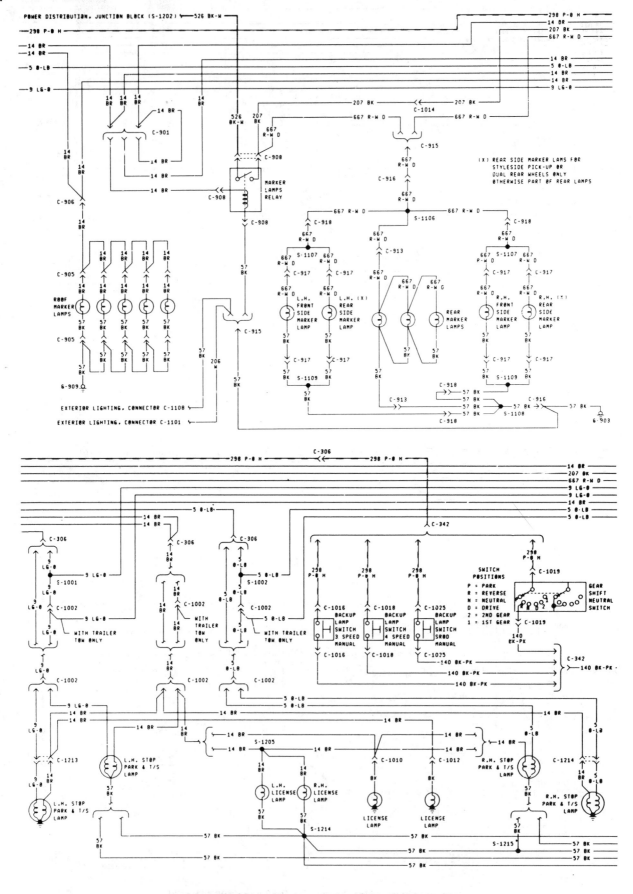

Exterior lighting wiring diagram for 1982 and 1983 (2 of 3)

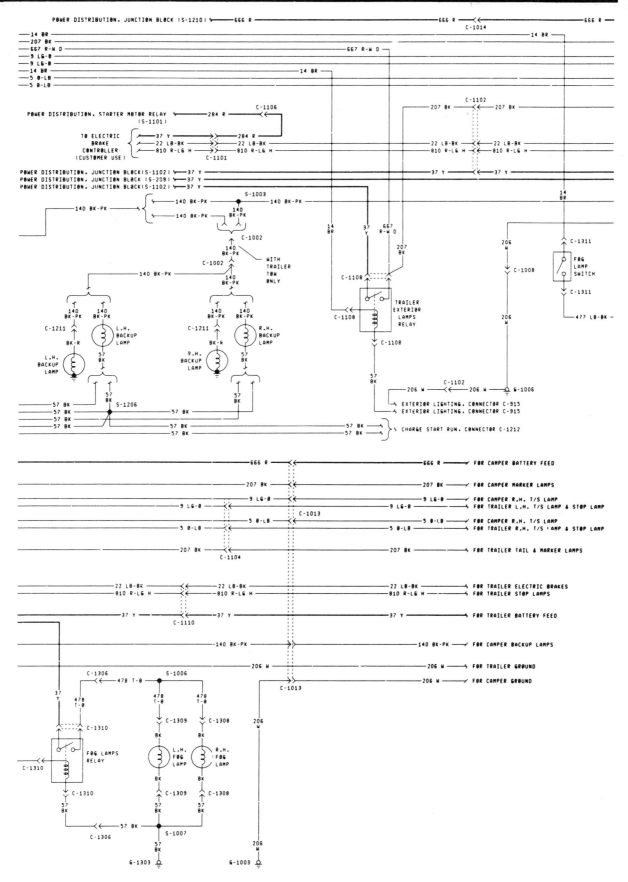

Exterior lighting wiring diagram for 1982 and 1983 (3 of 3)

POWER DISTRIBUTION, FUSE PANEL (F-1) ⇥ 19 LB-R ⇥ 19 LB-R

19 LB-R

19 LB-R

S-806

C-601

19 LB-R 19 LB-R 19 LB-R

C-208 OR C-208A

P.C.

C-601

W/S/W/WASHER CONTROLS ILLUMINATION LAMP

CLUSTER ILLUMINATION (5) LAMPS

P.C.

C-208 OR C-208A

A/C & HEATER CONTROLS ILLUMINATION LAMP

HEATER CONTROLS ILLUMINATION LAMP

57 BK

57 BK

19 LB-R

C-333

C-333 C-333 C-333 C-333 C-

19 LB-R 19 LB-R 19 LB-R 19 LB-R 19 LB-R

AM RADIO RECEIVER

AM/FM MONAURAL RADIO RECEIVER

AM/FM/MPX RADIO RECEIVER

STEREO TAPE/ AM/FM/MPX RADIO RECEIVER

57 BK

57 BK

57 BK

57 BK

57 BK

S-804

57 BK

S-805

57 BK

G-701

57 BK

57 BK

57 BK

57 BK

19 LB-R

19 LB-R

C-326

19 LB-R

19 LB-R

C-333

TO A/C OUTLET

TO A/C OUTLET

C-614

C-614

19 LB-R

ELECTRONIC RADIO

A B C

C B A

I/P ASH TRAY ILLUMINATION LAMP

C-615

C-615

STEREO INDICATOR LAMP (IN RADIO ASSY)

ENGINE BLOCK HEATER

ENGINE BLOCK HEATER

333

C-333

C-333

19 LB-R 19 LB-R

STEREO TAPE/ AM/FM/MPX RADIO RECEIVER

CASSETTE TAPE/ AM/FM/MPX RADIO RECEIVER

AM/FM/MPX SIGNAL SEEK RADIO RECEIVER

57 BK

PROTECTION & CONVENIENCE, CONNECTOR C-326

57 BK ⇥ CHARGE START RUN, THROTTLE ACTUATOR (C-327)

57 BK ⇥ PROTECTION & CONVENIENCE, CIGAR LIGHTER (C-708)

57 BK ⇥ PROTECTION & CONVENIENCE, CONNECTOR C-326

57 BK ⇥ PROTECTION & CONVENIENCE, SEAT BELT WARNING SWITCH (C-419) OR P.C.

57 BK ⇥ AIR COND. & HEATER, A/C OR HEATER SWITCH (C-607)

57 BK ⇥ CHARGE START RUN, FUEL GAUGE SENDER (C-336 OR C-340)

Illumination lamps and immersion heater wiring diagram for 1982 and 1983

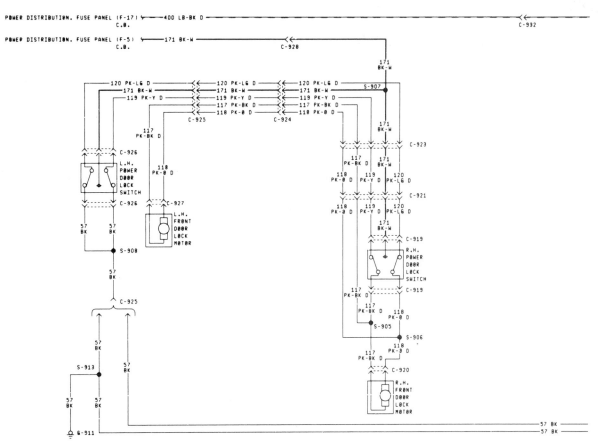

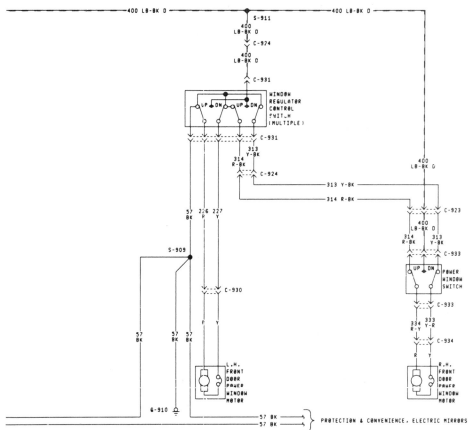

Power door locks and windows wiring diagram for 1982 and 1983

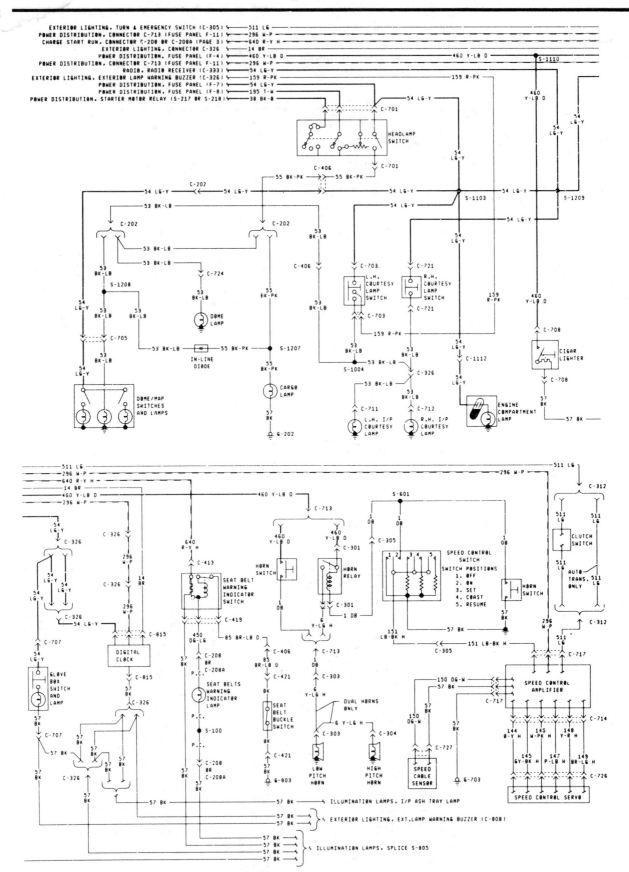

Protection and convenience, and horn/speed control wiring diagram for 1982 and 1983 (1 of 2)

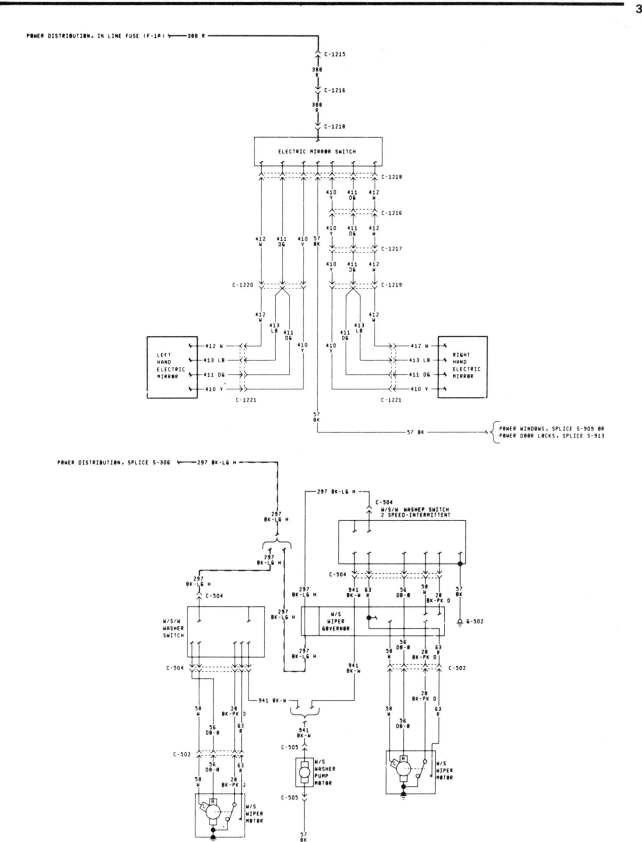

Protection and convenience, and horn/speed control wiring diagram for 1982 and 1983 (2 of 2)

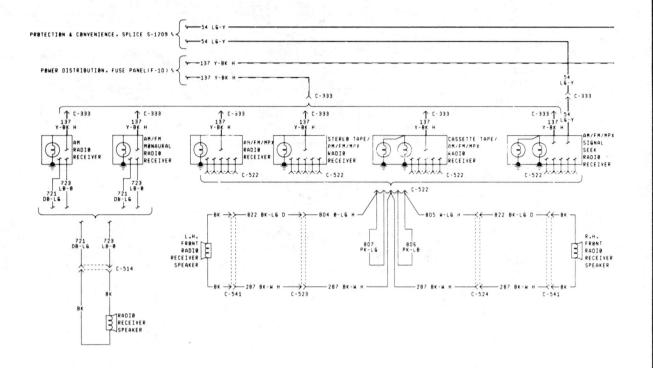

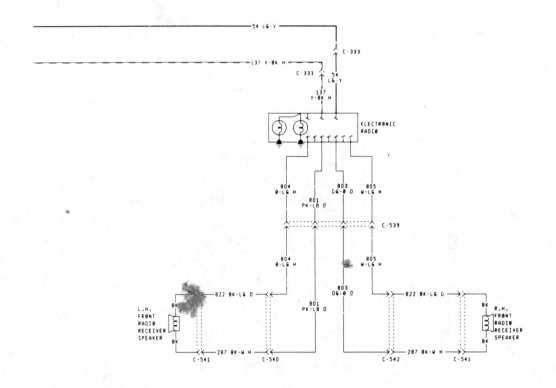

Radio wiring diagram for 1982 and 1983

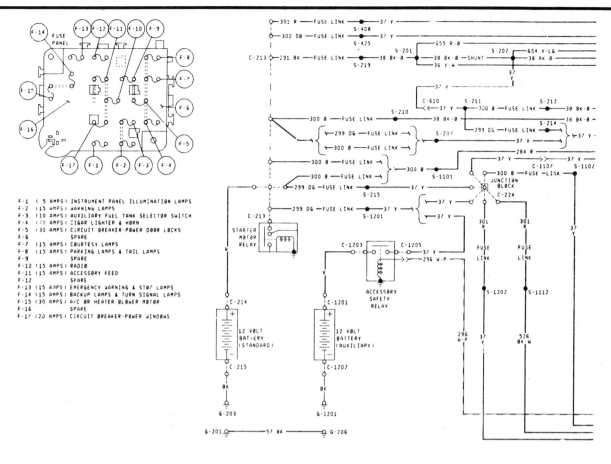

F-1 (5 AMPS) INSTRUMENT PANEL ILLUMINATION LAMPS
F-2 (15 AMPS) WARNING LAMPS
F-3 (10 AMPS) AUXILIARY FUEL TANK SELECTOR SWITCH
F-4 (20 AMPS) CIGAR LIGHTER & HORN
F-5 (30 AMPS) CIRCUIT BREAKER-POWER DOOR LOCKS
F-6   SPARE
F-7 (15 AMPS) COURTESY LAMPS
F-8 (15 AMPS) PARKING LAMPS & TAIL LAMPS
F-9   SPARE
F-10 (15 AMPS) RADIO
F-11 (15 AMPS) ACCESSORY FEED
F-12   SPARE
F-13 (15 AMPS) EMERGENCY WARNING & STOP LAMPS
F-14 (15 AMPS) BACKUP LAMPS & TURN SIGNAL LAMPS
F-15 (30 AMPS) A/C OR HEATER BLOWER MOTOR
F-16   SPARE
F-17 (20 AMPS) CIRCUIT BREAKER-POWER WINDOWS

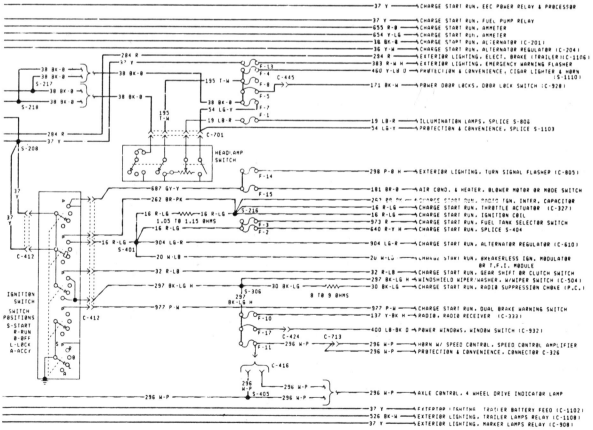

Power distribution wiring diagram, 1984 through 1986

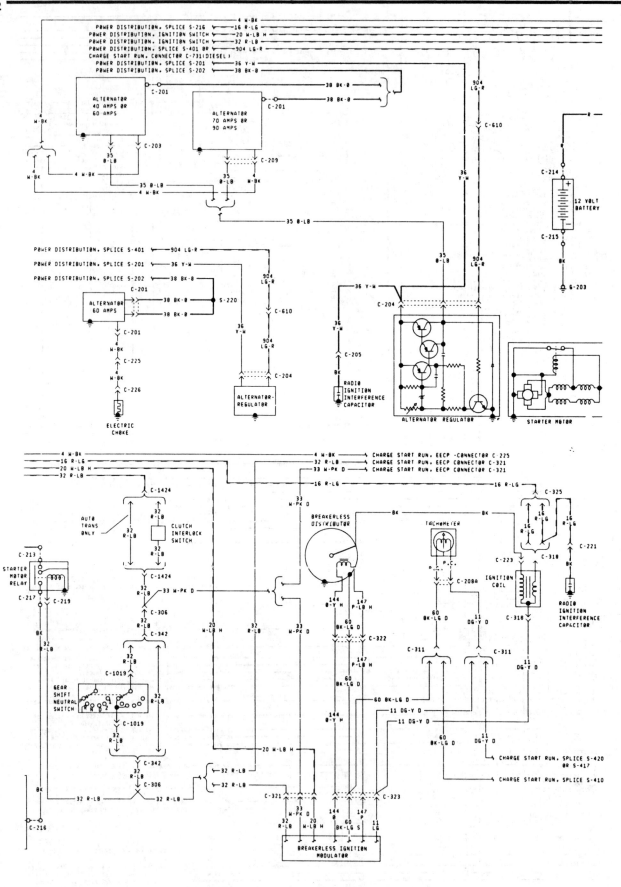

Charge, start, run wiring diagram, 1984 through 1986 (1 of 7)

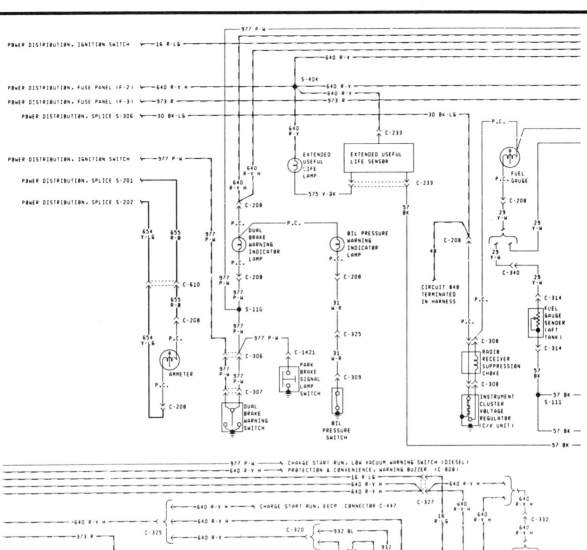

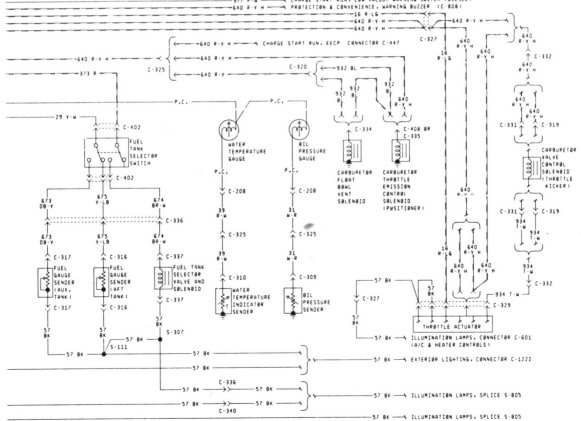

Charge, start, run wiring diagram, 1984 through 1986 (2 of 7)

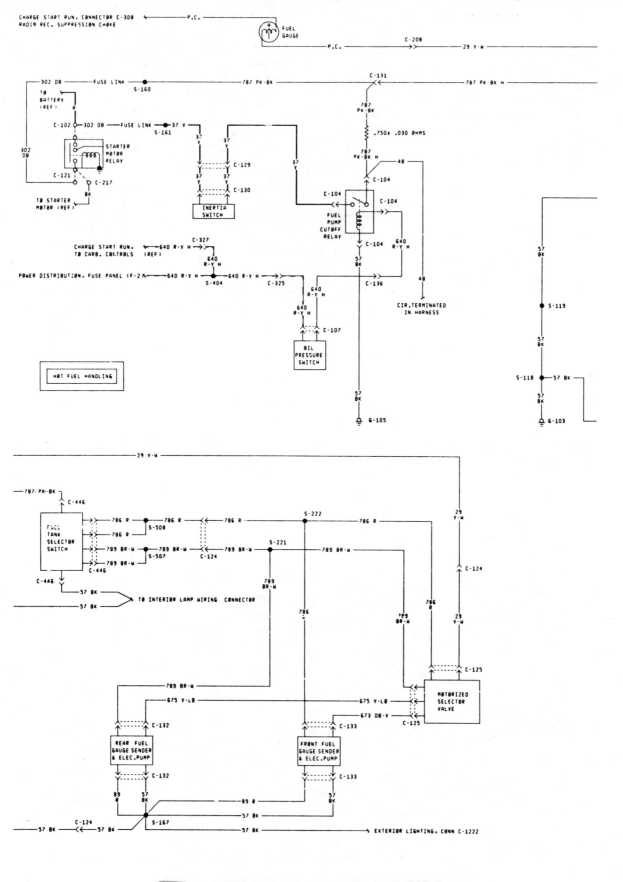

Charge, start, run wiring diagram, 1984 through 1986 (3 of 7)

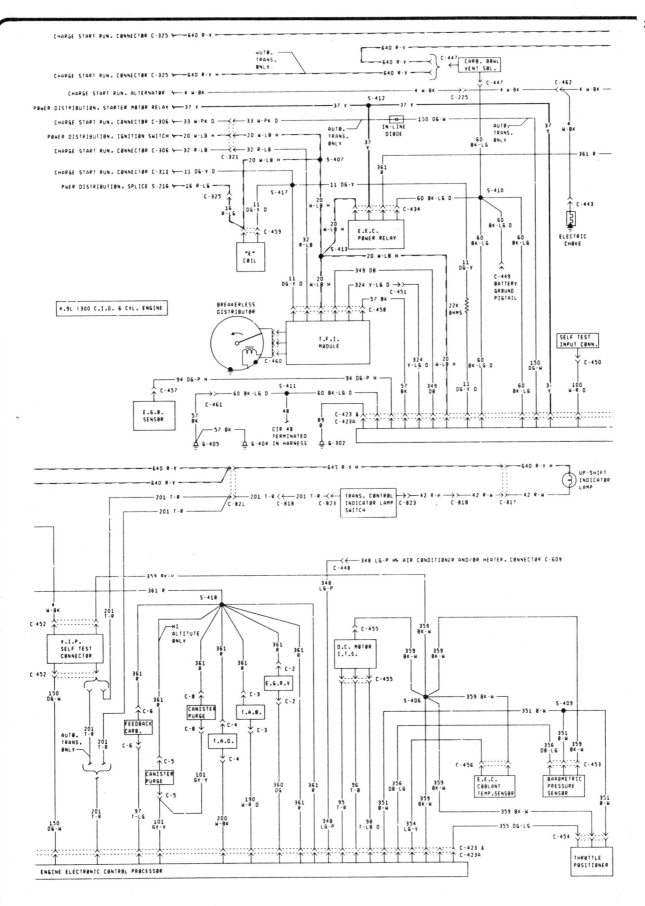

Charge, start, run wiring diagram, 1984 through 1986 (4 of 7)

356

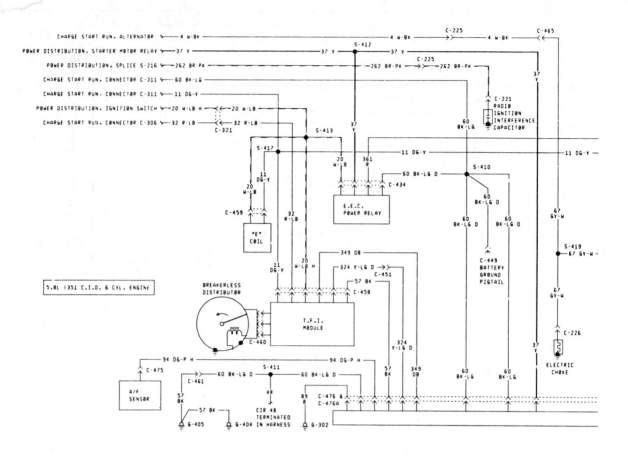

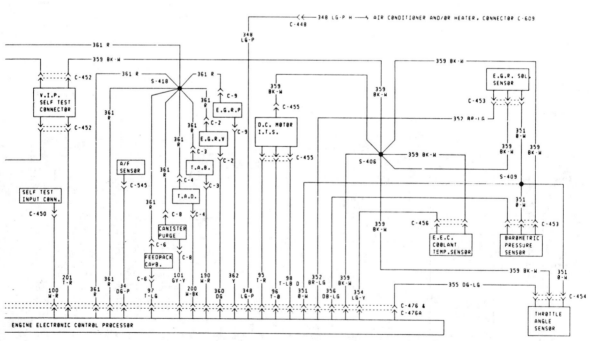

Charge, start, run wiring diagram, 1984 through 1986 (5 of 7)

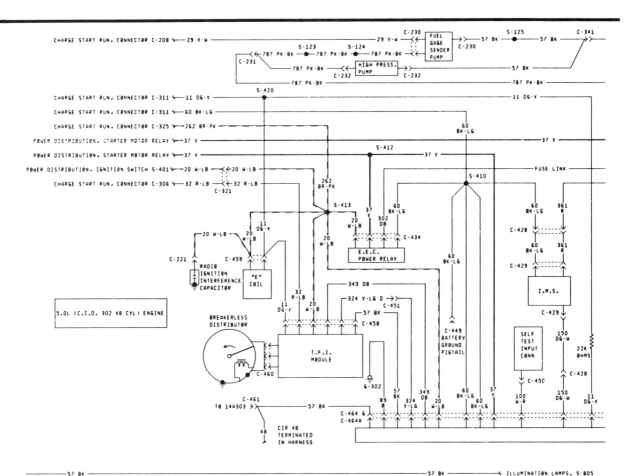

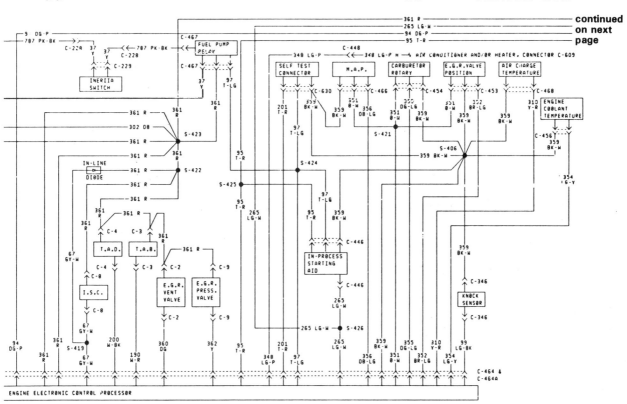

continued
on next
page

Charge, start, run wiring diagram, 1984 through 1986 (6 of 7)

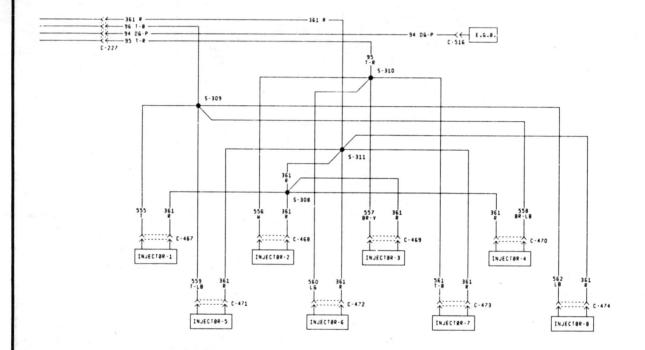

Charge, start, run wiring diagram, 1984 through 1986 (7 of 7)

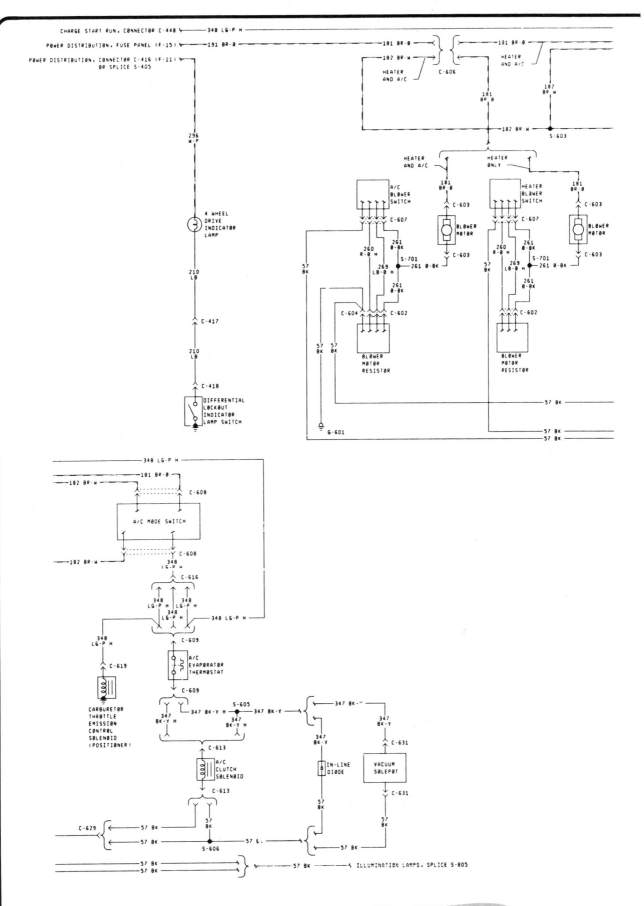

Axle control, air conditioning, heater wiring diagram, 1984 through 1986

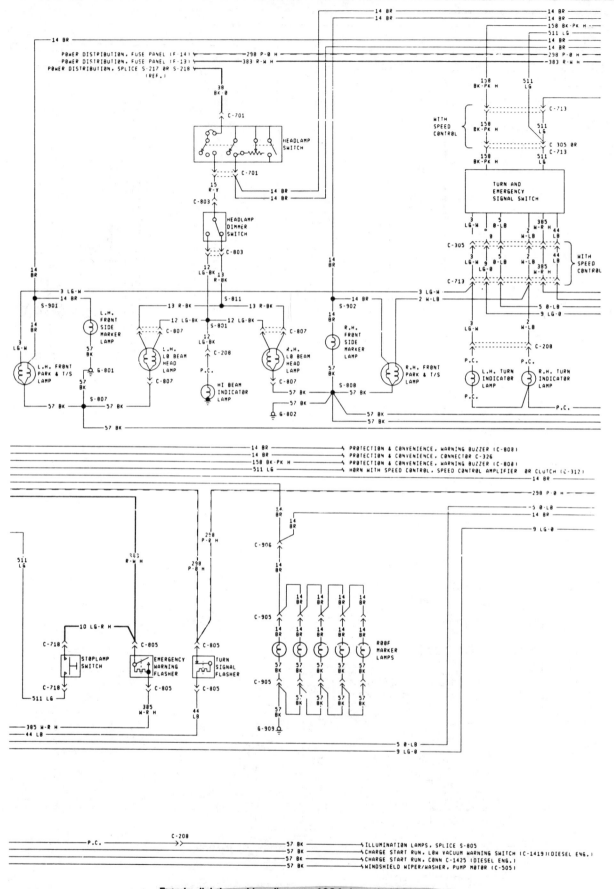

Exterior lighting wiring diagram, 1984 through 1986 (1 of 3)

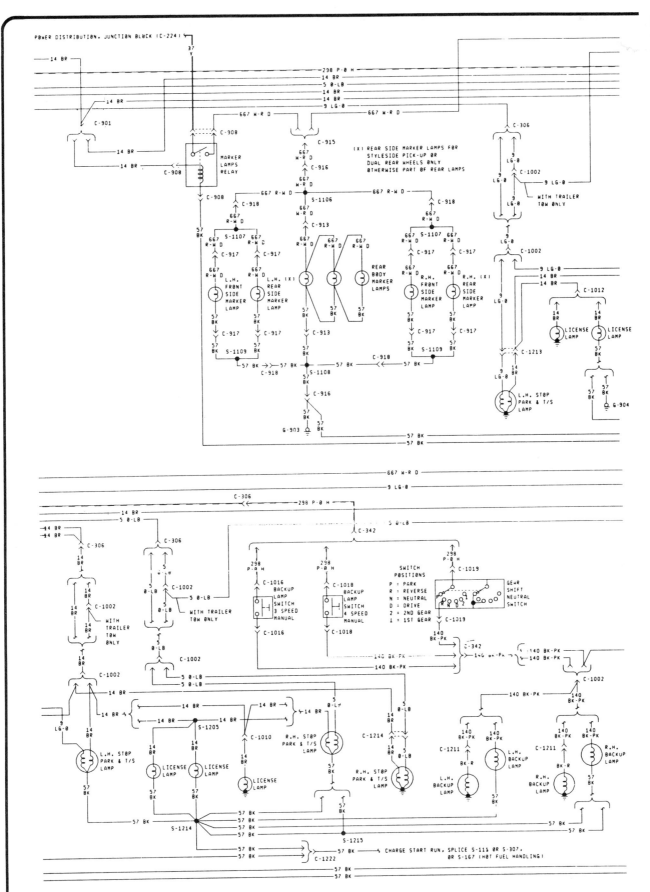

Exterior lighting wiring diagram, 1984 through 1986 (2 of 3)

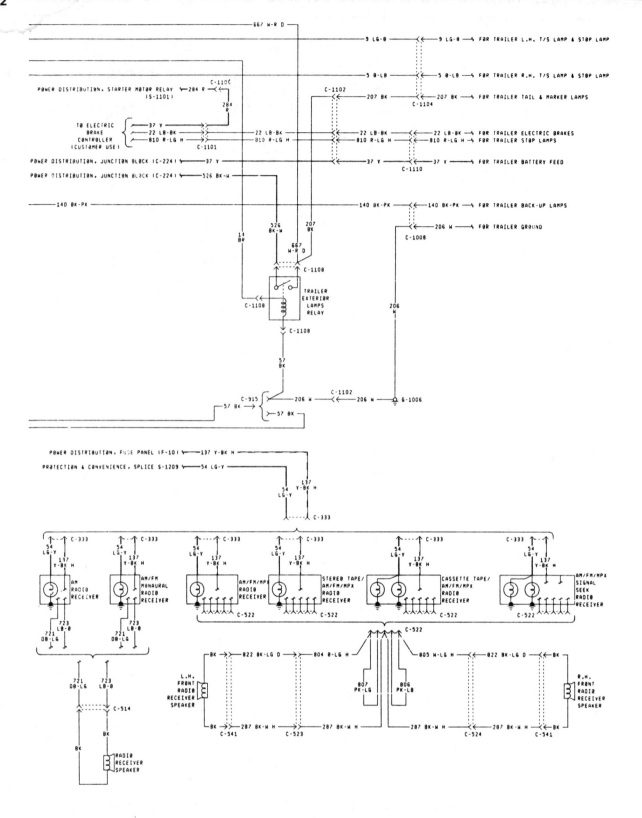

Exterior lighting wiring diagram, 1984 through 1986 (3 of 3)

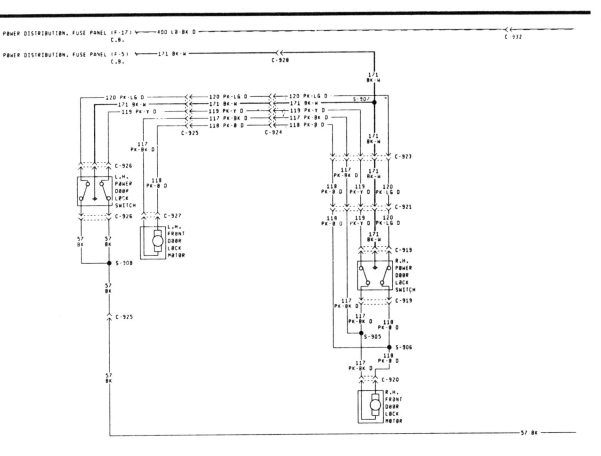

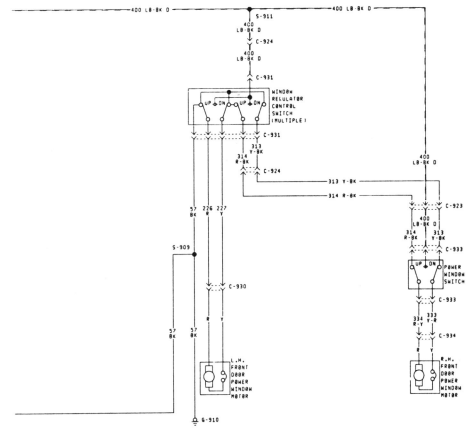

Power door locks, power windows wiring diagram, 1984 through 1986

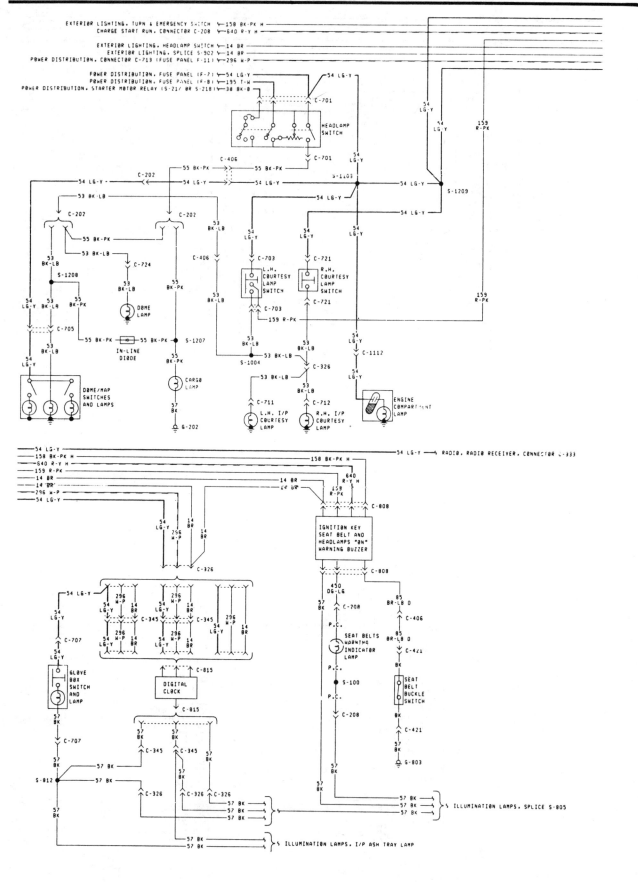

Protection and convenience wiring diagram, 1984 through 1986

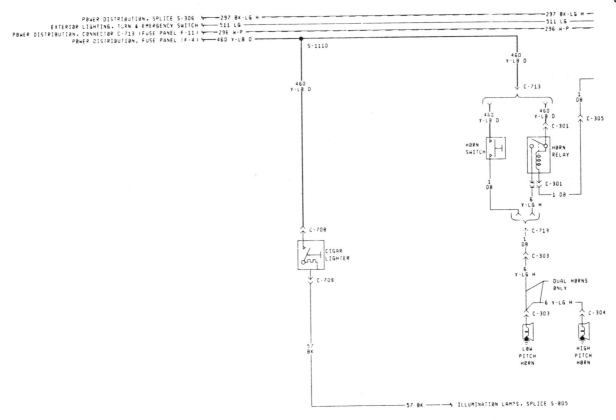

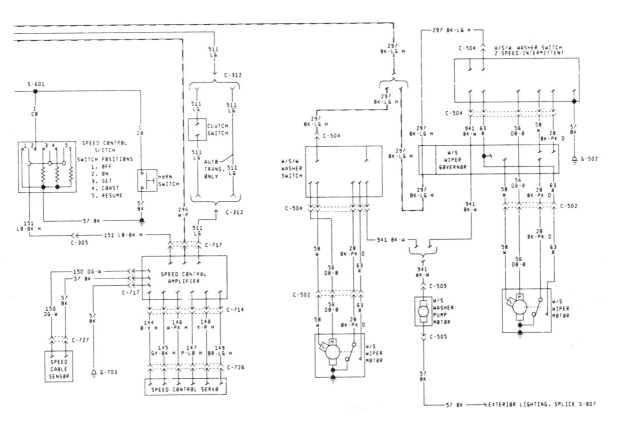

Protection and convenience, horn, speed control, windshield wiper/washer, 1984 through 1986

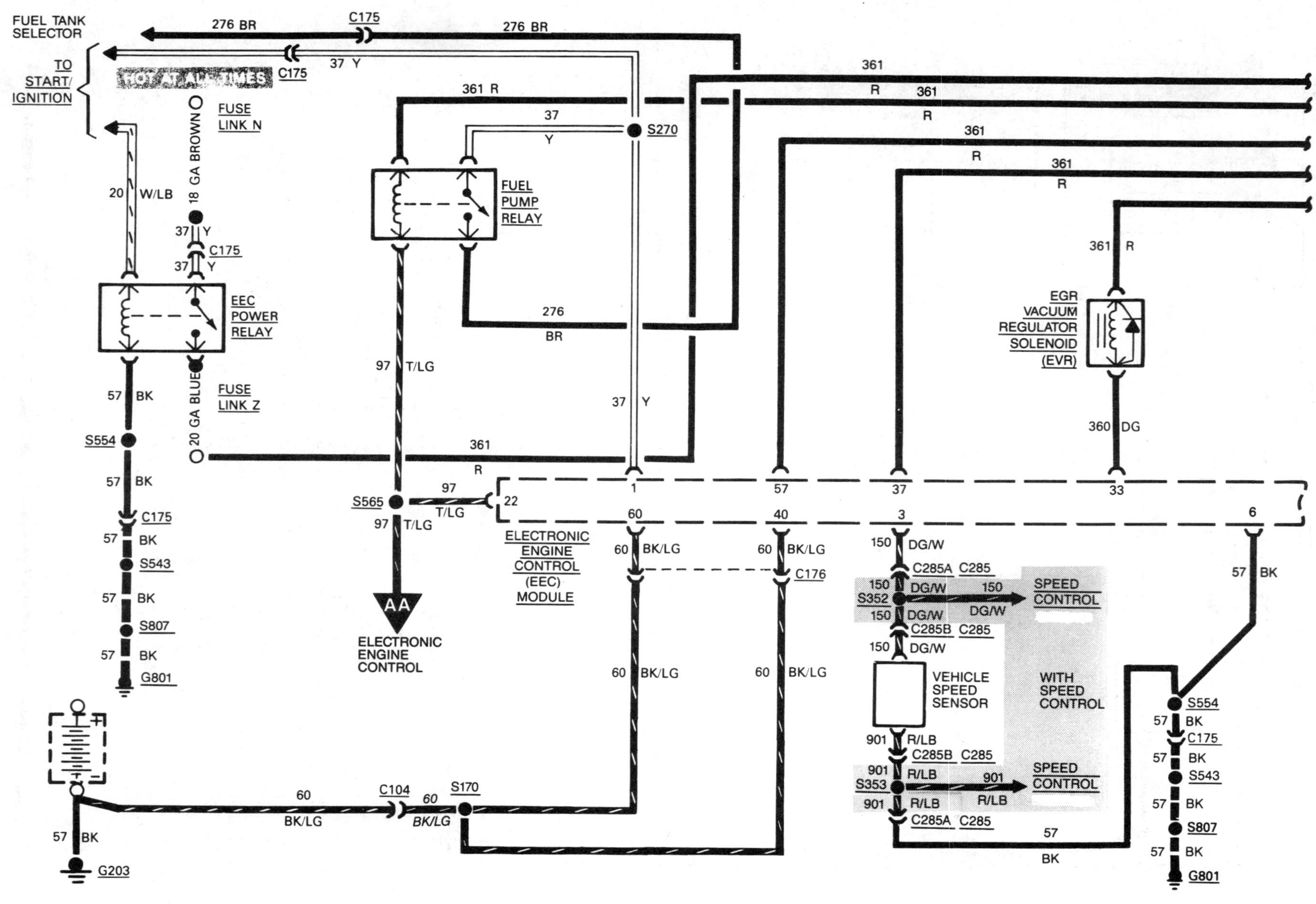

BK

57

S554 BK C175 BK S543 BK S807 BK G801

57 57 57 57

R
361

DG
360

33

SPEED CONTROL

WITH SPEED CONTROL

SPEED CONTROL

57 BK

EGR VACUUM REGULATOR SOLENOID (EVR)

361 R

361 R

361 R

361 R

DG/W C285A C285 DG/W 150 DG/W C285 DG/W

R/LB C285 R/LB 901 R/LB C285A C285

VEHICLE SPEED SENSOR

3

150 DG/W 150 C285B C285B 150 DG/W
150 S352 150 150

901 R/LB C285B 901 901 R/LB C285A
S353 901 901

37

BK/LG C176 BK/LG

57 40 60 60 60

276 BR

S270

BK/LG BK/LG

Y 37 1 60 60 60

37
Y

276 BR

FUEL PUMP RELAY

361 R

361 R

22

ELECTRONIC ENGINE CONTROL (EEC) MODULE

S170

BK/LG

97 T/LG

C104 60 BK/LG

C175

37 Y

97 T/LG S565 97 T/LG

AA

ELECTRONIC ENGINE CONTROL

60 BK/LG

276 BR C175

FUSE LINK N

EEC POWER RELAY

FUSE LINK Z

37 Y C175 Y

20 GA BLUE

C175 BK S543 BK S807 BK G801

18 GA BROWN

37 37

20 W/LB

57 S554 57 BK BK BK
57 57 57

G203

FUEL TANK SELECTOR

TO START/ IGNITION

57 BK

Electronic engine control wiring diagram — 4.9L engine — 1987 on (1 of 4)

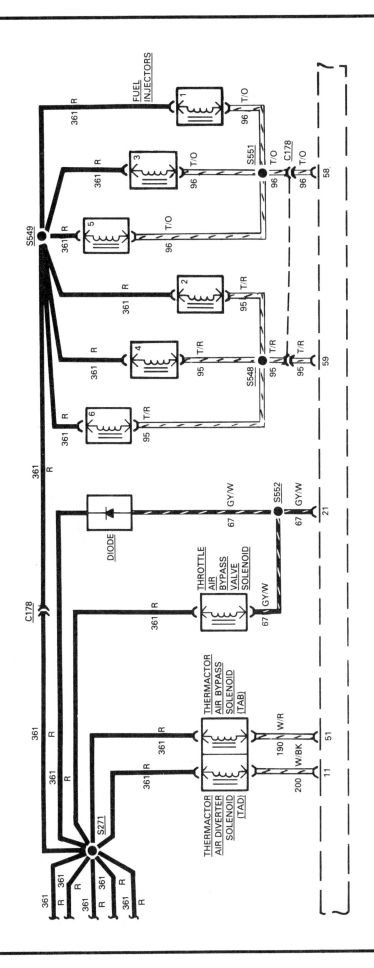

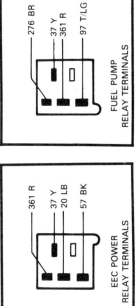

Electronic engine control wiring diagram — 4.9L engine — 1987 on (2 of 4)

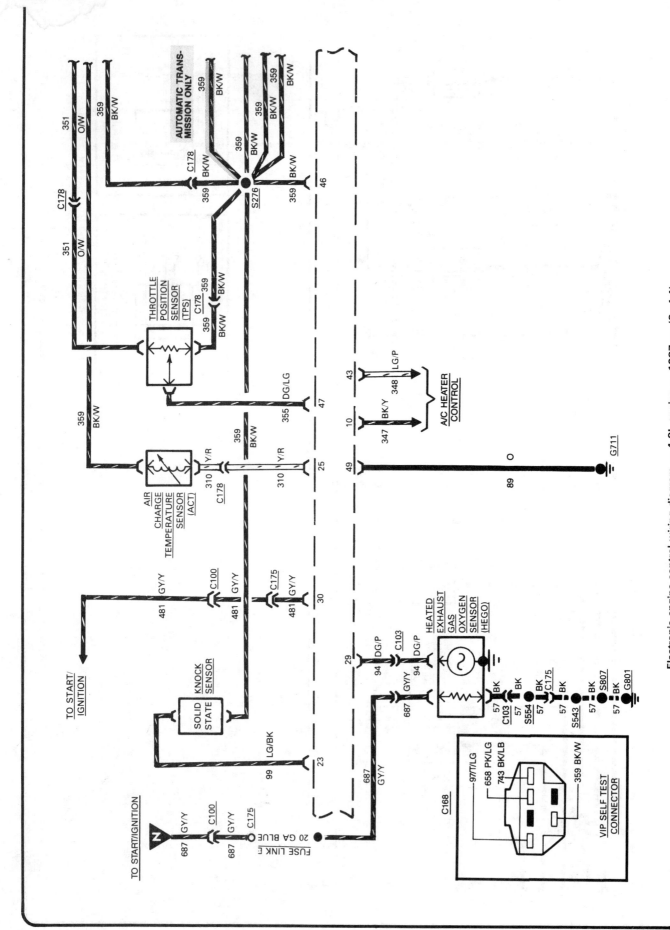

Electronic engine control wiring diagram — 4.9L engine — 1987 on (3 of 4)

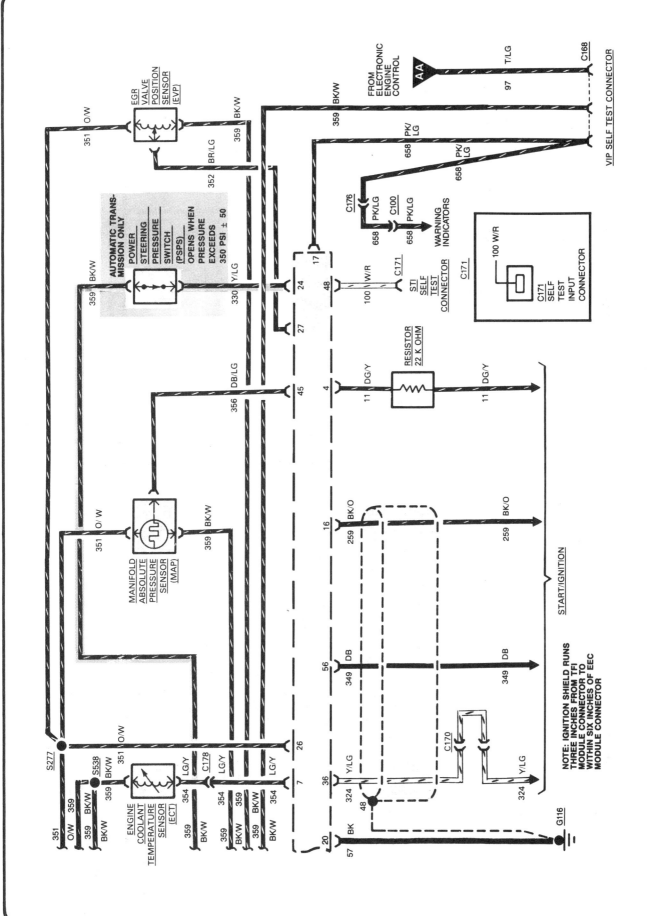

Electronic engine control wiring diagram — 4.9L engine — 1987 on (4 of 4)

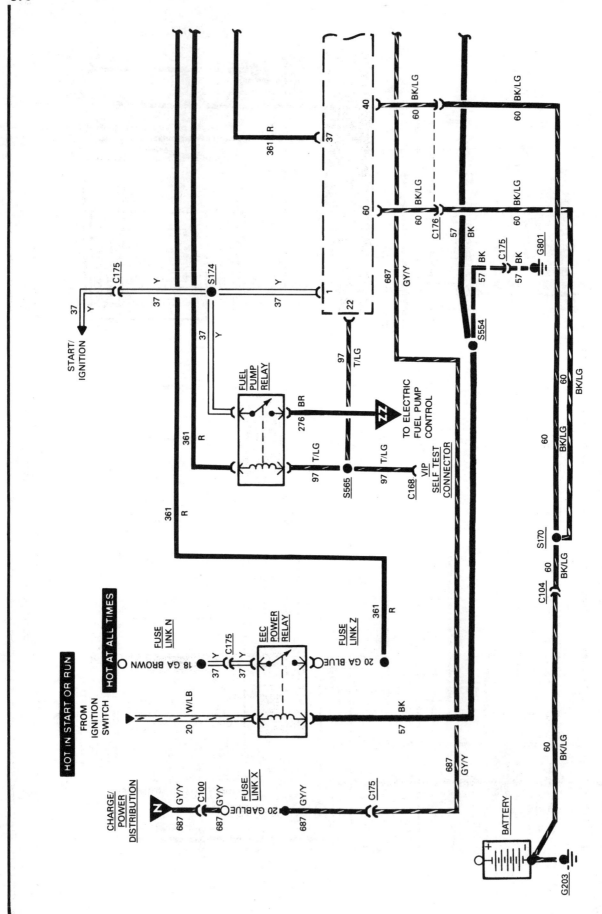

Electronic engine control wiring diagram — 5.0L, 5.8L and 7.5L engines — 1987 on (1 of 4)

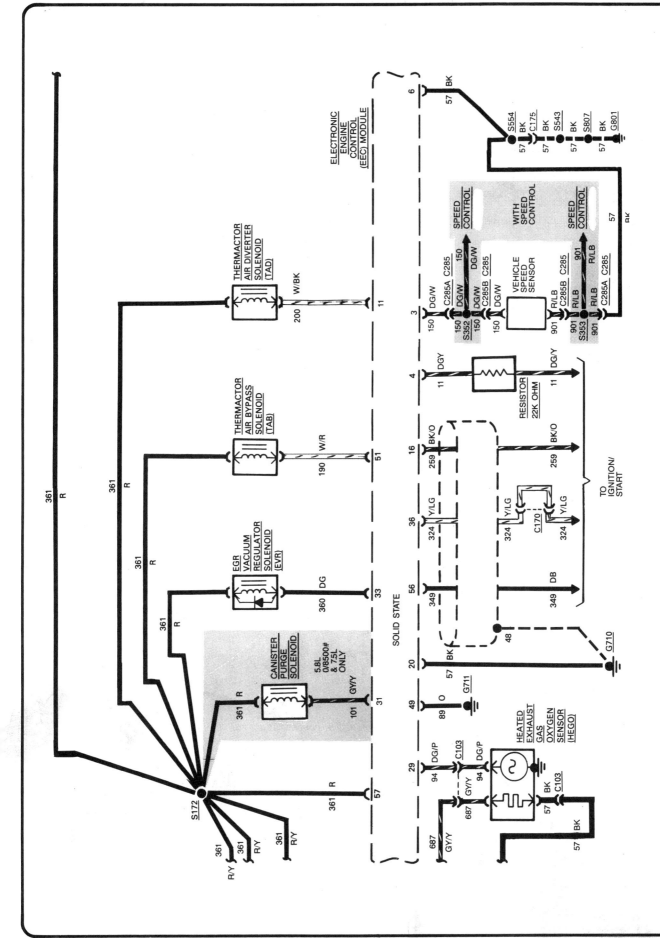

Electronic engine control wiring diagram — 5.0L, 5.8L and 7.5L engines — 1987 on (2 of 4)

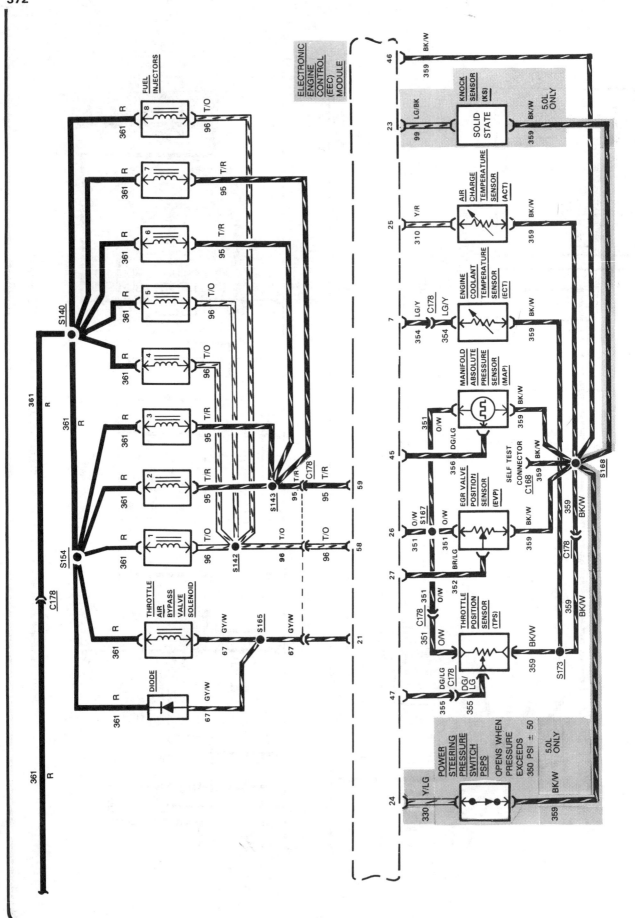

Electronic engine control wiring diagram — 5.0L, 5.8L and 7.5L engines — 1987 on (3 of 4)

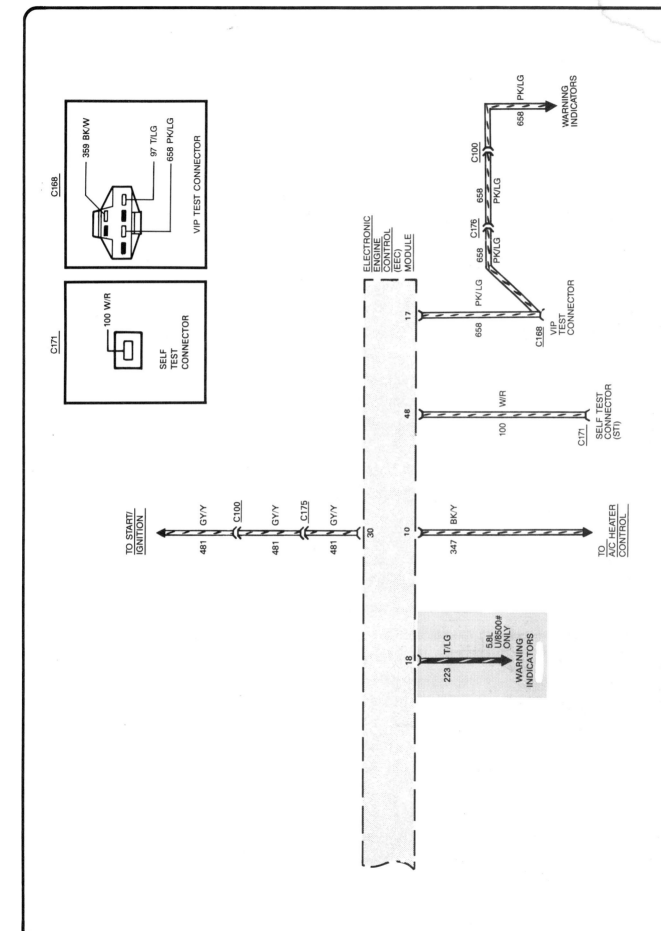

Electronic engine control wiring diagram — 5.0L, 5.8L and 7.5L engines — 1987 on (4 of 4)

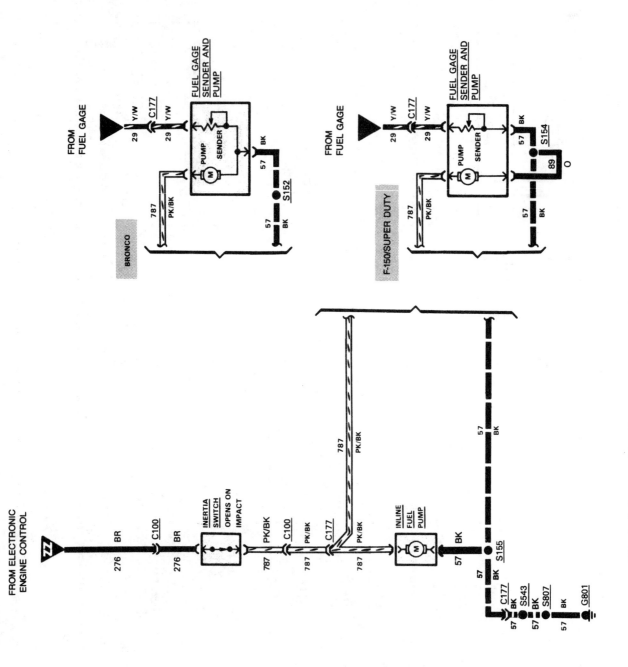

FUEL GAGE SENDER AND PUMP

FROM FUEL GAGE

29 Y/W | C177 | 29 Y/W

PUMP | SENDER | 57 BK | S152

787 PK/BK

57 BK

BRONCO

FUEL GAGE SENDER AND PUMP

FROM FUEL GAGE

29 Y/W | C177 | 29 Y/W

PUMP | SENDER | BK | 57 | S154 | 89

787 PK/BK

57 BK

F-150/SUPER DUTY

787 PK/BK

57 BK

FROM ELECTRONIC ENGINE CONTROL

276 BR | C100 | 276 BR

INERTIA SWITCH OPENS ON IMPACT

787 PK/BK | C100 | 787 PK/BK | C177 | 787 PK/BK

INLINE FUEL PUMP

57 BK | S155

57 BK | C177 | S543 | BK | S807 | BK | G801

57 | 57 | 57

Electric fuel pump wiring diagram — single tank, 1987 on with EFI

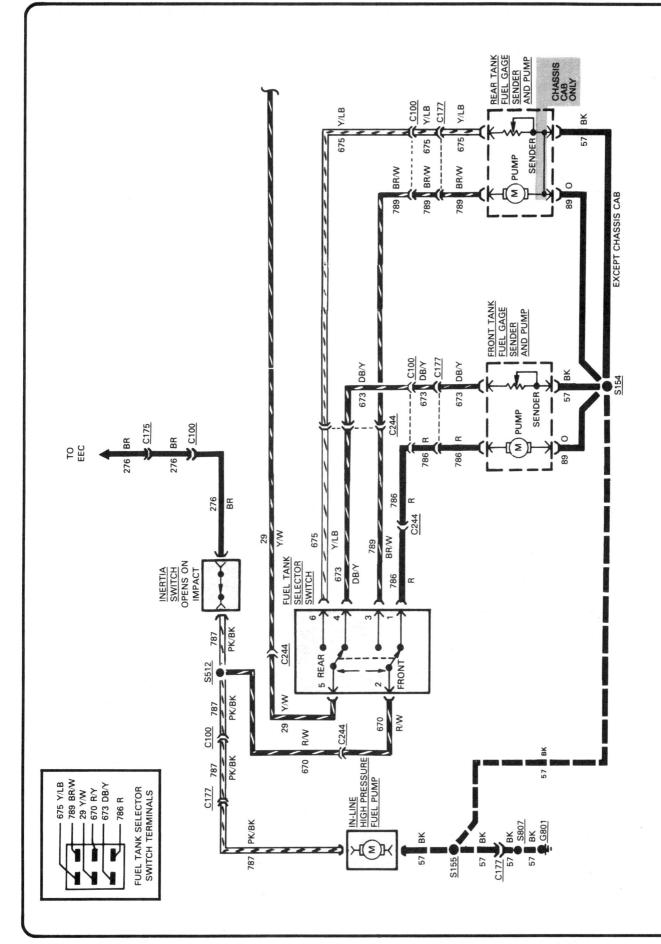

Fuel tank selector wiring diagram — dual tanks with EFI

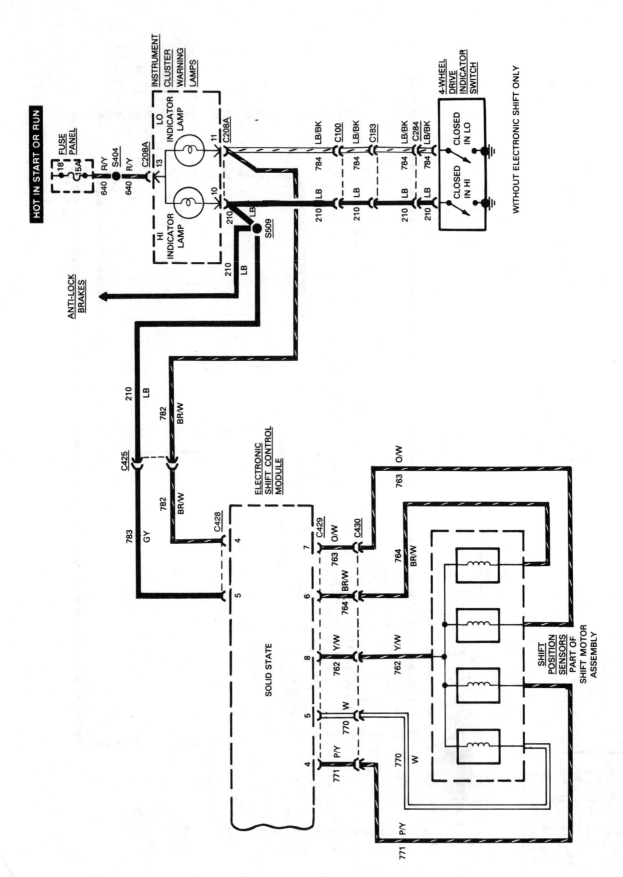

Electronic shift 4-wheel drive wiring diagram — 1988 on (1 of 2)

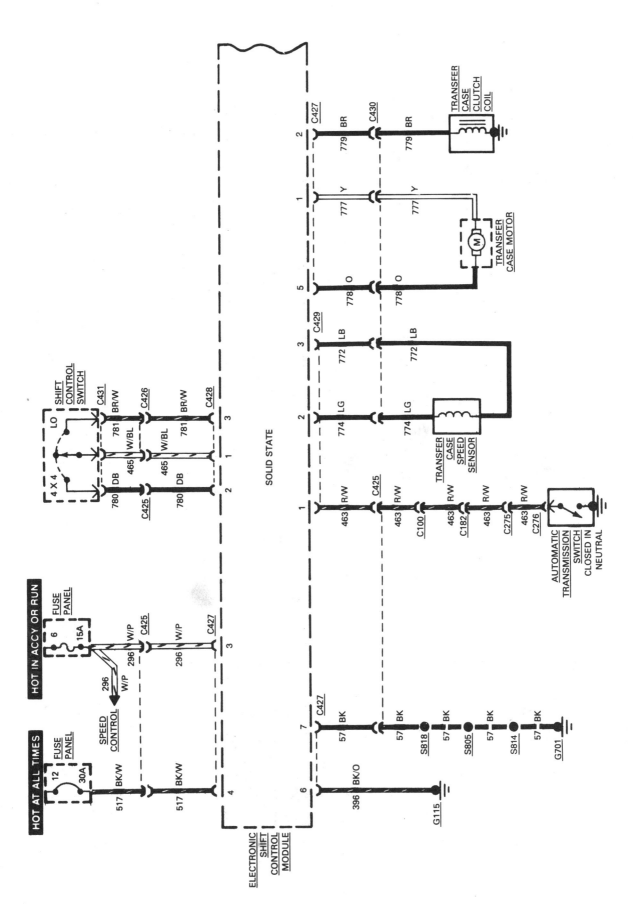

Electronic shift 4-wheel drive wiring diagram — 1988 on (2 of 2)

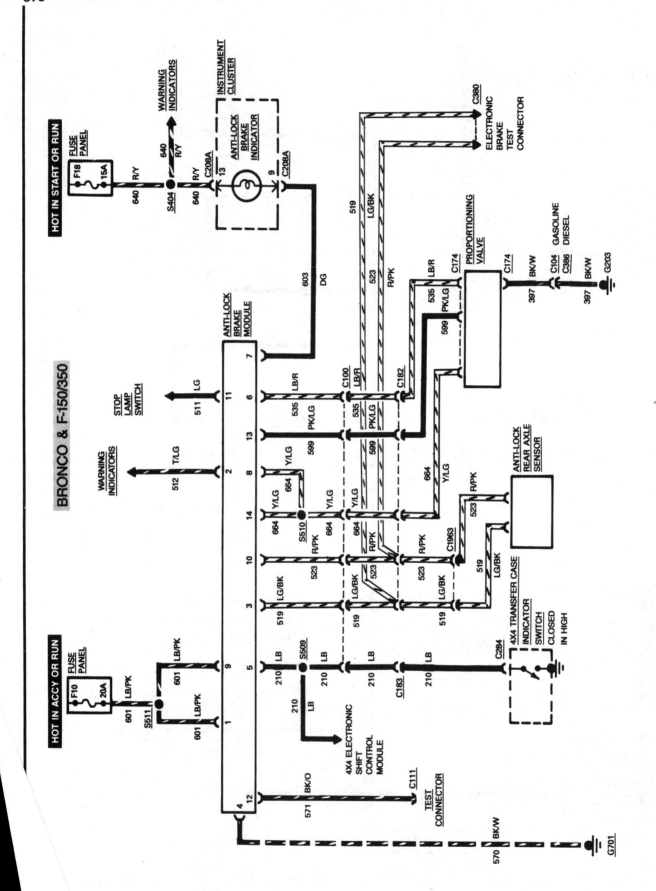

Rear anti-lock brake wiring diagram — 1988 on

Conversion factors

Length (distance)

Inches (in)	X	25.4	= Millimetres (mm)	X	0.0394	= Inches (in)
Feet (ft)	X	0.305	= Metres (m)	X	3.281	= Feet (ft)
Miles	X	1.609	= Kilometres (km)	X	0.621	= Miles

Volume (capacity)

Cubic inches (cu in; in³)	X	16.387	= Cubic centimetres (cc; cm³)	X	0.061	= Cubic inches (cu in; in³)
Imperial pints (Imp pt)	X	0.568	= Litres (l)	X	1.76	= Imperial pints (Imp pt)
Imperial quarts (Imp qt)	X	1.137	= Litres (l)	X	0.88	= Imperial quarts (Imp qt)
Imperial quarts (Imp qt)	X	1.201	= US quarts (US qt)	X	0.833	= Imperial quarts (Imp qt)
US quarts (US qt)	X	0.946	= Litres (l)	X	1.057	= US quarts (US qt)
Imperial gallons (Imp gal)	X	4.546	= Litres (l)	X	0.22	= Imperial gallons (Imp gal)
Imperial gallons (Imp gal)	X	1.201	= US gallons (US gal)	X	0.833	= Imperial gallons (Imp gal)
US gallons (US gal)	X	3.785	= Litres (l)	X	0.264	= US gallons (US gal)

Mass (weight)

Ounces (oz)	X	28.35	= Grams (g)	X	0.035	= Ounces (oz)
Pounds (lb)	X	0.454	= Kilograms (kg)	X	2.205	= Pounds (lb)

Force

Ounces-force (ozf; oz)	X	0.278	= Newtons (N)	X	3.6	= Ounces-force (ozf; oz)
Pounds-force (lbf; lb)	X	4.448	= Newtons (N)	X	0.225	= Pounds-force (lbf; lb)
Newtons (N)	X	0.1	= Kilograms-force (kgf; kg)	X	9.81	= Newtons (N)

Pressure

Pounds-force per square inch (psi; lbf/in²; lb/in²)	X	0.070	= Kilograms-force per square centimetre (kgf/cm²; kg/cm²)	X	14.223	= Pounds-force per square inch (psi; lbf/in²; lb/in²)
Pounds-force per square inch (psi; lbf/in²; lb/in²)	X	0.068	= Atmospheres (atm)	X	14.696	= Pounds-force per square inch (psi; lbf/in²; lb/in²)
Pounds-force per square inch (psi; lbf/in²; lb/in²)	X	0.069	= Bars	X	14.5	= Pounds-force per square inch (psi; lbf/in²; lb/in²)
Pounds-force per square inch (psi; lbf/in²; lb/in²)	X	6.895	= Kilopascals (kPa)	X	0.145	= Pounds-force per square inch (psi; lbf/in²; lb/in²)
Kilopascals (kPa)	X	0.01	= Kilograms-force per square centimetre (kgf/cm²; kg/cm²)	X	98.1	= Kilopascals (kPa)

Torque (moment of force)

Pounds-force inches (lbf in; lb in)	X	1.152	= Kilograms-force centimetre (kgf cm; kg cm)	X	0.868	= Pounds-force inches (lbf in; lb in)
Pounds-force inches (lbf in; lb in)	X	0.113	= Newton metres (Nm)	X	8.85	= Pounds-force inches (lbf in; lb in)
Pounds-force inches (lbf in; lb in)	X	0.083	= Pounds-force feet (lbf ft; lb ft)	X	12	= Pounds-force inches (lbf in; lb in)
Pounds-force feet (lbf ft; lb ft)	X	0.138	= Kilograms-force metres (kgf m; kg m)	X	7.233	= Pounds-force feet (lbf ft; lb ft)
Pounds-force feet (lbf ft; lb ft)	X	1.356	= Newton metres (Nm)	X	0.738	= Pounds-force feet (lbf ft; lb ft)
Newton metres (Nm)	X	0.102	= Kilograms-force metres (kgf m; kg m)	X	9.804	= Newton metres (Nm)

Power

Horsepower (hp)	X	745.7	= Watts (W)	X	0.0013	= Horsepower (hp)

Velocity (speed)

Miles per hour (miles/hr; mph)	X	1.609	= Kilometres per hour (km/hr; kph)	X	0.621	= Miles per hour (miles/hr; mph)

Fuel consumption*

Miles per gallon, Imperial (mpg)	X	0.354	= Kilometres per litre (km/l)	X	2.825	= Miles per gallon, Imperial (mpg)
Miles per gallon, US (mpg)	X	0.425	= Kilometres per litre (km/l)	X	2.352	= Miles per gallon, US (mpg)

Temperature

Degrees Fahrenheit = (°C x 1.8) + 32   Degrees Celsius (Degrees Centigrade; °C) = (°F - 32) x 0.56

*It is common practice to convert from miles per gallon (mpg) to litres/100 kilometres (l/100km), where mpg (Imperial) x l/100 km = 282 and mpg (US) x l/100 km = 235

Index

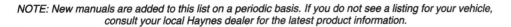 

HAYNES AUTOMOTIVE MANUALS

NOTE: New manuals are added to this list on a periodic basis. If you do not see a listing for your vehicle, consult your local Haynes dealer for the latest product information.

ACURA
1776 **Integra & Legend** '86 thru '90

AMC
Jeep CJ – *see JEEP (412)*
694 **Mid-size models,** Concord, Hornet, Gremlin & Spirit '70 thru '83
934 **(Renault) Alliance & Encore** all models '83 thru '87

AUDI
615 **4000** all models '80 thru '87
428 **5000** all models '77 thru '83
1117 **5000** all models '84 thru '88

AUSTIN
Healey Sprite – *see MG Midget Roadster (265)*

BMW
276 **320i** all 4 cyl models '75 thru '83
632 **528i & 530i** all models '75 thru '80
240 **1500 thru 2002** all models except Turbo '59 thru '77
348 **2500, 2800, 3.0 & Bavaria** '69 thru '76

BUICK
Century (front wheel drive) – *see GENERAL MOTORS A-Cars (829)*
*1627 **Buick, Oldsmobile & Pontiac Full-size (Front wheel drive)** all models '85 thru '93
Buick Electra, LeSabre and Park Avenue; **Oldsmobile** Delta 88 Royale, Ninety Eight and Regency; **Pontiac** Bonneville
*1551 **Buick Oldsmobile & Pontiac Full-size (Rear wheel drive)**
Buick Electra '70 thru '84, Estate '70 thru '90, LeSabre '70 thru '79
Oldsmobile Custom Cruiser '70 thru '90, Delta 88 '70 thru '85, Ninety-eight '70 thru '84
Pontiac Bonneville '70 thru '81, Catalina '70 thru '81, Grandville '70 thru '75, Parisienne '84 thru '86
627 **Mid-size** all rear-drive **Regal & Century** models with V6, V8 and Turbo '74 thru '87
Regal – *see GENERAL MOTORS (1671)*
Skyhawk – *see GENERAL MOTORS J-Cars (766)*
552 **Skylark** all X-car models '80 thru '85

CADILLAC
*751 **Cadillac Rear Wheel Drive** all gasoline models '70 thru '90
Cimarron – *see GENERAL MOTORS J-Cars (766)*

CAPRI
296 **2000 MK I Coupe** all models '71 thru '75
205 **2600 & 2800 V6 Coupe** '71 thru '75
375 **2800 Mk II V6 Coupe** '75 thru '78
Mercury Capri – *see FORD Mustang (654)*

CHEVROLET
*1477 **Astro & GMC Safari Mini-vans** all models '85 thru '91
554 **Camaro V8** all models '70 thru '81
*866 **Camaro** all models '82 thru '91
Cavalier – *see GENERAL MOTORS J-Cars (766)*
Celebrity – *see GENERAL MOTORS A-Cars (829)*
625 **Chevelle, Malibu & El Camino** all V6 & V8 models '69 thru '87
449 **Chevette & Pontiac T1000** all models '76 thru '87
550 **Citation** all models '80 thru '85
*1628 **Corsica/Beretta** all models '87 thru '92
274 **Corvette** all V8 models '68 thru '82
*1336 **Corvette** all models '84 thru '91

704 **Full-size Sedans** Caprice, Impala, Biscayne. Bel Air & Wagons, all V6 & V8 models '69 thru '90
Lumina – *see GENERAL MOTORS (1671)*
Lumina APV – *see GENERAL MOTORS (2035)*
319 **Luv Pick-up** all 2WD & 4WD models '72 thru '82
626 **Monte Carlo** all V6, V8 & Turbo models '70 thru '88
241 **Nova** all V8 models '69 thru '79
*1642 **Nova and Geo Prizm** all front wheel drive models, '85 thru '90
*420 **Pick-ups '67 thru '87 – Chevrolet & GMC,** all full-size models '67 thru '87; Suburban, Blazer & Jimmy '67 thru '91
*1664 **Pick-ups '88 thru '92 – Chevrolet & GMC** all full-size (C and K) models, '88 thru '92
*1727 **Sprint & Geo Metro** '85 thru '91
*831 **S-10 & GMC S-15 Pick-ups** all models '82 thru '92
*345 **Vans – Chevrolet & GMC,** V8 & in-line 6 cyl models '68 thru '92

CHRYSLER
*1337 **Chrysler & Plymouth Mid-size** front wheel drive '82 thru '89
K-Cars – *see DODGE Aries (723)*
Laser – *see DODGE Daytona (1140)*

DATSUN
402 **200SX** all models '77 thru '79
647 **200SX** all models '80 thru '83
228 **B-210** all models '73 thru '78
525 **210** all models '78 thru '82
206 **240Z, 260Z & 280Z Coupe & 2+2** '70 thru '78
563 **280ZX Coupe & 2+2** '79 thru '83
300ZX – *see NISSAN (1137)*
679 **310** all models '78 thru '82
123 **510 & PL521 Pick-up** '68 thru '73
430 **510** all models '78 thru '81
372 **610** all models '72 thru '76
277 **620 Series Pick-up** all models '73 thru '79
720 Series Pick-up – *see NISSAN Pick-ups (771)*
376 **810/Maxima** all gasoline models '77 thru '84
124 **1200** all models '70 thru '73
368 **F10** all models '76 thru '79
Pulsar – *see NISSAN (876)*
Sentra – *see NISSAN (982)*
Stanza – *see NISSAN (981)*

DODGE
*723 **Aries & Plymouth Reliant** all models '81 thru '89
*1231 **Caravan & Plymouth Voyager Mini-Vans** all models '84 thru '91
699 **Challenger & Plymouth Saporro** all models '78 thru '83
236 **Colt** all models '71 thru '77
610 **Colt & Plymouth Champ (front wheel drive)** all models '78 thru '87
*556 **D50/Ram 50/Plymouth Arrow Pick-ups & Raider** '79 thru '91
*1668 **Dakota Pick-up** all models '87 thru '90
234 **Dart & Plymouth Valiant** all 6 cyl models '67 thru '76
*1140 **Daytona & Chrysler Laser** all models '84 thru '89
*545 **Omni & Plymouth Horizon** all models '78 thru '90
*912 **Pick-ups** all full-size models '74 thru '91
*1726 **Shadow & Plymouth Sundance** '87 thru '91
*1779 **Spirit & Plymouth Acclaim** '89 thru '92
*349 **Vans – Dodge & Plymouth** V8 & 6 cyl models '71 thru '91

FIAT
094 **124 Sport Coupe & Spider** '68 thru '78

479 **Strada** all models '79 thru '82
273 **X1/9** all models '74 thru '80

FORD
*1476 **Aerostar Mini-vans** all models '86 thru '92
788 **Bronco and Pick-ups** '73 thru '79
*880 **Bronco and Pick-ups** '80 thru '91
268 **Courier Pick-up** all models '72 thru '82
789 **Escort & Mercury Lynx** all models '81 thru '90
*2046 **Escort & Mercury Tracer** all models '91 thru '93
*2021 **Explorer & Mazda Navajo** '91 thru '92
560 **Fairmont & Mercury Zephyr** all in-line & V8 models '78 thru '83
334 **Fiesta** all models '77 thru '80
754 **Ford & Mercury Full-size,** Ford LTD & Mercury Marquis ('75 thru '82); Ford Custom 500, Country Squire, Crown Victoria & Mercury Colony Park ('75 thru '87); Ford LTD Crown Victoria & Mercury Gran Marquis ('83 thru '87)
359 **Granada & Mercury Monarch** all in-line, 6 cyl & V8 models '75 thru '80
773 **Ford & Mercury Mid-size,** Ford Thunderbird & Mercury Cougar ('75 thru '82); Ford LTD & Mercury Marquis ('83 thru '86); Ford Torino, Gran Torino, Elite, Ranchero pick-up, LTD II, Mercury Montego, Comet, XR-7 & Lincoln Versailles ('75 thru '86)
*654 **Mustang & Mercury Capri** all models including Turbo '79 thru '92
357 **Mustang V8** all models '64-1/2 thru '73
231 **Mustang II** all 4 cyl, V6 & V8 models '74 thru '78
649 **Pinto & Mercury Bobcat** all models '75 thru '80
*1670 **Probe** all models '89 thru '92
*1026 **Ranger & Bronco II** all gasoline models '83 thru '92
*1421 **Taurus & Mercury Sable** '86 thru '92
*1418 **Tempo & Mercury Topaz** all gasoline models '84 thru '91
1338 **Thunderbird & Mercury Cougar/XR7** '83 thru '88
*1725 **Thunderbird & Mercury Cougar** '89 and '90
*344 **Vans** all V8 Econoline models '69 thru '91

GENERAL MOTORS
*829 **A-Cars** – Chevrolet Celebrity, Buick Century, Pontiac 6000 & Oldsmobile Cutlass Ciera all models '82 thru '90
*766 **J-Cars** – Chevrolet Cavalier, Pontiac J-2000, Oldsmobile Firenza, Buick Skyhawk & Cadillac Cimarron all models '82 thru '92
*1420 **N-Cars** – Buick Somerset '85 thru '87; Pontiac Grand Am and Oldsmobile Calais '85 thru '91; Buick Skylark '86 thru '91
*1671 **GM: Buick** Regal, **Chevrolet** Lumina, **Oldsmobile** Cutlass Supreme, **Pontiac** Grand Prix, all front wheel drive models '88 thru '90
*2035 **GM: Chevrolet Lumina APV, Oldsmobile Silhouette, Pontiac Trans Sport** '90 thru '92

GEO
Metro – *see CHEVROLET Sprint (1727)*
Prizm – *see CHEVROLET Nova (1642)*
Tracker – *see SUZUKI Samurai (1626)*

GMC
Safari – *see CHEVROLET ASTRO (1477)*
Vans & Pick-ups – *see CHEVROLET (420, 831, 345, 1664)*

(continued on next page)

---

* Listings shown with an asterisk (*) indicate model coverage as of this printing. These titles will be periodically updated to include later model years – consult your Haynes dealer for more information.

Haynes North America, Inc., 861 Lawrence Drive, Newbury Park, CA 91320 • (805) 498-6703

HAYNES AUTOMOTIVE MANUALS

NOTE: New manuals are added to this list on a periodic basis. If you do not see a listing for your vehicle, consult your local Haynes dealer for the latest product information.

HONDA
- 351 **Accord CVCC** all models '76 thru '83
- *1221 **Accord** all models '84 thru '89
- 160 **Civic 1200** all models '73 thru '79
- 633 **Civic 1300 & 1500 CVCC** all models '80 thru '83
- 297 **Civic 1500 CVCC** all models '75 thru '79
- *1227 **Civic** all models '84 thru '91
- *601 **Prelude CVCC** all models '79 thru '89

HYUNDAI
- *1552 **Excel** all models '86 thru '91

ISUZU
- *1641 **Trooper & Pick-up**, all gasoline models '81 thru '91

JAGUAR
- *242 **XJ6** all 6 cyl models '68 thru '86
- *478 **XJ12 & XJS** all 12 cyl models '72 thru '85

JEEP
- *1553 **Cherokee, Comanche & Wagoneer Limited** all models '84 thru '91
- 412 **CJ** all models '49 thru '86
- *1777 **Wrangler** all models '87 thru '92

LADA
- *413 **1200, 1300. 1500 & 1600** all models including Riva '74 thru '86

MAZDA
- 648 **626** Sedan & Coupe (rear wheel drive) all models '79 thru '82
- 1082 **626 & MX-6 (front wheel drive)** all models '83 thru '91
- 370 **GLC Hatchback (rear wheel drive)** all models '77 thru '83
- 757 **GLC (front wheel drive)** all models '81 thru '86
- *2047 **MPV** '89 thru '93
  Navajo – see FORD Explorer (2021)
- *267 **Pick-ups** '72 thru '92
- 460 **RX-7** all models '79 thru '85
- *1419 **RX-7** all models '86 thru '91

MERCEDES-BENZ
- *1643 **190 Series** all four-cylinder gasoline models, '84 thru '88
- 346 **230, 250 & 280** Sedan, Coupe & Roadster all 6 cyl sohc models '68 thru '72
- 983 **280 123 Series** all gasoline models '77 thru '81
- 698 **350 & 450** Sedan, Coupe & Roadster all models '71 thru '80
- 697 **Diesel 123 Series** 200D, 220D, 240D, 240TD, 300D, 300CD, 300TD, 4- & 5-cyl incl. Turbo '76 thru '85

MERCURY
For all PLYMOUTH titles see FORD Listing

MG
- 111 **MGB** Roadster & GT Coupe all models '62 thru '80
- 265 **MG Midget & Austin Healey Sprite** Roadster '58 thru '80

MITSUBISHI
- *1669 **Cordia, Tredia, Galant, Precis & Mirage** '83 thru '90
- *2022 **Pick-ups & Montero** '83 thru '91

MORRIS
- 074 **(Austin) Marina 1.8** all models '71 thru '80
- 024 **Minor 1000** sedan & wagon '56 thru '71

NISSAN
- 1137 **300ZX** all Turbo & non-Turbo models '84 thru '89

- *1341 **Maxima** all models '85 thru '91
- *771 **Pick-ups/Pathfinder** gas models '80 thru '91
- *876 **Pulsar** all models '83 thru '86
- *982 **Sentra** all models '82 thru '90
- *981 **Stanza** all models '82 thru '90

OLDSMOBILE
- **Custom Cruiser** – see BUICK Full-size (1551)
- 658 **Cutlass** all standard gasoline V6 & V8 models '74 thru '88
- **Cutlass Ciera** – see GENERAL MOTORS A-Cars (829)
- **Cutlass Supreme** – see GENERAL MOTORS (1671)
- **Firenza** – see GENERAL MOTORS J-Cars (766)
- **Ninety-eight** – see BUICK Full-size (1551)
- **Omega** – see PONTIAC Phoenix & Omega (551)
- **Silhouette** – see GENERAL MOTORS (2035)

PEUGEOT
- 663 **504** all diesel models '74 thru '83

PLYMOUTH
For all PLYMOUTH titles, see DODGE listing.

PONTIAC
- **T1000** – see CHEVROLET Chevette (449)
- **J-2000** – see GENERAL MOTORS J-Cars (766)
- **6000** – see GENERAL MOTORS A-Cars (829)
- 1232 **Fiero** all models '84 thru '88
- 555 **Firebird** all V8 models except Turbo '70 thru '81
- *867 **Firebird** all models '82 thru '91
- **Full-size Rear Wheel Drive** – see Buick, Oldsmobile, Pontiac Full-size (1551)
- **Grand Prix** – see GENERAL MOTORS (1671)
- 551 **Phoenix & Oldsmobile Omega** all X-car models '80 thru '84
- **Trans Sport** – see GENERAL MOTORS (2035)

PORSCHE
- *264 **911** all Coupe & Targa models except Turbo & Carrera 4 '65 thru '89
- 239 **914** all 4 cyl models '69 thru '76
- 397 **924** all models including Turbo '76 thru '82
- *1027 **944** all models including Turbo '83 thru '89

RENAULT
- 141 **5 Le Car** all models '76 thru '83
- 079 **8 & 10** all models with 58.4 cu in engines '62 thru '72
- 097 **12 Saloon & Estate** all models 1289 cc engines '70 thru '80
- 768 **15 & 17** all models '73 thru '79
- 081 **16** all models 89.7 cu in & 95.5 cu in engines '65 thru '72
- **Alliance & Encore** – see AMC (934)

SAAB
- 247 **99** all models including Turbo '69 thru '80
- *980 **900** all models including Turbo '79 thru '88

SUBARU
- 237 **1100, 1300, 1400 & 1600** all models '71 thru '79
- *681 **1600 & 1800** 2WD & 4WD all models '80 thru '89

SUZUKI
- *1626 **Samurai/Sidekick and Geo Tracker** all models '86 thru '91

TOYOTA
- *1023 **Camry** all models '83 thru '91
- 150 **Carina Sedan** all models '71 thru '74
- *2038 **Celica** Front Wheel Drive '86 thru '92
- 935 **Celica** Rear Wheel Drive '71 thru '85
- *1139 **Celica Supra** '79 thru '92
- 361 **Corolla** all models '75 thru '79
- 961 **Corolla** all models (rear wheel drive) '80 thru '87
- *1025 **Corolla** all models (front wheel drive) '84 thru '91
- *636 **Corolla Tercel** all models '80 thru '82
- 230 **Corona & MK II** all 4 cyl sohc models '69 thru '74
- 360 **Corona** all models '74 thru '82
- *532 **Cressida** all models '78 thru '82
- 313 **Land Cruiser** all models '68 thru '82
- 200 **MK II** all 6 cyl models '72 thru '76
- *1339 **MR2** all models '85 thru '87
- 304 **Pick-up** all models '69 thru '78
- *656 **Pick-up** all models '79 thru '92

TRIUMPH
- 112 **GT6 & Vitesse** all models '62 thru '74
- 113 **Spitfire** all models '62 thru '81
- 322 **TR7** all models '75 thru '81

VW
- 159 **Beetle & Karmann Ghia** all models '54 thru '79
- 238 **Dasher** all gasoline models '74 thru '81
- *884 **Rabbit, Jetta, Scirocco, & Pick-up** all gasoline models '74 thru '91 & **Convertible** '80 thru '91
- 451 **Rabbit, Jetta & Pick-up** all diesel models '77 thru '84
- 082 **Transporter 1600** all models '68 thru '79
- 226 **Transporter 1700, 1800 & 2000** all models '72 thru '79
- 084 **Type 3 1500 & 1600** all models '63 thru '73
- 1029 **Vanagon** all air-cooled models '80 thru '83

VOLVO
- 203 **120, 130 Series & 1800 Sports** '61 thru '73
- 129 **140 Series** all models '66 thru '74
- *270 **240 Series** all models '74 thru '90
- 400 **260 Series** all models '75 thru '82
- *1550 **740 & 760 Series** all models '82 thru '88

SPECIAL MANUALS
- 1479 **Automotive Body Repair & Painting Manual**
- 1654 **Automotive Electrical Manual**
- 1480 **Automotive Heating & Air Conditioning Manual**
- 1762 **Chevrolet Engine Overhaul Manual**
- 1736 **Diesel Engine Repair Manual**
- 1667 **Emission Control Manual**
- 1763 **Ford Engine Overhaul Manual**
- 482 **Fuel Injection Manual**
- 1666 **Small Engine Repair Manual**
- 299 **SU Carburetors** thru '88
- 393 **Weber Carburetors** thru '79
- 300 **Zenith/Stromberg CD Carburetors** thru '76

See your dealer for other available titles

---

* Listings shown with an asterisk (*) indicate model coverage as of this printing. These titles will be periodically updated to include later model years – consult your Haynes dealer for more information.

Over 100 Haynes motorcycle manuals also available

1-93

Haynes North America, Inc., 861 Lawrence Drive, Newbury Park, CA 91320 • (805) 498-6703